2015
The Supreme Court Review

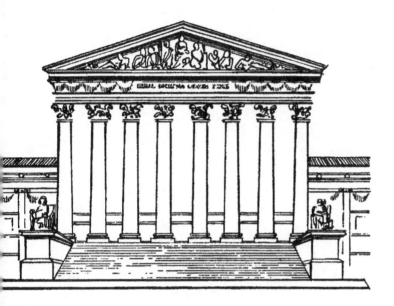

2015
The

"Judges as persons, or courts as institutions, are entitled to no greater
immunity from criticism than other persons or institutions . . .
[J]udges must be kept mindful of their limitations and
of their ultimate public responsibility by a vigorous
stream of criticism expressed with candor however blunt."
—*Felix Frankfurter*

". . . while it is proper that people should find fault when
their judges fail, it is only reasonable that they should recognize the
difficulties. . . . Let them be severely brought to book,
when they go wrong, but by those who will take the trouble
to understand them."
—*Learned Hand*

THE LAW SCHOOL

THE UNIVERSITY OF CHICAGO

Supreme Court Review

EDITED BY

DENNIS J. HUTCHINSON

DAVID A. STRAUSS

AND GEOFFREY R. STONE

 THE UNIVERSITY OF CHICAGO PRESS

CHICAGO AND LONDON

INTERNATIONAL STANDARD BOOK NUMBER: 978-0-226-39221-9

LIBRARY OF CONGRESS CATALOG CARD NUMBER: 60-14353

THE UNIVERSITY OF CHICAGO PRESS, CHICAGO 60637

THE UNIVERSITY OF CHICAGO PRESS, LTD., LONDON

© 2016 BY THE UNIVERSITY OF CHICAGO, ALL RIGHTS RESERVED, PUBLISHED 2016

PRINTED IN THE UNITED STATES OF AMERICA

IN MEMORIAM

Indelible figure—in the classroom,
on the bench,
on the printed page

CONTENTS

SAIKRISHNA BANGALORE PRAKASH

ZIVOTOFSKY AND THE SEPARATION OF POWERS

Zivotofsky v Kerry[1] concerns disputed borders, territorial and constitutional. Is Jerusalem part of Israel? May Congress force the President to issue passports that are premised on the conviction that Jerusalem is within Israel? The Court disclaimed any desire to opine on the first question.[2] On the second, it declared that the Constitution grants the President an exclusive power to recognize other nations, governments, and their territorial claims.[3] Based on its conclusion that the presidency had exclusive authority over recognition, the Court held that Congress could not command the President to issue documents that intimated that Jerusalem was part of Israel.[4]

Saikrishna Bangalore Prakash is James Monroe Distinguished Professor of Law and Horace W. Goldsmith Research Professor of Law, University of Virginia.

AUTHOR'S NOTE: Thanks to Jared Kelson, Steven Kessler, and Nicholas Suellentrop for able research assistance and comments. Gratitude to Will Baude, Curtis Bradley, Ashley Deeks, Jack Goldsmith, John Harrison, Marty Lederman, Michael Ramsey, Paul Stephan, and David Strauss for comments and criticisms. Thanks to the University of Virginia for summer research funds and to the superb law librarians at the University of Virginia for research support.

[1] 135 S Ct 2076 (2015). Two Supreme Court cases bear the name "Zivotofsky." The first concluded that the subject of the underlying dispute was not a political question. *Zivotofsky v Clinton*, 132 S Ct 1421 (2012). In this article, the shorthand "*Zivotofsky*" always refers to the second opinion, *Zivotofsky v Kerry*, 135 S Ct 2076 (2015).

[2] *Zivotofsky*, 135 S Ct at 2081.

[3] Id at 2087.

[4] Id at 2095–96.

The Court's opinion drew sharp dissents from the late Justice Antonin Scalia and Chief Justice John Roberts and a somewhat critical opinion from Justice Clarence Thomas.

While the Court will have no trouble distinguishing or limiting *Zivotofsky*, the case will likely reverberate for years because it touches on numerous aspects of foreign relations law and the separation of powers. The case generated a series of insightful opinions, each of which adds to our understanding of the Constitution's allocation of foreign affairs powers. Lawyers, judges, and scholars will dissect these opinions, extracting arguments and drawing analogies. Perhaps more importantly, the Court's opinion has many elements favoring presidential power, even as it takes pains to reassure that Congress retains considerable authority over foreign affairs. Finally, the opinion marks the first instance in which the Court struck down a federal law on the grounds that it impermissibly infringes upon the President's foreign affairs powers. *Zivotofsky* will stand alongside *United States v Klein*,[5] *Myers v United States*,[6] and *I.N.S. v Chadha*[7] as a case in which the Court sided with the presidency over Congress.

Though we can learn from each of the opinions, each has shortcomings. The majority opinion mistakenly inferred an exclusive presidential authority over recognition when it seems quite likely that in certain instances only Congress can recognize foreign nations, governments, and their territorial claims. Moreover, the majority inferred executive exclusivity without actually considering, in any genuine way, the scope of congressional power in foreign affairs, an approach that is flawed. Justice Thomas's treatment of congressional authority was more careful but he failed to see that the statute in question was not actually designed to help identify citizens naturalized at birth. Instead, the absurdly narrow scope of the statute makes it evident that Congress crafted it to alter recognition policy, something wholly unrelated to its authority over naturalization. Finally, Justice Scalia and Chief Justice Roberts failed to identify plausible sources of congressional authority for the statute that Congress actually passed.

I believe that Congress attempted to alter recognition policy via an artfully drafted statute, that its statutory command of the President

---

[5] 80 US (13 Wall) 128 (1871).

[6] 272 US 52 (1926).

[7] 462 US 919 (1983).

was unconstitutional because Congress was not exercising any of its enumerated powers, but that the President lacks an exclusive power to recognize foreign nations, governments, and territorial claims. Part I recounts the case and the opinions. Part II discusses the merits, including what the statute sought to accomplish, why authority over recognition is likely shared, and why Congress had no authority to enact the statute. Part III considers *Zivotofsky*'s future impact.

I. The Case

On October 17, 2002, Menachem Binyamin Zivotofsky was born to U.S. citizens in Jerusalem.[8] Less than a month before, Congress had passed the 2003 Foreign Relations Authorization Act, Section 214 of which concerned "United States Policy with Respect to Jerusalem as the Capital of Israel."[9] Section 214(d) declared that for purposes of birth registration, certificates of nationality, and passports issued to U.S. citizens born in Jerusalem, the Secretary of State shall, upon request, list "Israel" as the place of birth.[10] This was contrary to prevailing executive policy, under which the Secretary of State had omitted reference to any nation and merely listed "Jerusalem" for all American citizens born in that city after 1948.[11] According to the State Department, this rule of omission enabled the United States to serve as a neutral broker in Middle East peace efforts.

In a signing statement, President George W. Bush construed Section 214 as if it were merely advisory on the grounds that it otherwise would "impermissibly interfere with the President's constitutional authority to formulate the position of the United States, speak for the Nation in international affairs, and determine the terms on which recognition is given to foreign states."[12] Because reading Section 214(d) as merely advisory was implausible, this was a means of announcing that the executive branch was going to ignore it.

---

[8] Brief for Petitioner, *Zivotofsky v Kerry*, 135 S Ct 2076, *3 (filed July 15, 2014) ("Pet Br").

[9] Foreign Relations Authorization Act, Fiscal Year 2003, Pub L No 107-228, § 214, 116 Stat 1350 (2002).

[10] Id § 214(d).

[11] Department of State, 7 Foreign Affairs Manual ("FAM") § 1383.4–1383.6 (1987).

[12] Statement on Signing of the Foreign Relations Authorization Act, Fiscal Year 2003, Public Papers of the Presidents, George W. Bush, vol 2, Sept 30, 2002, at 1698 (2005).

In December 2002, Menachem's mother went to the U.S. Embassy in Tel Aviv to obtain a passport and a consular report of birth for her son.[13] She sought documents that listed "Israel" as the nation of birth.[14] Citing long-standing U.S. policy, embassy clerks refused.[15] Menachem's parents subsequently brought suit on behalf of their son. After interesting jurisdictional tussles that made their way to the Supreme Court,[16] the D.C. Circuit, on remand, declared the statute unconstitutional.[17] Zivotofsky successfully secured Supreme Court review a second time.

In a 5-1-3 split, the Court struck down the statute as unconstitutional. Justice Kennedy's opinion for the Court discussed the concept of recognition under modern international law, saying that it encompassed recognition of statehood, regimes, and their territorial claims.[18] The Court admitted that the Constitution, as a textual matter, never specifically assigns recognition authority to the President.[19] Nonetheless, the President must receive ambassadors, a constitutional directive that "would be understood to acknowledge his power to recognize other nations."[20] Moreover, the Court noted that the powers to make treaties and to send emissaries, both of which may be used to acknowledge foreign nations and governments, also rest with the President.[21] At this point, the Court extrapolated from these specific powers and spoke of the President enjoying a "recognition power,"[22] one that could be exercised even when no treaty was made or ambassadors exchanged. Having reached that conclusion, the Court saw no need to decide whether the Article II Vesting Clause ("The executive Power shall be vested in the President of the United States of America") also granted the President authority over recognition.

Next, the Court asserted that Congress lacked a "similar power" over recognition and that, for functional reasons, the nation needed

---

[13] Pet Br at *3.

[14] Id.

[15] Id.

[16] *Zivotofsky v Clinton*, 132 S Ct 1421 (2012).

[17] *Zivotofsky v Sec'y of State*, 725 F3d 197 (DC Cir 2013).

[18] *Zivotofsky v Kerry*, 135 S Ct at 2096.

[19] Id at 2084.

[20] Id at 2085.

[21] Id.

[22] Id at 2085–86.

to "have a single policy regarding which governments are legitimate in the eyes of the United States" and that such decisions cannot be "equivocal."[23] The "Nation must 'speak ... with one voice'" and that "voice must be the President's."[24] As compared to Congress, the executive has "unity at all times," can engage in "delicate" and "secret diplomatic contacts" and can take the decisive steps necessary to recognize another nation.[25] Wary that such reasoning might be read as unduly minimizing Congress, the Court mentioned congressional authority in various areas of foreign affairs and insisted that only Congress could make law.[26] The Court also maintained that though the President has an implied monopoly on recognition, the chambers of Congress are not obliged to facilitate ties with recognized nations or governments. For instance, the Senate could choose not to consent to treaties with nations the President recognized.[27]

The Court then considered its caselaw, contending that a "fair reading" reveals that the President's role in recognition is "central and exclusive."[28] Citing *Williams v Suffolk Insurance Co.*,[29] *United States v Belmont*,[30] *United States v Pink*,[31] and *Banco Nacional de Cuba v Sabbatino*,[32] the Court concluded that most of its sundry statements on the topic reinforced the notion that the President has an exclusive recognition power. The majority dismissed Zivotovsky's argument that the Court's cases had acknowledged that the recognition power was shared. Rather, those cases merely reflected a desire to leave recognition questions to politicians and rested upon the reasonable assumption that Congress customarily supports the executive's recognition determinations.[33]

The Court then turned to historical practice and asserted that "the weight of historical evidence" largely supports the notion that rec-

---

[23] Id at 2086.

[24] Id (quoting *American Insurance Association v Garamendi*, 539 US 396, 424 (2003)).

[25] Id.

[26] Id at 2087.

[27] Id.

[28] Id at 2088.

[29] 38 US (13 Pet) 415 (1839).

[30] 301 US 324 (1937).

[31] 315 US 203 (1942).

[32] 376 US 398 (1964).

[33] *Zivotofsky*, 135 S Ct at 2091.

ognition rests exclusively with the President and that Congress has "accepted" this exclusivity.[34] Presidents have repeatedly made recognition decisions with no congressional input. Congress has occasionally interceded, but only after Presidents had sought advice. Before Section 214(d) Congress had never enacted a statute that contradicted the President's previous recognition decisions, or so claimed the Court.[35]

The Court accordingly held that Section 214(d) encroached upon the President's recognition power, a power which includes authority to make a recognition determination and to maintain it without contradiction. Agreeing with an argument advanced by the executive, the Court concluded that Section 214(d) required the executive to contradict its policy of not recognizing Israel's claim to Jerusalem. If Congress could force the executive to contradict its prior decisions, in passports or reports of birth abroad, Congress would effectively enjoy the power to recognize. Indeed, Section 214's caption—"United States Policy with Respect to Jerusalem as the Capital of Israel"—signaled that Congress sought "to infringe on the recognition power."[36]

The majority closed by insisting that it was not questioning Congress's "wide" authority over passports.[37] The Court merely denied that such power could be used to usurp the President's exclusive recognition power. In other words, any congressional power over passports could not be wielded "to aggrandiz[e]" Congress vis-à-vis the President.[38]

Justice Thomas wrote separately, concurring in part and dissenting in part. His opinion distinguished passports from reports of birth abroad. As to passports, he maintained that the President had residual foreign affairs authorities by virtue of the grant of "[t]he executive power" in Article II, Section 1 and that this power extended to the content of passports. Further, he argued that Congress had no enumerated power to enact Section 214(d) insofar as it pertained to passports. Because the President had foreign affairs powers that ex-

---

[34] Id at 2091, 2094.

[35] Id at 2091.

[36] Id at 2095.

[37] Id at 2096. The Court did not separately consider congressional authority over reports of birth abroad because it concluded that Zivotofsky had waived any arguments that they should be treated differently from passports. Id at 2083.

[38] Id at 2096 (quoting *Freytag v Commissioner*, 501 US 868, 878 (1991)).

tended to passport issuance and because Congress could not regulate passports (at least not in this manner), Justice Thomas found Section 214(d) unconstitutional as applied to passports. Yet reports of birth abroad merited different treatment, said Justice Thomas. These reports effectuated Congress's naturalization laws and were beyond the President's residual, executive foreign affairs powers. Because Congress had enumerated power over birth reports, the President had to honor Section 214(d) with respect to such reports.[39]

Justice Scalia, in an opinion joined by Chief Justice Roberts and Justice Alito, penned a confident and vigorous dissent, one that was little different from the many that characterized his celebrated tenure. Justice Scalia argued that both branches could act on their respective views regarding Jerusalem, so long as they exercised powers granted to them by the Constitution. The naturalization power, said Justice Scalia, grants Congress authority to issue documents to those born abroad that authenticate their American citizenship. Using such authority, Congress could specify that people born in Jerusalem were born in Israel.

The majority's extended discussion of recognition was irrelevant, argued Justice Scalia, because Section 214(d) had nothing to do with recognition. The Justice explained that "[i]t is utterly impossible for [the statute's] deference to private requests to constitute an act that . . . manifests an intention to grant recognition."[40] The section, Justice Scalia said, was about identification and fraud prevention and merely showed "symbolic support" for Israel's claim.[41]

Chief Justice Roberts penned a separate dissent, one joined by Justice Alito. The Chief Justice stressed the unprecedented nature of the majority opinion—the Court had never before held that the President could "defy an Act of Congress in the field of foreign affairs"—and asserted that the President's claims bore a heavy burden.[42] The Chief Justice also echoed Justice Scalia's assertion that the case did not implicate recognition.

In sum, six Justices believed that Section 214(d) was void as applied to passports. Five of those six concluded that it was also invalid

---

[39] Id at 2109–11 (Thomas, J, concurring in part and dissenting in part).

[40] Id at 2119 (Scalia, J, dissenting).

[41] Id at 2120 (Scalia, J, dissenting).

[42] Id at 2116 (Roberts, CJ, dissenting).

as applied to reports of birth abroad. The same five held that the recognition power rests exclusively with the executive, that Congress can neither exercise that power nor compel the executive to contradict its own recognition policies, and that Section 214(d) had unconstitutionally directed the executive to reverse its stance on Jerusalem.

II. THE MERITS

Contrary to the claims of the dissents, Congress designed Section 214 to alter recognition policy, either by forcing the executive to issue documents that recognized Israel's claim or by requiring the executive to take steps that would eventually lead to recognition. Moreover, I believe that Congress lacks constitutional authority to compel the executive to issue passports and overseas birth records that intimate that Jerusalem was in Israel.

A. THE STATUTE

Section 214(d) was embedded in a provision entitled "United States Policy with Respect to Jerusalem as the Capital of Israel."[43] Section 214(a) reiterated Congress's desire to move the U.S. embassy "in Israel" to Jerusalem, thereby affirming the view that Jerusalem was part of Israel.[44] Section 214(b) required that any consulate in Jerusalem be under the direct control of the U.S. ambassador to Israel, another signal that Jerusalem was in Israel.[45] Section 214(c) forbade the use of federal funds to publish documents that listed the capitals of foreign states unless Jerusalem was recorded as the Israeli capital.[46] The last provision, Section 214(d), gave Americans born in Jerusalem an option to list "Israel" as their place of birth on various official documents.[47]

---

[43] Pub L No 107-228 § 214, 116 Stat at 1365.

[44] Id § 214 (a).

[45] Id § 214 (b).

[46] Id § 214 (c).

[47] Id § 214 (d). To be clear, the statute did not require listing "Jerusalem, Israel" or even "Jerusalem" as a place of birth. It only provided that if an American was born in Jerusalem, she had the right to demand that "Israel" be listed as the place of birth. While Zivotofsky's parents originally sought "Jerusalem, Israel" as the birthplace, they amended their complaint to seek only "Israel" as provided for in the statute.

Every Justice agreed that Section 214(d) did not itself recognize Israel's claim over Jerusalem. Yet there was sharp disagreement regarding the effect and purpose of the section. The majority cast a jaundiced eye, asserting that it was an "undoubted fact that the purpose of the statute was to infringe on the recognition power."[48] Section 214(d) sought to force the executive to issue documents that would have contradicted its existing policy.[49] Moreover, the title of Section 214 was troubling, as was the House Conference Report, which observed that the section contained "four provisions related to the recognition of Jerusalem as Israel's capital."[50] The Court also noted that foreigners believed that the section had altered U.S. policy regarding Jerusalem.[51] "To allow Congress to control the President's communication in the context of a formal recognition determination is to allow Congress to exercise that exclusive power itself."[52]

The Scalia and Roberts dissents claimed that Section 214(d) did not concern recognition at all. The statute never declared that it was a formal act of recognition. Moreover, forcing the executive to list "Israel" on various documents would in no way recognize Israel's claim because passport entries had apparently never been used to confer recognition. As Justice Scalia noted, Section 214(d) is entitled

---

The executive consistently maintained that it had constitutional authority to publish "Jerusalem" in government documents without any reference to the entity that properly enjoyed sovereignty over it. From one perspective, the executive could have complied with Section 214(d) without issuing any documents specifying that Jerusalem was in Israel. After all, declaring that someone was born in Israel without mentioning Jerusalem as the city of birth might not have signaled that the executive (or the United States) was acknowledging that Jerusalem was in Israel. During oral argument, the executive admitted that there would be many who read such passports and have no idea that the person was born in Jerusalem. Oral Argument, *Zivotofsky v Kerry*, 135 S Ct 2076, *45 (Nov 3, 2015) ("Oral Arg"). Yet the executive must have concluded that issuing passports with "Israel" marked as the place of birth for those born in Jerusalem in the context of a statute that clearly sought recognition of Jerusalem would have suggested to knowledgeable foreign officials that the executive had acquiesced in the view that Jerusalem was in Israel. Those most attuned to Jerusalem's status would have received some sort of message that the United States had at least inched closer to recognizing Israel's claim.

[48] *Zivotofsky*, 135 S Ct at 2095.

[49] As noted, the statute itself did not force the executive to do anything. Rather it merely gave those born in Jerusalem an option to list "Israel" as the place of birth. But members of Congress knew with certainty that some Americans born in Jerusalem would exercise the option. Hence, Congress was essentially compelling the President to issue documents that implied that Jerusalem was in Israel.

[50] Foreign Relations Authorization Act, HR Conf Rep No 107-671, 107th Cong, 2d Sess 123 (2002).

[51] *Zivotofsky*, 135 S Ct at 2095–96.

[52] Id at 2096.

"Record of Place of Birth as Israel *for Passport Purposes.*"[53] According to the Justice, the section merely permitted the inclusion of extra information in government documents, thereby facilitating the identification of U.S. citizens. Knowing whether a Menachem Zivotofsky was born in Jerusalem, New York[54] enables the government to distinguish him from any Menachem Zivotofskys born in ancient Jerusalem. The law merely evinced "symbolic support for Israel's territorial claim."[55]

Justice Scalia had a point—recognition is a "type of legal act" and not merely *any* "statement."[56] If Congress required a private citizen to issue a document that said that the United States recognizes Israeli sovereignty over Jerusalem and that citizen complied, that would surely not constitute *United States* recognition of Israel's claim. Moreover, if Congress clandestinely passed a law that forced the President to author a document declaring that the "United States recognizes Israel's sovereignty over Jerusalem" and also directed the President to never reveal the document to the world, the creation of the document would not constitute recognition because the latter would seem to require an action that *manifests* a decision to recognize. If there is no document or action that publicly signals recognition, no recognition has taken place.

But Justice Scalia pressed his point too far, for some statements may amount to recognition. If Congress required the President to issue a document entitled "United States Policy with Respect to Jerusalem as the Capital of Israel" to foreign ambassadors resident in America and the document declared that "Henceforth, the United States recognizes Israel's claim to Jerusalem," this would surely be an attempt to force the President to recognize Israel's claim. Likewise, if Congress openly enacted a law that asserted the "United States recognizes that Jerusalem is in Israel" this would at least be an attempted recognition by Congress.

Admittedly, Section 214(d) does not go as far as these examples. Still, there should be no doubt that members of Congress were

---

[53] Id at 2120 (Scalia, J, dissenting) (emphasis in original).

[54] There are three cities named "Jerusalem" in the United States. So far as I can tell, only one exists outside the United States.

[55] *Zivotofsky*, 135 S Ct at 2120 (Scalia, J, dissenting).

[56] Id at 2121 (Scalia, J, dissenting).

attempting to alter recognition policy. The section's title and the House Conference report indicate as much. The fact that documents implying recognition were to come from the Secretary of State pursuant to a statute declaring that Jerusalem was the capital of Israel should leave little doubt that the issuance of those documents was meant to revise "United States" policy toward Jerusalem.

Justice Scalia failed to appreciate that any document, no matter its nominal title and its dominant purpose, can be used for seemingly odd ends. The passport has long served as a request for protection directed toward foreign sovereigns. Yet, today it also serves as a means of facilitating reentry into the country, tracking international travel, and authenticating identity within the United States.

Passports can also function as a means of instilling patriotism and as a tool for propagating American values. The U.S. passport reproduces quotations from the Constitution's Preamble, Lincoln's Gettysburg Address, and Martin Luther King, Jr. It contains iconic images, from Mount Rushmore to Diamond Head.[57] Such propaganda not only stirs Americans, it may influence foreigners as well. It quotes John F. Kennedy's "[l]et every nation know...that we will bear any burden...to assure the survival and the success of liberty."

The United States is not alone in using passports as an instrument of foreign policy. For instance, passports of the People's Republic of China (PRC) make and reinforce territorial claims. PRC passports contain a map of China that extends to disputed areas of the South China Sea and the Himalayas.[58] These passports annoy Vietnam, India, and many Asian nations. Vietnam refuses to issue visas in these passports; India stamps its preferred map over the Chinese one. Both actions signal disagreement. China is making a territorial claim and other states are disputing it, all within the context of passports.

Recording country of birth may seem inconsequential in the context of documents that originally served as a means of requesting protection from foreign sovereigns. Yet as we have seen, the original, narrow function of passports has little bearing on their supplementary uses today. Take the case of recognition. As Justice Kennedy

---

[57] Neil MacFarquhar, *Stars, Stripes, Wrapped in the Same Old Blue*, New York Times WK7 (Apr 29, 2007).

[58] Max Fisher, *Here's the Chinese Passport Map That's Infuriating Much of Asia*, Washington Post (Nov 26, 2012).

noted, the executive had long treated the "place-of-birth section as an official executive statement implicating recognition."[59] The executive "will not list a sovereign that contradicts the President's recognition policy in a passport."[60] Given that foreign nations knew that the executive had consistently hewed to the recognition policies of the United States in its passports, and given that the statute was designed to alter recognition policy, the advent of a new passport stance with respect to Jerusalem would have been seen as a change in policy toward that city's status.

The "Israel" designation also seems more consequential when one keeps in mind that Congress enacted a one-sided rule. Those born in Jerusalem after 1948 had no option of insisting upon "Palestine" or "Jordan" as their place of birth. Nor could they express a desire for negotiations to settle the status of Jerusalem. Given the context of Section 214(d), it is little wonder that foreigners thought it concerned U.S. recognition of Israel's claim.[61]

In sum, rather than declaring that the United States was "hereby recognizing" Israel's claim, Congress chose an indirect path. It sought to alter recognition policy by piggybacking on the fact that U.S. passports conform to the recognition stances of the United States.

The claims of Justice Scalia and Chief Justice Roberts that the statute did not concern recognition may seem plausible if one assumes that both were implicitly invoking the avoidance canon[62] as a means of sidestepping the constitutional question regarding recognition. Yet neither invokes that canon. Moreover, even if that is the best way of reconceiving their arguments, I think they still fail. The avoidance canon can be invoked only if an alternative, reasonable interpretation is available.[63] I believe it is *un*reasonable to read the statute as anything but an attempt to change recognition policy. Again, the statute repeatedly states that Jerusalem is "in Israel" and

---

[59] *Zivotofsky*, 135 S Ct at 2095.

[60] Id.

[61] Brief for Respondent, *Zivotofsky v Kerry*, 135 S Ct 2076, *54 (filed Sept 22, 2014) ("Resp Br").

[62] See, for example, *Crowell v Benson*, 285 US 22, 62 (1932) ("When the validity of an act of Congress is drawn into question, and even if a serious doubt of constitutionality is raised, it is a cardinal principle that this Court will first ascertain whether a construction of the statute is fairly possible by which the question may be avoided."). For general discussion of the avoidance canon, see Caleb Nelson, *Statutory Interpretation* 146–64 (Foundation, 2011).

[63] *Crowell*, 285 US at 62.

explicitly concerns the "United States Policy with Respect to Jerusalem as the Capital of Israel." As the House Conference Report put it,
Section 214 contained "four provisions related to the recognition of
Jerusalem as Israel's capital." Given this context, to conclude that the
statute did not concern recognition is to blink reality.

This still leaves unresolved the manner in which Congress was
seeking to alter recognition policy. Neither the Court nor the executive was entirely clear about what the section's implementation
would have accomplished. One could suppose that Section 214(d)
sought to force the Secretary of State to recognize Israel's claim. The
executive suggested this, arguing that if it had complied with Section
214(d), the resulting "passports [would have] acknowledge[d] Israel's
sovereignty over Jerusalem."[64] The executive's objection, expressed
in its brief, that Congress was trying to force it to contradict itself
could also be understood as a claim that enforcement of the statute
would reverse the existing nonrecognition of Jerusalem.

At times, the Court seemed to endorse this view. For instance, the
majority said that if Congress could compel the President to issue the
passports, it would have forced a contradiction upon the executive
and that Congress would enjoy the recognition power. The latter two
claims imply that the President *would have recognized Israel's claims*
had he complied with the statute, for if the statement required of
the President did not constitute recognition, there would be neither
a contradiction nor warrant for asserting that Congress effectively
exercised the recognition power.

Yet the Court also emphatically declared "the statement required
by § 214(d) would not itself constitute a formal act of recognition."[65]
How can we square the Court's various statements? Perhaps the
Court had in mind an alternative way of thinking about recognition,
one supposing that recognition might not always consist of a single,
discrete act but sometimes might consist of a series of measures. The
executive may have advanced this theory when it suggested the statute
compelled it to take "steps" toward recognition.[66]

In other words, perhaps Congress was muddying the President's
clear policy of nonrecognition by pressuring the executive branch

---

[64] Resp Br at *52.

[65] *Zivotofsky*, 135 S Ct at 2095.

[66] Resp Br at *52.

(and therefore the United States) to gradually recognize Israel's claim. Congress might have supposed that faithful compliance with Section 214(d) (and the rest of Section 214) would have had the tendency to bring the United States closer to the point of recognizing Israel's assertion. A frog placed in a pot of water will, as the cook raises the water's temperature, eventually boil to death. Similarly, if Congress can force the executive to take a series of steps related to recognition of Jerusalem, eventually the United States will have acknowledged Israel's claim.

Whether compliance with the statute would have instantly recognized Israel's claim or would have been a step toward such recognition, Congress was endeavoring to alter "United States Policy with Respect to Jerusalem." The statute was not a mere legislation resolution, like those that establish "National Asbetos Awareness Week" or "Wreaths Across America Day," that offered no more than "symbolic support" for Israel's claim. Rather it sought to establish that the United States regarded Jerusalem "as the Capital of Israel."

B. THE CONSTITUTION

If perceiving the effects and purposes of Section 214(d) is somewhat challenging, the sledding is tougher still once we turn to the constitutional questions. Does the President enjoy power to recognize nations, governments, and territorial limits? Does Congress enjoy concurrent authority over recognition? Can Congress force the executive to issue documents that are designed to alter U.S. policy over Jerusalem?[67]

Writing for the Court, Justice Kennedy asserted that Congress could not demand the issuance of documents signifying that Je-

---

[67] The command to include Israel as the place of birth fell upon the Secretary of State and not the President. The Secretary of State has but two constitutional rights or powers, ex officio, and certainly lacks a constitutional right to refuse to list Israel as the place of birth for those born in Jerusalem (one constitutional right of the Secretary is to offer independent opinions to the President upon the latter's request—the Opinions Clause of Article II implies as much—and the other relates to the Secretary of State's ability, grounded in the Twenty-Fifth Amendment, to decide whether the President is able to discharge the duties of his office). Yet no Justice dismissed the executive branch's constitutional arguments. Apparently, the Court treated the Secretary as the President's alter ego, at least for purposes of this statute. The Court must have supposed that directing the Secretary in this context was tantamount, for constitutional purposes, to directing the President. If the President had constitutional rights at stake, the President's invocation of them could serve as an aegis for the Secretary.

rusalem is in Israel because the President has exclusive authority to make that judgment himself. Citing implications from the Reception and Treaty Clauses and the President's ability to send ambassadors to foreign nations, Justice Kennedy credibly argued that some authority over recognition rested with the President.

Yet because the Justice's ultimate goal was to establish that the authority to recognize nations, governments, and territorial claims rested exclusively with the executive, he was under the burden of establishing that the President had a comprehensive recognition power. This he never did. Instead, Justice Kennedy extrapolated, concluding that because the President had authority to recognize foreign nations and governments via treaties and ambassadors, he had a generic, comprehensive recognition power that could be wielded outside of those contexts. But the conclusion does not follow. Even if the President has some power over recognition, to be wielded when he negotiates treaties and sends and receives ambassadors, it hardly follows that he has a generic power to recognize nations and governments that can be exercised outside those contexts. Moreover, even if the President's authority over ambassadors and treaties implies authority to recognize foreign governments and nations, it is hard to see why such authority necessarily includes power to recognize claims over disputed territory. When the President receives an ambassador, that reception carries no implications for whether the ambassador's nation controls disputed regions. Likewise, no one should suppose that making an arms control treaty with Russia somehow implies recognition of the latter's annexation of Crimea.[68]

Justice Kennedy's exclusivity claims were more troubled. The difficulty with establishing exclusivity is that because the Constitution does not expressly convey a recognition power it contains no specific rule about whether that power rests exclusively with one branch. Faced with the task of establishing implied exclusivity, Justice Kennedy asserted that Congress was poorly suited to exercise such authority, that concurrent recognition authority would generate con-

---

[68] These weaknesses in Justice Kennedy's argument were perhaps masked by the dissent's indifference to the matter. Neither Justice Scalia nor Chief Justice Roberts seemed interested in questioning the extent to which the President might enjoy recognition authority. They were instead focused on the scope of congressional authority, for even if the President had comprehensive recognition authority, if Congress had authority as well, the will of Congress, as expressed in statutes, would prevail. In other words, they sought to poke holes in Justice Kennedy's conclusion that presidential power over recognition was exclusive.

fusion, and that Congress had never unilaterally recognized nations or governments.

The Court's first two arguments cannot bear much weight. The majority's functional claim that Congress is poorly situated to exercise the recognition power can hardly be dispositive because the Constitution may reflect a contrary conclusion. At most, institutional competence arguments should count as a weak factor in disputes about the allocation of authority. Regarding the confusion that might arise from multiple branches with overlapping recognition authority, the Court overstated its case. Treaties and statutes overlap because both are means for adopting rules about commerce and the law of nations. The fact of concurrent authority does not give rise to endemic confusion about the state of the federal law relating to foreign commerce or the law of nations. The possibility of confusion is a function of how often the two branches generate conflicting rules. If conflicts are kept at a minimum, because one branch (Congress) exercises its authority only sparingly, there will be little cause for confusion. Relatedly, any legislative recognition faces the prospect of a veto, suggesting that if the President is vigilant Congress will wade into recognition disputes only rarely.

The Court's third argument about congressional practice suffers because it seems inconsistent with the historical record. For instance, Congress recognized Cuba's independence of Spain in 1898, as part of its protodeclaration of war against Spain.[69] While the bill was enacted with President McKinley's signature, he had, just days before, opposed recognizing Cuba's independence.[70] On two occasions, Congress ordered the President to recognize the independence of the Philippines.[71] In 1933, President Herbert Hoover had vetoed such a bill, only to have Congress override his objections.[72] When that 1933 law proved ineffective, President Franklin Roosevelt sought changes

---

[69] See Act of Apr 20, 1898, ch 24, 30 Stat 738 (1898) (declaring the people of Cuba "free and independent"); Kenneth E. Hendrickson, Jr., *The Spanish-American War* 22–23 (Greenwood, 2003). At a minimum, Congress asserted the authority to derecognize Spain's sovereignty over Cuba.

[70] Hendrickson, *The Spanish-American War* at 22–23 (cited in note 69).

[71] See, for example, William Nimmo, *Stars and Stripes Across the Pacific: The United States, Japan, and the Asia/Pacific Region, 1985–1945* at 152–54 (Greenwood, 2001).

[72] Herbert Hoover, *Veto of a Bill Providing for the Independence of the Philippine Islands*, January 13, 1933, archived at http://www.presidency.ucsb.edu/ws/?pid=23409. See also H. W. Brands, *Bound to Empire: The United States and the Philippines* 153 (Oxford, 1992).

from Congress.[73] The resulting 1934 statute also compelled the President to recognize the Filipino nation and government.[74] Roosevelt apparently did not object to the recognition directive.[75]

The greatest shortcoming of the Court's approach was its cursory consideration of congressional power. The Court first concluded that executive power was exclusive and then, at the end of its opinion, belatedly considered congressional power. But one cannot conclude that the Constitution implicitly vests with the President an exclusive power over recognition without also thoroughly considering whether (and to what extent) the Constitution conveys recognition authority to Congress. As Jack Goldsmith has argued, in denying congressional power "based on an analysis of Article II alone . . . the Court prejudged all that was to come."[76]

The Court's placement of the cart before the horse—finding that presidential power is exclusive before considering congressional power—perhaps explains why the Court's belated discussion of congressional authority was so shallow. The Court acknowledged that Congress has broad authority over passports but never grappled with its scope because the Court had already determined that the President's recognition power was exclusive. Having so concluded, the Court quickly asserted that Congress, by attempting to force the executive to contradict itself, was improperly aggrandizing itself.

I rather doubt that the recognition power rests exclusively with the President. Consider the reception of a foreign ambassador. The Court wrote as if the President had an absolute right to receive any foreign ambassador. But what if the reception of a foreign ambassador could constitute a declaration of war?[77] In the eighteenth century, receiving an ambassador from a rebel faction might be understood as a declaration of war against the nation attempting to subdue the revolutionaries. In other words, the reception of a rebel ambassador could constitute both recognition *and* a declaration of war, much in

---

[73] Franklin D. Roosevelt, *Message to Congress Regarding Independence for the Philippine Islands*, Mar 2, 1934, archived at http://www.presidency.ucsb.edu/ws/?pid = 14818.

[74] See, for example, Nimmo, *Stars and Stripes* at 152–54 (cited in note 71).

[75] Id.

[76] Jack Goldsmith, *Zivotofsky II as Precedent in the Executive Branch*, 129 Harv L Rev 112, 120 (2015).

[77] Robert Reinstein, the foremost expert on recognition, discusses the interaction of the declare-war power and recognition authority. Robert Reinstein, *Is the President's Recognition Power Exclusive?*, 86 Temple L Rev 1, 14, 15, 28–29, 39 (2013).

the same way that making a treaty of alliance with rebels might be construed as constituting recognition and a declaration of war.[78] The President has power to receive ambassadors, but Congress has the exclusive power to declare war. How are we to reconcile the two in a context when one decision implicates the other? Andrew Jackson faced this quandary. He declined to recognize the Texas Republic's independence on his own authority likely because he knew that Mexico might regard such recognition as a war declaration.[79] Hence, he sought congressional authority for recognizing Texas.[80]

There is no untroubled solution to this puzzle. Nonetheless I believe that a duty to receive ambassadors—for that is what the Reception Clause imposes—takes a back seat to a power to decide whether to wage war. The Reception Clause is generally "more a matter of dignity than authority."[81] It was added to ensure that America properly received foreign ministers with the pomp befitting a relatively new and (hopefully) potent nation.[82] It was not meant to signal that the President could choose to embroil the nation in wars by recognizing rebels or recognizing new governments.

Vesting the power to declare war in Congress reflected a decision that only Congress may authorize measures that could be construed as declarations of war.[83] Many of the founders understood the clause as not only vesting Congress with authority to decide to wage war but also implicitly *divesting* the executive of its traditional power to declare war.[84] This was a fundamental decision, one not to be undone by implications of presidential duties. If the Constitution chains the "dog of war" by stripping the executive's traditional prerogative of declaring war, we ought not to read a clause that imposes reception

---

[78] See Saikrishna Prakash, *Unleashing the Dogs of War: What the Constitution Means by "Declare War,"* 93 Cornell L Rev 45, 72–73 (2007).

[79] Andrew Jackson, *Special Message to the Senate and House of Representatives,* Dec 21, 1836, archived at http://www.presidency.ucsb.edu/ws/?pid=67012.

[80] Id.

[81] Federalist 69 (Hamilton), in Jacob E. Cooke, ed, *The Federalist* 457, 468 (Wesleyan, 1961) (X). Hamilton would later claim it included the power to recognize foreign nations. See *Pacificus No. 1,* in Morton J. Frisch, ed, *The Pacificus-Helvidius Debates of 1793–1794* at 8, 14–15 (Liberty Fund, 2007).

[82] See Saikrishna Bangalore Prakash, *Imperial from the Beginning* 133 (Yale, 2015).

[83] See Prakash, 93 Cornell L Rev at 50–51 (cited in note 78); Saikrishna Bangalore Prakash, *Exhuming the Seemingly Moribund Declaration of War,* 77 Geo Wash L Rev 89, 91 (2008).

[84] See Saikrishna Bangalore Prakash, *The Separation and Overlap of War and Military Powers,* 87 Tex L Rev 299, 313–15 (2008).

duties as if it implicitly creates an exception to the declare-war monopoly granted to Congress.

If the above argument rings true, whenever recognition of a nation, a regime, or its territorial claims could be construed as a declaration of war, the authority to recognize can be exercised by Congress, via its statutes, and not the President acting unilaterally. In other words, in some contexts, the decision to recognize rests *exclusively with Congress*.

This understanding helps explain the congressional recognition of Cuba's independence from Spain. The 1898 recognition was an exercise of the declare-war power and was accompanied by orders to attack Spanish military forces.[85] Congress, speaking on behalf of the "United States," demanded that Spanish military and civil officials withdraw from Cuba and directed the President to use the military to "carry these resolutions into effect."[86] Congress knew that recognizing Cuba's independence was a decision exercisable under the war power. The statute usually seen as the American declaration of war was a congressional reaction to the Spanish formal declaration of war.[87] But Congress already had declared war by recognizing Cuba's independence.

The Court also failed to consider how some of its statements suggested that Congress has some authority over recognition. For instance, in the course of distinguishing certain Supreme Court cases, the Court declared that "the political branches" could determine the territorial boundaries of the United States.[88] If the Court meant that Congress, by statute, may determine the territory of the United States, Congress will have some authority over recognition of foreign territorial claims. For instance, if Congress asserts in its statutes that Ciudad Juarez is in the United States, it is unavoidably rejecting Mexico's assertion of sovereignty. It is *denying recognition* of Mexico's claim.

Talk of a unitary "recognition power" suffuses the majority opinion in *Zivotofsky*. This subtly influences us to suppose that either an institution has the (entire) recognition power or has no part of it. But because the Constitution never expressly conveys or mentions the

---

[85] See Act of Apr 20, 1898, 30 Stat 738 (1898).

[86] Id.

[87] An Act Declaring that War Exists Between the United States of America and the Kingdom of Spain, 30 Stat 364 (1898).

[88] *Zivotofsky*, 135 S Ct at 2091.

"recognition power," we should be open to the possibility that the recognition power is shared, in the sense that the power is granted partly to Congress and partly to the President. To reach that conclusion, however, one would have to consider congressional authority, something the majority opinion never really did.

Unlike the majority, Justice Thomas canvassed both executive *and* congressional powers. He began with a lengthy discussion of the grant of executive power and why it conveyed residual authority over foreign affairs. He noted that Presidents had long exercised authorities not traceable to any specific grant of Article II, Section 2 authority and that founders such as Washington, Jefferson, Madison, and Hamilton had read the grant of executive power as conveying residual foreign affairs authorities to the President.

Turning to passports, Justice Thomas observed that early Presidents had issued them for almost three-quarters of a century and that their authority arose from the "executive power" rather than from statutes. In contrast, Congress lacked a freestanding "passport power."[89] He further asserted that Section 214(d) did not relate to foreign commerce because listing Israel in passports was unrelated to any commercial activity. Congressional naturalization authority was "unavailing" because passports request protection for the bearer and do not confer citizenship. Finally, the Justice argued that Section 214(d) was an "improper" means of carrying federal power into execution and hence the Necessary and Proper Clause did not authorize Congress to demand the inclusion of "Israel" in passports.

As noted earlier, Justice Thomas concluded that birth reports merited a different conclusion. First, reports of birth abroad had no historical connection to the "executive power" and were not communications directed to foreign powers. Hence, the President had no constitutional authority over them. Second, these reports were within Congress's purview. The naturalization power encompasses authority to determine who is eligible to become a citizen and the process one must undertake. The report of birth abroad—a naturalization certificate, essentially—is "well suited" to implementing the naturalization power, claimed the Justice. The report is the "primary means by which children born abroad" obtain official at-

---

[89] Id at 2103–04 (Thomas, J, concurring in part and dissenting in part).

testation of their citizenship.[90] Regulation of the report was thus necessary and proper for executing the naturalization power.

Justice Thomas is surely on to something. Passports and naturalization papers are meaningfully different. As he noted, Presidents granted passports for over a century prior to any meaningful congressional involvement.[91] Presidents must have thought they were exercising constitutional authority because no statute authorized their passport issuances. In contrast, naturalization is not associated with the executive power. While the Crown could make denizens of foreigners, it could not naturalize anyone. Only Parliament could naturalize.[92] On this side of the Atlantic, there seems little warrant for supposing that the President has any constitutional authority to naturalize or to issue proof of naturalization. Congress has an express grant of authority over the subject and, to my knowledge, no one has ever asserted that the President has an executive power of naturalization. Hence, if the children of U.S. citizens must be naturalized when born abroad, then only Congress may naturalize them.

Further, Congress can dictate that naturalized citizens receive documents from the executive validating their status because such documents help carry into execution Congress's naturalization authority. In such documents, specifying country of birth is useful in identifying naturalized citizens. While there are diminishing returns from requiring ever more information in naturalization documents, specifying country of birth hardly seems excessive. In fact, it seems entirely normal, especially since the executive normally includes country of birth on passports and reports of birth abroad.

Yet Section 214(d) was not designed to identify citizens. It does not mandate the recording of certain personal traits, for example, height, weight, eye color, etc., that could be used to identify naturalized citizens. Indeed, it does not even require country of birth on any documents. It gave applicants an *option* to list one country, Israel. It only granted that option to those born in Jerusalem, one city in the entire world. Realistically speaking, it granted that option only to those who wished to note Israel on their passports. Because Section 214(d) had an exceedingly narrow ambit, Congress could not possibly

---

[90] Id at 2111 (Thomas, J, concurring in part and dissenting in part).

[91] Id at 2101–02 (Thomas, J, concurring in part and dissenting in part).

[92] William Blackstone, 1 *Commentaries on the Laws of England* 362 (Oxford, 1765).

have been motivated by a desire to further the more precise identification of those naturalized at birth.

Section 214(d) was significant not as a means of identifying naturalized citizens but as a method of revising the foreign policy of the United States. Congress wanted to alter existing recognition policy. Such a desire, however, is far removed from anything having to do with naturalization. In fact, the two have no connection, other than the congressional attempt to leverage the naturalization power into authority over recognition.

If the statute's ends were orthogonal to naturalization, then the Naturalization and Necessary and Proper Clauses cannot justify the statute. More precisely, that Congress has authority to regulate the content of naturalization certificates hardly means that it may leverage its power to force the President to speak on matters related to international relations, such as U.S. policy toward the Crimea or Jerusalem. By granting a narrow set of people an option to personalize their reports of birth abroad, and only in a way that favored Israel's claim to Jerusalem, I believe that Congress pursued ends not committed to its care under the naturalization power. Congress does not carry into execution the naturalization power when it attempts to force the executive to alter its recognition policy.

Could Congress have imposed a set of rules with respect to place of birth? I believe so. Congress might have crafted a rule that declared that *every* certificate of birth abroad must mention both the city and the country *currently exercising sovereignty over that city.* This would have suggested that Congress was not commenting on which nations had legitimate claims over some city or area, unless one supposed that Congress always favored recognition of de facto sovereignty over a territory. Yet, Congress created no such neutral rule because in passing Section 214(d) it did not care about identifying the country in which U.S. citizens were born or in distinguishing among naturalized citizens. To this day, there is no statute obliging the executive to note the country of birth in passports or reports of birth abroad.

Justice Scalia's dissent was blind to Congress's true goal. He argued that Congress was exercising its naturalization power when it granted a few American citizens an option to insist that their passports and reports of birth abroad include "Israel." But American passports have no connection to naturalization; one can be naturalized and yet not have a passport, just as one can hold a passport and not be naturalized. Moreover, those passports have never conveyed citizenship. If passport authority flows from the naturalization power, early Presidents invaded congressional authority for decades.

Justice Scalia's similar claims regarding reports of birth abroad would have been plausible if it were true that Congress was actually trying to distinguish "people with similar names but different birth-places" or helping to uncover "identity fraud."[93] But, as discussed, Congress was attempting to alter recognition policy, or, as Justice Scalia put it, to fashion a "better foreign policy."[94] Moreover, neither the naturalization power nor any other legislative power empowers Congress to further a "[passport] bearer's conscientious belief that Jerusalem belongs to Israel"[95] any more than these powers could be used to advance my sincere belief that *Star Trek* is better than *Star Wars*. This is not to trivialize strong convictions about Jerusalem. Rather, it is to say that the naturalization power is a rather unlikely fount of authority to further the personal expressions of private citizens.

More generally, the enumerated powers found within the Constitution exist to further certain ends and not others. Perceiving those ends is sometimes easy, sometimes difficult. To take a fanciful example, could a billionaire President exploit his State of the Union duty to promote his private real estate empire? I rather doubt it. None of the President's constitutional powers can be wielded to further a President's private ends, and hence neither the State of the Union Clause nor anything else in Article II would authorize any attempt to flog a business before Congress. Congressional and judicial powers work the same way. Neither Congress nor the courts can further every end, because not all ends are committed to their care.[96]

As noted earlier, Justice Scalia was on much firmer ground when he suggested that perhaps Congress may recognize via other grants. I've

---

[93] *Zivotofsky*, 135 S Ct at 2117 (Scalia, J, dissenting).

[94] Id.

[95] Id.

[96] There are, of course, differences of opinion about the proper ends of congressional power. For instance, early- to mid-twentieth-century Commerce Clause cases can be seen as reflecting different perspectives on the scope of permissible ends that Congress may pursue under the Commerce Clause. Compare *Hammer v Dagenhart*, 247 US 251 (1918) (Commerce Clause does not grant Congress authority to regulate commerce as a means of regulating manufacture and labor) with *United States v Darby*, 312 US 100 (1941) (describing Commerce Clause authority as extending to any activity that substantially affects interstate commerce).

already spoken about the reception of ambassadors and why Congress has a monopoly when reception would constitute a declaration of war. Let me add a parallel example about treaties. Suppose the United States has a treaty of alliance with Great Britain that includes an obligation to defend British territory. Suppose further that Argentina tries to recapture the Falkland Islands. Should Congress declare war against Argentina in order to satisfy the treaty, Congress would be implicitly recognizing Great Britain's claim to the Falklands.

But that Congress has some authority over recognition hardly means that it has generic authority to recognize states, governments, and their territorial claims. By enacting Section 214(d), Congress sought to alter recognition policy in a context in which the most relevant governmental authorities (the combination of Naturalization and Necessary and Proper Clauses) cede no authority to recognize foreign nations.

What of the other powers cited by Justice Scalia in support of Section 214(d) as it relates to passports? As noted earlier, the commerce power is neither necessary for passports nor a sufficient warrant for issuing them. Despite lacking any legislative authority over commerce, the Continental Congress issued passports.[97] Moreover, not everyone seeking the protection of the United States overseas will engage in commerce overseas, and the thousands of passports the executive routinely issues (and has issued for over two hundred years) are not so limited in scope.

Justice Scalia also cited the citizenship provisions of the Fourteenth Amendment and the Property Clause of Article IV as possible founts of authority over the content of passports. The Fourteenth Amendment declares "[a]ll persons born or naturalized in the United States . . . are citizens of the United States" and grants Congress authority to enforce the amendment. But it is rather unclear how Section 5 grants any more authority over passports than does the Necessary and Proper Clause in conjunction with the Naturalization Clause. Because passports are federal property, the Property Clause of Article IV seems to provide a better source of authority to specify the contents of passports. Yet, this sort of claim proves too much.

---

[97] *Zivotofsky*, 135 S Ct at 2102 (Thomas, J, concurring in part and dissenting in part).

May the Congress regulate the use of all federal property and prevent the President from using the White House premises to make legislative recommendations or to veto legislation? Can Congress bar courts from using federal property (courthouses) to strike down federal statutes? The Property Clause is not some caustic acid that Congress may wield to dissolve the Constitution's separation of powers.

In sum, while Congress has vast legislative power, it does not have power to do everything. In *McCulloch v Maryland*,[98] Chief Justice Marshall uttered a warning:

> Should Congress, in the execution of its powers, adopt measures which are prohibited by the constitution; or should Congress, under the pretext of executing its powers, pass laws for the accomplishment of objects not entrusted to the government; it would become the painful duty of this tribunal . . . to say that such an act was not the law of the land.

I believe a third category is warranted: Should Congress enact laws meant to further ends not entrusted to it, the courts must say that those laws are not the law of the land. In enacting Section 214(d), Congress was trying to alter recognition policy in a context where it was neither exercising any of its powers nor pursuing any ends committed to its care.

III. Implications

Though foretelling what will come of a Supreme Court decision is speculative, certain consequences seem certain. After *Zivotofsky*, the executive can ignore foreign affairs statutes that it judges to be unconstitutional, with the courts making the ultimate judgments. A corollary is that congressional authority over foreign affairs is clearly limited and not merely by the few express constitutional grants to the President. Moreover, the majority opinion will embolden executive branch lawyers to assert that other foreign affairs statutes infringe the President's exclusive powers. Finally, to preserve its initiative in foreign affairs Congress will interpret *Zivotofsky* narrowly.

Less certain are the scope of recognition power and the continued willingness of the Court to recognize implied executive authorities. Lower courts may be the ones to initially sketch out what counts as

---

[98] 17 US 316, 423 (1819).

"recognition" and which other foreign affairs authorities rest exclusively with the President.

A. CONGRESS AND FOREIGN AFFAIRS

In holding that the recognition power rests exclusively with the President, the Court implicitly acknowledged that congressional authority over foreign affairs is limited. It would seem that if implied executive authority (recognition) can be exclusive, express executive powers might be as well. Indeed, the Court seems to suppose that the treaty power is exclusive (it had already found that the appointment power rests with the President alone).[99]

Beyond this, the Court left the confines of congressional power in foreign affairs undefined. On the one hand, the Court's opinion could be read to permit Congress to legislate in foreign affairs whenever executive power is not exclusive. Louis Henkin once argued the Congress enjoyed a "foreign affairs power."[100] His claim rested in part on the array of foreign affairs statutes and on doctrinal support from the Supreme Court.[101] Perhaps the idea of a congressional "foreign affairs power" remains viable, save for the finite set of instances in which courts hold that executive foreign affairs powers are exclusive.

On the other hand, the Court's opinion could be read to suggest that Congress lacks a "foreign affairs" power that can be used to legislate on all foreign matters. The opinion's lauding of one voice, unity, and decisiveness and its implied denigration of Congress could be thought to imply that "Congress does not have a general foreign affairs power."[102] Instead, to legislate on foreign affairs it must be exercising one of its specific foreign affairs powers or be carrying into execution some federal power.[103] Only time will tell which of these two readings will prevail.

---

[99] *Zivotofsky*, 135 S Ct at 2085–86.

[100] Louis Henkin, *Foreign Affairs and the United States Constitution* 70 (Oxford, 2d ed 1996).

[101] See *Perez v Brownell*, 356 US 44, 59 (1958) (asserting that Congress had power "to deal with foreign relations").

[102] Michael D. Ramsey, *The Constitution's Text in Foreign Affairs* 208 (Harvard, 2007).

[103] Id.

B. THE SCOPE OF THE RECOGNITION POWER

The Court said that Congress could not force the executive to contradict its own policy. Given that Section 214(d) did not actually demand that the executive expressly repudiate its nonrecognition policy and did not even require that the executive issue a document with the wording "Jerusalem, Israel," the Court had a capacious understanding of "contradict." Apparently, forcing the executive to issue documents that, in the context of Section 214, imply that Jerusalem is in Israel is enough to conclude that Congress tried to force the executive to contradict existing policy. One is left to wonder what other sorts of legislative diktats regarding Jerusalem the courts will regard as forcing the executive to "contradict" existing policy.

A greater uncertainty lies in the scope of "the recognition power." Declaring its exclusivity did little to reveal its breadth. Beyond saying that territorial recognition is part of the "recognition power," the Court never specified what constitutes an exercise of recognition authority.

Suppose Congress dictates unequivocally that the U.S. Embassy to Israel be moved to Jerusalem immediately. Would that invade the President's exclusive authority? Maybe, insofar as it might imply that the United States thought that Jerusalem was part of Israel. Maybe not, because foreign embassies need not be located within the territory they are meant to serve. Neither the Vatican nor Lichtenstein has embassies within its borders.[104]

The Court also took pains to note that Congress had exclusive authority to make law, mentioning the Commerce Clause in particular. What does that suggest about congressional power? Can Congress pass a commercial statute for Tibet, when the President does not recognize the latter as a nation? If so, why wouldn't Congress be exercising the power to recognize given that Congress's Foreign Commerce Clause extends to commerce with "foreign *nations*"? Alternatively, can Congress regulate foreign commerce only with those nations that the President has already recognized?

---

[104] The OLC has previously opined that Congress lacks legislative authority to specify the siting of American diplomatic offices. See Memorandum Opinion for the Counsel to the President on Bill to Relocate United States Embassy from Tel Aviv to Jerusalem, 19 Op Off Legal Counsel 123 (1995). But given that recognition of Israel's claim to Jerusalem would not logically follow from moving the embassy to Jerusalem, *Zivotofsky* does not necessarily support the OLC's position.

With respect to Jerusalem, can Congress pass a commerce statute that declares that "because Jerusalem is part of Israel, goods from Jerusalem face the same tariff as goods from other parts of Israel"? If Congress cannot do that, may it instead declare that goods from Jerusalem should merely be treated "as if they were from Israel"? And if Congress can do the latter, can it declare that for purposes of all U.S. statutes, "Jerusalem shall be considered to be part of Israel"?

Because the "impact of a Supreme Court decision depends very much on the institution that interprets and applies it,"[105] count on Congress to continue to grasp for greater foreign affairs powers. Saying that Congress cannot recognize foreign nations, governments, or territorial claims leaves a world of foreign relations powers within reach. Relatedly, expect Congress to continue to press for recognition of Israel's claim. Rather than trying to compel the executive to recognize and thus running the risk that courts will hold that Congress sought to force the executive to contradict itself, Congress will attempt to drive toward recognition by relying wholly on powers clearly within its purview and by speaking itself. Commerce statutes may supply an obvious mechanism.

Expect the executive to give *Zivotofsky* a profoundly different spin. Count on executive branch lawyers, who generally have an "institutional predilection in favor of presidential power,"[106] to read the opinion in a way that maximizes executive authority and minimizes congressional sway. The executive will insist that Congress cannot use any of its enumerated powers in a manner that implies recognition because that is what Congress was doing in Section 214(d).[107] Moreover, these lawyers now have a Supreme Court citation for the proposition that the President has some exclusive authorities in foreign affairs, a citation that they will use in a bid to expand the universe of exclusive presidential authorities.

C. YOUNGSTOWN: THE "LOWEST EBB" IS HIGH ENOUGH

As in perhaps no other case since *Dames & Moore v Regan*,[108] Justice Robert Jackson's *Youngstown* concurrence seemed to be central

---

[105] Goldsmith, 129 Harv L Rev at 114 (cited in note 76).

[106] Id at 133.

[107] Id at 136–38.

[108] 453 US 654 (1981).

in *Zivotofsky*.[109] Jackson articulated a test that divided presidential actions into three categories. First were those cases where the President acted consistently with the express or implied will of Congress. In these cases presidential power was at its zenith because the President would prevail unless the federal government as a whole lacked authority to take the act. The second category consisted of situations where the President acted in the absence of any congressional grant (or denial) of authority. In the third category, where the President acted contrary to the express or implied will of Congress, the President could only prevail if he had exclusive authority over a subject such that Congress could not legislate. Here the President's power was at its "lowest ebb."[110]

Jackson's test is like a submarine, surfacing and submerging from time to time, but with no apparent pattern. Courts seldom cited it until *Dames & Moore*,[111] when Chief Justice Rehnquist simultaneously elevated it above Justice Hugo Black's more formalist majority opinion and sought to strip away some of its artificial rigidity.[112] Since then, the Court has cited Justice Jackson's approach more often, but not in any consistent way.[113] For instance, in *Hamdi v Rumsfeld*,[114] only one of the four opinions (Justice Thomas's) cited the three-part test.

The three-part structure has always been quite vacuous. It is something of a doctrinal Rorschach test, telling us more about those earnestly applying it than it does about anything else. There is the initial question of whether to apply it at all. Does it apply to all disputes about the reach of presidential power? Or only ones involving foreign affairs or military matters? It has never been clear. Justice Jackson's opinion addressed a mixed question involving foreign and domestic matters (the seizure of domestic steel plants in time of a war when hostilities were confined overseas). *Dames & Moore*

---

[109] See *Youngstown Sheet & Tube Co. v Sawyer*, 343 US 579, 634 (1952) (Jackson, J, concurring).

[110] Id at 637 (Jackson, J, concurring).

[111] See Thomas A. O'Donnell, *Illumination or Elimination of the "Zone of Twilight"? Congressional Acquiescence and Presidential Authority in Foreign Affairs*, 51 U Cinn L Rev 95, 99 (1982).

[112] Justice Rehnquist said that Jackson's test was more aptly understood not as three distinct categories but as a more fluid continuum. See *Dames & Moore*, 453 US at 668–69.

[113] See id; *Medellin v Texas*, 552 US 491 (2008); *Hamdan v Rumsfeld*, 548 US 557 (2006).

[114] 542 US 507, 583 (2004) (Thomas, J, dissenting).

likewise involved a mixed question of foreign and domestic subjects (the domestic effects of a sole executive agreement). And yet, as noted above, the *Hamdi* plurality opinion never cited Jackson's framework even though *Hamdi* was about the war on terror. In *Hamdan v Rumfeld*,[115] another war-on-terror case, a terse discussion was relegated to a footnote.[116] In *Noel Canning*,[117] a case involving appointments to a domestic agency, there was no discussion of category 3.

There is also the difficulty of discerning the most appropriate category, a process that sometimes seems a matter of discretion. If a judge can say that Congress has not spoken to the issue—a claim that is often easy to assert—she essentially has carte blanche to decide which category applies. And if one supposes that the categories actually matter, then categorization is quite consequential.

But do the categories matter? Not so much. In all three, one must consider what the executive may do by virtue of the Constitution and statutes. One also may have to ask what Congress may do using its constitutional powers. These are the sorts of formalist questions that Justice Hugo Black highlighted in his *Youngstown* majority opinion. While in some ways Justice Jackson's opinion is functionalist—particularly category 2 with its rejection of "abstract theories of law" in favor of "imperatives of events and contemporary imponderables"—the other two categories seem to require at least some formalist inquiry.[118]

In *Zivotofsky*, Justice Kennedy admitted that this was a category 3 case and that the President's power was at its "lowest ebb"; acknowledged that the President's claim must be "scrutinized with caution"; and observed that if the executive was to succeed, it would have to show that its constitutional power was "exclusive" and "conclusive."[119] Kennedy then proceeded to declare that the recognition power was solely vested in the President and that Congress could not direct the executive to contradict a prior nonrecognition decision.

At times, Chief Justice Roberts wrote as if he supposed that being in category 3 ought to have mattered to the particular case at hand.

---

[115] 548 US 557 (2006).

[116] Id at 593 n 23.

[117] *N.L.R.B. v Noel Canning*, 134 S Ct 2550 (2014).

[118] *Youngstown*, 343 US at 637 (Jackson, J, concurring).

[119] *Zivotofsky*, 135 S Ct at 2084 (quoting Jackson's concurrence in *Youngstown*, 343 US at 637–38).

Like some scholars,[120] the Chief Justice seemed to act as if the President ought to lose in category 3 cases. As support for this reading, Chief Justice Roberts said that Jackson had instructed that the category "leave[s] the Executive 'in the least favorable of possible constitutional postures'" and that such claims must be "'scrutinized with caution.'"[121] But the *Youngstown* categories do not resolve cases and these Jacksonian statements about category 3 cases do not mean the President ought to lose. While it may be true that as compared to category 1 situations, more cases in category 3 will get resolved against the President, that fact does not tell one how a particular case ought to be decided. Moreover, one might suppose that *all* constitutional claims made by litigants in constitutional cases ought to be examined cautiously, a stance that should have little bearing on the actual disposition. After all, if the "constitutional equilibrium" is at stake whenever Congress and the President clash, why should only the *President's* constitutional claims be examined with "caution"? Cannot "the impetuous vortex,"[122] more politely called the legislative branch, upset the supposed "equilibrium"? Indeed, has not the Court found instances in which Congress has unconstitutionally encroached upon the executive?

As noted earlier, *Zivotofsky* is the first foreign affairs case where the Supreme Court has held that the President can act contrary to the express will of Congress—an unmistakable acknowledgment that the President does not automatically lose in category 3 cases. "Equilibrium" sounds good; "caution" is always warranted. But sometimes Presidents prevail over Congress.

D. CURTISS-WRIGHT—FROM SOLE ORGAN TO A UNIQUE, AUTONOMOUS ONE

Relying upon *United States v Curtiss-Wright Export Corp.*,[123] a case involving the constitutionality of a foreign affairs delegation to the President, the government had argued that the President had the "exclusive authority to conduct diplomatic relations" and

---

[120] See Patricia L. Bellia, *The Story of the Steel Seizure Case*, in Christopher H. Schroeder and Curtis A. Bradley, eds, *Presidential Power Stories* 271 (Foundation, 2008) (discussing the congressional primacy view that the President should lose in category 3).

[121] *Zivotofsky*, 135 S Ct at 2113 (Roberts, CJ, dissenting).

[122] Federalist 48 (Madison), in *The Federalist* at 332, 333 (cited in note 81).

[123] 299 US 304 (1936).

enjoyed the "bulk of foreign-affairs powers."[124] *Curtiss-Wright* had spoken of the "very delicate, plenary and exclusive power of the President as the sole organ of the federal government in the field of international relations,"[125] language often relied upon by executive branch lawyers to bolster presidential power. The *Zivotofsky* majority responded that there was no need to address the government's broad claims.

Nonetheless, the Court attacked *Curtiss-Wright* and then, even more curiously, seemingly embraced it. Justice Kennedy criticized *Curtiss-Wright* for describing the President as having the exclusive "'power to speak or listen as a representative of the nation,'" noting that this "was not necessary" to its holding.[126] Later, however, Justice Kennedy wrote of the President's role in "conducting foreign relations," a characterization untethered to the particular provisions in Article II, Sections 2 and 3 and no different than the executive branch's claim that the President "conduct[s] diplomatic relations."[127] Moreover, Justice Kennedy admitted that "the President does have a unique role in communicating with foreign governments."[128] Many would read the latter statement as acknowledging that the President speaks for the nation in some way (or ways) that Congress cannot. Sole organ or not, the Presidency is at a minimum a "unique" communicative organ.

Finally, by characterizing the statute as a demand that the President contradict a previous position on Jerusalem, the Court might have been suggesting that Congress lacks the power to insist that the President say anything on foreign affairs. During oral argument, Justice Kagan thought it would be absurd to suppose that Congress could compel the President to convey to all foreign ministers an official letter announcing that an American was born in Israel whenever a U.S. citizen was born in Jerusalem.[129] If others shared her view, it seems possible that the Court thought that Congress could not

---

[124] Resp Br at *16, 18.

[125] *Curtiss-Wright*, 299 US at 320.

[126] *Zivotofsky*, 135 S Ct at 2089–90. Ironically, Kennedy's critique of *Curtiss-Wright* suffers from the same flaw, for it too "was not necessary" to *Zivotofsky's* holding.

[127] Id at 2095.

[128] Id at 2090.

[129] Oral Arg at *20.

command the executive to serve as the organ of legislative viewpoints or messages.

E. IMPLIED EXECUTIVE AUTHORITY

Zivotofsky marks yet another instance in which the Court has held that presidential powers go beyond those specifically enumerated in Article II. In previous cases, the Court has declared that the President has the powers to protect Supreme Court Justices, preserve public property, shield executive communications and papers, remove officers, and preempt state law.[130] After *Zivotofsky*, we must add recognition to this list.

The broader lesson is that the Court has exhibited an enduring inclination to understand presidential power in much broader terms than the narrowly couched grants of Article II, Section 2 might imply. To borrow from *McCulloch*, the Court has read Article II as if it only marked the presidency's "great outlines" and designated "its important objects," with the "minor ingredients" to "be deduced from the nature of the objects themselves."[131] What is sauce for the legislative goose is sauce for the executive gander. At times, the Court acts as if the presidency has its own Necessary and Proper Clause to draw upon.[132]

F. GLOSSING OVER THE GRANT OF "EXECUTIVE POWER"

And yet the Court's embrace of an implied recognition power was unnecessary. The Solicitor General had argued that the "executive power" and its "historical gloss" encompassed vast authority over foreign affairs.[133] The Court sidestepped the Article II Vesting Clause, preferring to rely upon structural implications and policy arguments. The majority neither relied upon some original sense of the Vesting

---

[130] *In re Neagle*, 135 US 1 (1890); *United States v Midwest Oil*, 236 US 459 (1915); *United States v Nixon*, 418 US 683 (1974); *Myers v United States*, 272 US 52 (1926); *American Insurance Association v Garamendi*, 539 US 396, 424 (2003).

[131] *McCulloch*, 17 US at 407.

[132] But see William Van Alstyne, *The Role of Congress in Determining Incidental Powers of the President and of the Federal Courts: A Comment on the Horizontal Effect of "The Sweeping Clause,"* 36 Ohio St L J 788 (1975) (denying that President has necessary and proper authority).

[133] Resp Br at *16–17 (citing the Article II Vesting Clause and *American Insurance*, 539 US 396).

Clause nor explicitly adverted to the gloss that history may have added to the clause over time.[134]

This dodge was scarcely inevitable. In *Myers v United States*, the Court argued that the Vesting Clause authorized the President to remove officers.[135] In *Free Enterprise Fund v Public Company Accounting Oversight Board*,[136] the Court led with the clause, quoting with approval James Madison's 1789 discussion of executive authority and removal.[137] Most tellingly, in *American Insurance Association v Garamendi*, the Court asserted that the President's "'vast share of responsibility for the conduct of foreign affairs'" arose from "the historical gloss on the 'executive Power' vested in Article II," thereby construing the Vesting Clause as ceding foreign affairs authorities.[138]

Perhaps anxiety drove *Zivotofsky*'s avoidance. In particular, if the Court had declared that recognition authority flows from the clause, would the lower courts discover other foreign affairs authorities under the executive power penumbra? Relatedly, the Court might have dreaded the potential mischief-making of lawyers within the executive branch. Long ago, Charles Thach cited the clause as a potential "joker,"[139] to be played as a wild card.

But as should be obvious, if there were any such fears they were overblown or misplaced. First, Justices Kennedy and Breyer were part of the *Garamendi* majority that expressly relied upon the Vesting Clause and yet had no difficulty sidestepping that clause in *Zivotofsky*. This fairly proves that had the *Zivotofsky* majority cited the clause its members would hardly have been bound to rely upon it in future cases involving foreign affairs. Second, *Zivotofsky* could have relied

---

[134] Jack Goldsmith has argued that the failure of the majority to rely upon the Vesting Clause is telling because it suggests that its members do not believe the clause grants authority. See Jack Goldsmith, *Zivotofsky II and the Vesting Clause Theory of Presidential Foreign Relations Power* (Lawfare, Sept 18, 2015), archived at https://www.lawfareblog.com/zivotofsky-ii -and-vesting-clause-theory-presidential-foreign-relations-power. I believe that Professor Goldsmith is perhaps reading too much into the failure to rely upon the clause. See paragraph accompanying notes 140–42.

[135] *Myers*, 272 US at 163–64.

[136] 561 US 477 (2010).

[137] Id at 492.

[138] *American Insurance Association v Garamendi*, 539 US 396, 414 (2003) (quoting Justice Frankfurter's concurrence in *Youngstown*, 343 US at 610–11). *Garamendi* involved whether executive agreement and policy preempted state laws relating to insurance disclosure.

[139] Charles C. Thach, Jr., *The Creation of the Presidency 1775–1789: A Study in Constitutional History* 138 (Johns Hopkins, 1922).

upon the Vesting Clause and yet been easily distinguished in the future. *Myers*, for example, was limited by *Humphrey's Executor v United States*,[140] *Wiener v United States*,[141] and *Morrison v Olson*.[142] Third, declaring that the clause grants foreign affairs powers has no necessary implications regarding whether such powers rest exclusively with the President. *Zivotofsky* was less about the scope of presidential power than it was about whether Congress enjoyed concurrent, superseding authority. Fourth, in refusing to decide whether the Vesting Clause was relevant, the Court left lower courts at liberty to rely upon it and to cite the Court's reasoning in *Garamendi*, reasoning that the Court has not undermined much less discarded. Finally, the failure to rely upon the Vesting Clause does little to constrain executive officials. They can still cite *Zivotofsky* (along with *Garamendi*) for the proposition that the executive has considerable authority over foreign affairs and they can still make hay of the Vesting Clause. In my view, *Zivotofsky* neither advances nor retards scholarly claims regarding the Vesting Clause.

Not all were unwilling to rely upon the Vesting Clause. At great length, Justice Thomas's opinion argued that the clause grants residual foreign affairs authorities to the President. Citing work by Michael Ramsey and myself,[143] Justice Thomas asserted that the Vesting Clause vested a host of executive powers over foreign affairs. He also maintained that the clause explains why Presidents have long issued passports despite the absence of any congressional authorization.

Justice Scalia pointedly said that Justice Thomas's embrace of "broad, unenumerated 'residual powers' in the President" countenanced an executive that resembled George III,[144] leading the latter to reply that Justice Scalia's opinion imagined that Congress enjoyed the total sovereignty of the eighteenth-century English Parliament. Justice Scalia's assertion is especially interesting because he previously had insisted that the Vesting Clause was a grant of "*all* of the

---

[140] 295 US 602 (1935).

[141] 357 US 349 (1958).

[142] 487 US 654 (1988).

[143] See Saikrishna B. Prakash and Michael D. Ramsey, *The Executive Power over Foreign Affairs*, 111 Yale L J 231 (2001). My views on the allocation of recognition authority have evolved since that article.

[144] *Zivotofsky*, 135 S Ct at 2126 (Scalia, J, dissenting).

executive power."[145] Some will find a tension between his previous stances and the vision he laid out in *Zivotofsky*. Others may see a latent ambiguity, one that mitigates or resolves the tension. Perhaps Justice Scalia was merely opposed to a *broad* reading of the clause and favored reading it as conveying a narrow set of foreign affairs authorities. After all, the Justice did not deny that the clause vested *some* foreign affairs authority. Moreover, he would have been well aware that Presidents have long exercised foreign affairs authorities not attributable to Article II's specific clauses and that early Presidents and statesmen cited the Vesting Clause as a source of such authorities.

However to best understand his criticisms of Justice Thomas, Justice Scalia seemed dedicated to the proposition that rather than having separated powers, the Constitution contemplates shared powers. As he put it, the American people "did not entrust either the President or Congress with sole power to adopt uncontradictable policies about *any* subject—foreign-sovereignty disputes included."[146] His approach was in sharp contrast to the Court's, one that utterly denied that Congress could contradict the President on recognition matters.

The clashing visions bring to mind the Pacificus and Helvidius debates. After George Washington's Neutrality Proclamation suffered criticism on the grounds that it was illegal, Alexander Hamilton came to its defense as "Pacificus." Hamilton insisted that Congress *and* the President could speak to neutrality in the course of their respective functions.[147] James Madison, writing as "Helvidius," argued that the power to declare neutrality could not be held concurrently, lest chaos and confusion ensue, and that the power rested with Congress alone.[148] Some two centuries later, something of the same

---

[145] See *Morrison*, 487 US at 705 (emphasis in original). See also Antonin Scalia, *Originalism: The Lesser Evil*, 57 U Cinn L Rev 849, 860 (1989) (arguing that one "could reasonably infer" that grant of executive power to the President includes Crown's prerogatives save for those that are patently incompatible with republican principles); Antonin Scalia, Authority of the President to Enter into Executive Agreements in Congressional Oversight of Executive Agreements—1975, Hearings before the Subcommittee on Separation of Powers of the Committee on the Judiciary, 94th Cong, 1st Sess 302, 303 (1975) (saying that President has foreign affairs powers by virtue of "executive power" and noting "[a]uthorities since Alexander Hamilton have found within this the power to conduct foreign relations.").

[146] *Zivotofsky*, 135 S Ct at 2126 (Scalia, J, dissenting) (emphasis in original).

[147] *Pacificus No. 1*, in *The Pacificus-Helvidius Debates* at 8, 13 (cited in note 81).

[148] *Helvidius No. 2*, in id at 65, 69.

argument played out with Scalia as Pacificus and Kennedy as Helvidius.

G. THE PRESIDENT AS CONSTITUTIONAL INTERPRETER

Three modern fault lines regarding presidential power relate to signing statements, refusing to enforce statutes that are, in the executive's opinion, unconstitutional, and declining to defend the constitutionality of statutes. *Zivotofsky* might be read as implicitly endorsing presidential power in each instance.

First, the vocal concerns about signing statements now seem a distant memory. During the George W. Bush Administration, an American Bar Association ("ABA") Task Force Report denounced the tradition of signing bills into law that contain, under the President's view, unconstitutional provisions, saying that the practice was redolent of Charles II. The commission was quite critical of President Bush and the practice, which predated him.[149] Though *Zivotofsky* cited the executive's signing statement, it was silent about the practice and about President Bush's far-fetched reading of Section 214(d). The failure to address the practice in a context of a particularly implausible executive branch reading perhaps hints that signing statements do not trouble the Justices.[150]

Second, *Zivotofsky* advances the idea that the President can be an independent force in constitutional interpretation and disregard federal statutes that he regards as unconstitutional.[151] After all, the executive flouted Section 214(d), a stance that provoked no dismay from the majority. To be sure, *Zivotofsky* concerned the President's

---

[149] American Bar Association, *Task Force on Presidential Signing Statements and the Separation of Powers Doctrine, Recommendation and Report* (2006), available at http://www.americanbar .org/content/dam/aba/publishing/abanews/1273179616signstatereport.authcheckdam.pdf.

[150] During oral argument, Chief Justice Roberts seemed troubled by the fact that one executive had signed Section 214(d) into law and another was arguing that it was unconstitutional. Yet even he omitted any reference to the signing statement or its dubious reading of Section 214(d). In previous work, I have argued that the executive's duty to defend the Constitution obliges the President to veto bills that contain provisions the President regards as unconstitutional. See Saikrishna Prakash, *Why the President Must Veto Unconstitutional Bills*, 16 Wm & Mary Bill Rts J 81 (2007).

[151] For a defense of the claim that the Constitution *requires* the President to ignore unconstitutional statutes, see Saikrishna Bangalore Prakash, *The Executive's Duty to Disregard Unconstitutional Laws*, 96 Georgetown L J 1613 (2008). For a more qualified view, one that argues that the executive has some flexibility, see Presidential Authority to Decline to Execute Unconstitutional Statutes, 18 Op Off Legal Counsel 199 (1994) (memorandum from Assistant Attorney General Walter Dellinger).

disregarding a statutory directive that supposedly infringed executive authority and not a situation where the refusal to enforce was meant to vindicate the constitutional rights of private citizens. Still, the more often Presidents ignore unconstitutional statutes the more presidential review becomes an accepted feature of modern separation of powers.

Third, with respect to the executive's supposed duty to defend the constitutionality of federal statutes, *Zivotofsky*'s silence intimates that there is no ironclad duty. In *United States v Windsor*, Justice Kennedy's opinion for the Court expressed misgivings about the executive's refusal to defend a congressional statute.[152] Yet in *Zivotofsky*, Justice Kennedy's majority opinion was mute about the failure to defend Section 214(d). Conceivably Section 214(d)'s regulation of the executive justified the failure to defend. Or maybe the Court thought it would be odd to stay mum about the failure to honor Section 214(d) but simultaneously declare that the President should ordinarily defend the constitutionality of federal statutes. Whatever the case may be, some will read the Court as evincing greater acceptance of failures to defend.

Because many members of the current Court once served in the executive,[153] it seems quite likely that at least some of them have grown at least somewhat accustomed to the ideas that the President can sign bills into law even if he believes them unconstitutional and that the President can refuse to enforce and defend statutes when he believes them unconstitutional. While Justice Robert Jackson was confident enough to repudiate an opinion he had authored as Attorney General,[154] many people, academics included, find it hard to abandon views previously expressed and perspectives previously held.

IV. Conclusion

There is a prevailing fear of an imperial executive, a sense that modern Presidents have flouted the rule of law, usurped constitu-

---

[152] See *United States v Windsor*, 133 S Ct 2675, 2688–89 (2013).

[153] By my count, six of the *Zivotofsky* Justices served in the executive branch prior to being appointed to the Supreme Court. See Biographies of Current Justices of the Supreme Court at http://www.supremecourt.gov/about/biographies.aspx (recounting that Chief Justice Roberts and Justices Thomas, Breyer, Alito, and Kagan all worked in the executive). Justice Scalia had previously served as the head of the Office of Legal Counsel in the Department of Justice.

[154] *Youngstown*, 343 US at 647.

tional powers belonging to Congress, and ignored or twisted statutes. The anxiety goes back at least as far as Richard Nixon, with Arthur Schlesinger's *The Imperial Presidency* being one of the most prominent expressions of it.[155] There is, of course, an older tradition, one familiar to readers of the Federalist Papers.

> Its constitutional powers being at once more extensive, and less susceptible of precise limits, [the legislative branch] can, with the greater facility, mask, under complicated and indirect measures, the encroachments which it makes on the co-ordinate departments. It is not unfrequently a question of real nicety in legislative bodies, whether the operation of a particular measure will, or will not, extend beyond the legislative sphere.[156]

The Supreme Court's majority viewed this case in Madisonian, rather than Schlesingerian, terms. Though Congress had tried to "mask" its encroachment,[157] most of the Court saw through the camouflaging and refused to enforce the statute, thereby vindicating executive power.

---

[155] Arthur M. Schlesinger, Jr., *The Imperial Presidency* (Houghton Mifflin, 1973).

[156] Federalist 48 (Madison), in *The Federalist* at 332, 334 (cited in note 81).

[157] Id.

CASS R. SUNSTEIN AND
ADRIAN VERMEULE

THE NEW COKE: ON THE PLURAL AIMS
OF ADMINISTRATIVE LAW

In the early twenty-first century, public law is being challenged by a fundamental assault on the legitimacy of the administrative state, under the banner of "the separation of powers." Mainly found in academia, but with some support on the bench, the challengers frequently refer to the specter of Stuart despotism, and they valorize a (putatively) heroic opponent of Stuart despotism: the common-law judge, symbolized by Edward Coke. As we understand it here, the New Coke is a shorthand for a cluster of impulses stemming from a belief in the illegitimacy of the modern administrative state. The New Coke sometimes takes relatively modest forms, which would merely push existing doctrine in directions consistent with those impulses. But it occasionally takes far more aggressive forms, which would invoke heavy constitutional artillery either to invalidate existing practices or to transform them in light of what its advocates see as background principles for statutory interpretation.

Despite its historical guise, the New Coke is a living-constitutionalist movement, a product of thoroughly contemporary values and fears—clearly prompted by continuing rejection, in some quarters, of the

Cass R. Sunstein is Robert Walmsley University Professor, Harvard University. Adrian Vermeule is John H. Watson Professor of Law, Harvard Law School.

Authors' note: We are grateful to John Manning and David Strauss for valuable comments and to Maile Yeats-Rowe and Vishal Iyer for superb research assistance.

New Deal itself, and perhaps prompted by a reaction, on the part of some of its advocates, to controversial initiatives from more recent presidents. In two important decisions in 2015, however, a supermajority of the Court refused to embrace the New Coke, and properly so. Instead, the Court issued the long-awaited *Vermont Yankee II*, insisting that courts are not authorized to add procedures to those required by the Administrative Procedure Act (APA), and implicitly reaffirmed the validity of *Auer* deference[1] to agency interpretations of their own regulations. The Court's approach promises to honor the multiple goals of administrative and constitutional law without embracing novel, ungrounded claims that betray basic commitments of the public legal order. For now, the center holds.

The New Coke is best seen as analogous to other periods in American public law, in which a form of "normal science" has been opposed by a vigorous movement, both academic and political, from an identifiable ideological direction. Intellectual insurgencies are not hard to find. In the first third of the twentieth century, for example, Supreme Court scrutiny of economic legislation ran into severe objections from Justices Oliver Wendell Holmes and Louis Brandeis, who spoke on behalf of judicial restraint, endorsed at the time by many progressive commentators. In the middle of the twentieth century, the Court's occasionally cautious approach to civil liberties and civil rights was vigorously challenged by Justices William O. Douglas and Hugo Black, who generally argued for a more aggressive posture than the Court's majority was willing to support. In the 1970s and 1980s, Justices William Brennan and Thurgood Marshall—accompanied by a chorus of academic theorists—made similar arguments on behalf of a large-scale overhaul of constitutional law.

In the early twenty-first century, a fundamental assault on the legitimacy of the administrative state, under the banner of "the separation of powers," is playing a growing role in separate opinions. On occasion, it finds its way into majority opinions as well. Justice Clarence Thomas is the principal advocate, and his views are quite extreme, even eccentric; on the Court, he speaks only for himself. But on some prominent occasions, Justices Antonin Scalia and Samuel Alito, along with Chief Justice John Roberts, have also shown significant concern about what they see as the constitutionally ques-

---

[1] *Auer v Robbins*, 519 US 452, 461 (1997).

tionable discretionary authority wielded by contemporary administrative agencies. Those who express this concern sometimes appeal to putative principles of the Anglo-American constitutional order, particularly resistance to executive "prerogative"—the lawless despotism of the Stuart kings. We have said that the heroic opponent of Stuart despotism is the common-law judge, symbolized by Edward Coke. Where there are newly enthroned Stuarts, there must also be a New Coke.[2]

Our aims in this essay do not involve English constitutional history. We pay little attention to whether the lurid account of that history, implicit in the New Coke, is actually true—although we are skeptical.[3] Instead, our aims are to illuminate both the specific legal commitments and the broader constitutional theory of the New Coke, and to bring them in contact with what we see as a more sober view of American public law, above all as reflected in the Administrative Procedure Act and the Constitution.

We will undertake several tasks. One is to describe the growing presence of the New Coke in the Supreme Court, especially in the opinions of Justices Thomas and Scalia, and to a lesser extent in those of Justice Alito and the Chief Justice. On some occasions, these Justices have argued, in various ways and to different degrees, for constraining executive discretion, on the basis of grand theoretical commitments to the separation of powers, strongly rooted in a New Coke sensibility. Prominent targets include the idea that courts should defer to agency interpretations of ambiguous regulations and also of ambiguous statutes.

Another task is to show that despite this apparently growing presence, the New Coke has not yet had any significant victories; so far, the center holds. Most of the Justices, including most importantly Justice Kennedy, seem to find that the New Coke is not at all to their taste, and on prominent occasions even Justices Scalia and Alito, along with Chief Justice Roberts, have pointedly refused to embrace its more extreme forms. Finally, we will explain why the New Coke is

---

[2] For those who know that in Commonwealth countries, Coke (the judge) is often pronounced "Cook": imagine a counterfactual paper structured around a different image, that of the new cook who serves inedible dishes.

[3] See, for example, Adam Tomkins, *Our Republican Constitution* 5–88 (Hart, 2005) (detailing the conflicts between the Stuarts and the common-law judges before the English Civil War, and explaining that the common-law judges largely *supported* the monarch's legal claims).

legally unjustified, with special attention to the questions of delegation and administrative procedure at issue in the Court's 2015 rulings
in *American Railroads*[4] and *Perez*.[5]

One of our central claims is that the New Coke, like most previous
attacks on "normal science," is largely a product of very contemporary values and fears. Notwithstanding its claimed historical pedigree, its use by judges and Justices is methodologically of a piece with
such presentist decisions as *Roe v Wade*,[6] *Obergefell v Hodges*,[7] and
(arguably) *District of Columbia v Heller*.[8] In these decisions—whether
or not written in nominally originalist terms—such values and fears
also played a central role.[9]

At bottom, the New Coke rests on the overriding fear that the
executive will abuse its power.[10] That fear was, of course, entirely
familiar to those who designed the US Constitution. But the US
constitutional order in general, and administrative law in particular,
attend to other goals and risks as well, and do not take prevention of
executive abuses as the overriding goal or master principle. Such
abuses are not to be strictly minimized, either as a matter of original understanding or optimal institutional design. Instead, public law
in effect trades off the risks of executive abuse against other goals
and commitments. These include democratic participation and accountability, which will sometimes lead to a stronger executive; efficiency in government, which can lead in the same direction; rational and coordinated policymaking; and (the primary Hamiltonian
theme) the promotion of overall welfare, often by means of executive
action from public officials, who sometimes display constitutionally
legitimate "energy."[11]

---

[4] *Department of Transportation v Association of American Railroads*, 135 S Ct 1225 (2015).

[5] *Perez v Mortgage Bankers Association*, 135 S Ct 1199 (2015).

[6] 410 US 113 (1973).

[7] 135 S Ct 2584 (2015).

[8] 554 US 570 (2008). We acknowledge that there are plausible arguments for *Heller* that do
not rest on contemporary values.

[9] We do not mean, of course, to take a stand on whether one, two, or all of those decisions
might ultimately be justified.

[10] For a vigorous statement, see Charles Murray, *By the People: Rebuilding Liberty without
Permission* (Crown Forum, 2015) (calling for widespread civil disobedience to counteract
agency abuse).

[11] See Federalist 70 (Hamilton) in Jacob E. Cooke, ed, *The Federalist* 471, 471–76 (Wesleyan, 1982).

In the service of these multiple goals, the Constitution and the administrative state attempt to channel and constrain rather than eliminate or minimize executive discretion.[12] The New Coke is inherently limited and one-sided, a reflection of a subset of the relevant concerns,[13] and for that reason it offers an irremediably partial (and sometimes downright odd) account of both administrative and constitutional law. It is true, of course, that broad propositions about plural aims cannot dispose of concrete questions, such as the appropriate degree of deference to be given to agency interpretations of agency regulations. But an understanding of plural aims can, we think, dispel central assumptions of the New Coke that treat executive discretion as a kind of large-scale departure from the constitutional plan, or that see heightened judicial scrutiny as a cure for what ails us.

Part I gives background on the New Coke, both inside and outside the courts, and illustrates its influence on a number of opinions in *American Railroads* and *Perez*. Part II documents our claim that the center holds, with reference to the nondelegation doctrine, rulemaking procedure, and *Auer* deference to agencies' interpretation of their own regulations. Most important for doctrinal purposes, we show that *Perez* is the long-awaited *Vermont Yankee II* and should be celebrated as such. Part III examines the myopic, one-sided commitments of the New Coke and offers a general assessment. A brief conclusion follows.

I. Background

We begin with some brief and deliberately selective background on the New Coke, both without and within the courts, and then describe its flowering in *American Railroads*[14] and *Perez*.[15]

---

[12] See generally Adrian Vermeule, *Optimal Abuse of Power*, 109 Nw U L Rev 673 (2015). See also Adrian Vermeule, *The Constitution of Risk* 58–72 (Cambridge, 2013).

[13] By making this point, we do not suggest that the relevant fears initially appeared in (say) 2015, or 2009, or 2001; they have been with us from the beginning of the American republic. But we believe that their current influence, within the legal culture and the courts, is very much a product of a particular historical moment.

[14] *Department of Transportation v Association of American Railroads*, 135 S Ct 1225 (2015).

[15] *Perez v Mortgage Bankers Association*, 135 S Ct 1199 (2015).

A. OUTSIDE THE COURTS

Outside the courts, academics have been formulating the recipe for the New Coke for well over a decade. In the George W. Bush administration, civil libertarians of both left and right—but especially left—invoked the rhetoric of tyranny with respect to Guantánamo Bay and the Patriot Act, calling the president "George III" or otherwise citing the risk or reality of large-scale overreaching.[16] Roughly simultaneously, but with a marked acceleration once the Obama administration came into office, a broad and ill-defined movement in libertarian and conservative legal scholarship offered a wholesale critique of modern exercises of executive power. Leaders of the movement, devoted to restoring the "Lost Constitution"[17] or the "Constitution-in-Exile,"[18] began to suggest that the administrative state or the presidency, or the "Executive" loosely defined, threatened to accumulate tyrannous strength and to threaten the very rule of law itself.

The Constitution-in-Exile Movement, as it has been rightly called, draws attention to a supposedly lost set of constitutional commitments and asks the courts to return them to their rightful place. Books appeared with titles like *The Once and Future King: The Rise of Crown Government in America*[19] and *Is Administrative Law Unlawful?*,[20] both of which argued explicitly that the administrative state re-created a type of Stuart prerogative, albeit in a light disguise. There is an unmistakable overlap between the rise of the Tea Party, focused in part on executive power, and the rise of the New Coke (a point that supports, though it certainly does not prove, our claim that that rise is a product of twenty-first-century concerns rather than eighteenth-century ones).

At the same time, the conservative legal movement showed definite fault lines, which could also be found across parties and ideo-

---

[16] See, for example, Geoffrey R. Stone, *King George's Constitution*, U Chi L Sch Fac Blog (U Chi L Sch, Dec 20, 2005), online at http://uchicagolaw.typepad.com/faculty/2005/12/king_georges_co.html.

[17] See generally, for example, Randy E. Barnett, *Restoring the Lost Constitution: The Presumption of Liberty* (Princeton, 2013).

[18] See, for example, Douglas H. Ginsburg, book review, *Delegation Running Riot*, 1995 Reg 83–84 (1995).

[19] F. H. Buckley, *The Once and Future King: The Rise of Crown Government in America* (Encounter, 2015).

[20] Philip Hamburger, *Is Administrative Law Unlawful?* (U Chicago, 2014).

logical commitments. While some conservatives expressed anxiety about presidential power—especially under President Obama—others expressed anxiety about the swelling power of the administrative bureaucracy, seen as insufficiently accountable to anyone, including the president. Some expressed anxiety about both. As *Free Enterprise Fund*[21] had underscored, however, those two anxieties sometimes stood in mutual tension. The Chief Justice's essay in praise of the unitary executive, under which the president has a constitutional entitlement to remove all executive officers at will, emphasized the need for the president to have broad power to control the bureaucracy. The strong presidency is, in American constitutional law, perhaps the main check on the bureaucracy;[22] the Headless Fourth Branch flourishes where presidential control ends. More broadly, as Justice Scalia and the Chief Justice illustrate, the broadly conservative legal movement contains both libertarians and government-lawyer types; the latter are, chronically, far more cautious and hence somewhat ambivalent about the New Coke and its suspicion of executive power.

B. INSIDE THE COURTS

1. *Tensions over executive power.* With respect to questions of executive power, the Roberts Court has been fraught with tensions and conflicts. The record of that Court includes both unprecedented decisions rejecting claims of executive power, such as *Boumediene v Bush*[23] and *Medellin v Texas*,[24] and an unprecedented decision affirming the paramount constitutional claims of executive power, even in the face of clear contrary legislation, in *Zivotofsky v Clinton*.[25]

Indeed, the tensions even appear to lie within some of the Justices themselves. Just as "the line dividing good from evil runs through the heart of every human being,"[26] so too with executive power; a number of the Justices have issued opinions that seem to be in tension with other opinions by the same Justice, or perhaps even internally con-

---

[21] *Free Enterprise Fund v Public Co. Accounting Oversight Board*, 561 US 477 (2010).

[22] See, for example, Max Weber, *The Reich President*, 53 Social Research 125, 128–32 (1986) (Gordon Wells, trans).

[23] 553 US 723 (2008).

[24] 552 US 491 (2008).

[25] 132 S Ct 1421 (2012).

[26] Aleksandr I. Solzhenitsyn, 1 *The Gulag Archipelago* 131 (Basic, 1997).

flicted. The most obvious cases are the Chief Justice and Justice Scalia, both of whom served in the executive branch before ascending to the bench. As to Justice Scalia, a Martian observer would never guess that the same Justice had written both a remarkably broad affirmation of agencies' authority to determine the limits of their own jurisdiction, in *City of Arlington v FCC*,[27] and also impassioned separate opinions that criticize judicial deference to agency interpretations of their own regulations, on the ground that such deference makes agencies judges in their own cause.[28] As to the Chief Justice, the observer would be hard pressed to guess that the same Justice had authored both the remarkable essay in praise of the Unitary Executive, in *Free Enterprise Fund*,[29] resting on the virtues of political accountability through the executive, and also attempted to limit the scope of deference to agencies[30]—deference often justified by reference to political accountability.[31] These positions may be reconcilable,[32] but they do seem animated by quite different concerns.

2. *Development of the New Coke.* Amid the swirl of precedent, however, a consistent trend has been the growth of New Coke rhetoric.[33] A place to start, clearly linked to the emergence of the New Coke, is the Second Amendment. In *District of Columbia v Heller*,[34] the majority—in an opinion written by Justice Scalia—grounded an individual right to keep and bear arms for purpose of self-defense in a larger rationale: prevention of executive tyr-

---

[27] *City of Arlington, Texas v Federal Communications Commission*, 133 S Ct 1863 (2013) (Scalia, J).

[28] See, for example, *Talk America, Inc. v Michigan Bell Telephone Co.*, 131 S Ct 2254, 2265 (2011) (Scalia, J, concurring); *Decker v Northwest Environmental Defense Center*, 133 S Ct 1326, 1338–39 (2013) (Scalia, J, concurring in part and dissenting in part).

[29] 561 US at 494–95 (Roberts, CJ).

[30] See, for example, *City of Arlington*, 133 S Ct at 1877 (Roberts, CJ, dissenting); *Decker*, 133 S Ct at 1339 (Roberts, CJ, concurring) (expressing willingness to reconsider *Auer*).

[31] See *Chevron, USA, Inc. v Natural Resources Defense Council, Inc.*, 467 US 837, 865–66 (1984).

[32] It might, for example, be possible to say that the Take Care Clause supports the Chief Justice's position in *Free Enterprise Fund*, and that Article III supports his position in *Decker*.

[33] Very much including rhetoric that explicitly valorizes Coke himself. See, for example, *Perez*, 135 S Ct at 1220 (Thomas, J, concurring in the judgment); *American Railroads*, 135 S Ct at 1243 (2015) (Thomas, J, concurring in the judgment). Ironically enough, the earliest formulation of judicial deference to executive interpretation comes from the same judge. "[I]n a doubtful thing, interpretation goes always for the king." Sir Edward Coke, House of Commons, July 6, 1628. Tomkins, *Our Republican Constitution* at 70–71, 74 (cited in note 3).

[34] 554 US 570 (Scalia, J).

anny. The specter of the Stuarts was explicitly invoked.[35] In the majority's words, "[i]f . . . the Second Amendment right is no more than the right to keep and use weapons as a member of an organized militia . . . it does not assure the existence of a 'citizens' militia' as a safeguard against tyranny. . . . It guarantees a select militia of the sort the Stuart kings found useful, but not the people's militia that was the concern of the founding generation."[36] Yet the context of *Heller*, however attention grabbing it may be, was somewhat unusual and indeed limited. The case involved a particular right—the individual right to bear arms—and that very right was, according to *Heller* itself, subject to "reasonable" restrictions;[37] lower courts, by and large, have declined to expand the right to the limits of its logic.

An even larger question, hovering in the background, was whether tyranny prevention would be invoked in the setting of legal limitations on the administrative state. Justice Scalia was also a pioneer in that setting. In a widely discussed concurrence in *Decker*, in which he declared that he would no longer afford agencies so-called *Auer* deference[38] on the interpretation of their own regulations, Scalia argued from the risk of tyranny. For an agency to "resolve ambiguities in its own regulations" would, he wrote,

> violate a fundamental principle of separation of powers—that the power to write a law and the power to interpret it cannot rest in the same hands. "When the legislative and executive powers are united in the same person . . . there can be no liberty; because apprehensions may arise, lest the same monarch or senate should enact tyrannical laws, to execute them in a tyrannical manner." Montesquieu, Spirit of the Laws . . . . *Auer* is . . . a dangerous permission slip for the arrogation of power.[39]

As we will see, the perceived risk of tyranny or of executive abuse—a hallmark of the New Coke—becomes even more prominent in *American Railroads* and *Perez*. For Scalia, it will spill over from a concern about *Auer* deference to an even more consequential concern about *Chevron* deference itself; for Thomas, it will support a broader indictment of the whole administrative state.

---

[35] Id at 592 (Scalia, J).

[36] Id at 600 (Scalia, J).

[37] Id at 622 (Scalia, J).

[38] *Auer v Robbins*, 519 US 452, 461 (1997) (Scalia, J).

[39] *Decker*, 133 S Ct at 1341 (Scalia, J, dissenting).

Meanwhile, judges in the lower courts were contributing to the New Coke, albeit not in ways that the Supreme Court—or at least a clear majority of it—approved. A group of judges on the Court of Appeals for the District of Columbia Circuit were advancing a distinctive brand of libertarian administrative law,[40] often rooted in New Coke-style concerns about unchecked delegation and executive aggrandizement at the expense of common-law baselines.[41] Libertarian administrative law resulted in a number of doctrinal innovations within that circuit—including both the extraordinary invalidation on nondelegation grounds that gave rise to *American Railroads*, and the creation of a novel common-law restriction on agency rule-making that gave rise to *Perez*. But the Circuit's entrepreneurial libertarianism fared poorly in the Supreme Court. *Perez* emphatically repudiated the Circuit's common-law procedural innovation, while *American Railroads* vacated the Circuit's decision and returned it for another round of proceedings. As we will suggest, *American Railroads* and *Perez*, taken both separately and together, should be seen as a major rebuke to the DC Circuit and a severe blow to both libertarian administrative law and the New Coke.

C. AMERICAN RAILROADS AND PEREZ

The two cases we will examine in detail were granted around the same time and decided on the same day. It was not hard to see a common message in the pairing. In both cases, adventurism by the DC Circuit was overturned, in one case for good, in the other provisionally. In both, Justice Thomas wrote separately to state views that are pure distillations of the New Coke. And in both, although individual Justices expressed more diluted versions of the New Coke, the Court as a whole showed no enthusiasm for what Thomas was offering.

1. *American Railroads.* At issue in *American Railroads* was the Passenger Rail Investment and Improvement Act, enacted in 2008. The statute's basic aim was to improve Amtrak's performance, in part by helping Amtrak enforce a statutory preference, granted elsewhere in federal law, over freight traffic in the use of shared track and fa-

---

[40] See Cass R. Sunstein and Adrian Vermeule, *Libertarian Administrative Law*, 82 U Chi L Rev 393, 400 (2015).

[41] See id at 415.

cilities. In broad outline, the statute gives Amtrak and the Federal
Railway Administration joint authority to set metrics and standards
that will be incorporated in Amtrak's contracts with freight carriers
and that will be used to assess compliance. The Surface Transportation Board is charged with investigatory and enforcement duties.

The Association of American Railroads challenged the statute on a
number of grounds, including the claim that Amtrak was a private
party and that the statute effected an invalid delegation to a private
party—a claim that the Supreme Court had accepted as an alternative
holding as to the National Industrial Recovery Act in *ALA Schechter
Poultry Corp. v United States*[42] in 1935, but had roundly rejected in a
half dozen subsequent cases.[43] In a flagship decision for libertarian
administrative law, a panel of the DC Circuit declared the statute
invalid on nondelegation grounds, in an opinion written by Judge
Janice Rogers Brown.[44]

In a narrow resolution, the Supreme Court vacated the decision
below and remanded. The Court held that Amtrak was not a private
entity in the first place, at least for purposes of the separation of
powers.[45] For that reason, Justice Kennedy's opinion effectively
rejected the nondelegation holding of the lower court, though it left
other constitutional issues undecided, including a different nondelegation question. More ambitious were two opinions by Justices
clearly skeptical of the statute's constitutionality, Justices Alito and
Thomas. Justice Alito wrote the equivalent of a draft brief for the
challengers, explaining how they might attack the statute on Appointments Clause grounds.[46] Justice Thomas's remarkable concurrence in the judgment, however, is the more important for present
purposes, as it is a principal example of the influence of the New
Coke.[47]

---

[42] 295 US 495, 537 (1935).

[43] See, for example, *Sunshine Anthracite Coal Co. v Adkins*, 310 US 381, 392 (1940); *United States v Rock Royal Co-op, Inc.*, 307 US 533, 574 (1939).

[44] *Association of American Railroads v United States Department of Transportation*, 721 F3d 666, 670 (DC Cir 2013), vac'd and rem'd by *Department of Transportation v Association of American Railroads*, 135 S Ct 1225, 1234 (2015).

[45] *American Railroads*, 135 S Ct at 1233.

[46] Id at 1237–38 (Alito, J, concurring).

[47] See id at 1252 (Thomas, J, concurring in the judgment).

Thomas more or less adopted wholesale the view, laid out in an academic book, that the "executive power" could not include the power to make rules that are binding on private parties, even under an express statutory grant of power to engage in such rulemaking, and even if the grant of authority supplied a perfectly "intelligible principle." (This rationale, of course, has nothing to do with private entities; Thomas was offering a framework for the case on remand, in which it would be law of the case that Amtrak is a public body for nondelegation purposes.) The underlying book, Philip Hamburger's *Is Administrative Law Unlawful?*, as we have seen, explicitly called for a return to a (quite possibly imaginary) Anglo-American common-law order, cast as an alternative to Stuart tyranny founded on monarchical prerogative.

Thomas followed suit, rooting his understanding of the non-delegation doctrine in principles announced by Coke in his conflict with James I. For Congress to give *any* executive entity the power to make rules binding on private parties, no matter how intelligible the principle, would abolish individual liberty in the United States.[48] "At the heart of [the Framers' conception of] liberty were the Lockean private rights: life, liberty, and property. If a person could be deprived of these private rights on the basis of a rule (or a will) not enacted by the legislature, then he was not truly free."[49]

  2. *Perez. Perez* too arose out of an exercise in libertarian administrative law on the part of the DC Circuit. Here the experiment had a longer pedigree. Since 1997, in a panel decision known as *Paralyzed Veterans*,[50] the Circuit had imposed upon agencies a requirement unknown to Supreme Court caselaw: where an agency issued an interpretive rule that represented its "definitive position," the agency could not change that position by means of a subsequent interpretive rule, but would have to proceed through notice-and-comment rulemaking. Almost twenty years later, the administration finally took the validity of the *Paralyzed Veterans* doctrine to the Supreme Court.

In a brusque and analytically crushing rebuke, the Court ruled—unanimously on this point—that the DC Circuit's doctrine was im-

---

[48] See id at 1252–55 (Thomas, J, concurring in the judgment).

[49] Id at 1245 (Thomas, J, concurring in the judgment).

[50] *Paralyzed Veterans of America v DC Arena LP*, 117 F3d 579 (DC Cir 1997), abrogated by *Perez v Mortgage Bankers Association*, 135 S Ct 1199 (2015).

possible to square with the Administrative Procedure Act.[51] The act makes it quite clear that the process for revoking or modifying an interpretive rule is the same as the process for creating it in the first place. Although the DC Circuit had attempted to ground the *Paralyzed Veterans* doctrine in the reliance interests of regulated parties, the Court observed that such interests could, under existing law, be taken into account through arbitrary and capricious review of the agency's justifications for changing its interpretive rule; no further procedural barrier to such changes was either necessary or permissible.[52]

Although the Court was unanimous on that point—the only one on which review had been granted—several Justices with affinities for the New Coke took the opportunity to write separate opinions, mini-addresses on the state of the administrative state, especially on the issue of judicial deference to agency interpretations. Their concerns included both agency interpretations of their own regulations (*Auer*) and agency interpretations of the underlying organic statutes (*Chevron*). Because the relevant questions were not before the Court, this was an unusual and gratuitous step, attesting to the intensity of the underlying concerns.

Justice Thomas wrote a long concurrence in the judgment that was heavily reminiscent of his separate opinion in *American Railroads*. This one, like that one, prominently featured Hamburger's work, and offered an account of the conflict between James I and Edward Coke.[53] His point was that judges have a constitutional duty to interpret the law de novo, without deference to executive interpretations, so that *Auer* deference is unconstitutional. The logic, of course, impeaches *Chevron* as well, although Thomas did not mention that explicitly.[54] (He did so later in the Term, attacking *Chevron* on constitutional grounds.[55]) Justice Scalia also wrote against *Auer* deference,[56] as he had in the past, but went beyond his past statements by

---

[51] *Perez*, 135 S Ct at 1203–06.

[52] Id.

[53] Id at 1220 (Thomas, J, concurring in the judgment).

[54] But see id at 1217 (Thomas, J, concurring in the judgment) (implying that judges must exercise "independent judgment" even in ordinary cases in which agencies interpret their enabling statutes).

[55] See *Michigan v Environmental Protection Agency*, 135 S Ct 2699, 2712 (2015) (Thomas, J, concurring).

[56] *Perez*, 135 S Ct at 1211–13 (Scalia, J, concurring in the judgment).

expressing ambivalence about *Chevron*—this despite his ringing defense, two Terms before, of judicial deference even to agencies' decisions about the scope of their own jurisdiction. Justice Alito, in a separate opinion, called for reconsideration of *Auer* by the whole Court.[57]

Notably, however, neither the Chief Justice—who had in the past indicated willingness to reconsider *Auer*[58]—nor Justice Kennedy joined any of these separate writings. So far, there is no evidence at all that the Justices opposed to *Auer* can assemble five votes. The center seems to be holding, on this question and on many others. Let us explain this claim in more detail.

II. The Center Holds—For Now

We begin with the law. Despite the salience of the New Coke concurrences and dissents in the two cases, by Justices Scalia, Thomas, and Alito, respectively, it is important to be clear that none of them represents the current law. Nor do they have any great prospect of becoming the law any time soon, at least judging by the votes in these cases. Even the controversial *Auer* doctrine[59] seems, for now, to be surviving well; Justice Kennedy joined in full the main opinion in *Perez*, which implicitly reaffirmed *Auer*, and which channeled the underlying objections into other doctrines (for example, by saying that reliance interests should be taken into account through arbitrariness review). But we are getting ahead of ourselves; first let us examine the Court's blunt repudiation of the DC Circuit, and its reaffirmation of the primacy of the APA over administrative common law.

A. THE SECOND COMING OF VERMONT YANKEE

1. *Formalism, pragmatism, and APA fundamentalism.* One of the very few defining cases of modern administrative law is, of course, *Vermont Yankee Nuclear Power Corp. v NRDC*,[60] above all because of its celebrated insistence that courts may not impose procedural re-

---

[57] See id at 1210 (Alito, J, concurring in part and concurring in the judgment).

[58] See, for example, *Decker*, 133 S Ct at 1339 (Roberts, CJ, concurring).

[59] *Auer v Robbins*, 519 US 452, 461 (1997).

[60] *Vermont Yankee Nuclear Power Corp. v Natural Resources Defense Council, Inc.*, 435 US 519 (1978).

quirements that go beyond those mandated by the APA. *Vermont Yankee* embraces a kind of APA fundamentalism, resting on a view—derived from Justice Jackson in *Wong Yang Sung v McGrath*[61]—that the APA "settled 'long-continued and hard-fought contentions, and enacts a formula upon which opposing social and political forces have come to rest.'"[62]

Though *Vermont Yankee* was unanimous, and is now widely regarded as unquestionably correct, it was highly controversial when it was decided. The reaction of administrative law specialists was generally negative. Professor Kenneth Culp Davis described the decision as "one of the few occasions in which a unanimous Supreme Court speaks with little or no authority."[63] Professor Richard Stewart derided the decision as myopic and formalistic, and wildly inconsistent with the long-standing path of the law, which had treated the APA (in his view wisely and appropriately) as a foundation for "evolving judge-made law."[64] Professor Antonin Scalia said that he approved of the Court's insistence on fidelity to statutory text, but nonetheless lamented the decision, insisting that changed circumstances, including the unanticipated rise of notice-and-comment rulemaking as the principal vehicle for agency decision making, meant that the Court was undermining, rather than enforcing, the original legislative compromise. In his most telling words, Scalia wrote, "[t]he opening passage of the opinion ('In 1946, Congress enacted the Administrative Procedure Act'), redolent of the opening passage of the Gospel of St. John ('In the beginning was the Word'), characterizes an approach that attributes to the APA a fundamentality which, it seems to me, the statute can no longer bear."[65]

It was hardly impossible for the decision to be otherwise. A majority of the Court could have ruled, with a straight face, that lower courts do, in fact, have the authority to require procedures beyond the APA minima, which could have been described as floors but not

---

[61] 339 US 33 (1950).

[62] *Vermont Yankee*, 435 US at 523, quoting *Wong Yang Sung*, 399 US at 40.

[63] Kenneth Culp Davis, *Administrative Common Law and the Vermont Yankee Opinion*, 1980 Utah L Rev 3, 17 (1980).

[64] Richard B. Stewart, *Vermont Yankee and the Evolution of Administrative Procedure*, 91 Harv L Rev 1805, 1815 (1978).

[65] Antonin Scalia, *Vermont Yankee: The APA, the DC Circuit, and the Supreme Court*, 1978 Supreme Court Review 345, 375 (1978).

ceilings. And as Davis, Stewart, and Scalia saw, APA fundamentalism would have disrupted a great deal more than the Court itself seemed to understand. Perhaps most important, there is a legitimate question whether so-called "hard look" review, which is said to demand detailed explanations from agencies, is authorized by, or fits with, the APA's seemingly modest requirement of "a concise general statement of their basis and purpose"[66] for rules.[67] Other aspects of contemporary administrative law, including still-murky judicial restrictions on ex parte contacts, seem to run afoul of *Vermont Yankee*.[68] Noticing the disconnect between the APA and some established doctrines, a significant number of commentators have argued for a kind of *Vermont Yankee* II, III, or IV[69]—one that would remind the lower courts, in no uncertain terms, that with respect to administrative procedure, they are not permitted to be inventive.

An argument of this kind could be justified in two different ways. The first would be formalistic, and unapologetically so: The APA is a statute, and courts may not defy it. Adding to its procedural requirements is a form of defiance. The second would be pragmatic and consequentialist: In deciding on appropriate procedures, agencies have to balance numerous variables and values, including resource constraints, and they are in the best position to identify the right balance. To be sure, a genuinely arbitrary procedural choice, no less than an arbitrary substantive choice, should not be upheld. But in general, agencies should have a great deal of room to maneuver. While *Vermont Yankee* itself is largely formalist, it has an unmistakable pragmatic strand, suggesting that "if courts could continually review agency proceedings to determine which were, in the court's

---

[66] 5 USC § 553(c).

[67] None of this is meant to endorse hard look review. One of us thinks that it is neither faithful to the APA, nor even an accurate description of the case law. See Jacob E. Gersen and Adrian Vermeule, *Thin Rationality Review*, Mich L Rev (forthcoming), online at http://papers.ssrn.com/sol3/papers.cfm?abstractid= 2639644. The other one of us has written on its behalf. See Cass R. Sunstein, *Deregulation and the Hard-Look Doctrine*, 1983 Supreme Court Review 177, 187–88 (1983), though he has become less enthusiastic over time. See Cass R. Sunstein, *The Arithmetic of Arsenic*, 90 Georgetown L J 2255, 2258–60 (2002).

[68] See Gary Lawson and Jack M. Beermann, *Reprocessing Vermont Yankee*, 75 Geo Wash L Rev 856, 883–88 (2007).

[69] See, for example, Paul R. Verkuil, *Judicial Review of Informal Rulemaking: Waiting for Vermont Yankee II*, 55 Tulane L Rev 418, 418 (1981); Richard J. Pierce Jr., *Waiting for Vermont Yankee II*, 57 Admin L Rev 669, 683 (2005); Lawson and Beermann, 75 Geo Wash L Rev at 858 (cited in note 68).

opinion, perfectly tailored to reach what the court perceives to be the 'best' or 'correct' result, judicial review would be totally unpredictable."[70] That idea could be applied to a number of judge-made doctrines, including several that have survived the period of a quarter century (and counting) since *Vermont Yankee*.

In some cases, the APA does have sufficient ambiguity to support doctrines that might seem in tension with the underlying rationale and pragmatic concerns of *Vermont Yankee*, and in our view, Professor Scalia was correct to note the relevance of changed circumstances, which may make it important to be cautious about certain forms of APA fundamentalism. For example, there is a good argument that in 1946, Congress did not merely anticipate notice-and-comment rulemaking to be relatively rare; it also thought that when it occurred, reviewing courts might engage in de novo fact finding.[71] In *Overton Park*,[72] however, the Court essentially turned cases of de novo review into a null set—in part, we suspect, for pragmatic reasons. But how, exactly, should courts now approach rulemaking if they were originally supposed to review it de novo? That is not an easy question. But some cases are straightforward; we now turn to one of them.

B. EASY CASES MAKE GOOD LAW

1. *The folly of 1997.* The APA recognizes the existence of two kinds of rules: (1) legislative rules, which are generally a product of either formal ("on the record") or informal ("notice and comment") rulemaking processes;[73] and (2) interpretive rules, which agencies can issue without invoking such processes. Formal rulemaking involves something like a trial, and for that reason, it is now relatively rare. Notice-and-comment rulemaking, celebrated by Professor Davis as

---

[70] *Vermont Yankee*, 435 US at 546.

[71] See Nathanial L. Nathanson, *Probing the Mind of the Administrator: Hearing Variations and Standards of Judicial Review under the Administrative Procedure Act and Other Federal Statutes*, 75 Colum L Rev 721, 755–56 n 172 (1975); Nathanial L. Nathanson, *The Vermont Yankee Nuclear Power Opinion: A Masterpiece of Statutory Misinterpretation*, 16 San Diego L Rev 183, 191 (1979).

[72] *Citizens to Preserve Overton Park, Inc. v Volpe*, 401 US 402 (1971), abrogated by *Califano v Sanders*, 430 US 99 (1977).

[73] We put aside "excepted" legislative rules, such as those issued with "good cause" for bypassing the normal procedures. See 5 USC § 553(b)(3)(A)–(B).

"one of the greatest inventions of modern government,"[74] is supposed to be far less cumbersome. But because of a range of developments, it is rarely expeditious. Within the executive branch, internal review, coordinated by the Office of Information and Regulatory Affairs, can introduce substantial delays.[75] A large number of officials within the executive branch are often involved in the assessment of rules before they are either proposed or finalized—and their involvement can slow things down considerably. In addition, the process of seeking and responding to public comments often requires a substantial investment of time and resources. Adequate responses might take a long time, even if negative comments are ultimately unconvincing. (We note that those who wrote and voted for the APA could not easily have anticipated either of these developments.)

If an agency wants to avoid the notice-and-comment process, it might be able to do so; perhaps it can show "good cause" in the sense of an immediate need for action. But even without good cause, agencies can issue interpretive[76] rules, which lack the force of law, and which can be promulgated immediately. Such a rule might set out the agency's understanding of what its organic statute or its own prior legislative rule means. (There is a separate question, taken up below, whether that rule will receive the deference accorded to legislative rules under *Chevron*, some other kind of deference, or no deference at all.[77]) To be sure, agencies cannot *change* legislative rules

---

[74] Kenneth Culp Davis, *Judicial, Legislative, and Administrative Lawmaking: A Proposed Research Service for the Supreme Court*, 71 Minn L Rev 1, 5 (1987).

[75] For an overview, see generally Cass R. Sunstein, *The Office of Information and Regulatory Affairs: Myths and Realities*, 126 Harv L Rev 838 (2013).

[76] The APA calls them "interpretative" rules, but lawyers have conspired to ignore that inelegant term. We do not discuss here the question whether agencies may issue guidance documents, interpretive rules, or other documents that are *practically* binding, but that have not gone through notice-and-comment rulemaking. There is a good argument that under the APA, agencies are not compelled to use notice-and-comment procedures unless they have issued *legally* binding rules. See, for example, Jacob E. Gersen, *Legislative Rules Revisited*, 74 U Chi L Rev 1705, 1713 (2007). That argument gains strength from *Vermont Yankee* and *Perez*. But there is a very strong pragmatic argument that if guidance documents (for example) are practically binding, they should have to be preceded by notice-and-comment procedures— and that argument gains strength from the unanticipated growth and importance of documents of that kind. See *Community Nutrition Institute v Young*, 818 F2d 943, 946 (DC Cir 1987); *Appalachian Power Co. v Environmental Protection Agency*, 208 F3d 1015, 1021 (DC Cir 2000). And as a matter of sound practice, it often makes sense for agencies to use notice-and-comment procedures voluntarily for such documents, as they often do, whether or not this is a legal requirement.

[77] See text at notes 125–64.

simply by issuing interpretive rules; any such change must be preceded by the notice-and-comment process. But on all of these questions, the APA is not ambiguous.

It is puzzling but true that since 1997, the DC Circuit has been
challenged by this question, which is really not at all hard: What if an
agency rescinds an interpretive rule and replaces it with a new interpretive rule? Suppose that the Environmental Protection Agency
(EPA) issues a legislative rule at Time 1 (say, 1985), then issues an
interpretive rule at Time 2 (say, 1992) to clarify its understanding of
its own prior legislative rule. Then at Time 3 (say, 1996), the EPA
rescinds the old interpretation and issues a new interpretive rule,
perhaps reflecting changed circumstances, perhaps reflecting a new
assessment of relevant facts, perhaps reflecting the values of a new
administration. Must the new interpretive rule be preceded by some
kind of APA process?

The answer is straightforwardly and even self-evidently "no." The
APA does not require any such process. It authorizes agencies to issue
interpretive rules immediately and without notice-and-comment or
any other kind of process.[78] It is hard to imagine more explicit text
than § 553(b)(3)(A), which states that "this subsection"—that is, the
requirement of notice-and-comment rulemaking—"does not apply—
(A) to interpretative rules. . . ."[79] If courts required a notice-and-
comment process for interpretive rules that revise previous interpretive rules, they would be imposing a procedural requirement beyond
those contained in the APA—a clear violation of the restrictions explicitly laid down in *Vermont Yankee*.

Nonetheless, the DC Circuit spoke unambiguously, until it was
abruptly reversed in *Perez*. Circuit panels held that agencies must
use notice-and-comment procedures in order to change interpretive
rules that construe the agency's own prior legislative rules, at least so
long as the agency previously took a clear position.[80] In *Paralyzed
Veterans*, the court concluded that so long as the original interpretive
rule was "definitive," the agency could not change it without full
notice-and-comment.[81] The court squarely rejected the government's

---

[78] 5 USC § 553.

[79] Id.

[80] See *Paralyzed Veterans of America v DC Arena LP*, 117 F3d 579, 584 (DC Cir 1997).

[81] Id.

argument that "an agency is completely free to change its interpretation of an ambiguous regulation so long as the regulation reasonably will bear the second interpretation."[82]

In 2009, the court gave an apparent signal that it would at least qualify the principle, suggesting the possibility that those who invoke *Paralyzed Veterans* would have to show that significant reliance interests were at stake.[83] With this signal, the court indicated that a showing of reliance interests might amount to a separate requirement, independent of the requirement that the original interpretive rule be "definitive."[84] Imposition of such a requirement would narrow the reach of the principle, though it would amount to an additional epicycle on the misconceived idea. But in *Mortgage Bankers Association v Harris*,[85] the court unambiguously reaffirmed the *Paralyzed Veterans* principle, ruling that definitiveness is the sole requirement, and that reliance is relevant only insofar as it might inform the question of definitiveness.[86]

The lower court's decision invalidated an interpretive rule from the Obama administration, which would have expressed a more expansive view of the coverage of the Fair Labor Standards Act than had been announced by the Bush administration.[87] The court, in an opinion by Judge Janice Rogers Brown, stated the rule plainly: "Once a court has classified an agency interpretation as such, it cannot be significantly revised without notice and comment rulemaking."[88] And in explaining the practical effect of that rule, the court said that it "may very well serve as a prophylactic that discourages agencies from attempting to circumvent notice and comment requirements in the first instance."[89] Similarly, in an earlier case in the sequence, the court

---

[82] Id at 586.

[83] See *MetWest Inc. v Secretary of Labor*, 560 F3d 506, 511 & n 4 (DC Cir 2009).

[84] See id at 511 ("A fundamental rationale of *Alaska Professional Hunters[, Inc. v Federal Aviation Administration*, 177 F3d 1030 (DC Cir 1999)] was the affected parties' substantial and justifiable reliance on a well-established agency interpretation."); id at n 4 ("This is a crucial part of the analysis. To ignore it is to misunderstand *Alaska Professional Hunters*.").

[85] 720 F3d 966, 969 (DC Cir 2013), rev'd by *Perez v Mortgage Bankers Association*, 135 S Ct 1199 (2015).

[86] See *Mortgage Bankers*, 720 F3d at 970 ("[R]eliance is but one factor courts must consider in assessing whether an agency interpretation qualifies as definitive or authoritative.").

[87] Id at 970–72.

[88] Id at 971.

[89] Id at 969 n 4.

said that "[w]hen an agency has given its regulation a definitive interpretation, and later significantly revises that interpretation, the
agency has in effect amended its rule, something it may not accomplish without notice and comment."[90] Thus, the stage was set for
Supreme Court intervention.

   2. *Restoration.* Justice Sotomayor's opinion for the Court reads
like the long-awaited *Vermont Yankee II.* The principal holding is that
the *Paralyzed Veterans* principle is not consistent with the APA. Indeed, it is a violation of its "clear text."[91] In insisting that courts may
not impose procedural requirements beyond those in the APA, the
Court spoke emphatically against an administrative common law of
procedure—especially on the part of the lower courts.[92] It acknowledged that agencies must use notice-and-comment procedures when
they repeal legislative rules, but a change in an interpretive rule does
not amount to a repeal of any legislative rule. "Because an agency is
not required to use notice-and-comment procedures to issue an
initial interpretive rule, it is also not required to use those procedures
when it amends or repeals that interpretive rule."[93]

   The Court emphasized that the *Paralyzed Veterans* doctrine runs
directly into *Vermont Yankee*'s prohibition on judge-made procedural
rights. And in a paragraph that borrowed directly from the key passage in *Vermont Yankee,* the Court said that imposing the obligation
to notice-and-comment "is the responsibility of Congress or the
administrative agencies, not the courts."[94] To the claim that a change
in the interpretation of a regulation is a change in the regulation itself, the Court responded with incredulity. If an original interpretive
rule does not itself change a regulation, then why does a *change* in the
interpretive rule do so?[95] To be sure, an interpretive rule might re-

---

[90] *Alaska Professional Hunters Association, Inc. v Federal Aviation Administration,* 177 F3d
1030, 1034 (DC Cir 1999), abrogated by *Perez v Mortgage Bankers Association,* 135 S Ct 1199
(2015).

[91] *Perez,* 135 S Ct at 1206.

[92] But see generally Kathryn E. Kovacs, *Pixelating Administrative Common Law in Perez v
Mortgage Bankers Association,* 125 Yale L J F *31 (2015), online at http://www.yalelawjournal
.org/forum/pixelating-administrative-common-law-in-perez-v-mortgage-bankers-association
(criticizing the *Perez* court for failing to do just this). Stipulating to the validity of Kovacs's
aims, many of which we share, we believe that she goes wrong in not recognizing that *Perez*
does most or all of what she urges the Court to do.

[93] *Perez,* 135 S Ct at 1206.

[94] Id at 1207.

[95] Id at 1206.

ceive deference under the *Auer* doctrine, but that principle supplies no defense of *Paralyzed Veterans*. The validity of *Auer* is a logically independent question, one that we take up below.

The Court acknowledged that agencies might issue an interpretive rule in order to avoid the notice-and-comment process. If so, agencies face "a variety of constraints."[96] For example, their decisions might be found arbitrary and capricious on judicial review. The Court reaffirmed an earlier pronouncement that "the APA requires an agency to provide more substantial justification when 'its new policy rests upon factual findings that contradict those which underlay its prior policy; or when its prior policy has engendered serious reliance interests that must be taken into account. It would be arbitrary and capricious to ignore such matters.'"[97] (We bracket for now the fact that by its terms, the APA imposes no such requirement.) In addition, the Court acknowledged the possibility that an interpretive rule might be, in fact, a legislative rule. But that argument had been waived; the decision below rested upon the premise that the relevant rule was interpretive, not legislative.[98]

Perez was an easy case—indeed, it could have been written in just a few pages—and the absence of dissenters is no surprise. If no one else had spoken, the analogy to *Vermont Yankee* would have been very close; it would have been the same univocal rebuke to the DC Circuit, decades later. But three concurrences, showing a taste for the New Coke, could not have easily been anticipated. Justice Alito took the occasion to note the "understandable concern about the aggrandizement of the power of administrative agencies as a result of the combined effect of (1) the effective delegation to agencies by Congress of huge swaths of lawmaking authority, (2) the exploitation by agencies of the uncertain boundary between legislative and interpretive rules, and (3) this Court's cases holding that courts must ordinarily defer to an agency's interpretation of its own ambiguous regulations."[99] The most revealing phrase here is "huge swaths."

Justice Scalia offered an elaborate discussion of doctrines involving judicial deference to agency interpretations of law, even though

---

[96] Id at 1209.

[97] Id at 1209, quoting *Federal Communications Commission v Fox Television Stations, Inc.*, 556 US 502, 515 (2009).

[98] See *Mortgage Bankers*, 720 F3d at 969, rev'd by *Perez*, 135 S Ct 1199.

[99] *Perez*, 135 S Ct at 1210 (Alito, J, concurring).

those doctrines were not at issue in the case. A longtime defender of *Chevron*, and author of an important opinion rejecting a non-delegation challenge and affirming the legitimacy of broad agency discretion,[100] he seemed to question *Chevron* itself, noting that under the APA, the reviewing court, and not the agency, is to interpret statutory provisions. And he lamented the idea that agencies receive deference in interpreting ambiguities in their own regulations: "there are weighty reasons to deny a lawgiver the power to write ambiguous laws and then be the judge of what the ambiguity means."[101] Justice Thomas agreed, but he invoked the Constitution itself, complaining that *Auer* deference "represents a transfer of judicial power to the Executive Branch, and it amounts to an erosion of the judicial obligation to serve as a 'check' on the political branches."[102] We will take up these questions below.

C. NONDELEGATION AND ITS DISCONTENTS

For the time being, at least, the center holds not only with respect to APA procedure, the main issue in *Perez*, but also with respect to nondelegation. Of course, any assessment must be premature, given the narrow disposition of *American Railroads*. But it is significant that neither Justice Scalia nor Justice Alito joined Justice Thomas's concurrence in the judgment, with its startlingly broad criticism of nondelegation, adapted from academic work by Philip Hamburger. There seems to be little appetite on the Court for that unhappy meal, even among the Justices with an occasional taste for the New Coke.

Although Thomas's view-for-one should attract no more attention than it deserves, it is worth a brief look, if only better to understand the enduring view that has commanded the center of the Court over time. The centerpiece of the Court's nondelegation jurisprudence is the "intelligible principle" test,[103] which rests on a particular theory of the distinction between legislative and executive power. The theory holds that executive power always and necessarily includes discretion to bring statutes down to the ground, to implement them through

---

[100] See *Whitman v American Trucking Associations, Inc.*, 531 US 457 (2001).

[101] *Perez*, 135 S Ct at 1212–13 (Scalia, J, concurring in the judgment).

[102] Id at 1217 (Thomas, J, concurring in the judgment).

[103] *J. W. Hampton Jr. & Co. v United States*, 276 US 394, 409 (1928).

interpretation and even rulemaking,[104] so long as the interpretations and rules remain within the bounds of the granted statutory authority and so long as the legislature specifies the main aims for which discretion is to be exercised (the "intelligible principle").

On this view, it is therefore neither possible nor constitutionally desirable to exclude all executive discretion in the implementation of statutes. What is necessary is to ensure that the legislature at least sets the policy aims or overall ends, while the executive supplies the means. The "intelligible principle" test therefore attempts to sort the legitimate discretion of executive actors to choose the means by which to implement policy, on the one hand, from legislative power to specify the ends. An intelligible principle is one that gives the executive (enough) policy guidance as to ends.[105]

Within this framework, a conventional criticism of the Court's nondelegation cases—after *Schechter Poultry* in 1935, the last case in which the Court invalidated a federal statute on nondelegation grounds—is that the Court has been far too permissive in its application of the "intelligible principle" test. The DC Circuit's last adventure with the nondelegation doctrine, before *American Railroads*, involved Clean Air Act provisions giving the EPA authority to act as "requisite to protect the public health," with an "adequate margin of safety."[106] The panel invalidated the provisions on nondelegation grounds, reasoning, as many 1Ls do, that because the provisions did not specify exactly what margin of safety is adequate (or the meaning of "requisite to protect the public health"), they conferred excessive discretion.[107] (Oddly, however, the panel then remanded to the

---

[104] See *United States v Grimaud*, 220 US 506, 518 (1911).

[105] To be clear, one of us (Vermeule) thinks that the "intelligible principle" test is too restrictive (the opposite of Thomas, who thinks that it is too permissive). See Eric Posner and Adrian Vermeule, *Interring the Nondelegation Doctrine*, 69 U Chi L Rev 1721, 1727 (2002). On this view, the constitutional vesting of "executive power" demands compliance only with the *Youngstown* constraint—the basic principle of legality, that the executive must act on the basis of either a constitutional or statutory grant of authority. See *Youngstown Sheet & Tube Co. v Sawyer*, 343 US 579, 585–89 (1952) (Black, J). Putting aside cases of independent constitutional authority of the executive under Article II, if the executive stays within the legal limits of the granted statutory authority, there is no *further* question whether the grant supplies "too much discretion"; executive power just is the power to execute grants of statutory authority. However, we bracket that possibility for purposes of our discussion here.

[106] *American Trucking Associations, Inc. v United States Environmental Protection Agency*, 175 F3d 1027, 1033 (DC Cir 1999), opinion modified on reh'g, 195 F3d 4 (DC Cir 1999), aff'd in part, rev'd in part by *Whitman v American Trucking Associations, Inc.*, 531 US 457 (2001).

[107] *American Trucking*, 175 F3d at 1034–37.

agency to promulgate new regulations, the theory being that the agency could constrain its own discretion and thereby cure the unconstitutionality.[108]) The Supreme Court overturned the decision, ruling that the discretion conferred by the Clean Air Act was no greater than that conferred by many other statutes the Court had upheld since 1935. As the Court put it, "we have almost never felt qualified to second-guess Congress regarding the permissible degree of policy judgment that can be left to those executing or applying the law."[109] For some critics, of course, that is exactly the problem; the Court has been far too supine in its application of the intelligible-principle test, upholding even bare grants of authority to agencies to act in "the public interest."[110]

But this conventional criticism is emphatically not Thomas's criticism; indeed, he specifically repudiates the whole "intelligible principle" test altogether.[111] His view is from a different universe of discourse, in which any administrative authority to "bind" private parties—no matter how interstitial the issue, how clear the policy guidance from the legislature, or how specific the grant of authority—represents a revival of Stuart prerogative.[112] If the agency binds through rulemaking, it is exercising the lawmaking power; if it binds through adjudication, it is exercising the judicial power. In either case, it is going beyond the constitutional limits of executive power. The consequence is that huge stretches of the administrative state would be unconstitutional—very possibly, all grants of binding authority that go beyond the internal management and proprietary functions of government. (Perhaps administrative government could be salvaged by recasting administrative agencies as adjuncts to congressional committees, and having more or less pro forma legislative

---

[108] Id at 1034. See also Lisa Schultz Bressman, *Schechter Poultry at the Millennium: A Delegation Doctrine for the Administrative State*, 109 Yale L J 1399, 1422–31 (2000); Kenneth Culp Davis, *A New Approach to Delegation*, 36 U Chi L Rev 713, 725 (1969).

[109] *Whitman*, 531 US at 474–75 (quotation marks omitted), quoting *Mistretta v United States*, 488 US 361, 416 (1989) (Scalia, J, dissenting).

[110] See *City of Arlington, Texas v Federal Communications Commission*, 133 S Ct 1863, 1879 (2013) (Roberts, CJ, dissenting).

[111] *Department of Transportation v Association of American Railroads*, 135 S Ct 1225, 1251 (2015) (Thomas, J, concurring in the judgment) ("Our reluctance to second-guess Congress on the *degree* of policy judgment is understandable; our mistake lies in assuming that *any* degree of policy judgment is permissible when it comes to establishing generally applicable rules governing private conduct.").

[112] See id.

votes on the large quantity of regulations that any administrative regime must produce—but it is entirely speculative whether the resulting system would function at all.)

Elsewhere we have indicated our own, different views of the proper scope and limits of legislative grants of authority, from both constitutional and welfarist perspectives.[113] We will not belabor those views here, except to say that Thomas's opinions—whatever the dubious merits of their account of Stuart history[114]—offer a deeply unconvincing account of American constitutional and administrative law. In Thomas's narrative frame, the Court betrayed the deep principles of the Anglo-American constitutional order by licensing the administrative state. Yet in 1911—only six years after *Lochner v New York*[115] was decided, at the height of the Old Court—the Justices ruled *unanimously* in *United States v Grimaud* that a statutory grant of authority to the executive to make rules binding on private parties was not only valid, but had *always been* valid:

> From the beginning of the government, various acts have been passed conferring upon executive officers power to make rules and regulations,— not for the government of their departments, but for administering the laws which did govern. None of these statutes could confer legislative power. But when Congress had legislated and indicated its will, it could give to those who were to act under such general provisions "power to fill up the details" by the establishment of administrative rules and regulations, the violation of which could be punished by fine or imprisonment fixed by Congress, or by penalties fixed by Congress, or measured by the injury done.[116]

The view that the "executive power" inherently includes the power to complete legislative programs,[117] to "fill in the details" of legislative grants, through law interpretation (necessarily effected through either adjudication or rulemaking, which might bind private parties),

---

[113] See Posner and Vermeule, 69 U Chi L Rev at 1725 (cited in note 105); Cass R. Sunstein, *Is OSHA Unconstitutional?*, 94 Va L Rev 1407, 1410 (2008).

[114] A question as to which we are somewhere between agnostic and skeptical, for reasons that would take us too far afield from the present discussion.

[115] 198 US 45 (1905).

[116] *United States v Grimaud*, 220 US 506, 517 (1911), quoting *Wayman v Southard*, 23 US 1, 43 (1825). Hamburger attempts to confine *Grimaud* to federal management of the government's own property, but that is no part of the Court's rationale.

[117] See Jack Goldsmith and John F. Manning, *The President's Completion Power*, 115 Yale L J 2280, 2303–08 (2006).

is as old as the hills.[118] Even if there is room for reasonable debate about the originalist credentials of the "intelligible principle" test, certainly any constitutional theory that contains any scope for "liquidat[ion],"[119] practice,[120] custom, or tradition must recognize that the administrative state has venerable credentials, extending back well beyond the twentieth century, into the founding era itself.[121]

Thomas labors to show that *Wayman v Southard*, the 1825 decision that initially blessed legislative grants of authority to "fill in the details" and to bind private parties, does not actually stand for what it seems to say, but instead "strongly suggests that rules of private conduct were not the proper subject of rulemaking by the courts."[122] *Wayman* is a Delphic decision that has produced a great deal of interpretive controversy.[123] Here are three observations that should be uncontroversial, however: (1) Even if Thomas is correct that rules of private conduct were not the proper subject of rulemaking by the courts, it may still be true, as a logical matter, that rules of private conduct were and are the proper subject of rulemaking by executive bodies; (2) later cases like *Grimaud* read *Wayman*'s "fill in the details" theory as the foundation for what we have called the mainstream view of delegation and executive power;[124] (3) whatever the success of his defensive maneuvers, Thomas gives no *affirmative* precedent whatsoever, from the Supreme Court or any other American court, for the proposition that the legislature may never grant the executive authority to make binding rules. If Thomas indeed captures a deep

---

[118] See Jerry L. Mashaw, *Creating the Administrative Constitution: The Lost One Hundred Years of American Administrative Law* 53–65 (Yale, 2012).

[119] See Caleb Nelson, *Originalism and Interpretive Conventions*, 70 U Chi L Rev 519, 527 (2003); Federalist 37 (Madison), in Jacob E. Cooke, ed, *The Federalist* 231, 236 (Wesleyan, 1982) (cited in note 11).

[120] See Curtis A. Bradley and Trevor W. Morrison, *Historical Gloss and the Separation of Powers*, 126 Harv L Rev 411, 417 (2012); Curtis A. Bradley and Trevor W. Morrison, *Presidential Power, Historical Practice, and Legal Constraint*, 113 Colum L Rev 1097, 1103 (2013).

[121] Mashaw, *Creating the Administrative Constitution* at 12 (cited in note 118). A valuable discussion of the issuance of binding rules, but with a more modern time frame, is Thomas W. Merrill and Kathryn Tongue Watts, *Agency Rules with the Force of Law: The Original Convention*, 116 Harv L Rev 467 (2002).

[122] *American Railroads*, 135 S Ct at 1249 (Thomas, J, concurring in the judgment).

[123] Compare Posner and Vermeule, 69 U Chi L Rev 1721 (cited in note 105), with Gary Lawson, *Delegation and Original Meaning*, 88 Va L Rev 327, 359 (2002).

[124] See, for example, *Grimaud*, 220 US at 518; *Mistretta*, 488 US at 387; *American Railroads*, 135 S Ct at 1237 (Alito, J, concurring).

principle of Anglo-American constitutionalism, wouldn't he have a citation for it, beyond general propositions about the separation of powers?

In the end, Thomas's Hamburgerism fits well with the New Coke. Both are distasteful innovations. The rhetorical frame Thomas adopts from Hamburger—that the Court has betrayed ancient principles of the Anglo-American constitutional order—not only offers an unconvincing reading of American law, but also fails to give an accurate description of the theory behind the "intelligible principle" test that Thomas criticizes. The test is not some raw compromise with practicality, a betrayal of the Constitution that must be tolerated, if at all, solely for the sake of expediency. Rather, the test derives from an affirmative theory of the nature of executive and legislative power, and of their relationship, which sees the executive as constitutionally empowered to carry legislative policies into execution. *Pace* the New Coke, that theory has far better credentials in American administrative and constitutional law than does the view that the executive can never bind citizens to anything.

D. AUER'S HOUR?

1. *Problems and approaches.* Consider the following cases:

- An agency issues a legislative rule requiring employers to report occupational diseases within two weeks after they are "diagnosed." An employer asks the agency to clarify what counts as a "diagnosis." The agency answers, in an interpretive rule, that chest x-rays that "score" above a specified level of opacity count as a diagnosis.[125]
- An agency issues a regulation that imposes federal tariffs on "diaries" and "bound books." In an interpretive rule, it announces that "diaries" include daily journals, but not calendars, and that "bound books" refers only to formal bookbinding.[126]
- An agency issues a legislative rule that requires certain pens used to contain dangerous animals to be "structurally sound." In an interpretive rule, the agency specifies the height of the walls that

---

[125] See *American Mining Congress v Mine Safety & Health Administration*, 995 F2d 1106, 1108 (DC Cir 1993).

[126] See *United States v Mead Corp.*, 533 US 218, 221–24 (2001).

should be used, in the relevant pens, in order to count as structurally sound.[127]

- An agency issues a legislative rule that exempts "waiting time"
  from the requirements of its overtime regulations. In an interpretive rule, it says that certain emergency services employees are
  engaged in "waiting time," rather than "working time," if they are
  not required to perform job-related tasks, even if they have to be
  accessible by phone and available to come into work on ten minutes' notice.[128]

- An agency issues a rule requiring swimming pools, at hotels, to be
  "fully accessible" to people who use wheelchairs through "lifts,"
  which make pools easy to use. In an interpretive rule, the agency
  makes it clear that to qualify, a lift need not be a permanent part of
  the pool. It can be mobile and simply available to those who ask.[129]

Let us stipulate that whenever an agency's interpretive rule is
clearly inconsistent with the underlying regulation, it is unlawful for
that reason. Let us also stipulate that if the interpretive rule is, in
fact, a legislative rule, it will be unlawful if it has not been promulgated with the proper procedures. The question is this: If the legislative rule is ambiguous, should a court interpret it on its own, or
should it give deference to the agency's interpretation, and uphold
that interpretation so long as it is reasonable?

To sharpen the question, let us assume that in each one of our
cases, the legislative rule really is ambiguous. "Diagnosis" could mean
one or another level of opacity; the agency has chosen among several
plausible alternatives, taken as such by doctors. "Diaries" and "bound
books" have several definitions, and the agency has chosen two.
"Structurally sound" could mean one or another height, and one or
another set of materials; on the basis of practical considerations, the
agency has made some sensible judgments, but others are imaginable.
"Working time" might include being on call for one's employer, or it
might not; the agency's judgment depends on a mix of policy con-

---

[127] See *Hoctor v United States Department of Agriculture*, 82 F3d 165, 167–68 (7th Cir 1996).

[128] See *Skidmore v Swift & Co.*, 323 US 134, 136 (1944).

[129] But see *Questions and Answers: Accessibility Requirements for Existing Swimming Pools at Hotels and Other Public Accommodations* (US Department of Justice Civil Rights Division, May 24, 2012), online at http://www.ada.gov/qa_existingpools_titleIII.htm (discussing this issue but coming out the other way via "questions and answers").

siderations. "Fully accessible" could include mobile lifts, or it could exclude them. The agency's decision to include them—on the ground that even if people who use wheelchairs must ask, they are being treated equally—is consistent with the regulation's text, but it is not mandated by it. Reasonable people disagree, concluding that if people who use wheelchairs have to ask, the pools are not "fully accessible."

At least since the *Seminole Rock* case, decided in 1945, the Supreme Court has said that so long as the legislative regulation is genuinely ambiguous, courts should defer to reasonable agency interpretations. The result is the *Seminole Rock* principle, or as it is more often called, the *Auer* principle, after a post-APA case that seems to entrench it.[130] And let us be very clear that in *Perez*, the center held with respect to *Auer* as well. Six Justices—including, critically, the Chief Justice and Justice Kennedy—signed on to the *Auer* discussion in the majority's footnote 4. That note catalogs the checks and constraints on agency interpretation built into *Auer* and into administrative law generally, principally (1) judicial authority to enforce clear texts and (2) arbitrariness review, which can take into account the reliance interests of regulated parties.[131] The Court's treatment of *Auer* strongly suggests, even if it does not quite spell out, that six Justices would reject any wholesale challenge to the doctrine. The drama of the New Coke criticisms should not obscure that a solid (super)majority seems to like *Auer* just fine.

We should immediately notice a possible objection to *Auer*, in the spirit of the New Coke, which runs this way: The regulation sets out the law, and it is binding. But within the constraints of the law, regulated classes are authorized to do whatever they like. In the cases above, the agency interpretation is essentially irrelevant, because the legislative rule has given the regulated classes (some) room to maneuver. No additional constraints can come from an interpretive rule, which would effectively amend the legislative rule by imposing further restrictions.

It is true that some regulations are best interpreted in this way. If and when a regulation is properly understood as a grant of discretion to the private sector, then no interpretation can eliminate that dis-

---

[130] See generally *Auer v Robbins*, 519 US 452 (1997).

[131] *Perez*, 135 S Ct at 1219 n 4 (2015).

cretion. But however much one likes or does not like the New Coke, this approach cannot be understood as a *general* attack on interpretive rules as such; in fact, it is expressly repudiated by *Perez*, which says that an otherwise legitimate interpretive rule, sorting out an ambiguity, simply does not change or somehow "effectively" amend the regulation it interprets.[132] Ambiguities in regulations should not necessarily be taken as authorizations, as licenses of private conduct; they might simply be ambiguities. If they are indeed clearly authorizations of private choice, there is no problem; the court should hold that an interpretation inconsistent with a clear legislative authorization of private choice is unlawful, regardless of the deference rule. But suppose that a regulation is genuinely unclear and requires interpretation. If so, the question remains: Who interprets it, court or agency? Does the agency's view deserve some weight?

2. *Congress's ultimate authority?* We should agree, with Justice Scalia, that Congress has the authority to answer that question (subject to constitutional constraints, taken up below). Suppose that the national legislature expressly said that the EPA has the power to interpret ambiguities in its own regulations—or expressly denied it that authority. That direction should be authoritative (again, subject to constitutional constraints). For that reason, the question is this: Has Congress in fact exercised that authority, either globally or in particular statutes?

Justice Scalia appears to think so. He points to section 706 of the APA, which states that the "reviewing court shall . . . interpret constitutional and statutory provisions, and determine the meaning or applicability of the terms of an agency action."[133] In his view, the APA therefore "contemplates that courts, not agencies, will authoritatively resolve ambiguities in statutes and regulations."[134] But as Justice Scalia is aware, that conclusion raises a serious problem, which is that it would require rejection of the *Chevron* principle itself, on the ground that it defies the APA. Justice Scalia attempts (seemingly half-heartedly?) to rescue that principle as "in conformity with the long history of judicial review of executive action,"[135] even

---

[132] Id at 1207–08.

[133] 5 USC § 706.

[134] *Perez*, 135 S Ct at 1211 (Scalia, J, concurring in the judgment).

[135] Id at 1212 (Scalia, J, concurring in the judgment).

though it is apparently in tension with the APA (at least on the view Justice Scalia is endorsing). By contrast, his reasoning seems to run, *Auer* must be rejected on the ground that the APA forbids it—and no such long history justifies it.

But this argument moves far too quickly. Does the text of the APA really require independent judicial interpretations of law? If so, it would seem to repudiate any "long history," which would therefore be irrelevant. On many approaches to interpretation, a long history, preceding enactment of a contrary text, cannot overcome that text, so long as the text is indisputably clear.

In other writings, however, Justice Scalia has offered a different justification of *Chevron*, one that (in his view, as expressed in those writings) does not violate any statute or threaten the separation of powers. More particularly, he has contended that *Chevron* does not violate the APA at all. The question is what the APA commands, and the statement that the court shall "interpret" questions of law is not decisive in favor of independent judicial review, if it is also the case *that under organic statutes, the correct interpretation of law depends on the agency's interpretation of law.*[136] If an organic statute says "source (as defined by the EPA)," then the law is what the agency says (so long as the agency's interpretation is reasonable). But suppose that Congress has not said anything explicit but has generally given an agency the authority to issue regulations. Has it also given the agency the authority to interpret ambiguities in the underlying statute? If so, then *the law is, to that extent, what the agency says it is*—and in faithfully applying the APA, the reviewing court had better say so. On this view, courts do not violate the APA by deferring to reasonable agency interpretations; such deference just is, itself, part of the law that courts declare.[137]

But when has Congress given agencies interpretive authority? Justice Scalia saw that as a difficult question, answered in *Chevron* by a (good) legal fiction, one that is superior to the legal fiction that preceded it. He wrote:

> An ambiguity in a statute committed to agency implementation can be attributed to either of two congressional desires: (1) Congress intended

---

[136] See Henry P. Monaghan, *Marbury and the Administrative State*, 83 Colum L Rev 1, 6 (1983).

[137] See id. Here, too, we do not at all mean to endorse this justification for *Chevron*, only to elicit its implications for the *Auer* question.

a particular result, but was not clear about it; or (2) Congress had no particular intent on the subject, but meant to leave its resolution to the agency. When the former is the case, what we have is genuinely a question of law, properly to be resolved by the courts. When the latter is the case, what we have is the conferral of discretion upon the agency, and the only question of law presented to the courts is whether the agency has acted within the scope of its discretion—i.e., whether its resolution of the ambiguity is reasonable. As I read the history of developments in this field, the pre-*Chevron* decisions sought to choose between (1) and (2) on a statute-by-statute basis. Hence the relevance of such frequently mentioned factors as the degree of the agency's expertise, the complexity of the question at issue, and the existence of rulemaking authority within the agency. All these factors make an intent to confer discretion upon the agency more likely. *Chevron*, however, if it is to be believed, replaced this statute-by-statute evaluation (which was assuredly a font of uncertainty and litigation) with an across-the-board presumption that, in the case of ambiguity, agency discretion is meant.[138]

He added:

If the *Chevron* rule is not a 100% accurate estimation of modern congressional intent, the prior case-by-case evaluation was not so either—and was becoming less and less so, as the sheer volume of modern dockets made it less and less possible for the Supreme Court to police diverse application of an ineffable rule. And to tell the truth, the quest for the "genuine" legislative intent is probably a wild-goose chase anyway. In the vast majority of cases I expect that Congress *neither* (1) intended a single result, *nor* (2) meant to confer discretion upon the agency, but rather (3) didn't think about the matter at all. If I am correct in that, then any rule adopted in this field represents merely a fictional, presumed intent, and operates principally as a background rule of law against which Congress can legislate. If that is the principal function to be served, *Chevron* is unquestionably better than what preceded it.[139]

We think that this argument, relying on "a fictional, presumed intent," is essentially correct, so long as it is understood that the choice of fiction depends on the consequences of adopting one or another. *Chevron* recognizes that Congress has ultimate control of the deference question, and that in the face of uncertainty as to how Congress should be understood to have resolved that question, presumptive deference is the best instruction to attribute to the national

---

[138] Antonin Scalia, *Judicial Deference to Administrative Interpretations of Law*, 1989 Duke L J 511, 516 (1989).

[139] Id at 517.

legislature. And the reasons that such an instruction should be deemed best are principally the consequentialist reasons *Chevron* itself gave, involving the agency's comparative competence with respect to fact-finding and policymaking,[140] and its comparative political accountability.[141] When a statute is unclear, and especially when a complex modern regulatory statute is unclear, resolution of the ambiguity will inevitably require policymaking competence—which courts lack and which agencies have.[142] In 1989, Justice Scalia emphasized that precise point as well.[143]

3. *High theory, and reality.* Which brings us directly to *Auer*. If the APA required courts not to defer to agency interpretations of their own regulations, the problem would be solved, and *Auer* would be wrong. But, of course, it does no such thing. Nothing in the APA either endorses or rejects *Auer*, at least in express terms. True, courts are instructed to "determine the meaning or the applicability of the terms of an agency action," but perhaps Congress has said, in general or in particular cases, that the meaning of a regulation turns on the agency's interpretation of its meaning, where ambiguity exists. In that case, courts fulfill their duty "to determine the meaning" by deferring to that view. If so, courts might say that where legislative rules are ambiguous, the law is what the agency says it is (through an interpretive rule).

---

[140] See Cass R. Sunstein, *The Most Knowledgeable Branch*, U Pa L Rev (forthcoming 2016), online at http://papers.ssrn.com/sol3/papers.cfm?abstract_id=2630726.

[141] *Chevron, USA, Inc. v Natural Resources Defense Council, Inc.*, 467 US 837, 865–66 (1984). There are other considerations in support of *Chevron*. See Peter L. Strauss, *One Hundred Fifty Cases per Year: Some Implications of the Supreme Court's Limited Resources for Judicial Review of Agency Action*, 87 Colum L Rev 1093, 1121 (1987).

[142] See Sunstein and Vermeule, 82 U Chi L Rev at 444 n 251 (cited in note 40). Note, however, the interesting qualification in *King v Burwell*, stressing that in extraordinary cases, involving issues of great economic and social significance, the presumption should be reversed, and Congress should be presumed to want independent judicial judgment. *King v Burwell*, 135 S Ct 2480, 2488–89 (2015). For discussion, see Cass R. Sunstein, *Chevron Step Zero*, 92 Va L Rev 187, 236–42 (2006).

[143] See Scalia, 1989 Duke L J at 516–18 (cited in note 138). There is a competing view, which would invoke background principles of separation of powers, and perhaps concerns about agency self-dealing, to generate a different presumption. See Cynthia R. Farina, *Statutory Interpretation and the Balance of Power in the Administrative State*, 89 Colum L Rev 452, 456 (1989). See also Stephen Breyer, *Judicial Review of Questions of Law and Policy*, 38 Admin L Rev 363, 394–95 (suggesting a multifactor balancing test). In our view, Scalia's position in 1989 is essentially correct. For discussion, see Adrian Vermeule, *Introduction: Mead in the Trenches*, 71 Geo Wash L Rev 347, 347–61 (2003); Sunstein, 92 Va L Rev at 202–05 (cited in note 142).

It is true that just as in *Chevron*, Congress has not issued any such express instruction. But it has not issued a contrary instruction either. In this field, any rule again "represents merely a fictional, presumed intent"[144] which must be defended as the best instruction to attribute to the national legislature. In that light, *Auer* itself might be defended in two different ways. Perhaps the agency has the best understanding of what the underlying legislative rule actually meant. If Jones says, "go to the store around the block," he is in the best position to know which store he had in mind. In some cases, this rationale is indeed an exceptionally strong point for *Auer*, at least when the agency has issued an interpretive rule in relatively close temporal proximity to the legislative rule. (It might well work in the swimming pools case above, and it would work as well for a number of interpretations issued in the aftermath of legislative rules under the Affordable Care Act.) But when an agency has *changed* its interpretation, this particular argument will fail. And in many cases, an agency will not be uncovering an antecedent intention. It will be interpreting a term on which it had not previously focused. (That might well be true of the diagnosis case above.)

A second defense of *Auer* points, not to the agency's superior understanding of what it originally meant, but to pragmatic considerations. On this view, agencies have technical expertise as well as political accountability, and so long as a regulation is ambiguous, it should be interpreted by them, not by courts, which lacks those advantages. To be sure, the "traditional tools of statutory construction"[145] can be used to determine whether there is ambiguity at all. If the agency interprets its regulation to mean that for swimming pools to be accessible, people who operate them must provide the collected works of Philip K. Dick to people who use wheelchairs, that interpretation would be struck down. But where there is genuine ambiguity, the agency has comparative advantages—precisely parallel to its advantages in the *Chevron* setting. Just as, on Scalia's view in 1989, *Chevron* is the best fictional default rule for statutory construction, so too *Auer* is the best fictional default rule for interpretation of agency regulations.

---

[144] Scalia, 1989 Duke L J at 517 (cited in note 138).

[145] *Chevron*, 467 US at 843 n 9.

In 2015, Justice Scalia objects that "the purpose of interpretation is to determine the fair meaning of the rule," and "[n]ot to make policy."[146] (In 1989, by contrast, Scalia had rightly observed that the traditional tools of statutory construction "include not merely text and legislative history but also, quite specifically, the consideration of policy consequences."[147]) In his account, agency enactments must be taken "as written," thus giving "the Executive . . . a stable background against which to write its rules and achieve the policy ends it thinks best."[148] The second point is correct but irrelevant; *Auer* is not at all inconsistent with the view, which it does not contest, that regulations must be taken as written. And for reasons stated by Justice Scalia in 1989, the first point misses the mark. *Auer* is right for the same reason that *Chevron* is right: Where Congress has not been clear, deference to the agency, in the face of genuine ambiguity, is the best instruction to attribute to it.

4. *Misplaced concerns.* Critics of *Auer*, including Justice Scalia, have two independent concerns. One is that *Auer* creates an unfortunate and even dangerous incentive for agencies, which "is to speak vaguely and broadly, so as to retain a 'flexibility' that will enable 'clarification' with retroactive effect."[149] In the abstract, the concern is certainly intelligible, but the idea that *Auer* results in motivated and nefarious obscurity—"a dangerous permission slip for the arrogation of power"—strikes us as one of the New Coke's phantasmal terrors. Indeed, we are unaware of, and no one has pointed to, any regulation in American history that, because of *Auer*, was designed vaguely and broadly.[150]

We do not deny that such a thing might occur, but in deciding on the optimal level of clarity and specificity, agencies have a wide range of incentives, and the most important of these have nothing at all to do with *Auer*. Internal pressures often create an incentive toward clarity, so that everyone inside government knows what the regula-

---

[146] *Decker v Northwest Environmental Defense Center*, 133 S Ct 1326, 1340 (2013) (Scalia, J, concurring in part and dissenting in part).

[147] Scalia, 1989 Duke L J at 515 (cited in note 138).

[148] *Decker*, 133 S Ct at 1340.

[149] Id at 1341 (Scalia, J, concurring in part and dissenting in part).

[150] In nearly four years in the federal government, one of us (Sunstein) dealt with over two thousand rules, and he never heard even a single person suggest, or come close to suggesting, that a regulation should be written vaguely or ambiguously in light of *Auer*, or so that the agency could later interpret it as it saw fit.

tion means. External pressures often cut in exactly the same direction, with multiple requests for clarity from the regulated sector. To be sure, external and internal pressures might also call for deliberate ambiguity (though we believe that this is far less common). But when ambiguity exists, it is rarely, if ever, because of *Auer*. After all, few people who are involved in writing regulations think a great deal about *Auer*; some of them have no idea what *Auer* is. (It doesn't sound like a word at all.)

A recent study finds that *Auer* was less well known to agency drafters of regulations than *Chevron*, *Skidmore*, and *Mead*; drafters knew about *Auer* only about half of the time.[151] There is a further point: If an agency leaves a regulation ambiguous, it cannot be certain that a subsequent interpretation will be made by an administration with the same or similar values. For agencies, ambiguities are a threat, not only an opportunity.

Auer's critics also have a more fundamental objection, one that apparently has intuitive appeal, which is that *Auer* produces a constitutionally suspect combination of the power to make law with the power to interpret law. *Chevron* preserves that separation, because agencies interpret what Congress enacts, but *Auer* obliterates it, because agencies interpret what agencies enact. Quoting Montesquieu, Justice Scalia insists that this is a serious problem, because when "legislative and executive powers are united in the same person . . . there can be no liberty."[152] He concludes: "He who writes a law must not adjudge its violation."[153]

Justice Thomas's concerns are also constitutionally grounded, but somewhat different—and as we will see, their implications are even more sweeping. In his view, *Auer* "subjects regulated parties to precisely the abuses that the Framers sought to prevent," and so it is "constitutionally suspect."[154] It is, after all, the power of courts to issue authoritative interpretations in judicial proceedings. The critical problem with *Auer* is that it substitutes the agency's power of interpretation for that of the courts. "Because the agency is thus not prop-

---

[151] Christopher J. Walker, *Inside Agency Statutory Interpretation*, 67 Stan L Rev 999, 1007 (2015).

[152] *Decker*, 133 S Ct at 1341 (Scalia, J, concurring in part and dissenting in part).

[153] Id at 1342 (Scalia, J, concurring in part and dissenting in part).

[154] *Perez*, 135 S Ct at 1213, 1215 (Thomas, J, concurring in the judgment).

erly constituted to exercise the judicial power under the Constitution, the transfer of interpretive judgment raises serious separation-of-powers concerns."[155]

In these constitutional objections we find the genuine flavor of the New Coke. Unfortunately, it is undrinkable. The New Coke critique of *Auer* proves far too much. First, if the combination of lawmaking and law-interpreting functions in agencies really is constitutionally suspect as such, then there are much larger problems than *Auer* to discuss. The FCC, FTC, SEC, and a myriad of other agencies would seem to be constitutionally suspect as well; all of these agencies write binding rules, bring enforcement actions, and adjudicate violations. Justice Thomas may think these agencies distinguishable. Or he may indeed think they have to go and be willing to take the consequences (or rather to inflict them on others). But it is most doubtful that Justice Scalia, "the faint-hearted originalist,"[156] would go so far. The Supreme Court has repeatedly said that the combination of functions is not in itself a constitutional problem[157]—in part because executive power itself includes the power to make and to interpret rules, as the Court recently reiterated through the pen of . . . Justice Scalia.[158]

In any event, the analytic point is that there is a severe mismatch between the sweeping constitutional critique, on the one hand, and on the other the narrow context of *Auer*. If it is right, the critique actually amounts to an indictment not merely of *Auer* but indeed much of the contemporary administrative state, and its proponents should have the candor to argue for it on those terms. Perhaps those proponents, or some of them, believe that the constitutionality of agencies that combine lawmaking with law interpretation is too entrenched to deserve rethinking, while *Auer* is fair game. But—to presage a point to which we will return—is it really a good or even intelligible use of the separation-of-powers principle to insist that judges must, entirely on their own, interpret the meaning of words like "diagnosis" or "diaries"? Does constitutional liberty depend on an affirmative answer?

---

[155] Id at 1220.

[156] Antonin Scalia, *Originalism: The Lesser Evil*, 57 U Cin L Rev 849, 862 (1989).

[157] See, for example, *Marcello v Bonds*, 349 US 302, 311 (1955); *Federal Trade Commission v Cement Institute*, 333 US 683, 702 (1948); *Withrow v Larkin*, 421 US 35, 54 (1975).

[158] *City of Arlington*, 133 S Ct at 1873 n 4.

Second, Justice Thomas offers the somewhat different theory that Congress may not delegate "binding" interpretive power to agencies construing their own regulations, because as a constitutional matter Congress does not possess the "judicial power" in the first place, and therefore cannot give it away. The theory does have the virtue of novelty. But the problems that afflict it are so many, and so transparent, that one stares puzzled at Thomas's opinion—can it really be saying what it seems to be saying? The theory sweeps beyond agencies' interpretation of their own regulations, to include any "binding" agency interpretation at all, including agency interpretations of organic statutes, suggesting that those interpretations cannot be deemed binding. The theory would invoke the Constitution to bar not only *Auer* deference, but also *Chevron* deference, *even if explicitly required by Congress*—here too an outcome that is congenial to Justice Thomas, but not to Justice Scalia. Congress often uses terms and then says something like "as defined by the Secretary." It would be implausible to think that this approach violates separation-of-powers principles; it is simply a shorthand way of giving agencies, within the limits of an intelligible principle, some authority to specify policy.

Let us end with the Court's simple, emphatic, and powerful response to New Coke criticisms of *Auer*, based on separation of powers: the criticisms overlook the fact that the judiciary always retains the whip hand. When the underlying regulation is clear, the agency must comply, and it is ultimately up to the judges to decide when the regulation is clear.[159] It is instructive in this regard to compare the New Coke's view of *Auer* with the decision in *City of Arlington v FCC*— written by Justice Scalia only two Terms ago. *City of Arlington* upheld the authority of agencies to determine, through statutory interpretation, the scope of their own "jurisdiction," within the bounds of statutory ambiguity—an abomination to the traditional legal mind, and a holding that prompted vehement New Coke objections from the Chief Justice in dissent. For agencies to interpret the scope of their own jurisdiction would strengthen the "potent brew of executive, legislative and judicial power"[160] that agencies already mix together. (Again, let us be clear that the Court has steadily held that agencies implementing statutory grants of authority always and only exercise

---

[159] See *Perez*, 135 S Ct at 1219 n 4 (Thomas, J, concurring in the judgment).

[160] *City of Arlington*, 133 S Ct at 1877 (Roberts, CJ, dissenting).

executive power, which includes subsidiary powers to make and inter-pret rules.[161]) Justice Scalia's reply was strong and simple:

> The fox-in-the-henhouse syndrome is to be avoided not by establishing an arbitrary and undefinable category of agency decisionmaking that is accorded no deference, but by taking seriously, and applying rigorously, in all cases, statutory limits on agencies' authority. Where Congress has established a clear line, the agency cannot go beyond it; and where Con-gress has established an ambiguous line, the agency can go no further than the ambiguity will fairly allow.[162]

But this argument applies, *mutatis mutandis*, to *Auer* deference equally well. The putative separation-of-powers problem with the combination of lawmaking and law-interpreting power in the same hands—the fox put in charge of the henhouse—is exactly the same in both the *Auer* setting and the setting of agency self-determination of jurisdiction. And the remedy Scalia proposes, judicial enforcement of clear texts, is the same as well.

It is not as though there are no checks on agency built into the *Auer* framework. The New Coke summons the specter of unchecked agency self-dealing, but that abstract concern loses reality when put in the context of real-world problems. The regulation that is being interpreted provides the law, and any interpretation must comply with it. We have noted that in some cases, an ambiguity should be taken as a clear authorization to the private sector. An agency in-terpretation might also be arbitrary and capricious—perhaps because it defeats reliance interests. But as the Court noted in *Perez*, these points fit comfortably within both the *Auer* framework itself and the current law of arbitrariness review.

There is something overheated, wildly disproportionate, about the New Coke's critique of *Auer*. Return to the cases with which we

---

[161] Id at 1873 n 4 (majority): The Chief Justice's discomfort with the growth of agency power, see *post* at 1877–79, is perhaps understandable. But the dissent overstates when it claims that agencies exercise "legislative power" and "judicial power." *Post* at 1877–78; see also *post* at 1885–86. The former is vested exclusively in Congress, US Const, Art I, § 1, the latter in the "one supreme Court" and "such inferior Courts as the Congress may from time to time ordain and establish," Art III, § 1. Agencies make rules ("Private cattle may be grazed on public lands X, Y, and Z subject to certain conditions") and conduct adjudications ("This rancher's grazing permit is revoked for violation of the conditions") and have done so since the beginning of the Republic. These activities take "legislative" and "judicial" forms, but they are exercises of—indeed, under our constitutional structure they *must be* exercises of—the "executive Power." Art II, § 1, cl 1.

[162] *City of Arlington*, 133 S Ct at 1874.

began. Is constitutional liberty really at risk if an agency is allowed to interpret the word "diagnosis," within the bounds of textual meaning? "Bound books"? "Diaries"? Is liberty less at risk if, in the face of ambiguity, courts, composed of generalist judges, interpret such terms on their own? Does it matter that agency interpretations often increase, rather than confine, the freedom of the regulated class, by telling its members that they may in fact do what they want to do? Does it matter that interpretation of ambiguities often entails political judgments, as reflected in the different views of Republican and Democratic appointees, even under *Chevron*?[163] Does it matter that we are typically speaking of interstitial and highly technical judgments, in which agencies understand an ambiguous term ("diaries") in a linguistically permissible way? The whole class of questions seems to be pitched at a different level from the grand issues of constitutionality and prerogative on which advocates of the New Coke tend to focus.

In our view, the strongest objections to *Auer* do not involve Montesquieu or Madison or even the APA. They suggest, far more modestly, that when an agency is interpreting its own regulation, the best legal fiction is that ambiguities are for courts, not administrators. On this view, it would be possible to approve of *Chevron* but to disapprove of *Auer*, contending that if those who write laws (regulations) can also interpret them, there is a risk of bias or self-dealing. If we distrusted the agency's expertise, or believed that it was systematically biased, and if we thought that judges could be better trusted to resolve questions that often involve policy judgments, we might indulge that particular fiction. Some version of that view clearly underlies the bafflingly intense opposition to *Auer*.

But return to the cases with which we began, and ask whether a judgment about institutional competence really justifies the conclusion that the relevant ambiguities are best resolved through independent judicial judgment. Because of the need to resolve technical issues, and because of the plain advantages of accountability, the balance cuts hard in the direction of *Auer*.

Some critics of *Auer* plainly fear that agencies will seek to expand their own authority, interpreting ambiguous regulations in a way that increases their power over the private sphere. Here some

---

[163] See Cass R. Sunstein and Thomas J. Miles, *Depoliticizing Administrative Law*, 58 Duke L J 2193, 2202 (2009).

version of the New Coke is clearly relevant, even if it appears in modest forms. But even on its own terms, the fear depends on a wildly mistaken factual predicate, indeed a naive picture of what interpretive rules are *for*. One of the primary functions of interpretive rules has been *to confine agency authority rather than to expand it*, often in response to questions and concerns from the regulated community. *Auer* in effect allows agencies to clarify how they intend to exercise their discretion, without fear of judicial second-guessing (within the limits of relevant ambiguity). It accommodates the many agencies who respond to the questions and concerns of regulated parties by saying that the agency does not mean, and has no intention, to invade the private sphere in the relevant way. Would it be better for courts to second-guess agency judgments on this count?

III. The Risk of Executive Abuse

The New Coke is obviously animated by a fear of executive abuse. In our view, however, those who embrace the New Coke focus too myopically and selectively on one set of risks, and neglect the full universe of them. We can make this point in strictly legal terms, by focusing on legal documents, or more pragmatically, by focusing on the set of relevant values and how best to accommodate them.

We have emphasized the Court's recognition—in *Wong Yang Sung*, *Vermont Yankee*, and *Perez*—that the APA was a "formula upon which opposing . . . forces have come to rest."[164] More particularly, the APA settlement reflects a particular effort to balance a range of variables, including stability, constraints on executive power, accountability, and the need for expedition and energy—for vigorous government.[165] For the theorists and architects of the modern administrative state, "private" power, exercised through delegation of legal powers and entitlements by the common law and by "market" ordering, was itself a threat to individual liberty.[166] Hence vigorous

---

[164] *Perez*, 135 S Ct at 1207.

[165] For a classic statement, see generally James M. Landis, *The Administrative Process* (Yale, 1938).

[166] See Robert L. Hale, *Coercion and Distribution in a Supposedly Non-Coercive State*, 38 Pol Sci Q 470, 478 (1923). See generally Cass R. Sunstein, *The Second Bill of Rights: FDR's Unfinished Revolution and Why We Need It More Than Ever* (Basic, 2006); Daniel R. Ernst, *Tocqueville's Nightmare: The Administrative State Emerges in America, 1900–1914* (Oxford, 2014).

government, checking the abuse of corporate power and other "private" power, was just as indispensable for liberty as constraints on executive abuse.[167]

Of course the APA settlement did not by any means reflect a wholesale victory for the proponents of vigorous government. The defenders of private liberty played an important role in that settlement. But part of the balance involved a national recognition— prominent in the New Deal era—of the multiple values served by modern administrative agencies. The opponents of the New Deal did not win.[168] In the APA compromise, Congress created procedural safeguards to reduce the risk of executive abuse, and also recognized and in some ways fortified the judicial role, above all with the "substantial evidence" test.[169] But the APA does not embrace anything like the New Coke—on the contrary, it pointedly declines to do so.

No one doubts that the APA leaves gaps and ambiguities, and consistent with its terms, courts might move in the direction of strengthening those constraints on executive action that they see as infringing on liberty. But they cannot possibly claim that the APA, taken as a whole, calls for the kind of role sketched by Justice Thomas and his occasional allies. The New Dealers—villains, according to those who embrace the New Coke[170]—were willing to accept the APA, and they came to embrace it with some enthusiasm. Taken seriously, the New Coke vision stands opposed to the APA. It brands the accommodation of the administrative state as fundamentally wrong.[171]

What of the Constitution, the allegedly authentic source of the New Coke? We think that broadly speaking and on the relevant counts, the founding document is analogous to the APA. It too is a compromise, a balance among competing values and views,[172] including protection of private liberty, and it does not speak single-

---

[167] Vermeule, 109 Nw U L Rev at 678–79 (cited in note 12).

[168] Matthew D. McCubbins, Roger Noll, and Barry R. Weingast, *The Political Origins of the Administrative Procedure Act*, 15 J L Econ & Org 180, 182–83 (1999).

[169] See *Universal Camera Corp. v National Labor Relations Board*, 340 US 474, 477–88 (1951).

[170] See Murray, *By the People* at 63 n 9 (cited in note 10).

[171] See Hamburger, *Is Administrative Law Unlawful?* at 15 (cited in note 20); Lawson, 88 Va L Rev at 332–33 (cited in note 123).

[172] For one of many discussions, see generally Joseph J. Ellis, *The Quartet: Orchestrating the Second American Revolution, 1783–1789* (Knopf, 2015).

mindedly of constraining the executive. Of course the Framers were intensely concerned with the dangers of creating a monarchy, and the antifederalists vigorously objected to the document in part on the ground that they had not sufficiently counteracted that danger. Of course private liberty mattered. But the founding generation also deplored the absence of executive power in the Articles of Confederation. In part under the influence of Alexander Hamilton, they sought to ensure an energetic and coordinated executive branch, one that would be able to get things done.[173] They sought a degree of efficiency in government, and they wanted to create a framework that would overcome the weakness and the paralysis that they found under the Articles.

In Hamilton's own words, "A feeble Executive implies a feeble execution of the government. A feeble execution is but another phrase for a bad execution; and a government ill executed, whatever it may be in theory, must be, in practice, a bad government."[174] As Hamilton put it, "all men of sense will agree in the necessity of an energetic Executive," and so the only question is, "what are the ingredients which constitute this energy"?[175] In his terms, they include "first unity, secondly duration, thirdly an adequate provision for its support, fourthly, competent powers."[176] We do not contend that Hamilton's abstract claims can resolve particular questions; they hardly prove that *Chevron* or *Auer* is correct. But they have negative significance: at the very least, they raise serious doubts about the claimed constitutional pedigree of the New Coke, and about the view that executive discretion, for the founding generation, was a central constitutional evil to be averted, a reminder of the monarchical legacy.

The existence of broad grants of discretion to the executive in the earliest days of the Republic testify to this point,[177] as do a wide range of practices in the early period, which recognize the impor-

---

[173] See Saikrishna Bangalore Prakash, *Imperial from the Beginning: The Constitution of the Original Executive* 12–13 (Yale, 2015); Frank Bourgin, *The Great Challenge: The Myth of Laissez-Faire in the Early Republic* 54–56 (George Braziller, 1989).

[174] Federalist 70 (Hamilton), in Jacob E. Cook, ed, *The Federalist* 471, 471–72 (Wesleyan, 1982) (cited in note 11).

[175] Id at 472.

[176] Id.

[177] See Posner and Vermeule, 69 U Chi L Rev at 1227 (cited in note 105).

tance and advantages of executive authority for promoting the general welfare.[178] Those who think that the Constitution is inconsistent with the modern administrative state have yet to grapple with the historical materials, elaborated in great detail by Jerry Mashaw.[179] On the broadest questions, the constitutional settlement cannot easily be taken to favor the New Coke. Those who invoke the founding document as the basis for large-scale attacks on administrative agencies seem to us to be speaking less for history and the original understanding than for early twenty-first-century views and convictions.[180] Their methodology sounds far less in originalism than in current social movements and common-law constitutionalism, based on very contemporary values and fears—not less contemporary than those that have brought us *Roe v Wade*,[181] *District of Columbia v Heller*,[182] and more recently *Obergefell v Hodges*.[183]

To say this is not to say that the words of the founding document strictly rule the New Coke out of bounds. Though we do not favor it, a heightened version of the intelligible principle test would not obviously be inconsistent with the text of the document itself. Though we do not favor it, Justice Thomas's disapproval of binding regulations is not a textually unintelligible understanding of Article I taken by itself, in a vacuum. Though we do not favor it, background principles, involving the separation of powers, have been invoked with a straight face to challenge both *Chevron* and *Auer*.[184] We do not reject

---

[178] See Mashaw, *Creating the Administrative Constitution* at 53 (cited in note 118).

[179] Id at 29.

[180] In our view, the expansion of power of national government is the unanticipated development. The growth of the administrative state should be counted as unanticipated *only insofar as it reflects that expansion*—but not insofar as agencies wield discretion or have "binding" interpretive and rulemaking authority. We acknowledge that we cannot defend this controversial view in this brief space.

[181] 410 US 113 (1973).

[182] 554 US 570 (2008).

[183] 135 S Ct 2584 (2015).

[184] Indeed, one of us once did exactly that. See Cass R. Sunstein, *Constitutionalism after the New Deal*, 101 Harv L Rev 421, 467 (1987) ("*Chevron* suggests that administrators should decide the scope of their own authority. That notion flatly contradicts separation-of-powers principles that date back to *Marbury v. Madison* and to The Federalist No. 78. The case for judicial review depends in part on the proposition that foxes should not guard henhouses—an injunction to which *Chevron* appears deaf. It would be most peculiar to argue that congressional or state interpretations of constitutional provisions should be accepted whenever there is ambiguity in the constitutional text; such a view would wreak havoc with existing constitutional law. Those limited by a provision should not determine the nature of the limitation."). (Oh, the folly of youth.)

the claim that standing by itself the text could be taken to call for restrictions on executive authority that would move in the direction of the New Coke.

But those who call for such restrictions are, we think, engaged in a living-constitutionalist enterprise. The New Coke hovers somewhere between free-form constitutional law, ultimately based on the judges' own policy preferences, and Dworkin's conception of law as integrity,[185] which attempts to fit the existing legal matters but also to justify them by casting them in what seems (to the interpreters) to be the best or most appealing light. There is a deep irony here, because the New Coke is often defended as a necessary or at least faithful reading of the founding materials. We have noted that while Justice Thomas's approach to the nondelegation doctrine is not foreclosed by the text, it is hard to square with early American history, including the history of the founding era itself. The same is true of a strict version of the intelligible principle test. For the reasons we have sketched, what Thomas offers is hardly a necessary reading of the text, and history does not offer much support for it.

To the extent that the Constitution leaves gaps or ambiguities, and to the extent that the relevant legal materials[186] allow them, should judges embrace the New Coke, or at least take steps in its direction? Everything depends on the particular question. Our claim is just that constraining executive discretion is not the only goal of a sensible legal order. Constraints have costs as well, and they might even endanger liberty, however it is understood. The problem is greatly heightened if constraints on *executive* discretion amount, in practice, to increases in *judicial* discretion, allowing the political values of judges to play a significant role, as James Landis[187] and others argued[188]—a shift that should be especially unwelcome when technocratic expertise and political accountability greatly matter. We think that an ironic consequence of the New Coke would be to produce

---

[185] See Ronald Dworkin, *Law's Empire* 94 (Belknap, 1986).

[186] Of course, there is a question of how to identify them; some originalists would downplay history and precedent.

[187] James M. Landis, *Administrative Policies and the Courts*, 47 Yale L J 519, 528 (1938).

[188] See Thomas J. Miles and Cass R. Sunstein, *Do Judges Make Regulatory Policy? An Empirical Investigation of Chevron*, 73 U Chi L Rev 823, 841 (2006). Note that the finding in this essay is that political preferences play a role in the post-*Chevron* era; without *Chevron*, the role of those preferences would undoubtedly be magnified.

large-scale shifts of that kind, and in some singularly unappealing contexts.[189]

Would it be best for judges, rather than agencies, to decide on the meaning of the word "source" in the Clean Air Act (the issue in *Chevron* itself)? Would it be a good idea for judges, rather than agencies, to stare at dictionaries, or to consult their own policy preferences, to decide the meaning of terms like "diagnosis" and "diaries" and "waiting time," where those words are genuinely ambiguous? Some questions really do answer themselves.

IV. CONCLUSION

We have had three goals here. The first is to show that in *Perez*, the Court issued the long-awaited *Vermont Yankee II*, insisting that courts are not authorized to add procedures to those required by the APA. On the issue at hand, the Court's ruling was clearly correct; changes in interpretive rules need not be accompanied by notice-and-comment rulemaking. On other issues, the meaning of *Vermont Yankee II* remains less than entirely clear, because some judicial innovations have a more plausible connection to APA requirements, and because the Court is unlikely to want to undo the fabric of settled law (for example, by ruling that courts may not require agencies to respond to the most important public comments). But any such innovations—past, present, or future—will have to reckon with the language of *Perez*. Some or even a great deal of current doctrine, elaborated by courts through policing supposed notice-and-comment requirements, may ultimately be vulnerable.[190]

Our second goal has been to show that in both *Perez* and *American Railroads*, the center held. The Court ruled in narrow, legally supportable ways, and without embracing large-scale attacks on the administrative state. An approach of this kind, we suggest, promises to honor the multiple goals of public law without embracing partisan claims from the twenty-first century, resting on dubious tales from English history or current prejudices dressed up in the ill-fitting garb of the founding era.

---

[189] See the list at note 25 of cases in which rejection of *Auer* deference would call for a heightened judicial role.

[190] See *American Radio Relay League, Inc. v Federal Communications Commission*, 524 F3d 227, 246 (DC Cir 2008) (Kavanaugh concurring in part, concurring in the judgment in part, and dissenting in part).

Our third and largest goal has been to explore the New Coke, an approach that seems increasingly influential in academic circles, and that has made its presence felt on the Court—above all in Justice Thomas's extraordinary pronouncements, but also in more modest form in the opinions of several other Justices, who offer expressions of large-scale concern with the exercise of executive discretion. Not unlike the modern right to choose abortion, the right to same-sex marriage, and (at least arguably[191]) the right to individual gun ownership, the New Coke is a product of thoroughly contemporary values and fears—perhaps prompted by continuing rejection, in some quarters, of the New Deal itself,[192] and perhaps prompted by a reaction of some of its advocates to controversial initiatives from more recent presidents. Whatever the origins of the New Coke, the Court's failure to embrace it, and its calm, steady path this Term, are occasions for celebration, even if not quite dancing in the streets.[193]

---

[191] See generally *District of Columbia v Heller*, 554 US 570 (2008). The constitutional materials are of course disputed. See generally Mark V. Tushnet, *Out of Range: Why the Constitution Can't End the Battle over Guns* (Oxford, 2007); Reva B. Siegel, *Dead or Alive: Originalism as Popular Constitutionalism in Heller*, 122 Harv L Rev 191 (2008).

[192] See Douglas H. Ginsburg, *On Constitutionalism*, 2002–2003 Cato S Ct Rev 7, 16–17 (2003). See generally Murray, *By the People* (cited in note 10); Barnett, *Restoring the Lost Constitution* (cited in note 17).

[193] See Harry Kalven Jr., *The New York Times Case: A Note on "the Central Meaning of the First Amendment,"* 1964 Supreme Court Review 191, 221 (1964) (quoting Alexander Meiklejohn to the effect that *New York Times v Sullivan* is "an occasion for dancing in the streets").

OWEN FISS

TIERS OF STANDING

The Supreme Court is charged with protecting the Constitution, but it is not a roving commission. It must wait for a case to arrive at its doorstep before determining whether the Constitution has been violated. Someone must claim that a policy or practice is unconstitutional and, in addition, show that he or she has been, or is likely to be, injured by it. Without this showing of injury, the Court will dismiss the suit on the theory that the party who initiated the suit or the plaintiff lacked "standing," without ever addressing the merits of the claim advanced.

The standing requirement has, for generations, been a steadfast feature of our constitutional tradition.[1] Doctrinally, it has been understood as an extrapolation of Article III of the Constitution, which limits the jurisdiction of the federal judiciary to "cases" or "controversies." In turn, the Court has read these terms to extend solely to those disputes in which the plaintiff is actually injured.

Text aside, the standing requirement has also been defended on the ground that it serves the constitutional principle requiring separation of powers. Cabining the jurisdiction of the judiciary to disputes where

Owen Fiss is Sterling Professor Emeritus of Law, Yale University.

AUTHOR'S NOTE: I am grateful to the extraordinary research and editorial assistance of Daniel Rauch.

[1] Although the term "standing" first appears in Supreme Court decisions around the start of the twentieth century, it is rooted in concerns as old as the Constitution itself. See Daniel E. Ho and Erica L. Ross, *Did Liberal Justices Invent the Standing Doctrine? An Empirical Study of the Evolution of Standing, 1921–2006*, 62 Stan L Rev 591 (2010).

the plaintiff faces a threat of actual injury will, so it is argued, limit the judiciary to the task of adjudication and prevent it from usurping the functions of the legislative and executive branches of government, branches that also have the prerogative, even the duty, of construing the Constitution.

Others defend the standing requirement on more pragmatic grounds. It has been argued that it prevents the judiciary from wasting time on purely academic inquiries—matters of no practical import either for the operation of government or the lives of ordinary citizens. The standing requirement is also said to facilitate and strengthen the operation of our adversarial system, on the assumption that parties threatened with personal hardship will make more forceful presentations of the facts and law than litigants with merely abstract interests at stake.

In practice, the rigors of the standing requirement have shifted over time. During the 1960s, the heyday of the Warren Court, the standing requirement was read permissively—much in keeping with the broad conception of judicial power prevalent at that time. Starting in the mid-1970s, though, the Court became increasingly stringent in applying the standing requirement to all manner of cases, including constitutional ones. In particular, the Court became wary of citizen-initiated lawsuits in which plaintiffs alleged no personal injury beyond a concern that the government had acted or might soon act unlawfully. To curtail such challenges, the Supreme Court increasingly required that plaintiffs' injuries, or threats of injuries, be palpable and particularized.

In February 2013, more than a decade into the War on Terror, the Court continued along the same trajectory, but took a giant leap forward when it refashioned the standing requirement and gave it a new and special stringency in national security cases. This occurred in *Clapper v Amnesty International USA*,[2] where the Court was confronted with a constitutional challenge to a 2008 statute that had vastly enlarged the surveillance power of the federal government. The challenge raised vital constitutional questions, but the Court never reached them. Instead it dismissed the suit for lack of standing, even though doing so would virtually insulate the 2008 statute from judicial review. In reaching this result, *Clapper* fashioned an approach to justiciability that created "tiers of standing": a higher and more

---

[2] 133 S Ct 1138 (2013).

stringent standing requirement—a new tier—should govern national security cases.[3]

In other contexts, most notably equal protection and free speech, the concept of "tiers of scrutiny" is familiar. In these cases, the Court often uses three different standards for reviewing the constitutionality of statutes: strict scrutiny (the most exacting tier), intermediate scrutiny, and rational basis review (the most permissive). In equal protection cases, for instance, strict scrutiny is reserved for statutes that employ a suspect category (such as race) or that curtail the exercise of a fundamental right (such as the right to vote). Likewise, in free speech cases, strict scrutiny is reserved for measures that regulate speech on the basis of its content, while lesser scrutiny is applied for measures that merely regulate speech on the basis of its time, place, or manner. In either instance, in the heightened tier the government is required to show that the statute in question is designed to serve a compelling purpose and that the means is narrowly tailored, indeed, the least restrictive way of achieving that purpose. Not surprisingly, in practice, strict scrutiny has usually turned out to be "fatal in fact":[4] laws falling in this tier are overwhelmingly struck down.

In just the same way, *Clapper* seems to have created a special, heightened tier of standing for national security cases—a tier analogous to strict scrutiny. Yet in the standing context, this strict or more demanding tier dictates an opposite result: the suit is dismissed and the statute challenged is kept in force without a ruling on the merits. The doors of the courthouse are shut and, as a result, the Court declines to resolve or even address crucial constitutional questions raised by a policy, provided it is designed to further national security. In adopting this new, tiered approach, the Court has failed in its responsibility, as essential in times of war as well as peace, to hold the legislative and executive branches accountable to the law.

THE 2008 STATUTE

The 2008 statute at issue in *Clapper* had its origins in the initial phases of the War on Terror. In the fall of 2001, President George W. Bush issued a secret executive order establishing the

---

[3] The term "tiers of standing" was coined by Julie Verloff in my spring 2013 seminar on law and terrorism.

[4] Gerald Gunther, *Foreword: In Search of Evolving Doctrine on a Changing Court: A Model for a Newer Equal Protection*, 86 Harv L Rev 1, 17 (1972).

so-called Terrorist Surveillance Program. This order directed the National Security Agency to tap international telephone calls between persons in the United States and persons abroad who were suspected of having links to Al Qaeda or its allies. Initially, the president's order was hidden from public view. In December 2005, however, the program was publicly disclosed by the *New York Times* and became the subject of a heated controversy.[5]

Although some objections to the program were based on the Fourth Amendment, the main objection arose from the president's failure to abide by the requirements of the Foreign Intelligence Surveillance Act (FISA).[6] This law was adopted by Congress in 1978 in the wake of revelations about the far-reaching, and largely uncontrolled, surveillance activities of American intelligence agencies. To address these concerns, FISA set out new protocols for the interception of electronic communications to or from foreign nationals within the United States.

As originally enacted, FISA applied to any electronic surveillance of "agents"—defined as an "officer or employee" of a "foreign power," when used to gather "foreign intelligence information."[7] "Foreign power" was defined to include foreign nations and, crucially, any "group engaged in international terrorism." "Foreign intelligence information," in turn, was defined to include information about "clandestine intelligence activities," "sabotage," "international terrorism," and "the conduct of the foreign affairs of the United States."[8] The 1978 law also provided that, before conducting any electronic surveillance governed by the statute, the executive must obtain permission from a special court—the Foreign Intelligence Surveillance Court (FISC). This court was to consist of eleven sitting federal judges, each designated for this special assignment by the Chief Justice of the United States. Each of these judges was authorized to act alone, and both their identities and their proceedings were to be kept secret. FISA declared that the procedures that it established were to be the exclusive avenue

---

[5] James Risen and Eric Lichtblau, *Bush Lets U.S. Spy on Callers Without Courts*, NY Times (Dec 16, 2005), archived at http://www.nytimes.com/2005/12/16/politics/bush-lets-us-spy-on-callers-without-courts.html.

[6] Pub L No 95-511, 92 Stat 1783, 50 USC ch 36.

[7] 92 Stat at 1783–84, § 101 (a)–(b).

[8] Id at § 101(b)(2), 92 Stat 1784.

by which the executive could gather foreign intelligence from electronic communications.

In launching the Terrorist Surveillance Program, Bush wholly bypassed the FISC, thus apparently violating FISA. His Attorney General, Alberto Gonzalez, initially defended this strategy on the theory that it was authorized by the congressional resolution of September 18, 2001.[9] Gonzalez claimed that this resolution—which authorized the use of military force against those responsible for September 11—implicitly modified FISA, such that FISC review was no longer the exclusive procedure for conducting electronic surveillance of agents of Al Qaeda, the foreign power that directed the terrorist attacks of September 11.[10]

Gonzalez also treated the September 18 resolution as a declaration of war against Al Qaeda and maintained that requiring the president to submit to FISA's procedures unduly interfered with his constitutional prerogative to act as commander-in-chief of the armed forces. Article II of the Constitution vests the president with the authority and responsibility to act as commander-in-chief. Implicit in this power, accordingly to Gonzalez, is the authority to override any statute—including FISA—that unduly interferes with the discharge of his duties as commander-in-chief. Just as Congress cannot tell the president how to deploy the armed forces, Gonzalez claimed, it could not instruct the president on how to gather the intelligence needed for its war against Al Qaeda.

By 2007, however, the administration had changed its strategy and decided that it would no longer bypass FISA. Instead, Gonzalez turned to FISC to get what was wanted. In a letter to the chairman and ranking minority member of the Senate Judiciary Committee, Gonzalez reported that on January 10, 2007, a FISA judge had issued orders broadly authorizing the wiretapping that had previously been conducted through the clandestine Terrorist Surveillance Program. As Gonzalez put it, the FISA judge issued orders "authorizing the Government to target for collection international communications into or out of the United States where there is probable cause to believe that one of the communicants is a member or agent of al-

---

[9] Authorization for Use of Military Force (AUMF), Pub L No 107-40, 115 Stat 224 (2001).

[10] See Evidence to Committee on the Judiciary, US Senate, Wartime Executive Power and the National Security Agency's Surveillance Authority, 109th Cong, 2d Sess (2006) 10–15, archived at http://perma.cc/N8M6-Z2F4.

Qaeda."[11] In light of this turn of events, Gonzalez said that there would be no need to continue the Terrorist Surveillance Program (though he reaffirmed his belief that the program "fully complies with the law").

By April 2007, the administration grew uneasy with the strategy announced only months earlier. It felt that FISA, as it then stood, did not provide it with adequate tools to meet the threat of international terrorism. A decisive point came in March 2007, when, in the context of reviewing the original January orders, a FISA judge ruled that the authorization for wiretaps under the statute had to be made on a particularized or person-to-person basis, not on the broad grounds previously accepted.[12] This proved unacceptable to the Bush administration, which then turned to Congress for new legislation to "modernize" FISA—or, put differently, to give the intelligence agencies all the power that they thought they needed.

Congress responded favorably to the administration's overtures. On August 5, 2007, it passed the Protect America Act.[13] By its very terms, this law was set to expire in just six months, and in fact did expire (after a short extension) on February 16, 2008. Then, on July 10, 2008, Congress passed a replacement statute. This measure was presented as an amendment to the 1978 FISA statute, and was appropriately named the FISA Amendments Act of 2008.[14] Originally it was scheduled to expire at the end of 2012. As expected, however, during the pendency of the *Clapper* case, it was renewed for another five years and will remain in effect until 2017—subject of course to further renewal.

The principal innovation wrought by the FISA Amendments Act concerns foreign nationals located abroad. As originally enacted, FISA only governed calls in or to the United States, or calls routed through the United States. While this feature of the 1978 law remained, the 2008 amendments reduced, almost to a vanishing point, the requirements for approval by a FISA judge for interceptions where the target of the investigation was a foreign national located

---

[11] Letter from Alberto R. Gonzales, Attorney General, to Senator Patrick Leahy and Senator Arlen Specter (Jan 17, 2007), archived at http://perma.cc/GWU8-JXWP.

[12] Michael Isikoff, *Terror Watch: Behind the Surveillance Debate*, Newsweek (July 31, 2007), archived at http://perma.cc/69GQ-U5YM.

[13] Pub L No 110-155, 121 Stat 552, codified at 50 USC §§ 1801, 1803, 1805.

[14] Pub L No 110-261, 122 Stat 2436, codified at 50 USC § 1881a.

abroad. When such individuals are investigated, the government need only allege that the target is a foreign national located abroad and that a purpose of the interception is to gather foreign intelligence information. Crucially, it mattered not that the other party on the line is an American citizen or a foreign national lawfully admitted to residence in the United States.

The 2008 amendments also authorized FISC to grant blanket permissions for interceptions that covered groups of persons. The statute also compelled the court to act promptly (within 30 days) and to grant the government's request for an interception if, in its application, "all the required elements" were present.[15] No independent factual inquiries were to be undertaken by the FISA court.

CONSTITUTIONAL OBJECTIONS TO THE 2008 STATUTE

The *Clapper* suit was filed immediately after the enactment of the 2008 FISA amendments. The complaint largely focused on Congress's failure to require the government to obtain a judicial warrant prior to intercepting telephone conversations between American citizens and foreign nationals located abroad. Although the government was required to obtain prior judicial approval for electronic surveillance, the plaintiffs complained that the standards for granting this permission fell well below those specified by the Fourth Amendment. Specifically, the government was not required to show, as the Fourth Amendment mandates, "probable cause," which has long been construed to mean a reason to believe that the specific person whose calls are to be intercepted had committed, was committing, or would commit a crime.

Resolving this challenge to the 2008 statute would have required the Supreme Court to answer difficult constitutional questions. In particular, the Court would have had to determine whether the warrant requirement of the Fourth Amendment applies to electronic surveillance aimed at gathering foreign intelligence information. This was a question that the Court had avoided for decades and which was itself the product of an even earlier reluctance on the part of the Supreme Court to decide whether warrants are required for electronic surveillance designed to protect national security.

---

[15] Pub L No 110-261, 122 Stat 2436, 2444, codified at 50 USC § 1881a(a)(i)(3)(A).

The Court first extended the Fourth Amendment warrant requirement to wiretapping or electronic surveillance in its decision
Katz v United States in 1967.[16] In crafting its opinion, the Court was
careful to note that the case before it arose from an investigation into
gambling, an ordinary domestic crime, and that no view—one way or
the other—was being expressed on whether a warrant satisfying the
strictures of the Fourth Amendment would be needed if the investigation were instead aimed at protecting national security.[17]

The Court returned to this unresolved issue in the so-called *Keith*
case of 1972, a case that arose from the bombing, as part of the
sometimes violent protests against the Vietnam War, of a CIA office
in Ann Arbor, Michigan.[18] The telephone calls of one of the
defendants had been tapped without a warrant and the attorney
general defended this action on the ground that he had been investigating a threat to national security. The Court rejected the attorney
general's defense. In so doing, the Court denied that there was an
exception to the Fourth Amendment warrant requirement for
investigations aimed at protecting national security. However, the
Court went on to distinguish between two types of national security
threats—domestic and foreign—and made clear that its ruling applied only to the first category. The Court said that it was leaving
open the question of whether a warrant would have been required for
gathering foreign intelligence.[19]

Rather than wait for the Court to return to the issue left dangling in
Keith, in 1978 Congress took the lead and enacted FISA. In Fourth
Amendment terms, the 1978 act was a compromise: it required judicial approval for surveillance aimed at gathering foreign intelligence information, but it did not require the link to criminality
entailed by the Fourth Amendment's insistence on probable cause.
Indeed, the government only had to file an affidavit showing that the
purpose of the surveillance was to gather foreign intelligence and that
the person whose calls would be intercepted was an agent of a foreign
power. The 2008 measure built on, and in fact extended, the breadth
of the 1978 act. In cases where the target was a foreign national lo-

---

[16] 389 US 347 (1967).

[17] Id at 358 n 23.

[18] *United States v United States District Court*, 407 US 297 (1972).

[19] Id at 308.

cated abroad, the 2008 amendments enlarged the government's surveillance powers by dispensing with the requirement that it show that the target is an agent of a foreign power.

While the Supreme Court never ruled on the constitutionality of the 1978 act, a number of circuit courts upheld the law, so long as the "primary purpose" of the interception was to gather foreign intelligence (as opposed to advancing a criminal prosecution).[20] These lower-court rulings, in turn, led to the emergence of the so-called primary purpose test, a halfway measure intended to preserve the integrity of the rules announced by the Court in *Katz* and *Keith*. For decades, this rule was followed, not only by the lower federal courts, but also by the executive branch itself.

Matters changed after September 11, 2001. In the USA PATRIOT Act,[21] originally adopted soon after those terrorist attacks, Congress abandoned the primary purpose test, directing FISC to allow government interceptions as long as the gathering of foreign intelligence was a significant (as opposed to the primary) purpose of the interception. This particular statutory change compromised the protections of *Katz* and *Keith*, since any wiretap might have any number of purposes—including the gathering of foreign intelligence and supporting a criminal prosecution—and each of them might be "significant." The 2008 FISA amendments incorporated this enlargement of the FISA regime effectuated by the PATRIOT Act. It then compounded this dilution of the protection of privacy afforded by *Katz* and *Keith* by dispensing with the requirement that the target of the interception be an agent of a foreign power.

Apart from questions about the warrant requirement and its applicability to investigations aimed at gathering foreign intelligence or protecting national security, the *Clapper* suit also raised issues about the scope of persons protected by the Fourth Amendment. True, the standards for obtaining permission from FISC for an interception were significantly lowered by the 2008 act, but this new rule applied only in cases where the target of an investigation was a foreign national living abroad. What protections, if any, do these individuals have under the Fourth Amendment?

---

[20] See, for example, *United States v Pelton*, 835 F2d 1067, 1075–76 (4th Cir 1987); *United States v Badia*, 827 F2d 1458, 1464 (11th Cir 1987); *United States v Megahey*, 553 F Supp 1180 (E D NY 1982), aff'd under name *United States v Duggan*, 743 F2d 59 (2d Cir 1984).

[21] Pub L No 107-56, 115 Stat 272 (2001).

At first blush, the answer of Chief Justice William Rehnquist, writing for the Court in *United States v Verdugo-Urquidez* in 1990,[22] seems decisive: none. In that case, Rehnquist ruled that a warrantless search by U.S. officials of the home in Mexico of a Mexican citizen did not offend the Fourth Amendment, and that therefore evidence seized as part of the search could be used in the trial of that Mexican citizen to take place in the United States. Rehnquist had focused on the introductory phrase of the Fourth Amendment, which referred to "the right of the people" when it spoke about the guarantee against unreasonable searches and seizures. According to Rehnquist, the "people" consisted only of persons with a voluntary connection to the United States, such as American citizens or foreign nationals lawfully admitted to residence in the United States. The Fourth Amendment would protect no others.

Although Rehnquist claimed to be speaking for the Court, one of the Justices, Anthony Kennedy, who was needed to form a majority, wrote a separate concurrence in which he espoused a more cosmopolitan conception of the Constitution.[23] Kennedy said that he joined the Chief Justice's opinion, but nonetheless insisted that U.S. officials must always act reasonably, no matter where they were acting or against whomever they were acting. He rejected the Mexican citizen's Fourth Amendment claim, not because the individual had no Fourth Amendment rights, but only because the U.S. officials had, within the meaning of the Fourth Amendment, acted reasonably.

Later developments only further diminished the force of Rehnquist's stark stance in *Verdugo-Urquidez*. In the 2008 Supreme Court decision in *Boumediene v Bush*,[24] Kennedy, now writing the opinion of the majority, concluded that a federal statute that denied the writ of habeas corpus to foreign nationals detained at Guantánamo violated the Constitution. On the surface, Kennedy seemed less motivated by a regard for the constitutional rights of the prisoners than by a regard for separation of powers—the need to preserve the judiciary's role in reviewing the legality of executive detentions. Yet the implication of *Boumediene* for the rights of the Guantánamo prisoners was unmistakable, for there would be no point to protecting the authority of the

---

[22] 494 US 259 (1990).

[23] Id at 275.

[24] 553 US 723 (2008).

judiciary to review the legality of executive detentions, and thus for preserving the writ of habeas corpus, unless it could further be assumed that the Guantánamo prisoners—all of whom were foreign nationals originally apprehended abroad and now imprisoned abroad—possessed some constitutional rights.

Ultimately, the lawyers bringing the *Clapper* suit decided not to test the limits of *Verdugo-Urquidez*. Instead, they chose to name as plaintiffs American citizens residing and working in the United States—a category of persons unquestionably protected by the Fourth Amendment. Although the specific surveillance powers that they challenged were limited to cases in which the target of the investigation was a foreign national abroad, any telephone call or electronic communication must have another party on the line, and this party might well be an American. Under the 2008 act, the American citizen cannot be the target of the investigation and, for this reason, might be referred to as an "incidental victim" of the interception. Yet this is purely a technical classification, and it does not lessen the significance of the interception or the invasion of his or her right to privacy. The incidental victim's personal or private information is as vulnerable as that of the target.

From the very beginning, FISA sought to regulate interceptions that required access to facilities located in the United States. It created a procedure for granting the executive authority to tap telephone calls to and from the United States as well as calls between parties located in foreign nations but which were routed through the United States. The authors of the original legislation were mindful of the risks that such a grant of authority created for the privacy rights of Americans. Therefore, they required the attorney general, in seeking authorization from FISC for an interception, to attest under oath that there would be "no substantial likelihood that the surveillance would acquire the contents of any communication to which a United States person is a party."[25] ("United States persons" is a category that includes American citizens and foreign nationals lawfully admitted to residence in the United States.)

Following the 2008 FISA amendments, however, the attorney general did not need to meet this standard. Instead, he only needed to assure the FISA judge that procedures were in place to "prevent the

---

[25] Pub L No 95-511, 92 Stat 1783, at 1787, § 102 (a)(1)(B).

intentional acquisition of any communication in which the sender and all intended recipients are known at the time of acquisition to be located in the United States."[26] The introduction of an intentionality requirement and the use of the word "all" (as opposed to "any") profoundly diminished the protection of privacy interests of persons living and working in the United States, including American citizens.

Strategically, shifting the focus from foreign nationals located abroad to Americans working and living in the United States was intended to avoid the need to reexamine *Verdugo-Urquidez*. Yet it created a difficulty from another branch of Fourth Amendment doctrine: it has long been established, at least in ordinary criminal prosecutions, that although probable cause must be shown for the target of the interception, the statement of anyone who engages in a conversation with a target properly covered by a warrant might be used by the government in a criminal prosecution against those other persons.[27] In other words, the so-called incidental victims of a properly authorized wiretap are not protected by the exclusionary rule.

The question remains, however, whether this rule, fashioned in the context of a criminal prosecution, would apply in *Clapper*, where the issue was not the exclusionary rule, but a grant of authority, one that posed a much greater danger to the privacy of those American citizens whose calls would be intercepted on the theory that they were mere incidental victims of the interception. In particular, under the 2008 amendments, the target of the FISA interception need not be an individual—it can instead consist of broad categories or groups of foreign nationals, such as "Afghans affiliated with Al Qaeda." The amendments also removed the need to establish for the target the probable cause—suspicion of criminality—contemplated by *Katz* and *Keith*. Instead the government would only have to give reasons for believing the targets were foreign nationals located abroad, and that

---

[26] Pub L No 110-261, 122 Stat 2439, § 702(d)(1)(B), codified at 50 USC § 1881a(d)(1)(B).

[27] See, for example, *United States v Perillo*, 333 F Supp 914, 919–21 (D Del 1971), citing *Alderman v United States*, 394 US 165, 175 n 10 (1969) (deeming constitutional the government's use of conversations between the target of surveillance and a third party in a subsequent criminal prosecution of the third party, where the surveillance was conducted pursuant to a warrant applying only to the target of surveillance). See also *United States v Kahn*, 415 US 143, 157 (1974) (holding that the government's interception of incriminating telephone calls by the wife of a target of surveillance, and the subsequent use of those calls in a criminal prosecution against the wife, did not violate the Fourth Amendment even though the government had not established probable cause regarding the wife before beginning surveillance).

a significant purpose of the interception was to gather foreign intelligence information. The threshold for an interception is dramatically lower than that of the original 1978 act and, as a consequence, the so-called incidental victims—American citizens or foreign nationals lawfully residing in the United States who speak to foreign nationals abroad—are more exposed than ever to interceptions of their private conversations.

The Plaintiffs and Their Injury

The plaintiffs—all American citizens residing and working in the United States—had professional interests that led them to be in touch on a regular basis with persons who were in the Middle East. As part of the War on Terror, these individuals were each likely targets of government surveillance and wiretapping. Some of the plaintiffs were human rights researchers; others were journalists; still others were attorneys. In fact, one of the lawyers was, at the time the suit was filed, representing before a military commission in Guantánamo, Khalid Sheik Mohammad, the alleged mastermind of the September 11 attacks.

Most Fourth Amendment challenges arise in a criminal prosecution where the accused seeks to exclude or suppress evidence obtained in violation of the Constitution. Such cases present no doubt about justiciability: whatever the merits of the claim, the individual complaining of the Fourth Amendment violation surely has been personally and directly injured and thus has standing. Beyond these cases, however, Fourth Amendment challenges have also been made against statutes granting the government authority to engage in certain surveillance practices.[28] In such instances, the question is whether the statutory grant of authority itself offends the Fourth Amendment because the legislation fails to limit the authority to engage in surveillance to the circumstances that the Fourth Amendment permits.

In such cases, plaintiffs might seek a judgment declaring the grant of authority unconstitutional. Additionally, as happened in *Clapper*, plaintiffs can seek an injunction preventing the government from exercising the power the statute conferred. Typically, an injunction

---

[28] See, for example, *Berger v State of N.Y.*, 388 US 41 (1967).

prohibits a defendant from engaging in a certain course of conduct and implicitly threatens contempt for violations of that prohibition. The prohibition and threat of contempt are in effect from the moment the injunction is issued and they remain in effect until the judge dissolves the injunction. In this sense, the injunction governs the future, and that is why it is often deemed a prospective remedy. A distinction needs to be made, however, between the action that is governed by the injunction and the allegedly wrongful act that serves as the predicate for the issuance of the injunction.

The wrongful act that is the basis for the issuance of the injunction can be one that, at the time of the suit, is likely to occur in the future. An example of this type of injunctive suit can be found in the lawsuit brought to prevent the targeted killing of Anwar Al-Aulaki. He was an American citizen living and working in Yemen who, on September 30, 2011, was killed as a result of a drone attack launched by the United States. The year before this attack, Naser Al-Aulaki, Anwar's father, fearing that his son was on a "kill list" maintained by the U.S. government, brought a suit in the federal district court in Washington, D.C., seeking an injunction to prevent this act from ever occurring.[29] The complaint charged that such a killing would deprive Anwar of his life without due process of law.

Although an injunction could be predicated, as in the *Aulaki* case, on a future wrong, it need not be. Sometimes the wrongful act might have already occurred and the injunction would then seek to prevent that wrong from recurring and to eradicate the effects of that wrong. For example, an individual rejected from a job on the basis of race might seek an injunction prohibiting such discrimination from recurring. The injunction might also order the firm to grant this individual seniority in the firm that would be backdated to the time of the initial rejection.

The act the plaintiff seeks to declare unlawful and prohibit from occurring might also take place at the time the suit is filed (or perhaps a moment before). In such a case, the injunction sought would seek to restrain a present wrong. For example, imagine an injunctive suit filed immediately after a state enacts a law prohibiting abortions. In that case, the present wrong would consist of the threat a doctor confronts

---

[29] *Al-Aulaqi v Panetta*, 35 F Supp 3d 56 (D DC 2014).

if he or she performs an abortion, regardless of exactly when that abortion is performed, either a moment after the enactment of the statute or sometime in the future.

The plaintiffs in *Clapper* brought their suit soon after the enactment of the 2008 statute and, as in the imagined abortion case, they were complaining of a present wrong. To succeed on the merits, they would have to show that the grant of authority contained in the 2008 act was unlawful—that it authorized surveillance on conditions weaker than those permitted by the Fourth Amendment. To establish that they had standing to complain of this wrong, they would also need to show that the grant of authority was likely to be used by the government. Given the history of the 2008 statute and its origins in the Terrorist Surveillance Program, there could be little doubt on this issue.

President Bush fought hard for the enactment of the 2008 statute, insisting that without this enlargement of its powers, the government would not have adequate means to identify and respond to terrorist threats. His successor shared this view. As a senator, Barack Obama voted for the measure, and as president he has acted in ways indicating that he, too, believed the government needed the powers granted under the 2008 statute. Indeed, even as the *Clapper* case was pending before the Supreme Court, the 2008 statute was, at the urging of Obama, renewed for another five years. Power granted under these circumstances is likely to be used.

To be sure, the standing requirement, as conventionally understood, not only requires that the power granted be used; it also requires that plaintiffs show that this power will be used against them. In *Clapper*, this meant proving, with sufficient likelihood, that the newly created power would be used to intercept telephone calls in which plaintiffs were a party. Importantly, the conjecture implied by this understanding of the burden the plaintiffs face—we can only speak of likelihoods—derives not from the fact that their claim concerns what the government might do at some future time, but rather from the secrecy of the government's action: as a general matter, no one knows whether his or her calls are being intercepted, and as a result, the plaintiffs can only make a guess—albeit a good or informed guess—about whether their calls are being tapped. In such circumstances, all that can be reasonably required of plaintiffs is that they show there is a substantial risk that some of their calls would be intercepted by the government under the procedures established by the 2008 act.

In *Clapper*, this burden seemed amply met. The professional activities of the plaintiffs—lawyers, journalists, human rights researchers—were described with particularity in the complaint. These activities required that the plaintiffs regularly communicate with persons in the Middle East who were suspected members of terrorist groups, or with the friends and relatives of members of terrorist organizations, or with persons who might be familiar with the recruitment practices or planned attacks of terrorist organizations. Such communications most commonly occurred by phone. So, even if it were assumed the plaintiffs were not themselves targets of the government's taps, the persons abroad with whom they are in touch over the telephone are likely to be targets of the FISA approved interceptions. As a result, the *Clapper* plaintiffs routinely confronted the risk—a substantial risk—that the government would hear what they were saying and what was being said to them.

Admittedly, the government has many different ways of conducting terrorist investigations and may not, in any given case, use the specific powers granted by the 2008 act when investigating individuals abroad with whom plaintiffs abroad regularly communicate. In the world of secret surveillance, anything is possible. But when the executive branch pushed for the 2008 measure and its renewal, it did so on the ground that the powers it already possessed were inadequate, and that more was needed. This insistent demand for new forms of surveillance authority should be taken as a reliable indication that the authority eventually created by the 2008 enactment would, in all likelihood, be used, and that given the particular focus of the War on Terror, it would be used against people with whom the plaintiffs regularly speak on the telephone.

In principle, the government may criminally prosecute one of the parties to a telephone conversation intercepted under the authority created by the 2008 act, even if he or she were not the original target. During oral argument before the Supreme Court, the solicitor general assured the Justices that if such a prosecution ensued, the accused would be informed of the interception, and then any Fourth Amendment objections to the interdiction could be aired and, if they had merit, evidence obtained from the interdiction could be excluded from the trial. As it turned out, it proved difficult for the solicitor general to deliver on his promise—his control of the staff attorneys in charge of security prosecutions was more attenuated than he imagined.[30] Eventually, though, his assurance to the Justices became departmental policy, and in two prosecutions, one in Colorado[31] and the other in Oregon,[32] defendants were notified that their calls had been intercepted under the provisions of the 2008 act. In both cases, the validity of the 2008 statute was raised in motions to suppress evidence derived from these interceptions, but these motions were denied. Yet even if the motions had been granted, this would not obviate the core constitutional danger posed by the 2008 act, for the Fourth Amendment seeks to protect the privacy of telephone conversations— not just the use in a criminal trial of the evidence gathered through an interdiction of such a conversation.

Although a great deal of Fourth Amendment litigation arises from the exclusion of evidence in criminal trials, the exclusionary rule that renders evidence unconstitutionally obtained inadmissible at trial should be seen only as a means to enhance the Constitution's protection of private information. Deny the government the benefits of Fourth Amendment wrongdoing, it is reasoned, and the government will have far less incentive to transgress constitutionally protected privacy. Yet the protection provided by the exclusionary rule does

---

[30] Charlie Savage, *Door May Open for Challenge to Secret Wiretaps*, NY Times (Oct 17, 2013), archived at https://www.nytimes.com/2013/10/17/us/politics/us-legal-shift-may-open-door-for -challenge-to-secret-wiretaps.html (detailing some of the challenges of ensuring compliance with the Solicitor General's announced policy change).

[31] This case involved pretrial notification given to a defendant accused of providing material support to an Uzbekistan-based terror group. Order Denying Motion to Suppress Evidence Obtained or Derived Under FISA Amendments Acts or for Discovery, No l:12-cr-00033-JLK (D Colo, Nov 19, 2015).

[32] In this case, a student at Oregon State University was convicted for attempting to use a weapon of mass destruction. *United States v Mohamud*, 941 F Supp 2d 1303 (D Or 2013). Months after his conviction, the defendant was told that information obtained or derived from traditional FISA might have been augmented by information gathered under the 2008 act's provisions. Government's Supplemental FISA Notification, *United States v Mohamud*, No 3:10-CR-00475-KI (D Or, Nov 19, 2013). The ruling denying the motion is presented in Opinion and Order, *United States v Mohamud*, No 3:10-CR-00475-KI (D Or, Mar 19, 2014).

In a third case involving an individual accused of providing material support to a terrorist organization, the government provided the requisite notice after the accused had already pled guilty, but Loretta Lynch, then U.S. Attorney for the Eastern District of New York, on the theory that he had forfeited his right to appeal by pleading guilty, refused this individual the opportunity to withdraw his plea or otherwise attack the conviction. Letter from Loretta E. Lynch, United States Attorney, E D NY, to Agron Hasbajrami (Feb 24, 2014), available at https://www.documentcloud.org/documents/1028728-hasbajrami-supplemental-notice-2 -24-2014.html. For further discussion of these cases, see Laura K. Donohue, *Section 702 and the Collection of International Telephone and Internet Content*, 38 Harv J L & Pub Pol 117, 251 n 565 (2015).

little to shield the privacy of all those American journalists, lawyers, and activists who are "incidental victims" of eavesdropping aimed at foreign nationals suspected of terrorism or having links to terrorists.

At the time their suit was brought, the plaintiffs feared that their calls would be intercepted and adjusted their behavior accordingly— forgoing telephone conversations altogether or significantly limiting them. The chance that a motion to suppress might eventually be granted in a criminal prosecution that has not yet been brought, and that might not involve any of the plaintiffs, does little to reduce the substantiality of the danger posed by an interception and the loss of privacy that these individuals faced when they filed their suit, and continued to face over the five years during which their case wound its way through the federal courts. Such speculative protection from the exclusionary rule would not be a reason for denying them standing. In sum, traditional concepts of standing would suggest the *Clapper* plaintiffs were clearly entitled to a ruling on the merits.

Reformulating the Test for Standing?

In a sharply divided, five-to-four ruling, the *Clapper* Court reached a different conclusion, denying the plaintiffs standing. Justice Samuel Alito wrote the opinion for the five. Yet even this bare majority was internally splintered: although five Justices agreed on dismissing the suit for lack of standing, there was disagreement among them on the proper standard to apply.

Throughout much of his opinion, Justice Alito maintained the plaintiffs lacked standing because they did not establish that their claimed injury was "certainly impending."[33] This formula, and in particular, the word "impending," suggests the wrong the *Clapper* plaintiffs complained about was one they feared would occur in the future. But this was not in fact the case. Instead, the plaintiffs were concerned with the harms they experienced in the present from surveillance practices instituted by the government at the time the suit was filed. They were complaining of a current wrong. These practices may continue into the future or in fact might be commenced at some later date, but the plaintiffs' conjecture was not about the future. Rather, given the secrecy of the surveillance program, their

---

[33] For example, *Clapper v Amnesty Int'l USA*, 133 S Ct 1138, 1143 (2013) (internal citation omitted).

conjecture derives from the inevitable, currently felt fear that people the plaintiffs regularly spoke with were, in fact, targets of wiretaps allowed under the 2008 statute. Yet even if the plaintiffs' claim were intended to describe a future wrong—thus making the word "impending" proper—the word "certainly" would seem misplaced. As Justice Breyer said in his dissent, no one can be certain about the future.

In any event, it is doubtful that Alito's "certainly impending" standard had the backing of a majority of the Justices. At least one Justice who supported the dismissal—there may have been more—seemed unwilling to subscribe to this test. This is tellingly revealed by footnote 5 of Alito's opinion, which declares: "Our cases do not uniformly require plaintiffs to demonstrate that it is literally certain that the harms they identify will come about."[34] Importantly, the substance of this footnote, its literary style, the fact that it quotes language used in the body of Alito's opinion, and then refers to the test rejected as "clearly impending" rather than "certainly impending," each suggest that the footnote was not written by Alito himself, but another Justice, one who insisted that it be appended to Alito's opinion as a condition for obtaining his vote.

After distancing itself from the "certainly impending" test, footnote 5 invokes what might be regarded as the "substantial risk" test, though there is an ambiguity as to what the risk might be. Given that

---

[34] In its entirety, the footnote reads as follows:

> Our cases do not uniformly require plaintiffs to demonstrate that it is literally certain that the harms they identify will come about. In some instances, we have found standing based on a "substantial risk" that the harm will occur, which may prompt plaintiffs to reasonably incur costs to mitigate or avoid that harm. *Monsanto Co. v Geertson Seed Farms*, 561 US 139, ——, 130 S.Ct. 2743, 2754–2755, 177 L.Ed.2d 461 (2010). See also *Pennell v City of San Jose*, 485 US 1, 8, 108 S.Ct. 849, 99 L.Ed.2d 1 (1988); *Blum v Yaretsky*, 457 US 991, 1000–1001, 102 S.Ct. 2777, 73 L.Ed.2d 534 (1982); *Babbitt v Farm Workers*, 442 US 289, 298, 99 S Ct 2301, 60 L.Ed.2d 895 (1979). But to the extent that the "substantial risk" standard is relevant and is distinct from the "clearly impending" requirement, respondents fall short of even that standard, in light of the attenuated chain of inferences necessary to find harm here. See supra, at 1148–1150. In addition, plaintiffs bear the burden of pleading and proving concrete facts showing that the defendant's actual action has caused the substantial risk of harm. Plaintiffs cannot rely on speculation about "'the unfettered choices made by independent actors not before the court.'" Defenders of Wildlife, 504 US, at 562, 112 S.Ct. 2130.

Clapper v Amnesty Int'l USA, 133 S Ct 1138, 1150 n 5 (2013).

the suit was brought upon the enactment of the statute, in my view, the risk that needs to be ascertained is the risk that the plaintiffs are currently being harmed. Footnote 5, however, speaks of the risk that the plaintiffs *will be* harmed, as though what the plaintiffs feared was a future wrong. "In some instances," the footnote explains, "we have found standing on a 'substantial risk' that the harm will occur."[35] This version of the "substantial risk" test is then applied and the footnote concludes that the plaintiffs have failed that test.

The doctrinal significance of footnote 5 is unclear. At a minimum, we can say it means that Alito lacked a majority for the "certainly impending" test, and that at least one Justice who joined his opinion instead applied the more appropriate "substantial risk" test (which was elaborately defended by Justice Breyer in his dissent). On the other hand, in applying the "substantial risk" test, the Justice or Justices who insisted on the inclusion of footnote 5 agreed with Alito's ultimate conclusion, namely, that the plaintiffs lacked standing. And in explaining why the risk the plaintiff complained about was not substantial, the author of footnote 5 relied on the same two factors Justice Alito had used for explaining why the harm was not "certainly impending": (1) the plaintiffs' claim involved too attenuated a chain of inferences to find harm, and (2) the plaintiffs' allegations depended too heavily on speculations about the choices of independent actors not before the Court. In my view, however, neither of these factors— whether considered under the "certainly impending" or the "substantial risk" test—offers adequate ground for denying standing to the plaintiffs.

The first factor used to justify the dismissal for lack of standing is that plaintiffs rely on an "attenuated chain of inferences necessary to find harm."[36] In truth, however, the chain of inferences needed to show harm to plaintiffs—the interception of private telephone calls of plaintiffs under the procedures authorized by the 2008 statute—is not nearly as attenuated as either Alito or the Justice or Justices responsible for footnote 5 would have us believe. Granted, the interception of a telephone conversation depends on a decision by the government to utilize the powers given to it by the 2008 statute, and to do so in a way that targets persons the plaintiffs regularly speak with

---

[35] Id.

[36] Id.

by the telephone. But there is nothing improbable about this claim. It is based upon a concrete understanding of the origins of the 2008 statute, the imperatives of the War on Terror, and the professional activities of the plaintiffs. Although the War on Terror may have the global scope that President Bush had originally claimed for it, the operations of Al Qaeda, the principal adversary in that war, are centered in the Middle East and in the mountainous region between Afghanistan and Pakistan. The *Clapper* plaintiffs regularly make calls to these regions, and regularly speak with people who are likely suspected of links to Al Qaeda or other terrorist organizations.

The second factor used to deny plaintiffs' standing, under both Alito's "certainly impending" test and the footnote 5 "substantial risk" standard, was the charge that the plaintiffs depended on "speculation about 'the unfettered choices' made by independent actors not before the court."[37] This argument is also unpersuasive. The so-called "independent actors" referred to were presumably the FISA judges to whom the government must, under the 2008 statute, apply before intercepting plaintiffs' calls. It is true that the plaintiffs' calls could not be intercepted without the approval of a FISA judge, and that these judges possess the full powers of Article III judges. And while I would not say FISA judges, or any other Article III judge, have "unfettered discretion," FISA judges do have the authority to withhold the permission the government seeks. Although by its very terms, the 2008 statute ostensibly constrains the freedom of FISA judges—they must grant the government's request if all the elements required for an interception are present—FISA judges could declare this constraint invalid under either the Fourth Amendment or the doctrine guaranteeing separation of powers (on the ground that it is an impermissible interference with the judicial power).

Yet while the theoretical power of FISA judges to make such a ruling cannot be denied, in practice, the chances of such an exercise of power are quite remote. This conclusion does not rest on cynical speculations—inflamed by the fact that FISA judges are handpicked by the Chief Justice—about the capacity of federal judges to resist the executive in its effort to investigate international terrorism. Rather, it is derived from two essential features of the FISA scheme. One is that FISA judges act ex parte—they hear from only one side (the gov-

---

[37] Id.

ernment).[38] The other is that FISA judges are not obliged to abide by the strictures of public reason—they do not publicly announce the decision nor are they required or expected to justify their decisions on the basis of principle. In acting this way, FISA judges are no different than any other federal judge (or magistrate) passing on applications for search warrants. Still, the failure to abide by the procedural rules that generally govern the exercise of the judicial power makes it deeply unlikely that the constitutional power possessed by FISA judges will be exercised in such a way to protect the privacy interests of plaintiffs that are guaranteed by the Fourth Amendment.

For these reasons, the two factors—the attenuated chain of causation and the role of independent actors in this chain—offered by the author of footnote 5 to explain why, even under the substantial risk test, the *Clapper* suit should be dismissed for lack of standing seem unpersuasive. On top of this, I am troubled, as indeed the Justices should be, by the practical consequences of the application of this test, for it would effectively insulate the 2008 statute from any judicial review. In the body of his opinion, Justice Alito addresses this contingency and his willingness to do so is entirely appropriate, for the prospect of insulating the 2008 statute from judicial review seems even more evident under his "certainly impending" test. By its very terms—by its use of the word "certainly"—Alito's test would inevitably have this effect.

In confronting this objection, Alito's first strategy is to minimize the chance that the danger would ever materialize. To this end, he conjured several scenarios that might provide for judicial review of the statute—a constitutional judgment by a FISA judge when the government seeks permission to tap a telephone; a ruling by a federal judge presiding over a criminal trial granting a motion to suppress when a party in an intercepted conversation is criminally prosecuted; or a proceeding before the FISA court when an electronic communication services provider objects to an order granting access to its facilities. Yet while all of these imagined scenarios are possible, they could arise only in the most unusual of circumstances, and even if

---

[38] Two years after *Clapper*, new legislation was enacted that authorized FISA judges to designate civil liberties experts as amicus curiae to articulate "legal arguments that advance the protection of individual privacy and civil liberties." Uniting and Strengthening America by Fulfilling Rights and Ensuring Effective Discipline Over Monitoring Act of 2015 (USA Freedom Act), Pub L No 114-23, 129 Stat 268, § 401(4)(C).

they someday did, the 2008 statute would have already taken its toll on the plaintiffs and others in the plaintiffs' position. Fearing that their telephone conversations will be intercepted, the plaintiffs will be especially guarded or perhaps may decide to forgo the telephone conversation altogether and arrange their lives in a way to have key conversations face to face.

After trying to minimize the risk that the Court's ruling and his "certainly impending" test would insulate the 2008 statute from judicial review, Alito then expressed an indifference to such a result. Alito said that even if he were to concede that the dismissal of the plaintiffs' suit would in effect insulate the 2008 statute from judicial review, such a consequence, if it materialized, would be a legal irrelevance, reasoning that "the assumption that if respondents have no standing to sue, no one would have standing, is not a reason to find standing."[39]

As a purely technical matter, Justice Alito is correct: standing, under traditional doctrine, is an independent legal requirement. Yet the practical consequences of such an outcome offer good reason to scrutinize all the steps in the reasoning that led to it—the chosen test for standing and the way it was applied. Alito should be troubled, not indifferent, to the likely practical consequences of the test he applies and the decision to dismiss the plaintiffs' suit for lack of standing.

What might justify such indifference? Alito viewed his extravagant application of the standing requirement as furthering separation of powers. According to Alito, separation of powers dictates that the judiciary be careful not to intrude on the other branches of government. Such a reading views separation of powers as a "negative" principle—a restraint on judicial power. From this perspective, a ruling that has the effect of insulating the 2008 statute from judicial review coincides with what Alito takes as the principal requirement of separation of powers—that the judiciary should leave the other branches of government alone—and this coincidence may well explain his indifference to the practical consequence of his ruling or the "certainly impending" test itself.

In taking this view, however, Alito ignored the crucial "affirmative" dimensions of the separation-of-powers doctrine. Separation of pow-

[39] 133 S Ct 1138, 1154 (2013), quoting *Valley Forge Christian Coll. v Americans United for Separation of Church & State, Inc.*, 454 US 464, 489 (1982).

ers does not only work to preserve the boundaries between the three branches, to prevent one branch of government from usurping the function of another. It also serves a positive function: assuring that each branch perform its assigned function. So while the judiciary must not usurp the functions of the other branches, it is equally important that the judiciary perform its assigned duty, namely, to protect and safeguard the Constitution and to determine whether the action of political branches is in accord with that law. Thus, I would say that a ruling that has practical effect of insulating a statute from judicial review interferes with the discharge of that duty and should be viewed accordingly—skeptically.

Alito's emphasis on the negative dimensions of separation of powers and his willingness to embrace a standing rule that would have the effect of insulating the 2008 FISA amendments from judicial rule may well reflect a familiar deference that the judiciary has shown the political branches in matters of national security. Indeed, soon after announcing that the standing requirement prevents the judicial process from usurping the power from political branches, Alito added a crucial statement: "we have often found a lack of standing in cases in which the Judiciary has been requested to review actions of the political branches in fields of intelligence gathering and foreign affairs."

Following this statement, Alito cites three cases from the early 1970s—handed down at the same time as *Keith*—in which suits were dismissed for lack of standing. One involved a challenge to a statute that blocked congressional review of CIA expenditures;[40] the second involved a challenge to the army's intelligence gathering program;[41] and the third challenged the practice of allowing members of Congress to serve in the armed forces reserve.[42] None of these cases sought to apply Alito's "certainly impending" test. (That formula was derived from a case in which one prisoner challenged a death penalty that was to be imposed on a fellow prisoner.)[43] Moreover, none of these cases suggested that a higher or stricter standing requirement should be applied to cases involving intelligence gathering or foreign affairs. Alito is careful in his choice of words, as though he were merely de-

---

[40] *United States v Richardson*, 418 US 166 (1974).

[41] *Laird v Tatum*, 408 US 1 (1972).

[42] *Schlesinger v Reservists Comm. to Stop the War*, 418 US 208 (1974).

[43] *Whitmore v Arkansas*, 495 US 149 (1990).

scribing a practice (he uses the word "often"). In context, though, the message conveyed is prescriptive; it is as though Alito is announcing a rule that should henceforth govern the Court for assessing standing in national security contexts. Indeed, this announcement, heralding a heightened tier of standing for national security cases, may well be the takeaway point of *Clapper*.

In many contexts, we are accustomed to demands for judicial restraint when reviewing the work of the other branches in national security cases. According to this familiar rule, in the conflict between freedom and security, the judiciary should defer to the balance struck by the political branches. Alito defines the domain of deference a little differently—he speaks of "intelligence gathering" and "foreign affairs" as opposed to national security[44]—but little turns on that difference. In either case, the demand for deference to the political branches can be countered, or at least tempered, by an understanding of the affirmative dimensions of separation-of-powers doctrine—so forcefully vindicated by *Boumediene v Bush*.[45] As that case teaches, although it may be the responsibility of the political branches to determine the nature and magnitude of the threat the nation faces and what the appropriate response to that threat might be, it remains the responsibility of the judiciary to determine whether the course of action chosen by the political branches is in accord with the Constitution.

In charting their course of action, the legislative and executive branches must inevitably take a view on the meaning of the Constitution, for as members of Congress and the president well understand, their actions are limited by the grants of authority and overreaching principles contained in it. The right of the judiciary to second-guess the judgments of the political branches on the meaning of the Constitution does not arise from any moral expertise possessed by those who wield the judicial power—in the moral domain, they do not differ in any significant respect from those who serve in Congress or work in the White House. Rather, the right to review the judgments of the political branches on issues of law stems from the fact that judges are limited, in the exercise of this extraordinary power, by the strictures of public reason: They must confront grievances they might otherwise prefer to ignore, hear from all aggrieved persons, remain

---

[44] *Clapper v Amnesty Int'l USA*, 133 S Ct 138, 1147 (2013).

[45] *Boumediene v Bush*, 553 US 723 (2008).

insulated from political agencies, conduct their affairs in public, and justify their decisions on the basis of principle.[46] Adherence to the strictures of public reason entitles the judiciary to review a judgment about the law that undergirds the action of the political branches, and under our scheme of government this right has become a responsibility.

When, in the context of national security, the Court defers to the judgment of the political branches on a constitutional question, it is failing in the discharge of this responsibility of judicial review. When it applies a more exacting test for standing in national security cases and then dismisses the suit for lack of standing, it may seem that the Court is committing the same error. In fact, however, I believe the error is much worse, for the Court is dismissing the suit without ever considering the merits of the claim before it. This outcome not only frustrates and disappoints the plaintiffs, but, more importantly, constitutes an offense to the polity, for, in effect, the Court has refused to address in any way the disputed question of law before it—whether the 2008 FISA amendments violate the Fourth Amendment—and thus relieves itself of any responsibility for the operation of the statute or the infringement of the Constitution that the statute might well represent. In so doing, the Court may be protecting its sway in certain circles, including those interested in preserving the Court's so-called political capital, which arguably might be needed for other ventures.[47] That objective, however, should never be achieved at the expense of defaulting on its responsibility—long thought its primary responsibility, even in times of war—of holding the political branches accountable to the law.

---

[46] For more on the role of public reason and the judicial role, see generally Owen M. Fiss, *The Law as It Could Be* (NYU Press, 2003).

[47] See, for example, Justice Robert Jackson's famous dissent in *Korematsu v United States*, 323 US 214, 248 (1944) (Jackson, J, dissenting), and Alexander M. Bickel, *The Least Dangerous Branch: The Supreme Court at the Bar of Politics* (Bobbs-Merrill, 1962).

LOUIS MICHAEL SEIDMAN

THE TRIUMPH OF GAY MARRIAGE AND
THE FAILURE OF CONSTITUTIONAL LAW

Writing in these pages more than four decades ago, Harry Kalven, Jr. referred to the Supreme Court's decision in *New York Times v Sullivan*[1] as "an occasion for dancing in the streets."[2] Contemporary news accounts fail to indicate that anyone actually took advantage of the occasion. In contrast, there was actual dancing, in the streets among many other places, when the Court announced its decision in *Obergefell v Hodges*.[3]

The Court's much anticipated invalidation of gay marriage bans improved the personal lives of millions of ordinary Americans. It vindicated the courageous leaders who struggled for years on behalf of an unjustly despised, ridiculed, and persecuted minority. It made the country a more decent place. Even Chief Justice Roberts, at the conclusion of his otherwise scathing dissent, acknowledged that the decision was a cause for many Americans to celebrate.[4]

Louis Michael Seidman is Carmack Waterhouse Professor of Constitutional Law, Georgetown University Law Center.

AUTHOR'S NOTE: Thanks to Mary Anne Case, Martin Lederman, Eric N. Lindblom, Allegra McLeod, Sherally Munshi, Mark Tushnet, and participants at the Georgetown Law Center Summer Workshop for comments on an earlier draft and to Marc Gersen and Richard Kelley for outstanding research assistance.

[1] 376 US 254 (1964).

[2] Harry Kalven Jr., *The New York Times Case: A Note on the Central Meaning of the First Amendment*, 1964 Supreme Court Review 191, 221 n 125 (quoting Alexander Meiklejohn).

[3] 135 S Ct 2584 (2015).

[4] See id at 2626.

But although the Chief Justice thought that advocates of gay marriage should "by all means celebrate today's decision," he admonished them "not [to] celebrate the Constitution." The Constitution, he said, "had nothing to do with it."[5]

This article has three parts. Part I quarrels with the Chief Justice's assertion that the Constitution "had nothing to do with it." I argue that it is the dissenting Justices, rather than their colleagues in the majority, who have ignored the traditions of American constitutional law. Part II argues that the Chief Justice was exactly right when he said that we should celebrate the *Obergefell* decision, but not the Constitution, but he was right for reasons that he, himself, would disagree with. The Court's *decision* marks a partial and flawed but nonetheless important advance toward inclusion and decency. The majority's *opinion*, replete with invocations of the supposedly binding force of constitutional obligation, belittling of the large and growing number of Americans who are unmarried, and mischaracterization of the nature of the movement for gay rights, is exclusionary, reactionary, and authoritarian. Even as the Court demonstrates its (concededly limited) capacity to advance the cause of social justice, it unwittingly also demonstrates the failure of constitutional law to serve its core purpose of providing a just ground for cooperation among people who disagree about fundamentals. A brief concluding part discusses the implications of that failure.

I. "[N]OTHING TO DO WITH IT"?

Contrary to the Chief Justice's assertion, and for better or worse, *Obergefell* fits comfortably within the constitutional law canon. The decision is no more audacious than *Marbury v Madison*,[6] no more inconsistent with original understanding than *Brown v Board of Education*,[7] no more contrary to tradition than *Roe v Wade*,[8] no more antimajoritarian than *Miranda v Arizona*.[9]

---

[5] Id.

[6] 5 US (1 Cranch) 137 (1803).

[7] 347 US 483 (1954).

[8] 410 US 113 (1973).

[9] 384 US 436 (1966). And, it must be said, the opinion is no more audacious, inconsistent with the original understanding, contrary to tradition, or antimajoritarian than decisions

True, the opinion lacks the analytic paraphernalia that too often clutters the Court's contemporary work. There is no discussion of tiers of review, suspect classes, strict scrutiny, or narrow tailoring. These matters were also left undiscussed in *Marbury*, *Brown*, *Roe*, and *Miranda*. Perhaps the Chief Justice thinks that these cases were also wrongly decided, but he cannot deny that they were decided in the way that they were. Unless he wishes to embark on the radical project of saving "the Constitution," understood in a purely abstract sense, from generations of constitutional tradition, his claim will not withstand analysis. Embarking on this project would require not only overruling *Marbury*, *Brown*, *Roe*, and *Miranda*, but also disavowing many of his own opinions on subjects like affirmative action and executive power, which are no more grounded in text, original understanding, tradition, and majority acquiescence.[10]

Thus, the claim that *Obergefell* marks a break with the tradition of American constitutionalism will not withstand analysis. One need not look far to find opinions that are in conflict with that tradition, however. In ways that are sometimes jarring but often subtle and obscured, the dissenters demonstrate their own disdain for well-understood strands of constitutional jurisprudence.

There is an inverse relationship between the vitriol and abuse dished out in these opinions and their analytic content. At one extreme—really in a class by itself—is Justice Scalia's diatribe. The opinion is filled with the sort of personal abuse and invective that unfortunately has become his trademark.[11] Even as measured by Justice Scalia's own

authored in recent years by conservatives but not (yet?) in the canon. See, for example, *Bush v Gore*, 531 US 98 (2000), *District of Columbia v Heller*, 554 US 570 (2008), and *Citizens United v Federal Election Commission*, 558 US 310 (2010).

[10] See, for example, *Parents Involved in Community Schools v Seattle School Dist. No. 1*, 551 US 701 (2007) (Roberts, CJ) (invalidating decision by political branches to utilize race to promote desegregation of schools despite absence of clear textual prohibition on the practice, evidence drawn from the original understanding of the text, or a well-established tradition prohibiting the practice); *Free Enterprise Fund v Public Company Accounting Oversight Board*, 561 US 477 (2010) (Roberts, CJ) (inventing a new rule prohibiting political branches from establishing "double insulation" of removal of inferior office from the President despite the absence of textual support for the rule and no prior tradition establishing it).

[11] See, for example, *King v Burwell*, 135 S Ct 2480, 2496, 2506 (2015) (Scalia, J, dissenting) (accusing the majority's opinion of being "quite absurd" and asserting "the discouraging truth that the Supreme Court of the United States favors some laws over others, and is prepared to do whatever it takes to uphold and assist its favorites"); *Romer v Evans*, 517 US 620, 653 (Scalia, J, dissenting) ("Today's opinion has no foundation in American constitutional law, and barely pretends to."); *United States v Windsor*, 133 S Ct 2675, 2709 (2014) (Scalia, J, dissenting) ("I promise you this: The only thing that will 'confine' the Court's holding is its sense of what it can get away with.").

standards, though, the opinion is extraordinary. In the entire history of the Supreme Court, there is nothing that rivals it for petulance, name calling, and disrespect.

According to Justice Scalia, the Court's decision amounts to a "judicial Putsch."[12] It is "egotistic,"[13] reflects "astound[ing] ... hubris,"[14] lacks "even a thin veneer of law,"[15] is "profoundly incoherent,"[16] and relies on "the mystical aphorisms of the fortune cookie."[17] In place of actual argument against the majority's opinion, Justice Scalia makes observations about the religious affiliation of the Justices ("[n]ot a single Evangelical Christian ... or even a Protestant of any denomination")[18] and criticizes Justice Kennedy's writing style (noting that he would "hide my head in a bag" if "even as the price to be paid for a fifth vote" he joined an opinion containing the Court's rhetoric[19]).

It is hard to know how one should treat this outburst. The sad fact is that Justice Scalia has become a caricature of his earlier self. He embarrasses even many of his ideological friends. Perhaps the discreet and humane thing to do is to ignore him. The problem is that it is not easy to ignore one of the nine people making constitutional policy for the country, and constitutional pundits rarely make the effort. Instead, people who should know better routinely praise Justice Scalia for his brilliance, integrity, and scintillating writing style. It therefore seems necessary to point out that in recent years he has made a habit of substituting vitriol for anything resembling reasoned analysis.

When they are on their best behavior, Supreme Court Justices exhibit generosity of spirit, tolerance of disagreement, and respect for

---

[12] *Obergefell*, 135 S Ct at 2629 (Scalia, J, dissenting).

[13] Id at 2630.

[14] Id at 2629.

[15] Id at 2628.

[16] Id at 2630.

[17] Id at 2630 n 22.

[18] Id at 2629. In fairness, the statement is made to demonstrate that the Court lacks diversity, and Justice Scalia makes clear that lack of diversity would not matter if the Court were merely interpreting the law; he claims that it is not. Still, the argument makes sense only if he is asserting that the majority's decision is influenced by the religious beliefs of the Justices—an extraordinary charge that is supported by no evidence. For whatever it is worth, two of the five Justices in the majority have self-identified as Roman Catholics, and the Catholic Church has been a steadfast opponent of same-sex marriage.

[19] *Obergefell*, 135 S Ct at 2630 n 22.

their intellectual opponents. It has been a long time since Justice Scalia has been on his best behavior. Just as his ideological friends fear, and perhaps unfairly, he discredits the very causes that he wishes to advance.

Justice Thomas's dissent is more substantive and less vitriolic, but no less idiosyncratic. All of the dissenting opinions, including Justice Thomas's, are studded with odes to humility, caution, history, and tradition.[20] Yet Thomas himself seems remarkably cavalier about our legal tradition. On his view, "it is hard to see how the 'liberty' protected by the [Due Process Clause of the Constitution] could be interpreted to include anything broader than freedom from physical restraint."[21] If adopted, this interpretation would lead to wholesale overruling of scores of cases extending over almost a century, on subjects ranging from incorporation of Bill of Rights protections against the states,[22] to procedural due process cases,[23] to decisions protecting against government prohibitions on contraception,[24] abortion,[25] private schooling,[26] and family living arrangements.[27] Justice Thomas is nothing if not consistent. He seems to have a more or less worked-out theory, applied over a wide range of cases, for why virtually all of modern constitutional law has gone off track. Still, one must ask: who is the real radical on the Supreme Court?

Perhaps it would make sense to dispose of all these decisions if Justice Thomas's rival theory were coherent and attractive. But it is not.

---

[20] See, for example, id at 2612 (Roberts, CJ, dissenting); id at 2629 (Scalia, J, dissenting); id at 2631 (Thomas, J, dissenting); id at 2640 (Alito, J, dissenting).

[21] Id at 2633.

[22] See, for example, *Cantwell v Connecticut*, 330 US 296 (1940) (holding that the Free Exercise Clause was applicable to the states through the liberty protections of the Fourteenth Amendment's Due Process Clause).

[23] See, for example, *Perry v Sindermann*, 408 US 593 (1972) (holding that interest in continued employment was part of liberty entitled to procedural protection under the Fourteenth Amendment's Due Process Clause).

[24] See, for example, *Griswold v Connecticut*, 381 US 479 (1965) (holding that right of married person to contraception is guaranteed against state infringement by liberty provision in Due Process Clause of Fourteenth Amendment).

[25] See, for example, *Roe v Wade*, 410 US 113 (1973) (holding that abortion right is guaranteed against state infringement by liberty provision in Due Process Clause of Fourteenth Amendment).

[26] See *Pierce v Society of Sisters*, 268 US 510 (1925) (holding that state statute prohibiting private education violated liberty provision of Fourteenth Amendment).

[27] See, for example, *Moore v City of East Cleveland*, 431 US 494 (1977) (holding that municipal ordinance restricting occupancy in any dwelling to members of the same, narrowly defined family violated liberty provision of Fourteenth Amendment).

Justice Thomas claims that this killing field for precedent is required by the original understanding of the Fourteenth Amendment. Even on the flawed assumption that unadulterated originalism is either an important part of our constitutional tradition or an attractive methodology, it is hard to reconcile it with Thomas's defense elsewhere in his opinion of natural law as a check on unjust positive law.

The tension is most apparent when Thomas turns to his criticism of the majority for relying upon human dignity. Citing the Declaration of Independence, Thomas complains that the majority undermines a key premise of the natural law tradition—that "dignity is innate and [does not come] from the Government."[28] As Thomas puts the point:

> Slaves did not lose their dignity...because the government allowed them to be enslaved. Those held in internment camps did not lose their dignity because the government confined them. And those denied governmental benefits certainly do not lose their dignity because the government denies them benefits. The government cannot bestow dignity, and it cannot take it away.[29]

These jurisprudential musings are deeply confused. Of course, there is nothing confused about the claim that human dignity and rights are prepolitical. That claim is at the center of an honorable and venerable natural law tradition that has played an important role in our constitutional history. But no one identified with that tradition, including presumably Justice Thomas, would claim that because government cannot deprive people of their intrinsic dignity, we should therefore defer to political decisions that are inconsistent with dignity. Indeed, the whole point of the Declaration of Independence, which Thomas relies upon, is that political decisions inconsistent with human dignity do not deserve our respect or obedience.

If the government enforced slavery or established internment camps, would Justice Thomas really give it a free pass on the theory that these actions could not and did not take away human dignity? Perhaps he would if there were no constitutional text that governed the practice, but then one must ask who is it whose theory is not attendant to human dignity? The more conventional understanding of the natural law tradition is that claims to dignity give courts a place to

---

[28] *Obergefell v Hodges*, 135 S Ct 2584, 2631 (2015) (Thomas, J, dissenting).

[29] Id at 2639.

stand when they invalidate government decisions that are inconsistent with human dignity. And if courts should do this for slaves and internees, then why not for gay men and lesbians? Justice Thomas's invocation of natural law is therefore in tension with his own criticism of the majority for not deferring to positive law and the political process.

Justice Alito's worry about the "rights of conscience"[30] of people who oppose same sex marriage suffers from a similar contradiction. His opinion, like those of the other dissenters, includes a criticism of the majority for "usurp[ing] the constitutional right of the people to decide whether to keep or alter the traditional understanding of marriage,"[31] and ignoring "[t]he system of federalism [that] provides a way for people with different beliefs to live together in a single nation."[32] I will have more to say about these claims later.[33] For now, though, it is worth considering the tension between them and the argument, which he also advances, that the Court has ignored the "rights of conscience" of those who disagree with gay marriage. He claims that if the Court had not intervened, states might have tied recognition of same sex marriage to protection for "conscience rights" and that "[t]he majority today makes that impossible."[34]

Perhaps Justice Alito means to confine this criticism to instances where government officials are required to enforce the Court's decision. If so, the complaint is at odds with the Supreme Court's long-standing insistence on its own primacy in constitutional interpretation. We do not generally recognize the "conscience rights" of officials to violate the Constitution as interpreted by the Supreme Court. Would Justice Alito excuse a police officer who, out of conscience, searched a suspect in violation of the Supreme Court's interpretation of the Fourth Amendment? Would he accommodate a school superintendent who conscientiously opposed racial desegregation[35] or a department of motor vehicles employee who refused to provide

---

[30] Id at 2642 (Alito, J, dissenting).

[31] Id.

[32] Id at 2643.

[33] See text at notes 49–61 below.

[34] *Obergefell*, 135 S Ct at 2643 (Alito, J, dissenting).

[35] Compare James M. Oleske Jr., *The Evolution of Accommodation: Comparing the Unequal Treatment of Religious Objections to Interracial and Same-Sex Marriages*, 50 Harv CR-CL L Rev 99 (2015).

licenses to women on the ground that the Koran, properly understood, prohibits women from driving?[36]

It seems more likely that Alito is concerned about private individuals—the much discussed wedding caterer—who might be forced
to participate in gay marriages. But if this is his concern, then his assertion that the majority makes protection for these people "impossible" is flatly wrong. Nothing in the Court's opinion requires states
to provide gay couples with the legal right to force private individuals
to participate in gay weddings. If individual states do decide to provide this right, nothing in the Court's opinion prevents them from
tying the protection to exemptions for people conscientiously opposed to gay marriage. And if states do provide antidiscrimination
protection and decline to provide conscience exemptions, then the
fault—if, indeed, there is fault—lies not with the Supreme Court but
with the very democratic majority that Justice Alito elsewhere in his
opinion claims should resolve matters related to gay marriage. Justice
Alito leaves no doubt as to his personal judgment that same-sex marriage opponents should not be "labeled as bigots and treated as such
by governments, employers, and schools."[37] Of course, he is entitled
to that judgment, but if local majorities disagree with him, his own
embrace of democratic federalism leaves him with no standing to
object.

Invocations of majoritarianism, judicial restraint, and respect for
different views also lie at the heart of Chief Justice Roberts's opinion, the most extensive and carefully reasoned of the four dissents.
The opinion nonetheless overflows with ironies and contradictions.
Perhaps the most disturbing is his analogy between the majority opinion and the Court's decision upholding slavery in *Dred Scott v Sandford*.[38] The comparison will strike many as morally obtuse. Put simply,
requiring states to permit free individuals to choose gay marriage
is nothing like allowing states to enslave African Americans. Indeed,
among the many fundamental rights denied to slaves was the right
to marry and form families. How can the Chief Justice invoke a de-

---

[36] In *Davis v Miller*, 2015 WL 5097125, the Court, without any Justice noting a dissent,
denied a stay of a lower court order holding a clerk in contempt of court for refusing on
religious grounds to issue marriage licenses to gay couples.

[37] *Obergefell v Hodges*, 135 S Ct at 2643 (Alito, J, dissenting).

[38] 60 US (18 How) 393 (1857). Chief Justice Roberts discusses the comparison at *Obergefell
v Hodges*, 135 S Ct at 2616–17 (Roberts, CJ, dissenting).

cision that cruelly withheld the right to marry to criticize a decision that grants the right?

There is a second reason why Chief Justice Roberts's *Dred Scott* analogy fails. Unlike the majority opinion in *Obergefell*, Chief Justice Taney's opinion in *Dred Scott* did not purport to rest on controversial claims about human flourishing. On the contrary, Taney insisted that it was "not the province of the court to decide upon the justice or injustice, the policy or impolicy of these laws. The decision of that question belonged to the political or law-making power."[39]

In the most notorious passage in his opinion, Taney referred to African Americans as "beings of an inferior order, and altogether unfit to associate with the white race, either in social or political relations; and so far inferior, that they had no rights to which the white man was bound to respect."[40] But, importantly, Taney did not assert that these views were his own. On the contrary, he distanced himself from them. These were the views that others held "more than a century before."[41] According to Taney, "[i]t is difficult at this day to realize the state of public opinion in relation to that unfortunate race, which prevailed in the civilized and enlightened portions of the world at the time of the Declaration of Independence, and when the Constitution of the United States was framed and adopted."[42]

For Taney, racist views about African Americans were relevant not because they were correct (although, at least in slightly diluted form, he thought that they were), but because they helped interpret the original understanding of constitutional text. Taney purported to do precisely what Chief Justice Roberts chastises the *Obergefell* majority for failing to do. At least on his own account, Taney scrupulously abstained from injecting his own moral and political judgments into the decisional calculus and modestly deferred to judgments made by the Framers.

Modern historians continue to argue about whether Taney's interpretation of the text was correct,[43] but that argument is not at the

---

[39] *Dred Scott v Sandford*, 60 US (18 How) 393, 403 (1857).

[40] Id at 407.

[41] Id.

[42] Id.

[43] Compare Donald E. Fehrenbacher, *The Dred Scott Case: Its Significance in American Politics and Law* 335–88 (1978) (arguing that Taney misinterpreted the Constitution) with Mark A. Graber, *Dred Scott and the Problem of Constitutional Evil* 12 (2006) (arguing that "slavery unambiguously pervaded the antebellum constitutional order.").

heart of why *Dred Scott* is so reviled today. The opinion is part of our constitutional anti-canon not because Taney departed from original text and understanding, but because his insistence on adhering to his reading of the text led him to ignore the huge moral issue at stake. Of course, slavery is a greater evil than the failure to recognize gay marriage, but if the analogy between *Dred Scott* and *Obergefell* is useful at all, it undermines rather than supports Chief Justice Roberts's point.

Roberts's invocation of the other famous decision in the anti-canon—*Lochner v New York*[44]—better serves his argument. *Lochner* might more plausibly be interpreted as an example of the Court's confusion of its own stunted moral and political judgments for those embodied in constitutional text. Just as use of the word "liberty" in the Fourteenth Amendment did not "enact Mr. Herbert Spencer's Social Statics,"[45] so too, it might be thought, use of the word did not enact the views of the Human Rights Campaign.

But although the *Lochner* analogy is more on point, it, too, has problems. One problem is that it is no longer so clear that *Lochner* is part of the anti-canon. A growing number of conservatives are prepared to embrace *Lochner* as embodying important constitutional principles.[46] Moreover, in an odd way, some of *Lochner*'s opponents agree with these conservatives. They, too, think that the Court could not escape taking a stand on issues of economic justice. The problem, in their view, was not that *Lochner* adopted a contestable set of political and economic assumptions, but that it adopted the *wrong* political and economic assumptions.[47] If one holds this view, *Obergefell* is easily distinguishable because it adopts the *right* assumptions.

Of course, both the embrace and critique of *Lochner* on substantive grounds runs into the difficulty that people disagree about which assumptions are right and wrong. How can constitutional law retain

---

[44] 198 US 45 (1905).

[45] Id at 65 (Holmes, J, dissenting).

[46] See, for example, David E. Bernstein, *Rehabilitating Lochner* (2011); Randy E. Barnett, *Restoring the Lost Constitution: The Presumption of Liberty* 260–69 (2004). See generally Thomas B. Colby and Peter Smith, *The Return of Lochner*, 100 Cornell L Rev 527 (2015).

[47] See, for example, Cass Sunstein, *Lochner's Legacy*, 87 Colum L Rev 873 (1987). Compare *Planned Parenthood of Southeastern Pennsylvania v Casey*, 505 US 833, 860 (1992) ("In the meantime, the Depression had come and, with it, the lesson that seemed unmistakable to most people by 1937, that the interpretation of contractual freedom protected by [Lochner era cases] rested on fundamentally false factual assumptions about the capacity of a relatively unregulated market to satisfy minimal levels of human welfare.").

the respect of "people of fundamentally differing views"[48] if the correctness of a decision rests on the merits of those views? I return to this problem in Parts II and III of this article. For now, it is enough to see that Chief Justice Roberts's "judicial activism" critique of both *Lochner* and *Obergefell* misconceives not only the problem but also the solution.

The critique misperceives the problem because it assumes that *Lochner* and *Obergefell* impose a contestable judgment on people who disagree. For Justice Holmes, dissenting in *Lochner*, the Court "decided [the case] upon an economic theory which a large part of the country does not entertain."[49] Similarly, for Chief Justice Roberts and the other *Obergefell* dissenters, the Court "closed the debate and enacted their own vision of marriage as a matter of constitutional law."[50]

The first difficulty with this criticism, at least as applied to *Obergefell*, is that it misrepresents the obstacle to a political resolution of the problem. In fact, it is Chief Justice Roberts and his dissenting colleagues who are out of step with a large and growing majority that favors gay marriage.[51] The main obstacle to political resolution is state constitutional measures that prohibit gay marriage. If Chief Justice Roberts and his colleagues had their way, in many states, gay marriage would have to gain supermajority support in order to overturn these constitutional provisions much as supermajority support would be necessary to overturn *Obergefell*. To use Chief Justice Roberts's own words, state constitutions "closed debate and enacted their own vision of marriage as a matter of constitutional law."[52] There is a sense, then, in which it is the Court and not the dissenters who stand for majority rule.

But there is a more fundamental problem with Chief Justice Roberts's criticism. It is simply not true that, as the Chief Justice claimed,

---

[48] *Lochner v New York*, 198 US 45, 76 (1905) (Holmes, J, dissenting).

[49] Id at 65 (Holmes, J, dissenting).

[50] *Obergefell v Hodges*, 135 S Ct 2584, 2612 (2015) (Roberts, CJ, dissenting).

[51] For example, according to a *Washington Post*/ABC News Poll taken within two months of *Obergefell*, 61 percent of Americans favored gay marriage while 35 percent were opposed. See Scott Clement and Robert Barnes, *Poll: Gay-Marriage Support at Record High*, Wash Post (April 23, 2015), available at http://www.washingtonpost.com/politics/courts_law/poll-gay -marriage-support-at-record-high/2015/04/22/f6548332-e92a-11e4-aae1-d642717d8afa_story .html.

[52] *Obergefell*, 135 S Ct at 2612 (Roberts, CJ, dissenting).

the Supreme Court "enacted [its] own vision of marriage as a matter of constitutional law" any more than it is true that the *Lochner* Court mandated long working hours. Ironically, these criticisms would be more powerful if the laws invalidated in *Lochner* and *Obergefell* had been upheld. New York imposed mandatory maximum hour restriction on all New York bakery owners and bakery workers because of the controversial view that working more than ten hours per day was harmful and wrong. Similarly, the states that outlawed state-sanctioned gay marriage adopted a particular view of marriage that was not universally shared and imposed it on everyone. It was not the *Lochner* and *Obergefell* majorities that were forcing everyone to adhere to a uniform view. The decisions forced no one to work for more than ten hours or to marry a partner of the same sex. Instead, it left the choice to individuals.

Viewed in this way, it becomes clear that Chief Justice Roberts's criticism of *Lochner* and *Obergefell* not only has things backward; it also rests on a non sequitur. The argument starts with the accurate premise that people disagree about maximum hours legislation and gay marriage, but then jumps to the fallacious conclusion that therefore the disagreement should be settled for everyone by majoritarian institutions. To see that the conclusion does not follow from the premise, we need only transfer the argument to a different sphere. No one says that because people disagree about the nature of God, therefore, the United States should use democratic processes to adopt a uniform religion for everyone. On the contrary, disagreement about religion leads most people to the conclusion that individuals should be free to decide for themselves what they think about God.

The important dispute, then, is not between courts on the one hand and political institutions on the other, but between public decisions that bind everyone and private decisions that permit individual choice. People who believe, as Chief Justice Roberts claims to, that everyone should not be forced to accept a particular, controversial conception of marriage should embrace rather than oppose *Obergefell*.

Of course, it does not follow that people *should* believe that the marriage question ought to be resolved privately rather than publicly. The choice between public and private resolution rests on the answers to controversial questions about issues like the appropriate role for constitutional text, whether the Constitution establishes a presumption in favor of individual or political choice, the extent of externalities produced by individual decisions, the extent to which these decisions are truly "free," and whether paternalism is a legitimate basis for collective action. Although the *Obergefell* Court is not deciding for everyone how "marriage" should be conceived, it is implicitly resolving at least some of these issues.

Making the right choice between public decision and private choice is a problem, alright, but it is at this point that Chief Justice Roberts misconceives the solution. He and the other dissenters insist that the solution is to remit all questions to majority rule unless the Constitution leaves them to individuals. On this view, the Court should remain aloof from the battle between the contending forces. It should enforce only constitutional judgments, not its own. Unfortunately, though, this sort of neutrality is a logical impossibility.

To understand why this is so, we need to examine the microstructure of the plaintiffs' argument in *Obergefell*. Although the majority focused primarily on the plaintiffs' due process argument, the point is easiest to see with regard to their equal protection claim. That claim can be reduced to a simple assertion: The government has left decisions about forming heterosexual unions to individual, private choice; it treats gay men and lesbians unequally when it forces them to accept a collective, public decision about their unions.

The claim is plausible, but only if gay marriages are relevantly the same as straight marriages. The Equal Protection Clause requires that likes be treated alike, but when two things are not alike, it violates rather than vindicates equality to treat them in the same way. Are gay and straight marriages relevantly alike? All of the hard work must be done by defining the word "relevantly." Gay and straight marriages are both alike and unalike along an infinite number of dimensions. The key point is that it is impossible to decide which dimensions are relevant without making a contestable moral judgment about the institution of marriage.

Justice Alito's dissent makes the point with startling clarity. He apparently concedes, at least arguendo, that on a "consent-based" conception of marriage, gay men and lesbians have a legitimate claim to marriage, but, he insists, their claim is much less powerful on a "conjugal" conception of marriage.[53] Suppose we put aside questions about whether the "conjugal" conception really justifies our rules about

---

[53] See id at 2641 (Alito, J, dissenting). Justice Alito discusses the distinction at greater length and utilizes this terminology in *United States v Windsor*, 135 S Ct 2675, 2717 (2013).

heterosexual marriage and really rules out homosexual marriage.[54] Whether or not he has the right categories, Alito is certainly right that we cannot resolve issues about whether heterosexual and homosexual marriage are relevantly alike without making a judgment about what marriage is for.

But what follows from this observation? It emphatically does not follow that heterosexual marriage is for the private sphere while homosexual marriage is for the public sphere. The Equal Protection Clause requires that likes be treated alike, so a Court that reached this conclusion would have to believe that gay and straight marriage are not alike. It would have to embrace the "conjugal" conception (or some other conception that distinguished between the two forms of marriage) as the right one. But embracing that conception would violate the neutrality that the dissenters insist upon.[55]

In many cases, the Court resolves this problem by paying substantial deference to the political branches on questions of sameness and difference. With regard to ordinary social and economic legislation, the Court sometimes asks only whether the legislature was "rational," although more exacting scrutiny is required for other sorts of classifications.[56] The dissenters present no argument why mere rationality should be sufficient in this case, and there is strong reason to believe that the choice of level of scrutiny is, itself, the result of contestable moral and political views. For example, Chief Justice Roberts thinks that affirmative action measures should be viewed with suspicion because "divvying us up by race" is a "sordid business"[57] that is "pernicious,"[58] and "odious to a free people."[59] Justice Thomas

---

[54] The argument for these propositions must deal with the obvious facts that many people in heterosexual marriages do not raise children and many people in homosexual marriages do.

[55] We might come closer to neutrality if we completely privatized marriage. One could imagine a regime where anyone could marry anyone else without state sanction. Even this radical reform could not escape state involvement, however. State and federal governments would still need to decide which marriages were eligible for the various legal benefits and obligations that attach to marital status.

[56] See, for example, *Massachusetts Bd. of Retirement v Murgia*, 427 US 307, 314 (1976) ("legislative classifications are valid unless they bear no rational relationship to the State's objectives"); *Dandridge v Williams*, 397 US 471, 485 (1970) (state legislation "does not violate the Equal Protection Clause merely because the classifications [it makes] are imperfect.").

[57] *League of United Latin American Citizens v Perry*, 548 US 399, 511 (2008) (Roberts, CJ, concurring in part, concurring in the judgment in part, and dissenting in part).

[58] *Parents Involved in Cmty. Schools v Seattle School Dist. No. 1*, 551 US 701, 720 (2007) (Roberts, CJ).

[59] Id at 745–46 (Roberts, CJ).

has reached a similar conclusion because of his belief that African Americans can succeed without it.[60] If these Justices thought that discrimination against gay men and lesbians was similarly problematic, they would presumably utilize the same level of scrutiny.

Moreover, even when scrutiny is minimal, the Justices do not altogether forgo enforcement. It follows that even if the dissenters were to apply rational basis review, they would have to decide whether a particular conception of marriage was "rational." For example, the dissenters would almost certainly invalidate a statute that prevented couples unable to conceive a child or from different ethnic or economic groups from marrying. But that holding, like the holding in *Obergefell*, requires a moral judgment about the appropriate nature of marriage.

The Court might avoid moral judgment if it completely forwent enforcement. There is much to be said for this approach, and some have said it. It seems improbable, to say the least, but perhaps Chief Justice Roberts and his dissenting colleagues wish to join the small but growing chorus of rebels opposing the orthodoxy of constitutional obligation and Supreme Court supremacy.[61] What seems more likely is that the dissenters' distaste for gay marriage leads them to make an exception to the conventional rules of American constitutionalism for this case. Obviously, such an exception is also inconsistent with the dissenters' claim to neutrality in our culture wars.

There is still another reason why judicial deference does not solve the underlying problem. Deference to the political branches should not be confused with the view that constitutional commands should simply be ignored. When the Court defers, it assumes that constitutional commands will be enforced by legislative and executive officials. For reasons explained above, these officials would then have to incorporate controversial moral judgments into the Constitution. That fact shines a very different light on the dissenters' complaint about taking the same-sex marriage question away from the people. A conscientious legislator who is serious about enforcing the Constitution should not obey the commands of the people. Instead, he should obey the commands of

---

[60] See *Grutter v Bollinger*, 539 US 306, 349 (2003) (Thomas, J, concurring in part and dissenting in part) ("I believe blacks can achieve in every avenue of American life without the meddling of university administrators.").

[61] See, for example, Jeremy Waldron, *The Core Case against Judicial Review*, 115 Yale L J 1346 (2006); Mark V. Tushnet, *Taking the Constitution Away from the Courts* (1999); Louis Michael Seidman, *On Constitutional Disobedience* (2012).

the Constitution—including the controversial moral judgment about marriage that gives content to those commands. Either way, Justice Alito's choice between conceptions of marriage would not be open to democratic contestation.

Of course, few believe that political officials take seriously their supposed obligation to obey the Constitution, at least in this context. If that is the outcome that the dissenters favor, then we should not take seriously their rhetoric about adherence to constitutional limits. In that event, the Constitution would, indeed, have "nothing to do with it."

II. "Celebrate the Constitution"?

It will not do, then, to claim that the Constitution has "nothing to do" with *Obergefell*. It has everything to do with it. Neither does it follow, though, that we should celebrate either the Constitution or *Obergefell*'s embrace of our constitutional tradition.

Obergefell, like scores of other constitutional decisions, rests on a syllogism the structure of which is as fallacious as it is familiar:

> Major premise: We have a duty to adhere to the commands of the Constitution.
> Minor premise: The Constitution commands X.
> Conclusion: At least until the Constitution is changed, we have a duty to do X.

The truth of the major premise rests on the belief that properly understood, the Constitution provides a just basis for resolving disputes among people who would otherwise disagree. The truth of the minor premise rests on the belief that we can discern the meaning of the Constitution without presupposing an extra-constitutional resolution of that disagreement. Because both of these beliefs are false, the conclusion does not follow.

Consider first the major premise. People often claim that we have a duty to obey the Constitution because it produces good results— for example, a right to gay marriage. Unfortunately, this claim involves a conceptual mistake. A person who would do something anyway even if not commanded to do it is not obeying the command. No one would say that a Jew who keeps Kosher is obeying the Koran. The test for obedience comes when the command requires us to do something that we would not otherwise do.

It follows that people who say that we should obey the Constitution because of the good outcomes it produces are actually insisting that *others* obey, not that they themselves should obey. Their own obedience is conditional on the command producing results that they favor, yet they want others to obey even though it produces the wrong result from their point of view. It is an uphill climb to say the least to explain why others should have an obligation from which the person insisting on the obligation exempts herself.

To test the first premise, then, we have to imagine a constitutional command that clearly requires something that we would otherwise strongly oppose. For most readers of this article, the test requires turning the Court's holding in *Obergefell* inside out. Imagine, then, that provisions in the Constitution, written over two hundred years ago, unambiguously commanded that gay people should not be allowed to marry. Imagine as well (actually imagination is unnecessary here) that the mechanisms for changing the constitutional command are so cumbersome as to be virtually useless. Does this command, standing by itself, provide a just basis for resolution of the dispute about gay marriage? Does it provide a good reason why people who favor gay marriage should change their minds and now oppose efforts (short of constitutional amendment) to implement it?

I have written a book and several articles about why I think the answers to these questions are "no."[62] Nothing would be gained by repeating all those arguments here. Suffice it to say that it is far from self-evident that a document written by others containing a noxious command that, as a practical matter, cannot be changed should definitively resolve a dispute about whether the command should be obeyed.

Nor does it solve the problem to argue that even if this particular command is noxious, the Constitution does more good than evil. That argument still rests on a claim that, overall and all things considered, the Constitution commands what the person making the argument thinks of as the right results and would favor even if there were not a constitution. Put differently, the command is doing no work for the person making the argument, even though that person insists that it should do work for others.

---

[62] See Seidman, *On Constitutional Disobedience*; Louis Michael Seidman, *The Secret History of American Constitutional Skepticism: A Recovery and Preliminary Evaluation*, 17 U Pa J Const L 1 (2014); Louis Michael Seidman, *Why Jeremy Waldron Agrees with Me*, 127 Harv L Rev F 159 (2014); Louis Michael Seidman, *Constitutional and Political Obligation*, 93 BU L Rev 1257 (2013).

Matters are made much worse because the belief underlying the second premise is also false. If the command is, in fact, contained in the Constitution, then the many people who are unconvinced by my arguments will think that we must obey it. But for reasons that I have already set out,[63] we cannot determine whether the Constitution contains the command without judging for ourselves its correctness. One must hold some controversial conception of marriage in order to decide whether gay and straight marriage are relevantly similar. More broadly, it is simply not possible to give determinate content to commands like "don't deny equal protection" or "provide due process" without first resolving the very moral and political controversy that the Constitution is supposed to settle.

Because I have done so elsewhere, I won't bore readers with elaborate argumentation supporting this proposition either. Instead, in what follows, I explore some of the pernicious consequences that flow from this failed logic.

The first and perhaps most serious consequence is that disputants forced into a procrustean mold of constitutional argument end up alienated from their own, deeply held positions. Consider in this regard the plight of opponents of gay marriage. At least in its most defensible form, their opposition is rooted in a simple argument: There is no right to gay marriage because it is immoral, inconsistent with human flourishing, degrading, and unnatural.[64]

To be clear, I have no sympathy for this argument. I think that it is question-begging, unconvincing, and, indeed, barely comprehensible. Still, it is a view honestly held by millions of Americans, and it is at the center of the debate about same-sex marriage.

What happens to this argument when it gets fed into our constitutional law machine? Recall that the major premise rests on the position that constitutional law provides a just basis for resolving disputes among people who would otherwise disagree. Perhaps that position could be sustained if it were shown that the Constitution was somehow neutral as between rival views. As we have already seen, though, there is no way to supply the content of the particular substantive command invoked in the minor premise without taking a

---

[63] See text at notes 53–61 above.

[64] See, for example, Robert P. George and Gerard V. Bradley, *Marriage and the Liberal Imagination*, 84 Georgetown L J 301 (1995); John M. Finnis, *Law, Morality, and "Sexual Orientation,"* 69 Notre Dame L Rev 1049 (1994).

position on the very issue in dispute. To make the syllogism plausible, then, a court must demonstrate that it has given content to that command through the use of presuppositions that are very widely shared.

The chief such presupposition concerns means-ends rationality. Because we disagree about many ends and because this disagreement threatens the unanimity that the major premise requires, we are forced into assuming ends that are uncontroversial and then arguing about whether the chosen means really advance those ends.

Judge Posner's widely admired opinion for the Seventh Circuit Court of Appeals striking down gay marriage bans in Wisconsin and Indiana demonstrates what happens to constitutional argument when this process is operationalized.[65] Judge Posner notes that neither Wisconsin nor Indiana "make[s] a moral argument against permitting same-sex marriage."[66] Instead, the states made consequentialist arguments, like the assertion that "the only reason government encourages marriage is to induce heterosexuals to marry so that there will be fewer 'accidental births,' which when they occur outside of marriage often lead to abandonment of the child to the mother (unaided by the father) or to foster care."[67] Same-sex couples, in contrast "don't need marriage because [they] can't *produce* children, intended or unintended."[68]

With characteristic verve and acuity, Judge Posner proceeds to demolish this argument, demonstrating that it "is so full of holes that it cannot be taken seriously."[69] And the argument is indeed silly. But whose fault is that? The states can hardly be blamed for not making the argument that gay relationships are immoral. By the time the Seventh Circuit case was argued, the Supreme Court had already taken that argument off the table.[70] Having been deprived of the ar-

---

[65] See *Baskin v Bogan*, 766 F3d 648 (2014).

[66] Id at 668.

[67] Id at 664.

[68] Id at 656.

[69] Id.

[70] See *Lawrence v Texas*, 539 US 558, 569 (2003):

> The condemnation [of homosexuality] has been shaped by religious beliefs, conceptions of right and acceptable behavior, and respect for the traditional family. For many persons these are not trivial concerns but profound and deep convictions accepted as ethical and moral principles to which they aspire and which thus determine

gument that motivated them, gay marriage opponents were left with no alternative but to make substitute arguments that, not surprisingly, ill-fit the position they were defending.

There is little mystery about why the Supreme Court disallowed the morality argument. It is, at best, controversial, and the prospect of resolving the controversy by resort to presuppositions that are widely shared is nil. And so, in order to preserve the first premise, courts ignore the argument and replace it with another argument about rational means to an uncontroversial end. Judge Posner then gets to make fun of the litigants for defending a means that any intelligent person would see is completely disconnected from the posited end. Often, this display is coupled with dark hints that this disconnect demonstrates lack of good faith and candor. Perhaps the litigants are merely stupid, but if we assume that they are intelligent, then their seeming irrationality must be caused by the effort to advance some secret end that they are not revealing.

Playing this game is no doubt satisfying to the winners and demonstrates their intellectual and moral superiority, at least to their own satisfaction. The problem, though, is that the game is rigged. One can always win an argument if one starts by disqualifying the principal position of one's opponent.[71] It will not do to claim that moral arguments in general cannot justify laws. All laws have moral substrates. The Court remains blind to this fact in the same way that many white people think that they have no race. Requirements imposed by means/ends rationality, the harm principle, and welfare maximization themselves rest on moral presuppositions that the Court treats as neutral and "just there" only because they are familiar to the Justices. If one starts instead with a different set of premises, the wrongness of gay relations might be "just there," and then the pro-

---

the course of their lives. These considerations do not answer the question before us, however. The issue is whether the majority may use the power of the State to enforce these views on the whole society through operation of the criminal law. Our obligation is to define the liberty of all, not to mandate our own moral code.

[71] The phenomenon extends beyond the gay marriage debate and has become an important feature of constitutional law. For example, advocates of affirmative action are forced to make sometimes unconvincing arguments about diversity because the Supreme Court has taken the aim of ending racial subjugation off the table. Similarly, advocates of campaign finance regulation must make sometimes unconvincing arguments about quid-pro-quo corruption because the Supreme Court has taken the aim of equalizing political power without regard to wealth off the table. For my argument that substitution is a defining characteristic of constitutional law, see Louis Michael Seidman, *Substitute Arguments in Constitutional Law*, Va J L & Pol (forthcoming, 2016).

hibition of gay marriage would be a completely rational means that uncontroversially advances the end of discouraging immoral behavior.

All this is sufficiently obvious that there is a risk that the sham will be seen for what it is. For this reason, the basic moves of the game need to be supplemented with other rhetorical tropes. At this point, a second pernicious consequence of constitutional argument emerges. In order to make the argument plausible, the losing position must be painted as not only wrong, but also outside the bounds of reasonable discourse. The winning position, in turn, must be painted as not only right but also uncontroversial, and to make it uncontroversial, it must be distinguished from other positions that might raise problems.

That effort, in turn, gives the recognition of new constitutionally protected groups a curious, double-edged quality. Even as the Supreme Court extends the bounds of empathy and connection to the previously excluded, it frequently does so against the backdrop of other disfavored groups that are left all the more isolated.

There is a history to this. When the first Justice Harlan wrote his celebrated dissent in *Plessy v Ferguson*[72] deploring the forced segregation of African Americans, he felt called upon to distinguish them from the "[Chinese] race so different from our own that we do not permit those belonging to it to become citizens of the United States."[73] Generations later, when Harlan's grandson defended the right of married couples to use contraceptives, he coupled the defense with the statement that "I would not suggest that ... homosexuality ... [is] immune from criminal enquiry, however privately practiced."[74] Years after that, Justice Kennedy wrote an opinion striking down a provision that erected special barriers that prevented gay men and lesbians from securing passage of antidiscrimination laws that benefited them.[75] Coming full circle from the first Justice Harlan's dissent, Justice Kennedy subsequently made clear that this decision had nothing to do with provisions that similarly obstructed passage of affirmative action laws benefiting African Americans.[76]

---

[72] 163 US 539 (1896).

[73] Id at 561 (Harlan, J, dissenting).

[74] See *Poe v Ullman*, 367 US 497, 552–53 (1961) (Harlan, J, dissenting), incorporated by reference *Griswold v Connecticut*, 381 US 479, 500 (1965) (Harlan, J, concurring).

[75] See *Romer v Evans*, 517 US 620 (1996).

[76] Compare id with *Schuette v Coalition to Defend Affirmative Action*, 134 S Ct 1623 (2014) (Kennedy, J).

Who are the disfavored groups victimized by *Obergefell*? The most obvious candidates are religious and cultural conservatives. In fairness to the majority, it goes out of its way to express respect for these groups. There is, moreover, a difference between merely losing and being effectively excluded from the political community. Still, a necessary consequence of resting the decision on the duty to obey constitutional commands is that people on the other side are painted as not just wrong but as opposing the fundamental commitments under which our society is organized. Yes, "[m]any who deem same-sex marriage to be wrong reach that conclusion based on decent and honorable religious or philosophical premises"[77] but that does not change the fact that their position is not just wrong, but denies "the liberty promised by the Fourteenth Amendment."[78]

Perhaps more disturbing is the majority's marginalization of people—gay and straight—who cannot or choose not to marry. The belittling of the millions of Americans who fall into this category begins in the first paragraph of the Court's analysis and does not end until the last paragraph. At the beginning of the opinion, we learn that "marriage is essential to our most profound hopes and aspirations,"[79] apparently leaving the unmarried hopeless and without aspirations (at least of the profound variety). At the end, we are told that gay people must be allowed to marry so as "not to be condemned to live in loneliness"[80] as if unmarried people necessarily lack human connection and companionship.

In between, the Court informs us that marriage "fulfils yearnings for security, safe haven, and connection that expresses our common humanity."[81] It allows persons to find "expression, intimacy, and spirituality,"[82] "supports a two-person union unlike any other in its importance to the committed individuals,"[83] and "responds to the universal fear that a lonely person might call out only to find no one there."[84] Without the right to marry, gay men and lesbians are "out-

---

[77] *Obergefell v Hodges*, 135 S Ct 2584, 2602 (2015).

[78] Id.

[79] Id at 2594.

[80] Id at 2608.

[81] Id at 2599.

[82] Id.

[83] Id.

[84] Id at 2600.

cast."[85] Children of unmarried people suffer "stigma."[86] Worse yet, there is at least an implication that unmarried people are not quite full citizens. This is so because "marriage is a keystone of our social order" and "remains a building block of our national community."[87]

All this rhetoric takes no account of the fact that for many victims of spousal abuse, marriage is a cage that denies them "security, safe haven, and connection." Nor does it recognize that many unmarried people are quite capable of finding fulfillment, happiness, and civic engagement. Nor does the Court's blithe assumption that "[m]arriage ... affords the permanency and stability important to children's best interests"[88] take into account the fact that something like half of all marriages end in divorce.[89]

The valorization of marriage and attack on the unmarried is also deeply reactionary. It comes at a moment when, as just noted, a huge percentage of marriages end in divorce—often acrimonious and wrenching—and when fewer and fewer Americans are choosing marriage in the first place.[90]

This lack of empathy and understanding for a choice that many make and a necessity that many face is especially incongruous in an opinion that purports to argue for inclusion and understanding. The majority is on firm ground when it points to the human misery caused by insisting on a limited number of social scripts to which people must conform whether or not it suits their circumstances. It is therefore especially unfortunate that the very opinion that lauds the virtues of inclusion and respect also thoughtlessly contains an implicit attack on a central feature in the lives of so many.

Ironically, the majority's characterization of the unmarried also oversimplifies the experience of the gay Americans it purports to defend. The opinion effectively reads out of the gay rights movement

---

[85] Id.

[86] Id.

[87] Id at 2601.

[88] Id at 2600.

[89] According to the Center for Disease Control and Prevention, the marriage rate is 6.8 per 1,000 in the population, while the divorce rate is 3.6 per 1,000 in the population. The statistics are available at http://www.cdc.gov/nchs/fastats/marriage-divorce.htm.

[90] Center for Disease Control and Prevention statistics show that between 2000 and 2012, the annual marriage rate declined from 8.2 per 1,000 in population to 6.8 per 1,000 in population. The statistics are available at http://www.cdc.gov/nchs/nvss/marriage_divorce_tables.htm.

those who advanced a radical critique of mainstream sexual mores. Moreover, from reading the opinion, one might suppose that before being rescued by a beneficent Court, gay men and lesbians were "outcast[s]"[91] condemned to a lonely existence without hope or aspiration.

Of course, no one should deny the history of oppression, violence, and exclusion suffered by the gay community. But gay people, like other oppressed minorities, managed to develop a sustaining culture in the face of that oppression. Part of what made the culture sustaining was that it stood in opposition to the majority culture. Contrary to the implication of the majority opinion, all gay people were not isolated and miserable. They formed communities, had fun, lived productive lives, and gained sustenance from their association with each other.[92] The majority's condescending pity toward their oppositional culture is inconsistent with the very inclusive pluralism that it purports to embrace.

Constitutional argument distorts the experience of the gay community in yet another way. As I have argued above, the constitutional dispute about gay marriage revolves around whether the issue should be resolved publicly or privately. Because the Court's opinion defended private choice, its rhetoric necessarily celebrated the virtue of unfettered individualism and autonomy. On the Court's view, "the right to personal choice regarding marriage is inherent in the concept of individual autonomy."[93]

Few today would deny that individual choice is an important aspect of marriage. It should be obvious as well that liberty and autonomy are an important part of what gay liberation is about. But the fight for gay liberation also involved instilling the kind of group solidarity necessary to overcome the huge collective action problem posed by the closet.[94]

The story is a familiar one. So long as gay people saw themselves as atomized individuals, there was little hope for effective political

---

[91] *Obergefell v Hodges*, 135 S Ct at 2600.

[92] For a detailed revisionist history emphasizing the vibrancy and visibility of a gay community before World War II, see George Chauncey, *Gay New York: Gender, Urban Culture, and the Making of the Gay Male World, 1890–1940* (1994).

[93] *Obergefell v Hodges*, 135 S Ct at 2589.

[94] For one account, see Michael J. Klarman, *From the Closet to the Altar: Courts, Backlash and the Struggle for Same-Sex Marriage* (2013).

action. If left to the kind of individual choice that the *Obergefell* Court celebrates, it made little sense to many gay people to take the huge risks associated with coming out. With exit a plausible option, voice was foolhardy.

The solution to this dilemma was not individual, unfettered choice, but collective action. The most extreme strategy for promoting collective empowerment was the practice of "outing." Defenders of the practice argued that closeted gay people were not simply making an individual choice. Their failure to give voice inflicted externalities on others by reducing the political power of the gay community. For the good of the collective, their individual choice had to be countermanded by revealing their sexual identity against their will.[95]

For obvious reasons, "outing" is problematic, but there were other less troubling strategies that eventually succeeded in creating the kind of collective consciousness that made gay liberation a real possibility. Remarkably courageous leaders provided examples and role models. Iconic events like Stonewall provided causes to rally around. Gay pride parades and demonstrations showed that coming out could be empowering and joyful. These were not decisions made by individuals concerning how to lead their private lives. They were public manifestations of solidarity.

The public character of gay liberation involves not just means but also ultimate ends. Although *Obergefell* makes passing reference to the Equal Protection Clause,[96] the Court places its primary emphasis on due process rights. The distinction is important because the Due Process Clause is the natural home for individualist claims. As the dissenting opinions point out, the dominant strain of our constitutional tradition emphasizes the negative right of the individual to be shielded from the collective, not the positive right of groups to collective protection.[97]

Equality claims, in contrast, provide the one constitutional mechanism through which the government can be forced to extend positive protection to groups. If one group is denied things that others are granted, an equal protection argument can force the state into a choice of denying the benefit to everyone or granting it to the deprived group. Often, the government will choose to extend the ben-

---

[95] For a discussion, see Kenji Yoshino, *Covering*, 111 Yale L J 769, 821 (2002).

[96] *Obergefell v Hodges*, 135 S Ct 2584, 2590 (2015).

[97] See id at 2634 (Thomas, J, dissenting); id at 2620 (Roberts, CJ, dissenting).

efit. And although the Court has recognized the conceptual possibility of an equal protection "class of one,"[98] equality claims prototypically involve groups of people who are treated differently from each other.

Occasionally, the Supreme Court has utilized the Equal Protection Clause to mandate collective, positive rights, but the dissenting Justices are correct when they insist that this is not the dominant strain of American constitutionalism. The majority therefore needed to shield itself from the claim that it was embracing this strain. It did so by recasting the problem for gay Americans as the frustration of an individual choice to marry that was part of the "liberty" that the Due Process Clause protects.

That is part of the problem faced by gay Americans, but it is nothing like the whole problem. As Chief Justice Roberts points out, individual people face all sorts of restrictions on marital choice, including, most prominently, the restriction on polygamy.[99] The majority provides no answer to the Chief Justice's complaint that its opinion opens the door to constitutional protection for polygamists. To provide an answer, the majority would have had to acknowledge the public, group nature of the claim to gay marriage.

That claim is not premised solely on the frustration of individual choice (a characteristic it shares with polygamy), but on the fact that restrictions on gay marriage are part of a system of laws, practices, customs, and beliefs that subjugate gay men and lesbians as a group in a way that individuals who want more than one spouse are not subjugated. People who would like to be married to more than one spouse are not routinely beaten up, ridiculed, despised, and excluded from employment or public accommodations.[100] Nor are they part of a group formed by genetic or at least very deeply rooted characteristics that go to the core of their identity and that are not subject to change.

---

[98] See *Village of Willowbrook v Olech*, 528 US 562 (2000) (recognizing a "class of one"); but compare *Engqist v Oregon Dept. of Agriculture*, 553 US 291 (2008) (refusing to recognize "class of one" in cases where government is acting as employer).

[99] *Obergefell v Hodges*, 135 S Ct 2584, 2622 (2015) (Roberts, CJ, dissenting).

[100] The difference is significant now, but was less so when polygamy was associated with the Church of the Latter Day Saints, which was a group and suffered from oppression. Today, people who wish to marry more than one spouse find their choice frustrated, but they do not suffer widespread discrimination, violence, subjugation, or hatred so long as they do not violate the laws against their marital preferences. One could imagine that at some point in the future, polygamists would regain a group identity and solidarity that would make them more similar to gay men and lesbians.

Moreover, the solution to the problem involves much more than just recognizing the right of gay men and lesbians to be "let alone." As Chief Justice Roberts rightly points out, bans on gay marriage

> create no crime and impose no punishment. Same-sex couples remain free to live together, to engage in intimate conduct, to raise their families as they see fit. . . . [T]he laws in no way interfere with the "right to be let alone."[101]

After years of official oppression, a commitment by government to leave gay men and lesbians in peace is no doubt an advance. But it is far from all that is required. Much of the most serious oppression of gay Americans stems from private violence, hatred, and discrimination. To ward that off, positive government intervention to control private sphere is required. Most obviously, the protection consists of punishment of private violence, but there is more to it than that. Just as the dissent complained, gay marriage is important because it provides affirmative government endorsement of relationships that were once scorned. It is a symbolic part of the project of tearing down the closet that hid individual gay Americans from view. It turns them into visible, public citizens worthy of public respect.

It is similarly fallacious to suppose that this transformation produces no externalities. Contrary to the claims its defenders must make to fit within our constitutional tradition, same-sex marriage decisions are not solely self-regarding. Of course, the assertion that straight people will no longer marry because gay people do is ludicrous, but the assertion that the end of the closet will have an impact on American culture is not. Does anyone suppose that one can shield oneself from the profound effects of television and computers on everyday life by not purchasing these products? These innovations transformed our entire society, whether one personally used them or not. So, too, the end of the closet affects all of us, gay or straight, in sometimes subtle but pervasive ways.

These are changes that can only be defended on the merits. The defense ultimately rests on the assertion that gay intimacy is a good and that suppression of it is an evil. Conventional constitutional argument lacks the resources to defend that assertion. There is not some neutral principle contained in the text of the Constitution or in a tradition that everyone is bound to accept that establishes its truth. In-

---

[101] *Obergefell v Hodges*, 135 S Ct 2584, 2620 (2015) (Roberts, CJ, dissenting).

stead, the truth comes from lived experience, from a sense of solidarity and empathy, and from the pull of fundamental decency—or at least so it seems to me. It will not seem that way to religious and cultural conservatives, who think that homosexuality offends the natural order. Anyone who supposes that constitutional law can bridge that gap misunderstands its nature and depth.

Truly respecting the losers in *Obergefell* entails recognizing that fact. We should not trivialize their objections by pretending that they are relying on an argument that we have forced them into making or by insisting that their actual argument is inconsistent with a neutral and objective reading of our founding document. The governors, clerks, attorney generals, and justices of the peace who resist *Obergefell* should not be told that they have a constitutional duty to comply regardless of the moral rightness of the decision. From their perspective, they have a duty to resist. What they should be told instead is that their perspective is wrong—at least from our perspective.

Of course, telling them this will not resolve the dispute, but neither should constitutional law. It is just a fact that our society is divided about questions that matter. If the divide is to be bridged at all, it will have to be by a sense of cooperation and solidarity that comes from engaging in a joint enterprise. Vague words in an ancient text should not be allowed to do the trick.

III. What to Do?

No doubt, the governors, clerks, attorney generals, and justices of the peace will come around, albeit after some symbolic, short-lived unpleasantness. We are unlikely to see the kind of massive resistance that followed *Brown* or even the sustained political opposition that followed *Roe*. There are a variety of reasons for this acquiescence. Gay marriage does not disrupt an entrenched system in the way that *Brown* did. The Court did not embrace and, indeed, effectively isolated the strands of the gay rights movement that might have posed a challenge to the reigning ideology. The decision does not provide the numerous possibilities for evasion that existed after both *Brown* and *Roe*. And whereas the country was narrowly divided about both desegregation and abortion, there is a large and growing majority favoring gay marriage.[102]

---

[102] See note 51 above.

It must be conceded, though, that acquiescence also stems in part from a widespread belief that when the Supreme Court speaks in constitutional tones, its dictates appropriately settle the issue, at least until the decision is overruled. People who challenge the Court are said to be violating the rule of law and the Constitution itself, and many people think that that is a very bad thing.

The confluence of these forces has produced an undeniable, if partial and tainted victory. The day after *Obergefell*, there was indeed cause for dancing in the streets. People who had suffered years of exclusion and oppression finally achieved some recognition of their basic humanity. If Chief Justice Roberts cannot bring himself to begrudge them their celebration, then neither can I.

Still, when the dancing stops, we are left with some disturbing questions. Constitutionalism helped produce a victory in this case, but it did so through mechanisms we should be ashamed of. Should we embrace constitutionalism and use its tools so as to preserve this victory and, perhaps, win others as well? Put differently, if you or I were a Justice on the Supreme Court, should we sign Justice Kennedy's opinion? What if our vote was necessary to secure a majority?

It is worth emphasizing again that the test for authentic constitutional obedience comes only when it produces bad outcomes. In this case, the outcome was good, and the substantive "rightness" of *Obergefell* means that it cannot pose such a test, at least for those of us who believe that the outcome is substantively right. The real question, then, is whether the substantive rightness of this particular outcome provides sufficient reason to associate ourselves with a discourse that is corrupt and obfuscatory.

One could (barely) imagine a Justice writing an opinion that reached the same result but that did not implicate the Court in this dirty business. An honest opinion would make no claim that the result was dictated by impersonal commands from the past or that others had a duty to obey resting on the fundamental obligations of citizenship. Instead, it would acknowledge that Justices were making a choice in the here and now—a choice that seemed right to them, but that had no foundation in uncontroversial first principles that everyone is bound to accept. The opinion would express the hope that others would agree, but it would not speak in the language of duty and of the rule of law.

An opinion like this would preserve the personal integrity of those signing it, but at what cost? On some level, perhaps, most Americans understand that the Supreme Court regularly reads its own contestable views into the Constitution. Still, it is one thing to understand this in a general way and another for the Justices themselves to acknowledge these unsettling facts in the context of a particular case. There is no small risk that an opinion like this would undermine judicial authority, not just in this case, but across the board. Does the pull of integrity and honesty demand that we pay that price?

The question is most difficult if one assumes that not just in this case, but over the range of cases, American constitutionalism produces or is likely to produce substantively good outcomes. There is a huge literature that I cannot do justice to here arguing that the Court has only rarely stood for progressive social change and that, when it has attempted to do so, it has only rarely been successful. Much more frequently, the Justices have stood with the forces of reaction and privilege or backed down when confronted with opposition to progressive change.[103]

The gay rights story provides a partial corrective to this general narrative. The Court's decisions hastened the advent of gay marriage, and, for reasons I have just discussed, it seems quite likely that the reforms will stick. Still, even in this instance, judicial intervention was facilitated by exogenous social change that had little to do with constitutional litigation. By the time the Court finally got around to recognizing a right to gay marriage, the political and cultural isolation of gay men and lesbians was already quickly disappearing. It is probable that gay marriage would have been recognized almost everywhere within a decade or two even if the Justices had not intervened. The Court's very gradual advance toward mandating gay marriage, extending over several decades, amounted to an admission that it felt unable to act until the point when its efforts were largely unnecessary.

Moreover, as argued above, the victory for gay marriage came at the cost of distorting the argument for and against it and further isolating others who do not live within the territory of empathy that the Supreme Court has bounded. And against the ambiguous and partial advance that protection for gay marriage represents, we must weigh

---

[103] For an introduction, see Michael J. Klarman, *Rethinking the Civil Rights and Civil Liberties Revolutions*, 82 Va L Rev 1 (1996); Gerald N. Rosenberg, *The Hollow Hope: Can Courts Bring About Social Change?* (1991); but compare Justin Driver, *Constitutional Outliers*, 81 U Chi L Rev 929 (2014) (rejecting view that Court only invalidates measures that are already deemed antiquated).

all the unjust settlements that the Court and our sense of constitutional obligation have forced upon us. For every *Obergefell*, we have many *Bush v Gore*s, *Heller*s, and *Citizens United*s. Is the game really worth the candle?

I think that it probably is not, and if it is not, then we may not face the hard choice between integrity and substantive justice. Unfortunately, though, that doesn't quite settle the matter. What if it is possible to use the tools of constitutionalism in bad faith to produce good results in this case while disowning them when they produce bad results in other cases? Should you or I then sign Justice Kennedy's opinion?

There is a risk, of course, that we will be caught at this dishonest game or outsmarted by our opponents. Even if we are not, there are obvious problems of political morality at stake. If skillfully deployed, the tactic might marginally help produce a more substantively just society, but it does so only by removing from debate issues that ought to be contestable. There is no good reason grounded in political justice why people who disagree about, say, campaign finance, gun control, or gay marriage should be bound to put aside their principles and accept a particular judgment just because the Supreme Court thinks that the Constitution requires it. In place of these good reasons, constitutional law provides dishonesty, mystification, debate that has little relationship to what people do or should care about, and the false closure of authoritarian pronouncement. These characteristics of constitutionalism cannot be reconciled with the ideals of a mature, deliberative democracy. They do not accord our political opponents the dignity that they deserve.

If one would nonetheless sign Justice Kennedy's opinion, it must be because substantive justice trumps principles of political justice. It must be because those who are on the "right" side can appropriately insist on obedience for others that they would not accept for themselves. Is substantive justice the kind of trump that justifies this hypocrisy?

I am far from certain, but I'm inclined to think that it is. Put differently, if I somehow found myself on the Supreme Court, yes, I would be tempted to join Justice Kennedy's dreadful opinion. On one side of the ledger, there is the real and daily human suffering resulting from the status quo. On the other side, it is not as if my abstaining from our constitutional practice means that others will as well. If the practice is going to continue anyway, why not claim the benefits of the just results it occasionally produces?

But none of this changes the fact that this is, indeed, a dirty business. It means resorting to deception and manipulation and giving up on the prospect of resolving disputes by means of authentic dialogue with a common vocabulary.

I cannot make myself be completely at peace with that outcome. If we are to avoid it, though, the only alternative is to embrace the hard and urgent work of imagining a different, less authoritarian, distorting, and exclusionary discourse that can justly bind us together.

RICHARD H. McADAMS

CLOSE ENOUGH FOR GOVERNMENT WORK? HEIEN'S LESS-THAN-REASONABLE MISTAKE OF THE RULE OF LAW

In *Heien v North Carolina*,[1] the Supreme Court held 8–1 that a search or seizure can be lawful under the Fourth Amendment despite its being founded on a government agent's mistake of law, as long as the mistake was "reasonable." The Court did not hold merely that a police officer's reasonable mistake of criminal law excused the state from the remedy Heien sought—the exclusion of evidence from his criminal trial—but that there was no Fourth Amendment violation, that is, that "the people" have no federal right to be secure against such searches or seizures.[2] The gist of the opinion was the simple virtue of symmetry: Just as probable cause and reasonable suspicion do not require the police to be correct about the facts, but merely to have the right level of justified factual suspicion, these objective

Richard H. McAdams is Bernard D. Meltzer Professor, University of Chicago Law School.

AUTHOR'S NOTE: I thank Will Baude, Justin Driver, Daniel Hemel, Aziz Huq, Andy Leipold, Jennifer Nou, Michael Pollack, John Rappaport, and David Strauss for insightful comments and discussions on an earlier draft. I thank Sony Rao for excellent research assistance and the Robert B. Roesing Faculty Fund for research support.

[1] 135 S Ct 530 (2014).

[2] Although the Court did not word its holding this way, that formulation tracks the text of the Fourth Amendment, which declares: "The right of the people to be secure in their persons, houses, papers, and effects, against unreasonable searches and seizures, shall not be violated. . . ."

standards do not require the police to be correct about the law, but only to have a reasonable belief about what the law forbids.[3] In either case, the suspect's ex post innocence does not disprove the ex ante probable cause or reasonable suspicion of guilt (as the particular doctrine requires) that renders the search constitutional.

Plausible sounding as it may be, *Heien* is a riches of embarrassment. The symmetry reasoning is superficial, as it ignores or fails to grasp the power of obvious counterarguments, including: (1) A search or seizure based on a mistake of law is the joint result of executive *and* legislative action; viewing a government as a whole, mistakes of law are never reasonable because a reasonable legislature writes criminal statutes clearly enough to allow reasonable police officers to know what the law is. (2) Indeed, a state legislature can hardly be said to provide citizens with constitutionally sufficient "fair notice" of criminal prohibitions if the meaning of a criminal statute is so ambiguous that we cannot even expect law enforcement officers to get the law right. (3) Just as reasonable "ignorance of the criminal law is no excuse" for citizens, it should not excuse or empower government officials, especially not for mistakes about the law they are tasked with enforcing. (4) The issue in *Heien* arises almost entirely in the context of traffic enforcement, which is the very last place in criminal law where the Court should grant the police an extra dose of discretion. We might summarize these four points with the simple proposition that government, being the creator of law, is always limited in power by the law it actually creates, a principle which distinguishes government mistakes of law from governmental mistakes of fact. On reflection, *Heien* is a misstep for the rule of law.

For the most part, *Heien* does not even acknowledge the existence of these counterarguments, much less refute them. The Court does, however, engage the possible parallel to the ancient maxim *ignorance of law is no excuse*, admitting that the analogy "has a certain rhetorical appeal."[4] As the Court describes the point: "it is fundamentally unfair to let police officers get away with mistakes of law when the citizenry

---

[3] *Heien*, 135 S Ct at 534. Although the case focuses on reasonable suspicion, I assume the same rule applies to probable cause, where that is the relevant standard, because *Heien* cites as authority nineteenth-century cases involving "reasonable cause," which the Court says is the same as probable cause. Id at 536–37. Subsequent cases have made the extension with no hesitation. See, for example, *United States v Diaz*, 122 F Supp 3d 165, 175 n 6 (SD NY 2015) (saying that the contrary argument "borders on frivolous").

[4] *Heien*, 135 S Ct at 540.

is accorded no such leeway."[5] But the Court's brief conceptual response to this point, described below, is deeply flawed and incomplete. For many reasons, we should expect professional law enforcement officers to know the criminal law it is their job to enforce. And if we must impose a different rule for police and citizens, it should be more demanding for the police, not less.

Heien is difficult to square with other principles of American criminal law, including basic precepts of the rule of law. One standard feature of our law that is conventionally described as implementing the principle of legality is the vagueness doctrine, the rule that excessively vague statutes are a violation of the Due Process Clause.[6] The twin rationales of the vagueness doctrine, and of legality in general, are to provide citizens with fair notice of the criteria of law enforcement coercion[7] and to constrain discretion to prevent arbitrary and discriminatory enforcement.[8] Yet *Heien* damages both values,

---

[5] Id.

[6] See John Calvin Jeffries, Jr., *Legality, Vagueness, and the Construction of Penal Statutes*, 71 Va L Rev 189, 196 (1985) (explaining why "the vagueness doctrine is the operational arm of legality"); Paul H. Robinson, *Fair Notice and Fair Adjudication: Two Kinds of Legality*, 154 U Pa L Rev 335, 357–63 (2005). See also Marc Ribeiro, *Limiting Arbitrary Power: The Vagueness Doctrine in Canadian Constitutional Law* (British Columbia, 2004).

[7] See, for example, *United States v Cardiff*, 344 US 174, 176 (1952) ("The vice of vagueness in criminal statutes is the treachery they conceal either in determining what persons are included or what acts are prohibited. Words which are vague and fluid . . . may be as much of a trap for the innocent as the ancient laws of Caligula."); *Connally v General Construction Co.*, 269 US 385, 391 (1926) ("[T]he terms of a penal statute creating a new offense must be sufficiently explicit to inform those who are subject to it what conduct on their part will render them liable to its penalties . . . ; and a statute which either forbids or requires the doing of an act in terms so vague that men of common intelligence must necessarily guess at its meaning and differ as to its application, violates the first essential of due process of law.").

[8] See *Kolender v Lawson*, 461 US 352, 357–58 (1983) ("Although the doctrine focuses both on actual notice to citizens and arbitrary enforcement, we have recognized recently that the more important aspect of vagueness doctrine 'is not actual notice, but the other principal element of the doctrine—the requirement that a legislature establish minimal guidelines to govern law enforcement.'"). See also *Papachristou v City of Jacksonville*, 405 US 156, 170 (1972) ("Where, as here, there are no standards governing the exercise of the discretion granted by the ordinance, the scheme permits and encourages an arbitrary and discriminatory enforcement of the law."); *Shuttlesworth v Birmingham*, 382 US 87, 90–91 (1965) ("Literally read . . . the second part of this ordinance says that a person may stand on a public sidewalk in Birmingham only at the whim of any police officer of that city. The constitutional vice of so broad a provision needs no demonstration. . . . It 'does not provide for government by clearly defined laws, but rather for government by the moment-to-moment opinions of a policeman on his beat.'"); *Smith v Goguen*, 415 US 566 (1974) ("Statutory language of such a standardless sweep allows policemen, prosecutors, and juries to pursue their personal predilections. . . . [W]e share [Justice Black's] concern [with] . . . entrusting lawmaking 'to the moment-to-moment judgment of the policeman on his beat.' . . . Where inherently vague statutory language permits such selective law enforcement, there is a denial of due process.").

particularly by compromising the most important constraint on enforcement discretion, central to the rule of law—the requirement that government use coercion against its citizens only to enforce actual law.[9]

Another doctrine instantiating legality is the interpretive canon of the rule of lenity.[10] For judging the meaning of ambiguous criminal statutes, and thus when government may criminally punish an individual, the rule of lenity favors the narrower over the broader interpretation. By contrast, for deciding when government may search or seize individuals or their property, *Heien* creates what we should call a "rule of severity": when a criminal statute is ambiguous, bearing two or more reasonable interpretations, citizens are subject to search and seizure based on the broadest reasonable interpretation of the statute unless and until a court reaches the issue and adopts a narrower interpretation.

As a result, *Heien* damages incentives underlying the rule of law. The decision indulges and condones carelessness in legislative drafting by ensuring that the police can be excused for misunderstanding the law, despite the fact that citizens are not. *Heien* also diminishes incentives (1) for municipalities to rigorously train police in the limits of the traffic law they enforce, (2) for alleged traffic violators to challenge the erroneous police interpretations of state law, and (3) for courts to clarify the meaning of ambiguous traffic statutes.

Heien is therefore an occasion to reconsider the Supreme Court's vision of legality in criminal law or, more generally, the rule of law. The Court often characterizes these values—fair notice and constrained police discretion—as central to Due Process and therefore as animating the decision to strike down a vague statute. And, yet, like many constitutional values, the concern for citizen notice and limited discretion is honored only inconsistently.[11] In some ways, there is never any surprise about a decision in which the Court rejects (here, implicitly) the citizen's claim to "fair notice" or the demand for limits on police discretion. What is surprising, however, is that in the same term as the Court decided *Heien*, it decided a vagueness case,

---

[9] See Herbert Packer, *The Limits of the Criminal Sanction* 90 (Stanford, 1968).

[10] See, for example, Lawrence M. Solan, *Law, Language, and Lenity*, 40 Wm & Mary L Rev 57 (1998).

[11] See Jeffries, 71 Va L Rev at 207–12 (cited in note 6).

Johnson v United States,[12] which struck down a Congressional sentencing statute in which neither concern—fair notice or limited discretion—was present by any but the most extravagant standard. Together, *Heien* and *Johnson* show that something is seriously amiss in the Court's vision of the rule of law.

There is much to say about each point.[13] Part I describes the holding and reasoning of *Heien*, and an important dictum. Part II examines how *Heien* undermines the legality value of constraining enforcement discretion. This part also explains how *Heien* is inconsistent with the centuries-old maxim about ignorance of criminal law. Part III examines how *Heien* disserves the legality value of fair notice, producing the rule of severity described above.

I. The Alluring Symmetry of Heien

As with much constitutional law, *Heien* begins with a traffic stop. A sheriff's officer assigned to drug interdiction sat in his car on the side of an interstate highway and observed a driver pass by shortly before 8 a.m. The officer entered traffic and followed the car. The Fourth Amendment does not require a justification for this particular decision because the simple act of following a car is not a search or seizure. But for the broader context it is worth noting that the officer offered an explanation anyway, which was his perception that the driver was "very stiff and nervous."[14] When asked at a hearing to explain the manner in which the suspect was "stiff and nervous," judged in the brief interval as the car lawfully passed his position at 60 mph, the officer's entire reply was: "He was gripping the steering wheel at a 10 and 2 position, looking straight ahead."[15] Such is the suspicious nature of American law enforcement.

The pertinent legal issue concerns the officer's subsequent decision to stop the car. "A few miles later," which presumably means a few minutes later, the officer observed that only one of the vehicle's

---

[12] 135 S Ct 2551 (2015).

[13] And much has been said. For the best pre-*Heien* treatment of these issues, see Wayne A. Logan, *Police Mistakes of Law*, 61 Emory L J 69 (2011).

[14] *Heien*, 135 S Ct at 534.

[15] *Heien*, Joint Appendix, at 15 (transcript of motion to suppress hearing held in the General Court of Justice, Superior Court Division, in Surry County, Dobson, North Carolina, on March 18, 2010, Criminal Session, before the Honorable V. Brad Long, Judge Presiding).

two brake lights was working. For this apparent infraction, the officer pulled over the driver, who turned out to be Maynor Javier Vasquez.[16] Almost like a parable, the facts match the common claim that an officer can always find some reason to stop an automobile by following it for a few minutes. It also presents the standard concern that police engage in racial profiling, as the race or national origin of Vasquez might resolve the mystery of why an officer claimed to be suspicious that Vasquez drove in textbook form and watched the road ahead.[17] In any event, for the nonfunctioning brake light, the officer issued Vasquez a warning ticket.

Commonly enough, the officer used this opportunity to ask for consent to search the vehicle, though this request was directed at the second man in the car, Nicholas Brady Heien, who turned out to be the actual owner.[18] Commonly enough, he agreed. The officer discovered cocaine in the car and arrested Heien. Before trial in state court, Heien argued that the stop that revealed the cocaine violated his Fourth Amendment rights and that the cocaine should be excluded. The trial court denied the motion, finding that the faulty brake light gave the officer reasonable suspicion for the stop.[19]

Everything unfolded in the most ordinary manner until the first appellate court gave the case a twist by holding that the North Carolina vehicle code did *not* actually require a vehicle to have more than one working brake light, so that Heien's vehicle was not operating in violation of law.[20] The court reasoned that the officer did not have reasonable suspicion for the stop, that is, that having reasonable factual grounds for believing the suspect was engaged in conduct that, in actuality, violates no law does not constitute reasonable suspicion. The stop was therefore unreasonable under the Fourth Amendment. The court held that the evidence had to be excluded and reversed the conviction.[21]

---

[16] *Heien*, 135 S Ct at 534.

[17] Of course, if the stop were based on race or national origin, the only constitutional violation is under the Equal Protection Clause; the Fourth Amendment judges the stop based on the objective facts, not the officer's actual motivation. See *Whren v United States*, 517 US 806, 813 (1996).

[18] *Heien*, 135 S Ct at 534.

[19] Id at 535.

[20] Id. See *State v Heien*, 714 SE2d 827 (NC Ct App 2011) (interpreting NC Gen Stat § 20-129(g), NC Gen Stat § 20-129(d), and NC Gen Stat § 20-183.3).

[21] *Heien*, 135 S Ct at 535.

The state appealed the Fourth Amendment issue without appealing the ruling on the meaning of the traffic code. The Supreme Court of North Carolina held that police could have reasonable suspicion despite an error about the law and that the stop in question was reasonable because the officer's interpretation of the ambiguous vehicle code was reasonable, despite being (it assumed) erroneous. The court therefore reversed and reinstated the conviction.[22] The North Carolina Supreme Court's decision contributed to a split among state and federal courts on the issue—whether police mistakes of criminal law could be consistent with probable cause or reasonable suspicion.[23]

The United States Supreme Court affirmed.[24] The Court said that the reasonableness of the officer's mistaken belief that the law required all brake lights to be operational, combined with a correct and justified factual belief that one brake light was inoperative, meant that the traffic stop was based on sufficient reasonable suspicion and, therefore, complied with the Fourth Amendment. It is well understood that a police search or seizure can be reasonable (based on either probable cause or reasonable suspicion, as the law requires) despite the fact that the police officer acts on the basis of *factual* errors, if the factual beliefs were sufficiently reasonable.[25] If the police stopped Heien because he and his car tightly matched the description of a fleeing felon, for example, the stop would be lawful even if it turned out that Heien was not the fleeing felon but someone who looked like him. In an opinion joined by all the Justices except Justice Sotomayor, who dissented, Chief Justice Roberts explicitly framed the case as asking whether a parallel "mistake of law can nonetheless give rise to the reasonable suspicion necessary to uphold the seizure."[26] He continues: "We hold that it can."[27]

The reasoning was based partly on precedent, though precedent did not control the case. The Court cited a line of nineteenth-century cases interpreting a statute that indemnified customs officials

---

[22] Id. See *State v Heien*, 737 SE2d 351 (NC 2012).

[23] See *Heien*, 135 S Ct at 544 & n 1 (Sotomayor, J, dissenting) (listing one circuit that agreed with the North Carolina Supreme Court and five federal circuit and five state courts that disagreed).

[24] Id at 540.

[25] Id at 536.

[26] Id at 534.

[27] Id.

for damages suits for unlawful seizures when those seizures were based on "reasonable cause," which the Court said was a synonym for probable cause.[28] A number of cases decided under the statute recognized "reasonable cause" to exist even when it was premised on the official's reasonable mistake of law. The majority conceded that these cases were "not directly on point. Chief Justice Marshall was not construing the Fourth Amendment, and a certificate of probable cause functioned much like a modern-day finding of qualified immunity, which depends on an inquiry distinct from whether an officer has committed a constitutional violation."[29] Still, the cases are suggestive because they refer in dicta to the Fourth Amendment idea of probable cause, which the Court says has not fundamentally changed over time.[30] The bottom line, however, is that the issue *Heien* presents—whether a search or seizure can be reasonable under the Fourth Amendment despite being predicated on a mistake of law— had not been previously decided by the Court.

The majority and dissent also discussed one modern precedent— *Michigan v DeFillippo*[31]—but it too is not controlling. In *DeFillippo* police officers arrested a man for violating a Detroit ordinance that, in certain circumstances, required suspects to prove their identity to police.[32] After the arrest, a state court declared the ordinance to be unconstitutional under the Due Process Clause on the grounds that it was excessively vague.[33] The Supreme Court held that there was nonetheless probable cause for the arrest, and no violation of the Fourth Amendment, when police relied on an ordinance only later ruled unconstitutional.[34] Here is how the majority in *Heien* uses the case to support its holding: "The officers were wrong in concluding that DeFillippo was guilty of a criminal offense when he declined to identify himself. That a court only *later* declared the ordinance un-

---

[28] Id at 536–37 (citing *United States v Riddle*, 9 US (5 Cranch) 311 (1809); *Locke v United States*, 11 US (7 Cranch) 339 (1813); *Stacey v Emery*, 97 US 642, 646 (1878); *The Friendship*, 9 F Cas 825, 826 (CCD Mass 1812); *United States v The Reindeer*, 27 F Cas 758, 768 (CCDRI 1848); *United States v The Recorder*, 27 F Cas 723 (CCSDNY 1849); *The La Manche*, 14 F Cas 965, 972 (D Mass 1863)).

[29] *Heien*, 135 S Ct at 537.

[30] Id.

[31] 443 US 31 (1979).

[32] Id.

[33] See *People v DeFillippo*, 262 NW2d 921 (Mich App 1977).

[34] *DeFillippo*, 443 US at 40.

constitutional does not change the fact that DeFillippo's conduct was lawful when the officers observed it."[35]

Yet this analysis is too quick. Just after discussing *DeFillippo*, the Court introduced a distinction between mistakes of *criminal* law and mistakes of *Fourth Amendment* law. The Court said: "An officer's mistaken view that the conduct at issue did *not* give rise to [a Fourth Amendment] violation—no matter how reasonable—could not change that ultimate conclusion. . . . Here, by contrast, the mistake of law relates to the antecedent question of whether it was reasonable for an officer to suspect that the defendant's conduct was illegal."[36] Justice Kagan's concurrence emphasized her agreement on this point: "an error about the contours of the Fourth Amendment itself can never support a search or seizure."[37] The Court thus distinguishes police mistakes of statutory criminal law from police mistakes of the Fourth Amendment itself.

The combination of *DeFillippo* and this *Heien* dictum demonstrates that one cannot generalize across different categories of mistake of law. Police reliance on a reasonable mistake of Due Process law does not violate the Fourth Amendment, but police reliance on a reasonable mistake of Fourth Amendment law does violate the Fourth Amendment. If we cannot even generalize across police mistakes of constitutional law, then surely the separate issue in *Heien*—whether police reliance on a reasonable mistake of statutory criminal law violates the Fourth Amendment—must stand on its own footing.[38] *DeFillippo* no more controlled the issue of police mistakes of traffic law than the *Heien* dictum controlled the issue in the opposite direction.[39]

---

[35] *Heien*, 135 S Ct at 538.

[36] Id at 539.

[37] Id at 541, n 1 (Kagan, J, concurring).

[38] In her *Heien* dissent, Justice Sotomayor attempted to distinguish *DeFillippo* on the grounds that the case "did not involve any police 'mistake' at all" because society wants police to rely on the presumed constitutionality of legislative enactments. See id at 546. I agree with the presumption, but that is the wrong way to distinguish the case. It *is* a legal mistake to enforce a legally invalid ordinance, even if the mistake is excusable because we want to encourage police to enforce the statutory law as written. The right distinction between *DeFillippo* and *Heien* is the source of the police error: criminal law in *Heien* and constitutional law in *DeFillippo*, specifically the Due Process Clause. But unlike the presumption of constitutionality, there is no reason to encourage police to enforce the broadest reasonable meaning of every statute.

[39] The Court blurs its own distinction when it says "DeFillippo's conduct was lawful when the officers observed it." *Heien*, 135 S Ct at 538. DeFillippo had actually violated the ordi-

In response, one might defend the Court's reliance on *DeFillippo* by saying that it and *Heien* both address the police officer's mistakes of law about the legality of the suspect's conduct, where the *Heien* dictum addresses the police officer's independent mistakes of law about the legality of his or her own conduct. Arguably, a reasonable mistake is pertinent in the former but not the latter case. But there was no hint of this classification before *Heien* and therefore no reason to view *DeFillippo* as controlling. One could instead have read *DeFillippo* as ensuring strong incentives for police to treat statutes as presumptively constitutional (by excusing constitutional mistakes) and view the *Heien* situation as calling for strong incentives for police to learn the law they enforce (therefore, giving no excuse for mistakes). Notably, the lower courts, most of which held that searches and seizures could not be based on reasonable mistakes of law, had not treated *DeFillippo* as dispositive.

Without controlling precedent, the primary rationale for the *Heien* opinion was symmetry. As the discovery, ex post, of factual errors does not rule out the possibility of ex ante reasonable suspicion or probable cause, the Court thought police mistakes of law should be treated in the same way. Indeed, the Court thought the issue obvious:

> [R]easonable suspicion arises from the combination of an officer's understanding of the facts and his understanding of the relevant law. . . . There is *no reason* under the text of the Fourth Amendment or our precedents, why this same result should be acceptable when reached by way of a reasonable mistake of fact, but not when reached by way of a similarly reasonable mistake of law.[40]

"No reason" is a strong statement, excessively so, I claim below, because the Court's precedents on the ignorance of mistake maxim, the vagueness doctrine, and the rule of lenity favor a different outcome.

After *Heien*, a fundamental question is what legal mistakes count as "reasonable." The North Carolina statute at issue was poorly drafted and ambiguous, and there was at least a respectable argument for reading it to require all "stop lamps" to be functional, an interpre-

---

nance as written, but his behavior was lawful only because he had violated an *invalid* ordinance, given its unconstitutional vagueness. By contrast, Heien did *not* violate the brake light statute as written. Given the dictum, the ultimate source of the police mistake of law seems to matter, as it does in criminal law. See Parts IID and IIE.

[40] *Heien*, 135 S Ct at 536 (emphasis added); see id at 539 (reasoning that legal issues, like factual issues, "suddenly confront[]" officers in the field).

tation embraced by the trial judge and an appellate dissent.[41] So the mistake at issue in *Heien* passed a high bar of objective reasonableness and the majority implied the bar is high when it said that "the inquiry is not as forgiving as the one employed in the distinct context of deciding whether an officer is entitled to qualified immunity."[42] Justice Kagan's concurrence emphasized this point, stating that "the test is satisfied when the law at issue is 'so doubtful in construction' that a *reasonable judge* could agree with the officer's view," as was true in *Heien*.[43] A slight puzzle here is that this demanding level of reasonableness seems inconsistent with the rationale of symmetry because mistakes of fact are not judged by the standards of experts.[44] In any event, since *Heien*, the lower courts have taken the requirement of reasonableness seriously, rejecting a number of governmental mistakes of law as unreasonable.[45]

The Court might have affirmed Heien's conviction on a different ground. The remedy at issue was the exclusionary rule. Starting with *United States v Leon*,[46] the Court has recognized a good-faith exception to the exclusionary remedy, which it has recently expanded

---

[41] See 737 SE2d at 358–59 (Hudson, J, dissenting, joined by CJ Parker and J Timmons-Goodson) (calling the Court of Appeals' majority statutory interpretation "surprising").

[42] 135 S Ct at 539 (Roberts, CJ).

[43] Id at 541 (Kagan, J, concurring) (emphasis added).

[44] See, for example, *Ornelas v United States*, 517 US 690, 695 (1996), citing *Illinois v Gates*, 462 US 213, 231 (1983) (stating that reasonable suspicion and probable cause "are commonsense, nontechnical conceptions that deal with 'the factual and practical considerations of everyday life on which reasonable and prudent men, not legal technicians, act.'"). To illustrate, assume that a 20 percent probability is usually enough for reasonable suspicion and that an officer is 20 percent confident that a car she now observes has just made an illegal U-turn. Perfect parity between mistakes of fact and law would treat identically these cases: (1) where the officer is 20 percent confident that the car made a U-turn at a particular intersection and 100 percent sure (and correct) that the law forbade U-turns at that intersection; and (2) where the officer was 100 percent sure in the fact of the U-turn and only 20 percent confident (and incorrect) that a legal rule prohibited such movement. Yet it seems that Justice Kagan's standard might reject case (2) as unreasonable.

[45] See, for example, *United States v Mota*, __ F Supp 3d __ (SD NY 2016) (interpreting state statute to require only two working brake lights, not a third in the middle of the rear window, and holding that mistake of law was unreasonable); *Darringer v State*, 46 NE3d 464 (Ind App 2015) (police error of law regarding placement of interim license plate was unreasonable); *United States v Sanders*, 95 F Supp 3d 1274 (D Nev 2015) (police were unreasonable in believing that air fresheners hanging from rearview mirror violated law); *United States v Alvarado-Zarza*, 782 F3d 246 (5th Cir 2015) (finding officer mistake of law unreasonable because signaling for 100 feet was required before a turn, not before a lane change); *United States v Flores*, 798 F3d 645 (7th Cir 2015) (finding police mistake about obstructing license plate, when frame did not actually block any writing, was unreasonable).

[46] *United States v Leon*, 468 US 897 (1984).

in several cases.[47] Of greatest relevance, *Davis v United States* held that it was erroneous to exclude evidence when police were searching in reliance on binding precedent of the relevant United States Court of Appeals.[48] *Heien* presents something different because the police were relying not on binding precedent determining the meaning of a criminal statute, but on the absence of precedent interpreting a statute. If we translate the problem from police error to the analogous situation of criminal defendants, *Davis* is similar to a defendant claiming a mistake of criminal law based on reasonable reliance on an official interpretation of the law that is afterward determined to be erroneous, which frequently operates as a defense.[49] *Heien* is similar to a defendant claiming a mistake of criminal law based on his own reasonable misreading of the statute, which is usually not a defense.[50] Of course, the Court might have extended the doctrine by saying that

---

[47] See *Davis v United States*, 131 S Ct 2419 (2011); *Herring v United States*, 555 US 135 (2009); *Arizona v Evans*, 514 US 1 (1995); *Illinois v Krull*, 480 US 340 (1987).

[48] *Davis*, 131 S Ct at 2419. The case involved a broad car search incident to arrest that the Courts of Appeals had interpreted the Supreme Court case of *New York v Belton* to permit, but which the Court later rejected in *Arizona v Gant*. See *New York v Belton*, 453 US 454 (1981), limited by *Arizona v Gant*, 556 US 332 (2009).

[49] For the statutory and common law doctrine, see Paul H. Robinson, Matthew G. Kussmaula, Camber M. Stoddard, Ilya Rudyak, and Andreas Kuersten, *The American Criminal Code: General Defenses*, 7 J Legal Analysis 37, 93–94 (2015) (stating that, even though "there is typically no general excuse for even a reasonable mistake of law," "a majority of American jurisdictions recognize an excuse for someone who reasonably relies upon an official misstatement of law. The arguments in support of such a rule are not just the blamelessness of the actor, but also—and perhaps more importantly—estoppel against a government that has brought about the offense by its own erroneous advice. A majority of thirty-six jurisdictions" follow *Model Penal Code* § 2.04(3)(b) (ALI 1962) and recognize this defense).

There is also a constitutional doctrine, sometimes called entrapment by estoppel, that reads the Due Process Clause as mandating a criminal law defense when a government actor misled the defendant as to the meaning of the law. See *Raley v Ohio*, 360 US 423 (1959); *Cox v Louisiana*, 379 US 559, 572 (1965); *United States v Laub*, 385 US 475 (1967); *United States v Pennsylvania Industrial Chemical Corp.*, 411 US 655 (1973). For a discussion, see Gabriel J. Chin, Reid Griffith Fontaine, Nicholas Klingerman, and Melody Gilkey, *The Mistake of Law Defense and an Unconstitutional Provision of the Model Penal Code*, 93 NC L Rev 139, 154 (2014) (summarizing lower courts as interpreting *Raley*, *Cox*, *Laub*, and *PICCO* to provide a mistake-of-law defense when "(1) a government official (2) told the defendant that certain criminal conduct was legal, (3) the defendant actually relied on the government official's statements, (4) and the defendant's reliance was in good faith and reasonable in light of the identity of the government official, the point of law represented, and the substance of the official's statement.").

[50] Robinson et al, 7 J Legal Analysis at 93–94 (cited in note 49) ("As a general rule, ignorance or mistake of the law is no defense unless it negates a required offense element. That is, there is typically no general excuse for even a reasonable mistake of law. Only one state, New Jersey, provides such a general excuse.").

there is no need for the distinction in legal mistakes—between relying on official interpretations of the law and relying on one's own judgment—in the context of the exclusionary rule, so that evidence is always admissible if the legal mistake is reasonable.[51]

Yet the remedy issue had not been argued below or briefed for the Court. The case was decided on the substance of the Fourth Amendment because North Carolina is one of fourteen states that have rejected the good-faith exception as a matter of state law, so that resolution would not necessarily leave the conviction intact. Of course, state courts might now avoid *Heien* as a matter of state constitutional law. This article suggests that state courts should take that path.[52]

II. The Rule of Law, Heien, and the Problem of Police Discretion

There are contested theories about what constitutes the rule of law,[53] but a common framing is the distinction from the "rule of men," or, more appropriately, the rule of persons.[54] Criminal law is thought to be a particularly important domain for the rule of law, as criminal enforcement involves the most severe forms of government coercion. In American criminal law, the principle of "legality" includes several ideas relevant to the evaluation of *Heien*: first, that crime must be declared legislatively and in advance of the conduct to be criminal;[55] and, second, "to make these prescriptions material and not merely formal, the definitions of criminal conduct must be pre-

---

[51] There would also likely be qualified immunity in such a situation because the reasonableness of the mistake would mean that the police were not violating a well-established right (since the right, narrowly understood, cannot be well established if the search would have been lawful had the crime extended as far as the police officer reasonably believed it did). See *Wilson v Layne*, 526 US 603 (1999); *Anderson v Creighton*, 483 US 635 (1987).

[52] Unfortunately, the Illinois and Wisconsin Supreme Courts have already rejected the argument that their state constitutions impose a rule different than *Heien*. See *People v Gaytan*, 32 NE3d 641 (Ill 2015); *State v Houghton*, 868 NW2d 143 (Wisc 2015).

[53] See, for example, Albert Dicey, *The Law of the Constitution* 194 (Macmillan, 9th ed 1950); Joseph Raz, *The Authority of Law: Essays in Law and Morality* 210–32 (Clarendon, 1979); Lon Fuller, *The Morality of Law* 46–90, 157–59 (Yale, 2d ed 1969); Brian Tamanaha, *On the Rule of Law: History, Politics, Theory* (2004); Richard H. Fallon, Jr., *"The Rule of Law" as a Concept in Constitutional Discourse*, 97 Colum L Rev 1 (1997); Jeremy Waldron, *Is the Rule of Law an Essentially Contested Concept (in Florida)?*, 21 Law & Phil 137 (2002).

[54] See *Marbury v Madison*, 5 US 137, 163 (1803) ("The government of the United States has been emphatically termed a government of laws, and not of men.").

[55] Packer, *The Limits of the Criminal Sanction* at 79–80 (cited in note 9).

cisely enough stated to leave comparatively little room for arbitrary application."[56] The first point prohibits retroactivity in crime definition; the second point motivates the vagueness doctrine and the rule of lenity.[57]

Nonretroactivity appears modest enough in the prohibition of ex post facto legislation,[58] but it also rules out a judicial power that existed for centuries in England, the power to create new crimes.[59] Why do we take it for granted that a court can continue to create torts and rules of contract liability, retroactively applying the rules to the parties before it, but not create crimes? An intuitive explanation is the importance of fair notice: the state should prospectively articulate a line of criminal liability to inform the citizen how to stay on the proper side of it. Perhaps that rationale suffices, but one can question it, as we allow retroactive judicial lawmaking in civil law, and people do not generally learn the criminal law from reading statutes.[60]

---

[56] Id at 73.

[57] The Supreme Court linked these three doctrines (with some redescription) in *United States v Lanier*, where it said:

> There are three related manifestations of the fair warning requirement. First, the vagueness doctrine bars enforcement of "a statute which either forbids or requires the doing of an act in terms so vague that men of common intelligence must necessarily guess at its meaning and differ as to its application." [citations omitted] Second, as a sort of "junior version of the vagueness doctrine," H. Packer, *The Limits of the Criminal Sanction* 95 (1968), the canon of strict construction of criminal statutes, or rule of lenity, ensures fair warning by so resolving ambiguity in a criminal statute as to apply it only to conduct clearly covered. [citations omitted] Third, although clarity at the requisite level may be supplied by judicial gloss on an otherwise uncertain statute, [citation omitted] due process bars courts from applying a novel construction of a criminal statute to conduct that neither the statute nor any prior judicial decision has fairly disclosed to be within its scope, [citations omitted]. In each of these guises, the touchstone is whether the statute, either standing alone or as construed, made it reasonably clear at the relevant time that the defendant's conduct was criminal.

520 US 259, 266–67 (1997). The Court has characterized nonretroactivity as a limit on judicial reinterpretation of criminal statutes, for example, *Bouie v City of Columbia*, 378 US 347 (1964); as a potential limit on judicial change in common law rules, for example, *Rogers v Tennessee*, 532 US 451 (2001) (upholding judicial abandonment of the year-and-a-day limitation to criminal causation only because it was not "unexpected"); and as a constraint on easing of constitutional limits on criminal statutes, for example, *Marks v United States*, 430 US 188, 191–92 (1977). I focus in the text on the conceptually simpler limit on judicial crime creation.

[58] See US Const, Art I, § 9, cl 3; id at § 10, cl 1.

[59] Jeffries, 71 Va L Rev at 192 (cited in note 6).

[60] Packer, *The Limits of the Criminal Sanction* at 88 (cited in note 9); Jeffries, 71 Va L Rev at 79–80 (cited in note 6).

Another theory is that advanced legislative definition of crime helps to control the discretionary power of police and prosecutors, to prevent arbitrary and discriminatory enforcement, which is also essential to the rule of law.[61] Police and prosecutors operate primarily in the enforcement of criminal law and thereby distinguish criminal from civil law. By limiting the court's power to create new crimes, the police and prosecutor are limited to enforcing crimes that already exist, rather than offering up citizens whose novel conduct might serve to induce the court to create new law. We limit courts, in other words, as an indirect way of limiting the power of those enforcers who bring people into court. As Herbert Packer puts the point: "*the most important single device*" for constraining the enormous inherent discretion of police and prosecutors "is the requirement . . . that the police and prosecutors confine their attention [toward citizens] to the catalogue of what has already been defined as criminal."[62] John Jeffries elaborates:

> Where judges stand ready to create new crimes . . . police and prosecutors will bring them new crimes to create. . . . [T]he resort to common-law methodology broadcasts to the law-enforcement community a potent message: the limits of official coercion are not fixed; the suggestion box is always open. The result is that lawmaking devolves to law enforcement, and police and prosecutors are invited to play too large a role in deciding what to punish.[63]

The requirement that legislatures have the exclusive power to define crimes is so uncontroversial as to be barely noticed. But a second aspect of legality—sufficient precision in the law—is frequently litigated. The primary law that enforces this notion of legality is the vagueness doctrine, derived from the Due Process Clause, and applied with particular force to criminal statutes.[64] The Supreme Court has frequently identified the two rationales of the vagueness doctrine: vague laws "fail to provide the kind of notice that will enable ordinary people to understand what conduct it prohibits" and "may authorize and even encourage arbitrary and discriminatory enforce-

---

[61] Packer, *The Limits of the Criminal Sanction* at 88 (cited in note 9) ("the principle of legality . . . operates primarily to control the discretion of the police and of prosecutors rather than that of judges").

[62] Id at 90.

[63] Jeffries, 71 Va L Rev at 222–23 (cited in note 6).

[64] See sources cited in notes 6 and 7.

ment."[65] The defect of an excessively vague statute is the same as the defect in having no statute and relying on judicial crime creation.

The Supreme Court has linked these legality rationales to a third doctrine, the rule of lenity,[66] a canon of construction for criminal statutes that favors narrower meanings, that is, those more "lenient" to the defendant.[67] Partly the idea is that the rule of law requires that we err on the side of liberty, which means on the side of interpreting criminal prohibitions too narrowly rather than too broadly.[68] In a more subtle way, lenity might constrain police and prosecutors by denying them the opportunity to augment their power by accidents of inartful legislative drafting.[69] The rule of lenity has been given less

---

[65] *City of Chicago v Morales*, 527 US 41, 56 (1999).

[66] See *Lanier*, 520 US at 266.

[67] See, for example, *Yates v United States*, 135 S Ct 1074, 1088 (2015), quoting *Cleveland v United States*, 531 US 12, 25 (2000), quoting *Rewis v United States*, 401 US 808, 812 (1971) (invoking the "interpretive principle" that "'ambiguity concerning the ambit of criminal statutes should be resolved in favor of lenity'"); *Liparota v United States*, 471 US 419, 427 (1985) ("Application of the rule of lenity ensures that criminal statutes will provide fair warning concerning conduct rendered illegal and strikes the appropriate balance between the legislature, the prosecutor, and the court in defining criminal liability."); *Adamo Wrecking Co. v United States*, 434 US 275, 285 (1978) (noting that "'where there is ambiguity in a criminal statute, doubts are resolved in favor of the defendant,'" quoting *United States v Bass*, 404 US 336, 348 (1971)); *United States v Universal C. I. T. Credit Corp.*, 344 US 218, 221–22 (1952) ("[W]hen choice has to be made between two readings of what conduct Congress has made a crime, it is appropriate, before we choose the harsher alternative, to require that Congress should have spoken in language that is clear and definite."); *United States v Gradwell*, 243 US 476, 485 (1917), quoting *United States v Lacher*, 134 US 624, 628 (1890) (stating that "before a man can be punished as a criminal under the federal law his case must be 'plainly and unmistakably' within the provisions of some statute.").

[68] See Packer, *The Limits of the Criminal Sanction* at 93 (cited in note 9); *Ex parte Davis*, 7 F Cas 45, 49 (NDNY 1851) ("'It was,' says Professor Christian, 'one of the laws of the twelve tables of Rome, that whenever there was a question between liberty and slavery, the presumption should be on the side of liberty. This excellent principle our law has adopted, in the construction of penal statutes; for whenever any ambiguity arises in a statute, introducing a new penalty or punishment, the decision shall be on the side of lenity and mercy. . . . '").

[69] See, for example, *United States v Standard Oil Co.*, 384 US 224, 236 (1966) (Harlan, J, dissenting) ("Moreover, this requirement of clear expression [in the doctrine of strict construction] is essential in a practical sense to confine the discretion of prosecuting authorities"); *United States v Valle*, 807 F3d 508, 523 (2d Cir 2015) ("The rule of lenity ensures that criminal statutes will provide fair warning of what constitutes criminal conduct, minimizes the risk of selective or arbitrary enforcement, and strikes the appropriate balance between the legislature and the court in defining criminal liability."); Solan, 40 Wm & Mary L Rev at 135 (cited in note 10) ("The system of criminal justice, however, is not concerned only with notice to the defendant, but also with notice to all those empowered to punish people on behalf of the government, especially prosecutors and judges. The notion of limited government based on the rule of law crucially depends on there actually being law.").

weight by the Supreme Court in recent decades,[70] but the doctrine still exists in the federal and state courts, sometimes proving important to particular interpretations of criminal statutes.

Heien is in tension with legality, by which I mean these particular three doctrines (no common law crime creation, the vagueness doctrine, and the rule of lenity) and especially their rationales—fair notice and constrained discretion. In this part, I focus on the tension between *Heien* and the rule-of-law value of limiting arbitrary and discriminatory enforcement. In Part III, I explore *Heien's* tension with the value of fair notice.

A. LEGAL MISTAKES ABOUT TRAFFIC STOPS: HEIEN GIVES POLICE
   MORE DISCRETION WHERE THEY ALREADY HAVE TOO MUCH

American commitment to the rule of law has never been translated into a free-floating constitutional doctrine about constraining enforcement discretion. Instead, the Court has crafted some particular doctrines, such as the one against vagueness. The vagueness doctrine addresses the part of excess discretion caused by statutory imprecision. But there is more to the problem. If enough people violate a criminal statute, its being precise rather than vague is irrelevant to the degree of police discretion. To take the most familiar example, if 90 percent of motorists drive above the precise posted speed limit on some road and the police stop and ticket only 0.2 percent of speeders, the police discretion is virtually unfettered by the clarity and precision of the statute. Or to put it differently, if the police are being consistent in selecting the 0.2 percent, it is because they are enforcing an unposted and unspecified speed limit (e.g., more than 12 mph above the posted limit), or stopping cars on the basis of some undefined and unpublished criteria (e.g., fitting the officer's idea of what a drug dealer looks like). So the "real law" is genuinely vague even though the formal law is perfectly clear and beyond the reach of the vagueness doctrine.

As a result, what Packer terms "the most important single device" for constraining enforcement discretion—the limitation to "the cata-

---

[70] See, for example, *Johnson v United States*, 529 US 694, 713 n 13 (2000) ("Lenity applies only when the equipoise of competing reasons cannot otherwise be resolved"); *Muscarello v United States*, 524 US 125, 138–39 (1998).

logue of what has already been defined as criminal"—is, to some degree, merely formal. Bill Stuntz made this point by emphasizing the interaction of criminal procedure with substantive criminal law.[71] The Fourth Amendment requires probable cause for some searches and seizures such as an arrest—probable cause that the person has committed a crime. But what is a crime? The Fourth Amendment leaves that decision to the legislature, which means the legislature can expand the situations where the police have probable cause by expanding the scope of substantive criminal law. In other words, the Fourth Amendment permits overcriminalization, which in turn allows the government broad scope to search and seize its citizens.

We need not be surprised that the Court's limited commitment to constraining discretion allows this "loophole." Many constitutional values receive only inconsistent support, and it would be difficult to develop a constitutional doctrine that generally limited the quantity of criminalization. But we should acknowledge the trade-off between this police discretion and the rule of law. A simple traffic stop is obviously toward the low end of search or seizure intensity, but traveling by car is a pervasive part of American life during which motorists expect to maintain some privacy and dignity.[72] Police stops are anxiety provoking, given the potential for escalation, and sometimes humiliating. Stops that appear to be motivated by race cause serious resentment of law enforcement. So even for simple car stops, the degree to which we leave police unconstrained by law is a degree to which we fall short of the rule-of-law ideal.[73]

Heien is another incremental step away from that ideal. As I demonstrate below, the main effect of *Heien* is to expand police discretion in traffic stops. I am not aware of any legal commentators who believed that, before *Heien*, police possessed *too little* discretion to stop motorists. To the contrary, if we were ranking legal domains

---

[71] See William J. Stuntz, *The Uneasy Relationship Between Criminal Procedure and Criminal Justice*, 107 Yale L J 1 (1997).

[72] See, for example, *Delaware v Prouse*, 440 US 648, 662–63 (1979) ("Undoubtedly, many find a greater sense of security and privacy in traveling in an automobile than they do in exposing themselves by pedestrian or other modes of travel. Were the individual subject to unfettered governmental intrusion every time he entered an automobile, the security guaranteed by the Fourth Amendment would be seriously circumscribed.").

[73] See id at 661 (stating that, to allow random police stops to check for license and registration would produce the "kind of standardless and unconstrained discretion [that] is the evil the Court has discerned when in previous cases it has insisted that the discretion of the official in the field be circumscribed, at least to some extent.").

where government officials have the most discretion, and where discretion is so unbounded that it puts us near the reality of the "rule of persons" instead of the rule of law, the discretion of police to stop drivers is high on the list.[74]

Compared to other legal domains, traffic and vehicle laws stand out in familiar ways. First, traffic regulations are unusually dense and comprehensive, permeating nearly every moment of driving and every physical aspect of one's vehicle. Second, traffic rules regulate relatively innocuous misbehavior, among the most innocuous conduct in the criminal law (and sometimes not even criminal[75]). Because the offenses are so low level, many ordinarily law-abiding citizens routinely commit them. Third, because traffic violations are unusually public, committed as they are on open roads, the police find them easy to detect.

When the density of regulation for common misbehavior is high and the violations are easily observed, the result is enormous police discretion. There are so many violators that the police cannot plausibly stop more than a small fraction, leaving police legally free to choose which few to stop on any grounds or whim other than a few formally proscribed ones, mostly race. In fact, it is difficult for individuals to prove unconstitutional racial profiling, so even that limitation is more formal than real.[76] More than that, not only can the police select which few of the many observed violators to stop and ticket; the police can also choose to spend time observing a *nonviola-*

---

[74] See William J. Stuntz, *The Collapse of American Criminal Justice* 3 (Harvard, 2011) ("In the United States, posted limits don't define the maximum speed of traffic; they define [as a practical matter] the *minimum* speed. So who or what determines the real speed limits, the velocity above which drivers risk traffic tickets or worse? The answer is: whatever police force patrols the relevant road. Law enforcers—state troopers and local cops—define the laws they enforce."); Stuntz, 107 Yale L J 1, 67 n 229 (cited in note 71) ("*Whren* permits the police to use traffic offenses in precisely the same way that the police used old-style vagrancy and loitering law: as a grant of discretionary power to stop, question, and (in jurisdictions that classify traffic offenses as crime) search and arrest suspects based on unarticulated suspicion of other crimes, or worse, based on the officer's whim or prejudice. The result is Fourth Amendment doctrine that appears to limit traffic stops but in practice does not."); William J. Stuntz, *O. J. Simpson, Bill Clinton, and the Transsubstantive Fourth Amendment*, 114 Harv L Rev 842, 843 (2001) ("The law governing traffic stops allows police to pull over anyone for any reason.").

[75] See Jordan Blair Woods, *Decriminalization, Police Authority, and Routine Traffic Stops*, 62 UCLA L Rev 672 (2015).

[76] See, for example, Frank Rudy Cooper, *The Un-Balanced Fourth Amendment: A Cultural Study of the Drug War, Racial Profiling and Arvizu*, 47 Vill L Rev 851 (2002); Angela J. Davis, *Race, Cops, and Traffic Stops*, 51 U Miami L Rev 425, 431–32 (1997).

tor—what appears to be a law-abiding driver—to find a violation. Recall the *Heien* facts: the officer started to follow the car with Heien in it because he thought the driver, Vasquez, appeared "very stiff and nervous."[77] That was not an adequate basis for a stop, but after a few minutes the officer discovered a putative traffic offense—the non-functioning tail light. In general, as a result of the multiplicity of driving rules, the conventional understanding is that the police can usually develop reasonable suspicion of some crime if they follow a car for a few minutes.[78]

If one were unfamiliar with the dynamics of traffic stops, one might guess that police discretion is not so important because police focus their attention on the most egregious violators of the traffic laws, not bothering with technical violations. But stopping a car has the potential for much bigger payoffs for the officer than issuing a ticket. Once stopped, police can look carefully into the car,[79] order the occupants out,[80] frisk the person or conduct a cursory inspection of the car if they have reasonable suspicion to believe a firearm is present,[81] or ask for consent to search the car, which is frequently given.[82] If, at any point, the police develop probable cause to believe the car contains evidence of a crime, they can warrantlessly search the car for the evidence.[83] As a result, police do not limit themselves to stopping the most dangerous drivers, but play their hunches.

A recent study of Kansas City, Missouri traffic stops confirms this analysis.[84] The researchers found it useful to distinguish "safety"

---

[77] *Heien*, 135 S Ct at 534.

[78] See David A. Sklansky, *Traffic Stops, Minority Motorists, and the Future of the Fourth Amendment*, 1997 Supreme Court Review 271, 273 ("Since virtually everyone violates traffic laws at least occasionally, . . . police officers, if they are patient, can eventually pull over almost anyone they choose").

[79] *Texas v Brown*, 460 US 730, 739–40 (1983) (Rehnquist, J) (plurality) (ruling that the shining of a flashlight through car window and the bending over to see better inside are not searches).

[80] *Pennsylvania v Mimms*, 434 US 106 (1977) (holding it reasonable, during a lawful traffic stop, for officer to order driver out of car); *Maryland v Wilson*, 519 US 408 (1997) (holding it reasonable, during a lawful traffic stop, for officer to order passenger out of car).

[81] See *Terry v Ohio*, 392 US 1, 20 (1968); *Michigan v Long*, 463 US 1032, 1049–50 (1983).

[82] See *Schneckloth v Bustamonte*, 412 US 218 (1973); *Ohio v Robinette*, 519 US 33 (1996). It would not be necessary that the person giving consent has legal authority to give it if the person has apparent authority. See *Illinois v Rodriguez*, 497 US 177 (1990).

[83] *Pennsylvania v Labron*, 116 S Ct 2485, 2487 (1996); *California v Acevedo*, 500 US 565, 569–70 (1991); *Chambers v Maroney*, 399 US 42 (1970).

[84] See Charles Epp, Steven Maynard-Moody, and Donald P. Haider-Markel, *Pulled Over: How Police Stops Define Race and Citizenship* 59–64 (Chicago, 2014).

stops, aimed at motorists whose driving behavior poses a risk to other motorists, from "investigatory stops," which are motivated not by the trivial infractions that give police the power to make the stop but by the police hunch of some nontraffic crime, such as drug possession.[85] Minority drivers were disproportionately the target of these pretextual, investigatory stops.[86] In sum, the Fourth Amendment formally requires reasonable suspicion of a legal violation to justify a stop,[87] a fairly low bar,[88] but the breadth and intensity of traffic regulation threatens to make this limitation meaningless. That government can gin up an objective basis for a traffic stop contradicts the premises of legality.

One might say that none of this is the fault of the Supreme Court because it is difficult to create a doctrine that bars states from tightly regulating driving and motor vehicles. Yet the Supreme Court has made the problem worse in a series of cases that push us farther from the rule-of-law ideal. The consent standard, for example, is lax enough to avoid giving dispositive weight to the fact that someone who apparently "consented" did not know they had any choice in the matter.[89] In addition, the Court might have developed a pretext doctrine

---

[85] Id at 59–64.

[86] Id.

[87] Not all traffic violations are crimes. See Woods, 62 UCLA L Rev 672 at 698 (cited in note 75) (stating that twenty-two states have decriminalized minor traffic offenses). One might read the Court's doctrine to provide that reasonable suspicion suffices for a routine traffic stop only if it pertains to a crime, where probable cause might be required when police suspect a noncriminal traffic violation. Compare *Navarette v California*, 134 S Ct 1683, 1687 (2014) ("The Fourth Amendment permits brief investigative stops—such as the traffic stop in this case—when a law enforcement officer has 'a particularized and objective basis for suspecting the particular person stopped of *criminal activity*.'") (emphasis added); and *United States v Arvizu*, 534 US 266, 273 (2002) ("Because the 'balance between the public interest and the individual's right to personal security,' tilts in favor of a standard less than probable cause [for brief investigative stops of vehicles], the Fourth Amendment is satisfied if the officer's action is supported by reasonable suspicion to believe that *criminal activity* 'may be afoot.'" (citations omitted; emphasis added)); with *Whren*, 517 US at 810 (noting, in a case where the car stop was based on a civil traffic offense: "As a general matter, the decision to stop an automobile is reasonable where the police have probable cause to believe that a traffic violation has occurred."). But in *Heien*, the Court cast doubt on this qualification when it said: "All parties agree that to justify this type of seizure [a traffic stop], officers need only 'reasonable suspicion'—that is, 'a particularized and objective basis for suspecting the particular person stopped' of *breaking the law*," *Heien*, 135 S Ct at 536 (emphasis added). See also *Rodriguez v United States*, 135 S Ct 1609, 1615 (2015) ("A seizure for a traffic violation justifies a police investigation of that violation. '[A] relatively brief encounter,' a routine traffic stop is 'more analogous to a so-called "Terry stop" . . . than to a formal arrest.'").

[88] See id.

[89] *Schneckloth v Bustamonte*, 412 US 218 (1973).

to bar the police from using traffic regulation to circumvent restrictions on their power to play hunches, but the Court has instead rejected the relevance of the officer's subjective motivation.[90] Then, the Court compounded the problem by repeatedly making it easier to arrest the driver for the traffic offense,[91] which in turn triggers other powers to search the person and the car.[92] All of this gives police officers greater reason to use traffic offenses to play hunches or satisfy whim.

These points have been made before.[93] Indeed, the cynical response is to say that, because of these decisions, there is nothing at stake in *Heien*. If I am right that *Heien* is mostly about traffic stops, and if police already have unfettered discretion to make traffic stops, then perhaps *Heien* cannot give police any more discretion. On this view, one would have commended the Court for candor had it overruled *Delaware v Prouse*[94] and simply held that the Fourth Amendment permits police to stop any automobile without any individualized suspicion toward the driver or passengers (presumably justified as some kind of administrative or programmatic search[95]). Perhaps that acknowledgment of discretion would reconcile the law on the books with the law on the ground.

Yet the factual predicate is not quite true. Despite appearances, Fourth Amendment law does constrain traffic stops to some degree. The best evidence and perhaps the only good evidence for this point,

---

[90] See, for example, *Whren*, 517 US at 813.

[91] In *Atwater v City of Lago Vista*, 532 US 318, 354 (2001), the Court rejected the claim that the police could not make a warrantless public arrest for a trivial, fine-only misdemeanor—the traffic offense of failing to wear a seat belt—committed in the officer's presence. In *Virginia v Moore*, 553 US 164 (2008), the Court said it was irrelevant to the Fourth Amendment that the police violated state statutory law when making an arrest because the state law did not authorize arrest for the particular crime.

[92] Under *United States v Robinson*, 414 US 218 (1973), given a valid arrest, the police can warrantlessly search the person of the arrestee, including any containers he possesses (except for a cell phone, which requires a warrant; see *Riley v California*, 134 S Ct 2473 (2014)). Under *Arizona v Gant*, 556 US 332 (2009), the police can search the vehicle of the arrestee if they have reason to believe it contains evidence of the crime of arrest. Moreover, in many cases, where there is a safety reason not to leave the car where it is, the police could impound the vehicle and expect some officer to conduct an inventory search of the car. See *Colorado v Bertine*, 479 US 367 (1987); *South Dakota v Opperman*, 428 US 364 (1976).

[93] See, for example, sources cited in notes 75, 76, and 78.

[94] 440 US 648 (1979).

[95] See, for example, Eve Brensike Primus, *Disentangling Administrative Searches*, 111 Colum L Rev 254 (2011).

however, *comes in cases that Heien effectively overruled*. *Heien* removed
an important final limitation on police discretion, making it truer than
ever that police possess the power to stop any and all motorists. Thus,
there was something at stake for the rule of law in *Heien*.

To establish this point, the first step is to note that *virtually all
the preexisting cases raising the Heien issue were traffic cases*.[96] I found

---

[96] These include eleven cases from the five federal circuits that had previously held against
the rule that prevails in *Heien*, all involving traffic stops. See *United States v Miller*, 146 F3d
274, 279 (5th Cir 1998) (nonexistent offense of flashing a turn signal without turning or
changing lanes); *United States v Lopez-Valdez*, 178 F3d 282, 288–89 (5th Cir 1999) (nonexistent offense of driving with a cracked tail light); *United States v McDonald*, 453 F3d 958, 962
(7th Cir 2006) (nonexistent offense of unnecessarily using a turn signal at a ninety-degree
curve of a continuous road); *United States v King*, 244 F3d 736, 741 (9th Cir 2001) (nonexistent offense of driving with a disability card hanging from rearview mirror); *United States v
Lopez-Soto*, 205 F3d 1101, 1106 (9th Cir 2000) (traffic stop based on the erroneous belief that
the foreign jurisdiction licensing the car required an updated sticker on the license plate,
which would then have made it an offense in Texas); *United States v Twilley*, 222 F3d 1092
(9th Cir 2000) (traffic stop based on the erroneous belief that the foreign state licensing the
car required two plates); *United States v Nicholson*, 721 F3d 1236, 1244 (10th Cir 2013)
(nonexistent offense of turning left from one road into the rightmost side of the other road,
when there were no road markers designating separate lanes); *United States v Valadez-Valadez*,
525 F3d 987, 991 (10th Cir 2008) (nonexistent offense of traveling a moderate amount below
the speed limit without impeding traffic); *United States v Tibbetts*, 396 F3d 1132 (10th Cir
2005) (traffic stop for possible violation of rules about size and position of mud flaps); *United
States v DeGasso*, 369 F3d 1139 (10th Cir 2004) (nonexistent offense of using fog lights during
a fogless day and for an actual offense concerning the partial obscuring of the license plate);
United States v Chanthasouxat, 342 F3d 1271, 1279–80 (11th Cir 2003) (nonexistent offense of
having no inside rearview mirrors when there were side mirrors).

Another three cases from different circuits had occasion to endorse the holding of the above
circuits—contrary to *Heien*—but found the search or seizure was not based on a mistake of law.
These all involved traffic stops. See *United States v Coplin*, 463 F3d 96, 101 (1st Cir 2006);
United States v Harrison, 689 F3d 301, 309 (3d Cir 2012); *United States v Booker*, 496 F3d 717,
722, 724 (DC Cir 2007), *vacated on other grounds*, 556 US 1218 (2009).

Five state courts of last resort held that a mistake of law "*cannot* provide objective grounds
for reasonable suspicion" and all were in the context of a traffic stop. See *Hilton v State*, 961
So2d 284, 298 (Fla 2007) (nonexistent offense of a cracked windshield that does not seem to
impair safety); *State v Louwrens*, 792 NW2d 649, 652 (Iowa 2010) (U-turn in the absence of a
sign prohibiting them when the law required signage); *Martin v Kansas Department of Revenue*,
176 P3d 938, 948 (Kan 2008) (nonexistent offense of one of three brake lights not functioning
when law required only two to work); *State v Anderson*, 683 NW2d 818, 824 (Minn 2004)
(nonexistent offense of not being two lanes away from a stopped emergency vehicle); *State v
Lacasella*, 60 P3d 975, 981–82 (Mont 2002) (nonexistent offense of placing front license plate in
windshield).

Of three Eighth Circuit cases and one D.C. Circuit case favoring the rule *Heien* later
announced, all involved traffic stops. See *United States v Martin*, 411 F3d 998, 1001 (8th Cir
2005) (nonexistent offense of one of two brake lights being nonfunctional when the law only
requires one); *United States v Washington*, 455 F3d 824, 827 (8th Cir 2006) (nonexistent offense of crack in windshield when law only required the absence of obstruction to one's view,
which was not present); *United States v Smart*, 393 F3d 767 (8th Cir 2005) (nonexistent offense of not having a front plate when Iowa law allowed cars from other states to have only
rear plates if the licensing state allowed only rear plates, as here); *United States v Southerland*,

twenty-eight state and federal appellate cases that discussed the issue before *Heien* and twenty-seven of them concerned traffic offenses.[97] For example—remarkably—three pre-*Heien* cases involved the same kind of legal error that the police made in *Heien*, stopping someone for having one of multiple brake lights inoperative or cracked, when such trivial impairment violated no statute.[98] Other examples were where the police stopped someone for the putative infraction of signaling unnecessarily,[99] driving with a disability card hanging from the rearview mirror,[100] having only external rearview mirrors,[101] driving ten miles below the speed limit without impeding traffic,[102] using fog lights during a fogless day,[103] driving with a crack in the windshield that did not impair the driver's vision,[104] and for failing to dim one's lights at night immediately after being overtaken by another car traveling in the same direction.[105] In all of these cases, the officer had reasonable suspicion or probable cause for behaviors that violated no

486 F3d 1355 (DC Cir 2007) (nonexistent offense of displaying front license plate on the front dashboard).

In addition to the North Carolina Supreme Court in *Heien*, five state cases favoring the rule that *Heien* later announced all involved traffic stops. See *Travis v State*, 959 SW2d 32, 34 (Ark 1998) (Arkansas officer erroneously believed that Texas law required a sticker showing an expiration date be placed on the license plate); *Moore v State*, 986 So2d 928, 935 (Miss 2008) (officer erroneously believed that having only one operative tail light violated the law); *State v Wright*, 791 NW2d 791, 798–99 (SD 2010) (officer erroneously believed that one must dim one's lights after being passed); *Stafford v State*, 671 SE2d 484, 485 (Ga 2008) (parking in middle of street, where law was unclear); *City of Bowling Green v Godwin*, 850 NE2d 698, 702 (Ohio 2006) (disobeying signs about what is not an exit, where signs might be invalid for not being approved by city council).

[97] The one nontraffic case I found involved a different highly discretionary crime—disorderly conduct—in the precise context where legality concerns are greatest—when the police officer was reacting to vocal criticism of his policing. See *In re T.L.*, 996 A2d 805, 816 (DC App 2010) ("[A]n officer's mistake of *law*, however reasonable, 'cannot provide the objective basis for reasonable suspicion or probable cause' needed to justify a search or seizure.").

[98] See *United States v Lopez-Valdez*, 178 F3d 282, 288–89 (5th Cir 1999); *Martin v Kansas Dep't of Revenue*, 176 P3d 938, 948 (Kan 2008); *United States v Martin*, 411 F3d 998, 1001 (8th Cir 2005); *Moore v State*, 986 So2d 928, 935 (Miss 2008).

[99] See *United States v McDonald*, 453 F3d 958, 962 (7th Cir 2006) (driver used a turn signal at a 90-degree curve of a continuous road).

[100] *United States v King*, 244 F3d 736, 741 (9th Cir 2001).

[101] *Chanthasouxat*, 342 F3d at 1279–80 (11th Cir 2003) (side mirrors were legally adequate).

[102] *United States v Valadez-Valadez*, 525 F3d 987, 991 (10th Cir 2008).

[103] *United States v DeGasso*, 369 F3d 1139 (10th Cir 2004) (also involving an actual offense concerning the partial obscuring of the license plate).

[104] *United States v Washington*, 455 F3d 824, 827 (8th Cir 2006).

[105] *State v Wright*, 791 NW2d 791, 798–99 (SD 2010).

law. After *Heien*, the pattern persists; the many published cases applying its new rule are also overwhelmingly about traffic stops.[106]

These cases, limited to federal and state appellate courts, are obviously only the tip of the iceberg; for every appellate court opinion
involving police mistakes of criminal law, there must be scores or
hundreds that do not produce an appellate opinion. And each of these
cases represents an instance where the police stopped a motorist and,
after the fact, prosecutors could assert no lawful basis for it, only a
reasonable mistake of criminal law.

On reflection, this connection between police mistakes of law and
traffic stops seems inevitable. First, the issue of police mistakes of law
is most likely to arise with technical, *mala prohibita* offenses. Among
regulatory offenses, police do not usually enforce those pertaining
to food handling or the environment, but they do routinely enforce
traffic regulations. And, as just explained, they have a powerful in-

---

[106] Of eighteen post-*Heien* published opinions I located that present a genuine *Heien* issue, fifteen involved mistakes of the law governing traffic: See *Williams v State*, 28 NE3d 293 (Ind 2015) (nonexistent offense of crack in brake light that let through some white light); *Mota*, __ F Supp 3d at __ (nonexistent offense of having the brake light in the middle of the rear window be inoperative, when the two rear lights were operative); *Darringer*, 46 NE3d at 464 (nonexistent offense of placing interim license plate in rear window rather than rear bumper); *Gaytan*, 32 NE3d at 641 (nonexistent offense of having trailer hitch partially obscure the license plate); *United States v Sanders*, 95 F Supp 3d 1274 (D Nev 2015) (nonexistent offense of having air fresheners hanging from rearview mirror); *State v Dopslaf*, 356 P3d 559 (NM App 2015) (nonexistent U-turn violation); *People v Guthrie*, 30 NE3d 880 (NY App 2015) (stop sign violation where stop sign was not officially registered and therefore legally void; unclear if mistake of law or fact); *Freeman v Commonwealth*, 778 SE2d 519 (Va App 2015) (nonexistent violation of having an air freshener hanging from a rearview mirror); *State v Houghton*, 868 NW2d 143 (Wisc 2015) (nonexistent violation of having air freshener and GPS device being visible in front windshield); *United States v Alvarado-Zarza*, 782 F3d 246 (5th Cir 2015) (nonexistent offense of failing to signal 100 feet before lane change; law required such signal only before turn); *United States v Flores*, 798 F3d 645 (7th Cir 2015) (nonexistent violation of obstructing license plate when frame did not render any writing unreadable); *United States v Stanbridge*, 79 F Supp 3d 881 (CD Ill 2015) (traffic stop for not signaling at least 100 feet before pulling to a stop at the curb; court did not decide if law included such a requirement); *United States v Morales*, 115 F Supp 3d 1291 (D Kan 2015) (traffic stop for not signaling when merging from two lanes into one; court did not decide if law included such requirement); *State v Hurley*, 117 A3d 433 (Vt 2015) (nonexistent offense of windshield obstructions that do not impair driver's vision); *Village of Bayside v Olszewski*, 2016 WL 121398 (Wisc App 2016) (unpublished) (traffic stop for crossing into pedestrian crosswalk at stop sign; in the alternative court found that any mistake was reasonable); *People v Campuzano*, 188 Cal Rptr 3d 587 (Cal App 2015) (stop of bicyclist for nonexistent offense of riding on sidewalk not in the vicinity of a business).

Just three post-*Heien* cases I located did not involve traffic stops. See *J. Mack LLC v Leonard*, 2015 WL 519412, *10 (SD Ohio, 2015) (mistake of law regarding legality of synthetic marijuana); *Flint v City of Milwaukee*, 91 F Supp 3d 1032, 1058 (ED Wisc 2015) (mistake of law regarding state endangered species act); *Diaz*, 122 F Supp 3d at 165 (stop for violation of open-container law; court assumes without deciding that the law was not violated).

centive to stop automobiles: to look inside the car for signs of criminality and to ask for consent to search. When police make mistakes
of law, it is almost always about traffic rules. *Heien* facially stands for a
general proposition—that reasonable suspicion can be grounded in a
police mistake of law. In reality, *Heien* is yet another case about traffic
regulation.

Where the state or lower federal courts had ruled that the error,
even if reasonable, negated reasonable suspicion, the case served as
an example in which the Fourth Amendment was, in fact, offering
some limit on police discretion to make traffic stops. Even though the
police observed the car for some time, the government could offer
no better reason for the stop than a reasonable mistake of law. We
could infer from this failure that police actually had to incur some real
cost to develop a legally sound basis for many investigatory stops they
wished to make. The Fourth Amendment was serving rule-of-law
values. Yet *Heien* now removes the constraint when the legal mistake
is reasonable. The police are no longer limited by the scope of existing
criminal statutes, however broad, but by the even broader boundaries
of the aggregate set of all the reasonable interpretations of those
statutes. The opinion is another incremental step toward the rule of
persons.

B. HYPOTHETICAL LAWS AND HYPOTHETICAL MOTIVES

Heien's expansion of discretion is even more damaging when we
consider its interaction with *Whren v United States*[107] and *Devenpeck
v Alford*.[108] *Whren* settled that the officer's motivation for a car stop
was irrelevant under the Fourth Amendment because the stop is
judged only on the facts that objectively appeared to the officer.[109]
Whren also explains why the litigants and courts in *Heien* do not
bother to discuss the possible racial profiling in the case—that would
matter if Heien brought an Equal Protection claim, but not to the
Fourth Amendment.[110]

Oddly, the *Heien* majority does not cite *Devenpeck*, which extends
Whren, even though *Devenpeck* also involved a police error of law in

---

[107] *Whren*, 517 US at 806.

[108] *Devenpeck v Alford*, 543 US 146 (2004).

[109] 517 US at 814.

[110] Id at 813.

the context of an automobile stop. The officer there arrested Alford for audiotaping his interactions with police, but a state appellate court had already "clearly established" that the privacy statute at issue did not apply to such taping.[111] So the police mistake of law was not reasonable. Yet the Supreme Court held that the arrest could be lawful because the officer was aware of *other facts* that provided probable cause that Alford had committed *a different crime*—impersonating a police officer—and it did not matter that the officer was not subjectively motivated to arrest on those grounds.[112] Indeed, given the Court's general emphasis on an objective perspective, it did not appear to matter whether the officer was even aware of the law prohibiting the impersonation of a police officer, merely knowledge of the facts.[113] Moreover, the Court explicitly held that the crime that objectively justifies the arrest need not be "closely related" to the crime the officer invoked at the time of arrest (as the Ninth Circuit had required).[114]

What *Devenpeck* means is that the government lawyer assigned to defend an arrest is not limited by the officer's motivation for the arrest, but is free to examine the criminal code to find some crime the arrestee might have committed, as long as the facts known to the officer (or, as a practical matter, which the officer later claims to have known at the time) would constitute probable cause for that crime. The logic of *Devenpeck* applies to investigative stops as well as arrests, as several courts have held.[115]

---

[111] *Devenpeck*, 543 US at 151 (citing *State v Flora*, 845 P2d 1355 (Wash App 1992)).

[112] Id at 156 (remanding so that lower courts could consider whether there was probable cause, based on the facts known to the officer, to believe Devenpeck was guilty of impersonating a law enforcement officer).

[113] See id at 152 ("Whether probable cause exists depends upon the reasonable conclusion to be drawn from the facts known to the arresting officer at the time of the arrest."). See also id at 153 (an officer's "subjective reason for making the arrest need not be the criminal offense as to which the known facts provide probable cause.").

[114] Id (finding the "closely related" limitation requires inquiry into officer's subjective motivation that is inconsistent with prior Supreme Court precedent).

[115] The Third Circuit cites *Devenpeck* for the proposition that "Reasonable suspicion and probable cause are determined with reference to the facts and circumstances within the officer's knowledge at the time of the *investigative stop* or arrest," and that "The arresting officer need not have contemplated the specific offense for which the defendant ultimately will be charged. The appropriate inquiry, rather, is whether the facts and circumstances within the officer's knowledge at the time of an *investigative stop* or arrest objectively justify that action." *United States v Laville*, 480 F3d 187, 194 (3rd Cir 2007) (emphasis added). See also *United States v Wingle*, 565 Fed Appx 265, 268–69 & n 4 (4th Cir 2014) (unpublished).

Devenpeck and *Heien* have a troubling synergy. Suppose, for example, that a police officer parked on the side of the road watches a car approach with its fog lights on during a clear day and, once it passes, observes that one of the two brake lights is cracked. The officer stops the driver, issues the driver a ticket for the broken tail light, and asks for consent to search the vehicle for contraband. The driver consents, the officer finds cocaine, and the driver is arrested. The driver argues that the officer lacked reasonable suspicion for the stop because the law does not require more than one working brake light, an interpretation that is, let us assume, either obvious from the statute's unambiguous text or subsequent judicial interpretation. The officer's mistake of law is unreasonable and the government appears destined to lose.

As a fallback, however, suppose the state prosecutor elicits from the police officer the fact that he also noticed the fog light. If the fog light use violated the traffic code, *Devenpeck* already meant that the stop was valid. But now, under *Heien*, even if the fog light use did not violate the code, the stop is lawful if the police could reasonably have thought that it did. Given an ambiguously worded fog light regulation, *the stop is legal* even though the officer did not stop the motorist because of the fog light and the regulation did not forbid its use.

Indeed, under *Heien*, there is no reason to think that it matters whether the police officer actually believed the fog light statute prohibited the motorist's conduct, or even believed that a fog light regulation existed. One might mistake the references in *Heien* to "the officer's mistake of law"[116] as implying that the officer must have had an actual belief that the law prohibited the suspect's conduct. But the majority rejects this view when it insists on the objective perspective that pervades Fourth Amendment doctrine, noting: "We do not examine the subjective understanding of the particular officer involved."[117] Justice Kagan concurs that "an officer's 'subjective understanding' is irrelevant."[118]

---

[116] *Heien*, 135 S Ct at 534 (restating the holding as "Because the officer's mistake about the brake-light law was reasonable, the stop in this case was lawful under the Fourth Amendment.").

[117] Id at 539 (citing *Whren*, 517 US at 813).

[118] Id at 541. She goes on to say that, therefore, "the government cannot defend an officer's mistaken legal interpretation on the ground that the officer was unaware . . . of the law." Id. But that just means that the government does not automatically win because the officer was unaware of the law, not that the government is limited to reasonable interpretations of statutes of which the officer was actually aware.

These statements were apparently made to fend off the concern that police reasonableness would be judged by what the individual officer knew of the law, in which case the government might gain power from an officer's unique ignorance. But the *Heien* opinions do not seem to realize that disregarding the officer's subjective beliefs also means that the holding applies even when the officer affirmatively believed that the law *permitted* the defendant's conduct. It is easy to miss the point if one ignores *Devenpeck*. But once *Devenpeck* permits government attorneys to defend searches and seizures for reasons other than those motivating the police officer, the question arises whether the officer's subjective belief about the law might constrain the government, allowing its lawyer to assert a reasonable mistake of law only when the police officer actually believed the law prohibited the defendant's conduct.[119] But no such limit exists.

To summarize, under *Devenpeck*, the objective factual and legal basis for reasonable suspicion is sufficient; the fact that the officer was not subjectively motivated to make the stop because of the fog light statute (the law ultimately used to justify the search) is irrelevant. Under *Heien*, its being reasonable to believe the statute prohibited the fog light used in this situation created reasonable suspicion for the stop; that the law did not actually forbid its use and that the officer did not actually believe that the fog light violated the law are irrelevant. *Devenpeck* already allowed a government lawyer defending a police action to roam creatively throughout the criminal code to find some crime for which there was probable cause or reasonable suspicion. *Heien* now adds the fact that the government lawyer is not limited to the crimes that the code actually creates.[120]

In practical terms, what would it be like to peruse a traffic code looking for plausible expansive meanings that retroactively justify

---

[119] A similar issue arises in the exceptional cases where ignorance of law *is* a defense for those charged with criminal acts, such as reliance on official misstatements discussed in note 49. The Model Penal Code is clear that the defense requires an actual, subjective belief in the legality of one's conduct, in addition to the reasonableness of the belief. See MPC § 2.04(3)(b) (requiring "a belief"). Perhaps the Court could follow this approach in a future case, but the language from the opinion unequivocally disclaiming the relevance of the officer's "subjective understanding" rules out the approach for lower courts.

[120] See *J. Mack LLC v Leonard*, 2015 WL 519412, *10 (SD Ohio, 2015) (combining *Heien* with *Devenpeck* to reason that a seizure of "synthetic marijuana" can be reasonable, even if based on a legal mistake that it was prohibited, if some statute could be reasonably understood to prohibit it, even if the seizing officer was not subjectively aware of the statute). But see *Flint v City of Milwaukee*, 91 F Supp 3d 1032, 1058 (ED Wisc 2015) (rejecting a reasonable mistake-of-law claim, without considering interpretive reasonableness, when the officer did not know the statute existed).

stops? If the clever government lawyer knows the police officer stopped the car on a mere hunch, say, the racially loaded reason of "being in the wrong neighborhood," how hard will it be to use the *Devenpeck/Heien* stratagem of matching reasonable but nonmotivating beliefs about facts to reasonable but erroneous interpretations of law?

Suppose, for example, police observed other vehicles ahead of the defendant's car before the stop and a statute commands that drivers shall not "follow another vehicle more closely than is reasonable and prudent, having due regard for the speed of such vehicles and the traffic upon and the condition of the highway."[121] One could use accident statistics to argue that the "reasonable and prudent" standard rejects the customary following distance in favor of a far more generous distance, under which the vast majority of drivers are guilty of violating the statue. If a court has never previously ruled against this argument, its likely reasonableness would justify the stop, even if the court ultimately decides to read the "reasonable and prudent" standard as incorporating and affirming the customary following distance.

Conversely, suppose there was traffic observed *behind* the defendant and a statute says that no one may "drive a motor vehicle at such a slow speed as to impede or block the normal and reasonable movement of traffic."[122] Perhaps the prohibition means that a driver may not go *any* slower than the maximum speed limit if there are other drivers on the road behind her who are going the speed limit, and who will therefore need to slow down or pass. If a driver is obeying the speed limit, then the need to slow down or pass a slower-moving vehicle does "impede" one's "normal and reasonable" movement. Even if this is wrong—and I assume that it is—*Heien* and *Devenpeck* let the prosecutor argue that the officer *would have been reasonable* for interpreting the somewhat ambiguous statute in this way. So the officer's observation that the driver was proceeding five miles under the speed limit could supply the reasonable suspicion for the stop, even though the officer had no concern over the speed and a court later decides that the speed does not violate the statute.

In both examples, the prosecutor can successfully defend traffic stops without regard to either the actual motives of the police nor the

---

[121] The proposed example is inspired by the language of Illinois Vehicle Code, 625 ILCS 5/11-710 (2015).

[122] The language is from 625 ILCS 5/11-606.

actual legal rules. The government gets the benefit of hypothetical motives and hypothetical law.

C. LEGAL DEVELOPMENT VERSUS LEGAL OSSIFICATION

The extra discretion that *Heien* grants the government in traffic enforcement, as just described, might appear to be short term because, each time the prosecutor asserts some possible but erroneous statutory meaning, the courts will announce the meaning is erroneous. The prosecutor will win the case at hand if the possible meaning is reasonable, but lose the opportunity to use that interpretation again in the future. Once the court says that the interpretation is erroneous, it will never again be considered reasonable.

Yet there is no guarantee that the courts will ever rule that these reasonable interpretations are wrong. First, the criminal defendant may never litigate the statute's meaning. Second, the courts may never declare the statute's meaning.

Few, if any, criminal defendants will litigate about the meaning of a traffic offense if the only thing at stake is paying a minor fine. Before *Heien*, several lower courts reached the issue of whether probable cause or reasonable suspicion could be grounded in a reasonable legal mistake, and in their opinions, the courts engaged in statutory interpretation and published an analysis of the meaning of a minor traffic offense. But in each of these cases, the police acquired evidence of more serious wrongdoing for which the motorist was now being prosecuted; the defendant's hope was to exclude the evidence the police obtained as the fruits of a Fourth Amendment violation and thereby avoid a serious penalty.[123]

Even in that situation, there was always some chance that a court might apply the good-faith exception to the exclusionary rule and refuse to exclude the evidence even if there was a constitutional violation.[124] But, pre-*Heien*, criminal defendants still sometimes won the exclusion remedy, which ensured an incentive to litigate. One reason is that fourteen states reject the good-faith exception under state

---

[123] See, for example, *United States v Miller*, 146 F3d 274, 279 (5th Cir 1998) (traffic stop leading to prosecution of marijuana possession with intent to distribute); *United States v Lopez-Valdez*, 178 F3d 282, 288–89 (5th Cir 1999) (traffic stop leading to prosecution for willfully transporting undocumented aliens); *United States v McDonald*, 453 F3d 958, 962 (7th Cir 2006) (traffic stop leading to prosecution for felon in possession).

[124] *Davis*, 131 S Ct at 2419.

law.[125] Another reason is that the closest federal good-faith case—
Davis[126]—is distinguishable, as previously suggested. In *Davis*, the
police conducted a search in reliance on binding precedent of the
relevant United States Court of Appeals. In cases like *Heien*, the police were not relying on binding precedent upholding a category of
search, but on the objective reasonableness of the officer's legal belief, given the ambiguity in a statute that no court has previously
interpreted. In *Davis*, the dissent worried about the disincentives the
Court was creating for litigating Fourth Amendment claims, but the
majority noted how limited the disincentive was—only to challenges
arguing for the overruling of binding precedent. The stronger disincentive in cases like *Heien* offered a way of distinguishing *Davis*.[127]

After *Heien*, it no longer matters if *Davis* is distinguishable, and it
no longer matters whether a state rejects a good-faith exception to
the exclusionary rule, because *Heien* has declared that there is no
Fourth Amendment violation if the police were reasonable in believing the law reached the defendant's conduct, even if the courts
ultimately say it did not. Where the statute is ambiguous, defendants
expect to lose even if their interpretive view is vindicated. Of course,
a mistake may be unreasonable. Yet often the statute is genuinely
ambiguous—poorly drafted or drafted without any foresight of the
current application—and any lawyer can see as much. This is the
precise situation where judicial interpretation has the most value, yet
here the attorney has no reason to expect a victory and therefore no
reason to press the argument. When they clarify the law, appellate
opinions are a public good, and public goods tend to be underpro-
duced, so it is a particularly bad idea to undermine the incentives for
their creation.[128]

---

[125] This is done usually under the state constitution's equivalent to the Fourth Amendment.
See *Heien*, 135 S Ct at 545 & n 2 (Sotomayor, J, dissenting) (listing state courts that do not
recognize a good-faith exception to the exclusionary rule as a matter of state law). North
Carolina is one of the fourteen, so there was no good-faith barrier to the exclusionary remedy,
had the Court found a Fourth Amendment violation.

[126] *Davis v United States*, 131 S Ct 2419 (2011).

[127] As explained above, if we translate the problem from police to the analogous situation of
criminal defendants, *Davis* is similar to a defendant claiming a mistake of criminal law based
on reasonable reliance on an official interpretation of the law afterward determined to be
erroneous, which is frequently a defense. (See sources cited in note 49.) *Heien* is similar to a
defendant claiming a mistake of criminal law based on his reasonable misreading of the
statute, which is usually not a defense.

[128] Other branches could clarify the law. But legislatures and state attorneys general are not
likely to enact or issue sufficient clarifying amendments or opinions, respectively, on a matter
as mundane as the traffic code.

As a result, it is entirely possible that the police could continue indefinitely to stop motorists based on an erroneous view of the law because no motorist has an incentive to litigate. The first to prove the police are wrong gets no remedial benefit other than to nullify a ticket, which is not sufficient to motivate appellate litigation. If the court ruled against the government's interpretation, subsequent motorists would benefit (because the interpretation is no longer reasonable once a court rejects it), but there will never be "subsequent" motorists because no one wants to go first. At the end of this part, I document an example of this phenomenon, where police ticketed motorists over a period of time for a nonexistent traffic offense before a court finally ruled that the police were mistaken and the ruling occurred only because the defendant was trying to exclude evidence for a crime more serious than a traffic offense.

Even if a defendant does litigate about the meaning of the statute, the courts might not resolve the issue. When the statute is ambiguous, the court can always say that, *if* the police were wrong about the law, their interpretation is at least reasonable, which means the traffic stop was valid. This way of resolving the case—assuming without deciding that the police *are* wrong—does not resolve what the statute means, just what it plausibly could mean. Had *Heien* come out the other way, a court would have to decide whether the police were wrong on the law to determine the Fourth Amendment claim, but under *Heien*, courts can and will frequently simply say that, because the statute is ambiguous, the government wins. Since *Heien*, this has already happened several times.[129]

These issues about incentives to litigate have arisen many times in the Supreme Court. Whenever the Court cuts back on the remedy for a constitutional violation, the effect might be to stifle legal in-

---

[129] See, for example, the alternative reasoning employed in *United States v Stanbridge*, 79 F Supp 3d 881, 887 (CD Ill 2015) ("In sum, if § 11-804 did apply and Stanbridge was required to signal at least 100 feet before pulling to a stop at the curb, his failure to do so was a violation of the Illinois Vehicle Code. If § 11-804 did not apply, Officer Bangert was reasonably mistaken in believing that it did. In either case, Officer Bangert had probable cause to initiate a valid traffic stop."); and *United States v Morales*, 115 F Supp 3d 1291, 1296 (D Kan 2015) (applying *Heien* without resolving whether ambiguous statute required signaling when two lanes merge into one: "this Court declines to decide whether Morales committed a traffic infraction. The result is the same whether the officer was right or wrong about the law"; court notes that officer testified he had "previously enforced" the law in these circumstances). See also *Diaz*, 122 F Supp 3d at 165 (applying *Heien* to uphold a search based on putative violation of open-container law by assuming without deciding that the law was not violated); *State v Dopslaf*, 356 P3d 559 (NM App 2015) (applying *Heien* to uphold search based on putative U-turn violation without deciding whether there was a violation).

novation as litigants will no longer have an incentive to advocate for a new legal rule. The Court addressed the point explicitly in *Davis*, discussed above, and *Pearson v Callahan*, where it overruled the requirement created in *Saucier v Katz* that courts decide the merits of a constitutional claim before deciding whether qualified immunity bars the remedy of damages.[130] But one could embrace *Pearson* and *Davis* and still find *Heien* wanting. In *Davis*, the Court rejected the argument that the good-faith exception would "stunt" the development of the law of the Fourth Amendment, leaving it "ossified,"[131] partly on the ground that the purpose of the exclusionary rule was to deter police from violating the Fourth Amendment, not to spur innovation in the law[132]—a point that does not apply in *Heien*, where the issue is not the remedy but the right. Given the reality of overcriminalization, the Fourth Amendment should strictly limit government to searches and seizures that are justified by the actual scope of broad or overreaching criminal statutes. And we should want to ensure innovation in the law, when it takes the form of clarifying and possibly narrowing the reach of those overly expansive statutes, thus advancing the rule-of-law value of constrained enforcement discretion.

The Court in *Davis* also said that any given judicial opinion rejecting a Fourth Amendment claim leaves the issue open for innovation in jurisdictions (such as another federal circuit, or another state) where the precedent is not binding. If innovation is valuable in a given context, one would expect some jurisdiction to condemn the search or seizure, creating a split in the circuits that the Supreme Court can resolve.[133] Here again, *Heien* presents a more serious problem. *Davis* will cause potential litigants to give up the legal argument only after someone in the same jurisdiction has lost the argument. *Heien* will cause potential litigants to give up *before the argument is*

---

[130] See *Pearson v Callahan*, 555 US 223 (2009), overruling *Saucier v Katz*, 533 US 194 (2001).

[131] See *Davis*, 131 S Ct at 2432 ("Davis also contends that applying the good-faith exception to searches conducted in reliance on binding precedent will stunt the development of Fourth Amendment law. With no possibility of suppression, criminal defendants will have no incentive, Davis maintains, to request that courts overrule precedent."); id at 2433 ("At most, Davis's argument might suggest that—to prevent Fourth Amendment law from becoming ossified—the petitioner in a case that results in the overruling of one of this Court's Fourth Amendment precedents should be given the benefit of the victory by permitting the suppression of evidence in that one case.").

[132] Id at 2427 ("For exclusion to be appropriate, the deterrence benefits of suppression must outweigh its heavy costs.").

[133] Id at 2433.

ever made. If the defense lawyer can see that the statute is ambiguous and there is a reasonable argument for the broader interpretation the prosecutor favors, there is no gain from proving that the prosecutor's interpretation is wrong. So courts never get the chance to say the prosecutor is wrong.

Pearson also presents a distinguishable concern. One reason the *Pearson* majority gave for disregarding *Saucier*'s concern with legal development is that qualified immunity is supposed to relieve governmental defendants of the burden not only of liability, but of expensive litigation. But *Saucier* had blocked what was often the simplest and cheapest way of resolving the suit: by ruling that qualified immunity would exist if there were a violation so that there is no need to decide if there is a violation.[134]*Pearson* also noted that *Saucier*'s rigid procedure violated the canon of constitutional avoidance, in which courts generally attempt to avoid reaching constitutional issues.[135]

Neither point applies in *Heien*. The point of the Fourth Amendment is not to relieve the state of litigation, but to protect the people's right to be secure against unreasonable searches and seizures. And the rule that *Heien* rejected—holding the government strictly accountable for mistakes of criminal law—would require courts only to determine the meaning of state criminal statutes, which violates no canon of constitutional avoidance.

Thus, *Heien* uniquely erodes much of the incentive for litigants to contest the government's interpretation of criminal statutes and undermines the incentive for courts to resolve the correctness of that interpretation. In other words, *Heien* makes it likely that police officers can continue to enforce nonexistent criminal prohibitions for a long time before any court declares their interpretation unreasonable.

D. THE ANALOGY TO THE "IGNORANCE-OF-LAW" MAXIM:
   THE COURT'S LOGICAL ERROR

For a final perspective on the tension between *Heien* and the legality value of constrained enforcement discretion, I turn to the ancient "ignorance-of-law" maxim of criminal law, a doctrine the Supreme Court has repeatedly embraced.[136] The Court recognized but

---

[134] *Pearson*, 555 US at 237.

[135] Id at 241.

[136] For the Court's adherence to the maxim, see *Bryan v United States*, 524 US 184, 193, 196 (1998) (applying "the background presumption that every citizen knows the law" and "the

rejected the analogy between citizen and police mistakes of criminal law. In the next part, I use the analogy to further illuminate *Heien*'s damage to governmental incentives to follow the rule of law. In this part, I simply address head-on the logical failures of the Court's efforts to avoid the analogy.

For criminal law defendants, the mistake-of-law maxim survives even though it generates unfair results on occasion. For example, many criminal law courses teach the case of *People v Marrero*, where a federal prison guard in Connecticut was convicted of a gun possession crime in New York.[137] "Peace officers" were exempt from the New York gun law and Marrero claimed that he was a "peace officer" under the statute. This position was strong enough to convince the trial judge and, on appeal, two more judges.[138] But three appellate judges ruled against him. So Marrero was not a peace officer.

Marrero then raised the fallback argument that he made a reasonable mistake of law in believing he was a peace officer and that he should be excused for it. This mistake was so reasonable as to meet the heightened standards of Justice Kagan, noted above, as it persuaded three of the six judges who heard the argument. Yet Marrero

---

traditional rule that ignorance of the law is no excuse"); *United States v International Minerals & Chemical Corp.*, 402 US 558, 563 (1971) ("The principle that ignorance of the law is no defense applies whether the law be a statute or a duly promulgated and published regulation."); *Reynolds v United States*, 98 US 145, 167 (1878) ("Ignorance of a fact may sometimes be taken as evidence of a want of criminal intent, but not ignorance of the law."); *Barlow v United States*, 32 US 404, 411 (1833) ("It is a common maxim, familiar to all minds, that ignorance of the law will not excuse any person, either civilly or criminally."). Even when the Court recognizes an exception to the rule, it acknowledges the rule. See, for example, *Cheek v United States*, 498 US 192, 199 (1991) (noting that "[t]he general rule"—that "ignorance of the law or mistake of law is no defense to criminal prosecution"—"is deeply rooted in the American legal system").

For a sense of the age of the maxim, see Courtney Stanhope Kenny, *Outlines of Criminal Law* 68–69 (13th ed 1929); Ronald A. Cass, *Ignorance of the Law: A Maxim Reexamined*, 17 Wm & Mary L Rev 671, 685 (1976). More generally, see 4 William Blackstone, *Commentaries on the Laws of England* *26 (1765–69); Matthew Hale, *Pleas of the Crown* 42 (1680); Jerome Hall, *General Principles of Criminal Law* 27–69 (Bobbs-Merrill, 2d ed 1947); Oliver Wendell Holmes, Jr., *The Common Law* 45–46 (Belknap, 2009); 2 James Fitzjames Stephen, *A History of the Criminal Law of England* 94–95 (Macmillan, 1883); Glanville Williams, *Criminal Law: The General Part* §§ 52–74 (Steven & Sons, 2d ed 1961).

Criminal law is not the only area that treats legal mistakes as generally providing "no excuse." In torts, it is not generally a defense to say that one was reasonably mistaken about the law creating the tort the plaintiff is claiming. In property, there is no general defense to nuisance or trespass that one did not know the relevant law. The same is true in constitutional law and habeas litigation. See *Connecticut v Barrett*, 479 US 523, 531–32 (1987); *Bowles v Russell*, 551 US 205, 207–08 (2007).

[137] *People v Marrero*, 507 NE2d 1068 (NY App 1987).

[138] See *People v Marrero*, 94 Misc 2d 367 (NYS Sup 1978), reversed by *People v Marrero*, 71 AD2d 346 (NY Sup 1979).

lost because the New York courts, including the Court of Appeals, read their statutes to follow the maxim, "ignorance of law is no excuse."[139] This was the general common law rule and is endorsed by the Model Penal Code.[140]

There has always been criticism of the maxim. In 1939, one commentator argued, against the maxim, that the law should recognize a defense in these circumstances: "If the meaning of a statute is not clear, and has not been judicially determined, one who has acted 'in good faith' should not be held guilty of a crime if his conduct would have been proper had the statute meant what he 'reasonably believed' it to mean," even if that turned out to be erroneous.[141] Notice how perfectly this proposal describes what the Court did in *Heien*, except that the context is not a defense against criminal liability but a limitation on the Fourth Amendment. The Court and courts generally continue to recognize the maxim, so why reach a different outcome in *Heien*?

The Court described and rejected the analogy in a passage I quote in its entirety:

> Finally, Heien and amici point to the well-known maxim, "Ignorance of the law is no excuse," and contend that it is fundamentally unfair to let police officers get away with mistakes of law when the citizenry is accorded no such leeway. Though this argument has a certain rhetorical appeal, it misconceives the implication of the maxim. The true symmetry is this: Just as an individual generally cannot escape criminal liability based on a mistaken understanding of the law, so too the government cannot impose criminal liability based on a mistaken understanding of the law. If the law required two working brake lights, Heien could not escape a ticket by claiming he reasonably thought he needed only one; if the law required only one, Sergeant Darisse could not issue a valid ticket by claiming he reasonably thought drivers needed two. But just because mistakes of law cannot justify either the imposition or the avoidance of criminal liability, it does not follow that they cannot justify an investigatory stop. And Heien is not appealing a brake-light ticket; he is appealing a cocaine-trafficking conviction as to which there is no asserted mistake of fact or law.[142]

With due respect, this analysis is facile and disappointing. Without saying anything about the rationales for the maxim, the Court

---

[139] *Marrero*, 507 NE2d at 1069.

[140] See MPC § 2.02(9).

[141] Rollin M. Perkins, *Ignorance and Mistake in Criminal Law*, 88 U Pa L Rev 35, 45 (1939).

[142] *Heien*, 135 S Ct at 540.

merely identifies what it regards as the relevant counteranalogy: the requirement that an individual cannot be convicted of a crime based on the government's mistake of law. Heien could not be *convicted* just because the officer reasonably believed the law required two working brake lights, because the law actually does *not* require two working brake lights. So the officer's "ignorance of law" would be no "excuse" for convicting Heien. So far, so good. Then the Court says: "[J]ust because mistakes of law cannot justify either the imposition or the avoidance of criminal liability, it does not follow that they cannot justify an investigatory stop."[143]

Put aside the point that one cannot logically avoid an analogy between *A* and *B* merely by identifying an analogy between *A* and *C*.[144] The important matter is that the Court did not reject Heien's call for consistency; the opinion did not seek to justify treating the legal mistakes of government officials more indulgently than those of its citizens. Instead, the Court reasoned that the maxim applies only when the context is a criminal *prosecution*, whereas *Heien* concerned the distinct context of a criminal *investigation* (search and seizure).

Of course, this distinction simply raises rather than answers the question: If the government is not allowed to *convict and punish* an individual based on its mistake of law, no matter how reasonable the mistake, why should it be allowed to use coercion to *search and seize* the individual based on a reasonable mistake of law? And, here, the Court fails to follow through on its own logic. If, as the Court says, the relevant and distinct context is criminal investigation, then we should compare police and citizen mistakes of law specifically *in the context of criminal investigation*. Figure 1 illustrates the four categories these distinctions create and—in the lower right—the new question they logically raise.

Is the citizen's mistake of criminal law relevant in the investigation context? *Heien* didn't recognize the question, but surely the answer is no. No one thinks that a citizen's reasonable but erroneous belief that *X* was legal in any way affects the government's power to search or seize the citizen based on probable cause or reasonable suspicion

---

[143] Id.

[144] For example, just as ignorance of the law is generally no excuse to crime, the state cannot convict an individual of a crime (not even an attempt crime) merely because the individual mistakenly believes he is committing a crime. But that additional comparison does not rob the Court's own analogy of power, any more than the Court's analogy robs Heien's analogy of power. More than one analogy can be apt.

	Context of Criminal Liability	Context of Criminal Investigation
Govt Official Reasonable Mistake of Law	Irrelevant	Excusing (*Heien*)
Citizen Reasonable Mistake of Law	Irrelevant (the maxim)	?

Fig. 1.

	Context of Criminal Liability	Context of Criminal Investigation
Govt Official Reasonable Mistake of Law	Irrelevant	*Excusing* (*Heien*)
Citizen Reasonable Mistake of Law	Irrelevant	Irrelevant

Fig. 2.

that he did *X*. The government could deprive Marrero of liberty and property by imprisoning and fining him, despite his reasonable mistake of law; surely the government could search and seize based on probable cause (and if necessary a warrant) that he had committed a firearms offense, despite his reasonable mistake of law.

Thus, the Court's claim of consistency is simply false. After *Heien*, when the government searches and seizes, its reasonable legal mistakes excuse, while the citizen's mistakes *in the same investigatory context* do not. The government gains power from the reasonable legal mistakes of its agents, who can justify more searches than the actual law would justify, but citizens gain no power or immunity from government investigation from their reasonable mistake of law. In short, citizens get the actual law; government, a bit more. Figure 2 fills in the missing cell and highlights the one rule that is not like all the others—*Heien*.[145]

---

[145] We could add one more comparison. The *Heien* dictum discussed above says that police mistakes of Fourth Amendment law cannot justify a search or seizure, no matter how reasonable. Surely, the same is true of citizen mistakes of Fourth Amendment law—they could never invalidate a search or seizure no matter how reasonable. Again, the sole case in which parallelism breaks down is *Heien*.

E. THE ANALOGY TO THE "IGNORANCE-OF-LAW" MAXIM:
   THE COURT'S ERROR IN PRACTICE

Moving from the logical to the practical, the real point of Heien's analogy to the mistake-of-law maxim was, surely, that the *rationale* in one domain might apply to the other. There is an area of law that has dealt with legal mistakes and has, for centuries, rejected claims of symmetry, treating legal mistakes as being fundamentally different from factual mistakes. So it is hasty for the Court to announce there is "no reason" to treat them differently in *Heien*, without pausing to consider *why* the criminal law, including the Court's own precedent,[146] treats them differently. Critics of the "ignorance-of-law" maxim would no doubt celebrate *Heien* if it could be read to reject the maxim. But *Heien* does not question the rule; it merely distinguishes its domain. The conceptual distinction *Heien* draws, however inadequate, makes it inevitable that lower courts will reject the claim that *Heien* is inconsistent with the maxim.

What are the reasons for the criminal law maxim? There is no simple agreement on the rationale, or even whether the maxim is justified in a modern society with a complex criminal code.[147] When criminal law was much simpler, it might be said that people already knew the law, so that claims of mistake were not credible, or that it was not worth sorting the tiny few that were credible from all the others that were not.[148] But that idea has become implausible. Because *mala prohibita* offenses densely regulate various realms, mistakes of criminal law are common and inevitable.[149] A second possibility is that the system cannot afford the costs of determining what law the defendant knew.[150] That point, however, is not convincing, given that

---

[146] See sources cited in note 136.

[147] For recent critiques of conventional doctrine, see Douglas Husak, *Mistake of Law and Culpability*, 4 Crim Law and Philos 135 (2010); Edwin Meese III and Paul J. Larkin, Jr., *Reconsidering the Mistake of Law Defense*, 102 J Crim L & Criminol 725 (2012).

[148] See, for example, *Cheek*, 498 US at 199 (stating that the maxim regarding ignorance of criminal law is "[b]ased on the notion that the law is definite and knowable"); 4 Blackstone, *Commentaries* at *27 (cited in note 136). Hall and Seligman tie this point to the vagueness doctrine, saying that it invalidates only the statutes that would fail to give fair notice and justify a mistake of law. See Livingston Hall and Selig Seligman, *Mistake of Law and Mens Rea*, 8 U Chi L Rev 641, 667 (1941).

[149] See Meese and Larkin, 102 J Crim L & Criminol at 738–48 (cited in note 147).

[150] See, for example, *Barlow v United States*, 32 US 404, 411 (1833) (explaining that the principle that mistake of law is not an excuse "results from the extreme difficulty of ascertaining what is, bonâ fide, the interpretation of the party"); 4 Blackstone, *Commentaries* at *46

the *mens rea* requirement frequently requires the determination of very complex questions about what facts the defendant knew.[151]

A third possibility is simple deterrence, that citizens are more likely to learn the law, which would make them more likely to obey the law, if they have no hope for a mistake of criminal law defense.[152] There is a lot one could say against this rationale, from general arguments against deterrence to arguments that strict liability deters no better than negligence liability, under which we would recognize a reasonable mistake of criminal law defense. Especially because there are exceptions of the "ignorance is no excuse" maxim, it seems strange to expect the maxim to motivate citizens to know the law when they might not even know of the maxim.

Nonetheless, the rationale of deterrence makes much more sense for police than it does for criminal defendants. The Court claims that its decision "does not discourage officers from learning the law" because it "tolerates only reasonable mistakes" and does not depend on "the subjective understanding of the particular officer involved."[153] Yet police mistakes of law seem far more deterrable than citizen mistakes because police are part of a professional organization that must, by necessity, train its personnel to know the law. Police departments are part of a municipal government that may be liable for constitutional violations caused by its failure to train its operatives.[154] Viewed from this professional and institutional framework, rather than naively focusing on the individual officer "suddenly confronted" by legal issues in the field,[155] the less forgiving the law is for mistakes of law,

---

(cited in note 136); 1 John Austin, *Lectures on Jurisprudence* 480–83 (Robert Campbell, 5th ed 1885).

[151] See Holmes, *The Common Law* at 47–48 (cited in note 136); Meese and Larkin, 102 J Crim L & Criminol at 749–55 (cited in note 147). Yet another possibility is that one can be blamed for not knowing the law, so it cannot provide a defense. Yet even if it is a sufficient basis for criminal liability, it seems unlikely that ignorance of law deserves to be treated as equally blameworthy or dangerous a crime as committing the criminal conduct knowing it is against the law. See Meese and Larkin, 102 J Crim L & Criminol at 759 (cited in note 147).

[152] See Holmes, *The Common Law* at 47–49 (cited in note 136). See *Barlow v United States*, 32 US 404, 411 (1833) (referring to "the extreme danger of allowing such excuses to be set up for illegal acts, to the detriment of the public. There is scarcely any law, which does not admit of some ingenious doubt; and there would be perpetual temptations to violations of the laws, if men were not put upon extreme vigilance to avoid them.").

[153] *Heien*, 135 S Ct at 539.

[154] See *Monell v New York Department of Social Services*, 436 US 658 (1978); *City of Canton v Harris*, 489 US 378, 390 (1989).

[155] *Heien*, 135 S Ct at 539.

plausibly the more these institutions will invest in training to avoid mistakes.[156] If a legal instructor for a metropolitan police force discovers that the ambiguous language of a criminal statute does not support the nonetheless reasonable interpretation common to officers in the force, on the basis of which they make stops and searches, there was an incentive before *Heien* to tell the officers of the legal constraint.[157] After *Heien*, it would be malpractice of a sort for the instructor to voice his or her concern, given that the police will not violate the Fourth Amendment by relying on their interpretation until some court rejects it.

Nor is there any reason to focus exclusively on police departments. One of the most blatant errors in *Heien* is the failure to note this simple point: a police mistake of law is jointly caused by the conduct of two branches of government: the executive officials—police—who misinterpret the criminal law and the legislature that creates the law that is misinterpreted. If the police misinterpretation is reasonable, then it is nearly inevitable that the legislature did a poor job of drafting the statute, that is, that the legislature made a drafting mistake that was not reasonable. One branch or the other was sloppy; *the government* as a whole is almost by definition "unreasonable" in stopping or arresting an individual based on a mistake of law. A reasonable legislature writes criminal statutes clearly enough to allow reasonable police officers to know what the law is.

One of the common arguments for textualism, as a method of statutory interpretation, is "its ability to stimulate legislators to perform

---

[156] Law and economics identifies a different advantage of the strict liability rule that *Heien* rejects in favor of a negligence rule for police mistakes of law. Unlike negligence, strict liability creates optimal incentives for "activity levels." See Steven Shavell, *Strict Liability versus Negligence*, 9 J Legal Stud 1, 2 (1980). As a standard example goes, optimal driving requires not only the optimal care in the *manner* of driving, but also the optimal *amount* of driving; given that even careful driving carries a risk of accident, it is inefficient for an individual to drive at all, even carefully, when the social risks exceed the driver's private benefits. Negligence liability is generally insensitive to activity levels, but strict liability gives an individual the incentive to minimize the activity to optimal levels. Applying this logic to the Fourth Amendment, strict liability would prod government to minimize the quantity of searches to the optimal point where the ex ante benefits of the search exceed the risk of searching the innocent (the equivalent to an accident). This is another reason to favor holding government strictly liable for its agents' mistakes of law.

[157] Admittedly, with qualified immunity to damages and good-faith exceptions to the exclusionary rule, the instructor's incentive before *Heien* was already weak. But if the Court meant to say that *Heien* did not undermine the incentive for police to learn the law because its prior decisions had already reduced that incentive to zero, it should have said so. To the contrary, a general concern for exclusion of evidence can motivate accuracy in the legal instruction of police officers.

their functions better, as by drafting statutes more precisely."[158] The idea is that the more attention the courts pay to legislative text, refusing to rescue the legislature from the plain meaning of its poor drafting, the more attention the legislature will pay to legislative text, aligning the plain meaning with its intent. Justice Scalia is famously associated with this view.[159]

The argument for courts holding legislature's "feet to the fire" when interpreting statutes applies with at least equal force to the context of *Heien*. The Court's decision rescued the North Carolina legislature from the effect of its drafting sloppiness. There was nothing ineffable about prescribing the number of brakes lights on a car that must be functioning. It would have been easy enough to have drafted a clear statute. So the legislature did a bad job, but *Heien* allocates the loss not on the legislature or any part of government, but on the citizen who is stopped for being suspected of something that is perfectly legal. Borrowing a simple idea from economics, if we want to avoid governmental errors, the Court should have assigned the "loss" from such errors to the government.

Presumably, the response to this argument is, again, to point back to the Court's good-faith analysis in the exclusionary rule context. The Court said in *Illinois v Krull* that the purpose of the remedy is to deter police violations of the Fourth Amendment, not to deter legislative violations.[160] But that reasoning was always limited to the particular remedy of exclusion, not to the content of the Fourth Amendment rights themselves. When we decide whether a search or seizure is reasonable, the question is whether the government's action, *taken*

---

[158] William N. Eskridge, Jr., *The New Textualism*, 37 UCLA L Rev 621, 677 (1990) ("Hence, Justice Scalia seems to argue, if Congress is aware that its statutes will be read with a strict literalism and with reference to well-established canons of statutory construction, it will be more diligent and precise in its drafting of statutes."). See also Einer Elhauge, *Statutory Default Rules: How to Interpret Unclear Legislation* 333 (Harvard, 2008); Adrian Vermeule, *Foreword: System Effects and the Constitution*, 123 Harv L Rev 4, 47 (2009) ("Increasing the number of textualist votes by one percent would then increase legislative incentives to draft responsibly by one percent.").

[159] See, for example, *United States v Taylor*, 487 US 326, 346 (1988) (Scalia, J, concurring in part) (stating that statutory interpretation should be conducted "in a fashion which fosters that democratic process"); Antonin Scalia and Bryan A. Garner, *Reading Law: The Interpretation of Legal Texts* 51 (West, 2012) ("The [textual] canons . . . promote better drafting. When it is widely understood in the legal community that, for example, a word used repeatedly in a document will be taken to have the same meaning throughout . . . you can expect those who prepare legal documents competently to draft accordingly.").

[160] 480 US 340, 350 (1987).

as a whole, is reasonable. In this analysis, there is no reason to ignore the unreasonableness of the legislative authorization of the police to search and seize under a statute that is so badly drafted that professional enforcers can't be expected to ascertain its meaning. As much as textualism wants to encourage clear legislative drafting, we should want the Fourth Amendment not to reward poor drafting by excusing searches and seizures based on avoidable mistakes of law.

Now consider a final (nonstandard) rationale for the ignorance-of-law maxim: to maintain the incentives for the development and clarification of law. In particular, if the criminal law statute is ambiguous, there is significant social value in using litigation to clarify the law. But if the criminal defendant can raise a mistake of criminal law defense to avoid conviction, then the courts need not decide what the statute actually means.

In *Marrero*, for example, the defendant lost his legal argument that he did not commit the offense because he was a "peace officer" entitled to carry a firearm. But if it had been established beforehand that reasonable mistakes of criminal law were a defense, it would have been easier for the court to avoid deciding the substantive legal issue. A judge could instead reason that the statutory definition of peace officer was ambiguous and that no prior precedent clearly established that a federal corrections officer from out of state was not a peace officer. Thus, Marrero would be entitled to prevail without deciding whether he was a peace officer. The court could, of course, reach the merits if it wished, but it would not need to.

Where the court renders a decision without reaching the merits, the rest of society loses the clarification of the law. Indeed, the expectation of losing to the reasonable-mistake argument may deter a prosecutor from ever bringing the charge that could clarify the law. If the right answer is that Marrero was not a peace officer, the only way to be certain that issue is decided is to prosecute him in a regime where ignorance of law is no defense.

There is more going for this law-development rationale than is immediately apparent. Consider that the ignorance-of-law maxim has always exempted mistakes of civil law.[161] The issue arises most

---

[161] Although I term this exception one for "mistakes of civil law," others have described it differently. See Gerald Leonard, *Rape, Murder, and Formalism: What Happens If We Define Mistake of Law?*, 72 U Colo L Rev 507, 537 n 88 (2001) (citing secondary literature using terms such as "different-law mistake," mistake of "non-penal law," mistake of "private law," etc.). See also MPC § 2.04(1).

commonly in connection with the meaning of "property of another" in theft prosecutions.[162] A criminal defendant who mistakenly believed the property he took was not the property of another has a defense, even if the source of his error is not a fact, but the legal rule of property, such as when the law recognizes personal property as being abandoned or as becoming part of the real property. The fact that the ignorance-of-law maxim does not apply to these mistakes suggests that there is a distinction between the mistake of criminal and civil law.

The law-development rationale explains why. A defense of mistake of criminal law will interfere with legal clarification in a way that a defense of mistake of civil law will not. If, for example, the term "peace officer" in New York's statute is not clarified in a prosecution brought under that statute, then it will not be clarified at all (unless by coincidence it occurs, and has the same meaning in, some other statute). By contrast, if a criminal statute refers to "property of another," it is clearly borrowing from another area of law; the law of property will decide the meaning of that term. We do not need criminal litigation to clarify its meaning; civil disputes over property will be sufficient.

The law-development rationale can also explain the *Heien* dictum, discussed above. The Court distinguished between different kinds of legal mistakes the police can make, a mistake of criminal statutory law, like the one in *Heien*, and a mistake of Fourth Amendment law, saying that reasonable mistakes of the latter sort are never a valid basis for a search or seizure.[163] Neither the majority nor concurrence explained this distinction.[164] One might suppose that we should more readily attribute to police the knowledge of their state's criminal law, *the law it is their job to enforce*, than knowledge of federal constitutional law.

---

[162] See, for example, *R v Smith (David Raymond)*, 1 All E R 632 (1974). See generally Williams, *Criminal Law* at 320–27 (cited in note 136) (reviewing cases finding a "claim of right" defense to larceny where the claim is based on a misunderstanding of the law of property).

[163] *Heien*, 135 S Ct at 539; id at 541, n 1 (Kagan, J, concurring).

[164] There is a precedent for an analogous distinction in *Cheek v United States*, 498 US 192 (1991). In *Cheek*, the Court recognized an exception to the ignorance-of-law maxim when the defendant's mistake concerned tax law, id at 204–05, but then refused to extend the exception to Cheek's mistakes of constitutional law, id at 205, where he claimed to believe that the tax laws were unconstitutional. The Court said that the constitutional claims were "of a different order" than the statutory ones. Id. Like *Heien*, however, *Cheek* did not offer much reason for treating mistakes of constitutional law more harshly than mistakes of statutory law.

Yet the law's development gives a simple justification. If the police were excused for making a mistake of Fourth Amendment law, so long as the mistake was reasonable, then litigants would have little incentive to raise a Fourth Amendment argument in any unresolved area. Consider, for example, the Court's recent innovation in *Riley v California*,[165] holding that a search incident to arrest of a cell phone found in the possession of the arrestee required a warrant (or warrant exception other than search-incident doctrine). Before *Riley*, police officers were plainly reasonable in thinking that the standard search-incident doctrine, allowing warrantless searches of containers found on arrestees, applied to cell phones.[166] If, accordingly, there was no Fourth Amendment violation in that case, a litigant would have no incentive to raise the issue—even if the Court were prepared to say that, in future cases, it would apply a new and contrary rule requiring a warrant. In general, courts would have less incentive to resolve close issues when they could just resolve the case by holding that, because the police view of the Fourth Amendment law was reasonable, there was no Fourth Amendment violation.

Similarly, the law-development rationale can explain one distinct category of legal mistakes that deserved the Court's indulgent treatment. In quite a few pre-*Heien* cases, the officer in one jurisdiction made a mistake of criminal law from another jurisdiction[167]—and those mistakes, unlike the one in *Heien*, *should* have been excused. For example, many states make relevant the law of other states by requiring the vehicle to display the license plate(s) as is required in the jurisdiction that issued the plate. So state *A* excuses a vehicle from state *B* from complying with the license plate requirements of state *A*, but does require, as a matter of the law of state *A*, that the driver

---

[165] *Riley*, 134 S Ct at 2485.

[166] See *United States v Robinson*, 414 US 218, 235 (1973).

[167] See *United States v Lopez-Soto*, 205 F3d 1101, 1106 (9th Cir 2000) (traffic stop based on the erroneous belief that the foreign jurisdiction licensing the car required an updated sticker on the license plate, which would then have made it an offense in Texas); *United States v Twilley*, 222 F3d 1092 (9th Cir 2000) (traffic stop based on the erroneous belief that the foreign state licensing the car required two plates); *United States v Smart*, 393 F3d 767 (8th Cir 2005) (traffic stop based on uncertainty as to what foreign jurisdiction licensed the car and whether it required a front as well as rear license plate); *United States v Southerland*, 486 F3d 1355 (DC Cir 2007) (traffic stop based on mistake about whether the state licensing the car permitted the front license plate to be displayed on the front dashboard); *Travis v State*, 959 SW2d 32, 34 (Ark 1998) (traffic stop because Arkansas officer erroneously believed that Texas law required a sticker showing an expiration date be placed on the license plate).

from state B comply with the license plate requirements of state B. In a number of cases involving this scenario, the officer from state A made a mistake about the law of state B, stopping a car for, say, not having a front plate, when the other jurisdiction's law did not require a front plate.

Under either plausible rationale for the ignorance-of-law maxim—deterrence and law development—the officer's error should be excused in this situation. It is less important to motivate the police to know the law of another jurisdiction, and there is no good reason for one jurisdiction to worry about the law development in another jurisdiction. The courts of state B will resolve ambiguities in the statutes of state B when their own drivers contest tickets or stops.

To return to the legal issue in *Heien*, this analysis actually reveals a new argument for the Court's result, one unrecognized in the opinion. One could simply say that the judicial cases that will resolve the meaning of the brake light rule in North Carolina are the cases where someone disputes the ticket received for having only one working brake light. Traffic courts can clarify traffic rules. By contrast, Heien was prosecuted for possessing cocaine, and seeks to suppress the cocaine under the Fourth Amendment exclusionary rule. Arguably, we do not need cocaine cases to hone the meaning of the brake light rule. Yes, they are both criminal law, but the meaning of the brake light rule is "collateral" to the law determining the cocaine offense. So we could excuse the officer's mistake of traffic law in all cases except those directly litigating the traffic offense, and get the clarification we need.

The contrary argument is obvious and, I think, more compelling. The law-development argument should be grounded in reality, not formalism. Drivers rarely hire a lawyer to contest a simple traffic ticket into the appellate courts. It is much cheaper to pay the ticket, and while people will sometimes litigate for principle over money, traffic tickets are not usually the place for grand gestures. That is the reason that nearly all these police mistake-of-law cases involve criminal defendants facing more serious charges litigating the statutory issue. If we want the courts to clarify traffic offenses and thereby limit police discretion, we will need to rely on cases where something larger is at stake, as a criminal defendant seeking to exclude evidence of a more serious crime obtained in a stop that was unjustified under the correct reading of the traffic law.

The point is empirical and contestable. As some evidence for my view, however, consider the Eleventh Circuit's decision in *United States v Chanthasouxat*, where a traffic stop for "failure to have an inside rearview mirror" resulted in the discovery of a large amount of cocaine.[168] The traffic code did not actually require an interior rearview mirror, so the van's side mirrors were sufficient. The government argued, however, that the officer's belief that the van was in violation of the law was reasonable because he had relied on advice from a city magistrate and his police training.[169] Amazingly, the government also contended the belief was reasonable because the officer had previously written "more than 100 tickets for this particular 'violation.'"[170]

In other words, a single officer had written over a hundred tickets for a nonexistent offense, and those drivers had apparently paid the tickets or suffered the consequences for not paying tickets, before this case occurred. I previously noted how American courts have abandoned common law crime creation, but here is evidence that, for a recent span of time, there existed in the state of Alabama *executive crime creation*. And the incentive for the litigant who finally put an end to it was not the desire to avoid a traffic ticket; it was the exclusion of evidence of a drug charge. The Eleventh Circuit agreed that the officer's "mistake of law was reasonable under the circumstances," but held that no mistake of law, "no matter how reasonable or understandable," can "provide reasonable suspicion or probable cause to justify a stop."[171] If, instead, *Heien* had been the law before 2003, it is likely that no one would have ever challenged the police officer's interpretation (and possibly courts would have avoided the issue when they did) and those officers would today still be stopping motorists and writing tickets for a nonexistent offense. What would we conclude about adherence to the rule of law in another nation in which police routinely stopped motorists and issued tickets for nonexistent offenses?

---

[168] *Chanthasouxat*, 342 F3d at 1272.

[169] Id at 1279.

[170] Id. There is another example in the same state. In *JDI v State*, 77 So3d 610 (Ala Crim App 2011), the Court held that "Alabama state law does not prohibit driving a vehicle with a cracked windshield," id at 616, but the officer testified that "he routinely stopped cars with cracked windshields." Id at 612.

[171] *Chanthasouxat*, 342 F3d at 1279.

In the aggregate, the breadth and depth of traffic regulations probably give police as much discretion to stop drivers as some unconstitutionally vague loitering laws would have given police to stop pedestrians. There is no easy constitutional solution to the problem of excess discretion, but one should at least avoid crafting other legal doctrines in a manner to make the problem worse. Unfortunately, *Heien* does make matters worse, granting police more traffic enforcement discretion when they already have too much. *Heien* empowers government attorneys to defend traffic stops by scanning the criminal code for hypothetical interpretations of traffic regulations that would justify the stop, undermines the incentives of municipalities and police forces to train individual officers in the strict limits of the traffic laws, damages the incentives of criminal defendants to challenge expansive and erroneous interpretations of the traffic laws, diminishes the incentives of courts to decide the issue when it is raised, and weakens the incentives of legislatures to avoid statutory ambiguity in the first place. Having law enforcement stop people and ticket them for nonexistent offenses is an embarrassment to the rule of law. That the stops are constitutional is even worse.

III. The Rule of Law, Heien, and the Problem of Fair Notice

The other rationale for the vagueness doctrine, also an important matter for the rule of law, is that citizens are entitled to fair notice of what the law prohibits. The Supreme Court has repeatedly stated the constitutional importance of fair notice to Due Process. Indeed, one might say that the "ignorance-of-law" maxim makes it all the more important that statutory language is sufficiently clear to provide notice, given that we take the statutory notice as being fully sufficient per se.[172] Fair notice has survived as a formulation of constitutional value despite being somewhat formalistic, in that the notice required is satisfied by the mere publication of a criminal

---

[172] Hall and Seligman say that the vagueness doctrine invalidates statutes that would fail to give fair notice and justify a mistake of law. See Hall and Seligman, 8 U Chi L Rev at 667 (cited in note 148). Packer, *The Limits of the Criminal Sanction* at 85 (cited in note 9), and Jeffries, 71 Va L Rev at 207–08 (cited in note 6), articulate how the discussion of fair notice feels fictional because citizens do not check statute books before deciding to commit crimes, which is why each emphasizes the other legality rationale—constraining enforcement discretion. Nonetheless, as both scholars recognize, notice is an important value because government should avoid criminal liability that is genuinely surprising (see, e.g., *Lambert v People of the State of California*, 355 US 225 (1957)) and because notice is a good proxy for whether the statute sufficiently limits enforcement discretion.

statute and most citizens (including most criminals) do not spend time parsing such texts. And, of course, even if they do, reasonable misinterpretations of the text are generally no excuse for violating the law. But the idea of fair notice still makes sense as a minimal kind of procedural formalism, a regularity of process that imposes a restraint on government power, partly as a protection against genuinely surprising government coercion, partly as a proxy for when the legislature has reasonably constrained enforcement discretion.

That fair notice is a constitutional value does not mean it always prevails. But *Heien* is, however implicitly, a surprising repudiation of its importance. Part A describes the basic inconsistency between notice and *Heien*. Part B illustrates that inconsistency by focusing on another case from last term.

A. THE RULE OF LENITY AND A NEW RULE OF SEVERITY

Nothing in the vagueness doctrine, nor in *Heien*, implies that North Carolina's poorly drafted brake light statute is unconstitutionally vague. One of the few black-letter principles of the vagueness doctrine is that vagueness is evaluated based not just on statutory text, but on subsequent judicial interpretation, including narrowing construction to save the statute.[173] Once the North Carolina appellate decision held that the state brake light statute required only one working brake light, no ambiguity remained. Moreover, if a simple dichotomous uncertainty about whether the statute required one or two functioning brake lights were sufficient to render the statute unconstitutional, then a large fraction of all criminal statutes would be unconstitutional, which is surely not the case.

The result is an ugly double standard: a statute can be sufficiently clear to give constitutionally adequate notice to citizens, but also sufficiently ambiguous to excuse police searches and seizures based on errors about its meaning. One expects the Court to work at strengthening the rule of law by creating at least the appearance of equal treatment for the government and the governed, but *Heien* expresses greater solicitude of government agents. If we are to distinguish the issues—citizen and police notice of law—one would more sensibly expect it to work in the opposite direction. Knowledge of the crimi-

---

[173] See, for example, *Boos v Barry*, 485 US 312, 329–30 (1988); *Village of Hoffman Estates v Flipside, Hoffman Estates*, 455 US 489, 494 n 5 (1982).

nal law falls within the employment responsibilities of police officers; they need to know the law in order to enforce it. Citizens generally
do not have jobs requiring them to acquire comprehensive knowledge
of the parameters of criminal law. So how can the legislature be providing citizens with sufficient "fair notice" of its criminal prohibitions
if the meaning of a statute is so ambiguous that we cannot even expect
law enforcement officers to get the law right?

Here, we reach another one of the most important but overlooked
features of the *Heien* reasoning. Legality and the vagueness doctrine
are not just about whether a statute is sufficiently clear to permit
conviction and punishment. They also require that individuals have
fair notice for how to avoid giving government enforcers cause to
subject them to techniques of coercive *investigation*—searches and
seizures. This is why Herbert Packer ties legality to limiting the
power, not just to punish crime, but "to call conduct *into question* as
criminal, with all the destruction of human autonomy that this power
necessarily imports."[174] Even if a criminal code were fair and clear
and the courts employed a fair and accurate process, citizens would
still face a nightmarish police state if the police were insufficiently
constrained, that is, if the stated law did not affect the circumstances
of an arrest or search, which depended instead on the whim of an
officer.[175] However imperfectly we achieve the goal, the standard
account of legality is that citizens should have fair notice of how not
to be treated by the state as a criminal, which includes how not to be
stopped, arrested, and searched, as well as how to avoid conviction
and punishment. This goal is all the more important when the criminal code contains a multitude of fine-only offenses, where the arrest
and search are far worse than the actual criminal punishment.[176]

Of course, there is no way to live one's life without risking a police
encounter that may involve a search or seizure. One might look like
the description of a recent perpetrator. Or one might need to "break
into" one's own car or house and give the appearance of being a car
thief or burglar. But one cannot even begin to take into account what
actions may *appear* suspicious if one does not have fair notice of what
the law prohibits. To the extent practical, the citizen wants fair no-

---

[174] Packer, *The Limits of the Criminal Sanction* at 94 (emphasis added) (cited in note 9).

[175] Compare id at 93 ("A good definition of a police state would be a system in which the law enforcers were allowed to be the judges of their own cases").

[176] See, for example, Malcolm M. Feeley, *The Process Is the Punishment* (Russell Sage, 1992).

tice of the criteria for arrest and search. A driver wants to know how to drive in such a lawful way that police have no grounds for a stop. *Heien* moves us further away from that goal.

One way to measure the failure of *Heien* on this score is to contrast the opinion with the rule of lenity: the rule that, in the interpretation of criminal statutes, courts should resolve ambiguity in favor of the defendant.[177] The Supreme Court appears to give less weight to lenity than in the past, but the Court still recognizes lenity as relevant at least where the text has more than one plausible meaning and the other canons of construction do not clearly resolve which one is best.[178] State courts continue to give lenity more weight.

The origin of the doctrine is in a very particular context of English criminal law, where courts sought doctrines to ameliorate the harshness of criminal sanctions.[179] The modern rationale is that we ensure notice by erring on the side of construing the statute too narrowly rather than too broadly.[180] Lenity creates a kind of clear-statement rule: if the legislature wants to prohibit something, it should say so clearly in the statute,[181] thereby giving the citizen fair notice.

Heien implicitly repudiates the rule of lenity in favor of a *rule of severity*.[182] Under *Heien*, if a criminal statute reasonably bears two

---

[177] See id; see also Solan, 40 Wm & Mary L at 57 (cited in note 10).

[178] See, for example, *Yates v United States*, 135 S Ct 1074, 1091 (2015) (relying on lenity to give narrow interpretation to meaning of "tangible thing").

[179] See Jeffries, 71 Va L Rev at 189 (cited in note 6).

[180] See *McBoyle v United States*, 283 US 25, 27 (1931) (Holmes, J). Another possibility is that the rule serves "a libertarian purpose of limiting the reach of criminal statutes . . . as well as the structural purposes of ensuring legislative primacy in the drafting of criminal statutes." Michael Coenen, *Spillover Across Remedies*, 98 Minn L Rev 1211, 1233 n 77 (2014). Regarding the latter, see Zachary Price, *The Rule of Lenity as a Rule of Structure*, 72 Fordham L Rev 885, 887 (2004) (arguing that lenity "compels legislatures to detail the breadth of prohibitions in advance of their enforcement, and . . . compels prosecutors to charge crimes with enough specificity to indicate to voters—and juries—what conduct has been treated as criminal.").

[181] See William N. Eskridge, Jr., *Overriding Supreme Court Statutory Interpretation Decisions*, 101 Yale L J 331, 413–14 (1991) ("[F]ew of the clear statement rules are as sensible as the rule of lenity.").

[182] Justice Scalia used this term to make a parallel point when administrative agencies claim *Chevron* deference for their interpretations of penal statutes. See *Chevron USA Inc. v Natural Resources Defense Council, Inc.*, 467 US 837 (1984). In *Crandon v United States*, 494 US 152 (1990), he wrote an opinion concurring in the judgment (and joined by Justices O'Connor and Kennedy) in which he stated that "we have never thought that the interpretation of those charged with prosecuting criminal statutes is entitled to [*Chevron*] deference." Id at 177. Justice Scalia noted that the context—giving advice to governmental employees—was one in which the Justice Department naturally erred on the side of being overinclusive. As a result,

meanings, the police are free to search and seize based on the broader interpretation, the one that disfavors the defendant. If the statute can be read as requiring merely one working brake light or requiring two, then the police can lawfully stop the car on the broader assumption that it requires two until a court interprets the statute to say otherwise. Since *Heien*, the Illinois Supreme Court has explicitly embraced this reasoning:[183] having found an ambiguity in the statute defining a license plate obstruction, it chose to apply the rule of lenity to adopt the narrower interpretation (that did not apply to an object, like a trailer hitch, that is not directly attached to the license plate). But the Illinois court nonetheless upheld under *Heien* a car stop based on the broader and erroneous view of the statute *because* its need to resort to the canon of lenity supported the reasonableness of the officer's legal mistake.[184] Putting aside the fact that the police might be expected to know, in a general sense, even the rule of lenity, the *Heien* Court never explains why the lenity regime governs convictions, but the severity regime governs searches and seizures. The Court does not even seem to recognize it is creating a disparate rule of severity and offers "no reason" that leniency should not apply to both settings.

"to give persuasive effect to the Government's expansive advice-giving interpretation of [the statute] would turn the normal construction of criminal statutes upside-down, *replacing the doctrine of lenity with a doctrine of severity*." Id at 178 (emphasis added).

More recently, in a statement respecting a denial of certiorari in *Whitman v United States*, 135 S Ct 352 (2014), Justice Scalia (joined by Justice Thomas) reiterated his opposition to judicial deference to administrative interpretations of penal statutes. Such deference, he said, "collide[s] with the norm that legislatures, not executive officers, define crimes." Id at 353. He continued:

> The Government's theory that was accepted here would . . . upend ordinary principles of interpretation. The rule of lenity requires interpreters to resolve ambiguity in criminal laws in favor of defendants. Deferring to the prosecuting branch's expansive views of these statutes "would turn [their] normal construction . . . upside-down, replacing the doctrine of lenity with a doctrine of severity." *Crandon v. United States*, 494 U.S. 152, 178 (1990) (Scalia, J., concurring in judgment). [The provision of] "fair warning" to would-be violators . . . is not the only function performed by the rule of lenity; equally important, it vindicates the principle that only the legislature may define crimes and fix punishments. Congress cannot, through ambiguity, effectively leave that function to the courts—much less to the administrative bureaucracy.

Id at 353–54.

[183] See *Gaytan*, 32 NE3d at 641. See also *U.S. v Flaven*, 2015 WL 2219779, *2 (D Nev) ("Although the ambiguity in the statute might favor Defendant in the context of a citation for an illegal lane change due to the rule of lenity, the ambiguity favors the Government in the context of a Fourth Amendment challenge.") (citing *Heien*).

[184] See *Gaytan*, 32 NE3d at 652–53.

One might try to distinguish between the interpretation of the statute for purposes of conviction and the interpretation for purposes of searches and seizures, but it is difficult to see what the argument would be. One might say that searching and seizing is not as serious a power as that of convicting and punishing, but certainly sometimes the reverse is true, when the authorized punishment is trivial (a fine only) but the search or seizure is very intrusive (arrest and temporary detention). In any event, the rule of law is general: if government powers should be limited by the law government creates, the limit should apply to all of its coercive powers, or at least to the seriously coercive ones, which searches and seizures certainly are. That is why they appear in the Bill of Rights.

B. THE PUZZLING COMBINATION OF HEIEN AND JOHNSON

In the usual run of cases, vagueness challenges fail except in two instances: where the law regulates or arguably regulates speech and when the law involves vagrancy, loitering, or similar crimes of "being suspicious." In all other contexts, the inevitability of ambiguity means that the Court will ignore it. We might explain this rule of thumb by noting (1) the special importance of free speech,[185] and the dangers of chilling speech through the uncertain application of law, and (2) that statutes that prohibit loitering create a particularly intense problem of arbitrary and discriminatory enforcement.[186] The rest of the criminal law has ambiguity, but doesn't present one of these special problems.

In this last term, however, the Court decided a case that departed from the ordinary pattern. *Johnson v United States*[187] struck down, as unconstitutionally vague, the residual clause of the Armed Career

---

[185] See *Goguen*, 415 US at 573 ("Where a statute's literal scope, unaided by a narrowing state court interpretation, is capable of reaching expression sheltered by the First Amendment, the doctrine demands a greater degree of specificity than in other contexts."); *Grayned v Rockford*, 408 US 104, 109 & n 5 (1972) (explaining the special import of the vagueness doctrine in a First Amendment context); see also Ronald D. Rotunda and John E. Nowak, 5 *Treatise on Constitutional Law* § 20.8–20.9 (West, 4th ed 2009).

[186] See Peter W. Poulos, *Chicago's Ban on Gang Loitering: Making Sense of Vagueness and Overbreadth in Loitering Law*, 83 Cal L Rev 379, 393 (1995) ("Vagueness and overbreadth challenges to loitering laws have received this special treatment. Although loitering is not expressly protected by the First Amendment, it is conduct affecting free speech and free movement, and, when engaged in by two or more persons, borders on the rights of association and assembly.").

[187] 135 S Ct 2551 (2015).

Criminal Act (ACCA), a law that provides a sentence enhancement for the commission of certain crimes, with an ambiguous catch-all provision.[188] Six Justices voted for the vagueness holding, while Justices Kennedy and Thomas concurred in the judgment on statutory grounds; Justice Alito dissented. Justice Scalia's majority opinion dutifully cited the twin rationales of the vagueness doctrine, that excessively vague statutes deny fair notice and invite arbitrary and discriminatory enforcement.[189]

Yet the opinion never attempts to connect the faults it found in the statute—the difficulty of interpretation—to the vagueness rationales. There is no attempt to describe any defendant, past or future, being unfairly surprised under the statute, nor any arbitrary or discriminatory enforcement that might arise, much less any innocuous behavior that would be chilled by this statutory ambiguity. The ordinary source of arbitrary enforcement—police—is not present here because prosecutors, not police, control the use of sentencing statutes. Prosecutors have unchallenged discretion to decline prosecutions, to accept plea bargains, and to make sentencing recommendations[190]—discretion that surely swamps what the ACCA gave them. And it is not clear why the ACCA, however confusing, provides less notice than other poorly drafted or technically convoluted statutes, such as the law of the federal sentencing guidelines. The opinion simply ignores these difficulties. Justice Scalia's opinion contents itself to describe how confused its ACCA law had become.

Large pockets of law are, for a time, confused and unpredictable, but we cannot generally live with a standard that declares such law unconstitutional. Consider the felony murder rule. State law often treats a killing that would otherwise be manslaughter or no crime as a murder, which dramatically affects the sentence, because the killing occurs in the course of an independent and "inherently dangerous"

---

[188] The ACCA raises the penalty for a violation of 18 USC § 922(g) to a minimum of fifteen years and a maximum of life. 18 USC § 924(e)(1); see *Johnson*, 135 S Ct at 2555.

[189] Id at 2556–57 (citations omitted).

[190] When the Supreme Court upheld the trial-penalty sentence (a higher sentence for refusing to plea bargain) in *Bordenkircher v Hayes*, 434 US 357 (1978), for example, it was not troubled by the fact that the prosecutor had the discretion whether to charge Hayes under the Kentucky Habitual Criminal Act, which carried a life term for an offense that, without the act, carried a maximum of ten years. See also *Ewing v California*, 538 US 11 (2003) (upholding life term under three-strikes law where prosecutor had discretion over whether "wobbler" crime was treated as felony triggering the life term or misdemeanor that did not).

felony.[191] Courts struggle over whether to judge inherent danger-
ousness from the perspective of the statute alone or the facts of the
particular case, or something in between.[192] Courts also struggle over
whether the felony is "independent" of the killing or "merges" with
it, especially killings from assaultive behavior.[193] The resulting cases
are famously tangled, confused, and counterintuitive, as much as the
prior ACCA cases. But before *Johnson*, the idea that a felon could
claim that the felony murder rule was void for vagueness would be
treated as laughable. We would have assumed that it was fully sufficient to give the individual fair notice of the definition of the underlying felony and fair notice of the general parameters of the felony murder rule.

Within the law of vagueness, *Johnson* is therefore a surprising victory.[194] The result may be defensible, but it is a deep puzzle to me how
the five Justices who joined both the vagueness holding in *Johnson* and
the majority in *Heien*[195] were able to detect concerns about fair notice and arbitrary enforcement in the former case, where they were
subtle at best, and not in the latter case, where they were substantial
and serious. *Johnson* was explicitly a vagueness challenge, while *Heien*
was not. Yet the vagueness doctrine has always been justified by the
need for fair notice and constrained enforcement discretion, both
of which were surely relevant in *Heien*. A cynic might observe that
the decision in *Johnson* will save the federal courts further struggle to
make sense out of the badly drafted ACCA, while *Heien* will make it
easier for federal courts to avoid the trouble of interpreting ambiguous traffic statutes.[196] There is certainly some symmetry in that.

---

[191] See Guyora Binder, *Felony Murder* 254 (Stanford, 2012).

[192] See Evan Tsen Lee, *Why California's Second-Degree Felony Murder Is Now Void for Vagueness*, 43 Hastings Const L Q 1 (2015).

[193] See, for example, *People v Robertson*, 95 P2d 872 (Cal 2004).

[194] See Peter W. Low and Joel S. Johnson, *Changing the Vocabulary of the Vagueness Doctrine*, 101 Va L Rev 2051, 2109 (2015) (offering a novel account of the vagueness doctrine, one that supports *Johnson*, but noting that "*Johnson* remains an unusual decision. It is rare that federal statutes are declared void for vagueness rather than construed . . . in a manner that will save them from that fate.").

[195] Justice Sotomayor dissented in *Heien* and Justice Alito dissented in *Johnson*. Justices Kennedy and Thomas joined both decisions but concurred in the judgment in *Johnson* on statutory grounds, not joining the vagueness holding. The remaining five Justices held both that the ACCA was unconstitutionally vague for failing to give notice and/or failing to con-strain discretion, but also that the Fourth Amendment need not limit police to searches and seizures based on the actual criminal law.

[196] Compare with Aziz Z. Huq, *Judicial Independence and the Rationing of Constitutional Remedies*, 65 Duke L J 1 (2015).

CONCLUSION

   Heien is a setback for the rule of law. Conceptually, *Heien* errs by focusing its analysis entirely on police officers. A search or seizure based on a mistake of law is the joint result of executive and legislative action. Viewing a government as a whole, government mistakes of law are never reasonable because a reasonable legislature writes criminal statutes clearly enough to allow reasonable police officers to know what the law is.

   Doctrinally, *Heien* is in tension with the Court's precedent concerning the ignorance of criminal law maxim, the rationales of the vagueness doctrine, and the rule of lenity. One cannot avoid the analogy to the "ignorance-of-law" maxim merely by noting that individuals may not be convicted based on a reasonable police (or prosecutorial) mistake of law. The correct parallel to a police mistake of criminal law in the context of searches and seizures is a suspect's mistake of criminal law in the same context. We would never say that police have violated the Fourth Amendment based on the suspect's reasonable but erroneous view of the criminal law; by the same logic, we should not say that police have complied with the amendment because of their own reasonable but erroneous view of the criminal law. If this analogy is imperfect, it is only because there is a weaker case for excusing police mistakes of law when it is the very law they are tasked with enforcing.

   Heien is also inconsistent with a central component of legality—that the discretion of law enforcers is limited by the existing law; the police may enforce only previously declared prohibitions. Legality is not just about limiting government power to convict and punish individuals for crime, but also about limiting government coercion for the purpose of investigating crime, including coercive searches and seizures. In vagueness cases, the Court has proclaimed the constitutional value of controlling law enforcement discretion, but *Heien*'s nearly exclusive effect is to grant extra discretion to police in a domain, traffic enforcement, where they already have too much. *Whren* and *Devenpeck* previously established that police are not judged by the motives they actually have for using coercive power; *Heien* adds that police are not judged by the limit of actual law, but by the broader set of possible reasonable interpretations of the law. The Court's vagueness doctrine also proclaims the importance of fair notice to criminal prohibitions, yet *Heien* implies that a criminal statute can provide citizens with constitutionally sufficient notice even though it is so ambiguous that we cannot expect law enforcement officers to get the law right.

Finally, *Heien* creates incentives for a variety of actors, all of them bad. By excusing the legal errors of the government but not the governed, *Heien* diminishes the incentives of legislatures to draft statutes precisely enough to avoid error. Even if the limitation of *Heien* to "reasonable" police errors does not give municipalities the incentive to make their police wholly ignorant of the law, the decision nevertheless undermines the incentives to carefully train officers in the law's limits. Combined with *Devenpeck*, *Heien* encourages police to give free range to their inarticulable hunches when making car stops, because government lawyers have wide latitude to find, ex post, a reasonable basis for the stop, should it be litigated. And, yet, because the actual criminal law is no longer dispositive of the Fourth Amendment issue, *Heien* damages the incentives of litigants and lower court judges to challenge and resolve, respectively, the statutory ambiguities that create error.

One might have predicted that the *Heien* case would have unified conservatives and liberals, traditionalists and libertarians, originalists and common law constitutionalists, to produce a lopsided win for the simple proposition that government, being the creator of law, is limited by the law it creates. If one accepts the simple principle that government coercion, including the power to search and seize its population, is limited by the actual law, one would never regard governmental mistakes of law as symmetrical to governmental mistakes of fact. Instead, the Court recognized as reasonable under the Fourth Amendment a category of searches and seizures aimed at enforcing nonexistent criminal prohibitions. I suspect this is less because the Justices reject the rule-of-law principles I have articulated than that they failed to notice that they were squarely at stake in the case. The rule of law demands better.

MATTHEW B. KUGLER AND
LIOR JACOB STRAHILEVITZ

ACTUAL EXPECTATIONS OF PRIVACY,

FOURTH AMENDMENT DOCTRINE,

AND THE MOSAIC THEORY

The mosaic theory of the Fourth Amendment holds that, when it comes to people's reasonable expectations of privacy, the whole is greater than the sum of its parts.[1] More precisely, it suggests that the government can learn more from a given slice of information if it can put that information in the context of a broader pattern, a mosaic. This insight, that the incremental privacy threat posed by the government's acquisition of information increases as more information is obtained, was given its most forceful articulation by

Matthew B. Kugler is Assistant Professor, Northwestern University Pritzker School of Law. Lior Jacob Strahilevitz is Sidley Austin Professor of Law, University of Chicago.

AUTHORS' NOTE: The authors thank Katerina Linos, Eric Oliver, and Peter Winn for helpful discussions; Adam Chilton, Paul Crane, Adam Feibelman, Lee Fennell, Barry Friedman, Jancy Hoeffel, Chris Hoofnagle, Orin Kerr, Richard McAdams, Pamela Metzger, Paul Ohm, Eric Posner, Richard Posner, John Rappaport, Richard Re, Christopher Slobogin, Geoffrey Stone, Matt Tokson, Heather Whitney, and Tal Zarsky; workshop participants at Tulane Law School, the University of Chicago Law School, Boston University Law School, UCLA Law School, and Emory Law School for constructive comments on earlier drafts; Michelle Hayner and Adam Woffinden for research assistance; plus the Russell J. Parsons and Bernard Sang Faculty Research Funds and the Coase-Sandor Institute for Law & Economics for generous research support.

[1] *United States v Maynard*, 615 F3d 544, 558 (DC Cir 2010) ("[T]he whole of one's movements is not exposed *constructively* even though each individual movement is exposed, because that whole reveals more—sometimes a great deal more—than the sum of its parts.").

Judge Douglas Ginsburg of the D.C. Circuit in the landmark case that ultimately became *United States v Jones*.[2]

Writing for the Court of Appeals, Judge Ginsburg used a mosaic theory to explain why long-term geolocation surveillance of a vehicle was categorically different from short-term surveillance:

> Prolonged surveillance reveals types of information not revealed by short-term surveillance, such as what a person does repeatedly, what he does not do, and what he does ensemble. These types of information can each reveal more about a person than does any individual trip viewed in isolation. Repeated visits to a church, a gym, a bar, or a bookie tell a story not told by any single visit, as does one's not visiting any of these places over the course of a month. The sequence of a person's movements can reveal still more; a single trip to a gynecologist's office tells little about a woman, but that trip followed a few weeks later by a visit to a baby supply store tells a different story.[3]

This analysis allowed the D.C. Circuit to reach an otherwise difficult conclusion. A controlling precedent, *United States v Knotts*,[4] had held that an individual driving a car on public roads has no expectation of privacy in her whereabouts.[5] Ginsburg nevertheless held that a lack of constitutional protection against being seen in public at any given moment in time does not preclude the possibility that the police would need to obtain a warrant to record someone's movements for several weeks. This approach stood in stark contrast to most prior Fourth Amendment thinking.[6]

Soon thereafter, the Supreme Court granted certiorari and agreed to hear the *Jones* case. The Court decided in favor of the defendant on narrow grounds, holding that the installation of the device was a trespass and therefore a search.[7] To the surprise of many, however, four Justices signed a concurring opinion that embraced much of Judge Ginsburg's mosaic theory.[8] Justice Alito, writing for Justices

---

[2] 132 S Ct 945 (2012).

[3] *Maynard*, 615 F3d at 562.

[4] 460 US 276 (1983).

[5] Id at 281. For an early and incisive critique of *Knotts*, see Richard H. McAdams, Note, *Tying Privacy in Knotts: Beeper Privacy and Collective Fourth Amendment Rights*, 71 Va L Rev 297 (1985).

[6] See David Gray, Danielle Keats Citron, and Liz Clark Rinehart, *Fighting Cybercrime After United States v. Jones*, 103 J Crim L & Criminol 745, 760 (2013).

[7] *Jones*, 132 S Ct at 949.

[8] See, for example, Daniel J. Solove and Paul M. Schwartz, *Information Privacy Law* 334 (Wolters Kluwer, 5th ed 2015) ("Both concurring opinions, involving five justices, embraced

Ginsburg, Breyer, and Kagan, wrote that warrantless geolocation surveillance for four weeks was unconstitutional, even though surveillance for a short period of time would not be. As he stated:

> Under this approach, relatively short-term monitoring of a person's movements on public streets accords with expectations of privacy that our society has recognized as reasonable. But the use of longer term GPS monitoring in investigations of most offenses impinges on expectations of privacy. For such offenses, society's expectation has been that law enforcement agents and others would not—and indeed, in the main, simply could not—secretly monitor and catalogue every single movement of an individual's car for a very long period. In this case, for four weeks, law enforcement agents tracked every movement that respondent made in the vehicle he was driving. We need not identify with precision the point at which the tracking of this vehicle became a search, for the line was surely crossed before the 4-week mark.[9]

As we demonstrate below, Justice Alito mostly grounded his short-term versus long-term distinction in the purported actual beliefs of reasonable people, referring in various places to "popular attitudes," "popular expectations," and "the average person's expectations."[10] In her separate concurring opinion, Justice Sotomayor expressed approval of mosaic-theory-style reasoning, focusing on the conclusions that could be drawn from prolonged surveillance.[11] She agreed with Justice Alito that "longer term GPS monitoring in investigations of most offenses" should be deemed a search, though she did not say whether a search warrant should also be required for short-term

---

a new theory of privacy. In previous cases, the Court has focused extensively on whether something . . . was exposed to the public. The concurrences recognize that extensive and aggregated surveillance can violate a reasonable expectation of privacy regardless of whether or not such surveillance occurred in public."); Orin S. Kerr, *The Mosaic Theory of the Fourth Amendment*, 111 Mich L Rev 311, 314 (2012) ("The concurring opinions in *Jones* raise the intriguing possibility that a five-justice majority of the Supreme Court is ready to endorse a new mosaic theory of Fourth Amendment protection."); but also see note 30 (identifying another possible explanation for the duration distinction).

[9] *Jones*, 132 S Ct at 964 (Alito, J, concurring) (citation omitted).

[10] See Part II.A.

[11] *Jones*, 132 S Ct at 955 (Sotomayor, J, concurring) ("GPS monitoring generates a precise, comprehensive record of a person's public movements that reflects a wealth of detail about her familial, political, professional, religious, and sexual associations. See, for example, *People v Weaver*, 12 NY3d 433, 441–42 (2009) ('Disclosed in [GPS] data . . . will be trips the indisputably private nature of which takes little imagination to conjure: trips to the psychiatrist, the plastic surgeon, the abortion clinic, the AIDS treatment center, the strip club, the criminal defense attorney, the by-the-hour motel, the union meeting, the mosque, synagogue or church, the gay bar and on and on' ")); Ryan Birss, Note, *Alito's Way: Application of Justice Alito's Opinion in United States v. Jones to Cell Phone Location Data*, 65 Hastings L J 899, 925 (2014).

geolocation monitoring.[12] In light of Alito's and Sotomayor's opinions, it seems likely that there are now five votes for the mosaic
theory and its "duration-sensitive" approach.[13]

Indeed, post-*Jones* cases indicate that nearly all the Justices are beginning to talk about privacy in mosaic-theory terms. *Riley v California*[14] made this particularly clear. Chief Justice Roberts, writing
on behalf of eight Justices, held that the police generally could not
search an arrestee's cell phone at the time of arrest without first
obtaining a warrant. Explaining why the arrestee's wallet could be
searched but his cell phone could not, Roberts offered an argument
that is much akin to the mosaic theory:

> [A] cell phone collects in one place many distinct types of information—
> an address, a note, a prescription, a bank statement, a video—that *reveal
> much more in combination than any isolated record.* . . . The sum of an indi-
> vidual's private life can be reconstructed through a thousand photographs
> labeled with dates, locations, and descriptions; the same cannot be said of a
> photograph or two of loved ones tucked into a wallet. [Finally], *the data on
> a phone can date back to the purchase of the phone, or even earlier.* A person
> might carry in his pocket a slip of paper reminding him to call Mr. Jones;
> *he would not carry a record of all his communications with Mr. Jones for the past
> several months,* as would routinely be kept on a phone.[15]

It is this aggregation of multifaceted information over a long time
period—which is purported to be qualitatively distinct from the mere
snapshot exposed by prior searches—that worried the Chief Justice. Because of this emphasis on quantity and time scale, *Riley* hints
that mosaic-theory reasoning about the Fourth Amendment may
have rapidly won over nearly all the Justices. And Antonin Scalia's
unexpected death means that the only Justice who has authored a
recent opinion openly skeptical of the mosaic theory is no longer on
the Court.[16]

---

[12] *Jones,* 132 S Ct at 955 (Sotomayor, J, concurring) ("I agree with Justice Alito that, at the
very least, 'longer term GPS monitoring in investigations of most offenses impinges on
expectations of privacy.' In cases involving even short-term monitoring, some unique attributes of GPS surveillance relevant to the *Katz* analysis will require particular attention.").

[13] See Laura K. Donohue, *Technological Leap, Statutory Gap, and Constitutional Abyss: Remote
Biometric Identification Comes of Age,* 97 Minn L Rev 407, 507 (2012); Gray et al, 103 J Crim L
& Criminol at 764 (cited in note 6); Kerr, 111 Mich L Rev at 313 (cited in note 8); Richard
M. Re, *The Due Process Exclusionary Rule,* 127 Harv L Rev 1885, 1963 (2014).

[14] 134 S Ct 2473 (2014).

[15] Id at 2489 (emphasis added).

[16] *Jones,* 132 S Ct at 954 (majority opinion) ("The concurrence posits that 'relatively short-
term monitoring of a person's movements on public streets' is okay, but that 'the use of

If embraced by the Court, the mosaic theory would upend decades of settled doctrine.[17] It is therefore hardly surprising that legal scholars have begun to explore a number of important questions posed by the sudden rise of the mosaic theory.[18] But at least one fundamental question remains unaddressed by the courts and in the literature so far: Does the mosaic theory, which is explicitly grounded in people's reasonable expectations of privacy, reflect the public's *actual* expectations? When presented with the kinds of scenarios that the Court was wrestling with in *Jones*—momentary geolocation surveillance, day-long surveillance, month-long surveillance, etc.— do ordinary Americans agree with Justice Alito that duration determines expectations of privacy?

The answer is that the public does not agree with him. Specifically, only a very small proportion of the respondents in our representative (census-weighted) national sample said that the duration of the surveillance affected whether they would expect privacy in their geolocation information. According to our survey data, a large majority of Americans always expect privacy in their geolocation information, a meaningful minority never expect privacy, and only a tiny remnant allow their expectations to depend on surveillance duration. Put another way: If we ask people whether they expect the police to be able to obtain geolocation information track-

---

longer term GPS monitoring in investigations *of most offenses*' is no good. (emphasis added). That introduces yet another novelty into our jurisprudence. There is no precedent for the proposition that whether a search has occurred depends on the nature of the crime being investigated. And even accepting that novelty, it remains unexplained why a 4-week investigation is 'surely' too long and why a drug-trafficking conspiracy involving substantial amounts of cash and narcotics is not an 'extraordinary offense' which may permit longer observation. What of a 2-day monitoring of a suspected purveyor of stolen electronics? Or of a 6-month monitoring of a suspected terrorist? We may have to grapple with these 'vexing problems' in some future case where a classic trespassory search is not involved and resort must be had to *Katz* analysis; but there is no reason for rushing forward to resolve them here.").

[17] See Monu Bedi, *Social Networks, Government Surveillance, and the Fourth Amendment Mosaic Theory*, 94 BU L Rev 1809, 1840–44 (2014); David Alan Sklansky, *Too Much Information: How Not to Think About Privacy and the Fourth Amendment*, 102 Cal L Rev 1069, 1072–73 (2014).

[18] See, for example, Bedi, 94 BU L Rev at 1809 (cited in note 17); Jace C. Gatewood, *District of Columbia Jones and the Mosaic Theory—In Search of a Public Right of Privacy: The Equilibrium Effect of the Mosaic Theory*, 92 Neb L Rev 504 (2014); David Gray and Danielle Citron, *The Right to Quantitative Privacy*, 98 Minn L Rev 62 (2013); Gray et al, 103 J Crim L & Criminol at 745 (cited in note 6); Kerr, 111 Mich L Rev at 311 (cited in note 8); Benjamin M. Ostrander, Note, *The "Mosaic Theory" and Fourth Amendment Law*, 86 Notre Dame L Rev 1733 (2011); Andrew B. Talai, Comment, *Drones and Jones: The Fourth Amendment and Police Discretion in the Digital Age*, 102 Cal L Rev 729 (2014).

ing someone's whereabouts over the course of a day or a month, the clear plurality say no to both, a sizable minority say yes to both, and a very small number of respondents provide the answer that is consistent with the mosaic theory and Justice Alito's gloss on it—yes for one day and no for one month. The percentage of respondents who believed that surveillance either definitely or likely violates a reasonable expectation of privacy rose by just *three* percentage points when the surveillance's duration was described as month-long rather than day-long. Following people's actual expectations of privacy would thus require overruling *Knotts* rather than trying to preserve it via the mosaic theory.

That duration was of such limited relevance took us by surprise. We believe it would take at least four Supreme Court Justices by surprise as well. Before we launched our first survey, we had expected that respondents would agree with Justice Alito that the duration of the surveillance was central to the question of whether police surveillance violates a reasonable expectation of privacy. After learning otherwise in Wave 1 of our survey, we supplemented Wave 2 so that respondents who believed that surveillance duration does not matter would be asked follow-up questions to explain their reasoning. Our results here were also surprising. The respondents who consistently felt that surveillance for a day, a week, or a month *did not* violate their reasonable expectations of privacy overwhelmingly embraced the third-party doctrine as the basis for their views.[19] Notwithstanding the criticism to which this doctrine has been subjected in recent years,[20] about 11% of our sample (and 65% of those with low privacy expectations) embraced it and its privacy-skeptical implications. Respondents who felt that both one-day and

---

[19] The third-party doctrine holds that individuals have no reasonable expectation that information voluntarily shared with third parties (like the bank, a telecommunications company, or passersby) will not be exposed to the government's agents. See, for example, *United States v Miller*, 425 US 435, 443 (1976).

[20] See, for example, Richard A. Epstein, *Privacy and the Third Hand: Lessons from the Common Law of Reasonable Expectations*, 24 Berkeley L & Tech L J 1199 (2009); Stephen E. Henderson, *Beyond the (Current) Fourth Amendment: Protecting Third-Party Information, Third Parties, and the Rest of Us Too*, 34 Pepperdine L Rev 975, 976–77 (2007); Erin E. Murphy, *The Case Against the Case for the Third Party Doctrine: A Response to Epstein and Kerr*, 24 Berkeley Tech L J 1239 (2009); Daniel J. Solove, *Digital Dossiers and the Dissipation of Fourth Amendment Privacy*, 75 S Cal L Rev 1083, 1089–1117 (2002); Matthew Tokson, *Automation and the Fourth Amendment*, 96 Iowa L Rev 581 (2011); text accompanying note 172. But see Orin S. Kerr, *The Case for the Third Party Doctrine*, 107 Mich L Rev 561 (2009) (defending the doctrine).

one-month surveillance *does* violate their reasonable expectations of privacy were far more numerous but slightly less unified in their rationales. The most commonly expressed bases for this view were (1) that the police are likely to abuse any power to obtain the geolocation of an individual's car,[21] and (2) that giving the police such power threatens personal freedom. Both responses commanded majority support among duration-insensitive respondents who believe the surveillance infringes on reasonable expectations of privacy.[22]

A third wave conducted almost a year later replicated the prior findings, showing an impressive level of stability in privacy expectations over time. This third collection also included separate questions on the perceived *intrusiveness* of searches. Though the doctrine emphasizes expectations in determining whether a law enforcement action implicates the Fourth Amendment, the perceived intrusiveness of a proposed search is relevant to the question of whether a particular privacy expectation is one that society is prepared to recognize as reasonable.[23] More participants drew duration distinctions in the domain of intrusiveness but, again, consistency was the rule.

In this article, we will argue that data about what the public expects (and regards as intrusive) are not only interesting but also doctrinally relevant. We proceed as follows. Part I provides some essential background on Fourth Amendment search and seizure law and then examines the post-*Jones* case law to see how the question of surveillance duration has played out. The lower courts have embraced inconsistent approaches to the question of how to treat the suggestion in Justice Alito's concurrence that warrantless surveillance becomes unconstitutional as its duration increases.

Part II offers several arguments about why drawing on reliable social science research about public sentiment lends itself to relatively predictable and workable rules of thumb for law enforcement and the citizenry to follow. We also parse the case law to suggest a framework that is more coherent than the ones proposed in the

---

[21] Notably these surveys were conducted in June and July 2014, prior to the prominent controversies surrounding Michael Brown, Eric Garner, and Laquan McDonald capturing public attention.

[22] Respondents were asked to select the one or two rationales that best explained their views. Among those with consistently low privacy expectations, 48.9% selected one option, 37.8% selected two, and the remainder selected three or more. Among those with consistently high expectations, 37.8% selected one option, 39.2% selected two options, and the remainder selected two or more.

[23] See notes 131–32 and accompanying text.

existing doctrinal literature. Under our proposed approach, inquiries concerning the scope of the Fourth Amendment would have a tripartite framework. First, courts would decide whether law enforcement actions violate a suspect's property rights. If so, the police conduct would amount to a search. This is consistent with the Court's opinion in *Jones*, which focused on whether law enforcement had trespassed on the suspect's property by installing a small tracking device on his car. Second, if there is no police trespass, then the courts would apply a clarified version of the framework from *Katz v United States*. *Katz* prong 1 would prompt courts to scrutinize survey research to determine whether people in general expect privacy against a particular law enforcement strategy. Third, *Katz* prong 2 would focus on the sensitivity of the information collected by the police, relying in part on survey research results about whether information revealed by a particular category of searches would be sensitive or embarrassing. Despite the enhanced role of survey research in our framework, the ultimate determination of whether a warrant is required in a given instance would, as now, involve balancing of a variety of costs and benefits. Survey data would help illuminate some of the costs associated with police searches, but there are other costs and benefits that would need to be evaluated using other strategies at the post-*Katz* reasonableness stage. Part II also provides a truncated normative defense of this approach.

Part III presents our empirical data, derived from census-representative surveys. Our main finding is that the duration of surveillance barely affects the extent to which the public regards geolocation tracking as invading their reasonable expectations of privacy. Whatever the policy merits of the mosaic theory, it does not resonate intuitively with ordinary Americans. Our data also indicate that younger Americans actually have stronger expectations of privacy in their geolocation data than older Americans, and that anti-authoritarian attitudes are strongly correlated with privacy expectations. Finally, our data give a clear answer to the question of whether Americans expect that the police will be able to monitor the location of citizens' vehicles remotely, without first obtaining a warrant. Most Americans who take a position regard such warrantless surveillance as a violation of their reasonable expectations of privacy. The rejection of the mosaic theory's duration sensitivity is therefore principally driven by those who have more robust privacy expectations than are accounted for in existing doctrine.

Part III concludes by offering new data on popular expectations regarding a number of presently controversial policing strategies, such as the use of stingray devices to determine citizens' geolocation or the examination of hotel guest registries. By presenting a census-representative sample of the population with various neutral scenarios, it is easy to spot those instances in which police tactics are fully consistent with or largely contrary to prevalent expectations of privacy.

I. SURVEILLANCE DURATION AFTER JONES

In 1967, the Supreme Court held that wiretaps are a search under the Fourth Amendment in *Katz v United States*.[24] Nearly half a century later, in 2012, the Court held in *United States v Jones* that month-long geolocation surveillance, effectuated by the installation of a GPS device on a vehicle, similarly amounted to a search.[25] Interestingly, in neither pathbreaking case is the Court's opinion the central focus of scholarly inquiry. Rather, it is the concurring opinions of Justice Harlan in *Katz* and Justice Alito in *Jones* that tantalize jurists and fascinate scholars.

Harlan's concurrence in *Katz* set out the reasonable expectations test for Fourth Amendment protections. He wrote that police conduct amounts to a search, thereby implicating the Fourth Amendment, when "a person [exhibits] an actual (subjective) expectation of privacy, and [when] the expectation [is] one that society is prepared to recognize as 'reasonable.'" In subsequent cases, this test was embraced by the Court as a whole and has become the key touchstone for determining whether any particular form of surveillance constitutes a "search" within the meaning of the Fourth Amendment.[26] Thus, for nearly fifty years courts have spoken of "reasonable expectations of privacy."

---

[24] 389 US 347, 362 (1967); see also Christopher Slobogin, *Privacy at Risk: The New Government Surveillance and the Fourth Amendment* 13 (Chicago, 2007) ("*Katz v. United States* [is] the most important judicial decision on the scope of the Fourth Amendment.").

[25] Jones, 132 S Ct at 949.

[26] 389 US 361 (Harlan, J, concurring). Anthony G. Amsterdam, *Perspectives on the Fourth Amendment*, 58 Minn L Rev 349, 382 (1974) (describing *Katz* as a "watershed in fourth amendment jurisprudence"). For an illuminating examination of *Katz*'s backstory, see Peter Winn, *Katz and the Origins of the "Reasonable Expectation of Privacy" Test*, 40 McGeorge L Rev 1 (2009). The Katz test is also used to determine whether a defendant's conduct is covered by federal wiretap statutes. See, for example, *Huff v Spaw*, 794 F3d 543, 548 (6th Cir 2015); *United States v Turner*, 209 F3d 1198, 1200 (10th Cir 2000).

Some courts and commentators have treated Justice Alito's opinion in *Jones* as a similarly important shift in Fourth Amendment jurisprudence. His focus on surveillance duration makes the combination of two discrete acts that are independently not searches—say, surveillance for one week and surveillance for the next week—a Fourth Amendment search. One federal court recently dubbed Alito's opinion "the shadow majority opinion in *United States v Jones*,"[27] and academic commentators have similarly referred to it as "*Jones's* second majority opinion,"[28] invoking Sotomayor's adoption of portions of Alito's reasoning as a justification for adding her vote to Alito's four. After *Jones*, the "vexing problems" raised by Alito's concurrence have become arguably the most important looming questions in Fourth Amendment law.[29] If Justice Alito's apparent[30] nod in the direction of the mosaic theory represents the future of *Katz*, then many settled assumptions about Fourth Amendment search doctrines may be called into question.

Though the Supreme Court has not revisited the issue of surveillance duration in the years since *Jones*, the issue has already arisen in a number of lower court cases. In *United States v Skinner*,[31] for example, the Sixth Circuit considered whether tracking a criminal suspect for three days by pinging his phone to determine the clos-

---

[27] *In the Matter of the Application of the United States of America for an Order Authorizing Disclosure of Historical Cell Site Information for Telephone Number [Redacted]*, 40 F Supp 3d 89, 92 (DDC 2014).

[28] Jonathan Siegel and Kate Hadley, *Jones' Second Majority Opinion: Justice Alito's Concurrence and the New Katz Test*, 31 Yale L & Policy Rev Inter Alia 1, 2 (2012) ("While the concurrence only gained four votes in *Jones*, Justice Sotomayor explicitly endorsed Justice Alito's approach in her own concurrence, providing the necessary fifth vote for a future majority opinion.").

[29] See note 16; see generally Caleb Mason, *New Police Surveillance Technologies and the Good-Faith Exception: Warrantless GPS Tracker Evidence after United States v. Jones*, 13 Nev L J 60, 61 (2012).

[30] We say "apparent" here because it is conceivable that Justice Alito and the Justices who signed his concurrence were implicitly adopting another rationale for their duration-sensitive shadow holding. Perhaps they believe that because law enforcement have long been able to tail suspects for a day using unmarked police cars, people expect such conduct, whereas tailing suspects for a month was impractical and therefore unexpected. If that was indeed Justice Alito's rationale, our survey data show that the rationale turns out not to be a good prediction of what the public actually expects. See Tables 1–3. Note also Table 5, which indicates that our respondents rarely think about expectations of privacy in ways tied to the state's expenditures on surveillance. In any event, our survey tests the congruence between expectations and the shadow holding in Justice Alito's opinion rather than testing sentiment regarding any particular rationale for that holding.

[31] 690 F3d 772 (6th Cir 2012).

est cell-phone towers amounted to a Fourth Amendment search.[32] The cell-tower information led them to the suspect's mobile home, where they discovered large quantities of marijuana and two semi-automatic weapons. The Sixth Circuit used at its starting point Justice Alito's opinion, and viewed the difference between twenty-eight-day tracking and three-day tracking as constitutionally dispositive:

> Justice Alito's concurrence and the majority in *Jones* both recognized that there is little precedent for what constitutes a level of comprehensive tracking that would violate the Fourth Amendment. Skinner's case, however, comes nowhere near that line. While *Jones* involved intensive monitoring over a 28-day period, here the DEA agents only tracked Skinner's cell phone for three days. Such "relatively short-term monitoring of a person's movements on public streets accords with expectations of privacy that our society has recognized as reasonable." Id. at 964 (Alito, J., concurring).[33]

In a subsequent case, a federal district court in Michigan applied *Skinner* and deemed real-time surveillance of several cell phones that lasted between thirty and forty-five days to be a search, requiring a warrant supported by probable cause.[34] The boundary between permissible and impermissible warrantless real-time surveillance of geolocation in the Sixth Circuit is therefore somewhere between three and twenty-nine days.[35] Another decision, also from a district court in Michigan, went even further than the Court in *Jones* and held that a warrant allowing for cell-phone GPS tracking for a thirty-day period was invalid for lack of particularity.[36] According to that court, such prolonged surveillance was so troublesome that, absent minimization procedures, "[t]he tracking warrants were akin to the general warrants condemned by the Founders and are repugnant to the Fourth Amendment."[37]

---

[32] Id at 776.

[33] Id at 780 (internal citations omitted).

[34] *United States v Powell*, 943 F Supp 2d 759, 774 (ED Mich 2013). Although the *Powell* Court found that warrants backed by probable cause were required, id at 778, 780, it nevertheless deemed the geolocation admissible under the good-faith exception to the exclusionary rule. Id at 783–84.

[35] See also *Commonwealth v Augustine*, 4 NE3d 846, 865 (Mass 2014) (applying the Alito *Jones* framework to historical cell-site tracking information and deeming the collection of two weeks' worth of geolocation information without a warrant to violate the state constitution).

[36] See *United States v White*, 62 F Supp 3d 614, 627 (ED Mich 2014).

[37] Id at 617. Again, however, the suppression motion was denied under the good-faith exception. See note 34.

In *United States v Graham*, the Fourth Circuit treated the government's collection of even two weeks' worth of cell-site location information as a Fourth Amendment search.[38] Dissenting in *Graham*, Judge Diana Gribbon Motz accused her colleagues of trying "to beat the Supreme Court to the punch" of overruling its prior precedents applying *Katz* and the third-party doctrine.[39] Other courts have been similarly divided over the implications of Justice Alito's opinion. In *United States v Davis*, an en banc decision in the Eleventh Circuit, the majority argued that the Alito and Sotomayor concurrences altered nothing, the dissenter argued that the game has permanently changed, and three separate concurring opinions expressed different understandings of the governing law.[40]

The Florida Supreme Court's opinion in *Tracey v State*[41] provides yet another approach to *Jones*. The court in *Tracey* reviewed the various concurring opinions in *Jones* and concluded that the duration of monitoring could not be constitutionally decisive.[42] Distinguishing the Supreme Court's 1983 decision in *Knotts*, the court found that tracking Tracey's cell phone in real time on public roads for one day without a warrant violated the Fourth Amendment.[43] Surveillance duration was therefore irrelevant because such police action was a search regardless of its duration. Other courts have held that warrantless cell-phone tracking for just one evening constitutes a search under their state constitutions.[44]

---

[38] *United States v Graham*, 796 F3d 332 (4th Cir 2015). The Fourth Circuit has voted to reconsider its opinion in *Graham* en banc. See *United States v Graham*, 2015 WL 6531272 (Oct 28, 2015).

[39] Graham, 796 F3d at 390 (Motz dissenting).

[40] *United States v Davis*, 785 F3d 498 (11th Cir 2015) (en banc). Indeed, the district court considering *Jones* on remand opined that Justice Alito's proposed distinction between short-term surveillance and long-term surveillance was not the law. See *United States v Jones*, 908 F Supp 2d 203, 213–14 (DDC 2012). The district court held the evidence admissible under the good-faith exception to the exclusionary rule. Id at 214–16.

[41] 152 So3d 504 (Fla 2014).

[42] Id at 520 ("[B]asing the determination as to whether warrantless real time cell-site location tracking violates the Fourth Amendment on the length of the time the cell phone is monitored is not a workable analysis. It requires case-by-case, after-the-fact, ad hoc determinations whether the length of the monitoring crossed the threshold of the Fourth Amendment in each case challenged.").

[43] Id at 525–26.

[44] See, for example, *State v Earls*, 70 A3d 630, 644 (NJ 2013) ("[W]e hold today that police must obtain a warrant based on a showing of probable cause, or qualify for an exception to the warrant requirement, to obtain tracking information through the use of a cell phone....

With these disparate approaches, we have seen the federal and state courts fragment every which way on the duration question foregrounded by Justice Alito's opinion in *Jones*. Some judges, like those in *Skinner*, apply the Alito framework and deem warrantless short-term geolocation surveillance constitutionally permissible and warrantless long-term surveillance impermissible.[45] Other judges, as in *Davis*, ignore the duration of geolocation surveillance, and hold both long- and short-term surveillance permissible.[46] Finally, still other judges, as in *Tracey*, reject the salience of surveillance duration by holding even very short-term warrantless geolocation tracking impermissible.[47] The Supreme Court will need to revisit the salience of duration in the constitutional analysis soon. In Part II, we argue that the Supreme Court should consider public opinion data when it does so.

II. The Katz Framework's Ambiguity

Under *Katz*, whether police conduct constitutes a "search" depends on whether it violates a person's actual expectation of privacy and whether society is prepared to recognize that subjective expectation as reasonable. Getting the target of surveillance to describe his own privacy expectations honestly is quite challenging, and there is little normative reason to care what any particular defendant thought.[48] One response to these problems is to ask a large number of disinterested people whether they would have expected privacy were they in the target's shoes. These responses can then become a good proxy for what the target of surveillance should have actually expected and, more importantly, provide law enforcement with direct evidence of what expectations are commonly held. As it happens, however, there are disputes among both jurists and scholars as

---

Our ruling today is based solely on the State Constitution. We recognize that *Jones* and *Smith*, to the extent they apply, would not require a warrant in this case.").

[45] See notes 31–37 and accompanying text.

[46] *United States v Wilford*, 961 F Supp 2d 740, 772 (D Md 2013) ("But the mosaic theory was not adopted as a holding by the Supreme Court, nor has it been endorsed by the Fourth Circuit. And, it appears somewhat unworkable in practice."); see also *United States v Barraza-Maldonado*, 879 F Supp 2d 1022, 1029 (D Minn 2012) (ignoring the duration of surveillance under *Katz* and *Jones* in deeming the police's use of GPS tracking on a vehicle constitutionally permissible); *State v Drayton*, 411 SC 533 (SC App 2015) (following the subsequently reversed district court opinion in *Graham*, not *Tracey*).

[47] See *Earls*, 70 A3d at 630.

[48] See note 148.

to whether it is appropriate to consult survey data in determining the meaning of "expectations of privacy" and the related question of whether those expectations are "reasonable." The debate is presently unresolved and it continues to preoccupy at least some Justices on the Court. In this part we highlight some prominent recent judicial and scholarly statements about Fourth Amendment methodologies. We also present a normative case for integrating survey research into *Katz* doctrine, building on important work previously done by Christopher Slobogin.

A. ARE ACTUAL BELIEFS ACTUALLY RELEVANT?

Justice Alito is the member of the Court who seems most interested in exploring the relevance of what ordinary people actually believe about searches. A recent exchange highlights his frustration with the present uncertainty over Fourth Amendment methodologies. In October Term 2013, the Court held that, absent exigent circumstances, it will usually be unreasonable for law enforcement to conduct a warrantless search of a suspect's cell phone incident to his arrest.[49] During the oral argument for what would become the Court's opinion in *Riley v California*, Justice Alito asked Judith Mizner, an Assistant Federal Public Defender, on at least four different occasions: "On what basis does the Supreme Court conclude that a reasonable expectation of privacy exists?"[50] The answer he was apparently sympathetic to, which Mizner never provided, appeared in Alito's *Jones* concurrence, where he equated Fourth Amendment reasonable expectations of privacy with "popular attitudes," and warned of the dangers that arise when judges gauge these attitudes by projecting their own beliefs onto those of the public as a whole.[51] In *Jones*, he referred at various times to reasonable expectations of pri-

---

[49] *Riley*, 134 S Ct at 3495.

[50] *United States v Wurie* (US April 29, 2014), Oral Argument Transcript, available at 2014 WL 1694920, at *39–*41. *Wurie* and *Riley* were consolidated into the *Riley* opinion. Justice Souter posed essentially the same question to Kenneth Lerner, the lawyer for Danny Kyllo in the landmark Fourth Amendment case of *Kyllo v United States*, 533 US 27 (2001). See Oral Argument Transcript in *Kyllo v United States*, 2001 WL 168056, at *19 (Feb 20, 2001) ("Justice Souter: So you're saying that reasonable expectation is in part based on fact, what you do, in fact, expect, and that informs, should inform the standard of reasonable expectation, is that the nub of what you're saying?" "Mr. Lerner: Yes. It is partly what we all expect.").

[51] Jones, 132 S Ct at 957, 962 (Alito, J, concurring) ("[J]udges are apt to confuse their own expectations of privacy with those of the hypothetical reasonable person to which the *Katz*

vacy as "the average person's expectations about the privacy of his or her movements,"[52] treated "popular expectations" and "popular attitudes" as synonymous,[53] and referenced the "circularity" of *Katz*'s reasonable expectation of privacy test. Of course, circularity is only an intelligible concern if public attitudes are the guiding force in the *Katz* test.[54] He also differentiated between what the public may prefer and what it may nevertheless believe and expect.[55] Finally, he criticized Justice Scalia's majority opinion for embracing a vision of the Constitution that treats technological surveillance as a search, but old-fashioned surveillance that yields the same quantum of information as a nonsearch.[56]

To be sure, there is some ambiguity about what methodology Justice Alito was applying in his concurring opinion.[57] But, on the

---

test looks. In addition, the *Katz* test rests on the assumption that this hypothetical reasonable person has a well-developed and stable set of privacy expectations. But technology can change those expectations. Dramatic technological change may lead to periods in which popular expectations are in flux and may ultimately produce *significant changes in popular attitudes.*") (emphasis added).

[52] Id at 963.

[53] Id at 962 ("Dramatic technological change may lead to periods in which popular expectations are in flux and may ultimately produce significant changes in popular attitudes.").

[54] Id ("The *Katz* expectation-of-privacy test avoids the problems and complications noted above, but it is not without its own difficulties. It involves a degree of circularity, and judges are apt to confuse their own expectations of privacy with those of the hypothetical reasonable person to which the *Katz* test looks.") (citations omitted). The circularity critique holds that popular attitudes dictate judicial pronouncements about the state of the law, which in turn dictate popular attitudes. See Michael Abramowicz, *Constitutional Circularity*, 49 UCLA L Rev 1, 60–62 (2001); Jed Rubenfeld, *The End of Privacy*, 61 Stan L Rev 101, 106–07 (2009). During oral arguments for *City of Los Angeles v Patel*, Justice Kennedy asked counsel: "If you prevail in this case and a member of the Court sits down to write the opinion, does he or she have to use the phrase "reasonable expectation of privacy" and say there is no reasonable expectation of privacy in our society, in our culture, in our day, or do we just forget that phrase? In a way, *as we all know it's circular, that if we say there is a reasonable expectation, then there is.*" See *City of Los Angeles v Patel* (Mar 3, 2015), Oral Argument Transcript, available at 2015 WL 888287, at *13 (emphasis added).

[55] *Jones*, 132 S Ct at 957, 962 (Alito, J, concurring) ("New technology may provide increased convenience or security at the expense of privacy, and many people may find the tradeoff worthwhile. And even if the public does not welcome the diminution of privacy that new technology entails, they may eventually reconcile themselves to this development as inevitable.").

[56] Id at 961 ("Second, the Court's approach leads to incongruous results. If the police attach a GPS device to a car and use the device to follow the car for even a brief time, under the Court's theory, the Fourth Amendment applies. But if the police follow the same car for a much longer period using unmarked cars and aerial assistance, this tracking is not subject to any Fourth Amendment constraints.").

[57] Most puzzlingly, Justice Alito writes: "The Court argues—*and I agree*—that 'we must "assure preservation of that degree of privacy against government that existed when the

whole, his oral argument questioning in *Riley* and his concurring opinion in *Jones* elevated the importance of the average member of the public's actual beliefs and suggested their centrality to the *Katz* inquiry.

We agree with Justice Alito's apparent approach to this basic jurisprudential question and we show how scientific polling can alleviate concerns that, in undertaking such an inquiry, judges will place undue weight on their own beliefs or on the beliefs of people in their social orbits. We posit that under *Katz*, the Court should recognize subjective expectations of privacy under the Fourth Amendment when it finds as an empirical matter that contemporary, ordinary Americans expect privacy in a particular context.

B. FOUR MODELS OF THE FOURTH AMENDMENT?

Katz's two-prong test focuses both on whether the target of surveillance has a subjective expectation of privacy and whether that expectation is one that society is prepared to recognize as reasonable.[58] Confusion has abounded in the decades since *Katz* about precisely what Justice Harlan meant when he articulated the test and what the Court itself took it to mean. The consensus in the scholarship on *Katz*'s first prong seems to be something like this. *Katz* prong 1 is nearly always a nonissue because it is generally safe to assume a criminal defendant would not have exposed incriminating information unless she believed she was not being monitored. This view is nicely encapsulated in a recent article by Orin Kerr, *Katz Has Only One Step: The Irrelevance of Subjective Expectations.*[59]

Most of the scholarly and judicial discussion of *Katz* has therefore focused on the second prong of the test: whether the privacy expectations are of a sort "that society is prepared to recognize as 'rea-

---

Fourth Amendment was adopted."' But it is almost impossible to think of late-18th-century situations that are analogous to what took place in this case." Id at 958 (emphasis added) (citation omitted). Justice Alito does not develop this thought any further, but there is little reason to expect continuity in attitudes between eighteenth-century Americans and twenty-first-century Americans.

[58] See note 26 and accompanying text.

[59] Orin S. Kerr, *Katz Has Only One Step: The Irrelevance of Subjective Expectations*, 82 U Chi L Rev 113 (2015); see also Renee McDonald Hutchins, *Tied Up in Knotts? GPS Technology and the Fourth Amendment*, 55 UCLA L Rev 409, 429 (2007) ("[I]n striking an appropriate balance between the two prongs of the *Katz* test, the Court has chosen to weigh far more heavily the objective reasonableness inquiry.").

sonable.'" Kerr has done important work in this area as well. In his 2007 article, *Four Models of Fourth Amendment Protection*, he identifies four distinct threads in Supreme Court jurisprudence that reflect divergent understandings of *Katz*'s second prong.[60] The first is what Kerr calls the "probabilistic model." This is a purely descriptive approach, one that "tries to assess the likelihood that a person will be observed or a place investigated based on prevailing social practices."[61] Kerr's second approach is the "the private facts model." This model focuses on the sensitivity of the information at issue—if "the government obtains information that is particularly private, then the acquisition of that information is a search."[62] A third possibility is the "positive law model." Under this approach, the courts are to determine whether the government's conduct would run afoul of some independent legal framework.[63] If the police enter the interior of a home, for example, that is a search because it is also a trespass. Kerr notes that, in addition to property law, federal regulations may also affect reasonable expectations of privacy under this model.[64] Finally, Kerr identifies the "policy model" under which the existence of a search depends on the answer to a utilitarian balancing inquiry. Under this approach, "[j]udges must consider the consequences of regulating a particular type of government activity, weigh privacy and security interests, and opt for the better rule."[65]

Kerr provides a long list of examples in which the Supreme Court has embraced, rejected, or ignored these four approaches to addressing *Katz*'s second prong.[66] Sometimes several models are applied to the same case by the Court, and sometimes the Court implausibly claims its cases are methodologically consistent. Kerr argues that this state of affairs, in which the Court decides in each case which of

---

[60] Orin S. Kerr, *Four Models of Fourth Amendment Protection*, 60 Stan L Rev 503 (2007). Kerr's article has already been cited by seven different courts, as of December 2014.

[61] Id at 508.

[62] Id at 512.

[63] Id at 516–18.

[64] Id at 517 (citing *Florida v Riley*, 488 US 445 (1989)).

[65] Id at 519.

[66] Id at 509–22. Kerr observes that the Court has never criticized the policy model, but they have ignored it plenty of times. Id at 521–22. Compare Thomas K. Clancy, *The Fourth Amendment's Concept of Reasonableness*, 2004 Utah L Rev 977, 1022–23 (identifying the Supreme Court's inconsistent approaches to determining the reasonableness of searches over time).

these four models to apply, is desirable.[67] We disagree, because this approach creates an undue risk of doctrinal incoherence and unpredictability.[68]

It is worth emphasizing that Kerr's helpful framework for analyzing Fourth Amendment expectations predates *Jones*. *Jones* itself removes the "positive law" model from the *Katz* framework, instead requiring that courts decide *before reaching the Katz questions* whether law enforcement conduct violated independent rights under applicable state property law.[69] After *Jones*, we might then regard the pre-*Katz* trespass/positive law inquiry as the precursor to *Katz*'s application. Justice Alito's opinion, on the other hand, argues in favor of integrating the question of what the positive law says into the *Katz* framework itself.[70] Finally, while Kerr is right that the Supreme Court often considers cost-benefit analysis germane to *Katz* prong 2 under the policy model, we believe the correct place to incorporate such analysis is the reasonableness inquiry that courts turn to if they decide that particular police conduct constitutes a Fourth Amendment search.[71] That reasonableness inquiry determines whether a warrant or something less is required before the search can commence.

The *Katz* framework has become incoherent and inconsistent, but it need not remain so. Under our approach, the positive law model would be applied to determine whether courts even need to reach

---

[67] Kerr, 60 Stan L Rev at 542 (cited in note 60).

[68] It has also been argued that all of these models collapse into an overall assessment of intrusiveness. See, for example, Christopher Slobogin, *Proportionality, Privacy, and Public Opinion: A Reply to Kerr and Swire*, 94 Minn L Rev 1588, 1603 (2010).

[69] *Jones*, 132 S Ct at 950–51. The same methodology was employed by a majority of the Court in the subsequent Fourth Amendment search case of *Florida v Jardines*, 133 S Ct 1409, 1417 (2013). The Court said that because the police's use of a drug-sniffing dog on Jardines's porch would have been a trespass and thus a search, it was unnecessary for the courts to consider the *Katz* framework. Id.

[70] *Jones*, 132 S Ct at 959–60 (Alito, J, concurring).

[71] For descriptions of the Supreme Court's turn toward cost-benefit balancing in Fourth Amendment reasonableness doctrine, see Slobogin, *Privacy at Risk* at 21–47 (cited in note 24) (developing a proportionality principle of the Fourth Amendment and showing how it is consistent with some of the Supreme Court's case law); Clancy, 2004 Utah L Rev at 1003–15 (cited in note 66) (discussing the courts' use of the balancing approach to Fourth Amendment reasonableness determinations); Morgan Cloud, *Pragmatism, Positivism, and Principles in Fourth Amendment Theory*, 41 UCLA L Rev 199, 223–47 (1993) (discussing the evolution of the case law during the Warren Court era); Cynthia Lee, *Reasonableness with Teeth: The Future of Fourth Amendment Reasonableness Analysis*, 81 Miss L J 1133, 1159–60 (2012) (advocating a balancing approach that is not deferential to government actors' asserted interests).

the *Katz* question, and the probabilistic model would become the *Katz* prong 1 inquiry—it asks whether people in general expect privacy in a given situation and uses this as a proxy for what the target of surveillance expected. Courts deciding whether society is prepared to recognize a subjective expectation of privacy as reasonable (*Katz* prong 2) would then apply the private-facts model; if the privacy expectation only serves to hide unlawful conduct and cannot reveal any other sensitive information, then it would not be a search. And, finally, if surveillance was deemed to be a search, courts would apply the policy model to determine whether it was reasonable for the state to conduct that search without a warrant. All four of the factors Kerr identified in the case law would remain relevant, but each would now have one doctrinal hook. This approach is clearer than the status quo, where courts selectively ignore factors or try to cram multiple factors into *Katz* prong 2 without explaining how they interact. In instances where the results of a judicial cost-benefit analysis were clear but the result of the *Katz* test was murky, the courts could continue to assume that there was a subjective expectation of privacy that society is prepared to recognize but find no Fourth Amendment violation on the basis of the reasonableness of the warrantless search. The Supreme Court did precisely that in the *Quon* case.[72]

Under our approach, *Katz* prong 1 would become more significant and *Katz* prong 2 would become less contentious and less frequently fatal to targets of surveillance. Compared to the muddled status quo, courts collectively would likely find there to be more searches. Put another way, prong 1 would be satisfied in many cases that are currently doctrinally marginal and prong 2 would treat more surveillance as searches than it presently does. But this shift would not drastically expand the warrant requirement. The constitution forbids only unreasonable searches, and judges would consider the benefits of surveillance in the post-*Katz* reasonableness inquiry. This would likely lead courts to bless an increased number of warrantless searches. This doctrinal reshuffle would have two major practical effects. First, judges would be forced to be explicit when they wish to override privacy expectations in the name of law enforcement efficiency. This would likely lead to more carefully considered and more limited divergences from actual privacy expectations. Second,

---

[72] *City of Ontario, California v Quon*, 560 US 746, 760–65 (2010).

there may be some cases in which the American people do not expect privacy but judges think they ought to. Under our approach, judges would not be able to override privacy expectations in that direction. As our data indicate, however, those instances in which the American public by and large does not expect privacy are ones in which current doctrine would almost certainly not provide protection. For example, Americans generally expect that if they are in a public park the police can use silent video surveillance to watch them.[73] This expectation lines up quite well with judicial interpretations of the Fourth Amendment.[74] Though we do not have enough data to know for sure, it may be that there are no cases in which current doctrine *would* protect privacy and the public's actual expectations would *not*.[75]

C. SURVEYS AS A MORE SATISFYING METHODOLOGY

Ordinary people's views sometimes help shape the Court's views of the Constitution's meaning. To offer a couple of high-profile examples, changing popular views about same-sex marriage mattered in *Obergefell*,[76] and shifting beliefs about the death penalty for juveniles, reflected in state-level legal changes, mattered in *Roper v Simmons*.[77] Indeed, although there are occasional instances in which the Court acts in a countermajoritarian fashion, the Supreme Court generally interprets the Constitution in a manner that is consistent with public opinion.[78] Against that backdrop, we think the case for

---

[73] See Table 9.

[74] See note 199.

[75] There may, however, be situations that would be searches under current doctrine but fail under our understanding of prong 2.

[76] *Obergefell v Hodges*, 135 S Ct 2584, 2603 (2015) ("[I]n interpreting the Equal Protection Clause, the Court has recognized that new insights and societal understandings can reveal unjustified inequality within our most fundamental institutions that once passed unnoticed and unchallenged.").

[77] 543 US 551, 564–68 (2005) (striking down the juvenile death penalty under the Eighth Amendment's "evolving standards of decency" test in light of shifting state practices).

[78] Robert G McCloskey, *The American Supreme Court* 260 (Chicago, 5th ed 2010) (revised by Sanford Levinson) ("One of the main points to emerge from this study is that the interests and values, and hence the role, of the Court have shifted fundamentally and often in the presence of shifting national conditions. . . . Indeed, the facts of the Court's history impellingly suggest a flexible and nondogmatic institution fully alive to such realities as the drift of public opinion and the distribution of power in the American republic. . . . [I]t is hard to find a single historical instance when the Court has stood firm for very long against a really clear wave of public demand."); Barry Friedman, *The Will of the People: How Public Opinion Has*

incorporating stable popular expectations into Fourth Amendment analysis is relatively strong. First, the Court has been doing this for decades in the context of figuring out what constitutes a search. Probabilistic model cases like *Bond v United States*,[79] *Minnesota v Olson*,[80] and *California v Carney*,[81] among many others,[82] make that plain enough. Writing on a blank slate, it would be sensible to argue that popular attitudes should influence surveillance law only to the extent that those attitudes affect the content of legislation. But adopting that view now, after the Court has repeatedly indicated that constitutional law will play a major role in regulating run-of-the-mill surveillance, after Congress had shown that it intends to defer often to the courts in this area, and after many Fourth Amendment decisions have elevated the salience of popular expectations, is less appealing. Second, the Fourth Amendment is designed to sort between surveillance that is costly enough to justify the imposition of a warrant requirement and surveillance whose privacy costs are less significant. It is theoretically possible to sort between serious and nonserious privacy harms without looking at what ordinary people want and expect. But, for reasons we discuss below, ignoring popular attitudes is less appealing than taking them into account.

That said, in our view, the role for survey data in Fourth Amendment analysis is important but limited. It is appropriate to ask laypeople whether they expect particular police conduct, how much it bothers them, and whether such conduct might reveal sensitive or embarrassing information. People can give meaningful and reasonably well-informed responses to these questions, and these are the kinds of data we will present in Part III. We think asking peo-

---

Influenced the Supreme Court and Shaped the Meaning of the Constitution 13–14 (Farrar, Straus and Giroux, 2009) ("[O]ver time, as Americans have the opportunity to think through constitutional issues, Supreme Court decisions tend to converge with the considered judgment of the American people. . . . On issue after contentious issue—abortion, affirmative action, gay rights, and the death penalty, to name a few—the Supreme Court has rendered decisions that meet with popular approval and find support in the latest Gallup Poll."). Gerry Rosenberg has articulated skepticism about claims that the Supreme Court's interpretations of the Constitution influence popular beliefs, a skepticism we share. See Gerald N. Rosenberg, Book Review, *The Wonder of It All*, 45 Tulsa L Rev 679, 686–87 (2009). Our hypothesis is that public views influence the Justices' views but that the Court's interpretations of the Constitution do little to influence public beliefs. See note 92.

[79] 529 US 334, 338–39 (2000).

[80] 495 US 91, 98–100 (1990).

[81] 471 US 386, 390–93 (1985).

[82] Kerr, 60 Stan L Rev at 508–10 (cited in note 60).

ple whether the benefits of police surveillance outweigh the costs is much less valuable. Most members of the public lack the expertise and information necessary to make those policy judgments.[83] Hence our doctrinal approach leaves those policy decisions in the hands of judges, who would continue to make post-*Katz* judgments about the reasonableness of a search, and legislatures, which could provide for greater privacy protections than the Fourth Amendment presently requires. We do think judges will do a better job of confronting these trade-offs when they have reliable information about the extent to which the public would be surprised and bothered by particular police tactics. The alternative is for judges to rely on their own intuitions and those of their clerks, which are unlikely to be representative.

In the remainder of this part we argue that public opinion data drawn from nationally representative samples of the population ought to be dispositive on the question of *Katz* prong 1. In our formulation, the question of whether there was a subjective expectation of privacy would be framed as whether people *in general* expect privacy in a given situation. Just as the *Jones* majority pulled the "positive law" question out of the *Katz* framework, we would pull the "probabilistic" inquiry out of prong 2, and make it the central question under *Katz* prong 1. A defendant wishing to claim that a surveillance strategy constitutes a search would need to show that the populace[84] generally regards the law enforcement conduct in question as a violation of privacy expectations. With positive law already consigned to a pre-*Katz* inquiry by *Jones*,[85] our approach would permit courts to distill *Katz* prong 2 down to the "private-facts" inquiry. This would allow for more objective results than the cost-benefit balancing inquiry (i.e., Kerr's "policy model") and, unlike the policy model, it isn't duplicated elsewhere in Fourth Amendment law.[86]

---

[83] Some other empirical research asks respondents to make these normative judgments. See note 113.

[84] See note 149 for elaboration on how the populace might be defined.

[85] After Justice Scalia's death there are only four remaining votes on the Supreme Court favoring the disaggregation of the positive law framework from the *Katz* approach. The law in this area may well hinge on the views of Justice Scalia's eventual replacement.

[86] See text accompanying notes 157–63.

We feel that focusing *Katz* prong 1 on an empirical question is normatively desirable.[87] The Fourth Amendment is designed to safeguard individuals against governmental overreach. When there is a sharp divide between what the courts describe as the Fourth Amendment's scope and what the people actually expect the Fourth Amendment's scope to be, various problems arise. Law-abiding people may take excessive precautions to protect their information, keeping it not only from the state's agents but also from third parties who could put the information to productive uses.[88] Or citizens might make inordinate investments in learning the contours of Fourth Amendment law, time and money that could be better spent elsewhere. Also, mistaken expectations limit the effectiveness of the democratic process as a check on law enforcement surveillance; the public may not move legislatively to protect privacy if they mistakenly believe it is already protected constitutionally. Disconnects between actual law and perceived law may also provide police officers and prosecutors with undue leverage over citizens. Although figuring out whether various possible interpretations of the Fourth Amendment enhance social welfare is a tricky business, we think there is a strong case to be made that misalignment between the law and social expectations is detrimental for both efficiency and fairness-related reasons. So even though an empirical vision of "reasonable expectations of privacy" isn't what Justice Harlan had in mind when he penned his *Katz* concurrence,[89] there are good reasons why ordinary citizens' actual beliefs have become more doctrinally salient in the years that followed.[90]

---

[87] See also text accompanying notes 123–25 for further development of our normative argument. For different, but largely congenial, accounts that argue for the centrality of privacy expectations in Fourth Amendment inquiries, see Christopher Slobogin, *A Defense of Privacy as the Central Value Protected by the Fourth Amendment's Prohibition on Unreasonable Searches*, 48 Tex Tech L Rev 143, 157–62 (2015); Slobogin, 94 Minn L Rev at 1602–04, 08 (cited in note 68).

[88] See Thomas P. Crocker, *The Political Fourth Amendment*, 88 Wash U L Rev 303, 368–78 (2010); William J. Stuntz, *Waiving Rights in Criminal Procedure*, 75 Va L Rev 761, 794 (1989); James J. Tomkovicz, *Beyond Secrecy for Secrecy's Sake: Toward an Expanded Vision of the Fourth Amendment Privacy Province*, 36 Hastings L J 645, 720 (1985).

[89] See text accompanying note 26; Kerr, 82 U Chi L Rev at 124 (cited in note 59).

[90] To be clear, while there are Fourth Amendment decisions like *Kyllo* and *Jardines* in which originalist considerations of what Founding Era citizens would have expected play a role, we do not regard the basic *Katz* test as remotely originalist. See generally *Kyllo v United States*, 533 US 27 (2001); *Florida v Jardines*, 133 S Ct 1409 (2013). Nor do we think that present jurists interpreting *Katz* owe a duty of fidelity to whatever Justice Harlan intended when he penned his concurrence in that case. Popular expectations of privacy do change over

Katz prong 1 is, of course, only part of the threshold Fourth Amendment calculus. Though we think that it should become the focal point for data-driven Fourth Amendment decision making, there are other places where incorporating survey results from nationally representative samples could improve judicial decision making. Namely, prong 2 of *Katz* asks whether society is prepared to recognize a subjective expectation of privacy as reasonable, and data about the degree to which Americans regard particular information as sensitive and embarrassing (Kerr's "private-facts" model) could figure in to this calculus.

It is important at this stage to underscore the difference between two related but distinct empirical questions. One involves the privacy *expectations* of ordinary Americans. The other examines the degree of perceived intrusion, embarrassment, and personal exposure created by the surveillance. These two inquiries are conceptually independent.[91] An example may help. A frequent flier will likely *expect* deeply intrusive searches at airport security, but may still be embarrassed by them and concerned that they will reveal sensitive personal information. Thus expectations are not violated, but intrusion still occurs. Conversely, a person might be greatly surprised if the government scrutinized his monthly natural gas utility bills for the last several years, but may not feel the search embarrassed him or revealed anything of importance about him. In our formulation, the perceived intrusiveness of a search is relevant under *Katz* prong 2, but the expectations of ordinary Americans should be dispositive under *Katz* prong 1.

How would researchers go about measuring the public's expectations of privacy? The most obvious approach would be the one we use here, which is to ask a representative sample of Americans such questions directly. There will inevitably be some heterogeneity

---

time, and under the *Katz* line of cases it is implicit that the scope of constitutional protections will similarly fluctuate. See Monu Bedi, *Facebook and Interpersonal Privacy: Why the Third Party Doctrine Should Not Apply*, 54 BC L Rev 1, 71 (2013). Even originalism-friendly opinions like *Jardines* devote more space to discussing contemporary norms than Founding Era norms, in part because evidence of the latter is so difficult to come by. *Jardines*, 133 S Ct at 1414–16. For a persuasive critique of Fourth Amendment originalism, see David A. Sklansky, *The Fourth Amendment and Common Law*, 100 Colum L Rev 1739 (2000). The question of how much privacy expectations change over time is part of a long-term project that we are just beginning. See note 146.

[91] As a practical matter, there are some connections between expectations and intrusiveness. See text accompanying note 158.

in responses, but we should expect to find broad consensus around many questions involving law enforcement surveillance.[92] There are at least two possible weaknesses to this approach. The first is that there may be a disconnect between actual and reported attitudes. Survey instruments rely on cheap talk by respondents. Respondents have no real skin in the game when we are asking them about their privacy expectations, and researchers employ no lie detectors. As a result, respondents might answer questions in a way that reflects their aspirations rather than their true expectations.[93]

The problem of insincere respondents can never be discounted completely, but it is one with which psychology and the other social sciences have come to terms. That isn't to say that data about the revealed preferences of Americans when it comes to privacy wouldn't be better. They may be,[94] but they are very difficult to collect,[95] especially in the same quantities that we are able to report here. Comfortingly, the available evidence from various well-designed surveys is broadly consistent with observational studies of revealed preferences.[96] In fact, there is a large empirical liter-

---

[92] See generally Christopher Slobogin and Joseph E. Schumacher, *Reasonable Expectations of Privacy and Autonomy in Fourth Amendment Cases: An Empirical Look at "Understandings Recognized and Permitted by Society,"* 42 Duke L J 727 (1993); Matthew B. Kugler, *The Perceived Intrusiveness of Searching Electronic Devices at the Border: An Empirical Study,* 82 U Chi L Rev 1165 (2014). In subsequent work, we will draw on other data we have collected to show that it is common for there to be lay consensus on Fourth Amendment questions. See Matthew B. Kugler and Lior Jacob Strahilevitz, *The Myth of Fourth Amendment Circularity* (in progress).

[93] Daniel J. Solove, *Fourth Amendment Pragmatism,* 51 BC L Rev 1511, 1522–23 (2010).

[94] One approach to collecting such data in the privacy domain is described in Lior Jacob Strahilevitz, *A Social Networks Theory of Privacy,* 72 U Chi L Rev 919, 934–39, 970–73, 983–85 (2005) (discussing whether for the purposes of invasion of privacy tort claims, "reasonable expectations of privacy" should be based on survey research results or observational studies of consumer behavior that utilize social network theory).

[95] The price system sometimes permits the analysis of revealed preferences through large data sets. Unfortunately, the price system does rather little to reveal the private value that Americans place on keeping the government from learning information about them. For example, when someone decides to build a fence around her home, it is difficult to determine the extent to which the purchase was driven by privacy concerns and the extent to which it was driven by security concerns (thwarting trespassers, deterring burglars, etc.). Disentangling the two likely requires surveying the purchaser, which brings us back to square one. The same entanglement can occur online, with nearly all privacy enhancements acting as simultaneous security enhancements.

[96] See Sampo V. Paunonen, *Big Five Factors of Personality and Replicated Predictions of Behavior,* 84 J Personality & Soc Psych 411, 413–21 (2003) (surveying the literature and reporting on the results of original experiments designed to test correlations between survey responses and observed behavior).

ature showing that sufficiently specific attitude measures are often very good predictors of behavior.[97] Social scientists also can use survey strategies to weed out disinterested or insincere respondents, thereby enhancing the correlation between survey responses and actual beliefs. We describe our use of this technique below.[98]

The second potential weakness is that consultation of public attitudes may lead to circularity. By this account, social expectations will change as the law does, so that expectations will eventually conform to policies that were initially rejected.[99] There are two variations on the circularity claim. The first is a story about information dissemination and public opinion updating. On this account, when courts make a good-faith interpretation of the law, members of the public hear about it and update their prior beliefs. To lay our cards on the table, we are unimpressed with this claim. As part of a future project, we have collected significant amounts of data about the extent to which well-publicized legal changes affect ordinary Americans' articulated expectations of privacy. Those data, which will form the core of our next paper, indicate that even prominent Fourth Amendment decisions respondents say they have heard about move the needle of Americans' articulated expectations of privacy very little.[100] A unanimous, well-publicized *Supreme Court* opinion on cell-phone privacy barely affected public expectations on the issue before the Court, and this was true whether respondents were questioned a week after the decision was handed down or nearly a year later. Based on the data we have collected, we would be surprised if any Fourth Amendment decision other than *Miranda*[101] has permeated popular culture and discourse enough to alter significantly the public's expectations about what the police can do.

---

[97] See Icek Ajzen and Martin Fishbein, *Attitude-Behavior Relations: A Theoretical Analysis and Review of Empirical Research*, 84 Psych Bull 888 (1977); Jens Hainmueller, Dominik Hangartner, and Teppei Yamamoto, *Validating Vignette and Conjoint Survey Experiments Against Real-World Behavior*, 112 Proceedings of the National Academy of Sciences 2395 (2015); Jason T. Siegel et al, *Attitude-Behavior Consistency, the Principle of Compatibility, and Organ Donation: A Classic Innovation*, 33 Health Psych 1084 (2014).

[98] See text accompanying note 164.

[99] *Jones*, 132 S Ct at 962 (Alito, J, concurring) ("The *Katz* reasonable expectation of privacy test . . . involves a degree of circularity.").

[100] See Kugler and Strahilevitz, *The Myth of Fourth Amendment Circularity* (in progress) (cited in note 92).

[101] *Miranda v Arizona*, 384 US 436 (1966).

A more sinister circularity story suggests that expectations of privacy can be conditioned. If the President announces on national television that all private residences are now subject to warrantless searches, then people will come to expect such searches.[102] The conditioned-expectations story posits that government actors will proceed in bad faith to expand their power at the expense of the citizenry. Not surprisingly, when the conditioned-response argument is made in the modern American context it is always articulated as a hypothetical. No court or credible scholar has pointed to an instance of a power-hungry elected official acting in such a manner and getting away with it. The conditioned-response story assumes away the inevitable popular counterreaction to transparent government overreaching. Individuals can no doubt be conditioned, but conditioning a hostile body politic in a democratic regime is extremely difficult.[103] And government officials in democracies understand that announcing broad, new, invasive searches that are deeply unpopular is foolhardy, which is why conditioning narratives remain hypothetical. In sum, proponents of the circularity hypothesis overestimate both the visibility and moral authority of government pronouncements with the public. Our data indicate that the real-world effects of the Fourth Amendment's supposed circularity problem are overblown.

Other scholars have previously advocated assessing "reasonable expectations of privacy" using a survey instrument. Christopher Slobogin is the legal scholar who has pioneered this approach.[104]

---

[102] *Smith v Maryland*, 442 US 735, 741 n 5 (1979); Kerr, 60 Stan L Rev at 532 (cited in note 60) ("[I]magine the government announced that the FBI is tapping every single telephone call in the United States to listen for evidence of criminal activity. The invasions of privacy would be extraordinarily severe but no reasonable person would expect privacy in their calls after learning of this fact.").

[103] Arguably Facebook has succeeded in conditioning its users over a lengthy period of time to have diminished expectations of privacy. Paul Ohm, *Branding Privacy*, 97 Minn L Rev 907, 919–22 (2013). Yet even Facebook, which benefits from strong network effects, is obviously constrained by its users' existing preferences. When it takes steps that flout its users' privacy expectation and receives a negative reaction it typically apologizes and backtracks. See Ira S. Rubinstein and Nathaniel Good, *Privacy by Design: A Counterfactual Analysis of Google and Facebook Privacy Incidents*, 28 Berkeley Tech L J 1333, 1392–1405 (2013).

[104] See, for example, Slobogin, *Privacy at Risk* (cited in note 24); Slobogin, 94 Minn L Rev at 1588 (cited in note 68); Slobogin and Schumacher, 42 Duke L J at 727 (cited in note 92).

Slobogin has surveyed students[105] and jury pool respondents[106] to gauge the perceived intrusiveness of various governmental surveillance techniques. A key finding from Slobogin's research is that while respondents' opinions typically track judicial attitudes about whether the technique at issue constitutes a "search" under the Fourth Amendment, scattered and important divergences do arise.[107] For example, under *Hoffa v United States*,[108] it is not a search for police to use undercover informants in criminal investigations, but respondents regard such government investigative techniques as more intrusive than other techniques that the courts have consistently held to be Fourth Amendment searches.[109]

An admitted problem with research by Slobogin and others is that it has not been conducted on a nationally representative sample of Americans.[110] Students obviously skew much younger than the general population, and the jury pool in a particular town will not reflect national sentiment. It is only in the last few years that legal scholars influenced by Slobogin's methods have begun examining the privacy preferences of Americans in a more empirically sound way. The trend owes much to the steeply declining costs of survey research. For example, in 2012 scholars at Berkeley commissioned a poll to assess the attitudes of Americans on the question of whether law enforcement should be required to get a warrant before searching a cell phone incident to an arrest.[111] Some of the same scholars followed up in 2014 with a nationally representative study of con-

---

[105] Slobogin and Schumacher, 42 Duke L J at 737 (cited in note 92). The identities of Slobogin's research subjects has troubled some, though the replication of several significant findings by other scholars using similar samples at different universities has alleviated a few concerns about the external validity of Slobogin's results. See Jeremy A. Blumenthal, Meera Adya, and Jacqueline Mogle, *The Multiple Dimensions of Privacy: Testing "Lay Expectations of Privacy,"* 11 U Pa J Const L 331, 344–45 (2009).

[106] Slobogin, *Privacy at Risk* at 111 (cited in note 24).

[107] Slobogin and Schumacher, 42 Duke L J at 739–42 (cited in note 92).

[108] 385 US 293 (1966); see also *United States v White*, 401 US 745, 752 (1971) (reaffirming *Hoffa*).

[109] Slobogin and Schumacher, 42 Duke L J at 740, 738 tbl 1 (cited in note 92) (noting that the use of a secretary as an undercover agent is deemed noticeably more intrusive by respondents than the search of an office drawer).

[110] See Orin S. Kerr, *Do We Need a New Fourth Amendment?*, 107 Mich L Rev 951, 964 (2009).

[111] Jennifer M. Urban, Chris Jay Hoofnagle, and Su Li, *Mobile Phones and Privacy* 10 (UC Berkeley Public Law Research Paper No 2103405, July 2012), archived at http://ssrn.com/abstract=2103405.

sumer privacy attitudes.[112] That said, no externally valid recent study delves deeply into Americans' Fourth Amendment attitudes.[113] While Slobogin himself has written about *Jones*, his paper on the subject did not draw on any new empirical research about public attitudes toward the mosaic theory, so he never posed Justice Alito's "duration sensitivity" question to research subjects.[114] As a result, there is a dearth of literature on what Americans actually believe with respect to the constitutional issues that the state and federal courts must decide every day. If a judge wanted to follow the probabilistic model in a given case, she would have to decide between relying on dated studies whose external validity has not been established[115] and

---

[112] Chris Jay Hoofnagle and Jennifer M. Urban, *Alan Westin's Privacy Homo Economicus*, 49 Wake Forest L Rev 261 (2014).

[113] We know of only one additional contemporary paper that uses a nationally representative sample to track changes in attitudes about legal questions pending in the courts. See Katerina Linos and Kimberly Twist, *The Supreme Court, the Media, and Public Opinion: Comparing Experimental and Observational Methods* (2015 unpublished working paper, on file with authors). Linos and Twist's sophisticated paper does not examine any Fourth Amendment issues.

Another paper, which postdates ours by a little while, analyzes the public's normative attitudes about Fourth Amendment issues. See Christine S. Scott-Hayward, Henry F. Fradella, and Ryan G. Fischer, *Does Privacy Require Secrecy? Societal Expectations of Privacy in the Digital Age* (July 20, 2015 unpublished working paper, on file with authors). Though the Scott-Hayward and coauthors' paper is well done in many respects, our research strongly suggests that it suffers from external validity problems. Because of budgetary limitations, the paper uses a Mechanical Turk sample as a proxy for ordinary Americans' attitudes. Id at *41–*42. As our research shows, Mechanical Turk respondents are significantly more privacy-protective than the general U.S. population, perhaps because they skew younger. See note 171 and accompanying text. The size of the discrepancy between our representative sample and Mechanical Turk findings was large. We therefore believe that one should not use Mechanical Turk samples to assess the base-rate support for privacy-related beliefs in the general population. It may, however, still be valid to use such samples to evaluate the *relative* intrusiveness of searches. We do not have data specifically on that point. The Scott-Hayward paper also argues that the public's normative beliefs, not its expectations, are relevant, relying on the circularity hypothesis that our subsequent work debunks. Id at *39–*40.

We also note Marc McAllister, *GPS and Cell Phone Tracking: A Constitutional and Empirical Analysis*, 82 U Cin L Rev 207 (2013), and Marc McAllister, *The Fourth Amendment and New Technologies: The Misapplication of Analogical Reasoning*, 36 SIU L J 475 (2012). Both studies have serious methodological problems relating to a lack of clarity about the sample composition, the unusual way results are reported, and the way questions were phrased.

[114] Christopher Slobogin, *Making the Most of United States v. Jones in a Surveillance Society: A Statutory Implementation of Mosaic Theory*, 8 Duke J Const L & Pub Pol 1 (2012). Slobogin's paper is more doctrinal than empirical, and it winds up proposing that surveillance lasting longer than 48 hours generally requires a warrant based on probable cause. Id at 24. The 48-hour threshold is not driven by his survey results. Our data show that this 48-hour distinction is not salient to American citizens. See Table 3 (showing very little difference in attitudes concerning one-day surveillance and one-week surveillance).

[115] Slobogin and Schumacher discuss the external validity of their research at Slobogin and Schumacher, 42 Duke L J at 745–51 (cited in note 92).

relying on guesswork, a straw poll of acquaintances, or other pseudo-scientific approaches.

Even setting aside questions about external validity, Slobogin's survey-based approach has been challenged on other grounds. Scholars wonder whether courts have the capacity to assess popular attitudes,[116] whether popular attitudes will fluctuate wildly from day to day,[117] why the content of constitutional provisions should hinge on those attitudes as opposed to doctrines grounded in prior constitutional and property-related precedents,[118] and whether popular attitudes about complicated legal and technological issues are meaningful.[119] Slobogin has responded to some of these criticisms, noting, for example, that courts routinely interpret survey results in other contexts, like trademark litigation.[120] And he points out that replication should alleviate concerns about random sample fluctuations.[121] We believe Slobogin acquits himself well in the debate, and our studies support many of his points. Notably, our own data on privacy expectations show nearly perfect stability over a time span of almost a year.[122]

That said, concerns about turning public opinion into constitutional doctrine remain. Absent the development of a public choice account for police practices and democratic failures, it is unclear why the content of constitutional law should depend on upholding popular sentiment. We have developed only a brief account here.[123] We do think that the case for placing real weight on survey responses is

---

[116] Kerr, 107 Mich L Rev at 965 (cited in note 110) ("How would judges know when public opinion has changed? And how should courts reconcile dueling surveys?").

[117] Id at 964 ("Results of a survey taken one day, with one audience, with questions phrased in a particular way may not match results from another day, another audience, and another set of questions.").

[118] See, for example, Solove, 51 BC L Rev at 1522 (cited in note 93); Daniel B. Yeager, *Search, Seizure, and the Positive Law: Expectations of Privacy Outside the Fourth Amendment*, 84 J Crim Law & Criminol 249 (1993).

[119] Solove, 51 BC L Rev at 1523 (cited in note 93).

[120] Slobogin, 94 Minn L Rev 1599–1600 (cited in note 68).

[121] Id at 1599.

[122] See Table 7A and Table 7B (comparing the results of Wave 3 to those of Waves 1 and 2); see also note 167 (noting that Wave 1 and Wave 2 of our surveys were statistically indistinguishable on questions concerning *Jones*).

[123] See text accompanying notes 87–90.

strongest when laypeople are being surveyed on issues that are familiar to them. For that reason, our surveys ask people about the
sorts of technologies that they are likely to have encountered in the
world, like email accounts, smartphones, car-based navigation sys-
tems, and computer webcams. With respect to less familiar technology, survey designers must do more work explaining the underlying
technology to respondents, increasing the danger that responses will
be influenced by the researchers' subjective judgments about how to
describe the technology.

In assessing our approach it is important to avoid the mistake
of comparing an admittedly imperfect survey-based methodology
to an idealized alternative. If all judges were well-informed phi-
losopher kings, then there would be good reasons to allow them
to decide all Fourth Amendment questions on purely normative
grounds. But judges are imperfect too. They have their own biases,
their own limitations, and their own misimpressions,[124] and there is
a danger that the effects of these biases will be magnified when
constitutional law is decided by just nine people, three people, or
one person. The system loses the benefits of aggregating the factual
impressions of a large sample,[125] and enhances the risk that the
idiosyncratic characteristics of the unrepresentative decision makers will systematically distort their assessments of the social trade-
offs. While we do not believe that laypeoples' naive priors are particularly useful to help courts resolve every constitutional question,
we do think that they are informative in this context, particularly
since the judges who are deciding Fourth Amendment cases are
less likely than the broader populace to have been targeted or feel
threatened by the surveillance techniques at issue. These naive priors
will be informative, not decisive, precisely because *Katz* has more
than one real prong under our approach.

Nevertheless, there are alternatives to basing "reasonable expectations of privacy" on what ordinary Americans actually say they

---

[124] See, for example, Lee Epstein, William M. Landes, and Richard A. Posner, *The Behavior
of Federal Judges: A Theoretical and Empirical Study of Rational Choice* (Harvard, 2013).

[125] See, for example, Dhammika Dharmapala and Richard H. McAdams, *The Condorcet Jury
Theorem and the Expressive Function of Law: A Theory of Informative Law*, 5 Am L & Econ Rev
1, 6–8 (2003); see also Cass R. Sunstein, *If People Would Be Outraged by Their Rulings, Should
Judges Care?*, 60 Stan L Rev 155, 183–92 (2007) (describing the implications of the Condorcet jury theorem to judicial decision making).

expect. To recall Kerr's framework, the law might use precedents derived from external sources of law, like state property law, to define reasonable expectations.[126] Alternatively, the law might focus on how sensitive the information sought by the government is. Finally, the courts could engage in a utilitarian balancing calculus, weighing the privacy costs and security benefits of requiring a warrant when the government seeks information of a particular kind.[127] As we note above, there is a role for each of these frameworks to play in Fourth Amendment law, but incorporating survey data about public expectations and the costs of surveillance will make each of these inquiries less dependent on the life experiences and ideological priors of judges who happen to be resolving a case.

Consider a controversial problem in contemporary law—does the Fourth Amendment prohibit the National Security Agency's (NSA) warrantless collection of metadata concerning email and telephone traffic from tens of millions of Americans?[128] Figuring out whether the NSA's program satisfies a cost-benefit calculus is close to impossible given the limits of available knowledge.[129] Public opinion, however, furnishes one relevant data point in such a calculus by providing a measure of the extent to which the program enhances or diminishes Americans' sense of freedom and safety. These sorts of data can be obtained at a relatively low cost through the surveys

---

[126] For a thoughtful and extensive argument along these lines, see William Baude and James Y. Stern, *The Positive Law Model of the Fourth Amendment*, 129 Harv L Rev (forthcoming 2016) (unpublished draft on file with authors).

[127] See text accompanying notes 60–65. Of course, the courts could substitute a deontological framework for a consequentialist one in assessing the propriety of government surveillance. See Sklansky, 102 Cal L Rev at 1110–15 (cited in note 17).

[128] See generally *Klayman v Obama*, 957 F Supp 2d 1 (DDC 2013) (holding that parts of the NSA program are searches); *Smith v Obama*, 24 F Supp 3d 1005 (D Idaho 2014) (argued before 9th Circuit on appeal, Dec 8, 2014).

[129] Assuming the program is challenged in court within a few years of its implementation, nobody is likely to have a handle on the extent to which the program produces actionable intelligence, the costs of security officials' time spent responding to false leads generated by the program, the extent to which its existence chills commerce, the effect the program may have on political expression and the consequences for democracy of marginally more inhibited communications, the danger that information stored in the database will eventually fall into the hands of America's enemies through espionage or hacking, and a host of other pertinent considerations. Courts do their best to muddle through these extremely difficult issues, but it appears likely that at the time of the suit they will have before them reasonably accurate information about the government's out-of-pocket expenditures on the NSA program, some statements from civil libertarians expressing alarm at the existence of the program, and little else of probative value.

we describe below.[130] It is a sensible place to start the analysis even if it does not provide all the necessary answers.

A final point about the policy model is worth repeating. There is already plenty of room elsewhere in Fourth Amendment doctrine for the courts to engage in a cost-benefit balancing process. The determination that police conduct amounted to a search does not resolve the Fourth Amendment questions. Rather, once police conduct is found to have amounted to a search, the courts then shift their attention to the question of whether the police's conduct was reasonable.[131] As it has evolved in recent decades, this judicial inquiry often focuses on a balancing approach that weighs the costs and benefits of the government conduct at issue.[132] Considering the utilitarian calculus with respect to both the scope of the Fourth Amendment *and also* the level of process that reasonableness requires has the effect of double counting utilitarian interests, potentially slanting the doctrine against finding violations of the Constitution.[133] We regard that essential part of Fourth Amendment analysis as the right spot for judges to evaluate the policy trade-offs associated with surveillance strategies.

Survey data also can play a role in applying the "private-facts" model that would become the core of *Katz* prong 2 under our framework. Determining what information counts as sensitive requires numerous subjective judgments. Sensitivity depends a great deal on context, on the identity of the recipient of the information, on the preferences of the data privacy subject, the risks posed by present or future disclosure, and the priors of the person evaluating the information.[134] People and even cultures are heterogeneous with respect to what information about themselves they are willing to share, with

---

[130] The out-of-pocket cost for Wave 3 of our large-sample survey was $4,550, but that survey instrument was used to generate results relevant to four separate research papers by the authors. Obviously, this figure does not include the authors' imputed wages for designing the survey and analyzing the results.

[131] See, for example, *Grady v North Carolina*, 135 S Ct 1368, 1371 (2015).

[132] See note 71.

[133] Some readers and courts might prefer to see a purely normative judicial inquiry in *Katz* step 2 and the incorporation of survey data about sensitivity and embarrassment into the reasonableness inquiry. We think there is a case to be made for that approach instead of the one we advocate in the text. What we object to is redundant double-counting.

[134] See, for example, Helen Nissenbaum, *Privacy in Context: Technology, Policy, and the Integrity of Social Life* (Stanford, 2009); Paul Ohm, *Sensitive Information*, 88 S Cal L Rev 1125 (2015).

whom they are willing to share it, and under what circumstances sharing is appropriate.[135] Differences in individuals' psychological worldviews contribute to this heterogeneity,[136] and the result is that it can be difficult to determine what counts as sensitive.

Yet this again leads us to public opinion data. Supreme Court cases are, as Kerr notes, inconsistent in their application of the private-facts model. Under that model, dog-sniff tests used to determine whether drugs are inside a tent or chemical tests that indicate whether a powder that has spilled outside a FedEx package en route do not amount to searches because all the tests do is help police sort between contraband and legal substances. The fact that an object is contraband is deemed nonsensitive.[137] But if the police open a package to determine its contents and find drugs inside or bring a drug-sniffing dog to someone's front porch, that *is* a search, with the private-facts model receiving little attention.[138] And if a police officer who is lawfully in a home nudges stereo equipment a few inches to see its serial number so he can check whether it has been reported stolen, that's a search, even though the serial number sought and seen is not sensitive.[139] The law's coherence is undermined by the fact that the cases variably veer between treating the sensitivity of the information sought as decisive and dismissing it as irrelevant.

Against this backdrop, a more objective and replicable way to address the question of sensitivity is to poll a representative sample of ordinary Americans and see what they say is sensitive in what context. Christopher Slobogin has shown exactly how this sort of research can be done, constructing a hierarchy of more- and less-sensitive data based on popular attitudes.[140] Taking a shortcut by substituting judicial hunches for the actual view of the populace seems

---

[135] See generally James Q. Whitman, *The Two Western Cultures of Privacy: Dignity Versus Liberty*, 113 Yale L J 1151 (2004); Adam M. Samaha and Lior Jacob Strahilevitz, *Don't Ask, Must Tell, and Other Combinations*, 103 Cal L Rev 919 (2015).

[136] Matthew B. Kugler, *Affinities in Privacy Attitudes: A Psychological Approach to Unifying Informational and Decisional Privacy*, available at http://papers.ssrn.com/sol3/papers.cfm?abstract_id=2469562.

[137] Kerr, 60 Stan L Rev at 513–15 (cited in note 60) (discussing *United States v Jacobson* and *Caballes v Illinois*).

[138] Id at 515; *Florida v Jardines*, 133 S Ct 1409, 1417 (2013).

[139] *Arizona v Hicks*, 480 US 321, 325–26 (1987); Kerr, 60 Stan L Rev at 514–15 (cited in note 60).

[140] See, for example, Slobogin, *Privacy at Risk* at 110–13, 183–84 (cited in note 24).

particularly misguided. To be sure, there may be some easy cases where judges will conclude, uncontroversially, that information is highly sensitive (take social security numbers, for example[141]), but in these easy cases survey respondents will get the answer right too.[142] Contemporary polling on sensitivity produces a hierarchy that many readers will find intuitive. Americans regard social security numbers, a list of medications they take, and the contents of their phone conversations as highly sensitive, the list of websites they have visited and queries they have run in search engines as moderately sensitive, and their basic purchasing habits and the sort of media they like to consume as not terribly sensitive.[143] Some readers may prefer to construct the hierarchy differently than the median citizen does, but the popular consensus reflects a level-headed judgment about what sort of information would be dangerous to the individual if broadly disclosed and (relatedly) what sort of information most people tend to guard closely. The principles underlying popular attitudes are more readily comprehensible than those underlying the Court's private-facts cases.[144] In presenting this article, we sometimes get accused of over-privileging the naive priors of laypeople. But when the judgments of the crowd are placed alongside those of jurists, the crowd doesn't seem less wise. Of course one can quibble with majoritarian judgments. Perhaps survey respondents underestimate the threat that is associated with people knowing what websites they visit, but if so the federal courts have erred in the same way.[145]

---

[141] See, for example, *Greidinger v Davis*, 988 F2d 1344 (4th Cir 1993).

[142] See, for example, Pew Research Center, *Public Perceptions of Privacy and Security in the Post-Snowden Era* at 7 (Nov 12, 2014), archived at http://www.pewinternet.org/files/2014/11/PI_PublicPerceptionsofPrivacy_111214.pdf (reporting that 90% of Americans surveyed describe their social security number as "very sensitive," a much higher rate than any other sort of information about which respondents were surveyed).

[143] Lee Rainie, *The State of Privacy in America: What We Learned*, Pew Research Center (Jan 20, 2016), archived at http://www.pewresearch.org/fact-tank/2016/01/20/the-state-of-privacy-in-america/.

[144] Indeed, the four dissenters in *Jardines* effectively point out the incoherence of the Court's conflicting approaches to dog sniffs. See *Florida v Jardines*, 133 S Ct at 1424–25 (Alito, J, dissenting). To make sense of the case law, it is necessary to either embrace a slippery act-omission dichotomy or make highly contestable assumptions about the dynamic effects of particular enforcement policies, along the lines of those suggested by Kerr, 60 Stan L Rev at 534–35 (cited in note 60).

[145] *See United States v Forrester*, 512 F3d 500, 510 (9th Cir 2008) (holding that there is no Fourth Amendment reasonable expectation of privacy in a list of IP addresses one has visited).

And here is the rub. We want law enforcement and security personnel to be able to assess the legality of such programs ex ante. Assessing the social welfare effects of a new investigative technique is even harder ex ante than it would be ex post, but decisions to greenlight an investigative strategy have to be made ex ante. Can a local police chief or CIA director commission a poll where she hires reputable survey researchers to figure out where public sentiment is on dozens of new investigative techniques that the department or agency is considering implementing? Yes, and she can do so on a tight budget these days. A good social scientist might be hired to design and run a survey for less than the price of ten or twenty outside counsel billable hours,[146] and if even that is too pricey our own aim is to collect lots of these data over time and make them freely available on the Internet. We provide some of these data in Table 9.

D. HOW SURVEY RESEARCH CAN RESTORE COHERENCE
TO KATZ DOCTRINE

This brings us to our final point before we dive into the data. Recall that the Supreme Court's *Katz* test is articulated as a two-prong inquiry—the courts are to look to subjective and objective expectations of privacy. Yet it appears that *Katz*'s subjective prong has atrophied. For this development, Orin Kerr blames a misreading of Justice Harlan's original *Katz* opinion by the Supreme Court in cases like *Smith v Maryland*, which articulated *Katz*'s subjective prong in terms of how much privacy a reasonable defendant would expect with respect to numbers he dialed into a land-line telephone's handset.[147] But what if there is a better way to be faithful to both *Smith* and the version of *Katz* that emerged from *Jones*?

Integrating *Smith v Maryland* with *Jones*, one could instead apply the *Katz* test in three steps. Beginning with *Katz*, through the lens of *Jones*, one would ask whether police conduct infringed on a suspect's property right. If the police committed a trespass, then the conduct amounts to a search and the courts need only ask whether

---

[146] The authors would like to conduct surveys like the ones we describe in this article on an annual basis and to make the results of our surveys available online for free. To the extent that courts begin relying on survey data in Fourth Amendment contexts, we would expect other academic survey researchers to launch similar efforts, creating a large repository of current public domain opinion research. See note 113.

[147] See Kerr, 82 U Chi L Rev at 128–33 (cited in note 59).

the warrantless search was reasonable. Second, assuming there was no trespass, a court would apply *Katz*'s two traditional prongs. For prong 1, it would examine whether privacy was expected in a particular situation. Because getting inside the defendant's head is neither easy nor helpful, and it will always be tempting for a defendant to claim falsely (for the benefit of an evidentiary motion) that he did, in fact, expect privacy,[148] the law should use the sentiments of the median American citizen as a proxy for the defendant's subjective expectation of privacy. If more Americans would have expected privacy in a particular situation than not, it is reasonable to assume that the defendant did too. Arguably even a lower threshold should be used, or courts could allow some consideration of heterogeneous privacy expectations across race and gender lines.[149]

Assuming the police acted in a way contrary to the expectations of the median American or the median American of a protected class, the court would shift its attention to *Katz*'s second prong—whether the defendant's subjective expectation of privacy is one society is prepared to accept as reasonable. Because *Jones* moved the "positive law" inquiry outside of *Katz* and our doctrinal suggestion moves the "probabilistic" model from *Katz* prong 2 to *Katz* prong 1, the second

---

[148] It is perhaps puzzling why the law should care inherently about the individual defendant's actual expectation of privacy. Given that courts articulate precedents that guide thousands of people who will never litigate, a generally applicable inquiry into whether most people actually would have expected privacy in a (recurring) circumstance is more helpful. From an ex ante perspective, improving the alignment between the law and expected outcomes reduces the costs associated with learning the law and modifying one's behavior. See notes 88–89 and accompanying text.

[149] One might argue that if most members of a minority group would expect privacy in a particular setting, then *Katz* prong 1 should be satisfied regardless of whether a particular defendant happens to be a member of that minority. In our data set, neither race nor gender has any measurable association with privacy expectations toward GPS tracking. But we can imagine situations in which race or gender could influence peoples' expectations, and in those instances society might want to make sure that the law protects potentially marginalized subgroup members. A good example is *Safford Unified School District #1 v Redding*, 557 US 364 (2009), a case involving a school's search of a thirteen-year-old girl's undergarments. Justice Ginsburg has said that during the Justices' arguments about the case, she was able to convince her colleagues that a thirteen-year-old girl has different concerns and expectations about being forced to remove her clothes than a thirteen-year-old boy. See Emily Bazelon, *The Place of Women on the Court*, NY Times MM22 (July 7, 2009). To do that in a manner consistent with the Fourteenth Amendment, Fourth Amendment doctrine likely needs to protect everyone. The existence of privacy expectations among some oddly configured and obscure subgroup—say, Buddhist soccer moms in suburban Nebraska—would be insufficient to create reasonable expectations of privacy for everyone. Were it otherwise, then data miners could always satisfy our *Katz* prong 1 test. Moreover, law enforcement cannot be required to anticipate every obscure subgroup's prevalent privacy expectations. For those reasons, a court open to minoritarian expectations of privacy might focus on categories like race and gender.

prong of *Katz* now gives the courts an opportunity to consider the "private-facts" model. Courts must have a sense of what information is considered "private" to assess whether a particular technique implicates sensitive "private facts."

We think this approach is basically what the Supreme Court was trying to do in *Smith v Maryland*,[150] though the Court's execution left much to be desired. In *Smith* the issue before the Court was whether law enforcement's use of a pen register to record all the numbers dialed on a suspect's phone amounted to a search. The Court began by examining *Katz*'s first prong. As the Court saw it:

> [W]e doubt that people in general entertain any actual expectation of privacy in the numbers they dial. All telephone users realize that they must "convey" phone numbers to the telephone company, since it is through telephone company switching equipment that their calls are completed. . . . Telephone users, in sum, typically know that they must convey numerical information to the phone company; that the phone company has facilities for recording this information; and that the phone company does in fact record this information for a variety of legitimate business purposes. Although subjective expectations cannot be scientifically gauged, it is too much to believe that telephone subscribers, under these circumstances, harbor any general expectation that the numbers they dial will remain secret.[151]

The Court recognizes the difficulty of figuring out what Smith thought, so it pivots to the question of what people in general think about the privacy of call information.[152]

Counsel for Smith argued to the Court that regardless of what "telephone users in general" thought when they dialed their numbers, Smith himself expected privacy because he placed the call from inside his residence.[153] The Court rejected this argument too,

---

[150] 442 US 735 (1979).

[151] Id at 742–43.

[152] To be sure, its empirical intuitions were likely off-base. It cited no evidence for its broad assertions about what "all telephone users" and "most people" believed in the 1970s, and some of its factual inferences seem to assume a higher level of sophistication than ordinary Americans typically possess. See *Smith*, 442 US at 748–49 & n 1 (Marshall dissenting). The Court played fast-and-loose with some facts. The majority notes that the phone call at issue was a local call, not a long-distance call. Given that many Americans at the time paid a flat monthly fee for local calls and saw no itemized bills for them, it is possible that many Americans would have believed the phone company kept no records of outgoing calls.

[153] Id at 743.

once again drawing on the views of telephone users in general to do so. As the Court wrote, "Regardless of his location, petitioner had to convey that number to the telephone company in precisely the same way if he wished to complete his call. The fact that he dialed the number on his home phone rather than on some other phone could make no conceivable difference, nor could any subscriber rationally think that it would."[154] With this sentence, the Court indicated that it hardly cared what Smith himself thought.[155] A rational subscriber could not expect that the numbers he dialed would remain private, so Smith would still lose under prong 1. The Court then noted that "even if petitioner did harbor some subjective expectation that the phone numbers he dialed would remain private," such an expectation would not satisfy *Katz*'s objective prong.[156]

In summary, then, we believe there is a good case to be made for interpreting Fourth Amendment law in a manner consistent with *Smith v Maryland* but in some tension with other pronouncements by the Court. Rather than throwing overboard the first prong of *Katz*'s canonical test, as many courts seem to be doing,[157] we would propose resuscitating it by making popular expectations an important part of the inquiry into whether an individual maintained reasonable expectations of privacy in a particular setting. The costs of obtaining reliable evidence about such expectation have fallen dramatically, and with those diminished costs come increased predictability. Under our approach, popular sentiment gauged by reliable social science methods would become a necessary (though not sufficient) element of a court's determination that a particular investigative technique amounted to a search. If survey results suggested that the use of technology violated people's expectations, then the courts would turn to an examination of the sensitivity of the information sought and obtained.

We want to make two final points before concluding this part. First, there will surely be some overlap between expectations and sensitivity. Police surveillance into the interior of a home is deeply

---

[154] Id.

[155] See also note 148.

[156] Id.

[157] See Kerr, 82 U Chi L Rev at 131 (cited in note 59).

troublesome to people both because of what the investigation looks like and what it reveals. Indeed, it is very interesting that while both Justice Alito and Justice Sotomayor arguably embraced the mosaic theory in *Jones*, Alito focused on popular expectations in his articulation of the mosaic theory and Sotomayor emphasized the sensitivity of the information gathered through long-term surveillance.[158]

Second, though both our approach and Slobogin's approach are driven by survey data, we use these data in different ways. Slobogin uses survey results to assemble a hierarchy of searches, scaled to the perceived intrusiveness of the search, and then balances the proportional costs of that intrusiveness against the security benefits of the surveillance.[159] His surveys invite normative judgments on the part of laypeople, and some subsequent researchers have done likewise.[160] We, by contrast, are primarily asking for descriptive assessment by laypeople—how unexpected would this be?—and then sliding their responses into the existing *Katz* framework for determining the Fourth Amendment's scope. So while there are important commonalities and areas of agreement, we are collecting more representative data, about different questions, and putting those data to a divergent doctrinal use. That said, we think a data-driven approach to determining sensitivity—along the lines suggested by Slobogin—would represent an improvement on current practice. In part to promote dialogue between his approach and ours, we asked the traditional Slobogin intrusiveness question in Wave 3 and describe how it relates to the expectation data in Part III.E.

Having made the case for survey research's relevance, we will now present the results of our research into the public's attitudes regarding the key doctrinal issue left open by *United States v Jones*. When law enforcement obtains geolocation information from a criminal suspect without effecting a trespass onto land or chattels, how long can the surveillance continue before a warrant is required?

---

[158] Compare *Jones*, 132 S Ct at 962–63 (Alito, J, concurring), with *Jones*, 132 S Ct at 955–56 (Sotomayor, J, concurring).

[159] Slobogin, *Privacy at Risk* at 180–96 (cited in note 24).

[160] See Scott-Hayward et al, *Does Privacy Require Secrecy?* at 39–40 (unpublished) (cited in note 113).

III. Empirical Data about Views on Surveillance Duration

So far we have shown how public opinion surveys can help resolve Fourth Amendment questions about what constitutes a search. Hard data about Americans' expressed beliefs are highly relevant to the constitutional inquiry. The data could be decisive in some cases. But this raises an obvious problem. What if the American people are as divided as the lower courts over the question of duration salience? Happily, it turns out that American citizens have coalesced around two clear points of consensus. First, the duration of geolocation tracking strikes the lion's share of Americans as irrelevant to the question of whether a reasonable expectation of privacy has been violated. Second, Americans are nearly two and a half times more likely to view geolocation surveillance of any duration as infringing a reasonable expectation of privacy as they are to reach the opposite conclusion.

A. PARTICIPANTS, PROCEDURE, AND MEASURES FOR WAVES 1 AND 2

A weighted sample of adult Americans was recruited by Toluna, a professional survey firm with an established panel.[161] The sample was drawn to mirror closely the American population as a whole across various demographic dimensions.[162] The panel was recruited in two waves but, as there are no differences between waves on any of the relevant measures, the results are combined for most of

---

[161] For discussion of demographically weighted panels and online versus telephone surveys, see generally J. Michael Brick, *The Future of Survey Sampling*, 75 Pub Opinion Q 872, 881–85 (2011); Dan Farrell and James C. Petersen, *The Growth of Internet Research Methods and the Reluctant Sociologist*, 80 Sociological Inquiry 114, 116–20 (2010); Robert P. Berrens et al, *The Advent of Internet Surveys for Political Research: A Comparison of Telephone and Internet Samples*, 11 Pol Analysis 1, 5–21 (2003).

[162] The sample was 51.3% female; 80.6% of the sample identified as White, 11.5% as Black, and 4.6% as South or East Asian. On a separate question, 16.7% reported identifying as Hispanic or Latino. The median age was 51 (range 18–95, $M = 48.56$, $SD = 16.80$). On a scale ranging from 1 (very liberal) to 7 (very conservative), the mean response was 4.23 ($SD = 1.72$), indicating a politically moderate sample. Slightly more of the sample than the national population as a whole had completed at least some college coursework. In the sample, 14.1% had graduate degrees, 28.7% had four-year college degrees, 23.3% had two-year degrees, 32.2% had high school degrees, and 1.6% had not completed high school. According to the U.S. Census Bureau, 12.7% of those 35–39 have graduate degrees, a further 22.6% have four-year degrees, 10.8% have two-year degrees, 42.8% have a high school degree but have not completed any college degree, and 11.2% do not have a high school degree. See United States Census Bureau, Educational Attainment in the United States: 2012—Detailed Tables, archived at http://www.census.gov/hhes/socdemo/education/data/cps/2012/tables.html.

our data analysis.[163] The final sample contained 1,461 participants, all of whom were adult U.S. citizens.[164]

For the key question, participants were asked, Would it "violate people's reasonable expectations of privacy if law enforcement" (1) used a car's onboard GPS system to locate it on public streets without the owner's permission? (2) used a car's onboard GPS system to track its movements on public streets for one day without the owner's permission? (3) same, but for one week? (4) same, but for one month?

Participants answered these four questions on response scales that ranged from 1 (definitely not) to 5 (definitely yes). The questions asked about the use of a car's own GPS system—rather than a GPS tracking device installed by police—to better reflect the types of nontrespass cases that have arisen in the wake of *Jones*.[165]

B. MAIN RESULTS

The participants were more likely than not to believe that this type of GPS tracking violated reasonable expectations of privacy. As can be seen in Table 1, roughly twice as many participants scored above rather than below the scale's midpoint on each question. Also, the response mean was significantly above the scale's midpoint for each of the four questions.[166] These data therefore provide a clear answer to whether GPS tracking violates reasonable expectations of privacy in the eyes of ordinary citizens.

In addition to this baseline expectation of privacy, there was a small yet discernible effect of tracking duration.[167] People were more

---

[163] Wave 1 data were gathered June 11–12, 2014. Wave 2 data were gathered July 1–2, 2014. There were differences between these waves on other measures, but those differences are not relevant to this project.

[164] The survey instrument contained a question directing participants to show that they were paying attention by selecting a particular answer choice. Only participants who responded correctly to this question were included in the analysis.

[165] See notes 31–44 and accompanying text. We avoided asking about the duration of geolocation tracking via cell-phone towers because we knew the *Riley* case, involving the privacy of cell-phone contents when the phone's owner is arrested, would be decided between Wave 1 and Wave 2.

[166] One-sample *t*-tests revealed that all mean scores were significantly above the scale's midpoint value of 3. The *t*-values for locate, one day, one week, and one month were 10.29, 13.42, 14.48, and 15.41, respectively. All are significant at $p < .001$.

[167] A mixed analysis of variance was conducted to examine whether there were consistent differences between participants' responses to the four GPS tracking questions. There were

Table 1

Effect of Duration on Privacy Expectation

	M	*SD*	% Below Midpoint	% Above Midpoint
Locate	3.41	(1.51)	28	51
Track 1 day	3.53	(1.51)	25	56
Track 1 week	3.57	(1.51)	25	58
Track 1 month	3.61	(1.51)	24	59

NOTE.—Responses were on a 1–5 scale with higher values corresponding with greater invasion of privacy. All pairwise comparisons are significant.

inclined to say that a person's reasonable expectation of privacy is violated by month-long tracking than by week-long, more by week-long than day-long, and more by day-long than instantaneous.[168]

This effect of duration on expectations hides an underlying consistency in responses across measure. Most participants give the same response to each of these four questions, and only a handful show the kind of rising trend pattern implied by the gradually increasing means. As can be seen in Table 2, nearly 40% of respondents consistently reported that people's expectations of privacy would be violated in all these situations (giving ratings of all fours or all fives).[169] A further 16.9% consistently reported that they believed expectations of privacy were not violated (all ones or all twos), and 11% consistently gave the middle response (all threes). Only 5.3% gave responses that started low—stating that expectations of privacy were not violated—and ended high. This is the pattern of responses that would be consistent with Justice Alito's view in *Jones* that surveillance duration is highly salient, and it was nearly eight times less popular than the view that all durations of geolocation tracking equally violate people's expectations of privacy.

The "none of these patterns" category represents a puzzle. A portion of the respondents in that category appeared to be particularly sensitive to the use of a GPS device to determine where a

---

no effects of wave and no interaction between wave and duration. Wave $F(1, 1459) = .82$, $p = .37$; interaction $F(1.98, 2884.80) = .16, p = .85$. A Greenhouse-Geisser correction was used for the within-subjects portion of this analysis because Mauchly's test revealed a sphericity violation.

[168] $F(1.98, 2884.80) = 33.62, p < .001, \eta 2 = .023$. All pairwise comparisons are significant at the $p < .05$ level.

[169] Fully 45.4% of respondents gave only fours or fives (in some combination) on this question, versus 19% who gave only ones or twos. This is a 2.39:1 ratio.

Table 2

Patterns of Privacy Responses

Response	%
Consistently high	39.5
Consistently middle	11.0
Consistently low	16.9
Rising trend that does not cross midpoint	11.8
Rising trend that crosses the midpoint	5.3
None of these patterns	15.5

NOTE.—Proportion of participants using each of the above response patterns.

vehicle is *right now*, reporting a high level of privacy invasion for that item and lower scores for longer duration monitoring. Others may have believed that long-term tracking would necessarily be less granular than short-term tracking, or simply been confused. The study was not designed to differentiate between these perspectives, so we cannot make any definitive statement about what was driving these relatively rare responses.

The level of consistency appears to be even higher if one looks question by question. Table 3 reports the percentage of people giving the same response to each possible pair of questions. Obviously there is more consistency between neighboring questions—locate is closer to one day than to one week, etc.—but the general theme is one of extreme consistency. As mentioned above, most courts that have tried to draw a duration distinction have put the line somewhere between a day and a month. Here, more than 81% of respondents gave the same scores to month- and day-long tracking. The expectations judgment, then, appears to be qualitative rather than quantitative: conduct is a search, or it is not. Duration is largely irrelevant.

In a follow-up study (reported in the Online Supplement OS.A), we tested variants of the question reported here that altered both the question text, whether it asked about "expectations of privacy," "reasonable expectations of privacy," or merely "privacy," as well as whether the question referred to "people's" privacy versus "your" privacy. The changes in privacy wording had no effect on the pattern of consistency reported above.[170] We therefore have reason to believe that our results are robust to minor variations in question

---

[170] The use of first-person wording only had the effect of slightly elevating privacy expectations across the board. This is consistent with a similar effect reported by Slobogin

Table 3

Percentage of Respondents Whose Scores Are
Identical Across Question Pairs

	1 Day (%)	1 Week (%)	1 Month (%)
Locate	77.9	72.4	71.6
1 day		83.4	81.2
1 week			91.2

wording. We also observed that the sample in that follow-up study, which was from Amazon's Mechanical Turk rather than a representative sample like the ones reported above, was substantially more privacy protective.[171] This leads us to be very concerned about the use of Mechanical Turk to establish base rates in this type of privacy research.

C. EXPLANATIONS

Respondents in Wave 2 who reported consistently low or consistently high privacy expectations were asked to report their reasoning on a subsequent page. This page noted that the participants had given consistent responses and gave a list of reasons that would support their doing so. They were asked to select the best one or two of the provided answers, or to contribute their own.

To our surprise, the dominant option among the minority who reported consistently low expectations of privacy is an articulation of the third-party doctrine: the car's driver is sharing the information of their location with a number of parties and, as such, assumes the risk that it will be shared with the government (see Table 4). As

and Schumacher, 42 Duke L J at 759 (cited in note 92). First- versus third-person wording did not affect the consistency pattern.

[171] The nationally representative sample gave mean expectation ratings for locate, one day, one week, and one month searches of 3.41, 3.53, 3.57, and 3.61, respectively (Table 1). The same numbers for the identically worded question (third person, reasonable expectations) from the Mechanical Turk collection were 4.02, 4.22, 4.32, and 4.35, respectively, an average difference of .70 on a five-point scale. To give some sense of magnitude, .70 is also roughly the difference in expectation ratings we observe between examining the content of a person's emails and inspecting a hotel guest registry (see Table 9). Similarly, the proportion of people with consistently high responses goes from 39.50% to 49.20%, while the proportion with consistently low responses goes from 16.90% to 5.88%. See also Ruogu Kang et al, *Privacy Attitudes of Mechanical Turk Workers and the U.S. Public*, USENIX Association Tenth Symposium on Usable Privacy and Security 37, 42 (2014), archived at https://www.usenix.org/system/files/conference/soups2014/soups14-paper-kang.pdf.

Table 4

Reasons Given by Those with Consistently Low Privacy
Expectations (16.9% of the Sample)

Reason	%
The driver of the car is already sharing the information from the GPS with several companies (e.g., OnStar, the car manufacturer, the company that owns the GPS satellites, etc.) so the driver should expect that the same information can be shared with law enforcement.	65.19
A car is being driven on public roads, so any police car in the vicinity already could lawfully determine a car's location or even follow the car for a month.	29.63
It is very important that the police be able to keep the population safe, and privacy interests should give way to public safety interests.	25.19
Only sensitive information like medical history, sexual behavior, or political beliefs should be private and someone's whereabouts during a particular day or month isn't sensitive.	20.00
Dangerous driving is an activity that puts others' lives at risk, and cars are often used to commit crimes, so drivers should not expect any privacy behind the wheel.	20.00
Privacy is a relic of the past. In 2014, people really should not expect privacy in any settings, especially when technology is involved.	17.04
Other	6.67

NOTE.—Numbers display the percentage of participants selecting each of the available options. Participants were asked to select the best one or two options, but were not prevented from checking more than two boxes.

it has been applied by the courts, the third-party doctrine has been routinely attacked for not being consistent with everyday under-standings of privacy.[172] It is therefore particularly interesting to see that most of those who express low privacy expectations actually do cite it as a driving force in their analysis. Less than half as many participants cite the explanation that the authors would have predicted: that the car is visible on public roads and could be monitored there by other means. This type of reasoning, suggestively endorsed by the Supreme Court in *United States v Karo*,[173] played a distinct second fiddle to the unexpectedly popular third-party doctrine. Other plausible theories did not attract high levels of support.

---

[172] See, for example, Slobogin and Schumacher, 42 Duke L J at 734, 740 (cited in note 92); Sonia K. McNeil, Note, *Privacy and the Modern Grid*, 25 Harv J L & Tech 199, 214–15 (2011); see also sources cited note 20.

[173] 468 US 705, 717–19 (1984).

Two concerns predominated among those who consistently exhibited high privacy expectations: (1) that the police would abuse GPS tracking if they were free to use it, and (2) that even locating a car through GPS tracking imposes substantial restrictions on personal freedom (see Table 5). The first of these concerns does not directly speak to privacy expectations and may indicate a general discomfort with granting the police the power to invade the privacy of citizens absent some type of process. The second echoes part of the concern expressed by Justice Sotomayor: that monitoring of GPS information is not harmless and may chill certain types of lawful behaviors.[174]

One theory rejected by these respondents was that the sheer impracticality of locating or tracking a random vehicle in a pre-GPS world—requiring a huge investment of resources—makes the tracking unexpected. Lest this idea be dismissed as an obvious straw man, consider Justice Sotomayor's view that long-standing resource constraints on government investigations continue to inform reasonable expectations of privacy,[175] and Justice Alito's discussion of the "very tiny constable" needed for eighteenth-century carriage tracking.[176] There is something appealing in the theory that it violates people's privacy expectations when law enforcement acquires a seemingly magical new ability to gather information about the activities of the citizenry. Yet less than 10% of even privacy-conscious participants think in those terms.

D. PERSONALITY DIFFERENCES

We approach the issue of Fourth Amendment law with a particular interest in the psychological underpinnings of privacy sentiment. Scholarly understandings of the psychology of privacy are in their infancy, and there have been only a few papers considering whether people with strongly protective privacy views are system-

---

[174] *Jones*, 132 S Ct at 955 (Sotomayor, J, concurring).

[175] Id at 956 (Sotomayor, J, concurring) ("[B]ecause GPS monitoring is cheap in comparison to conventional surveillance techniques . . . it evades the ordinary checks that constrain abusive law enforcement practices: 'limited police resources . . .'").

[176] In the majority, Justice Scalia analogized the state's action in *Jones* to "a constable's concealing himself in the target's coach in order to track its movements," which would amount to trespassing. 132 S Ct at 950 n 3. Justice Alito appeared to find this risible. See id at 958 n 3 (Alito, J, concurring) ("[T]his would have required either a gigantic coach, a very tiny constable, or both—not to mention a constable with incredible fortitude and patience.").

Table 5

Reasons Given for Consistently High Privacy Expectations (39.5% of the Sample)

Reason	%
If the police could do this to anyone at any time they would very likely abuse the power.	58.74
It really restricts personal freedom for the police to be able to locate a car whenever they feel like it, and that kind of privacy shouldn't be compromised.	54.55
It is wrong for the police to use a person's own GPS system to track them because it is their own property.	35.31
The police might learn just as much about a person from one day's monitoring as from one month's, so they're both equally intrusive.	21.33
Privacy interests are very important, and public safety interests should always give way to them.	19.58
The police could not track a car's location using officers in squad cars without spending lots of resources, so people don't expect it.	9.79
Other	4.20

NOTE.—Numbers display the percentage of participants selecting each of the available options. Participants were asked to select the best one or two options, but were not prevented from checking more than two boxes.

atically different than others.[177] Our survey instrument therefore contained several measures that are useful for mapping the effects of personality and political ideology on privacy attitudes. Results on some of these are reported here (see Table 6), and the rest are included in the Online Supplement OS.D. We analyzed responses using a between-subjects analysis of variance with the response categories described in Table 2 as the between-subjects factor.

The two most interesting effects we discovered were on age and authoritarian submission. The age effect was very simple: those in the low privacy expectation group were significantly older on average than people in the other three groups.[178] This was a moderate effect, with the difference between the consistently high and consistently

---

[177] See Sunil Hazari and Cheryl Brown, *An Empirical Investigation of Privacy Awareness and Concerns on Social Networking Sites*, 9 J Info Privacy & Security 31, 41–45 (2013); Deborah M. Moscardelli and Richard Divine, *Adolescents' Concern for Privacy When Using the Internet: An Empirical Analysis of Predictors and Relationships with Privacy-Protecting Behaviors*, 35 Family & Consumer Science Res J 232, 243–47 (2007); Mike Z. Yao, Ronald E. Rice, and Kier Wallis, *Predicting User Concerns about Online Privacy*, 58 J Am Soc Information Science & Tech 710, 718–20 (2007); Hoofnagle and Urban, 49 Wake Forest L Rev at 261 (cited in note 112); Kugler, *Affinities in Privacy Attitudes* (unpublished) (cited in note 136); Alan F. Westin, *"Whatever Works": The American Public's Attitudes Toward Regulation and Self-Regulation on Consumer Privacy Issues*, in *Privacy and Self-Regulation in the Information Age* ch 1, § F (1997), archived at http://www.ntia.doc.gov/page/chapter-1-theory-markets-and-privacy.

[178] All post-hoc tests described as significant are significant at least at the $p < .05$ level.

Table 6

Personality Characteristics as a Function of Privacy Views

	F (3,1229)	η^2	Consistently High	Consistently Low	Consistently Middle	Rising Trend
Liberalism-conservatism	1.23	.003	3.95 (1.70)	4.18 (1.75)	4.08 (1.51)	3.99 (1.63)
Authoritarianism	11.95***	.028	3.50_c (1.04)	3.94_a (.98)	3.60_{bc} (.73)	3.67_b (.92)
Age	8.84***	.021	47.58_b (16.59)	54.00_a (16.21)	48.97_b (16.44)	49.62_b (16.36)
Supreme Court knowledge	.87	.002	.51 (.33)	.53 (.33)	.48 (.32)	.52 (.33)

NOTE.—Group means are significantly different when they do not share subscripts. So for authoritarianism, the consistently high group (c) is significantly different than the low group (a) but not the middle group (bc).

*** $p < .001$.

low group means amounting to 6.42 years. This finding cuts strongly against the conventional wisdom that younger cohorts do not care about their privacy.[179]

Authoritarian submission requires a word of explanation. The social psychological theory of authoritarianism defines authoritarians as people who are especially willing to submit to authority, who believe that it is particularly important to yield to traditional conventions and norms, and who are hostile and punitive toward those who question authority or who violate such conventions and norms.[180] The Authoritarian Submission Scale, developed by John Duckitt and colleagues, is intended to measure the first of those impulses: the extent to which people believe that authority should be respected and obeyed rather than challenged and questioned.[181] Authoritarianism is one of the two major individual difference constructs in political psychology.[182] It has been shown to correlate with attitudes toward a wide array of political issues, including abortion, affirmative action, racial minorities in general, illegal drug use, the homeless, homosexuality, and, among men, hostility toward women.[183]

---

[179] See, for example, Teri Dobbins Baxter, *Low Expectations: How Changing Expectations of Privacy Can Erode Fourth Amendment Protections and a Proposed Solution*, 84 Temple L Rev 599, 609–14 (2012); Jo Bryce and Mathias Klang, *Young People, Disclosure of Personal Information and Online Privacy: Control, Choice, and Consequences*, 14 Info Sec Technical Rep 160, 160 (2009) ("It has been claimed that users, particularly young people, have a lack of interest in their online privacy. . . ."). But see Moscardelli and Divine, 35 Family & Consumer Science Res J at 246 (cited in note 177) (finding teens had higher levels of privacy vigilance than adults, as reflected on temporally distant survey responses); Chris Jay Hoofnagle et al, *How Different Are Young Adults from Older Adults When It Comes to Information Privacy Attitudes and Policies?* at *20 (unpublished article April 14, 2010), archived at http://papers.ssrn.com/sol3/papers.cfm?abstract_id=1589864 (finding younger respondents and older respondents largely in alignment with respect to privacy attitudes and concerns).

[180] See Bob Altemeyer, *The Other "Authoritarian Personality,"* in Mark Zanna, ed, 30 *Advances in Experimental Social Psychology* 47–92 (Elsevier, 1998).

[181] Items include "It's great that many young people today are prepared to defy authority" (reverse coded), and "What our country needs most is discipline, with everyone following our leaders in unity." The response scale ranged from 1 (strongly disagree) to 6 (strongly agree). Higher scores indicate stronger endorsement of authoritarian ideologies. John Duckitt et al, *A Tripartite Approach to Right-Wing Authoritarianism: The Authoritarianism-Conservatism-Traditionalism Model*, 31 Pol Psych 685–715 (2010). The other two authoritarianism scales developed by Duckitt and colleagues (authoritarian aggression and traditionalism) were also administered. We believe that authoritarian submission is a better measure of the ideology construct for these purposes, however.

[182] See generally John Duckitt and Chris G. Sibley, *A Dual Process Motivational Model of Ideological Attitudes and System Justification*, in John Jost et al, eds, *Social and Psychological Bases of Ideology and System Justification* 292 (2009); Altemeyer, *The Other "Authoritarian Personality"* at 47 (cited in note 180).

[183] Herbert L. Mirels and Janet B. Dean, *Right-Wing Authoritarianism, Attitude Salience, and Beliefs about Matters of Fact*, 27 Political Psych 839, 840–41 (2006) (reviewing studies).

The effect on authoritarian submission was similar to that on age: those with consistently low privacy expectations had significantly higher authoritarianism scores than those in any other category. The difference between the consistently high and consistently low groups was moderate, amounting to about half a standard deviation. These results are supported by prior work showing that those high in authoritarianism are consistently less supportive of both information and decision privacy protections.[184] In fact, the same Authoritarian Submission Scale has previously displayed a moderate correlation with a composite of criminal procedure privacy questions.[185]

Two other interesting factors did not differ across condition. First, there was no overall effect of political orientation. Despite the authoritarianism finding, those with lower privacy expectations did not tend to be more conservative. Second, Supreme Court knowledge, assessed with a four-question quiz, also had no effect.[186]

Our surprising finding about age has important implications for judicial behavior. Judges tend to be much older than the population at large. This means that the group entrusted with actually assessing expectations of privacy is unrepresentative on an important dimension. And those who endorse the third-party doctrine are significantly older than even others with low privacy expectations.[187] This disproportionate appeal of the third-party doctrine to older Americans could help explain its persistence in legal doctrine despite its apparent lack of resonance with younger Americans.

E. WAVE 3: REPLICATION, INTRUSIVENESS, AND SUGGESTIVE DATA
   ON OTHER SEARCHES

A third wave of data was collected between May 26 and June 2, 2015, approximately a year after Waves 1 and 2. Participants for this wave were also recruited by Toluna. The final sample con-

---

[184] See Kugler, *Affinities in Privacy Attitudes* (unpublished) (cited in note 136). This result may reflect the historical links between privacy protections and autonomy beliefs. Louis Henkin, *Privacy and Autonomy*, 74 Colum L Rev 1410, 1425 (1974).

[185] See Kugler, *Affinities in Privacy Attitudes* (unpublished) (cited in note 136). Table 3 of that paper shows a correlation of .37 between the criminal procedure composite and authoritarian submission. Importantly, the previous research in this area concerned privacy *attitudes* rather than privacy *expectations*. We suspect this difference in question type explains why the relationship between authoritarianism and privacy attitudes was stronger in the preceding paper.

[186] This is described in greater detail in the Online Supplement OS.D.

[187] $F(1,133) = 7.66, p = .006, \eta2 = .054$. Endorse third-party doctrine ($M = 58.45$ years old, $SD = 15.62$). Low privacy expectations but adopting other theories ($M = 50.57, SD = 16.02$)

tained 1,441 respondents, all of whom were adult U.S. citizens. The demographic breakdown was similar to that in the first two waves.[188] Participants in this study received one of four versions of the GPS tracking question. One version mirrored that used in Waves 1 and 2 in that it asked about reasonable expectations of privacy and provided participants with a five-point response scale. The new wave employed a slightly revised version of the locate question.[189]

The results of each wave are nearly identical; there are no significant differences in the means or the consistency categories (see Table 7A and Table 7B). Even after a year, a year that included any number of events arguably relevant to police-community relations,[190] almost nothing had changed. These data should therefore help alleviate concerns that privacy expectations be inconsistent over time.

The second version of the GPS tracking question asked three questions designed to assess the intrusiveness of GPS tracking rather than expectations. For each search duration, participants were asked to rate the intrusiveness, the likelihood the search would reveal sensitive information, and how embarrassing the search would be (see Table 8).[191] The intrusiveness question mirrors that used by Slobogin in his research. The separate questions involving the revelation of personal information and embarrassment are intended to be supplemental measures of the social cost of allowing a search. They are drawn from Kugler's prior work on searches of electronic devices.[192]

---

[188] Of the sample, 49.8% was female; 12.1% had graduate degrees, 28.2% had four-year college degrees, 23.1% had two-year degrees, 34.5% had high school degrees, and 2% had not completed high school; 79.7% of the sample identified as White, 13.1% as Black, and 4.2% as South or East Asian. On a separate question, 17.1% reported identifying as Hispanic or Latino. The median age was 46 (range 18–89, $M = 46.04$, $SD = 16.41$). On a scale ranging from 1 (very liberal) to 7 (very conservative), the mean response was 4.19 ($SD = 1.78$).

[189] It now reads "Used a car's onboard GPS system to locate it on public streets without the owner's permission?" We believe this is clearer than the previous version. Both versions were used in the wording test study reported in the Online Supplement OS.A, and the results did not differ.

[190] See, for example, Michael S. Schmidt and Matt Apuzzo, *South Carolina Officer Is Charged with the Murder of Walter Scott*, NY Times A1 (April 8, 2015).

[191] "If law enforcement used a car's onboard GPS system to locate it on public streets at a single moment in time without the owner's permission: How intrusive would this be? How likely would this be to reveal sensitive personal information? How embarrassing would this be?" All response scales ranged from 1 (not at all) to 5 (very), with no labels on the other points. Note that the midpoint is less inherently meaningful for these three questions. Whereas a below-midpoint answer to the expectation question can fairly be read as "not violating expectations," a below-midpoint response to the embarrassment item may be fairly read as "only somewhat embarrassing."

[192] See Kugler, 82 U Chi L Rev at 1194 (cited in note 92) (using these as measures of the privacy and dignity interests implicated by border searches of electronic devices).

Table 7A

Categorical Consistency Between 2014 and 2015 Waves

	Waves 1 and 2 (%)	Wave 3 (%)
Consistently high	39.5	37.8
Consistently middle	11.0	11.0
Consistently low	16.9	15.2
Rising trend/not cross	11.8	13.5
Rising trend/cross	5.3	6.4
None of these patterns	15.5	16.0

Table 7B

Distributional and Mean Consistency Between 2014 and 2015 Waves

	Waves 1 and 2			Wave 3		
	M	% Below	% Above	M	% Below	% Above
Locate	3.41 (1.51)	28	51	3.44 (1.50)	27	54
Track 1 day	3.53 (1.51)	25	56	3.55 (1.52)	24	57
Track 1 week	3.57 (1.51)	25	58	3.67 (1.46)	21	61
Track 1 month	3.61 (1.51)	24	59	3.73 (1.46)	19	63

NOTE.—Numbers in parentheses are standard deviations.

These data followed a somewhat different pattern in that there are larger shifts as the search duration lengthens. Though the expectation score increases by only .29 as the search lengthens from locate to 1 month, the intrusiveness score increases by .57, the sensitive information score by .61, and the embarrassment score by .45.[193] To the extent that the mosaic theory resonates at all with the public, that resonance has to do with the private-facts model and sensitivity, as Justice Sotomayor suggested, not the probabilistic model and expectations, as Justice Alito argued.[194] In our framework, surveillance duration is somewhat relevant under *Katz* prong 2 and irrelevant under *Katz* prong 1.

---

[193] This difference is reflected in the effect sizes for each measure. ANOVAs examining the effect of duration on expectations showed an effect size of only .048; $F(2.12, 765.77) = 18.02$, $p < .001$, $\eta 2 = .048$. The effect sizes for intrusion (.127), information (.127), and embarrassment (.090) were much higher: $F(2.14, 802.27) = 54.60$, $p < .001$, $\eta 2 = .127$; $F(1.92, 719.21) = 54.48$, $p < .001$, $\eta 2 = .127$; and $F(2.18, 815.45) = 36.98$, $p < .001$, $\eta 2 = .090$, respectively. Greenhouse-Geisser corrections used for all degrees of freedom.

[194] See note 158 and accompanying text.

Table 8

Mean Intrusiveness, Information, and Embarrassment
Scores for Each Duration of Search

	M	% Below	% Above
Intrusiveness:			
Locate	3.59 (1.38)	22	56
Track 1 day	3.95 (1.28)	15	69
Track 1 week	4.07 (1.26)	12	72
Track 1 month	4.16 (1.23)	12	76
Reveal sensitive information:			
Locate	3.37 (1.33)	25	47
Track 1 day	3.66 (1.22)	17	56
Track 1 week	3.86 (1.21)	13	63
Track 1 month	3.98 (1.20)	12	70
Embarrassment:			
Locate	3.34 (1.36)	25	45
Track 1 day	3.51 (1.30)	20	50
Track 1 week	3.66 (1.30)	18	55
Track 1 month	3.79 (1.32)	16	60

NOTE.—Numbers in parentheses are standard deviations. Results in
terms of the consistency categories are in the Online Supplement OS.C.

The final two versions of the GPS tracking questions presented the
same expectations or intrusion questions as the preceding two but gave
response scales that ranged from 0 to 100. These data are reported in
the Online Supplement OS.B. Results showed that even giving participants the ability to draw very finely grained distinctions resulted in
only minimal variation in expectations as durations increase.

Approximately half the sample, 739 respondents, were asked to
rate a series of other law enforcement activities on the same five-
point expectations-of-privacy scale used above. Though these results are not central to our project, they provide a sense of how the
approach we advocate in the GPS monitoring context would affect
the handling of other hot-button Fourth Amendment questions.

Our subjects differentiated sharply among these other types of law
enforcement surveillance. On some of these, the public was quite divided. Popular expectations regarding inspection of hotel guest registries, a topic visited by the Court in the 2015 case *City of Los Angeles
v Patel*,[195] were exactly evenly split. On tracking a person using cell-
site data, on the other hand, about half the participants thought this
was a violation of their expectations of privacy, and just under a third

---

[195] 135 S Ct 2443 (2015).

disagreed. This is a lopsided split, but reasonable people can disagree about whether it is lopsided enough to raise concern.

There were other instances, however, in which a very clear majority of the public either had or lacked expectations of privacy. A super-majority believes that the police's remote activation of the webcam on an individual's personal computer would violate a reasonable expectation of privacy. It is, surprisingly, not well established in the case law whether such tactics amount to Fourth Amendment searches or violations of federal law when engaged in by law enforcement.[196] An overwhelming majority also feels that the police obtaining emails from an internet service provider infringes a reasonable expectation of privacy. Federal law generally requires police to obtain a warrant to access recent email communications,[197] and one circuit court has ruled that the Fourth Amendment also requires the police to get a warrant in order to obtain any emails from an internet service provider.[198] By contrast, most survey respondents were comfortable with police tactics like the installation of a video surveillance camera in a public park where criminal activity had recently occurred. Those who believed such tactics definitely did not or probably did not infringe a reasonable expectation of privacy outnumbered those who had opposite feelings by a 58% to 29% margin (see Table 9). The case law is consistent with popular sentiment here as well.[199]

IV. CONCLUSION

This project has both empirical and doctrinal implications. As an empirical matter, we show that very large majorities of the American public do not conceptualize Fourth Amendment expectations

---

[196] See *Clements-Jeffrey v City of Springfield*, 810 F Supp 2d 857, 865–66, 874–77 (SD Ohio 2011).

[197] See, for example, 18 USC § 2703 (Stored Communications Act warrant requirement); 18 USC § 2518 (Wiretap Act super warrant requirement). The government may obtain emails that have been in electronic storage for longer than 180 days via subpoena, provided it gives advance notice to the email user. 18 USC § 2703(b).

[198] See *United States v Warshak*, 631 F3d 266, 288 (6th Cir 2010) (finding a reasonable expectation of privacy in email contents).

[199] See, for example, *United States v Brooks*, 911 F Supp 2d 836, 842–43 (D Ariz 2012). See also *United States v Houston*, 813 F3d 282 (6th Cir 2016) (holding that ten consecutive weeks of video surveillance of a suspect's trailer home and its surroundings via a camera installed on a nearby utility pole did not violate the owner's reasonable expectation of privacy); *United States v Wells*, 739 F3d 511, 522–25 (10th Cir 2014) (holding that someone invited to a guest's hotel room has no reasonable expectation of privacy against video surveillance in the room, and indicating that were the court to hold otherwise the police's ability to conduct such surveillance in public places would be cast into doubt).

Table 9

Results for Other Searches

	M	% Above	% Below	Ratio: Above/Below
Remote activate webcam	4.06 (1.37)	73	15	4.74
Obtain emails from ISP	3.73 (1.40)	63	20	3.16
Stingray cell-phone tracking	3.42 (1.42)	51	25	2.03
Cell site data	3.26 (1.50)	49	31	1.57
Inspect hotel guest registry	2.99 (1.51)	38	38	1.00
Facial recognition at Super Bowl	2.61 (1.54)	33	52	.63
Camera in public park	2.40 (1.55)	29	58	.49

NOTE.—Numbers in parentheses are standard deviations. The questions appeared in random order. Participants were asked, Would it violate people's reasonable expectations of privacy if law enforcement:

- Used remote activation software to turn on the webcam on their laptop without their permission?
- Obtained from their internet service provider copies of emails exchanged between them and someone else?
- Used a fake cell tower to trick their phone into giving the police more accurate information about where the phone is?
- Obtained from their cell-phone company stored information about whether their cell phone was near a particular location on a particular day?
- Searched a hotel's guest register to obtain the names, home addresses, and assigned hotel room numbers of the guests who stayed there on a particular night?
- Used facial recognition software to check whether any of the fans entering the Super Bowl stadium match images in a Department of Homeland Security database?
- Installed a video camera to watch a public park where criminal activity has recently occurred?

of privacy in a manner that is congenial to the "mosaic theory." Americans generally regard the police's use of car-based GPS devices to determine an individual's whereabouts as the sort of action that infringes on a reasonable expectation of privacy regardless of whether geolocation information is collected for a long or short period of time. These Americans mostly cite the potential for police abuse and infringements on personal freedom as the basis for their consistently high privacy expectations. A substantial minority of the population regards the use of such devices as unproblematic from a Fourth Amendment perspective and, again, the duration of surveillance does not appear to make much difference. Among members of this subgroup, the much-maligned third-party doctrine finds substantial numbers of adherents. Only a tiny percentage of respondents have differential responses based on the length of surveillance, and even among these respondents the "longer surveillance is more problematic" view is hardly universal. It is fair to say, then, that the people whose expectations of privacy are purportedly at issue when the Court considers the Fourth Amendment's scope are duration-insensitive with regard to geolocation surveillance.

Of course, the Fourth Amendment involves questions of privacy cost as well as expectations, and Americans do believe that longer duration searches are somewhat more intrusive and more likely to expose sensitive information than shorter duration searches. But even there, the salience of duration should not be overestimated. To the extent that courts wish to make surveillance duration relevant, however, the sensitivity/invasiveness calculus is the appropriate doctrinal hook.

Attitudes toward privacy and expectations of privacy are heterogeneous across the population, and this heterogeneity is predictable. Political psychology metrics like Duckitt's Authoritarian Submission Scale correlate with expectations of information privacy in police search contexts. Other demographic variables, like age, plausibly drive the resonance of the third-party doctrine. This article is an early step toward the broader goal of explaining the psychological basis of privacy expectations.

On the doctrinal front, our project offers a cleaner way for courts to resolve Fourth Amendment questions. Fourth Amendment doctrine has become an unpredictable jumble. Instead of a status quo where the courts inexplicably ignore considerations that have been treated as dispositive in previous cases, we offer a straightforward constitutional framework where the same questions are always relevant. First, did the government infringe on a protected property interest? If so, a search has occurred. Second, do Americans generally expect the government to conduct the kind of surveillance it performed in a particular case? If so, then no search has occurred. Third, is the type of search conducted meaningfully likely to reveal sensitive information? If not, then no search has occurred. And, finally, if a warrantless search has happened, do cost-benefit calculations justify permitting that search? Survey data would be irrelevant to the first inquiry, dispositive of the second, relevant to the third, and perhaps informative for the fourth.

We think that the science of survey research has now advanced to the point where analytical clarity is achievable in a manner that takes the idea of "reasonable expectations of privacy" seriously. It is not Justice Alito's fault, nor the fault of other Justices, that their sense of what people expect is occasionally out of line with what people actually expect[200]—the academy has failed to provide jurists with sufficiently trustworthy data about the public's perceptions. The price of gathering and analyzing survey results from a representative sample of Americans is declining toward zero, and this dropping pricepoint makes it increasingly feasible for social scientists in the academy to gather such data for the benefit of courts and police departments.

Having covered our empirical and doctrinal contributions, it is worth raising a normative question about whether it matters that the public and the Supreme Court Justices are in this instance out of step in their assessments when it comes to privacy expectations. Does the fact that the mosaic theory fails to resonate with the public's expectations render the theory bad law? We think the failure of duration sensitivity to resonate with the public presents a serious problem. The Fourth Amendment exists for instrumental purposes—it allows people to predict when an action will remain private and when it may become public, and to direct their behavior accordingly. When Fourth Amendment protections and popular expectations are misaligned, people are guarded when they should feel free and feel free when they should be guarded. This creates a real social cost.

One possible reaction to this problem is to conclude that advocates of the mosaic theory have a great deal of marketing and persuasion work ahead of them. If the doctrine is sound as a policy matter, perhaps the solution to our dilemma is to correct the expectations of ordinary Americans. Our other ongoing research makes us inclined to believe that, at least in the short run, such persuasion efforts would be largely futile.

Another possible reaction is to declare that reasonable expectations of privacy for Fourth Amendment purposes have nothing to do with what reasonable Americans expect. We also find this possibility unappealing. The practical costs of disagreement are very real. Absent an anchor to the opinions of ordinary Americans, the content of the Fourth Amendment becomes subject to the whims of unrepresentative legal elites. Given that our data show that basic personality and demographic factors, including age, strongly influence privacy

---

[200] See note 51; see also *Minnesota v Carter*, 525 US 83, 97 (1998) (Scalia, J, concurring) ("In my view, the only thing the past three decades have established about the *Katz* test . . . is that, unsurprisingly, those actual subjective expectations of privacy that society is prepared to recognize as reasonable bear an uncanny resemblance to those expectations of privacy that this Court considers reasonable.") (citation and internal quotation marks omitted).

expectations, it is inevitable that elite and popular opinion will diverge on these issues. At a time when the Court is famously homogeneous in so many respects,[201] we should not be comfortable if judges and Justices rely entirely on the limits of their personal experiences. Modern social science has developed to the point where the legal system need not and should not tolerate "this is what I think" or "this is what my law clerk thinks" being used as proxies for what members of society generally expect and value. Rather than adopt either of these answers, we have proposed what we think is a more sensible, data-driven approach to the morass that is Fourth Amendment search doctrine. We also note that, unlike in many other areas of law, looking to public expectations here would plausibly result in *increased* constitutional protections. The usual role of courts as protectors of minority rights is actually being inhibited by a failure to consider this evidence.

The mosaic theory emerged from the minds of judges who wanted to guarantee some measure of Fourth Amendment privacy in the digital age without overruling *Knotts*, which held short-term geolocation surveillance to be a nonsearch. We are personally sympathetic to the goals of the mosaic theory. Given how the Fourth Amendment precedents of the 1980s and 1990s interact with the realities of cheap electronic monitoring, some doctrinal innovation is needed to leave space for personal privacy. But we are concerned enough by this disconnect between what the people expect and how judges characterize those popular expectations to become skeptical about whether the revolution in Fourth Amendment jurisprudence that *United States v Jones* seems to foreshadow will prove to be an enduring endeavor. Given these data, rejecting *Knotts* is better than trying to translate the mosaic theory into workable and intuitive doctrine. Returning to the central issue emerging from *Jones*, then, we think it makes sense to stand with the very large group of citizens who label geolocation surveillance of any length an infringement of reasonable privacy expectations rather than with the very tiny group who say that the Fourth Amendment is implicated only if the surveillance lasts long enough.

---

[201] See, for example, Dahlia Lithwick, *The 2014 Supreme Court: An Ivy League Clan*, New Republic (Nov 13, 2014), archived at http://www.newrepublic.com/article/120173/2014 -supreme-court-ivy-league-clan-disconnected-reality.

FREDERICK SCHAUER

NOT JUST ABOUT LICENSE PLATES: WALKER v SONS OF CONFEDERATE VETERANS, GOVERNMENT SPEECH, AND DOCTRINAL OVERLAP IN THE FIRST AMENDMENT

It all depends on where you start. For free speech questions arising under the First Amendment, as for a cornucopia of other legal topics, a single set of facts or a single question may be placed in any of a number of different doctrinal categories, with the category selected determining not only the analytic approach but also often the outcome as well. Psychologists and other social scientists refer to this phenomenon as framing, and framing effects are as important in law as they are in most other aspects of our lives.[1]

Frederick Schauer is David and Mary Harrison Distinguished Professor of Law, University of Virginia School of Law.

AUTHOR'S NOTE: Special thanks to Geof Stone for editing that was careful, knowledgeable, justifiably critical, and unqualifiedly helpful.

[1] A useful overview of the psychological research is Scott Plous, *The Psychology of Judgment and Decision Making* 69–76 (McGraw-Hill, 1993). Prominent applications to law include Chris Guthrie, Jeffrey J. Rachlinski, and Andrew J. Wistrich, *Inside the Judicial Mind*, 86 Cornell L Rev 777 (2001); Jonathan Remy Nash, *Framing Effects and Regulatory Choice*, 82 Notre Dame L Rev 313 (2006); Jeffrey J. Rachlinski, *Cognitive Errors, Individual Differences, and Paternalism*, 73 U Chi L Rev 207 (2006). For a more skeptical view, see Gregory Mitchell, *Taking Behavioralism Too Seriously? The Unwarranted Pessimism of the New Behavioral*

The problem of framing in law often arises as a consequence of multiple doctrinal approaches being potentially applicable to a single event or problem. Such doctrinal multiplicity pervades the law, especially in messy common law environments, but it appears especially salient with respect to the First Amendment. We know that there is much case law and commentary about content regulation, about the public forum, about unconstitutional conditions, and about, more recently, government speech. But often we do not realize that a host of First Amendment controversies can be placed in any or all of the foregoing doctrinal baskets, with the one selected to drive the analysis often determining the outcome, even though there may be no conclusive doctrinal reason for selecting any one of them over any of the others.

The problem of doctrinal multiplicity, which more accurately might be understood as doctrinal overlap, was especially apparent in the Supreme Court's recent decision in *Walker v Texas Division, Sons of Confederate Veterans*.[2] The precise issue in the case—was Texas constitutionally permitted to deny specialty license plate status to the Sons of Confederate Veterans because of Texas's unwillingness to have the Confederate battle flag on state-issued license plates?— could be analyzed in one way if the focus was on what was unquestionably an act of viewpoint discrimination, in another way if the issue was framed in terms of whether Texas's specialty license plates constituted some sort of public forum, in still another way if the state's policy was seen as the imposition of an unconstitutional condition, and, finally, in yet another way if, as the Supreme Court

---

Analysis, 53 Wm & Mary L Rev 1907, 1961–63 (2002). In two respects my use of the idea of framing differs from the idea as it appears in much of the social science and legal literature. First, most (but not all, as in Guthrie et al, id) of the use of the idea of framing in the legal literature refers to the existence of framing effects on legal subjects, and much less on judges and other legal decision makers. Second, the central understanding of a framing effect, initially from Amos Tversky and Daniel Kahneman, *The Framing of Decisions and the Psychology of Choice*, 211 Sci 453 (1981), is that people may react differently (and thus irrationally) to the identical choice option depending on how it is framed. My usage here is looser, and thus I make no claim that the choice of doctrinal category is arbitrary, or that the multiple doctrinal categories applicable to a single question or set of facts are exactly equivalent. Rather, the different doctrinal categories applicable to a single legal judgment are different but overlapping, such that each of them may be at least plausibly applicable even if they are not identical. And thus the implication is that the choice among these plausible but not identical doctrinal options may have greater consequences than the actual differences between the doctrines might justify.

[2] *Walker v Texas Division, Sons of Confederate Veterans, Inc.*, 135 S Ct 2239 (2015).

majority saw the case, the Texas policy was analyzed as an example of government speech.

The fundamental problem is that placing the *Walker* facts into any of the just-listed frames or doctrinal categories would not be wrong, for each of them was at least plausibly applicable to the controversy in *Walker*. Thus, it is not that the Court majority was correct to see this as a case of government speech and Justice Alito in dissent was mistaken to understand it as a case of viewpoint discrimination. In fact, the case was both, just as it was also a case involving the distinction among a genuine public forum, a public forum by designation, a limited public forum, a nonpublic forum, and no forum at all, and just as it was a case arguably imposing an unconstitutional condition on the exercise of the citizen's right to have a customized license plate, a right that in decades past would have been called a privilege. *Walker* was all four of these, and the choice by the majority to frame it in one way and by the dissent to frame it in another may be the most significant doctrinal decision faced by the Justices, and may be the most important aspect of understanding what the decision should now be taken to represent.

The availability of multiple doctrinal frames, a problem hardly unique to the First Amendment or even to constitutional law more generally, raises two possibilities. One, and most obviously, is that selecting the correct frame is both difficult and important. But the other and less noticed consequence of the existence of multiple available doctrinal frames is that when multiple plausible frames are available, the selection of one rather than another might be a product, as the Legal Realists would have predicted, of some obscured factor that actually motivated the choice of the frame. Just as Karl Llewellyn famously observed that the selection between equally applicable but mutually exclusive canons of statutory construction might be the consequence of a judge's desired outcome rather than methodological preference,[3] so too might the selection of a frame of doctrinal analysis

---

[3] Karl N. Llewellyn, *Remarks on the Theory of Appellate Decision and the Rules or Canons about How Statutes Are to Be Construed*, 3 Vand L Rev 395 (1950). On understanding Legal Realism largely through the lens of the ubiquitous availability of multiple doctrines or sources for any single controversy, see especially Hanoch Dagan, *Reconstructing American Legal Realism and Rethinking Private Law Theory* 19–22 (Oxford, 2013). See also Brian Leiter, *Naturalizing Jurisprudence: Essays on American Legal Realism and Naturalism in Legal Philosophy* 22, 97 (Oxford, 2007); Frederick Schauer, *Editor's Introduction*, in Karl N. Llewellyn, *The Theory of Rules* 1, 14 (Frederick Schauer ed, Chicago, 2011).

be the consequence of a different kind of outcome preference, a preference whose own dimensions might at the same time be both complex and unrevealed. Insofar as *Walker* exemplifies this phenomenon, subjecting it to closer inspection might illuminate important dimensions of First Amendment doctrine, while also offering a useful glimpse at larger questions of constitutional and legal analysis.

I. The Walker Case Itself

The background to *Walker* is the increasingly common phenomenon by which owners of automobiles may use—for a fee—their license plate numbers and letters to make a personal statement. The statement is often the driver's name—HERBIE, for example—or the designation of the type of car—MUSTANG, or MYCHEVY—or an abbreviation or acronym for some message or self-identification—CATLOVR, or TPARTY76.[4] Typically the issuing state allows, subject to content-neutral prohibitions on duplication and content-based prohibitions on the vulgar or the obscene,[5] registrants to choose anything they wish for such "vanity" plates within the designated limits on the number and types of characters.

States have also long made available—again, for a fee—a limited number of specialty license plates traditionally focusing on one of the state's natural features. The standard issue Virginia license plate, for example, contains only the name of the state and the letters and numbers identifying the registrant, but the registrant may pay a fee and choose a license plate with, for example, a picture of a bear and an "advertisement" for the Shenandoah National Park, or a picture of a crab with a similar expression of appreciation for the natural and culinary virtues of the Chesapeake Bay.

Recently, the states, or at least most of them, have recognized the commercial possibilities of allowing a combination of these two models for customized license plates. As a result, Michigan residents, for example, may select not only license plates bearing the name and

---

[4] My wife, for example, displays her affection for our (well, really, her) Australian shepherd with the Virginia license plate OZSHEP. And even before Gary Trudeau created a character in the *Doonesbury* comic strip with this name, my New Hampshire license plate during my undergraduate years bore the letters PHRED.

[5] Vermont, for example, prohibits license plates that are "vulgar, scatological, or obscene, or constitute racial or other epithets," or that "connote breast, genitalia, pubic area, or buttocks or relate to sexual or eliminatory functions." Vt Stat Ann § 23.304 (2015).

logo of the University of Michigan or Michigan State University, but also, if there is sufficient demand, the name and logo of Harvard or Ohio State. Similarly, individuals can select specialty license plates announcing their sympathy with, or membership in, specific organizations, for example, the Boy Scouts, the Rotary Club, or the Daughters of the American Revolution.

Walker arose in the context of this latter type of customized or specialty license plates. As in most other states, Texas residents could select from among a wide range of off-the-rack options, or a non-profit entity could propose its own distinctive license plate. Thus, although many Texans have license plates announcing their affiliation with the University of Texas, Texas A & M University, and even the University of Oklahoma, a Texan who happened to be a graduate of, or sympathetic to, the University of Dubrovnik could also, upon an accepted proposal from a relevant nonprofit entity and the payment of the appropriate fee,[6] have her wishes accommodated with a license plate bearing the name and logo of that university as well.

Seeking to take advantage of this program, the Texas division of an organization called the Sons of Confederate Veterans proposed a license plate containing, along with the words "Texas" and the identifying letters and numbers, the name of the organization, the date of its founding (1896), and a picture of the Confederate battle flag, the flag often referred to simply as the "Confederate flag" or as the "Stars and Bars."

In response to this application, the Texas Department of Motor Vehicles Board twice refused the request, finding, after inviting public comment, that "the confederate flag portion of the design" was unacceptable "because public comments ha[d] shown that many members of the public find the design offensive, and because such comments are reasonable."[7] Moreover, the board said, "a significant portion of the public associate the confederate flag with organizations advocating expressions of hate directed toward people or groups that is demeaning to those people or groups."[8]

---

[6] An accepted specialty plate option would require payment of a fee in excess of $8,000, 135 S Ct at 2260–61 (Alito, J, dissenting), although obviously the individual driver selecting that option is not required to pay a fee of that magnitude.

[7] 135 S Ct at 2245.

[8] Id.

Sons of Confederate Veterans challenged the board's rulings on First Amendment grounds, but the United States District Court for the Eastern District of Texas upheld the board's decision. The District Court's ruling was reversed by the Fifth Circuit, however, with the Court of Appeals holding that in denying the application the board had engaged in unconstitutional viewpoint discrimination with respect to what the court characterized as an exercise of private speech by the Sons of Confederate Veterans.[9]

The Supreme Court reversed the Fifth Circuit, and upheld the board's decision to reject the Confederate battle flag license plate. Writing for a five-to-four majority, Justice Breyer saw the issue as substantially similar to that in the Court's 2009 decision in *Pleasant Grove City v Summum*,[10] which had characterized a privately funded and donated monument in a public park as government speech and thus not constrained by the First Amendment's general prohibition on government content or viewpoint discrimination. Relying heavily on *Summum*, Justice Breyer concluded in *Walker* that the state's license plates were the government's own speech, and that the First Amendment therefore imposed no restrictions at all on what the government could choose to say in its own voice, with its own facilities, and on its own property. Although the various designs for specialty license plates were proposed by private citizens or organizations, Justice Breyer emphasized that the license plates were the state's own registration system and were owned and controlled by the state.[11] The license plates could therefore, he insisted, be used by the state to convey any message the state wished to convey. The corollary of this, the Court concluded, was that the state could choose *not* to convey any message that it did not wish to convey, and thus that it was not required to convey a message the state believed to be offensive to many of its citizens.[12] In effect, the Court treated the case as if Texas was deciding for itself what messages to put on its license

---

[9] *Texas Division, Sons of Confederate Veterans v Vendergriff*, 759 F3d 388 (5th Cir 2014).

[10] 555 US 460 (2009).

[11] See 135 S Ct at 2248, observing that Texas law "dictates the manner in which drivers may dispose of unused plates" and "require[es] that vehicle owners return unused specialty plates to the State."

[12] Texas was seemingly concerned not only with the sensibilities of its citizens, but also with its own image. Although Texas had been a member of the Confederacy, that feature of the state's history is not one that Texas, for various reasons, appeared eager to emphasize or celebrate.

plates—or, more precisely, what messages *not* to put on its license plates—without any private involvement. In the Court's view, the fact of private initiation in the process of proposing possible messages was irrelevant to the characterization of the situation as government speech.

In dissent, Justice Alito, writing for himself, Chief Justice Roberts, and Justices Scalia and Kennedy, did not deny the basic principle that the government could speak in whatever manner *it* wished without being constrained by the First Amendment.[13] Thus, apart from the differences between the majority and dissent on the proper application of this principle to the Texas specialty license plate program, *Walker* is noteworthy for establishing the Court's unanimity on the core principle of government speech.[14] Although disputes in application will continue to arise, especially in the context of speech by government employees,[15] such disputes at the margins should not detract from the importance of the Court's unanimous assertion that the government, when speaking as the government, is free to say or not say whatever it wishes, and is free to express some viewpoints and not others.[16]

But although Justice Alito agreed with the majority about the existence and broad contours of the government speech doctrine, he denied that it controlled in this case, or, for that matter, that it was even applicable to the facts of *Walker*. What was at issue in *Walker*, he argued, was the privately generated message and the privately developed license plate design of the Sons of Confederate Veterans. And

---

[13] 135 S Ct at 2255 (Alito, J, dissenting).

[14] And, indeed, it was Justice Alito who wrote for the Court in *Pleasant Grove City v Summum*.

[15] Application of the "government speech" idea to public employees has generated voluminous litigation. See, for example, *Garcetti v Ceballos*, 547 US 410 (2006); *Lane v Franks*, 134 S Ct 2369 (2014); *Gibson v Kilpatrick*, 773 F3d 661 (5th Cir 2014); *Mpoy v Rhee*, 758 F3d 285 (DC Cir 2014); *Hays v LaForge*, 2014 WL 4087070 (ND Miss, July 6, 2015). It is likely that *Walker* will be relevant even if not directly applicable to similar cases arising in the future.

[16] Justice Alito described the board's decision as "blatant viewpoint discrimination," 135 S Ct at 2256, and observed that the same board that had rejected the Sons of Confederate Veterans plate had, at the same meeting, accepted a specialty plate honoring the Buffalo Soldiers, the African-American members of the army who had served in the nineteenth century. Id at 2262. But there was no dispute between the majority and the dissent about the existence of viewpoint discrimination. The dispute was about whether this was a decision and domain in which such viewpoint discrimination was permitted, as the majority maintained, or a decision and domain in which viewpoint discrimination was prohibited by the First Amendment, as Justice Alito's dissent insisted.

although the state might choose to express with the state's words the state's preference for one view about the Confederacy over another,[17] it could not, Justice Alito insisted, engage in viewpoint discrimination in choosing which *private viewpoints* to permit on license plates and which *private viewpoints* to exclude.

On the surface, then, *Walker* appears to be largely about application of a doctrine—the government speech doctrine—whose existence and fundamental principles were not a source of disagreement. Both the majority and the dissent agreed that government speech was not subject to First Amendment limitations, and the only question was whether the customized or specialized inscriptions on a license plate were government speech or private speech. When viewed in this manner, *Walker* may appear to be a small case. Presumably, it will apply to other license plate controversies, and, quite obviously, it appears to apply as well to the various Adopt-a-Highway signs on the nation's roadways designating the organizations who have either supported the roadway or agreed to clear litter from the shoulders.[18] And *Walker* will, when applied to such controversies, add texture to the basic issue in *Summum* of whether monuments, memorials, inscriptions, and the like that are donated to government and placed on government property are private speech or government speech. But apart from these and similar issues, the direct applications of *Walker* seem limited, and just as Justice Stevens memorably observed some years ago that few citizens would send their sons and daughters off to war to preserve an individual's right to see "Specified Sexual Activities" in the theaters of their choice,[19] perhaps so too would few of those citizens be willing to go to war to protect an individual's

---

[17] Thus it is clear that the state is free to use its license plates to convey its own messages. These messages may be largely innocuous commercial or tourism promotion, as with "Famous Potatoes" on Idaho's license plates or "Wild Wonderful" on West Virginia's, or expressions of historical pride, as in "First in Flight" on North Carolina's plate or "The First State" on Delaware's, or they may be more politically tendentious, as with "Taxation Without Representation" on the District of Columbia plate and "Live Free or Die" on New Hampshire's, the latter having been the impetus for *Wooley v Maynard*, 430 US 705 (1977).

[18] Compare *Robb v Hungerbeeler*, 370 F3d 735 (8th Cir 2004) (invalidating restriction on Ku Klux Klan sponsorship); *San Diego Minutemen v California Department of Transportation*, 570 F Supp 2d 1229 (2008) (invalidating restriction on anti-immigrant group's sponsorship), with *State of Texas v Knights of the Ku Klux Klan*, 58 F3d 1075 (5th Cir 1995) (upholding restriction as "reasonable" in light of location of sign near integrated housing project).

[19] *Young v American Mini Theatres, Inc.*, 427 US 50, 70 (1976).

right to display one's avocational or even political affiliation on state-issued license plates.

When seen this way, and especially when seen against the background of the earlier cases that had established the basic government speech doctrine in the context of various government employee free speech claims,[20] *Walker* seems almost trivial. What makes *Walker* interesting and important, however, is precisely the fact that it was not inevitable that the case would even be framed as a government speech case at all, and that in choosing to frame the case as a question about government speech the Court immediately found itself pretty far down one path of First Amendment doctrine. But it was not necessary that the Court take that path, and exploring the various paths the Court did not take, in whole or in part, reveals *Walker* to be an ideal example of the doctrinal overlap that may be even more apparent and more problematic with respect to the First Amendment than it is in other domains of constitutional law or legal doctrine more generally.

II. The Problems of Government Speech

A. THE OLD PROBLEM

For a period of time, especially in the late 1970s and early 1980s, mention of "government speech" referred largely to the claim that speech by the government ought to be subject to First Amendment constraints.[21] Because government speech was so powerful and per-

---

[20] See especially *Garcetti v Ceballos*, 547 US 410 (2006), and, subsequently, *Lane v Franks*, 134 S Ct 2369 (2014). See generally Helen Norton, *Constraining Public Employee Speech*, 59 Duke L J 1 (2009). The roots of the modern government speech doctrine are traceable at least as far back as *Rust v Sullivan*, 500 US 173, 193–94 (1991), with subsequent elaborations in *Legal Services Corp. v Velazquez*, 531 US 533 (2001), and *Johanns v Livestock Marketing Ass'n*, 544 US 550 (2005). See Caroline Mala Corbin, *Mixed Speech: When Speech Is Both Private and Governmental*, 83 NYU L Rev 101 (2008); Helen Norton, *The Measure of Government Speech: Identifying Expression's Source*, 88 BU L Rev 587 (2008); Helen Norton, *Not for Attribution: Government's Interest in Protecting the Integrity of Its Own Expression*, 37 U C Davis L Rev 1317 (2004).

[21] See Mark G. Yudof, *When Government Speaks: Politics, Law, and Government Expression in America* (California, 1983); Robert Kamenshine, *The First Amendment's Implied Political Establishment Clause*, 67 Cal L Rev 1104 (1979); Steven H. Shiffrin, *Government Speech*, 27 UCLA L Rev 565 (1980); Edward H. Ziegler, Jr., *Government Speech and the Constitution: The Limits of Official Partisanship*, 21 BC L Rev 578 (1980); Note, *Unconstitutional Government Speech*, 15 San Diego L Rev 815 (1978). And, earlier, see William W. Van Alstyne, *The First Amendment and the Suppression of Warmongering Propaganda in the United States: Comments and Footnotes*, 31 L & Contemp Probs 530 (1966).

vasive, it was argued, there was a risk that the government's speech could drown out the speech of nongovernment speakers. This dominance of speech by the government would, so the argument went, distort the marketplace of ideas, thus frustrating the goals of the First Amendment. If governmental intrusions into that marketplace could be in some way limited in the name of the First Amendment, it was said, then the various virtues of private speech would be allowed to flourish, thus fulfilling the First Amendment's deeper aspirations.

To be sure, there are some pathologies of government speech that, at the extremes, ought to generate First Amendment concern, and in fact they have done so. If the speech of government expresses a threat of legal action against those who voice or publish constitutionally protected but unpopular or even dangerous views, then the courts have been willing to intervene.[22] And if parties or officials in power use their control over government resources to secure their own re-election, the dangers to the democratic processes, and thus to larger First Amendment concerns, again seem apparent.[23]

Apart from such epiphenomenal examples, however, the courts have never been persuaded that speech by the government itself can or should be limited by the First Amendment.[24] Part of the problem is practical and doctrinal, because it seems impossible to craft a doc-

---

[22] See *Bantam Books, Inc. v Sullivan*, 372 US 58 (1963).

[23] Although the problems seem obvious, there appears never to have been a case setting forth exactly this proposition. In *National Endowment for the Arts v Finley*, 524 US 569, 596 n 3 (1998) (Scalia, J, concurring), Justice Scalia observed that "I suppose that it would be unconstitutional for the government to give money to an organization devoted to the promotion of candidates nominated by the Republican party—but it would be just as unconstitutional for the government itself to promote candidates nominated by the Republican Party, and I do not think that that unconstitutionality has anything to do with the First Amendment." Justice Scalia was perhaps thinking of the Article IV guarantee to every state of a "Republican form of government," but apart from that it is not clear why he was unwilling to locate his obvious conclusion in the First Amendment. At oral argument in *Walker*, Justice Kagan asked whether a state could issue a "Vote Republican" and not a "Vote Democrat" license plate, and Justice Scalia interjected in response his view from *Finley*. See http://www.supremecourt.gov/oral_arguments/argument_transcripts/14-144_5i36.pdf. In considering the issue, it may be useful to note Justice Brennan's observation in the context of school libraries in *Bd. of Educ., Island Trees Union Free School Dist. No 26 v Pico*, 457 US 853, 870–71 (1982) (plurality opinion), where he used a similar parade of horribles to distinguish "narrowly partisan or political" content or viewpoint control from other forms of content- or viewpoint-based governmental decision making.

[24] See, for example, *Muir v Alabama Educ. Television Comm'n*, 688 F2d 1033, 1044 (5th Cir 1982); *P.A.M. News Corp. v Butz*, 514 F2d 272, 276–78 (DC Cir 1975); *Joyner v Whiting*, 477 F2d 456, 461–62 (4th Cir 1973). Nor were some commentators. See Laurence Tribe, *Toward a Metatheory of Free Speech*, 10 Sw U L Rev 237, 244–45 (1978); Frederick Schauer, *Is Government Speech a Problem?*, 35 Stan L Rev 373 (1983) (book review).

trine that would respond to the concerns about the allegedly distorting effects of government speech without also limiting the ability of presidents and other government officials to promote the policies they were elected to pursue. A legal doctrine that would render unconstitutional[25] Franklin Roosevelt's highly effective "fireside chats" had no hope of getting off the ground, and indeed it is far from clear that public officials should or could be prohibited from condemning such constitutionally protected groups as the American Nazi Party and the Ku Klux Klan.[26]

More to the point, though, the claim that government speech should itself be unconstitutional was based on an empirical premise that appeared dubious then, and is far more so now. The primary claim of proponents of First Amendment limitations on government speech was that such speech could drown out private speech by its ubiquity or its authority, but neither of these premises is even close to sound. The voices of ABC, CBS, NBC, Fox, the *New York Times*, the *Washington Post*, the *Wall Street Journal*, Microsoft, Coca-Cola, Apple, and General Motors, to say nothing of the voices distributed on Facebook and Twitter, cannot plausibly, by whatever measure we choose, be seen to be at risk of being drowned out by government speech, and in an era in which political candidates seek to outdo each other in antigovernment rhetoric, it appears equally implausible to suppose that speech coming from the government, at whatever level, is treated with such inherent respect that it has such an authoritative advantage as to counteract its numerical and financial disadvantage. And thus the view that government should be restricted in the positions it takes or endorses, religion apart,[27] and however popular it was in the academic literature for a brief period of time, is now scarcely more than a relic of constitutional history.

---

[25] Or even subject to anything above mere rational basis scrutiny.

[26] This appears to be the lesson of *Meese v Keene*, 481 US 465 (1987), permitting the government to label certain constitutionally protected films as "propaganda." And although on its facts this case may be controversial, especially in requiring the speaker to convey the label selected by the government, the basic proposition that government can condemn that which the First Amendment protects is less so, and may well be the turning point for the "old" government speech doctrine.

[27] Government speech endorsing religion, of course, brings in an entirely different set of considerations under the Establishment Clause. See *Bd. of Educ., Westside Community Schools (Dist. 66) v Mergens*, 496 US 226, 250 (1990).

B. GOVERNMENT SPEECH NOW

The question of government speech did not disappear with the demise of the call for First Amendment restrictions on what government itself could say. The government speech issue has more recently reemerged, but in exactly the opposite way. In the contemporary incarnation, the issue is not whether government speech should be held to violate the First Amendment, but whether it stands outside the First Amendment entirely.

In its simplest form, this more recent doctrine of government speech as a type of government action that is unconstrained by the First Amendment seems self-evidently correct. Much that the government does involves advocating, imploring, criticizing, and condemning, and it is hard to imagine that it could be otherwise. The government urges us to drive carefully, to drink in moderation, to exercise, and to lose weight; it condemns ISIS, the Ku Klux Klan, drug dealers, and littering; and it takes all sorts of positions on issues of public policy. In so doing, it clearly engages in viewpoint-based communicative behavior, for the government does not feel any need to promote obesity, alcoholism, texting while driving, the virtues of Al Qaeda or the American Nazi Party, or positions on issues of public policy that it opposes.

As Justice Breyer observed in *Walker*, "How could a city government create a successful recycling program if officials, when writing householders asking them to recycle cans and bottles, had to include in the letter a long plea from the local trash disposal enterprise demanding the contrary?"[28] And as Justice Alito noted in *Pleasant Grove City v Summum*, "it is not easy to imagine how government could function if it lacked [the] freedom"[29] to "speak for itself."[30] In making its choices about what to say and what not to say, the state, like the rest of us, makes decisions that are invariably based on content and point of view.[31] And thus the United States of America is just as free

---

[28] 135 S Ct at 2246.

[29] 555 US at 468.

[30] *Board of Regents of Univ. of Wisconsin System v Southworth*, 529 US 217, 229 (2000). See also *Johanns v Livestock Marketing Ass'n*, 544 US 550, 553 (2005); *Rosenberger v Rector and Visitors of University of Virginia*, 515 US 819, 833 (1995); *Columbia Broadcasting System, Inc. v Democratic National Committee*, 412 US 94, 139 n 7 (1973) (Stewart, J, concurring).

[31] "It is the very business of government to favor and disfavor points of view." *National Endowment for Arts v Finley*, 524 US 569, 598 (1998) (Scalia, J, concurring in the judgment).

to condemn or support ISIS, the Ku Klux Klan, the Boy Scouts, actions to combat climate change, income redistribution, abortion, same-sex marriage, and affirmative action as individual citizens are free to applaud or condemn those same groups and policies.

As noted briefly above,[32] there seem obvious limits to the existing hands-off approach to government speech. Although government may use its voice and thus its resources to advocate fitness and criticize obesity and to promote equality and condemn discrimination, things look different if the question is whether government may use its voice and its resources to advocate for the Republican Party and condemn Democrats. Justice Scalia appears to believe that this would be a constitutional problem but not necessarily a First Amendment one,[33] but the resolution of this limiting case is more likely the one identified by Justice Brennan in *Island Trees v Pico*.[34] Although a public or school library may plainly select books about the Holocaust without using equivalent resources or shelf space for books denying the Holocaust's occurrence, and may engage in viewpoint-based preference for books and magazines opposing sexual violence over books and magazines endorsing it, a public library that chose only books written by Democrats and excluded those by Republicans appears very different. For Justice Brennan the distinction between what we might call "ordinary" viewpoint discrimination and partisan political discrimination was crucial, and thus the problem he first identified, and the one later noted by Justices Scalia and Kagan, is a problem largely a function of the crudeness of the category of viewpoint discrimination. Justice Brennan was right to distinguish partisan political viewpoint discrimination from other forms of viewpoint discrimination, and this distinction, whether located in the First Amendment or in other parts of the Constitution, appears to properly recognize the inevitability of frequent desirability of government viewpoint discrimination in what the government says and how it expends its resources while at the same time carving out a different approach for government speech and government expenditure that crosses the line into contested partisan electoral politics.[35]

---

[32] See note 23.

[33] Id.

[34] Cited in note 23.

[35] There may be other limiting cases as well. If government speaks to promote one religion and condemn another, the Establishment and possibly Free Exercise Clauses of the First

Because neither the federal government nor the states have a mouth with which to speak nor the fingers with which to wield a pen or tap a keyboard, however, the government must speak through its employees, all of whom enjoy First Amendment rights in their individual capacities.[36] And therein lies the problem. The modern question of government speech arises most commonly as a question about whether employees of government who speak in ways that anger or annoy their supervisors are protected by the First Amendment as private speakers, or whether instead the government is permitted to conscript their speech to ensure that they convey the government's own message.

In earlier times, the problem of the free speech rights of government employees was treated as no problem at all. But Oliver Wendell Holmes's statement, for the Massachusetts Supreme Judicial Court, that whatever Constable McAuliffe's rights he had as a citizen were forfeited upon his taking up public employment[37] has achieved iconic status in that category of cases that Jamal Greene has referred to as the "anticanon."[38] The notion that "the petitioner may have a con-

---

Amendment may come into play, and if government speaks to promote one race and condemn another there may, although less obviously, be Equal Protection issues. Indeed, if *Brown v Board of Education*, 347 US 483 (1954), is taken at face value, it is the segregating board of education's implicit *statement* of racial inequality that produces the inequality, thus suggesting another exception to existing government speech doctrine. But apart from such cases, it remains difficult to imagine how government can be restricted from expressing public positions on contested issues. That many people (erroneously) deny the human contribution to climate change, for example, cannot plausibly be understood as reason to disallow the government from taking the contrary position. And if there is a remedy for government taking an erroneous position, that remedy is located in the ballot box and not in the First Amendment.

[36] *Pickering v Bd. of Educ.*, 391 US 563 (1968). See also *Rankin v McPherson*, 483 US 378 (1987); *Givhan v Western Line Consolidated Sch. Dist.*, 439 US 410 (1979). Thus it has been suggested (Corbin, 83 NYU L Rev, cited in note 20) that the kind of speech at issue in *Walker* and many of the government employee cases is a form of "mixed" speech involving both governmental and individual components, and that such mixed speech should receive intermediate and not totally deferential First Amendment scrutiny. But because government does not have a mouth or a pen, it always speaks through the individuals whom it employs or funds. And except in the rare case in which a government employee is given a script to read, the employee or recipient of funds will always have at least some leeway about what to say and how to say it. As a result, virtually all government speech is mixed speech, and designating a particular class as "mixed" will not go very far in telling us which mixed speech should be considered as speech by the government and which as speech by the employee or funding recipient.

[37] "The petitioner may have a constitutional right to talk politics, but he has no constitutional right to be a policeman." *McAuliffe v Mayor of New Bedford*, 29 NE 517, 518 (Mass 1892).

[38] Jamal Greene, *The Anticanon*, 125 Harv L Rev 379 (2011).

stitutional right to free speech, but he has no constitutional right to be a policeman" is now little more than a laugh line, interred with the so-called right-privilege distinction that it embodied.[39] Whatever Holmes and the entire system of law and government may have believed in 1892, it is unimaginable in 2016 that a street-level employee of the sanitation department could be dismissed for criticizing the government or joining the Communist Party,[40] and equally unthinkable that a resident of public housing could now be evicted for engaging in the same behavior.[41]

But although Constable McAuliffe could no longer be dismissed for engaging in political advocacy, the mayor of New Bedford, the nominal defendant in that case, would even now be on much safer ground in seeking to dismiss the chief of police for his public advocacy of assault or bank robbery. Insofar as the policy of New Bedford was to oppose bank robbery, the modern government speech doctrine allows the city to take that position through the voices of its employees, and thus allows the city to demand that its employees, at least those at a certain level, do the job of espousing the government's position, if doing so is part of what the employee has been hired to do.[42]

The modern government speech doctrine, therefore, compels an inquiry into whether government employees are speaking as private citizens or whether they are speaking on behalf of the government as part of their jobs. And although the similarity may not be immediately apparent, this was much the same question the Court faced in *Walker*, despite the obvious differences between license plates and employees, or between citizens choosing license plates and employees choosing what to say. In the typical public employee speech case, of which *Pickering v Board of Education*[43] is exemplary, the employee is claiming that she is engaged in private speech—that despite her government employment she has the right as a citizen to *choose*

---

[39] William Van Alstyne, *The Demise of the Right-Privilege Distinction in Constitutional Law*, 83 Harv L Rev 1429 (1968).

[40] See *Keyishian v Board of Regents*, 385 US 589 (1967); *Elfbrandt v Russell*, 384 US 11 (1966).

[41] See *Chicago Housing Auth. v Blackman*, 122 NE2d 522 (1954); *Holt v Richmond Redevelopment & Housing Auth.*, 266 F Supp 397, 400 (ED Va 1966); Robert M. O'Neil, *Unconstitutional Conditions: Welfare Benefits with Strings Attached*, 54 Cal L Rev 443 (1966).

[42] See especially *Garcetti* and *Lane* (cited in note 20).

[43] 391 US 563 (1968).

what to say. And in response, as in *Garcetti v Cebalos*,[44] the government is typically saying that the citizen-employee's choice is subservient to the government's using that employee to convey the government's message. And so just as the question to be asked in the government employee context is whether the employee was speaking as a citizen or as an employee, so too was the question in *Walker* whether the government was speaking through its specialty plate program, as the majority concluded, or whether it was the individual license plate holder, and not the government, who was the speaker, as the dissent insisted. But once the issue had been framed as a government speech problem, it became clear, especially after *Garcetti* and *Pleasant Grove City*, that the weight of the argument was in favor of the Texas Division of Motor Vehicles. The modern doctrine of government speech is a doctrine of nonreview, and once the case is framed as a government speech case the result could hardly have been in doubt.

In challenging Texas's claim that it was speaking through its specialty license plate program, Justice Alito in dissent was troubled by what he perceived as a tension between the government's claim that it was speaking, on the one hand, and the wide range of the more than 350 specialty license plate designs that Texas had in fact permitted.[45] But this argument is weak. A parent who says to his teenage child that he can associate with whomever he wants but cannot join a gang is still making a strong statement against gangs, no matter how many other friendship options are open to the child, and the restaurant patron who tells the waiter to bring whatever he thinks best as long as it does not contain anchovies is still making a strong anti-anchovy statement, no matter how many food choices remain. Similarly, the fact that Texas chose to make an anything-you-want-except-this statement does not mean that Texas was not making a strong statement—speaking—against the one thing that was excluded from the otherwise "anything goes" policy. Indeed, by excluding only one variety of plate from an otherwise largely open program, Texas was making an especially strong statement by the very nature of what it excluded compared to what it did not. In allowing so much and prohibiting so little, Texas was undeniably speaking, and thus the question was not whether Texas was making a statement, but whether in making a

---

[44] 543 US 1186 (2005).

[45] 135 S Ct at 2255 (Alito, J, dissenting).

statement in this manner Texas came within the government speech doctrine. In holding that it did, the majority determined the outcome, but it is not so clear that putting the case within the government speech category at the outset was quite as inevitable as the majority made it out to be.[46]

III. DID TEXAS DISCRIMINATE?

In his *Walker* dissent, Justice Alito devoted a substantial portion of his opinion to challenging the majority's characterization of the specialty license plate program, seeing it as the plateholder's speech and not the government's. The main thrust of his dissent, however, was that Texas had engaged in an unconstitutional act of viewpoint discrimination. He can therefore be understood as arguing that this was not a government speech case at all, but a viewpoint discrimination case.

There is no question that Texas rejected the Confederate flag plate precisely because of the point of view it embodied, and no one claimed that a flag embodying the opposite viewpoint—the American flag—would have been excluded. There is thus no plausible argument that Texas's decision was not viewpoint-based.[47] The ques-

---

[46] The Court in *Walker* attempts to distinguish *Rosenberger v Rector and Visitors of University of Virginia*, 515 US 819 (1995), by characterizing *Rosenberger* not as a government speech case but as a "limited public forum" case. 135 S Ct at 2250. The *Rosenberger* Court would have obviated the tension had it decided that case on Establishment Clause and not Free Speech Clause grounds, but having chosen the latter course it was incumbent on the Court in *Walker* to explain why the license plates were not also a limited public forum. This the majority attempted to do, 135 S Ct at 2251, but in relying largely on the conclusion that Texas traditionally associated itself with license plate messages in a way that the University of Virginia did not associate itself with campus speech, the majority leaves us with the conclusion that *Rosenberger* would have been decided differently had the University of Virginia historically exercised more control over what was said in spaces on its campus. This may well be so, but more likely there is simply a tension between *Walker* and *Rosenberger*, a tension that the Court purports to resolve by choosing to see the case as a government speech case and not a forum case. But *Walker* was both, and its outcome was determined largely by the choice between more or less equally plausible analytic paths, but for reasons the Court scarcely explains. And that unexplained choice is the principal theme of this article.

[47] The Court's decision in the same Term in *Reed v Town of Gilbert*, 135 S Ct 2218 (2015), has seemingly softened some application of the distinction between viewpoint and other forms of content discrimination. In *Reed*, Justice Thomas for the majority described viewpoint discrimination as a "more blatant" and "egregious" form of content discrimination, 135 S Ct at 2230, quoting *Rosenberger v University of Virginia*, 515 US 819, 829 (1995), but emphasized that in most contexts content discrimination even without viewpoint discrimination would be constitutionally problematic in prohibiting "public discussion of an entire topic." 135 S Ct at 2230, quoting *Consolidated Edison Co. of N.Y. v Public Service Comm'n of*

tion was whether this was a form of viewpoint discrimination that the First Amendment prohibits.

Although the modern government speech doctrine expressly allows the government to espouse some viewpoints and decline to espouse others, the large-scale import of more than four decades of content discrimination jurisprudence[48] is that the act of government in authoritatively selecting one point of view over another lies at the center of what the First Amendment stands against. When Justice Powell in *Gertz v Robert Welch, Inc.*[49] famously observed that "[u]nder the First Amendment there is no such thing as a false idea,"[50] he articulated the long-central First Amendment theme that choosing between or among competing ideas is for the public, or for the so-called marketplace of ideas, and not for authoritative governmental selection. And from the perspective of the First Amendment's prohibition on viewpoint discrimination, for government to tell citizens that they can express one view but not the opposing view is a central violation of the very idea of freedom of speech.

An important aspect of content discrimination jurisprudence, as with equality doctrine and theory more generally, is that for government to draw an impermissible distinction is to trigger an equality-based prohibition without regard to the importance (or lack of importance) of the context in which the distinction is drawn. Just as the Equal Protection Clause is violated by racial discrimination even in the context of something as trivial (to some) as golf,[51] so too is the First Amendment's prohibition on content discrimination violated

---

N.Y., 447 US 530, 537 (1980). See Geoffrey R. Stone, *Restrictions of Speech Because of Its Content: The Peculiar Case of Subject-Matter Restrictions*, 46 U Chi L Rev 81 (1978). The implications of *Reed* and the reach of its conclusion about the distinction between subject-matter and viewpoint discrimination, especially in the context of commercial advertising, remain uncertain and contested. See *California Equity Partners v City of Corona*, 2015 WL 4163346 (CD Cal, July 9, 2015); *Citizens for Free Speech, LLV v County of Alameda*, 2015 WL 4365439 (CD Cal, July 16, 2015). But because the distinction in *Walker* was unquestionably viewpoint based, the important complexities and uncertainties added by *Reed* are largely beside the point in *Walker*.

[48] A plausible candidate for the starting point would be *Police Dept of City of Chicago v Mosley*, 408 US 92 (1972), with important early commentary including Kenneth Karst, *Equality as a Central Principle in the First Amendment*, 43 U Chi L Rev 20 (1975); Paul Stephen, *The First Amendment and Content Discrimination*, 68 Va L Rev 203 (1982); Geoffrey R. Stone, *Content Regulation and the First Amendment*, 25 Wm & Mary L Rev 189 (1983); Susan Williams, *Content Discrimination and the First Amendment*, 139 U Pa L Rev 201 (1991).

[49] 418 US 323 (1974).

[50] Id at 339.

[51] *Holmes v City of Atlanta*, 350 US 879 (1955).

even if the object of the discrimination is, in the grand scheme of things, comparatively unimportant. It clearly violates the First Amendment, for example, for the government to prohibit bumper stickers on cars only if they display the Confederate flag, or only if they refrain from displaying the Confederate flag. Thus if the appropriate frame for *Walker* is the aversion to content-based and viewpoint-based discrimination, as Justice Alito and the other dissenters insisted, then the fact that the discrimination occurred with reference to something as trivial as specialty license plates is entirely beside the point.

If, with Justice Alito, we frame *Walker* as a case about viewpoint discrimination, then the permissibility of such discrimination with respect to government's own speech can be seen as an exception to a general principle condemning viewpoint discrimination. Although we do not know from his opinion the sequence of Justice Alito's decisional processes, it is not implausible to hypothesize that he and his three dissenting colleagues first perceived Texas's decision to deny the Sons of Confederate Veterans specialty license plate as an example of viewpoint discrimination, and then characterized the license plate scheme as private speech in order to remove it from the government speech "exception,"[52] rather than first perceiving the case as being within the government speech doctrine. Presumptions, starting points, and frames matter, and the difference between the majority and the dissent may well depend on whether *Walker* is framed at the outset as a government speech case, in line with the majority's conclusion, or as a viewpoint discrimination case, as the dissenters saw it. But *Walker* is *both* a government speech case and a viewpoint discrimination case, and the different conclusions of the majority and the dissent are largely a product of the selection of different starting points—or frames.

IV. ARE LICENSE PLATES A FORUM?

Under still another way of framing the case, *Walker* raises the question of just what kind of forum license plates are understood to be. It is now well settled that true public forums, which guarantee access for speakers even against (most) state claims of inconsistent

---

[52] For the view that government speech is in some way an "exemption" from otherwise applicable First Amendment principles, see *The Supreme Court, 2014 Term*, 129 Harv L Rev 221, 230 (2015).

use,[53] are limited to the streets, the parks, and the sidewalks.[54] And under a simplified version of what was formerly the doctrine, pieces of state-owned property that did not qualify as public forums could be closed to speakers as long as the closing was content neutral.[55] The government could completely deny public access to a school, for example, but could no more allow access to those who supported the government and deny it to those who criticized it than the city of Atlanta, which was not required to build a municipal golf course, could choose to build one and then open it to whites and deny access to African-Americans.[56]

Initially, this doctrine was about as straightforward as these things get, but over the years it has become more complicated, and not necessarily for the better.[57] One complication is the creation of doctrine about the so-called public forum by designation.[58] Although the category of traditional public forums is limited to the streets, parks, and sidewalks, a community might (although it is not clear why) designate other spaces as public forums, in which case all of the rules about mandatory access to streets, parks, and sidewalks apply to these public forums by designation as well.

Even more important was the Court's creation of the category of limited purpose public forums. Speech in such forums, the Court has held, can be restricted on the grounds of relevance to the purpose of

---

[53] See *Hague v C.I.O.*, 307 US 496 (1939); *Schneider v Irvington*, 308 US 147 (1939); Geoffrey R. Stone, *Fora Americana: Speech in Public Places*, 1974 Supreme Court Review 233. See also *Forsyth County v The Nationalist Movement*, 505 US 123 (1992) (demonstrators in the public forum cannot be required to bear the entire cost of their demonstration).

[54] *International Society for Krishna Consciousness, Inc. v Lee*, 505 US 672 (1992).

[55] See *Cornelius v NAACP Legal Defense & Educ. Fund, Inc.*, 473 US 788 (1985); *United States Postal Service v Council of Greenburgh Civic Ass'ns*, 453 US 114 (1981); *Greer v Spock*, 424 US 828 (1976); *Southeastern Promotions, Ltd. v. Conrad*, 420 US 546 (1975); *Lehman v City of Shaker Heights*, 418 US 298 (1974). See generally Alan Brownstein, *The Nonforum as a First Amendment Category*, 42 U C Davis L Rev 717 (2009); Robert Post, *Between Governance and Management: The History and Theory of the Public Forum*, 34 UCLA L Rev 1173 (1987).

[56] *Holmes v City of Atlanta*, 350 US 879 (1955). See *Good News Club v Milford Central School*, 533 US 98 (2001) (unconstitutional viewpoint discrimination to disallow use of school facilities to religious groups while allowing it for others speaking about the same subjects).

[57] See Norman T. Deutsch, *Does Anybody Really Need a Limited Public Forum?*, 82 St John's L Rev 107 (2008); Daniel Farber and John Nowak, *The Misleading Nature of Public Forum Analysis: Content and Context in First Amendment Adjudication*, 70 Va L Rev 1219 (1984); Lyrissa Lidsky, *Public Forum 2.0*, 91 BU L Rev 1975 (2011); Matthew D. McGill, *Unleashing the Limited Purpose Public Forum: A Modest Revision of a Dysfunctional Doctrine*, 52 Stan L Rev 929 (2000).

[58] *International Society for Krishna Consciousness, Inc. v Lee*, 505 US 672 (1992).

the institution in which the forum was located, as long as the limitations are not based on viewpoint.[59] For example, a public school might choose to allow citizens to meet in school facilities to discuss issues related to the school, while refusing to permit them to use the school facilities to meet to discuss other issues.

Because it is rarely clear what the purpose of a limited purpose public forum is, the category of limited purpose public forums has long been criticized as providing an ex post rationale for decisions reached on other and rarely disclosed grounds.[60] The basic idea, however, is that the government may at times choose to open some of its facilities to communicative activity, but that in doing so it takes on additional obligations of viewpoint neutrality, in much the same way that the government takes on obligations of nondiscrimination when it chooses to create a municipal golf course or swimming pool. But because such limited purpose public forums are typically located in purpose-specific sites such as schools or auditoriums, the doctrine allows a range of subject matter restrictions that would be impermissible if imposed on the true public forums of streets, parks, and sidewalks.

Because the government is permitted to engage in even viewpoint discrimination with respect to government property that is not a forum at all,[61] the distinction between the nonforum and the limited purpose public forum is crucial, in that it generates a distinction between those state-owned domains in which all varieties of content (including viewpoint) discrimination are allowed and those domains in which only subject matter discrimination under a relevance standard is permitted.

If *Walker* is viewed through the forum analysis frame, the question then is whether Texas, by permitting a degree of public choice about what plateholders may put on their license plates, has created

---

[59] See *Rosenberger v Rector and Visitors of the University of Virginia*, 515 US 819 (1995). Under one view, the university in *Rosenberger* created a limited-purpose public forum as to which viewpoint and even some subject matter discrimination was prohibited. Under another, the university in *Rosenberger* had created a public forum by designation, such that all of the rules regarding traditional public forums applied. And on the relationship between forum doctrine and government speech principles, see Randall P. Bezanson and William G. Buss, *The Many Faces of Government Speech*, 86 Iowa L Rev 1377 (2001). See also, with particular reference to the subject matter and viewpoint discrimination questions, Kent Greenawalt, *Viewpoints from Olympus*, 96 Colum L Rev 697 (1996).

[60] See note 59.

[61] *Perry Education Ass'n v Perry Local Educators' Ass'n*, 460 US 37 (1983).

a limited purpose public forum in which the viewpoint discrimination undeniably existing in the case was fatal, or instead whether Texas has no more created a forum of any kind than it has when it establishes an internal mail system that, as in *Perry*,[62] is largely but not completely open as to the kinds of messages that can be transmitted through that system. And so although designating some government property as a nonforum produces outcomes similar or identical to treating the matter as one of government speech, once again presumptions and burdens of proof matter. If one starts with a government speech frame, then even a degree of citizen choice, as in *Garcetti*, *Summum*, and *Walker*, is likely to produce a rejection of the free speech claim. But if one starts instead with a forum analysis frame, then there appears to be more of a presumption that government property open to a wide variety of views and speakers is, at the very least, a limited purpose public forum in which viewpoint discrimination is prohibited. Starting with a government speech frame may consequently produce less protection than starting with a forum frame, even though, analytically, the category of the nonforum is essentially coextensive with the category of government speech.

Forum analysis is thus an additional potential starting point and analytic frame for the problem presented in *Walker*. Justice Breyer in his majority opinion does attempt briefly to engage with forum analysis, and he does so by going out of his way to say that the license plate is not a forum at all. In addition to observing, obviously, that "license plates are not traditional public forums for speech,"[63] he adds that they are not even a "nonpublic forum,"[64] the import of which is that not even the prohibition on viewpoint discrimination that applies to nonpublic forums applies to license plates.[65] In having earlier in his opinion concluded that this was government speech by Texas, Justice Breyer therefore answered *en passant* the forum question, and

---

[62] Id.

[63] 135 S Ct at 2249–50.

[64] Id at 2251.

[65] To Justice Breyer, therefore, the category of the nonpublic forum is different from the category of the nonforum, with license plates falling into the latter and not the former category. Forum analysis is thus now divided into five categories—public forums, designated public forums, limited purpose public forums, nonpublic forums, and nonforums—but sorting this out would go well beyond the focus of this article. For present purposes, the main point is that starting with forum analysis may produce a presumption against viewpoint discrimination that starting with government speech does not.

the discussion of forum analysis was for Justice Breyer simply an alternative characterization of the same conclusion. But if he had considered the license plate to be some sort of forum, as Justice Alito did in dissent, then the argument that the license plates are government speech would be more difficult. It is of course true that government itself often speaks in the forums that it creates, but in such forums the government cannot speak by that which it prohibits, even though it is permitted to do exactly that in those pieces of government property that are not forums at all. Starting with forum analysis may as a logical matter produce the conclusion that some piece of government property is not a forum at all, and thus open to viewpoint discrimination. But as a psychological or rhetorical matter, starting with forum analysis may involve a presumption in favor of the space being some kind of forum, and thus ineligible for viewpoint discrimination. Conversely, starting with government speech analysis may as a logical matter produce the conclusion that what looks like government speech is really a forum of some sort, and thus inappropriate for viewpoint discrimination. But, again as a psychological matter, starting with the frame of government speech may understand the forum—of any kind—as the exception, and thus incline the analysis in favor of just the kind of viewpoint discrimination that existed in *Walker*. Insofar as forum doctrine retains viability, therefore, it can be understood as providing that forums of a certain variety—not public forums, and not public forums by designation, but not nonforums—involve a presumption in favor of some citizen freedom, a conclusion that becomes irrelevant if the starting point, instead, is the modern doctrine of government speech.

V. Unconstitutional Conditions

And then there is the doctrine of unconstitutional conditions. Long before public forum doctrine turned from the straightforward to the baroque, somewhat before the prohibition on content discrimination became crystallized, and long before the modern version of the government speech issue emerged, the doctrine of unconstitutional conditions had been the vehicle for the interment of *McAuliffe v Mayor of New Bedford* and the right-privilege distinction.[66]

---

[66] Interestingly, the right-privilege distinction was not only embodied in Holmes's opinion in *McAuliffe*, but also in his not-quite-as-famous decision in *Commonwealth v Davis*, 39 NE

Because being a policeman was a privilege and not a right, Holmes had argued, it could be withdrawn for any reason or no reason at all, including McAuliffe's engagement in otherwise protected political activity.[67]

Starting in the 1950s, however, and significantly as part of the larger reaction against McCarthyism that culminated in *Yates v United States*,[68] *Scales v United States*,[69] *Noto v United States*,[70] and finally *Brandenburg v Ohio*,[71] the Court overturned a number of restrictions on the speech of public employees in the name of its newly created doctrine of unconstitutional conditions. If one was otherwise eligible for public employment, or some tax benefit, or any of a number of other government benefits, then conditioning that benefit on relinquishing what would have otherwise been the beneficiary's constitutional right to free speech amounted to an unconstitutional condition. If a New York schoolteacher had a constitutional right as a citizen to join the Communist Party or to advocate the overthrow of the government, then requiring her to give up those rights in order to secure or retain her job would be a classic unconstitutional condition.[72]

The unconstitutional conditions doctrine has over the years spawned a voluminous commentary, most devoted to attempting to locate a principle distinguishing those government benefits to which one had

---

113 (Mass 1895), concluding that even entry onto the Boston Common, a public park, was a privilege that could therefore be conditioned on relinquishing what would otherwise be a constitutional right. And because *Davis* is plainly inconsistent with classic public forum cases such as *Hague* and *Schneider* (note 53), the *Davis* manifestation of the right-privilege distinction died even before a similar fate befell *McAuliffe* and the use of the distinction in the context of public employment.

[67] See notes 37–40 and accompanying text.

[68] 354 US 298 (1957).

[69] 367 US 203 (1961).

[70] 367 US 290 (1961).

[71] 395 US 444 (1969) (per curiam). Unlike *Yates*, *Scales*, and *Noto*, *Brandenburg* was not on its facts directly about communism, socialism, or McCarthyism. But the Ohio Criminal Syndicalism Act at the center of *Brandenburg* was initially enacted not as a weapon against Klansmen like Clarence Brandenburg but precisely to deal with communists, socialists, anarchists, and others of similar antigovernmental proclivities. Moreover, the Court's language in *Brandenburg* makes clear that the Court saw the case more as part of the general *Yates*, *Scales*, *Noto*, and *Dennis v United States*, 341 US 494 (1951), cluster of issues than as anything about the Klan or even about racist speech or incitement to immediate violence.

[72] *Keyishian v Board of Regents*, 385 US 589 (1967). *Keyishian* had been preceded by several cases reaching similar results on the grounds of vagueness. *Baggett v Bullitt*, 377 US 360 (1964); *Cramp v Board of Public Instruction*, 368 US 278 (1961); *Shelton v Tucker*, 364 US 479 (1960).

a justified expectation independent of the condition from those in which the government was simply describing from the outset the contours of some government benefit.[73] Constable McAuliffe, for example, possessed an independent constitutional right to engage in political advocacy at, say, ten o'clock in the morning, but could constitutionally be required to relinquish that right upon taking a job that required him to be directing traffic at that hour. Similarly, although citizens are allowed to advocate the virtues of ineffective methods of weight loss, a government program providing funds for research into effective weight-loss measures need not provide such funds to an individual desiring funding for a demonstrably ineffective method.[74]

The unconstitutional conditions doctrine thus remains limited by two understandable, and indeed necessary, qualifications. First, if the right that the speaker is required to relinquish is one whose exercise is inconsistent with the benefit he seeks, then the unconstitutional conditions doctrine is inapplicable. Although a citizen has a right to advocate the position that the use of marijuana is both harmless and psychologically beneficial, a school district can presumably fire a teacher for advocating marijuana use to her students. Second, if the speech is dependent on and exercised in conjunction with the benefit, the state is permitted to specify conditions for the exercise of the benefit. As *Rust v Sullivan*[75] made clear, the government is not required by virtue of creating the National Endowment for Democracy to make funds available to those who would advocate fascism,[76] and the government can therefore condition its grants on the recipient's agreement not to use the grant to attack democracy

---

[73] See, for example, Lynn A. Baker, *The Prices of Rights: Toward a Positive Theory of Unconstitutional Conditions*, 75 Cornell L Rev 1185 (1990); David Cole, *Beyond Unconstitutional Conditions: Charting Spheres of Neutrality in Government-Funded Speech*, 67 NYU L Rev 675 (1992); Richard A. Epstein, *The Supreme Court, 1987 Term—Foreword: Unconstitutional Conditions, State Powers, and the Limits of Consent*, 102 Harv L Rev 4 (1988); Michael Herz, *Justice Byron White and the Argument That the Greater Incudes the Lesser*, 1994 BYU L Rev 227; Seth F. Kreimer, *Allocational Sanctions: The Problem of Negative Rights in a Positive State*, 132 U Pa L Rev 1293 (1994); Kathleen M. Sullivan, *Unconstitutional Conditions*, 102 Harv L Rev 1413 (1989).

[74] Combining the two examples, however, illustrates the other side of the problem, because it would almost certainly be unconstitutional under *Keyishian* and its progeny to deny public employment as a police officer to someone who on his own time advocated empirically dubious weight-loss programs.

[75] 500 US 173 (1991).

[76] 500 US at 194.

and promote fascism, however much the recipient has the right to do so with his own resources and on his own time.

When applied to *Walker*, the unconstitutional conditions doctrine in its simplest version would have come out in favor of the Sons of Confederate Veterans. As citizens, the Sons had the right to display the Confederate flag, and imposing a restriction on that right in exchange for securing a specialty plate would be deemed an unconstitutional condition. It is of course true that the Sons had no constitutional right to specialty plates, but nor did McAuliffe have a constitutional right to be a policeman, and nor do residents of public housing have a constitutional right to their housing. Rather, citizens, including the Sons, were granted a certain kind of nonconstitutional entitlement, just like McAuliffe and the residents of public housing, and the core of the unconstitutional conditions doctrine is that such an entitlement may not be conditioned on giving up what would otherwise be a constitutional right. And thus public housing might be the best analogy, because the question is whether we define the right in terms of speaking outside of one's public residence, which would be the clearest case of an unconstitutional condition if the resident were required to waive it in exchange for being allowed to benefit from public housing, or in terms of speaking within public housing. If the government were to allow occupancy in public housing only to those who agreed not to criticize the government while *in* that housing, then the case begins to resemble *Walker*. Under some circumstances, restrictions attached to the very entitlement are permissible if relevant to the nature of the entitlement, but if the restrictions are not relevant to the nature of the entitlement then the unconstitutional conditions doctrine comes into play even if the forced waiver is with respect to activity within the entitlement.

There is no point here in getting any further into the weeds of unconstitutional conditions doctrine, because my only point is that looking at *Walker* through an unconstitutional conditions frame would hardly be implausible once we recognize that unconstitutional conditions doctrine might apply even with respect to otherwise constitutionally protected activities that are being exercised inside of and not outside of the entitlement. And thus if the analogy with agreeing not to criticize the government while in public housing is persuasive, the Sons could with at least some degree of plausibility have argued that limiting their use of specialty license plates for what would be constitutionally protected speech in other settings is the same case as limiting the use of public housing for what would be constitutionally protected speech in other locations.

It is true that the unconstitutional conditions doctrine post-*Rust v Sullivan* would have distinguished the case in which the Sons were not allowed to have Confederate flags on their state-issued license plate—the benefit—from the case in which a condition of getting a specialty plate was a willingness not to have an image of the Confederate flag anywhere on one's vehicle, the former being a permissible condition and the latter plainly not. But it also seems true that even post-*Rust* there are limits to what conditions can be imposed even within the state-created program, as the foregoing public housing example may suggest, and as some of the cases involving on-the-job public employee speech may support as well.[77] And thus although the current version of the unconstitutional conditions doctrine might not have helped the Sons of Confederate Veterans, the very fact that *Rust* has been highly controversial[78] suggests that taking the entire *Walker* controversy through the unconstitutional conditions doctrine would not have been a preposterous approach. If one has an independent First Amendment right to place virtually any message of one's choosing on one's vehicle,[79] and if the state permits citizens to have vanity plates with virtually any message on them, then an argument starting with unconstitutional conditions doctrine might well have seemed plausible. And thus, without delving into the outcome that such an approach would have produced, the entire unconstitutional conditions history, from the 1950s to the present, offers still another lens through which we might have perceived the controversy,

---

[77] For example, *Givhan v Western Line Consol. Sch. Dist.*, 439 US 410 (1979), and those parts of *Connick v Meyers*, 461 US 138 (1983), and *Rankin v McPherson*, 483 US 378 (1987), holding it unconstitutional to require an employee to give up what would otherwise be off-the-job free speech rights even while on the job.

[78] For criticism, see, for example, David Cole, *Beyond Unconstitutional Conditions: Charting Spheres of Neutrality in Government-Funded Speech*, 67 NYU L Rev 675 (1992); Dorothy Roberts, *Rust v. Sullivan and the Control of Knowledge*, 61 Geo Wash L Rev 587 (1993). Much of the criticism of *Rust*, however, may have been based less on free speech principles and more on the question of abortion. See Abner S. Greene, *Government of the Good*, 53 Vand L Rev 1 (2000).

[79] Even Justice Douglas, staunch supporter of a very strong First Amendment, did not even consider the possibility that there might be a free speech dimension to the New York City restriction on vehicle advertising that was at issue in *Railway Express Agency v New York*, 336 US 106 (1949). But commercial advertising aside, whether now or in 1949, it is clear that posting even offensive political messages on one's vehicle is protected by the First Amendment. See *Baker v Glover*, 776 F Supp 1511 (M D Ala 1991) ("Eat Shit" bumper sticker protected by the First Amendment).

and still another frame on which the issue could have been structured. Here again the starting point may influence the outcome, and
seeing *Walker* in an unconstitutional conditions frame may well have
created a presumption more favorable to the free speech claim of the
Sons than was the case under one or more of the alternative available frames.

VI. Too Many Choices

The point of the foregoing doctrinal survey was not to say
anything definitive or original about government speech, content discrimination, forum analysis, or unconstitutional conditions. Rather,
this brief tour of four overlapping doctrinal categories was designed to
illustrate how the specialty license plate question presented in *Walker*
could have been analyzed through any of at least these four different
frames or doctrinal pathways. And although each of the four might
surpass what we can call a threshold of plausibility,[80] there are nine
Justices and many more commentators who would be happy to explain why, as a strictly doctrinal matter, one of these categories was
correct and the others were largely beside the point. Justice Breyer
and the majority were of course not unaware of the alternatives, but
nevertheless insisted that government speech was the correct starting point, thus rendering the question of content or even viewpoint
discrimination irrelevant, forum analysis decidedly secondary, and unconstitutional conditions not even worth considering.

At the same time, Justice Alito and the dissent insisted, with seemingly equal conviction and awareness of the alternatives, that *Walker*
presented a classic case of government viewpoint discrimination, with
Texas having decided that some viewpoints held by private citizens
are unacceptable and unworthy of state acknowledgment, a posture,
according to the dissenters, that is fundamentally at odds with the
basic premises of the First Amendment. And although thinking of
Walker as an unconstitutional conditions case is perhaps a bit more
of a reach, it is by no means preposterous, just as it is certainly imaginable that a Justice or commentator could frame the entire controversy in terms of forum analysis, then seeking to determine whether
the specialty license plates should be considered a public forum, a

---

[80] Or, to put it in modern vernacular, each of the four would pass the smell test.

designated public forum, a limited purpose public forum, a nonpublic forum, or a nonforum entirely.

The existence of disagreement is not, of course, dispositive or even very much relevant to the question whether there is in fact a right answer. People disagree about President Obama's birthplace, but one side of that disagreement is simply wrong. Similarly, people, and even Supreme Court Justices, have disagreed about whether racially separate but superficially equal public schools violate the Fourteenth Amendment, but, again, one side of that disagreement is mistaken, and was mistaken even before *Brown v Board of Education*[81] was decided.

But although the mere fact of disagreement is not conclusive evidence that multiple alternative doctrinal frames are available, there are plausible cases to be made in *Walker* for the relevance of each of these four different doctrinal frames. If this is so, then we are in a position to speculate about what might have led both the majority and the dissenting Justices to choose the frames that they did.

One possibility, of course, is that some or all of the Justices were genuinely wrestling with the ins and outs of each of these four frames, and were trying to decide, from the outset, which frame seemed most suited to the case at hand, and which frame would be most likely to produce the best set of results over a longer run of cases over a longer period of time.[82] For the sake of simplicity, we might label this the "doctrinal" approach to frame selection.[83] At some level, it seems

---

[81] 347 US 483 (1954).

[82] I assume, without wishing to provide a lengthy argument or analysis here, that good doctrinal analysis involves considering the implications for future controversies of any precedent created by, or rule set forth in, the case now being decided. See Kent Greenawalt, *The Enduring Significance of Neutral Principles*, 78 Colum L Rev 982 (1978); Frederick Schauer, *Do Cases Make Bad Law?*, 73 U Chi L Rev 883 (2006); Frederick Schauer, *Giving Reasons*, 47 Stan L Rev 633 (1995).

[83] A rich political science literature explores the existence and effect of so-called jurisprudential regimes in Supreme Court decision making. See, for example, Herbert M. Kritzer and Mark J. Richards, *Jurisprudential Regimes and Supreme Court Decision-Making: The Lemon Regime and Establishment Clause Cases*, 37 L & Soc Rev 827 (2003); Jeffrey R. Lax and Kelly T. Rader, *Legal Constraints on Supreme Court Decision-Making: Do Jurisprudential Regimes Exist?*, 72 J Politics 273 (2010); Mark J. Richards and Herbert M. Kritzer, *Jurisprudential Regimes in Supreme Court Decision-Making*, 96 Am Pol Sci Rev 305 (2002); Kevin M. Scott, *Reconsidering the Impact of Jurisprudential Regimes*, 87 Soc Sci Q 380 (2006). Apart from the question whether jurisprudential regimes have explanatory power with respect to free speech cases even if they do elsewhere (see Xun Pang et al, *Endogenous Jurisprudential Regimes*, 20 Political Analysis 417 (2012)), the perspective offered in this article takes place one step earlier. Even on the assumption that jurisprudential regimes—doctrinal categories or frames or pathways—matter, and even on the assumption that they matter in free speech cases, the question still

plainly to be part of the explanation of the decisional processes that produce the results in cases such as *Walker*. Some frames would simply be too preposterous to imagine, and at an unspoken and probably even subconscious level, no Justice and no commentator worth taking seriously would consider thinking of *Walker* in Dormant Commerce Clause, procedural due process, or even freedom of religion terms. And although *Chicago Police Department v Mosley* and some of the commentary that decision generated might in earlier years have suggested that *Walker* was really an equal protection case,[84] the equal protection dimension of concerns about content discrimination have been left so far behind[85] that once again, as a strictly doctrinal matter, the equal protection frame was no longer among the plausible candidates.

We can comfortably say, therefore, that some constitutional doctrines constitute plausible frames and others do not. And I am also comfortable in asserting as well that determining the initial plausibility of some doctrinal frame is itself largely a matter of understanding the doctrine and understanding what the doctrine is aimed at achieving. In the context of *Walker*, this would suggest an outcome-independent evaluation of the purposes and contours of each of the four frames described here, with the aim of seeing which frames, solely or largely as a matter of doctrinal analysis, should govern the matter at hand. Just as experienced lawyers will immediately be able to categorize a set of facts as involving, say, products liability and not bailment, or civil procedure and not conflict of laws, so too will experienced First Amendment lawyers and decision makers know, largely as a matter of traditional doctrinal knowledge and analysis, which frames make sense and which do not.[86]

---

remains about why one jurisprudential regime is chosen over other candidates when there are multiple jurisprudential regimes nonlaughably available.

[84] See note 48.

[85] See *Consolidated Edison Co. v Public Service Comm'n*, 447 US 530 (1980). It is true, however, that in one subsequent case—*Minnesota State Board for Community Colleges v Knight*, 465 US 271 (1984)—Justice Stevens in dissent, 465 US at 317–19, did refer to *Mosley* as an equal protection case, which might be sufficient to add this frame to the realm of nonlaughable doctrinal frames applicable to *Walker*.

[86] Implicit in the foregoing is the assumption that some of the Justices some of the time have policy-independent and outcome-independent methodological preferences. See Joshua B. Fischman, *Do the Justices Vote Like Policy Makers? Evidence from Scaling the Supreme Court with Interest Groups*, 44 J Legal Stud 269 (2015).

Once we have concluded, however, that multiple doctrinal frames are plausible, things get trickier. The traditional view, of course, is that the nature of the competing doctrines will be the primary driver in determining which of them should be employed. Under this view, the analysis in cases like *Walker* is principally doctrinal from beginning to end, for doctrine not only puts the four options on the table, but also leads Justice Breyer and the majority to select government speech as the controlling option, and leads Justice Alito and the dissenters to select the frame of viewpoint discrimination as the best choice.

But now let us consider an alternative possibility. This possibility is that doctrine gives the decision makers a set of plausible choices, but that selecting among the plausible choices is largely an extra-doctrinal matter. On this view, the driving force is something other than legal doctrine, even capaciously understood—although just what the "something else" is presents a range of possibilities.

One possibility is that the choice among competing plausible doctrinal frames is determined by a judge's or a commentator's simple preference for one outcome rather than another in the particular case. Perhaps, as particularist Realists, such as Jerome Frank[87] and Joseph Hutcheson,[88] would have predicted, the Justices in cases like *Walker* simply made an all-things-considered choice between the Texas Department of Motor Vehicles and the Sons of Confederate Veterans, and selected a frame of analysis that would produce their preferred outcome in this particular case between these particular parties.

Especially (but probably not only) in the context of the First Amendment, however, such a particularist understanding of the judicial process seems inaccurate. Although we can readily imagine a Justice having at least a modicum of sympathy with the historical preservation goals of even groups like the Sons of Confederate Veterans, such an explanation of First Amendment decision making seems bizarre in the context of such recent cases as *Snyder v Phelps*,[89] *United States v Stevens*,[90] and *Brown v Entertainment Merchants*,[91] to

---

[87] Jerome Frank, *Law and the Modern Mind* (Brentano's, 1930).

[88] Joseph C. Hutcheson, Jr., *The Judgment Intuitive: The Function of the "Hunch" in Judicial Decision*, 14 Cornell L J 274 (1929). On the particularist or party-focused branch of Legal Realism, see Frederick Schauer, *Thinking Like a Lawyer: A New Introduction to Legal Reasoning* 126–32 (Harvard, 2009).

[89] 562 US 443 (2011).

[90] 559 US 460 (2010).

[91] 132 S Ct 81 (20110.

say nothing of earlier cases involving the Ku Klux Klan[92] and the American Nazi Party,[93] all of which involve prevailing litigants who are probably even less attractive than the Sons of Confederate Veterans.

If sympathy or hostility to particular litigants is not doing much, if any, of the work in most free speech cases,[94] we can then hypothesize two alternative possibilities. One is that the choice of frame is motivated by a larger vision of what a system of freedom of speech is designed to do. It may be, for example, that Justice Alito is motivated on free speech questions by a pervasive distrust of governmental decision making with respect to speech,[95] a distrust that would lead him to be particularly alert to the possibility of government viewpoint discrimination. Conversely, Justice Breyer may even in free speech cases be motivated by a general deference toward regulation, a view that would lead him to be sympathetic with administrative regulation and expertise, and a view that would explain not only his majority opinion in *Walker* but also his dissent in *Brown v Entertainment Merchants*. All of this is wildly speculative, of course, but the idea is only that the Justices might have visions of the First Amendment, and of its place in the larger legal and constitutional system, that extend beyond any doctrinal frame and beyond any specific line of decisions. To the extent that they do, then this larger vision, rather than narrower doctrinal analysis, may be what is leading the Justices to select a particular frame in a particular case.

The second possibility is that the choice of frame is prompted by even broader and less First-Amendment-related political and ideological concerns. This is not a claim that the Justices are driven by raw politics in a partisan sense. Nor is it a claim that free speech decisions can be categorized on a conservative to liberal spectrum, with free speech protection being the so-called liberal position and allowing the state to regulate the so-called conservative one. Such an un-

---

[92] Most prominently *Brandenburg v Ohio*, 395 US 444 (1969) (per curiam). See also *Forsyth County v Nationalist Movement*, 505 US 123 (1992).

[93] *Collin v Smith*, 578 F2d 1197 (7th Cir 1978); *Village of Skokie v National Socialist Party*, 373 NE2d 21 (Ill 1978).

[94] But see *Hill v Colorado*, 530 US 703 (2000), in which Justice Scalia's angry dissent argued that just this kind of litigant preference was the only explanation for the outcomes in the Court's abortion clinic picketing cases.

[95] On distrust of government as an underlying explanation for much of free speech theory, see Frederick Schauer, *Free Speech: A Philosophical Enquiry* 80–85 (Cambridge, 1982).

derstanding does not in any way reflect the reality of the current Justices' votes in First Amendment cases.[96] The politics of free speech is
now far more complex than that. We can more easily imagine some
Justices being concerned, for example, with a political environment in
which a host of views are denigrated for largely political reasons, and
seeing the First Amendment as a reaction to this phenomenon. And
we can imagine other Justices recognizing the way in which speech is
largely continuous with action, and thus being more inclined than
others to uphold speech regulations in contexts in which they would
uphold regulations of the conduct that the speech is about.

These possibilities are no more than unsupported speculation,
but there is a structural point that is my principal concern here. The
structural point is that constitutional doctrine may be the driving
force in identifying a set of plausible doctrinal frames, but that selecting among the doctrinal frames may be largely an extradoctrinal
matter. What these extradoctrinal considerations are may well vary
from Justice to Justice and from commentator to commentator, but
the basic point is that there is reason to hypothesize a two-step process in which doctrine plays the major role in the first step and something else dominates at the second step, even though the something
else, in the context of freedom of speech, will be far more complex
than some of the cruder attempts to align free speech issues on a simple liberal to conservative scale would have it.

VII. LEGAL REALISM?

If the foregoing speculations have any resonance, then they
suggest a slightly different way of thinking about some of the classic
Legal Realist hypotheses about the nature of legal decision making,
at least in the context of Supreme Court First Amendment decision
making. Insofar as traditional Realist views would suggest that extradoctrinal considerations are the driving force from the outset, the
picture offered here is to the contrary. In a country and a legal culture
with deeply embedded free speech values, it seems counterintuitive
to suppose that those inside the culture—Supreme Court Justices

---

[96] Too much of the attitudinal political science literature labors under this misconception.
Whatever may have been the situation for free speech cases of the 1950s, 1960s, and 1970s, it
is no longer even close to accurate. See J. M. Balkin, *Some Realism About Pluralism: Legal
Realist Approaches to the First Amendment*, 1990 Duke L J 375; Frederick Schauer, *The Political
Incidence of the Free Speech Principle*, 64 U Colo L Rev 935 (1993).

most prominently—would have the ability or the desire to put free speech considerations aside at the point of initial perception. Legal knowledge strongly affects legal and even nonlegal perception, and just as First Amendment lawyers but not lay people might see Nazis, the Ku Klux Klan, and the civil rights demonstrators of the 1960s as all part of the same category of speakers prevailing against attempts at government restriction, so too might First Amendment lawyers and judges who are knowledgeable about the First Amendment see some part of the world through a free speech lens.[97] If this is so, then it would be a mistake to imagine that judicial perception of a free speech controversy could possibly be entirely or even largely a matter of extra-legal attitudes or ideology.

But although free speech values may frame how a Justice or a commentator would initially perceive or frame many questions, and although free speech doctrine may also suggest various subframes, it could still be the case in a world of doctrinal complexity—or doctrinal inconsistency or indeterminacy—that neither the initial perception of some case as a free speech case nor the secondary perception of the various available doctrinal frames would serve to resolve the matter before the Court. In those cases, extradoctrinal consider-ations, including non-case-specific outcome preferences, might well be among the most important factors. And perhaps it is at this third stage that the Realist focus on factual patterns or situations that may not themselves be derived from the doctrine will have the greatest explanatory force.

VIII. Conclusion: Is the First Amendment Different?

Walker is only one case, but it may be a case that both sug-gests the foregoing sequencing of decision making, and that provides one data point for its explanatory soundness. Because *Walker* presents a situation in which multiple overlapping but noncongruent doc-trinal frames all surpass some threshold of doctrinal and theoretical plausibility, because the majority and the dissent see the case through different doctrinal frames, and because the Confederate flag itself is connected with a larger range of highly salient public controversies

---

[97] See Barbara A. Spellman, *Judges, Expertise, and Analogy*, in David Klein and Gregory Mitchell, eds, *The Psychology of Judicial Decision Making* 149 (Oxford, 2010), focusing on legal knowledge as a source of legal perception.

about race, about history, about cultural sensitivities, and about so-called political correctness, *Walker* may well be a case in which constitutional doctrine tells us which frames are relevant, but in which factors other than constitutional doctrine play a significant role in selecting among the relevant frames and thus in determining the outcome.

Even if these speculations are sound, they may well be limited to the First Amendment. In the First Amendment, but less elsewhere, except with respect to criminal procedure,[98] doctrinal preferences may diverge to a significant extent from preferences about the parties involved in the controversy. And more for the First Amendment than for most other areas of law except, again, for constitutional criminal procedure, second-order constitutional values may have migrated into the universe of first-order political or ideological preferences. All of this is to say that for the First Amendment, possibly more than for most other areas of constitutional law, the line between legal doctrine and extralegal ideology may be especially elusive. Insofar as this is so, it will be especially difficult to determine what factors are at work when Justices select one from among the multiple overlapping frames that are so often available in First Amendment cases. But however difficult the task may be, it remains important to recognize that for most First Amendment cases, especially, the available doctrinal frames will be multiple and overlapping, and if we do not recognize the problem of multiple plausible analytic or doctrinal frames, we may remain too much in the dark about just what it is that best explains First Amendment decision making.

---

[98] To be more specific, freedom of speech and criminal procedure may be the two areas of constitutional law in which constitutional claims are most likely to be pressed by otherwise unappealing litigants. See Frederick Schauer, *Slippery Slopes*, 99 Harv L Rev 361 (1985).

HEIDI KITROSSER

THE SPECIAL VALUE OF PUBLIC
EMPLOYEE SPEECH

In its 2014 decision in *Lane v Franks*,[1] the Supreme Court held that a public employee deserved protection, under the First Amendment, for testifying under oath about financial fraud in the statewide youth program he directed. The Court rejected the lower court's view that, because the testimony consisted of information that Lane had learned in the course of performing his job, his employer should be free to sanction him for his speech.[2] The lower court's approach, the Supreme Court explained, is in tension with one of the core reasons that it accords public employees some First Amendment protection. That is, "speech by public employees on subject matter related to their employment holds special value precisely because those employees gain knowledge of matters of public concern through their employment."[3]

Lane's internal logic is eminently sound. If public employee speech is protected partly because employees gain unique insights on the job, it makes little sense to exclude from protection all speech reflecting

Heidi Kitrosser is Professor, University of Minnesota Law School.

AUTHOR'S NOTE: I am very grateful to Cindy Estlund, Pauline Kim, Helen Norton, Mary-Rose Papandrea, Geof Stone, and participants at the 2015 Freedom of Expression Scholars Conference at Yale Law School for wonderfully helpful comments.

[1] *Lane v Franks*, 134 S Ct 2369 (2014).

[2] *Lane v Central Alabama Community College*, 523 Fed Appx 709, 711–12 (11th Cir 2013).

[3] *Lane*, 134 S Ct at 2379 (2014).

those insights. This reasoning inspires both a hope and a lament about the Court's 2006 decision in *Garcetti v Ceballos*.[4] The lament is that *Garcetti*'s rule—that speech conducted pursuant to one's public employment is unprotected—itself is at odds with the notion that public employee speech has special value because of the distinctive insights and expertise it offers. The *Garcetti* rule also reflects an overly generous vision of the government interests at stake. The hope is that *Lane* provides occasion to dig more deeply into both the special value of public employee speech and the government interests at issue and thus to rethink *Garcetti* entirely. More modestly, *Lane* can point the way to means by which *Garcetti* can be limited.

In this article, I explore the yin and yang of *Lane*, both the lament and the hope. In lamentation mode, I argue that *Garcetti* is emblematic of the Court's failure to dig beneath the surface of its own long-standing acknowledgment that public employee speech holds special value. If one tunnels into that subterrane, one finds that the value of public employee speech is a function not just of content, but of form. Public employees play a special role under the First Amendment by virtue of their privileged access both to information and to communication channels for conveying it. The special communication channels to which employees have access—including internal channels—can be uniquely effective in supporting accountability and the rule of law, and thus in fulfilling core free speech values.

Public employees' special communication channels take two forms. The first encompasses avenues to raise grievances, such as when agencies provide employees with special complaint procedures or privileged access to inspectors general. The second is more subtle, encompassing the simple acts of employees doing their jobs conscientiously and in accordance with the norms of their professions. When employees engage in such behavior—for instance, when government auditors honestly and competently investigate and report in a manner consistent with professional auditing standards—they help to maintain consistency between the functions government purports to perform and those that it actually performs. In this sense, public employees are potential barriers against government deception. They can disrupt government efforts to have it both ways by purporting publicly to provide a service while distorting the na-

---

[4] *Garcetti v Ceballos*, 547 US 410 (2006).

ture of that service. When they do this through their speech acts—for example, by reporting the results of budgetary analyses or scientific studies—they engage in speech of substantial First Amendment value.

Apart from its cramped and under-theorized conception of special value, *Garcetti* also betrays confusion over the government interests at stake. *Garcetti* suggests both that public employers require managerial discretion to evaluate work product that takes the form of speech and that because public employees speak for the government their supervisors can dictate their speech content. Although the former is a legitimate concern, the latter is wildly overbroad. It applies legitimately to only a narrow subset of government jobs. The latter also reflects a profoundly underdeveloped conception of special value, as special value derives partly from employees making independent professional judgments. Indeed, a government speech rationale would swallow even a shallow vision of special value, overtaking employees' rights to disseminate any speech that supervisors deem unwelcome.

In my more hopeful mode, I consider how a fuller conception of special value might be reconciled with a more sharply defined government interest. I propose that, where work product speech can confidently be identified, courts should consider whether employees were disciplined based on a genuine, not pretextual assessment of work product quality. Only disciplinary actions based on such assessments should be exempt from further scrutiny. Crucially, in cases where employees were hired to render independent professional judgments, disappointment with those judgments, not because they reflect low quality, but because they are politically or personally inconvenient for employers, should *not* be deemed quality-based assessments. As a second-best, but perhaps more realistic near-term alternative, I also consider means to limit *Garcetti*'s reach.

In Part I, I unpack the Supreme Court's understanding of public employee speech value as reflected in the so-called "*Pickering*" cases,[5] which include *Garcetti* and *Lane*. In Part II, I turn to lower federal courts, summarizing lower court approaches, both before and after *Lane*, to the difficult, case-by-case determination that *Garcetti* requires them to make: when is speech engaged in pursuant to one's

---

[5] The cases are so named for the first in the series, *Pickering v Board of Education*, 391 US 563 (1968).

job and thus unprotected by the First Amendment? In Part III, I develop the concept of the special value of public employee speech, exploring its underpinnings in free speech theory and constitutional structure. In Part IV, I examine *Garcetti*'s major defenses and challenge the argument that *Garcetti* does not much impact free speech values because it mostly affects internal government speech. In Part V, I expand on what constitutes a judgment based on work product quality and on how courts can determine whether discipline was based on a genuine such judgment. Finally, in Part VI, I consider a more moderate, and perhaps more realistic, approach. That approach builds on *Lane* in order to narrow *Garcetti*'s reach.

I. Unpacking the Supreme Court's Understanding(s) of Public Employee Speech Value

This part summarizes the modern constitutional doctrine of public employee speech, with an emphasis on the Court's stated understandings of the free speech interests at stake. As I will show, one of the Court's two major rationales for protecting public employee speech—the goal of achieving parity between the free speech protections enjoyed by government employees and those enjoyed by others—does little explanatory work on its own. The Court is much more convincing insofar as it suggests that public employee speech warrants protection because it holds special social value. But the Court's failure to probe very deeply into the nature of this special value, and its tendency to vacillate between the parity and special value rationales, stunts the special value rationale's contributions to the doctrine. I also explain that an additional rationale for protecting public employee speech—one based on fears of government-imposed orthodoxy—can be found in the loyalty oath and antisubversion cases that are the modern doctrine's most immediate ancestors. This third rationale does little work in the decisions that comprise the modern doctrine, but if resurrected it could contribute to a richer and more coherent approach.

A. THE MODERN APPROACH TO PUBLIC EMPLOYEE SPEECH: AN OVERVIEW

The Court's 1968 decision in *Pickering v Board of Education* was the first in the line of cases comprising the modern doctrine of public employee free speech rights. In *Pickering*, the Court established

both that public employees have some protection from being ter-
minated or disciplined for their speech, and that the government has
broader discretion to punish speech when it operates as an employer
than when it acts as sovereign.[6] The government may constitutionally
punish its employees for their speech when justified by the "interests
of the State, as an employer, in promoting the efficiency of the public
services it performs through its employees."[7] The Court explained
that courts must weigh any such interests, case by case, against the
interests of employees, as "citizen[s], in commenting upon matters of
public concern."[8] In *Connick v Myers*, the Court clarified that employee speech is subject to protection under this standard (hereafter
the *Connick-Pickering* test) only when it involves a matter of public
concern.[9] In *Garcetti*, the Court added that speech is unprotected,
even if it involves a matter of public concern, when it is part of the
employee's job.[10]

Pickering and its progeny offer two main justifications for protecting employee speech. The first justification, aptly termed the "parity
theory" by Randy Kozel,[11] is that government employees should not
be robbed of "the First Amendment rights that they would otherwise enjoy as citizens to comment on matters of public interest."[12]
The goal of parity is not definitively linked to a single conception of
free speech value. In describing it, the Court evokes both free speech's
intrinsic value to the speaker and its social value.[13] The parity approach seems grounded in the notion that whatever values are served
by free speech presumptively apply to government employees just

---

[6] *Pickering*, 391 US at 568.

[7] Id.

[8] Id.

[9] *Connick v Myers*, 461 US 138, 142–43, 146–47 (1983). The Court later suggested that
public employees who speak or write on their own time about matters unrelated to their
jobs—whether or not those matters are of public concern—warrant protection stronger
than that accorded public employees who speak on or about their jobs. See Cynthia
Estlund, *Harmonizing Work and Citizenship: A Due Process Solution to a First Amendment
Problem*, 2006 Supreme Court Review 115, 128–29, 131–32 (2006) (citing *United States v
National Treasury Employees Union*, 513 US 454 (1995), *City of San Diego v Roe*, 543 US 77
(2004)).

[10] *Garcetti*, 547 US at 421.

[11] Randy J. Kozel, *Free Speech and Parity: A Theory of Public Employee Rights*, 53 Wm & Mary
L Rev 1985, 1990 (2012).

[12] *Pickering*, 391 US at 568.

[13] See id at 568, 571–72. See also, for example, *Roe*, 543 US at 82–83.

as they do to others. Deviations from ordinary free speech protections thus are warranted only when justified by the state's needs as
employer.[14]

The second justification, which I call the "special value" rationale,
is linked to speech's extrinsic value to the public. From this perspective, public employees deserve free speech protections not because they are just like everybody else, but because they have something *special* to contribute to the marketplace of ideas. As the Court
has observed, public employees "are often the members of the community who are likely to have informed opinions as to the operations
of their public employers, operations which are of substantial concern to the public."[15] This justification, too, must give way when
warranted by overriding employer needs.

B. A CLOSER LOOK AT THE PARITY RATIONALE

1. *Parity as independent justification.* Perhaps the most foundational
criticism that can be directed toward the parity rationale is that it
compares metaphorical apples and oranges. The approach's premise
is that public employees should not be robbed of "the First Amendment rights that they would otherwise enjoy as citizens to comment
on matters of public interest."[16] But when government fires or
disciplines its own employees, it exercises a power that by definition it
could not exercise over persons not in its employ.[17]

---

[14] See *Pickering*, 391 US at 568 (citing need to balance employee's interest "in commenting
upon matters of public concern and the interest of the State, as an employer, in promoting
the efficiency of the public services it performs"). See also Kozel, 53 Wm & Mary L Rev at
2011 (cited in note 11) (deeming "default of parity" the most logical implication of the
Court's rejection of the rights-privilege distinction and explaining that under "[p]arity
theory . . . the doctrine of employee speech should be reoriented around a single inquiry: Is
there a valid reason for permitting the government to treat the employee differently from
her peers in the citizenry at large?").

[15] *Roe*, 543 US at 82.

[16] *Pickering*, 391 US at 568. See also, for example, *Connick*, 461 US at 142 ("state cannot
condition public employment on a basis that infringes the employee's constitutionally
protected interest in freedom of expression").

[17] See Kermit Roosevelt III, *Not as Bad as You Think: Why Garcetti v. Ceballos Makes Sense*,
14 U Pa J Const L 631, 637 (2012) ("Government employees cannot be fined or thrown in
jail for speech any more than a private citizen"); Patrick M. Garry, *The Constitutional Relevance
of the Employer-Sovereign Relationship: Examining the Due Process Rights of Government Employees in Light of the Public Employee Speech Doctrine*, 81 St John's L Rev 797, 798 (2007)
(suggesting Supreme Court erred in equating "[G]overnment as employer" with "government as sovereign").

If parity between likes were the Court's concern, it might make more sense for it to compare public employers with private employers, rather than to compare government *qua* sovereign with government *qua* employer. This would return us to the approach that the Court took prior to the mid-twentieth century, when it drew a distinction between rights (such as free speech) and privileges (such as holding a job).[18] As Justice Holmes famously explained while sitting on the Supreme Judicial Court of Massachusetts, "The petitioner may have a constitutional right to talk politics, but he has no constitutional right to be a policeman."[19] Holmes's rights/privilege distinction seems grounded in a baseline norm of parity between private and public employers. As a government employee, one enters into an employer-employee relationship, just as one would do in a private enterprise. That the employer happens to be the government ought not to affect its discretion to supervise its employees. Only when the government operates as a sovereign—imposing civil or criminal penalties—does the Constitution restrain it.

The modern Court does not explain why, insofar as parity is its concern, it shifts from comparing public and private employers to comparing government *qua* sovereign with government *qua* employer.[20] Perhaps the answer inheres, simply enough, in the state action doctrine. After all, the First Amendment applies only to the government, not to private actors. Still, if the state action doctrine explains why public employers are constrained by the First Amendment, it does not guide us as to the type and degree of such constraints. In this respect, parity may be viewed simply as a logical starting point.

The notion that the free speech rights enjoyed by nonemployees should be the starting point, or default norm, for public employees' First Amendment rights seems closest to what the Supreme Court has actually said about parity. Yet the doctrine that the Court constructs—that is, the *Connick-Pickering* balance and its caveats—bears

---

[18] See Estlund, 2006 Supreme Court Review at 147–48 (cited in note 9) ("To anchor the free speech rights of public employees to those of private sector employees vis-à-vis their employers would ... take us back to the heyday of the 'rights-privileges' distinction.").

[19] *McAuliffe v City of New Bedford*, 155 Mass 216, 220 (1892).

[20] Kermit Roosevelt observes that the modern Court to some extent is motivated by both types of parity. See Roosevelt, 14 U Pa J Const L at 633 (cited in note 17) ("First, the Court wants to promote equality between government and private employers with respect to control over the workplace and employee performance.... Second, it wants to maintain equality between government employees and other citizens.").

little resemblance to the doctrine that applies when government restricts speech in its sovereign capacity. Recall, for example, that public employee speech is unprotected when it is not about a matter of public concern.[21] A categorical pass for government employers to punish speech not of public concern could not be further removed from the doctrine that restricts government's power to punish speech when it acts as sovereign. And the *Connick-Pickering* balance itself, with its deferential approach even to restrictions based on content, marks a far cry from the protections accorded persons when the government acts as sovereign. The concept of parity thus seems to do very little work beyond contributing to the view that public employee speech warrants some First Amendment protection.[22]

2. *Social value as a supplement to parity.* While the concept of parity in its own right contributes little to the public employee speech doctrine, other factors have greater explanatory value. The most obvious is government's interest in protecting its managerial control over employees. As for speech value, the factor that looms largest in the Court's reasoning is the social value of public employee speech.

The Court cites social value as among the reasons why it protects public employee speech. Of more practical consequence, it has concluded that only speech on matters of public concern is sufficiently valuable to displace employers' managerial discretion. Parity interests therefore are triggered only when public employees speak on matters of public concern. In *Connick v Myers*, in which the Court first declared that speech on "matters of personal interest" would not be protected "absent the most unusual circumstances,"[23] the Court observed that it "has frequently reaffirmed that speech on public issues occupies the 'highest rung of the hierarchy of First Amendment values,' and is entitled to special protection."[24]

---

[21] Employees retain some protection for conveying speech away from and unrelated to their job. See note 9.

[22] See Kozel, 53 Wm & Mary L Rev at 1989–90, 2013–22 (cited in note 11) (deeming parity rationale incompatible with modern public employee speech doctrine, describing what parity-based doctrine would look like). See also Estlund, 2006 S Ct Rev at 149 (cited in note 9) ("When we scratch the surface of the [*Garcetti*] majority's recurring references to the 'liberties the employee might have enjoyed as a private citizen,' they appear to be less an aid to analysis than a rhetorical trope.").

[23] *Connick*, 461 US at 147.

[24] Id at 145.

The Court in *Connick* did hedge its bets a bit, citing the heightened value of public affairs speech while also conflating private interest speech with speech "made as an employee," such as "employee grievances," for which there are no nonemployee analogues.[25] In this way, the Court hinted at two separate justifications for limiting protection to public interest speech: the greater social worth of such speech and the goal of parity in its own right. Subsequent cases made clear, however, that private interest speech is not limited to employee grievances.[26] This development, combined with the Court's invoking the heightened value of public affairs speech in *Connick* and elsewhere, suggests that the Court excludes private interest speech mainly because it is insufficiently valuable to offset employers' managerial control. The Court made this point explicit in *City of San Diego v Roe*:

> To require *Pickering* balancing in every case where speech by a public employee is at issue, no matter the content of the speech, could compromise the proper functioning of government offices.... This concern prompted the Court in *Connick* to explain a threshold inquiry ... that in order to merit *Pickering* balancing, a public employee's speech must touch on a matter of "public concern."[27]

C. THE SPECIAL VALUE RATIONALE

Beyond the parity rationale, the Court has recognized that public employees can add something special to the marketplace of ideas—something that other individuals cannot contribute—when they speak about their jobs. As the Court explained in *San Diego v Roe*, "[u]nderlying the decision in *Pickering* is the recognition that public employees are often the members of the community who are likely to have informed opinions as to the operations of their public employers, operations which are of substantial concern to the public."[28] This reasoning is prominent in several opinions in the *Pickering* line of cases, including *Pickering*, *Garcetti*, and *Lane*. The Court in these cases

---

[25] Id at 147.

[26] See, for example, *Roe*, 543 US at 78–79, 84 (deeming sexually explicit videos featuring uniformed police officer not of public concern); id at 83–84 ("public concern is something that is a subject of legitimate news interest; that is, a subject of general interest and of value and concern to the public at the time of publication").

[27] Id at 82–83.

[28] Id at 82.

has invoked this concept, in addition to parity, to explain why public employee speech warrants some protection.[29]

To be sure, it was not until *Lane* that the Court coined the term "special value" to capture this rationale.[30] Nor has the Court cited the special value rationale consistently.[31] Moreover, there are two significant shortcomings in the Court's discussion of special value, and both affect the contours of the doctrine. First, the Court's understanding of special value is incomplete. Second, the Court mixes its special value and parity discussions somewhat haphazardly, at times interjecting parity in a way that stunts the scope of the protections that might otherwise follow from special value.

As for the Court's incomplete understanding, although it recognizes the potentially high value of public employee speech content, it overlooks the value of employees' access to privileged channels through which to communicate that content. As the Court has recognized in the *Pickering* cases and elsewhere, the First Amendment serves partly to support self-government and the rule of law. It serves, in short, to support the constitutional structure. That structure depends on a variety of internal as well as external checks.[32] The special access that public employees have to a mix of channels, including internal channels, to convey dissenting views is as important to the constitutional design as the content of those views. It was the Court's failure to credit this aspect of special value that enabled it to deny protection to work product speech in *Garcetti*.[33]

---

[29] See *Pickering*, 391 US at 572 ("Teachers are, as a class, the members of a community most likely to have informed and definite opinions as to how funds allotted to the operations of the schools should be spent. Accordingly, it is essential that they be able to speak out freely on such questions"); *Waters v Churchill*, 511 US 661, 674 (1994) (plurality opinion) ("Government employees are often in the best position to know what ails the agencies for which they work"); *Roe*, 543 US at 82 (language quoted at text accompanying note 28); *Garcetti*, 547 US at 419–21 (citing with approval *Pickering* and *Roe* discussions of special value); *Lane*, 134 S Ct at 2379 ("speech by public employees on subject matter related to their employment holds special value precisely because those employees gain knowledge of matters of public concern through their employment").

[30] *Lane*, 134 S Ct at 2379.

[31] For example, the Court does not mention the rationale in *Connick*, despite the fact that the speech the Court deemed "of public concern" there involved the speaker's workplace. See *Connick*, 461 US at 149.

[32] See Part III(B) (explaining that federal executive branch is designed partly to facilitate internal checking).

[33] For instance, the *Garcetti* Court minimized *Garcetti*'s impact by observing that employees still can participate in "civic discourse" like other citizens. *Garcetti*, 547 US at 422–24.

The Court also wields the concept of parity in a way that stunts the reach of special value-based protections. It did this most notably in *Garcetti*. There, it based its decision to preclude protection for all work product speech partly on the fact that "such speech owes its existence to a public employee's official responsibilities." Suppressing it therefore "does not infringe any liberties the employee might have enjoyed as a private citizen."[34] While the Court elsewhere in *Garcetti* cited the special social value of public employee speech, it shifted its focus to parity just long enough to dismiss constitutional concerns over categorically denying protection to work product speech.

The parity-based aspect of *Garcetti*'s reasoning is in tension with the very notion of special value,[35] and it generated the uncertainty that led to *Lane v Franks*. Some lower courts, relying on *Garcetti*'s statement that speech is unprotected when it "owes its existence" to the speaker's public employment, leaned heavily against protecting speech consisting of information learned through such employment.[36] The Fourth Circuit took this view in *Lane*,[37] leading to its reversal by the Supreme Court.[38]

In *Lane*, the Supreme Court mitigated some of the damage caused by its incomplete conception of special value and its haphazard mixing of the special value and parity rationales. It did not, however, fully reverse that damage or eliminate the tension between *Garcetti* and the special value rationale. Indeed, *Lane* is potentially subject to a narrow reading, one that limits it to settings in which speech consists of "truthful subpoenaed testimony" that is not part of the speaker's ordinary job duties.[39] Under this reading, *Lane* would not necessarily

---

[34] *Garcetti*, 547 US at 421–22. See also Estlund, 2006 Supreme Court Review at 144–45 (cited in note 9) (citing "recurring motif in the *Garcetti* majority opinion: the effort to anchor the free speech rights of public employees to the 'liberties the employee might have enjoyed as a private citizen,'" and explaining motif's restrictive effects).

[35] See Estlund, 2006 Supreme Court Review at 119–20 (cited in note 9) (noting tension between parity and special value rationales).

[36] See Part II(A)(1).

[37] See note 56 (discussing Eleventh Circuit opinions in *Lane*).

[38] See text accompanying notes 2–3.

[39] The *Lane* majority notes that it granted certiorari to "resolve discord among the Courts of Appeals as to whether public employees may be fired—or suffer other adverse employment consequences—for providing truthful subpoenaed testimony outside the course of their ordinary job responsibilities." *Lane*, 134 S Ct at 2377.

preclude courts in other settings from weighing the fact that speech conveys information learned on the job heavily or even conclusively against First Amendment protection. To be sure, this would be a flawed interpretation of *Lane*. Although the Court in *Lane* deemed special value particularly evident in the factual setting before it, it invoked the concept more broadly.[40] It also cited earlier decisions embracing the special value rationale outside of the testimonial context.[41] Moreover, for reasons that I discuss later, a generous reading of *Lane* is most consistent with free speech theory. Nonetheless, *Lane* is open to a narrow interpretation that would sharply limit its significance in protecting speech of special value, and even a broad reading of *Lane* cannot fully erase the damage done by *Garcetti*.

D. GOVERNMENT DISTRUST

For better or worse, then, the modern public employee speech cases frame the free speech interests at stake predominantly in terms of (under-theorized) parity and special value rationales. A third rationale—one arising out of government's natural inclination to quell criticism about itself—can be gleaned from a string of earlier decisions. These ancestors to *Pickering* arose "from the widespread efforts in the 1950s and early 1960s to require public employees, particularly teachers, to swear oaths of loyalty to the state and reveal the groups with which they associated."[42] In several of these decisions, the Court characterized loyalty requirements as dangerous attempts by government to leverage its role as employer to enforce orthodoxy in its institutions and throughout American society.

The Court's opinion in *Wieman v Updegraff* reflects this view. Writing for the Court in 1952, Justice Clark cited the inevitable chilling effect of a state law conditioning public employment on an oath of nonaffiliation with subversive groups.[43] "There can be no dispute," he explained, "about the consequences visited upon a person excluded from public employment on disloyalty grounds. In the view of the community, the stain is a deep one; indeed, it has become a

---

[40] Id at 2377, 2379.

[41] Id.

[42] *Connick*, 461 US at 144 (calling these cases "the precedents in which *Pickering* is rooted.").

[43] *Wieman v Updegraff*, 344 US 183, 184–86 (1952) (describing state law).

badge of infamy."[44] The oath requirement "stifle[s] the flow of democratic expression and controversy at one of its chief sources."[45]

The Court suggested that the stakes were especially high where employment in public schools was at issue. In *Keyishian v Board of Regents*—a case decided just one year prior to *Pickering*, and cited in *Pickering* and throughout its progeny—"the Court invalidated New York statutes barring employment [in the New York State public school system] on the basis of membership in 'subversive' organizations."[46] Justice Brennan's opinion for the Court invoked "academic freedom, which is of transcendent value to all of us and not merely to the teachers concerned. That freedom is therefore a special concern of the First Amendment, which does not tolerate laws that cast a pall of orthodoxy over the classroom."[47]

Wieman itself was brought by faculty and staff members of Oklahoma Agricultural and Mechanical College.[48] Concurring in *Wieman*, Justice Frankfurter, joined by Justice Douglas, observed that "the case of teachers brings the safeguards of [the First Amendment] vividly into operation...."[49] Inhibitions such as loyalty and oath requirements have "an unmistakable tendency to chill that free play of spirit which all teachers ought especially to cultivate and practice."[50]

Pickering's most direct ancestors were thus rooted partly in fears that government will leverage its power as an employer to enforce a culture of political orthodoxy. In these decisions, the Court reasoned that employees might censor themselves to avoid retaliation from employers, and that restrictions on public employee speech could threaten the operation of government institutions that depend on open lines of inquiry and discourse.

These concerns provide another set of explanations for important aspects of *Pickering* and its progeny. First, they enhance the case for protecting public employee speech, supplementing the special value rationale with the concern that, left to its own devices, government will leverage its role as employer to skew public knowledge and

---

[44] Id at 190–91.

[45] Id at 191.

[46] *Connick*, 461 US at 144 (citing *Keyishian v Board of Regents*, 385 US 589, 605–06 (1967)).

[47] *Keyishian*, 385 US at 603.

[48] *Wieman*, 344 US at 184–85.

[49] Id at 195 (Frankfurter, J, concurring).

[50] Id at 195.

debate. Second, they suggest a further reason for the Court to focus on speech about public affairs. That is, government officials will be most tempted to manipulate knowledge and criticism about themselves rather than about purely private matters. Third, these concerns help make sense of the Court's acknowledgment in *Garcetti* that "[t]here is some argument that expression related to academic scholarship or classroom instruction implicates additional constitutional interests that are not fully accounted for by this Court's customary employee-speech jurisprudence," and its consequent caveat that it is not deciding "whether the analysis . . . [in *Garcetti*] would apply in the same manner to a case involving speech related to scholarship or teaching."[51]

The Court has not explicitly incorporated a government distrust rationale into its modern public employee speech doctrine, but it should. Such reasoning would improve the doctrine's coherence and content. For instance, *Garcetti*'s reference to academic freedom could be buttressed by analysis echoing that of the loyalty oath and antisubversion cases. The Court might also connect the dots between the academic freedom arguments of the earlier cases and broader "antidistortion" fears to the effect that government might leverage its employment relationships to manipulate the messages produced by its institutions. Indeed, the Court has hinted at an antidistortion rationale in First Amendment cases involving government subsidy conditions.[52]

In Parts III through VI, I will elaborate on how government distrust and the related antidistortion interest should factor into the doctrine and theory of public employee speech rights. Specifically, I will explain how a richer conception of special value might incorporate such concerns and help improve the doctrine. For the moment, though, suffice it to note that the rudiments of such reasoning can be found in the loyalty oath and antisubversion precedents that are the *Pickering* cases' most direct antecedents.

II. Lower Court Decisions Since Garcetti and Lane

In this Part I explore some of the approaches taken by lower courts in their efforts to determine when public employee speech

---

[51] *Garcetti*, 547 US at 425.

[52] See discussion at Part III(A)(2).

can be restricted after *Garcetti*. Some approaches reflect and even exacerbate *Garcetti*'s pathologies, while others mitigate them. Similarly, in the year since the decision in *Lane*, some lower courts have invoked *Lane* to narrow *Garcetti*'s reach, while others have essentially ignored it.[53]

A. THE CONTENT OF THE SPEECH

1. *Does the information relate to, or was it learned through, the speaker's job?* Prior to *Lane*, some courts and commentators adopted strong, even conclusive presumptions to the effect that speech is unprotected under *Garcetti* when it conveys information learned on the job.[54] Support for this view derived most directly from *Garcetti*'s parity-driven statement that "[r]estricting speech that owes its existence to a public employee's professional responsibilities does not infringe any liberties the employee might have enjoyed as a private citizen."[55] In the wake of *Garcetti*, some lower courts reasoned that speech relating to, or conveying information learned through, an individual's public employment would not have existed absent the employment. They weighed this factor heavily against protection.[56] Other courts

---

[53] *Lane* was issued on June 19, 2014. Using Westlaw, I researched opinions decided between that date and June 26, 2015. I used the search term (garcetti /2 ceballos) to search the entire text of opinions for all state and federal cases issued within the designated time frame. Given the number of cases that turned up (over 260), I looked only at federal appellate court cases. Some of the cases that I reviewed relied on pre-*Lane* developments in their jurisdictions. Where useful, I followed those leads and thus read and report here on some pre-*Lane* cases as well as post-*Lane* cases. I also conducted separate searches to find pre-*Lane* opinions on certain discrete issues, including the status of speech conveying information learned on the job.

[54] See cases cited at note 56. See also Stephen I. Vladeck, *The Espionage Act and National Security Whistleblowing After Garcetti*, 57 Am U L Rev 1531, 1540–41 (2008) (suggesting *Garcetti* precludes protection for speech conveying information learned through speaker's public employment); Garry, 81 St John's L Rev at 814 (cited in note 17) (same).

[55] *Garcetti*, 547 US at 421–22.

[56] See, for example, *Lane v Central Alabama Community College*, 523 Fed Appx 709, 712 (11th Cir 2013) (relying solely on fact that Lane's testimony was about acts performed in his official capacity, although stating that that fact was "not dispositive" of conclusion that the testimony was unprotected); *Abdur-Rahman v Walker*, 567 F3d 1278, 1279, 1283 (11th Cir 2009) (deeming reports unprotected because they concerned information learned through investigations performed "as part of [plaintiffs'] assigned duties"); id at 1289 (Barkett dissenting) ("the essence of the majority opinion, with its emphasis on *Garcetti*'s phrase 'owes its existence to,' appears to be that speech about anything a public employee learns about in the course of performing his job ... is unprotected, because the speech would not exist without the job activity"). See also, for example, *Gorum v Sessoms*, 561 F3d 179, 185 (3d Cir 2009) ("We have held ... that a claimant's speech might be considered part of his official duties if it relates to 'special knowledge' or 'experience' acquired through his job."). But see *Dougherty v*

implicitly rejected this reasoning by protecting speech relating to, or conveying information learned through, a speaker's public employment.[57] Still others explicitly rejected this reasoning, deeming it at odds with reasoning in the *Pickering* cases, including *Garcetti*, regarding the special value of public employee speech.[58]

In *Lane*, the Supreme Court made clear that, at a minimum, speech is not unprotected merely because it conveys information learned on the job, or otherwise relates to one's public employment, when it consists of truthful subpoenaed testimony outside of one's ordinary job responsibilities.[59] More broadly, the Court in *Lane* observed that "the mere fact that a citizen's speech concerns information acquired by virtue of his public employment does not transform that speech into employee—rather than citizen—speech."[60]

Since *Lane*, federal courts of appeal have continued to ask whether speech relates to the speaker's employment or concerns information learned in the course of the employment. Although they usually indicate that these factors are not dispositive, they differ appreciably in the weight they accord the factors. The most straightforward way for courts to limit the weight of these factors is to consider them only insofar as they shed light on the ultimate question articulated in *Lane*—that is, whether an employee spoke within "the scope of his ordinary job responsibilities."[61] The United States Courts of Appeals for the Third and Fifth Circuits both described their inquiries, post-*Lane*, as so circumscribed.[62] On the other hand, the Eleventh Circuit

---

School District of Philadelphia, 772 F3d 979, 989 (3d Cir 2014) (clarifying, post-*Lane*, that *Gorum* does not stand for proposition that the special knowledge factor alone makes speech unprotected).

[57] See Heidi Kitrosser, *Free Speech Aboard the Leaky Ship of State: Calibrating First Amendment Protections for Leakers of Classified Information*, 6 J Natl Sec Law & Policy 409, 436 nn 135–36 (2013) (citing post-*Garcetti* cases protecting speech conveying information learned on the job).

[58] See *Chrzanowski v Bianchi*, 725 F3d 734, 738 (7th Cir 2013); *Carl v City of Mountlake Terrace*, 678 F3d 1062, 1071–72 (9th Cir 2012).

[59] See note 39 and accompanying text.

[60] *Lane*, 134 S Ct at 2379.

[61] Id at 2378.

[62] See *Culbertson v Lykos*, 790 F3d 608, 618 (5th Cir 2015) ("First Amendment ... may still apply when the employees make statements *relating* to their public employment; the question 'is whether the speech at issue is itself ordinarily within the scope of an employee's duties, not whether it merely concerns those duties'"); *Flora v Luzerne*, 776 F3d 169, 178 (3d Cir 2015) ("whether an employee's speech 'concern[s] the subject matter of [his] employment' is 'nondispositive' under *Garcetti*.... In *Lane*, the Supreme Court clarified that "'[t]he critical

described the "central inquiry" as "whether the speech at issue 'owes its existence' to the employee's professional responsibilities." The Eleventh Circuit did not deem it "dispositive" that "the speech concerns the subject matter of the employee's job," although it allowed that that "may be relevant."[63]

It also is worth noting that, in a post-*Lane* unpublished opinion, the Fifth Circuit appeared to place substantial emphasis on whether information was learned in the course of the speaker's job, and neither cites *Lane* nor otherwise makes clear that the factor is not dispositive.[64] Similarly, the Ninth Circuit has issued a post-*Lane* unpublished opinion that does not cite *Lane*, and that gravitates between asking whether speech was made "pursuant to" an employee's duties or whether it simply "related to" or "owed its existence to" those duties.[65]

2. *Is the speech directed toward resolving problems that interfere with the employee's duties?* Both before and after *Lane*, a number of lower courts deemed the fact that speech is directed toward resolving problems that interfere with the speaker's duties to signal its status as work product speech. In *Weintraub v Board of Education*, for example, the Second Circuit held, in a pre-*Lane* case, that a teacher's union grievance "challeng[ing] the school assistant principal's decision not to discipline a student who had thrown books" at the teacher was unprotected under *Garcetti*.[66] The court cited Weintraub's argument that inaction posed a threat to himself, to other teachers, to students, and to the school's learning environment.[67] The court deemed the grievance "'pursuant to' [Weintraub's] official duties because it was 'part-and-parcel of his concerns' about his ability to 'properly execute his duties' ... as a public school teacher—namely,

---

question under *Garcetti* is whether the speech at issue is itself *ordinarily* within the scope of an employee's duties, not whether it merely concerns those duties'"); *Dougherty v School District of Philadelphia*, 772 F3d 979, 989 (3d Cir 2014) (rejecting notion that speech is unprotected because it relates to one's job or conveys information learned through it, explaining that prior case considered such factors but treated them as nondispositive).

[63] *Moss v City of Pembroke Pines*, 782 F3d 613, 618 (11th Cir 2015).

[64] *Tucker v Parish*, 582 Fed Appx 363, 365–66 (5th Cir 2014) ("even assuming his duties as a probation officer did not include reporting misconduct that occurred in his presence, Tucker's speech consisted of reporting information he gained because of his employment as a probation officer").

[65] *Smith v North Star Charter School, Inc.*, 593 Fed Appx 743, 744–45 (9th Cir 2015).

[66] *Weintraub v Board of Education*, 593 F3d 196, 198 (2nd Cir 2010).

[67] Id at 199, 203.

to maintain classroom discipline, which is an indispensable prerequisite to effective teaching and classroom learning."[68] The court cited opinions from several circuits using similar reasoning.[69]

In a post-*Lane* case, the Eleventh Circuit similarly took the view that an assistant fire chief engaged in *Garcetti* speech, largely because his comments were directed toward resolving problems that fell within his job responsibilities. The court found that the assistant chief's duties "encompassed every aspect of running the fire department," including budgetary matters.[70] The court also cited his testimony to the effect that his criticisms of the city on budget and pension matters—criticisms made in a pension board meeting, a staff meeting, and conversations with fire department employees—were "motivated by his belief that the City's actions would negatively impact the fire department's provision of services." This testimony, the court explained, "confirms that plaintiff's speech was made in furtherance of his self-described responsibilities."[71] The court was unmoved by the fact that he "was not required to provide the requested guidance" and that he had, in fact, "been instructed to keep his opinions [on these matters] to himself."[72]

Lower court decisions also identify factors that may indicate that speech was *not* directed toward resolving problems within a speaker's job responsibilities. For example, the more narrowly that an employee's job duties are defined, the more difficult it is to characterize speech as supporting them. To illustrate, the Second Circuit in *Matthews v City of New York* recently distinguished *Weintraub* and found that a police officer did not speak as an employee when he complained to his commanding officers about the precinct's arrest quota policy.[73] The court explained that the officer's "speech addressed a precinct-wide policy. Such policy-oriented speech was neither part of his job description nor part of the practical reality of his everyday work."[74]

---

[68] Id at 203.

[69] Id at 202–03.

[70] *Pembroke Pines*, 782 F3d at 618–19.

[71] Id at 619.

[72] Id at 620.

[73] *Matthews v City of New York*, 779 F3d 167, 169, 174 (2d Cir 2015).

[74] Id at 174.

Some of the Supreme Court's language in *Lane*—particularly its casting of the *Garcetti* inquiry as whether the employee spoke within "the scope of his ordinary job responsibilities"[75]—strengthened the case for defining speech that furthers one's job responsibilities narrowly. Indeed, while the court in *Matthews*—which was decided post-*Lane*—did not invoke *Lane* in this manner, its emphasis on whether speech addresses impediments to one's "day-to-day responsibilities" is consistent with such reasoning.[76] Other courts have expressly "speculated whether" *Lane*'s use of a "new adjective, ['ordinary'] signals a shift in the law that broadens the scope of First Amendment protection for public employees."[77] For example, the D.C. Circuit in *Mpoy v Rhee*, while not deciding the question, acknowledged that this aspect of *Lane* might require the court to narrow its "consistent[]" holding that "a public employee speaks without First Amendment protection when he reports conduct that interferes with his job responsibilities, even if the report is made outside his chain of command."[78]

3. *Does the speech convey information about government misconduct?* Another factor is whether speech conveys information about government misconduct. Both prior to and since *Lane*, the Fourth Circuit has invoked broad language suggesting that speech exposing public corruption warrants protection. In its 2015 decision in *Hunter v Mocksville*, the Fourth Circuit reiterated its statement from an earlier case that "'speech about serious governmental misconduct, and certainly not least of all serious misconduct in a law enforcement agency, is protected.'"[79] The court observed that the Supreme Court in *Lane* made statements in keeping with this view.[80] The Court in *Lane* had indeed explained that "[i]t would be antithetical

---

[75] See *Lane*, 134 S Ct at 2378.

[76] The *Matthews* court does cite *Lane* in passing in two places. *Matthews*, 779 F3d at 172, 175.

[77] *Flora*, 776 F3d at 179, n 11 (3rd Cir 2015) (citing *Mpoy v Rhee*, 758 F3d 285, 295 (DC Cir 2014)). See also *Gibson v Kilpatrick*, 773 F3d 661, 668 (5th Cir 2014) ("much of the treatment of *Lane* thus far has speculated that the insertion of 'ordinary' may signal a narrowing of the Supreme Court's position on *Garcetti*'s coverage").

[78] *Mpoy* at 291, 294–95. The court refrained from deciding whether the D.C. Circuit must indeed adjust its past holdings in light of *Lane*. It found that, at minimum, the defendant had qualified immunity because she could reasonably have believed prior to *Lane* that the plaintiff's speech was unprotected. Id at 295.

[79] *Hunter v Mocksville*, 789 F3d 389, 401 (4th Cir 2015).

[80] Id at 398.

to our jurisprudence to conclude that the very kind of speech necessary to prosecute corruption by public officials—speech by public employees regarding information learned through their employment—may never form the basis for a First Amendment retaliation claim."[81]

While the Fourth Circuit's expansive language could be interpreted to mean that speech exposing public corruption or abuse of authority intrinsically constitutes citizen speech, the Fifth Circuit in *Gibson v Kilpatrick* cautioned against reading *Lane* so broadly. It argued that "the passage [in *Lane*] must be read in the context of *Lane's* facts and in light of *Lane's* statement that the opinion does 'not address in this case whether truthful sworn testimony would constitute citizen speech under *Garcetti* when given as part of a public employee's ordinary job duties.'"[82] The court in *Gibson* only decided, however, that so expansive a reading of employee protections was not "clearly established" with respect to conduct that took place prior to *Lane*.[83]

B. HOW OR TO WHOM WAS THE SPEECH CONVEYED?

Lower courts have also considered, both before and since *Lane*, whether the audience to whom the speech was conveyed, or the medium through which the speech was conveyed, reflects the speaker's employment. A common way for courts to couch this inquiry is to ask whether the employee directed her speech "up the chain of command."[84] Others frame the inquiry by asking whether there is a

---

[81] *Lane*, 134 S Ct at 2380.

[82] *Gibson*, 773 F3d at 669.

[83] Id. See also id at 666 (explaining inquiry's significance: defendants possess qualified immunity for behavior infringing on rights not clearly established at the time of that behavior).

[84] See, for example, *Wilson v Tregre*, 787 F3d 322, 325 (5th Cir 2015) ("Wilson was acting in his official duties....he was simply reporting potential criminal activity up the chain of command"); *Flora*, 776 F3d at 177 (citing 2007 case in which Third Circuit "declined to extend First Amendment protection when the speech in question was directed 'up the chain of command'"); *Olendzki v Rossi*, 765 F3d 742, 749 (7th Cir 2014) (quoting 2010 Seventh Circuit case to effect that "a public employee's complaints 'made directly up the chain of command to his supervisors are not protected under the First Amendment'"); *Mpoy*, 758 F3d at 294 (DC Cir 2014) ("whether speech is made inside or outside a chain of command may be a contextual factor in determining *whether* the employee made it to report interference with his job responsibilities"); *Wetherbe v Smith*, 593 Fed Appx 323, 328 (5th Cir 2014) (quoting 2008 Fifth Circuit case for proposition that an employee "generally does not have First Amendment protection for communications that 'relate to his own job function up the chain of command'").

"civilian analogue" for the speaker's chosen medium or the speech recipient.[85]

Of course, what constitutes "the chain of command" or what possesses a "civilian analogue" can be defined broadly or narrowly, with significant consequences for the scope of speech protection. For example, the Fifth Circuit in *Gibson v Kilpatrick* took an expansive view of the "chain of the command"—or, more precisely, of its equivalent—in reasoning that a city's mayor (Kilpatrick) did not infringe the city police chief's (Gibson's) clearly established First Amendment rights. Gibson alleged that Mayor Kilpatrick had retaliated against him for reporting Kilpatrick's misuse of a city gas card to outside law enforcement agencies, including the FBI, the federal Drug Enforcement Agency (DEA), the state attorney general, and the Office of the State Auditor (OSA).[86] The court acknowledged that among the factors it typically considers in determining whether a speaker spoke as an employee "is whether the employee's complaint was made within the chain of command or to an outside actor, such as a different government agency or the media."[87] The court clarified, however, that reports to outsiders are not invariably citizen speech. It concluded that Gibson conveyed his reports to external agencies as an employee. The court relied partly on the fact that chain-of-command reporting would not have been a desirable option for Gibson. It explained:

> the only entities to which [Gibson] could have reported within the chain of command were [Mayor] Kilpatrick and the Board. Reporting to Kilpatrick—the suspected perpetrator—clearly was undesirable, while reporting to the Board might have required public disclosure of Gibson's suspicions, perhaps endangering the subsequent investigation. Indeed, it appears that once Board members learned of the investigation, one of them informed Kilpatrick.[88]

In *Gibson*, the Fifth Circuit thus defined the chain-of-command factor broadly enough to encompass reporting either through an employee's actual chain of command or through logical alternatives.

---

[85] *Matthews*, 779 F3d at 173, 175–76.

[86] *Gibson*, 773 F3d at 664–65.

[87] Id at 670.

[88] Id at 671. See also id at 670 ("where, as here, the employee is reporting the misconduct of his supervisor, an outside agency may be the most appropriate entity to which to report the misconduct").

The court also considered whether *Lane* should affect its reasoning.[89] While acknowledging that a few "aspects of the *Lane* opinion … appear to offer the prospect of new law,"[90] the court concluded that such aspects, at minimum, were not "'clearly established' at the time of the challenged conduct," which took place prior to *Lane*.[91] *Lane* thus did not affect the Fifth Circuit's finding that the defendants violated no clearly established rights and therefore had qualified immunity.[92]

In contrast to the Fifth Circuit in *Gibson*, the Second Circuit in *Matthews* recently rejected a very expansive take on the conditions under which a speaker's forum choice signaled that he spoke as an employee. The Second Circuit held that police officer Craig Matthews spoke as a citizen when he complained to his commanding officers about an arrest quota policy at his precinct.[93] Among the factors the court considered was whether the forum through which Matthews spoke had "a civilian analogue."[94] The Second Circuit found that Matthews "chose a path that was available to ordinary citizens who are regularly provided the opportunity to raise issues with the Precinct commanders."[95] It rejected the district court's reasoning that Matthews's speech lacked a civilian analogue because "Matthews had better access to his commanding officers than would ordinary citizens."[96] "Presumably," the Second Circuit explained, "employees always have better access to senior supervisors within their place of employment."[97] If an employee's relative "degree of access" were considered, "internal public employee speech on matters of public concern not made as part of regular job duties would be unlikely to receive First Amendment protection."[98]

---

[89] The Fifth Circuit had issued an initial decision in *Gibson* prior to *Lane*. The Supreme Court vacated and remanded after *Lane*. Id at 666.

[90] *Gibson*, 773 F3d at 668.

[91] Id at 669. See also id at 670.

[92] Id at 670–73.

[93] *Matthews*, 779 F3d at 169.

[94] Id at 173.

[95] Id at 176.

[96] Id.

[97] Id.

[98] Id.

Sounding a note similar to that of the Second Circuit, the Fourth Circuit recently emphasized that speakers can be protected for speech directed through internal as well as external channels.[99] The court cited *Lane*'s trumpeting of the special value of public employee speech and its warning against reading *Garcetti* too broadly.[100] The Fourth Circuit also cited Justice Stevens's concern, expressed in dissent in *Garcetti*, "that it would be 'perverse to fashion a new rule that provides employees with an incentive to voice their concerns publicly,'" rather than internally.[101]

III. The Special Value of Public Employee Speech

In this part, I develop the concept of the special value of public employee speech. The basic argument is that public employees have a crucial structural role to play in countering government's capacity for deception. As courts acknowledge, one aspect of special value consists of the unique insights that public employees gain through their work. But courts disregard two other facets of special value. First, to the extent that employees have special access to internal communication channels, this heightens their free speech value. Second, through the very act of doing their jobs conscientiously and in accordance with the norms of their professions, public employees help to maintain consistency between the functions in which government purports to engage and those that it actually performs. In this sense, public employees are potential barriers against government deception through distortion.

The remainder of Part III expands on these points by building their theoretical foundations. Subpart A sets forth the free speech theory based foundations and identifies judicial precedent consistent with the same. Subpart B draws support from constitutional structure, particularly the federal separation of powers.

A. INSIGHTS FROM FREE SPEECH THEORY

1. *Self-government, checking, and distrust.* The First Amendment's text simply does not, either on its face or through its original mean-

---

[99] *Hunter*, 789 F3d at 399, 402.

[100] Id at 396–97.

[101] Id at 402.

ing, tell us very much about its scope.[102] As a result, scholars and courts long have relied on theories about the values underlying the Free Speech Clause to help determine the scope of First Amendment protections.[103]

The case for protecting public employees' work product speech builds on several strands of free speech theory. At its most basic level, it starts with the notion that, whatever other purpose the Free Speech Clause serves, it undoubtedly protects the conveyance of information and opinion about government to support an informed and engaged citizenry. This point is of no real controversy.[104] It is closely tied to the notion that speech that facilitates oversight and checking of government has substantial value.[105] A corollary of both notions is that wariness is called for whenever government seeks to restrict speech about its own operations.[106]

Vigilance against government efforts to skew public knowledge and debate in its favor is central to the Supreme Court's understanding of the First Amendment. As already noted, in its Cold War era loyalty oath and antisubversion decisions the Court railed against government's leveraging its role as employer to enforce political orthodoxy in the workplace or the broader community.[107] Similar judicial concerns are evident in the "content distinction" rule, which creates a strong presumption against laws or law enforcement based on the viewpoint, subject matter, or communicative impact of speech.[108] The Court even has limited government's ability to punish content-based subcategories of otherwise unprotected speech, for

---

[102] I have elaborated on this point elsewhere. See Heidi Kitrosser, *Interpretive Modesty*, 104 Georgetown L J *nn 168–72, 183–85 and accompanying text (forthcoming, 2016) (on file with author); Kitrosser, 6 J Natl Sec L & Policy at 421–22 (cited in note 57).

[103] See note 102.

[104] Kitrosser, 6 J Natl Sec L & Policy at 422 n 63 (cited in note 57) (citing consensus that "whatever else the freedom of speech may encompass, it undoubtedly includes a right to convey information and opinion about government").

[105] The seminal work on the checking value in First Amendment theory is Vincent Blasi's article of that title. See Vincent Blasi, *The Checking Value in First Amendment Theory*, 2 Am Bar Found Res J 521 (1977). Blasi details the checking value and explores its relationship to other free speech values. Id at 548, 553–554, 557–65.

[106] Frederick Schauer demonstrated that all major free speech theories share a core distrust of government, and that this should be a central concern of free speech doctrine. Frederick Schauer, *Free Speech: A Philosophical Enquiry* 33–34, 44–46, 86, 162–63 (Cambridge, 1982).

[107] See discussion at Part (I)(D).

[108] See, for example, Heidi Kitrosser, *From Marshall McLuhan to Anthropomorphic Cows: Communicative Matter and the First Amendment*, 96 Nw U L Rev 1339, 1339–1342, 1345–49

fear that government will use unprotected speech categories as vehicles to discriminate based on "hostility—or favoritism—towards the underlying message expressed."[109]

2. *Distortion*. Self-government, checking, and distrust theories lend themselves to concerns that government will distort information no less than that it will suppress it. By "information distortion," I refer to the phenomenon whereby government purports to provide or subsidize information of a type that is defined by reference to professional or social norms, while manipulating the information in a manner antithetical to those norms. Distortion occurs, for example, where government hires climate scientists to make climate projections but insists that they alter their findings for political reasons as a condition of their continued employment. Distortion alters the very picture of reality against which the public or intragovernmental actors can assess and respond to government actions and decisions.[110]

This concern about distortion is linked to another concern: that courts tend to overstate the dichotomy between "government speech" and "citizen speech."[111] The government is free, of course, to express its own viewpoints, including through government employees and subsidy recipients. Few would argue, for example, that "[w]hen Congress established a National Endowment for Democracy to encourage other countries to adopt democratic principles ... it was ... constitutionally required to fund a program to encourage competing lines of political philosophy such as communism and fascism."[112] But not all government speech consists of policy messages that the

---

(2002) (summarizing the rule and citing cases, though noting that Supreme Court does not always treat communicative manner as content).

[109] *R.A.V. v St. Paul*, 505 US 377, 386 (1992).

[110] See, for example, Helen Norton, *Constraining Public Employee Speech: Government's Control of Its Workers' Speech to Protect Its Own Expression*, 59 Duke L J 1, 27–31 (2009) (explaining that free speech concerns are raised when government's role in crafting speech of employees or subsidy recipients is obscured); Caroline Mala Corbin, *Mixed Speech: When Speech Is Both Private and Governmental*, 83 NYU L Rev 605, 665–71 (2008) (making similar point); Randall P. Bezanson and William G. Buss, *The Many Faces of Government Speech*, 86 Iowa L Rev 1377, 1397–1401, 1450, 1460–61, 1487, 1491 (2001) (same).

[111] See text accompanying notes 114–16. See also, for example, Corbin, 83 NYU L Rev at 625–26 (cited in note 110) (suggesting that public employee speech typically mixes "citizen speech" and "government speech"); Estlund, 2006 Supreme Court Review at 151–53 (cited in note 9) ("The work [public] employees do for the public through their job may be a truer ... expression of their character and self-conception as citizens than their rare letters to the editor or statements at public meetings.").

[112] *Rust v Sullivan*, 500 US 173, 194 (1991).

government transparently acknowledges as such. In many cases the government purports to subsidize speakers—whether by employing them or by funding particular projects—precisely for the expertise that enables them to make sound independent judgments.

Accordingly, some scholars observe that when government hires certain types of employees—for instance, lawyers or scientists—or subsidizes particular types of speech—such as artwork or health-care guidance—it commissions work constrained by professional, artistic, ethical, or other norms. Courts artificially wipe away these aspects of expertise and judgment—these "private citizen" aspects, so to speak—when they treat the speech as government property subject to government's unfettered control. In so doing, courts con-flate speech that purports to deliver professional expertise with speech that transparently conveys the government's policy preferences. By placing both in the "government speech" category, the Court enables the government to claim that it has commissioned "professional" speech at the same time as it strips that speech of the very features that make it professional.

For example, Robert Post criticizes the Supreme Court's reason-ing in the 1991 case of *Rust v Sullivan*. In *Rust*, the Court upheld federal regulations barring family planning clinics from mention-ing abortion in the course of providing federally subsidized counsel-ing.[113] Post questions whether the Court erred by treating subsidized medical counseling as falling within the government's "managerial domain," subject to extensive government control. Post notes that "[p]hysicians are of course professionals, and ... professionals must always qualify their loyalty and commitment to the vertical hierarchy of an organization by their horizontal commitment to general pro-fessional norms and standards."[114]

Orly Lobel expresses similar concerns, using insights from orga-nization theory. Lobel invokes the concept of "enlightened loyalty," whereby a loyal employee exercises some independent judgment, rather than blind obedience, to further the good of their organiza-tion.[115] From this perspective, the Court in *Garcetti* misstepped by

---

[113] Id at 173, 191.

[114] Robert C. Post, *Subsidized Speech*, 106 Yale L J 151, 172 (1996). See also id at 170–76.

[115] Orly Lobel, *Citizenship, Organizational Citizenship, and the Laws of Overlapping Obliga-tions*, 97 Cal L Rev 433, 437–40, 477 (2009).

drawing too sharp a distinction between one's wisdom, judgment, and moral and legal commitments as a private citizen, and one's acts as a public employee.[116]

The Supreme Court expressly invoked antidistortion reasoning in the 2001 case of *Legal Services Corporation v Velazquez*. *Velazquez* involved a federal statutory restriction on the use of Legal Services Corporation (LSC) funds. LSC was established by Congress in 1974 "to distribute funds appropriated by Congress to eligible local grantee organizations 'for the purpose of providing financial support for legal assistance in noncriminal proceedings or matters to persons financially unable to afford legal assistance.'"[117] The restriction prohibited attorneys, in the course of LSC-funded representation, from challenging the constitutionality of state or federal welfare laws or the consistency of state welfare laws with federal statutes.[118] While LSC attorneys were free to argue that agents had interpreted or applied welfare statutes incorrectly in their clients' cases, they were forbidden from challenging the legality of the statutes themselves.[119]

The United States argued that the restriction did not abridge speech, but simply set the parameters of a program that Congress had created and funded. The Court rejected this position. It explained that "[w]here the government uses or attempts to regulate a particular medium, we have been informed by its accepted usage in determining whether a particular restriction on speech is necessary for the program's purposes and limitations."[120] The LSC program purported to use the legal system "to facilitate suits for benefits."[121] Yet the restriction distorted that system by interfering with the "traditional role" of attorneys, limiting the range of "arguments and analyses" that they may make to courts and the options that they may present

---

[116] Id at 433–34, 453–55.

[117] *Legal Services Corporation v Velazquez*, 531 US 533, 536 (2001).

[118] Id at 536–37.

[119] LSC interpreted the restriction to mean that "[e]ven in cases where constitutional or statutory challenges became apparent after representation was well under way ... its attorneys must withdraw." Id at 539.

[120] Id at 543. To support this point, the Court cited limited public forum cases invalidating restrictions that altered the nature of the forums at issue. It acknowledged that the forum cases, while instructive, "may not be controlling in a strict sense" since *Velazquez* "involves a subsidy." Id at 544.

[121] *Velazquez*, 531 US at 544.

to clients.[122] The Court cited the negative effects of this distortion on the separation of powers, particularly on the judiciary.[123]

The Supreme Court had hinted at similar antidistortion concerns in the Cold War era loyalty oath and antisubversion cases. As expressed by the majority in *Keyishian*, the fear was that the restrictions would distort the classroom's status as "peculiarly the 'marketplace of ideas.'"[124] Or, as Justice Frankfurter put it, concurring in *Wieman*, such restrictions might "chill that free play of spirit which all teachers ought especially to cultivate and practice."[125]

Of course, neither the antisubversion cases nor *Velazquez* constitute the Supreme Court's only wisdom regarding public employee speech or government-funded speech. *Garcetti* and *Rust* complicate the case law, and they have kindred precedent. Indeed, *Rust* was the first in a line of cases taking an expansive view of the government's power to control "government speech." These cases involved speech that was created at least partly by private actors and that was not transparently presented as having been shaped by the government. Nonetheless, the Supreme Court characterized the speech as the government's own and permitted the government to control its content, free from the constraints of the First Amendment.[126] While *Velazquez* and the antisubversion cases thus are hardly the Supreme Court's only word on the matter, they do reveal flashes of judicial insight consistent with a more robust conception of the special value of public employee speech. These shards of wisdom, combined with those in the academic literature, provide the foundation for a free speech theory that offers a more satisfying approach to public employee speech.

---

[122] Id.

[123] Id at 546.

[124] *Keyishian*, 385 US at 603.

[125] See note 50.

[126] See, for example, *Walker v Sons of Confederate Veterans*, 135 S Ct 2239 (2015) (holding that state engaged in speech when it issued specialty license plates designed by private groups and that state therefore could reject proposed designs without any First Amendment limits); *Pleasant Grove City, Utah v Summum*, 555 US 460 (2009) (holding that city engaged in speech by accepting privately donated monuments for a public park and that city therefore could reject donations without First Amendment constraint). See also, for example, Corbin, 83 NYU L Rev at 611–16, 639–40, 663–71 (cited in note 110) (discussing government speech doctrine and arguing that it takes an overly broad view of what constitutes government speech); Norton, 59 Duke L J at 25–32 (cited in note 110) (same).

B. A ROLE FOR CONSTITUTIONAL STRUCTURE

The First Amendment is not the only constitutional means to check government power.[127] The Constitution is filled with mechanisms that enable government actors and institutions to challenge one another. Most important for our purposes are those checks on presidential power that empower subordinates to dissent.

Elsewhere, I have discussed such checking mechanisms in depth.[128] I summarize them here, starting with those that draw directly on constitutional text.[129] A number of textual details—including but not limited to the division of the appointments power between the President and the Senate, Congress's constitutional ability to delegate some inferior officer appointments away from the President, and the Opinions Clause, which confirms that the President may require written opinions from executive department heads—suggest an executive branch in which the President has substantial but not unfettered supervisory authority and in which his subordinates are potential checks against abuse or incompetence.[130]

The textual indications are bolstered by history from the framing and ratification period. For example, supporters of the proposed Constitution insisted that the Framers, in declining to annex a council to the President, had intentionally deprived the President of a group that would do his bidding and hide his secrets. Alexander Hamilton argued that the President not only would lack a council behind which to hide, but that his appointed subordinates, who were subject to Senate approval, would be unlikely to shield his bad acts.[131]

These structural aspects of the Constitution and its history confirm the dual role of public employees in the federal system. On the one hand, government employees are a part of the executive branch and are charged with supporting its efficacy. On the other hand,

---

[127] As Charles Black observed, a free speech right might be inferable from the Constitution even without the First Amendment. See Charles L. Black, Jr., *Structure and Relationship in Constitutional Law* 41–50 (Louisiana State, 1969).

[128] See, for example, Heidi Kitrosser, *Reclaiming Accountability* at chap 7 (Chicago, 2015).

[129] Parts of this paragraph and the next two are drawn from Section II(C)(1) of *Leak Prosecutions and the First Amendment: New Development and a Closer Look at the Feasibility of Protecting Leakers*, 56 Wm & Mary L Rev 1221, 1244–46 (2015).

[130] For elaboration on these points see Kitrosser, *Reclaiming Accountability* at 147–62 (cited in note 128).

[131] Federalist 76 (Alexander Hamilton) in Lawrence Goldman, ed, *The Federalist Papers* 373 (2008).

government employees are crucial safety valves for protecting the people from abuse and incompetence, given their unique access to information and to a range of avenues for transmitting the same.

While the Constitution does not dictate the structure of state or local governments, the logic underlying the federal model—that internal checks are necessary to head off tyranny or incompetence by superiors—also bolsters the insights of free speech theory as it relates to the states and localities.

IV. Practical and Conceptual Objections to Accommodating Special Value

While academic opinion runs largely against *Garcetti*, some thoughtful opposing views have been articulated and warrant attention. *Garcetti*'s defenses fall into two rough categories. One set of arguments suggests that *Garcetti* does not pose much of a threat to free speech. The other stresses that public employers need ample discretion to manage employees and their work product.

A. FREE SPEECH VALUE BASED OBJECTIONS

Some commentators posit that *Garcetti*'s impact falls predominantly on internal workplace speech, and that this speech lacks much salience under the First Amendment.[132] It is only when employees take their concerns public, they argue, that the speech has significant First Amendment value. One scholar writes, for example, that "the First Amendment ... is intended to facilitate public oversight of government, and that purpose is not served by intra-governmental speech."[133] Another argues: "When a public employee brings heretofore concealed misconduct into public view, he enables the process of political accountability to function.... Public employees whose views remain hidden from public view, in contrast, contribute little to public discussion and debate."[134]

---

[132] See Roosevelt, 14 U Pa J Const L at 649 (cited in note 17) ("*Garcetti* does not reach speech to the public, unless producing such speech is the employee's job (in which case the speech is actually the government's speech))"; Lawrence Rosenthal, *The Emerging First Amendment Law of Managerial Prerogative*, 77 Fordham L Rev 33, 57 (2008) ("For public employees who take their concerns to the public, *Garcetti* should pose no bar to First Amendment protection.").

[133] Roosevelt, 14 U Pa J Const L at 653–54 (cited in note 17).

[134] Id at 59.

This position is belied by the tremendous importance of private discussions to free speech values, including checking values. In the context of public employment, effective checking may occur, for instance, where improprieties are reported up the chain of command, even if those reports never reach the public. Such checking also can help shape the information that does make its way to the public. It may, for example, stymie practices that punish honest or effective internal reporting that itself enters the public discourse.[135]

Nor does it resolve First Amendment concerns to suggest that employees can simply bring their information or complaints directly to the public or otherwise air them in a manner that falls outside of their job responsibilities. Public employees' special value as speakers stems partly from their capacity to choose from a number of forums, including those through which they perform their jobs or other avenues to which the public lacks access. This flexibility enables employees to make judgments about more or less effective or safe forums from the outset, and to adapt when government plays shell games with accountability, as when it purports to provide an avenue for redress that it fails to deliver or that becomes a retaliation trap.[136] Such flexibility also empowers employees to reconcile their checking roles with respect for bureaucratic protocol without forfeiting constitutional protection. It enables them, for instance, to attempt to report through internal channels rather than turning to the press as a matter of first resort.

The Supreme Court has made clear that speech communicated privately by government employees in the workplace warrants protection. In *Rankin v McPherson*, for example, the Court deemed unconstitutional the firing of McPherson, who worked as a clerical employee in a constable's office.[137] McPherson was fired for saying, in a private office conversation with a work colleague after the two had heard a radio bulletin about the attempt to assassinate President

---

[135] See Estlund, 2006 Supreme Court Review at 125 (cited in note 9) (citing democratic benefits of internal employee speech).

[136] For one striking example of an apparent retaliation trap, see Jane Mayer, *The Secret Sharer*, New Yorker (May 23, 2011) (describing simultaneous raid on homes of three persons—two former NSA employees and one former congressional staffer—who had filed what they believed to be a confidential complaint with the Pentagon's Inspector General).

[137] *Rankin v McPherson*, 483 US 378, 383 (1987).

Reagan, that Rankin disapproves of Reagan's policies and that "'if they go for him again ... [she] hope[s] they get him.'"[138] The Court deemed Rankin's statement to be about a matter of public concern because it related to President Reagan's policies and the attempt on his life.[139] In a footnote, the Court rejected the suggestion, made by the United States as amicus, that "[t]he private nature of the statement ... vitiate[s its status] as addressing a matter of public concern."[140] In rejecting this contention, the Court cited *Givhan v Western Line Consolidated School District*.[141] In *Givhan*, the Court had vacated a lower court's holding that a teacher was not constitutionally protected from termination for expressing concerns to her principal, in private meetings, about perceived race discrimination in their school district.[142] The Court in *Givhan* emphasized that the Constitution protects a speaker when she "arranges to communicate privately with [her] employer rather than to spread [her] views before the public."[143]

B. OBJECTIONS BASED ON MANAGERIAL DISCRETION

Garcetti's defenders also emphasize government's need to manage its employees.[144] *Garcetti* itself "gestures at" two facets of this view.[145] The first—the "government speech" rationale—is the position that "speech produced pursuant to official duties [is] in some sense government speech."[146] When employees speak as the government, their

---

[138] Id at 380–82.

[139] Id at 386–87.

[140] Id at 386 n 11. The majority also found, in applying *Connick-Pickering*, that the speech's private setting cut strongly against finding it disruptive. Id at 388–89 & 388 n 13. The majority "agree[d] with Justice Powell," who concurred, "that a purely private statement on a matter of public concern will rarely, if ever, justify discharge of a public employee." Id at 388 n 13. See also Estlund, 2006 Supreme Court Review at 123 (cited in note 9) (citing this aspect of *Rankin*).

[141] *Rankin*, 483 US at 386 n 11 (citing *Givhan v Western Line Consolidated School District*, 439 US 410, 414–16 (1979)).

[142] *Givhan*, 439 US at 412–13.

[143] Id at 415–16. See also Estlund, 2006 Supreme Court Review at 121–22 (cited in note 9) (discussing this aspect of *Givhan*).

[144] See Roosevelt, 14 U Pa J Const L at 652 (cited in note 17); Rosenthal, 77 Fordham L Rev at 38, 46–49 (cited in note 132).

[145] Roosevelt, 14 U Pa J Const L at 635 (cited in note 17).

[146] Id.

employers must have free rein to dictate or correct what they say.[147] The second managerial discretion argument—the "evaluation rationale"—is that spoken or written work product "should be conceptualized as job performance rather than speech,"[148] and that courts are in no position—either constitutionally or as a practical matter—to second-guess supervisors' job performance evaluations.[149]

1. *The government speech rationale.* The "government speech" rationale plainly fails to justify *Garcetti*'s categorical rule. The problem is not that this consideration is invalid in all cases, but that it is inapplicable to many public jobs. As discussed earlier, some types of public employment—let us call them "scripted jobs"—entail conveying messages crafted by the government.[150] The very nature of a scripted job demands full governmental control of the messages that the employee is hired to deliver. Helen Norton offers several examples of scripted jobs, including those generated "when a school board hires a press secretary or lobbyist to promote its anti-voucher position, a health department hires an employee to implement an antismoking promotional effort … or a mayor commissions a muralist specifically to create patriotic art for the Fourth of July."[151]

But as noted earlier,[152] and as Norton and others point out, many government positions, including the assistant district attorney job at issue in *Garcetti*, are not scripted jobs (let us call these "unscripted jobs"). Unscripted jobs call for employees to exercise a nontrivial degree of independent judgment.[153] Such judgment can manifest itself in spoken or written work product, whether in the form of reports to supervisors, scientific reports for public or internal distribution, or court briefings.

It is true that even unscripted employee speech is government speech in the narrow sense that the government has paid for it.

---

[147] It is on this basis that Kermit Roosevelt dismisses concerns about *Garcetti*'s impact on public speech. Though acknowledging that "[s]ome employees might have the job of communicating to the public," he concludes that "such an employee is probably best conceived of as speaking for the government, in which case the government would be allowed to dictate the content of the speech." See id at 647 & 647 n 62.

[148] Id.

[149] See Part IV(B)(2), (3).

[150] See text accompanying notes 111–12.

[151] Norton, 59 Duke L J at 30–31 (cited in note 110).

[152] See text accompanying notes 112–25.

[153] See notes 110–25 and accompanying text.

But by definition, the government has paid unscripted speakers to produce undistorted speech.[154] In these circumstances, *Garcetti*'s categorical rule cannot be justified by invoking the particularized case of the scripted public employee.

2. *The evaluation rationale: the accountability argument.* The evaluation rationale has both practical and constitutional dimensions. As a constitutional matter, Lawrence Rosenthal argues that "if public policymakers could not remove subordinates whom they regard as unwilling or unable to execute their duties as those policymakers wish—including duties that involve speech—then they cannot be fairly held politically accountable for the performance of their offices.... Preserving the process of political control and accountability over public offices is surely at the core of our Constitution."[155]

The argument from political accountability rests on a premise that is partly sound. Political actors undoubtedly must retain meaningful control over unelected bureaucrats and their work product in order to tie administration to political accountability. But meaningful control does not necessarily equal full and unfettered control. I have discussed this point at length in a different context, explaining that unitary executive theorists err in deeming unfettered presidential control over all federal executive actors necessary to preserve accountability. As I argue in that setting, the level of political control necessary to maintain accountability is a functional, fact-sensitive question. Its answer varies with the nature of both the employment and the restriction at issue.[156]

More importantly, as I have also emphasized in discussing unitary executive theory, unfettered supervisory control can defeat rather than enhance accountability. This is especially true where written or spoken work product is at issue. At the federal level, for example, "[u]nfettered presidential control can be used ... to keep truthful information from emerging from the executive branch through White House vetting of congressional testimony, pressure to alter scientific findings for political reasons, or secretive influence over agency

---

[154] See Part III(A)(2) for discussion of the concept of distortion.

[155] Rosenthal, 77 Fordham L Rev at 48 (cited in note 132). Another scholar ties employee speech protections themselves to political accountability, explaining that "[i]f the democratic community needs or desires free and open 'whistleblower' speech, it can enact the appropriate laws." Garry, 81 St John's L Rev at 815 (cited in note 17).

[156] See Kitrosser, *Reclaiming Accountability* at 165–66 (cited in note 128).

policy decisions."[157] Helen Norton makes a similar point in critiquing *Garcetti*, explaining that "the government's accountability for its performance may well be undercut by the carte blanche *Garcetti* gives government to discipline workers who truthfully report irregularities and improprieties pursuant to their official duties."[158]

3. *The evaluation rationale: arguments concerning judicial overreach and relative competence.* The most challenging defenses of *Garcetti* are based on notions of comparative institutional advantage. Specifically, they are grounded in arguments that public employers are better situated than judges to evaluate employee work product. The point is partly about competence. As Kermit Roosevelt puts it, "the employer is much better than a judge at deciding whether particular speech is good job performance or not."[159] Nor would it help for courts to apply the *Connick-Pickering* test and weigh, case by case, the public employer's efficiency interests against employees' interests in "commenting upon matters of public concern."[160] As Roosevelt explains, *Connick-Pickering*'s application "would prevent employers from firing or reassigning employees whose memos address issues of public concern and are nondisruptive, but are riddled with errors of legal analysis."[161] Roosevelt also suggests that the judiciary is not the constitutionally appropriate institution to judge work product quality. Such content-based judicial judgments, he explains, would themselves raise First Amendment concerns.[162]

Concerns over institutional roles and competence are serious, but they are overstated in important respects. For one thing, as lower court applications of *Garcetti* reflect, the lines separating work product speech from other public employee speech often are quite fuzzy. The *Garcetti* rule itself thus demands no easy judicial feat. More importantly, this means that there is no bright line separating what courts have done for years—apply the *Connick-Pickering* test to "non-work product" speech—from the task of applying *Connick-Pickering* to work product speech.

---

[157] Id at 144.

[158] Norton, 59 Duke L J at 33 (cited in note 110).

[159] Roosevelt, 14 U Pa J Const L at 653 (cited in note 17).

[160] See text accompanying note 8.

[161] Roosevelt, 14 U Pa J Const L at 652 (cited in note 17).

[162] Id.

Even when we can comfortably identify work product speech, institutionally based objections to judicial review rest on a faulty premise. They assume that judicial review must entail substantive assessment of work product quality, duplicating the review conducted by work supervisors. But, as I will show in subpart C, this need not be the case.

C. ACCOMMODATING SUPERVISORS' EVALUATIVE NEEDS WITHOUT SACRIFICING SPECIAL VALUE

Judicial review in the work product context can and should be designed not to second-guess supervisor assessments of work product quality, but to smoke out retaliation against work product speech *for reasons other than quality*. The need for managerial discretion is at its apex in the realm of work product quality review. And employers' nonpretextual, quality-based judgments do not pose a strong threat to special value. On the other hand, special value is deeply threatened by retaliation in response to inconvenient facts or analysis in work product speech. Although such retaliation is not the only proper target of judicial review, it ought to be its main target.

Under the approach suggested here, then, courts would effectively leave nonpretextual decisions based on work product quality untouched. For example, a government lawyer's supervisor would have free rein to discipline her for turning in a memorandum "riddled with errors of legal analysis."[163] Similarly, a government scientist's superior would be free to discipline her for sloppy research methods or poorly written reports. On the other hand, retaliating against a government lawyer for her internal legal advice, not because the advice is unsound but because it provides a politically inconvenient answer, is not a work quality-based judgment. Nor would it constitute a work quality-based decision were a government scientist's supervisors to discipline her for reaching scientific conclusions in tension with an administration's policy agenda. On the other hand, a scripted employee's failure to stick to her script could legitimately be deemed poor work quality warranting discipline.

At this point, some of my fellow *Garcetti* critics might question why one would draw any threshold distinction between work product speech and non-work product speech in the first place. They could

---

[163] See text accompanying note 161 (citing Roosevelt's use of this example).

point to the practical difficulties in making the distinction. They might add that, even if we could confidently identify work product speech, the best way to accommodate free speech and managerial needs is to evaluate all challenged discipline under the fact-sensitive *Connick-Pickering* test.

In response to these concerns, it is important first to acknowledge that it is no easy task to distinguish work product speech from other public employee speech made in the workplace. Lower court decisions betray both this difficulty and the risk that poor line-drawing will suppress speech. That said, some work product speech is relatively easy to identify as such. Examples include legal briefs or memoranda written by government lawyers in the course of litigating their assigned cases, or scientific reports written at the request of agency scientists' superiors.

Furthermore, the fact that discipline for work product speech is not immune from judicial review under my approach should conduce to greater definitional precision. Such discipline would be spared further review only after a judicial determination that it was based on work product quality. This may help to narrow judicial understandings of work product speech to speech of a type that could be reviewed for its professional quality in the first place. In Part VI, I elaborate further on tools that courts can use to focus their conceptions of work product speech. The fact that work product speech based discipline would not be immune from judicial review also lowers the stakes of questionable judicial judgments in identifying such speech.

In addition, my approach has advantages over one that draws no distinction between work product speech and other employee speech. It accommodates the most compelling managerial prerogative needs without sacrificing free speech value. On the other hand, applying *Connick-Pickering* to evaluative determinations poses some risk to free speech value. The test, already subject to very deferential applications, may become yet more diluted through its application to such decisions.

Of course, my approach could be criticized from another perspective—that of *Garcetti*'s supporters. Such critics might argue that it is infeasible for courts to assess whether managerial judgments are based on work product quality without themselves evaluating such quality. But courts have considerable experience conducting inquiries designed to smoke out illegitimate decision-making bases and to distinguish them from permissible rationales. While hardly perfect, such inquiries are intrinsically different from those that second-guess a decision maker's substantive judgments.

V. An Alternative to Garcetti

A. DETERMINING WHETHER DISCIPLINE IS BASED ON WORK PRODUCT QUALITY

1. *What is a work product quality based assessment?* Public employers should be free to discipline employees for poor work product quality. The difficulty is in providing that freedom without granting carte blanche to employers to retaliate against work product speech for other reasons. The most serious concern, in light of special value, is that employers will attempt to distort work product speech. In other words, as Cynthia Estlund puts it, they will punish employees for "doing the job [they were] hired to do—indeed, perhaps for doing the job too well."[164] This could entail "honestly criticizing the performance of [their] superiors or other public officials."[165] It could also entail honestly and competently issuing reports that reflect the professional norms of the position—whether legal, scientific, or otherwise—for which one was hired.

Estlund's work helps us to see how one might frame the distinction between distorting speech versus punishing speakers for poor quality speech. She explains that "[e]mployees whose jobs require the exercise and expression of judgment or the disclosure of information on matters of public concern should enjoy a reasonable expectation that they will not be penalized for expressing that judgment and disclosing that information in a responsible manner."[166] She also stresses that employers can defend themselves on the basis that the employee's "speech, though on matters of public concern and uttered in the course of her job constituted poor job performance."[167]

Estlund frames her approach as somewhat of a hybrid due process and First Amendment claim. Rather than having courts conduct the proposed inquiry, she would have courts require impartial ad-

---

[164] Cynthia Estlund, *Free Speech Rights That Work at Work: From the First Amendment to Due Process*, 54 UCLA L Rev 1463, 1475 (2007).

[165] Id.

[166] Id at 1477.

[167] Id at 1479.

ministrative hearings. The hearing right would stem from a "convergence of legitimate employee expectations and the constitutional value of speech on matters of public concern."[168] Estlund's proposal is an important one, and it is far preferable to a world in which public employees have no constitutional right to challenge work product speech based discipline. That said, administrative hearings suffer from potential shortcomings relative to judicial forums, as Estlund acknowledges.[169] Additionally, it is important to establish that a middle ground—one between adjudicators abstaining entirely from reviewing work product speech based discipline and their probing the substantive merits of work product quality—can be found in the judicial realm itself. And it is equally important to understand that the free speech value of public employee work product is strong enough to fuel a First Amendment claim in its own right, ideally toward the end of overturning *Garcetti* or, at a minimum, toward narrowing *Garcetti*'s reach. For that matter, even a hybrid due-process/ First Amendment analysis is stronger if underscored partly by free speech reasoning that could stand on its own.

Thus, while the inquiry that Estlund suggests can be justified partly through employees' reasonable expectations that they will not be punished for doing their jobs "too well," the same inquiry is warranted on First Amendment grounds alone in light of the special value of public employee speech and antidistortion concerns.

2. *How will courts determine whether discipline was based on quality?* The prospect of judges asking if employment decisions were quality based inevitably conjures concerns about judicial intrusion and competence. But the judiciary has a number of tools at its disposal to make this determination without either overreaching or rubber-stamping employer decisions.

The easiest case, of course, is when the fact of a non-quality-based decision can be discerned from the employer's own explanation. For instance, an employer might explicitly discipline a scientist hired to conduct research because he reached a conclusion incompatible with

---

[168] Id at 1480.

[169] Id at 1490–96. The point is not that administrative proceedings are clearly inferior. As Estlund details, each option entails trade-offs. The point is that, insofar as there are reasonable arguments in favor of judicial rather than administrative tribunals, it is important to understand the former's feasibility. Such understanding also sheds light on the capacity of courts to review any administrative proceedings.

an administration's policy goals. Or a public employer might discipline an employee charged with investigating internal corruption because she "ruffled feathers" by finding corruption by higher-ups. Such rationales would amount to admissions that employers punished employees for doing the very jobs for which they were hired. As such, they would not constitute quality-based determinations.

In some instances, a public employer might justify disciplining an employee for a legitimate reason, but the employee might contest the veracity of the explanation. In such situations, courts can consider whether the employer's claim is pretextual.

While establishing actual purpose is notoriously tricky, it is a task that courts take on in multiple contexts, including constitutional cases and employment cases. Courts regularly ask, for example, whether laws are based on the content of speech on their face or in their underlying purposes.[170] Indeed, then-professor Elena Kagan argued in 1996 that the most important aspects of First Amendment doctrine are "best understood and most readily explained as . . . [indirect] motive hunting" devices.[171] She suggested, for example, that the only sensible justification for the presumption against facially content-based laws is the view that "content-based regulation [usually] emerges from illicit motives."[172] By the same token, she deemed courts' application of strict scrutiny to such laws to be "best understood as an evidentiary device that allows the government to disprove the implication of improper motive arising from the content-based terms of a law."[173]

In the equal protection context, courts regularly make explicit inquiries into whether government intentionally discriminated on the basis of race or some other suspect or quasi-suspect category. Indeed, the Supreme Court has developed a robust body of constitutional doctrine to address challenges to the effect that laws or other acts that are neutral on their face are discriminatory in purpose and effect.[174] And in statutory cases, courts routinely examine whether neutral

---

[170] See, for example, *Bartnicki v Vopper*, 532 US 514, 526 (2001) (citing *Ward v Rock Against Racism*, 491 US 781, 791 (1989)).

[171] Elena Kagan, *Private Speech, Public Purpose: The Role of Governmental Motive in First Amendment Doctrine*, 63 U Chi L Rev 413, 414 (1996).

[172] Id at 451.

[173] Id at 453.

[174] See, for example, *Rogers v Lodge*, 458 US 613, 618 (1982).

explanations for employee discipline are pretexts for discrimination.[175] Courts thus are well versed in evaluating neutral explanations
by public and private entities, including employers, to determine
whether they are pretexts for forbidden purposes.

Among the factors to which an employer might point to rebut an
impermissible motive claim is that the employer's quality assessment
was made using standard evaluative procedures, including review by
supervisors with expertise in the relevant field. The employer might
also benefit from a workplace history of effective whistle-blower
protections to which the employee bringing suit had access. The very
fact of such procedures ought not to be decisive. But their availability
and efficacy can be material to a court's analysis.

This feature of the proposed inquiry has the obvious benefit of
incentivizing employers to create effective workplace speech protections. Among the more criticized aspects of the *Garcetti* decision
is its reference to statutory and regulatory whistle-blower protections. The Court suggested that any hole that its decision left in
workplace speech protections was covered in large part by statutory
and regulatory measures.[176] As critics—including the dissenters in
Garcetti—pointed out, this aspect of the majority opinion painted an
unrealistically rosy picture of the breadth and effectiveness of nonconstitutional whistle-blower protections.[177] The approach proposed
here, in contrast, makes no factual assumptions about the existence or
effectiveness of workplace speech protections. It simply recognizes
that such protections, where they do exist, may shed light on the sin-
cerity of employers' claims.

B. THE BIGGER DOCTRINAL PICTURE

The treatment of public employee speech that does not constitute work product is beyond the scope of this article. The only impact
that the approach set out in this article would have in this realm is
to increase the amount of speech labeled non-work product. Such
an increase would follow both from my admonition to err on the
side of deeming speech non-work product in questionable cases, and
from the constraint that work product speech must be conducive to

---

[175] See, for example, *Reeves v Sanderson Plumbing Products, Inc.*, 530 US 133, 141–43 (2000).

[176] *Garcetti*, 547 US at 425–26.

[177] See id at 439–41 (Souter, J, dissenting).

quality-based assessments. Once speech is deemed non-work product, though, I assume here that the *Connick-Pickering* test would continue to apply.

My proposed approach to work product speech itself intersects
with *Connick-Pickering* in two respects. First, when a court finds that
discipline for work product speech did *not* stem from a judgment of
work product quality, judicial review would simply proceed under the
Connick-Pickering test. Second, in performing the *Connick-Pickering*
test, courts should adopt a strong presumption against finding a sufficient efficiency interest when the claimed interest is based on the
communicative effects of an employee's conveying information or
opinion in conformity with her job requirements. This presumption
is called for in light of the strong free speech value of such con-
veyances, and the close relationship between punishing such speech
and distortion. The presumption also poses little risk to the legitimate
exercise of managerial discretion. Indeed, courts applying *Connick-
Pickering* necessarily will have concluded that discipline was not based
on work product quality.

VI. If All Else Fails: Coping with Garcetti

My proposed approach marks less of a break from the status
quo than would an approach that draws no distinction between work
product speech and other public employee speech. My approach's
chance of adoption by the Supreme Court, while still slim, thus may
be greater than that of a more radical alternative to *Garcetti*.

It seems most realistic, however, to expect *Garcetti* to stay with us
for some time. The most constructive suggestions for mitigating its
harms thus are those designed to limit its reach. The same arguments
that support *Garcetti*'s overruling support the lesser measure of narrowing its scope. *Lane v Franks* also provides a useful starting point
for limiting *Garcetti*. And the lower court cases explored in Part II
provide instructive examples—both positive and negative—of approaches to defining work product speech.

My primary suggestion is that courts should apply *Garcetti* only
to relatively clear cases of work product speech.[178] While defining

---

[178] Kermit Roosevelt, though mostly supportive of *Garcetti*, similarly concludes that it
should extend only to "work product." See Roosevelt, 14 U Pa J Const L at 645–49 (cited in
note 17).

such speech is a fact-sensitive exercise, courts could institutionalize the clarity requirement. They might, for instance, create a presumption against finding something to be work product speech whenever the question is a close one. Courts ought also to draw on *Lane*'s references to "ordinary job responsibilities," and conclude, as some lower courts have speculated, that speech activity must indeed be part of one's typical daily job responsibilities to qualify as work product speech. It is true that *Lane* did not turn solely on the fact that Lane's testimony was not among his ordinary job responsibilities. The Court in *Lane* referenced several material facts, concluding that "[t]ruthful testimony under oath by a public employee outside the scope of his ordinary job duties is speech as a citizen for First Amendment purposes."[179] Nonetheless, much of *Lane*'s reasoning—including its emphases on the dangers of employer efforts to suppress information damaging to itself, the special value of public employee speech content, and the risks of reading *Garcetti* so broadly as to undermine that value—conduces to such a reading.

Courts also might carve out an exception to *Garcetti*, a presumption against its application, or at least a factor weighing against its application whenever truthful reporting of corruption or serious governmental misconduct is at issue. In so doing, courts would be taking a page from the Fourth Circuit, which held that public employee "'speech about serious governmental misconduct . . . is protected.'"[180] There are two independent reasons for courts to adopt this approach. First, such speech plainly has high checking value. Second, courts should look skeptically upon governmental pleas to control speech about its own misconduct.

Courts ought also to reject some factors as irrelevant to defining work product speech. Most importantly, courts should deem the fact that information was learned on the job irrelevant to this inquiry. As we have seen, and as the *Lane* Court recognized, public employees' privileged access to information is a core part of their special First Amendment value. Furthermore, because most speech anywhere near the category of work product speech will include information learned on or through the speaker's job, it is hard to see how that factor will help courts to distinguish work product speech from other speech.

---

[179] *Lane*, 134 S Ct at 2378.

[180] See text accompanying note 79.

Additionally, the Court in *Lane* made clear that the *Garcetti* language on which lower courts have relied in considering information's origin—namely, *Garcetti*'s reference to speech that "'owes its existence to [the] employee's professional responsibilities'"[181]—does not mean what those lower courts have taken it to mean. Given the special value at stake, the factor's low probative worth, and the problematic reading of *Garcetti*'s language from which the factor is typically drawn, courts should stop treating the fact that information was learned through one's job as relevant to the *Garcetti* inquiry.

VII. Conclusion

While it is no easy task to situate the First Amendment within the context of public employee speech, it is not impossible to do so wisely. The Court in *Garcetti* erred insofar as it suggested that any level of judicial review over managerial discipline for employee work product speech would intolerably compromise managerial control. What is called for is employer autonomy for particular *types* of decisions about work product—specifically, those based on work product quality—with judicial review to determine if particular employer decisions fall into that category. This approach hones in on employers' most pressing managerial needs, but also protects those aspects of employee discretion and independence that are essential to preserving the special constitutional value of public employee speech.

---

[181] *Lane*, 134 S Ct at 2376. See also Part II(A)(1) (discussing this aspect of *Garcetti* and lower court interpretations of the same).

BARRY CUSHMAN

INSIDE THE TAFT COURT: LESSONS
FROM THE DOCKET BOOKS

For many years, the docket books kept by certain of the Taft Court Justices have been held by the Office of the Curator of the Supreme Court. Though the existence of these docket books had been brought to the attention of the scholarly community, access to them was highly restricted. In April of 2014, however, the Court adopted new guidelines designed to increase access to the docket books for researchers. This article offers a report and analysis based on a review of all of the Taft Court docket books held by the Office of the Curator, which are the only such docket books known to have survived.

For the years of Chief Justice Williams Howard Taft's tenure, the Office of the Curator holds Justice Pierce Butler's docket books for the 1922 through 1924 Terms, and Justice Harlan Fiske Stone's docket books for the 1924–29 Terms. Each of these docket books records the votes that each of the Court's Justices cast in cases when they met to discuss them in conference. Justice Stone's docket books also contain occasional notes of remarks made by colleagues during

Barry Cushman is John P. Murphy Foundation Professor of Law, University of Notre Dame.

AUTHOR'S NOTE: Thanks to Matthew Hofstedt, Devon Burge, Franz Jantzen, Lauren Morrell, Nikki Peronace, and Erin Huckle, all of the Office of the Curator of the Supreme Court of the United States, for their kind hospitality and splendid assistance with the Taft Court docket books; to Margaret Adema, Jon Ashley, Dwight King, Kent Olson, and Cathy Palombi for their cheerful and excellent research assistance; and to participants in the Notre Dame Law School Faculty Colloquium for valuable comments and conversation.

the conference discussion. Unfortunately, Stone's handwriting frequently is quite difficult to decipher, and as a result the content of these notes too often remains obscure. Justice Butler's handwriting is more readily understood, however, and fortunately he often used the pages of his docket books to keep remarkably detailed and informative notes of the conference deliberations.[1]

These docket books have been examined and reported on before, but for limited purposes and therefore to a limited extent. Dean Robert Post, who has been commissioned to write the volume on the Taft Court for the *Oliver Wendell Holmes Devise History of the Supreme Court of the United States*, has presented an illuminating statistical analysis of the aggregate conference vote data.[2] Yet Dean Post's scholarship addresses the particular and qualitative dimensions of the conference records for only a relatively small number of cases.[3] This article seeks to improve our qualitative understanding of the Taft Court by examining and analyzing the votes and conference discussions in cases of particular interest to legal and constitutional historians.

This article examines the available docket book entries relevant to what scholars commonly regard as the major decisions of the Taft

---

[1] The Butler and Stone docket books remained in the Supreme Court building after each of these Justices died while in office. It is not known why these volumes were retained, nor why the set of Butler docket books is not complete. In 1972 all of the "historic" docket books held in the Supreme Court building were boxed up by the Court's Marshal at the order of Chief Justice Warren Burger, and were later transferred to the Curator's Office. E-mail communication from Matthew Hofstedt, Associate Curator, Supreme Court of the United States, Aug 26, 2014.

[2] Robert Post, *The Supreme Court Opinion as Institutional Practice: Dissent, Legal Scholarship, and Decisionmaking in the Taft Court*, 85 Minn L Rev 1267, 1309–55 (2001).

[3] See Robert Post, *Federalism, Positive Law, and the Emergence of the American Administrative State: Prohibition in the Taft Court Era*, 48 Wm & Mary L Rev 1, 36 n 119 (2006) (discussing *Gambino v United States*, 275 US 310 (1927)); id at 101 n 343 (discussing *Byars v United States*, 273 US 28 (1927), and *Agnello v United States*, 269 US 20 (1925)); id at 111 n 368 (discussing *New York v Zimmerman*, 278 US 63 (1928)); id at 121 n 403 (again discussing *Byars*); id at 124 n 406 (discussing *Carroll v United States*, 267 US 132 (1925)); id at 134 n 442 (again discussing *Agnello*); id at 142 n 470 and n 471 (discussing *Olmstead v United States*, 277 US 438 (1927)); id at 160 n 537 (discussing *Donnelley v United States*, 276 US 505 (1928)); id at 161 n 537 (discussing *Ziang Sung Wan v United States*, 266 US 1 (1924)); see also Robert Post, *Federalism in the Taft Court Era: Can It Be "Revived"?*, 51 Duke L J 1513, 1535 n 84 (2002) (discussing *Metcalf v Mitchell*, 269 US 514 (1926)); id at 1565 n 181 (discussing *Chicago Board of Trade v Olsen*, 262 US 1 (1923)); id at 1595 n 288 (discussing *Black and White Taxicab and Transfer Co. v Brown and Yellow Taxicab and Transfer Co.*, 276 US 518 (1928)); id at 618 n 353 (discussing *Texas Transport and Terminal Co. v New Orleans*, 264 US 150 (1924)); Robert C. Post, *Defending the Lifeworld: Substantive Due Process in the Taft Court Era*, 78 BU L Rev 1489, 1497 (1998) (discussing *Chastleton Corp. v Sinclair*, 264 US 543 (1924)); id at 1501 n 77 (discussing *Jay Burns Baking Co. v Bryan*, 264 US 504 (1924)).

Court.[4] This examination includes 117 cases concerning areas of law as diverse as the Commerce Clause, the dormant Commerce Clause, substantive due process, equal protection, the general law, antitrust, intergovernmental tax immunities, criminal procedure, civil rights, and civil liberties. The information in the docket books sheds particularly interesting new light on decisions such as *Whitney v California*,[5] *Village of Euclid v Ambler*,[6] *Adkins v Children's Hospital*[7] and its successor minimum wage cases,[8] *Pierce v Society of Sisters*,[9] *Buck v Bell*,[10] *Frothingham v Mellon*,[11] *Wolff Packing v Court of Industrial Relations*,[12] *Fiske v Kansas*,[13] *Tyson & Brothers v Banton*,[14] *Coronado Coal v United*

---

[4] The cases selected as "major" or "salient" are those that appear regularly in scholarly treatments of the Taft Court. See, for example, Peter Renstrom, *The Taft Court: Justices, Rulings, and Legacy* (ABC-CLIO, 2003); Alpheus Thomas Mason, *William Howard Taft: Chief Justice* (Simon and Schuster, 1964); Alpheus Thomas Mason, *The Supreme Court from Taft to Warren* (Louisiana State, 1958); Alpheus Thomas Mason, *Harlan Fiske Stone: Pillar of the Law* (Viking, 1956); Henry F. Pringle, 2 *The Life and Times of William Howard Taft* (American Political Biography, 1939); Post, 48 Wm and Mary L Rev at 1 (cited in note 3); Post, 51 Duke L J at 1513 (cited in note 3); Post, 85 Minn L Rev at 1267 (cited in note 2); Post, 78 BU L Rev at 1489 (cited in note 3); Barry Cushman, *The Secret Lives of the Four Horsemen*, 83 Va L Rev 559 (1997). Scholars may differ concerning the inclusion or exclusion of particular cases from this category, and the statistical discussion in the Conclusion must be read with that caveat in mind. Notwithstanding such potential differences, however, my effort has been to select cases about which I believe there would be a broad measure of agreement. For other scholarship exploring judicial behavior in "major" or "salient" cases, see Forrest Maltzman and Peter J. Wahlbeck, *Strategic Policy Considerations and Voting Fluidity on the Burger Court*, 90 Am Pol Sci Rev 581, 589 (1996); Robert H. Dorff and Saul Brenner, *Conformity Voting on the United States Supreme Court*, 54 J Pol 762, 772, 773 (1992); Timothy M. Hagle and Harold J. Spaeth, *Voting Fluidity and the Attitudinal Model of Supreme Court Decision Making*, 44 Western Pol Q 119, 124 (1991); Saul Brenner, Timothy Hagle, and Harold J. Spaeth, *Increasing the Size of Minimum Winning Coalitions on the Warren Court*, 23 Polity 309 (1990); Saul Brenner, Timothy M. Hagle, and Harold J. Spaeth, *The Defection of the Marginal Justice on the Warren Court*, 42 Western Pol Q 409 (1989); Saul Brenner, *Fluidity on the Supreme Court: 1956–1967*, 26 Am J Pol Sci 388, 389 (1982); Saul Brenner, *Fluidity on the United States Supreme Court: A Reexamination*, 24 Am J Pol Sci 526, 530 (1980); Elliot E. Slotnick, *Who Speaks for the Court? Majority Opinion Assignment from Taft to Burger*, 23 Am J Pol Sci 60 (1979).

[5] 274 US 357 (1927).

[6] 272 US 365 (1926).

[7] 261 US 525 (1923).

[8] *Donham v West-Nelson Co.*, 273 US 657 (1927); *Murphy v Sardell*, 269 US 530 (1925).

[9] 268 US 510 (1925).

[10] 274 US 200 (1927).

[11] 262 US 447 (1923).

[12] 262 US 522 (1923).

[13] 274 US 380 (1927).

[14] 273 US 418 (1927).

Mine Workers,[15] *Corrigan v Buckley*,[16] *Miles v Graham*,[17] *Brooks v United States*,[18] and *Radice v New York*.[19] In addition, for these and the many other cases examined, this article reports on whether a unanimous decision also was free from dissent at conference or became so only because one or more Justices acquiesced in the judgment of their colleagues, and on whether nonunanimous decisions were divided by the same vote and with the same alliances at conference. The docket books also provide records of instances in which a case that initially was assigned to one Justice later was reassigned to another. These records afford us some insight into the kinds of cases in which this tended to occur, and provide an opportunity to document for the first time the long-held suspicion that the notoriously slow-writing Justice Willis Van Devanter frequently was relieved of his opinions by the Chief Justice.

An examination of the docket books yields a series of interesting and often surprising revelations. Among them, we learn that by 1925 five of the sitting Justices believed that the 1923 decision of *Adkins v Children's Hospital* invalidating a minimum wage law for women had been wrongly decided, and the precedent survived challenge only because four of those Justices continued to adhere to it as a matter of stare decisis. We discover that Justice Brandeis D. Brandeis initially was disposed to dissent from rather than to file his landmark concurrence in the First Amendment case of *Whitney v California*. We are informed that the Justices regarded as uncontroversial foundational decisions laying the constitutional groundwork for the modern welfare state. We learn that the Court's published opinions present Chief Justice Taft and Justices Oliver Wendell Holmes and James Clark McReynolds as more favorably inclined toward the protection of civil rights and civil liberties than their votes in conference would indicate. The docket books also help to resolve a set of lingering questions concerning the behind-the-scenes deliberations in the landmark zoning case of *Village of Euclid v Ambler*.

---

[15] 268 US 295 (1925).

[16] 271 US 623 (1926).

[17] 268 US 501 (1925).

[18] 267 US 432 (1925).

[19] 264 US 292 (1924).

A review of the Taft Court docket books also makes possible two contributions to the political science literature on judicial behavior. The first is to the scholarship on vote fluidity and unanimity norms in the Supreme Court. It is widely agreed that the period from the Chief Justiceship of John Marshall through that of Charles Evans Hughes was characterized by a "norm of consensus," "marked by individual justices accepting the Court's majority opinions."[20] It is generally believed that this norm of consensus collapsed early in the Chief Justiceship of Harlan Fiske Stone,[21] though some scholars have pointed to causes that antedate Stone's elevation to the center chair.[22] Still others have suggested that there may have been "an earlier, more gradual change in norms" on the late Taft and Hughes Courts.[23] Political

---

[20] Pamela C. Corley, Amy Steigerwalt, and Artemus Ward, *Revisiting the Roosevelt Court: The Critical Juncture from Consensus to Dissensus*, 38 J Sup Ct Hist 20, 22 (2013); Mark S. Hurwitz and Drew Noble Lanier, *I Respectfully Dissent: Consensus, Agendas, and Policymaking on the U.S. Supreme Court, 1888–1999*, 21 Rev Pol Research 429, 429 (2004); Lee Epstein, Jeffrey A. Segal, and Harold J. Spaeth, *The Norm of Consensus on the U.S. Supreme Court*, 45 Am J Pol Sci 362, 376 (2001); John P. Kelsh, *The Opinion Delivery Practices of the United States Supreme Court 1790–1945*, 77 Wash U L Q 137, 161–62 (1999); Gregory A. Caldeira and Christopher J. W. Zorn, *Of Time and Consensual Norms in the Supreme Court*, 42 Am J Pol Sci 874, 874–75 (1998); Thomas G. Walker, Lee Epstein, and William J. Dixon, *On the Mysterious Demise of Consensual Norms in the United States Supreme Court*, 50 J Pol 361, 361–62 (1988).

[21] Herman C. Pritchett, *The Roosevelt Court: A Study in Judicial Politics and Values, 1937–1947* 40, 251 (1948) ("In 1941 divisive forces of some kind hit the Court full force"); Corley, Steigerwalt, and Ward, 38 J Sup Ct Hist at 47 (cited in note 20); Caldeira and Zorn, 42 Am J Pol Sci at 874–75 (cited in note 20); Walker, Epstein, and Dixon, 50 J Pol at 362 (cited in note 20); David Danelski, *The Influence of the Chief Justice in the Decisional Process*, in Joel B. Grossman and Richard S. Wells, eds, *Constitutional Law and Judicial Policy Making* 175 (Wiley, 1972).

[22] Compare Stephen C. Halpern and Kenneth N. Vines, *The Judges' Bill and the Role of the U.S. Supreme Court*, 30 Western Pol Q 471, 481 (1977) (arguing that the enactment of the Judges' Bill of 1925, which made the Court's docket almost entirely discretionary, increased the proportion of cases that were legally or politically salient and thus less likely to elicit acquiescence from colleagues inclined to disagree with the majority), with Walker, Epstein, and Dixon, 50 J Pol at 365–66 (cited in note 20) (agreeing that "it is possible that a discretionary docket may be one factor, and a necessary one at that, in maintaining high levels of conflict once such patterns are established," but disputing the contention that the 1925 statute was "the primary factor in the alteration of the Court's consensus norms," pointing out that "significant escalation in both the dissent and concurrence rates did not occur until almost fifteen years" after the dramatic increase in the discretionary share of the Court's docket); accord, Caldeira and Zorn, 42 Am J Pol Sci at 875 (cited in note 20); Post, 85 Minn L Rev at 1319–31 (cited in note 2) (rejecting the Halpern and Vines hypothesis on the ground that unanimity rates in certiorari cases were higher than in those falling under the Court's mandatory jurisdiction, and offering alternative reasons, such as changes in external circumstances, in Court personnel, and in the quality of Taft's leadership for the decline in unanimity on the late Taft Court).

[23] Caldeira and Zorn, 42 Am J Pol Sci at 892 (cited in note 20). See also Aaron J. Ley, Kathleen Searles, and Cornell W. Clayton, *The Mysterious Persistence of Non-Consensual Norms on the U.S. Supreme Court*, 49 Tulsa L Rev 99, 106 (2013) ("the proportion of unanimous decisions was declining prior to Stone's Chief Justiceship"); Marcus E. Hendershot, Mark S. Hurwitz, Drew Noble Lanier, and Richard L. Pacelle Jr., *Dissensual Decision Making: Re-*

scientists who have had access to the docket books of various Justices have demonstrated that much of the consensus achieved by the Court throughout its history has resulted from the decision of Justices who had dissented at conference to join the majority's ultimate disposition. A large body of literature shows that Justices commonly have changed their votes between the conference and the final vote on the merits.[24]

Of the different types of vote fluidity between the conference vote and the final vote on the merits in major Taft Court cases, by far the most common was for a Justice to move from a dissenting or passing vote to a vote with the ultimate majority. An examination of the docket books permits us to illuminate several features of this phenomenon: the major cases in which it occurred; how frequently it occurred; its comparative frequency in major cases as opposed to those of lesser salience; the frequency with which each of the Justices did so, and the comparative frequency with which they did so in non-salient cases; and the comparative success of Taft Court Justices in preparing majority opinions that would either enlarge the size of the ultimate winning coalition or produce ultimate unanimity from a di-

---

visiting the Demise of Consensual Norms within the U.S. Supreme Court, 20 Pol Res Q 1, 8 (2012) ("the Court's norm of consensus was first challenged by growing levels of dissent in the later years of the Hughes Court"); David M. O'Brien, *Institutional Norms and Supreme Court Opinions: On Reconsidering the Rise of Individual Opinions*, in Cornell W. Clayton and Howard Gillman, eds, *Supreme Court Decision-Making: New Institutionalist Approaches* (Chicago, 1999) ("the demise of the norm of consensus preceded Stone's chief justiceship"); Stacia L. Haynie, *Leadership and Consensus on the U.S. Supreme Court*, 54 J Pol 1158 (1992) (arguing that Stone consolidated a shift in behavioral expectations that began under Hughes). See also Kelsh, 77 Wash U L Q at 162 (cited in note 20) ("The most unusual thing about the nonunanimity rate for the 1864–1940 period is that the last ten years saw a sustained increase. This rate was to shoot up dramatically in the first years of the Stone Court, but the beginnings of the rise can be seen around 1930"); Kelsh, 77 Wash U L Q at 173 (cited in note 20) ("By the 1930s ... Justices had fully accepted the view that separate opinions had a legitimate role in the American legal system."). Compare Benjamin N. Cardozo, *Law and Literature* 34 (Harcourt Brace, 1931) (characterizing dissenters as "irresponsible").

[24] See, for example, Epstein, Segal, and Spaeth, 45 Am J Pol Sci 362 (cited in note 20) (Waite Court); Maltzman and Wahlbeck, 90 Am Pol Sci Rev 581 (cited in note 4) (Burger Court); Dorff and Brenner, 54 J Pol 762 (cited in note 4) (Vinson, Warren, and Burger Courts); Hagle and Spaeth, 44 Western Pol Q 119 (cited in note 4) (Warren Court); Brenner, Hagle, and Spaeth, 23 Polity 309 (cited in note 4) (Warren Court); Brenner, Hagle, and Spaeth, 42 Western Pol Q 409 (cited in note 4) (Warren Court); Brenner, 26 Am J Pol Sci 388 (cited in note 4) (Warren Court); Saul Brenner, *Ideological Voting on the U.S. Supreme Court: A Comparison of the Original Vote on the Merits with the Final Vote*, 22 Jurimetrics 287 (1982) (Vinson and Warren Courts); Brenner, 24 Am J Pol Sci 526 (cited in note 4) (Vinson and Warren Courts); Woodford Howard Jr., *On the Fluidity of Judicial Choice*, 62 Am Pol Sci Rev 43 (1968) (Stone and Vinson Courts).

vided conference. Among the more interesting findings here is that
the member of the Court who most commonly acquiesced in major
decisions that he had declined to join at conference was the famously
irascible Justice McReynolds.

The second contribution concerns the behavior of newcomers to
the Court. In 1958, Eloise C. Snyder published an article in which she
concluded that new members of the Court tended initially to affiliate
with a moderate, "pivotal clique" before migrating to a more clearly
ideological liberal or conservative bloc.[25] Seven years later, J. Woodford Howard argued that Justice Frank Murphy's first three terms on
the Court were marked by a "freshman effect" characterized by an
"instability" in his decision making that rendered the Justice "diffident
to the point of indecisiveness."[26] These studies in turn spawned a literature on the "freshman" or "acclimation" effect for Justices new to
the Court. These studies generally characterize the freshman effect "as
consisting of one or more of the following types of behavior: (1) initial
bewilderment or disorientation, (2) assignment of a lower than average
number of opinions to the new justices, and (3) an initial tendency on
the part of the new justice to join a moderate block of justices."[27] While
some studies have confirmed the existence of some feature or another
of the freshman effect,[28] others have cast significant doubt on the

[25] Eloise C. Snyder, *The Supreme Court as a Small Group*, 3 Social Forces 232, 238 (1958).

[26] Woodford Howard, *Justice Murphy: The Freshman Years*, 18 Vand L Rev 473, 474, 476,
477, 484, 488, 505 (1965).

[27] Timothy M. Hagle, *"Freshman Effects" for Supreme Court Justices*, 37 Am J Pol Sci 1142,
1142 (1993). See also Leigh Anne Williams, *Measuring Internal Influence on the Rehnquist
Court: An Analysis of Non-Majority Opinion Joining Behavior*, 68 Ohio St L J 679, 718–19
(2007); Saul Brenner and Timothy M. Hagle, *Opinion Writing and Acclimation Effect*, 18 Pol
Behav 235 (1996); Paul C. Arledge and Edward W. Heck, *A Freshman Justice Confronts the
Constitution: Justice O'Connor and the First Amendment*, 45 Western Pol Q 761, 761–62 (1992);
Edward V. Heck and Melinda Gann Hall, *Bloc Voting and the Freshman Justice Revisited*, 43 J
Pol 852, 853–54 (1981); Elliot E. Slotnick, *Judicial Career Patterns and Majority Opinion As-
signment on the Supreme Court*, 41 J Pol 640, 641 (1979).

[28] See, for example, Lee Epstein et al, *On the Perils of Drawing Inferences about Supreme
Court Justices from Their First Few Years of Service*, 91 Judicature 168, 179 (2008) (finding
evidence of ideological instability in the merits voting of "virtually all" freshman Justices);
Mark S. Hurwitz and Joseph V. Stefko, *Acclimation and Attitudes: "Newcomer" Justices and
Precedent Conformance on the Supreme Court*, 57 Pol Res Q 121 (2004) (finding freshman effect
with respect to conformity to precedent); Charles R. Shipan, *Acclimation Effects Revisited*,
40 Jurimetrics 243 (2000) (finding evidence of ideological instability in the merits voting of
some but not most freshmen Justices on the Warren and Burger Courts); Sandra L. Wood
et al, *"Acclimation Effects" for Supreme Court Justices: A Cross-Validation, 1888–1940*, 42 Am J
Pol Sci 690, 694 (1998) (finding "some evidence of an acclimation effect for at least some of
the justices" with respect to ideological instability in merits voting); Brenner and Hagle, 18
Pol Behav 235 (cited in note 27) (finding freshman effect with respect to opinion output);

hypothesis, maintaining that it is either nonexistent or confined to limited circumstances.[29] Studies of the freshman period for individual Justices on the whole have not lent much support to the hypothesis.[30]

Professor Howard suggested that the freshman effect might also be manifested by a tendency of new Justices to change their votes between the conference vote and the final vote on the merits. Howard

---

Timothy M. Hagle, *A New Test for the Freshman Effect*, 21 Southeastern Pol Rev 289 (1993) (finding evidence of ideological instability in the merits voting of some freshman Justices on the Burger and Rehnquist Courts); Hagle, 37 Am J Pol Sci 1142 (cited in note 27) (finding evidence of ideological instability in the merits voting of some Justices joining the Court between 1953 and 1989); S. Sidney Ulmer, *Toward a Theory of Sub-Group Formation in the United States Supreme Court*, 27 J Pol 133, 151 (1965) (finding some evidence of freshman effect in bloc voting for Justices joining the Court between 1946 and 1961).

[29] See, for example, Paul J. Wahlbeck, James F. Spriggs II, and Forrest Maltzman, *The Politics of Dissents and Concurrences on the U.S. Supreme Court*, 27 Am Pol Q 488, 503–04 (1999) ("Contrary to the freshman effect hypothesis, freshman justices are no less likely to join or author a concurring or dissenting opinion than their more senior colleagues"); Richard Pacelle and Patricia Pauly, *The Freshman Effect Revisited: An Individual Analysis*, 17 Am Rev Pol 1, 6, 15 (1996) (finding no freshman effect with respect to ideological instability in merits votes in the aggregate, and "only limited evidence" of such an effect with respect to individual Justices joining the Court between 1945 and 1988); Terry Bowen, *Consensual Norms and the Freshman Effect on the United States Supreme Court*, 76 Soc Sci Q 222, 227 (1995) (finding no freshman effect for separate opinion writing on the Hughes and Taft Courts, but finding such a freshman effect during the 1941–92 period); Terry Bowen and John M. Scheb II, *Freshman Opinion Writing on the U.S. Supreme Court, 1921–1991*, 76 Judicature 239 (1993) (finding no freshman effect with respect to opinion assignments); Robert L. Dudley, *The Freshman Effect and Voting Alignments: A Reexamination of Judicial Folklore*, 21 Am Pol Q 360 (1993) (finding no freshman effect with respect to bloc voting even when using Snyder's data); Terry Bowen and John M. Scheb II, *Reassessing the "Freshman Effect": The Voting Block Alignment of New Justices on the United States Supreme Court, 1921–90*, 15 Pol Behav 1 (1983) (finding no freshman effect with respect to bloc voting); Heck and Hall, 43 J Pol 852 (cited in note 27) (finding very little evidence of a freshman effect in bloc voting on the Warren and Burger Courts); Slotnick, 41 J Pol 640 (cited in note 27) (finding no freshman effect with respect to opinion assignments). For efforts to explain the divergences in scholarly findings, see Hagle, 21 Southeastern Pol Rev 289 (cited in note 28); Hagle, 37 Am J Pol Sci 1142 (cited in note 27); Albert P. Melone, *Revisiting the Freshman Effect Hypothesis: The First Two Terms of Justice Anthony Kennedy*, 74 Judicature 6, 13 (1990); Heck and Hall, 43 J Pol at 859–60 (cited in note 27).

[30] See, for example, Thomas R. Hensley, Joyce A. Baugh, and Christopher E. Smith, *The First-Term Performance of Chief Justice John Roberts*, 43 Idaho L Rev 625, 631 (2007) (finding no freshman effect with respect to bloc voting); Christopher E. Smith and S. Thomas Read, *The Performance and Effectiveness of New Appointees to the Rehnquist Court*, 20 Ohio N U L Rev 205 (1993) (finding a freshman effect with respect to Justice Souter but not with respect to Justice Thomas); Arledge and Heck, 45 Western Pol Q 761 (cited in note 27) (finding no freshman effect); Melone, 74 Judicature 6 (cited in note 29) (finding a freshman effect only with respect to majority opinion assignments); Thea F. Rubin and Albert P. Melone, *Justice Antonin Scalia: A First Year Freshman Effect?*, 72 Judicature 98 (1988) (finding a freshman effect only with respect to majority opinion assignments); John M. Scheb II and Lee W. Ailshie, *Justice Sandra Day O'Connor and the Freshman Effect*, 69 Judicature 9 (1985) (finding evidence of a freshman effect only with respect to majority opinion assignments in her first Term); Edward V. Heck, *The Socialization of a Freshman Justice: The Early Years of Justice Brennan*, 10 Pac L J 707, 714–16, 722–25 (1979) (finding little evidence of a freshman effect).

listed a number of considerations that might prompt a Justice to shift ground in this manner, but first among them were "unstable attitudes that seem to have resulted from the process of assimilation to the Court." For instance, he remarked, "Justice Cardozo, according to one clerk's recollection of the docket books ... frequently vot[ed] alone in conference before ultimately submerging himself in a group opinion."[31] Howard reported that Justice Murphy exhibited "a similar instability" during his freshman years on the Court.[32] Subsequent studies from the Vinson, Warren, and Burger Court docket books have produced divergent conclusions with respect to this reputed feature of the freshman effect.[33]

A review of the voting behavior of newcomers to the Taft Court does not disclose any appreciable freshman effect with respect to voting fluidity. Instead, one finds that in the major cases examined here, those who were early in their judicial tenures were not more likely than were their senior colleagues to change their positions between the conference vote and the final vote on the merits.

This article proceeds as follows. Part I briefly introduces the Taft Court Justices and their voting practices. Part II discusses the major Taft Court cases that were unanimous both at conference and in the

---

[31] Howard Jr., 62 Am Pol Sci Rev at 45 (cited in note 24). The clerk to whom Howard referred was Paul Freund. See Paul Freund, *A Tale of Two Terms*, 26 Ohio St L J 225, 227 (1965) ("I was struck in the 1932 Term with the number of occasions on which what came down as unanimous opinions had been far from that at conference. I had access to the docket book which the Justice kept as a record of the conference vote—these books are destroyed at the end of each term—and I was enormously impressed with how many divisions there were that did not show up in the final vote. I was impressed with how often Justice Cardozo was in a minority, often of one, at conference, but did not press his position.").

[32] Howard Jr., 62 Am Pol Sci Rev at 45 (cited in note 24).

[33] Compare Maltzman and Wahlbeck, 90 Am Pol Sci Rev at 589 (cited in note 4) (finding that "freshmen justices are significantly more likely to switch than are their more senior colleagues"), Saul Brenner, *Another Look at Freshman Indecisiveness on the United States Supreme Court*, 16 Polity 320 (1983) (finding that between the 1946 and 1966 Terms freshman Justices exhibited on average greater fluidity between the conference vote and the final votes on the merits than did senior Justices, and that this fluidity tended to diminish between a Justice's first and fourth terms on the Court), and Dorff and Brenner, 54 J Pol at 767, 769–71 (cited in note 4) (finding that freshman Justices were "more likely to be uncertain regarding how to vote at the original vote on the merits and more likely to be influenced by the decision of the majority at the final vote") with Hagle and Spaeth, 44 Western Pol Q 119 (cited in note 4) (finding that the voting fluidity of freshman Justices on the Warren Court did not differ significantly from that of their more senior colleagues, and that the voting fluidity of such freshman Justices had not diminished by their third and fourth Terms on the Court). See also Timothy R. Johnson, James F. Spriggs II, and Peter J. Wahlbeck, *Passing and Strategic Voting on the U.S. Supreme Court*, 39 L & Society Rev 349, 369 (2005) (finding that freshman Justices on the Burger Court did not pass more frequently than their senior colleagues).

published report of the decision. Part III examines cases that were not unanimous at conference but became unanimous by the time the Court announced its decision. Part IV analyzes the Court's non-unanimous cases. Part V reports on the Taft Court's opinion reassignment practices. Part VI concludes.

I. The Taft Court Justices and Their Voting Practices

Justice Stone was the last Justice to be appointed to the Taft Court, replacing Justice Joseph McKenna in 1925. The Court that he joined consisted of Chief Justice Taft, and Associate Justices Holmes, Devanter, McReynolds, Brandeis, George Sutherland, Butler, and Edward Terry Sanford. Because Justice Butler did not take his seat until January of 1923, we have no docket book records for cases decided during the 1921 Term, which was Taft's first as Chief Justice. Also lacking are docket records for cases decided early in the 1922 Term, including some of considerable interest.[34]

Taft is famous for his "consuming ambition" to "mass the Court"— to build unanimity so as to give "weight and solidity" to its decisions.[35] The Taft Court did achieve unanimity in a remarkable percentage of its cases. For the 1921–28 Terms, 84% of the Court's published opinions were unanimous;[36] taking into account all of its decisions for the entirety of Taft's tenure, the unanimity rate was 91.4%.[37] Though this rate of unanimity was in line with the rates achieved by the White Court,[38] certain characteristics of the Taft Court may have contributed to its maintenance. First, Taft discouraged dissents, believing that most of them were displays of egotism that weakened the Court's

---

[34] These include *Ozawa v United States*, 260 US 178 (1922) (holding that a Japanese national born in Japan was not Caucasian and was therefore ineligible for naturalization); *Yamashita v Hinkle*, 260 US 199 (1922) (same); *Heisler v Thomas Colliery Co.*, 260 US 245 (1922) (upholding a state tax on coal to be shipped in interstate commerce against a dormant Commerce Clause challenge); *United States v Lanza*, 260 US 377 (1922) (holding that prosecutions by both state and federal authorities for violations of their respective liquor laws did not violate the prohibition against Double Jeopardy); and *Pennsylvania Coal Co. v Mahon*, 260 US 393 (1922) (holding that a state law impairing an owner's subsurface mining rights constituted a taking).

[35] Mason, *William Howard Taft* at 198 (cited in note 4); Mason, *Taft to Warren* at 57 (cited in note 4); Alpheus Thomas Mason, *The Chief Justice of the United States: Primus Inter Pares*, 17 J Pub L 20, 31–32 (1968).

[36] Post, 85 Minn L Rev at 1309 (cited in note 2).

[37] Lee Epstein et al, *The Supreme Court Compendium: Data, Decisions, and Developments* 147, 161 (1994).

[38] Post, 85 Minn L Rev at 1310 (cited in note 2).

prestige and contributed little of value.[39] As a consequence, he worked hard to minimize disagreement, often sacrificing the expression of his own personal views.[40] This is illustrated by a comparison of the percentage of cases accompanied by written opinions in which various Chief Justices have dissented over the course of the Court's history. Taft dissented in only 0.93% of such cases. By contrast, his predecessor, Edward White, dissented in 1.53%; his successor, Charles Evans Hughes, did so in 2.24%; and Harlan Fiske Stone did so in 13.49% of all such cases handed down during his Chief Justiceship. Indeed, of all of the Chief Justices to serve from John Marshall through Earl Warren, only Marshall could boast a dissenting percentage lower than Taft's.[41] Van Devanter shared Taft's distaste for public displays of discord, and strongly lobbied his colleagues to suppress their dissenting views.[42] Butler similarly regarded dissents as exercises of "vanity" that "seldom aid us in the right development or statement of the law," and instead "often do harm."[43] He therefore commonly "acquiesce[d] for the sake of harmony & the Court."[44] McReynolds, Sutherland, Sanford, and McKenna expressed similar views and suppressed dissenting opinions accordingly.[45] Even the "great dissenters," Holmes and Brandeis, believed that dissents should be aired sparingly, and often "shut up," as Holmes liked to put it, when their views departed from those of their colleagues.[46]

---

[39] Id at 1310–11, 1356; Mason, *William Howard Taft* at 198 (cited in note 4); Mason, 17 J Pub L at 31–32 (cited in note 35); William Howard Taft to Harlan F. Stone, Jan 26, 1927, Box 76, Harlan F. Stone Papers, Manuscript Division, Library of Congress, quoted in Walter F. Murphy, *Elements of Judicial Strategy* 47 (Chicago, 1964); Danelski, *The Influence of the Chief Justice* at 174 (cited in note 21).

[40] 2 Pringle at 1049 (cited in note 4) (Taft "shrank from all dissents, including his own"); Post, 85 Minn L Rev at 1311–12 (cited in note 2).

[41] S. Sidney Ulmer, *Exploring the Dissent Patterns of the Chief Justices: John Marshall to Warren Burger*, in Sheldon Gordon and Charles M. Lamb, eds, *Judicial Conflict and Consensus: Behavioral Studies of American Appellate Courts* 53 (1986).

[42] Post, 85 Minn L Rev at 1318, 1340, 1341, 1343 (cited in note 2).

[43] Henry J. Abraham, *The Judicial Process: An Introductory Analysis of the Courts of the United States, England, and France* 214–15 (Oxford, 2d ed 1968); Murphy, *Elements of Judicial Strategy* at 52 (cited in note 39); Post, 85 Minn L Rev at 1340 (cited in note 2).

[44] Post, 85 Minn L Rev at 1341–43 (cited in note 2).

[45] Id at 1341–44; James C. McReynolds to Harlan F. Stone, Apr 2, 1930, Box 76, Harlan F. Stone Papers, Manuscript Division, Library of Congress, quoted in Corley, Steigerwalt, and Ward, 38 J Sup Ct Hist at 30 (cited in note 20); Murphy, *Elements of Judicial Strategy* at 52–53 (cited in note 39).

[46] Post, 85 Minn L Rev at 1341–42, 1344–46, 1349–51 (cited in note 2); Mason, *Taft to Warren* at 58 (cited in note 4) ("For the sake of harmony staunch individualists such as

A variety of factors may have contributed to this "norm of acquies-cence."[47] First, the literature of the period illustrates among the bench and bar a widely held aversion to dissents as excessively self-regarding, and as weakening the force of judicial decisions by unsettling the law.[48] This conviction found expression in Canon 19 of the American Bar Association's Canons of Judicial Ethics, which exhorted judges not to "yield to pride of opinion or value more highly his individual reputation than that of the court to which he should be loyal. Except in cases of conscientious difference of opinion on fundamental principle, dis-senting opinions should be discouraged in courts of last resort." In-stead, "judges constituting a court of last resort" were admonished to "use effort and self-restraint to promote solidarity of conclusion and the consequent influence of judicial decision."[49] It is worthy of note that Taft was the chair of the committee that drafted the Canons, and that Sutherland was a committee member before his appointment to the Court.[50] Second, in the early years of the Taft Court, new Justices came to the Court who were more likely to vote with the majority than some

---

Holmes, Brandeis, and Stone, though disagreeing, would sometimes go along with the ma-jority"); *Northern Securities Co. v United States*, 193 US 197, 400 (1904) (Holmes, J, dissenting) ("I think it useless and undesirable, as a rule, to express dissent"); Alexander M. Bickel, ed, *The Unpublished Opinions of Mr. Justice Brandeis* 18 (Chicago, 1957) ("'Can't always dissent,' [Brandeis] said ... 'I sometimes endorse an opinion with which I do not agree'"); Arthur M. Schlesinger Jr., *The Supreme Court: 1947*, 35 Fortune 78, 211–12 (1947) ("In the time of Chief Justice Taft, even Holmes and Brandeis might vote against a decision in conference without writing a dissent, and sometimes without even formally registering their disagree-ment.").

[47] Post, 85 Minn L Rev at 1344 (cited in note 2). See Mason, *Taft to Warren* at 58 (cited in note 4) ("Sometimes as many as three Justices would reluctantly go along with the majority because no one of them felt strongly enough about the issue to raise his voice in protest. During the early years of Taft's Chief Justiceship, it was not unusual for Justices to write on the back of circulated slip opinions: 'I shall acquiesce in silence unless someone else dissents'; or 'I do not agree, but shall submit.'").

[48] Post, 85 Minn L Rev at 1344, 1348–49, 1354, 1356–57 (cited in note 2); Evan A. Evans, *The Dissenting Opinion—Its Use and Abuse*, 3 Mo L Rev 120, 123–26 (1938) (quoting various criticisms of dissents made by members of the bench and bar); Alex Simpson Jr., *Dissenting Opinions*, 71 U Pa L Rev 205, 205–06 (1923) (quoting various professional criticisms of dissenting opinions); William A. Bowen, *Dissenting Opinions*, 17 Green Bag 690, 693 (1905) ("the Dissenting Opinion is of all judicial mistakes the most injurious").

[49] ABA Canons of Judicial Ethics, Canon 19 (1924), in Lisa L. Milord, *The Development of the ABA Judicial Code* 137 (ABA, 1992). In 1972, the American Bar Association replaced the Canons with a *Code of Judicial Conduct*, which does not contain a provision similar to Canon 19. Wahlbeck, Spriggs II, and Maltzman, 27 Am Pol Q at 508 n 1 (cited in note 29).

[50] Post, 85 Minn L Rev at 1284 n 55 (cited in note 2).

of their predecessors had been.[51] Third, there was an impulse among the Justices to show a united front in order to "fend off external attacks" from progressive senators like Robert LaFollette and William Borah, who shared the American Federation of Labor's dissatisfaction with some of the Court's recent decisions, and proposed legislation that would have limited the Court's power to review congressional legislation.[52] Fourth, the norm of acquiescence promoted a collegiality and reciprocity among the Justices that smoothed over potential conflicts.[53] And fifth, during this period nearly all of the Justices had only one clerk rather than the four that Justices typically have today, and most of the Justices wrote their own opinions.[54] With such comparatively limited resources at their disposal, the cost of preparing a dissenting opinion was considerably higher.[55]

In discussing the postconference voting behaviors of the Taft Court Justices, I will be using several defined terms. I shall use the term *acquiescence* to denote instances in which a Justice who either dissented or passed at conference ultimately joined in the majority's disposition.[56] In other words, acquiescence denotes instances in

---

[51] Id at 1313.

[52] Id at 1314–18.

[53] Id at 1345. See also Caldeira and Zorn, 42 Am J Pol Sci at 877 (cited in note 20); Murphy, *Elements of Judicial Strategy* at 61 (cited in note 39) ("A Justice who persistently refuses to accommodate his views to those of his colleagues may come to be regarded as an obstructionist. A Justice whose dissents become levers for legislative or administrative action reversing judicial policies may come to be regarded as disloyal to the bench. It is possible that either appraisal would curtail his influence with his associates.").

[54] During this period, Justices were authorized to employ a law clerk and a secretary. Pierce Butler used each to perform the duties of a law clerk, and one of them, John Cotter, wrote first drafts of most of Butler's opinions. The other Justices, however, tended to employ only one law clerk, and to do their own drafting. See Barry Cushman, *The Clerks of the Four Horsemen, Part I*, 39 J Sup Ct Hist 386 (2014); Barry Cushman, *The Clerks of the Four Horsemen, Part II*, 40 J Sup Ct Hist 55 (2015); Melvin I. Urofsky, *Louis D. Brandeis: A Life* 465 (2009). Congress did not authorize the Justices to hire two law clerks until 1941, though most of them continued to employ only one clerk until 1946. See Artemus Ward and David L. Weiden, *Sorcerer's Apprentices: 100 Years of Law Clerks at the United States Supreme Court* 36–37 (NYU, 2006).

[55] See Bradley J. Best, *Law Clerks, Support Personnel, and the Decline of Consensual Norms on the United States Supreme Court 1935–1995* 214, 232 (LFB, 2002) (finding "a positive, statistically significant relationship between the number of law clerks on the Court and the frequency of dissenting and concurring opinions"); Ley, Searles, and Clayton, 49 Tulsa L Rev at 112–13, 121 (cited in note 23) (concluding that "the opportunity for cost-lowering effects of law clerks" is "significant to our understanding of the persistence of non-consensual norms.").

[56] This is also sometimes referred to as "conformity voting," see, for example, Dorff and Brenner, 54 J Pol at 763 (cited in note 4), or "minority-majority voting," see, for example,

which a Justice who was not with the majority at conference moved *toward* the majority. I will refer to movements from dissent at conference to the majority in the final vote on the merits[57] as instances of *strong acquiescence*; I will refer to movements from a passing vote at conference to the majority in the final vote on the merits as instances of *weak acquiescence*.[58] Of course, such movement might have occurred either because the Justice in question became persuaded that the majority was correct, or because, though remaining unpersuaded, he elected to go along with the majority for the sake of some other consideration such as collegiality or public perception.[59] The information contained in the docket books does not enable us to discriminate between these two possibilities, and therefore I shall not attempt to do so here. I will use the term *nonacquiescence* to denote instances in which a Justice who dissented at conference remained steadfast in his opposition to the majority's disposition. In cases of nonacquiescence, there was no postconference change in the vote of the Justice in question. I will use the term *quasi-acquiescence* to denote a situation in which a Justice who was inclined in conference to oppose the majority's disposition withheld his dissent and instead publicly concurred in the result with the written statement that he was doing so only because he felt bound by the authority of an earlier decision with which he disagreed. Finally, I will use the term *defection* to denote instances in which a Justice who was either a member of the conference majority or passed at conference later dissented from the published opinion.[60] In other words, defection denotes instances in which the Justice in question moved *away* from the majority. Again, I will refer to movements from the majority at conference to dissent in the final vote on the merits as instances of *strong defection*; I will refer to movements

---

Saul Brenner and Robert H. Dorff, *The Attitudinal Model and Fluidity Voting on the United States Supreme Court: A Theoretical Perspective*, 4 J Theoretical Pol 195, 197 (1992).

[57] I borrow this term from Professor Saul Brenner, 22 Jurimetrics at 287 (cited in note 24). What he calls the "original vote on the merits" I refer to as the "conference vote."

[58] These two terms are adapted from Brenner, 26 Am J Pol Sci at 388 (cited in note 4), and Brenner, 24 Am J Pol Sci at 527 (cited in note 4) (referring to such movements as "strong fluidity" and "weak fluidity," respectively).

[59] See, for example, Brenner and Dorff, 4 J Theoretical Pol at 200 (cited in note 56) (concluding that Justices acquiesce "for non-attitudinal reasons, including small-group reasons"); Howard Jr., 62 Am Pol Sci Rev at 45 (cited in note 24) (same).

[60] This is also sometimes referred to as "counterconformity voting," see, for example, Dorff and Brenner, 54 J Pol at 763 (cited in note 4), or "majority-minority voting," see, for example, Brenner and Dorff, 4 J Theoretical Pol at 197 (cited in note 56).

from a passing vote at conference to the majority in the final vote on the merits as instances of *weak defection.*[61]

II. Unanimous Cases with No Vote Changes

The docket books contain vote tallies for 1,200 of the 1,381 cases in which the Court published a full opinion during the 1922–28 Terms. Eighty-six percent of these 1,200 cases, or 1,028, were decided unanimously. In 58% of these 1,028 unanimous cases, the vote also was unanimous in conference. Put another way, the conference vote was unanimous in 50% of the 1,200 cases for which we have conference records.[62] A number of these were decisions of considerable and lasting import. For example, *Massachusetts v Mellon* and *Frothingham v Mellon*[63] were unanimous 1923 decisions upholding the Sheppard-Towner Maternity Act of 1921 against constitutional challenge and articulating the taxpayer standing doctrine. Under these decisions, the constitutionality of congressional appropriations from general revenue could not be challenged by taxpayers, nor could states challenge the constitutionality of cooperative federal grant-in-aid programs. These precedents later would immunize billions of dollars in New Deal federal relief and public works spending from constitutional attack.[64] And the votes in conference were unanimous. Butler's notes record the disposition as "Dismiss 24 OR [*Massachusetts v Mellon*] as suit v U.S. No *int*[erest]. Dismiss on no right to sue. Not hurt. 962 [*Frothingham v Mellon*] Dismissed below. '*Affirmed*' by *all*. No interest to sue."[65]

---

[61] See, for example, Brenner and Dorff, 4 J Theoretical Pol at 197 (cited in note 56). There also are instances in which a docket book entry does not record a vote for a particular Justice. Often that was because the Justice was absent from the conference, and where that was the case, I do not treat that Justice as having engaged in any of the defined voting behaviors.

[62] Post, 85 Minn L Rev at 1332 (cited in note 2).

[63] 262 US 447 (1923).

[64] See Benjamin F. Wright, *The Growth of American Constitutional Law* 184 (Holt, 1967); Carl B. Swisher, *American Constitutional Development* 838–39 (Praeger, 2d ed 1954); Joel F. Paschal, *Mr. Justice Sutherland: A Man Against the State* 212 (Princeton, 1951); Edward S. Corwin, *Twilight of the Supreme Court: A History of Our Constitutional Theory* 176 (Shoe String, 1934).

[65] Butler OT 1922 Docket Book. Two other important Taft Court decisions concerning the separation of powers also were unanimous both at conference and in the announced judgment. See *J. W. Hampton Jr. and Co. v United States*, 276 US 394 (1928), a landmark in the development of the nondelegation doctrine, Stone OT 1927 Docket Book, and the *Pocket Veto Case*, 279 US 655 (1929), Stone OT 1928 Docket Book.

In *Florida v Mellon*,[66] the Court unanimously upheld a provision of the federal estate tax granting a credit against the tax for inheritance taxes paid to a state. An attractive package of mild winters and no state inheritance taxes had induced a number of wealthy residents from northern states to relocate to the sunshine state. The federal tax credit was designed to level the playing field so that there would be no estate tax advantage gained by moving from a state with an inheritance tax to a state without one. In either case, the total tax on the transmission of wealth at death would be the same. One predictable consequence of this would be that states with inheritance taxes would be less likely to repeal them, and states without such taxes might be more likely to enact them. This mechanism, of granting a credit against a federal tax for a comparable tax paid to a state, would provide the blueprint for the unemployment compensation provisions of the Social Security Act. Those provisions were crafted with the guidance of Justice Brandeis, and with *Florida v Mellon* very much in mind.[67] And the conference vote in that decision, like the conference vote in *Frothingham*, was unanimous.[68] The docket books indicate that these two major building blocks of the modern welfare state met with no objection from the Justices of the Taft Court.

Chas. Wolff Packing Co. v Court of Industrial Relations of the State of Kansas,[69] also decided in 1923, unanimously invalidated as violating

---

[66] 273 US 12 (1927).

[67] See, for example, Joseph P. Lash, *Dealers and Dreamers: A New Look at the New Deal* 244–45 (Doubleday, 1988); Philippa Strum, *Louis D. Brandeis: Justice for the People* 386–87 (Harvard, 1984); Lewis J. Paper, *Brandeis* 354–57 (Prentice-Hall, 1983); Bruce Allan Murphy, *The Brandeis/Frankfurter Connection: The Secret Political Activities of Two Supreme Court Justices* 165–77 (Oxford, 1982); Melvin I. Urofsky, *A Mind of One Piece: Brandeis and American Reform* 131 (Scribner, 1971); Arthur M. Schlesinger Jr., 3 *The Age of Roosevelt: The Politics of Upheaval* 301–03, 305–06 (Houghton Mifflin, 1960); David J. Danelski, *The Propriety of Brandeis's Extrajudicial Conduct*, in Nelson L. Dawson, ed, *Brandeis and America* 11, 26–27 (Kentucky, 1989); Nelson L. Dawson, *Brandeis and the New Deal*, in Dawson, ed, *Brandeis and America* 38, 48; Thomas H. Eliot, *The Advent of Social Security*, in Katie Louchheim, ed, *The Making of the New Deal* 150, 159, 160–61 (Harvard, 1983); Paul Freund, *Mr. Justice Brandeis*, in Allison Dunham and Philip B. Kurland, eds, *Mr. Justice* 177, 190 (Chicago, 1964); Melvin I. Urofsky and David W. Levy, eds, 5 *Letters of Louis D. Brandeis* 520, 523, 526–27 (State Univ NY, 1978); Franklin Roosevelt to Felix Frankfurter, June 11, 1934, in Max Freedman, annot, *Roosevelt and Frankfurter: Their Correspondence, 1928–1945* at 122–23 (Atlantic Monthly, 1968); Tom Corcoran and Ben Cohen to Felix Frankfurter, June 18, 1934, Freedman, annot, *Roosevelt and Frankfurter* 123–26; 79 Cong Rec 9287 (1935) (remarks of Senator Wagner); *Steward Machine Co. v Davis*, 301 US 548, 557, 559 (1937) (oral argument of Charles Wyzanski); *Steward Machine Co. v Davis*, 301 US at 562, 564 (oral argument of Assistant Attorney General Robert Jackson).

[68] Stone OT 1926 Docket Book.

[69] 262 US 522 (1923).

the Due Process Clause a wage order issued pursuant to the Kansas Court of Industrial Relations Act's statutory scheme of compulsory industrial arbitration. The vote again was unanimous at conference.[70] The case returned to the Court in 1925 under the same style, this time involving the constitutionality of an order concerning working hours. The Court again unanimously invalidated the order,[71] and the vote in conference similarly was unanimous. In arguing for reversal of the lower court, Taft lamented that "our mandate" in the earlier decision was "not obeyed." "The whole jud[gment] should go," he argued. "*Also*," he added, "that fixing of hours is bad *here*." Butler records Holmes and Van Devanter as following with "Yes," while McReynolds agreed that the "order is bad as to hours."[72]

Chastleton Corp. v Sinclair,[73] which unanimously held that the postwar emergency that had justified residential rent control in the District of Columbia had ended, also was unanimous at conference. Butler's notes indicate that Van Devanter, McReynolds, Sutherland, Butler, Sanford, and perhaps Taft expressed the view that the "Act [is] bad."[74] *Yeiser v Dysart*,[75] a 1925 decision unanimously upholding regulation of the compensation of lawyers representing workmen's compensation claimants in Nebraska courts, likewise was unanimous at conference. Butler's notes record Taft as stating that the regulation was a "Reasonable provision. Law applies to a class," and that a lawyer representing such a client was an "Officer of [the] Court."[76] This reasoning was faithfully reflected in Holmes's opinion.[77] *Weller v New York*[78] considered the constitutionality of a statute regulating theater ticket brokers. In 1927, a closely divided Court would invalidate a provision of the statute limiting the price that such brokers could

---

[70] Butler OT 1922 Docket Book.

[71] *Charles Wolff Packing Co. v The Court of Industrial Relations of the State of Kansas*, 267 US 552 (1925).

[72] Butler OT 1924 Docket Book.

[73] 264 US 543 (1924).

[74] Butler OT 1923 Docket Book. For a bit more detail about the conference discussion, see Post, 78 BU L Rev at 1497–98 (cited in note 3).

[75] 267 US 540 (1925).

[76] Butler OT 1924 Docket Book.

[77] 267 US 540 (1925).

[78] 268 US 319 (1925).

charge for resale tickets,[79] but in *Weller* the Court unanimously upheld a section of the statute requiring that such brokers be licensed. The vote at conference also was unanimous.[80] Butler records the Chief Justice as stating, "Within power to license brokers. Doubt as to price." Holmes remarked, "Stat. good," and Van Devanter added, "Good as to license."[81] In *Asakura v Seattle*,[82] the Court unanimously held that a Seattle ordinance excluding noncitizens from the business of pawn brokerage violated the terms of a treaty with Japan guaranteeing the rights of each nation's citizens or subjects to reside in the other in order "to carry on trade." The vote at conference was unanimous, with Taft stating, "Treaty gives right to carry on Trade & Pawn-broking is 'trade as old as business itself.'"[83]

There also were several important dormant Commerce Clause cases in which the unanimity generated in conference held firm. This was true in *Real Silk Hosiery Mills v Portland*,[84] which struck down an ordinance imposing a license tax on solicitors of orders to be filled by an out-of-state manufacturer;[85] in *Clark v Poor*,[86] which upheld a state requirement that common carriers obtain a permit and pay a tax to help maintain highways;[87] and in *Leonard & Leonard v Earle*,[88] which upheld state licensure and regulation of oyster-packing establishments.[89] Other significant economic regulation cases that were unanimous both at conference vote and at the final vote on the merits include *Miller v Schoene*,[90] which upheld a state statute requiring destruction of

---

[79] *Tyson and Bro. v Banton*, 273 US 418 (1927).

[80] Butler OT 1924 Docket Book; Stone OT 1924 Docket Book.

[81] Butler OT 1924 Docket Book. As was often the case, here Butler ceased recording the remarks of his colleagues after the first few had spoken.

[82] 265 US 332 (1924).

[83] Butler OT 1923 Docket Book.

[84] 268 US 325 (1925).

[85] Butler OT 1924 Docket Book; Stone OT 1924 Docket Book. Butler records Taft as presenting the case to the conference with the assertion that "The business is interstate commerce. The interference is direct."

[86] 274 US 554 (1927).

[87] Stone OT 1926 Docket Book.

[88] 279 US 392 (1929).

[89] Stone OT 1928 Docket Book.

[90] 276 US 272 (1928). It appears, however, that Butler may have harbored reservations. On his return of Stone's opinion he wrote, "I acquiesce." Justice Butler, Return of *Miller v. Schoene*, Box 55, Harlan Fiske Stone MSS, Manuscript Division, Library of Congress.

cedar trees infected with disease;[91] *Tagg Bros. & Moorhead v United States*,[92] which upheld federal regulation of fees charged by commission salesmen working in major stockyards under the Packers and Stockyards Act of 1921;[93] and *Roschen v Ward*,[94] which upheld a New York statute making it unlawful to sell eyeglasses at retail in any store unless a duly licensed physician or optometrist was in charge and in personal attendance.[95] *Roschen* would serve as the principal authority for the highly deferential 1955 decision in *Williamson v Lee Optical Co.*, in which the Court rebuffed the due process and equal protection claims of Oklahoma opticians who objected to a state statute making it unlawful for anyone other than a licensed optometrist or ophthalmologist to fit lenses to a face, or to duplicate or replace lenses without a written prescription from a licensed optometrist or ophthalmologist.[96]

A number of high-profile civil rights and civil liberties decisions also were unanimous from wire to wire. *Pierce v Society of Sisters*,[97] which unanimously invalidated an Oregon measure requiring children in the state to attend public schools, also was unanimous at conference.[98] Taft stated that the "Act deprives parents and children of liberty under the 14th Am." The Chief "Quoted Meyer v Nebraska," which two years earlier had invalidated a Nebraska statute prohibiting the teaching of any modern foreign language to children in the eighth grade or younger. Butler records that Taft "Couples" this precedent "with 'religious liberty' of par. & child—public schools

---

[91] Stone OT 1927 Docket Book. McReynolds was absent from the conference.

[92] 280 US 420 (1930).

[93] Stone OT 1929 Docket Book.

[94] 279 US 337 (1929).

[95] Stone OT 1928 Docket Book. Sutherland was absent from the conference.

[96] 348 US 483 (1955). Other regulatory cases that were unanimous both at the conference vote and at the final vote on the merits include *Sprout v City of South Bend*, 277 US 163 (1928) (invalidating city license tax for commercial carrier conducting an interstate business), Stone OT 1927 Docket Book; *Hygrade Provision Co. v Sherman*, 266 US 497 (1925) (upholding against a dormant Commerce Clause challenge a state law imposing criminal penalties on companies misrepresenting foods as kosher), Butler OT 1924 Docket Book, Stone OT 1924 Docket Book; and *The New England Divisions Case*, 261 US 184 (1923) (expansively reading the Interstate Commerce Commission's power to set rates), Butler OT 1922 Docket Book. *United States v American Linseed Oil Co.*, 262 US 371 (1923) (sustaining a conviction under the Sherman Act), may also fall into this category. There were no dissenting votes recorded at the conference, though it is not clear whether Holmes, Brandeis, or Sutherland actually voted. Butler OT 1922 Docket Book.

[97] 268 US 510 (1925).

[98] Butler OT 1924 Docket Book; Stone OT 1924 Docket Book.

cannot [illegible] it."[99] The Chief also cited to "Adams v Tanner, 244 U.S.,"[100] a 1917 decision invalidating a law prohibiting the receipt of fees by employment agents, which suggests that he was thinking of the case not only as a protection of religious liberty, but also in terms of the occupational liberty of the instructors. Taft also invoked "Harlan's diss. Berea College 211,"[101] which intimates that he also considered the statute an infringement of what Justice John Marshall Harlan I there had described in dissent as the constitutionally protected "right to impart and receive instruction not harmful to the public."[102] Holmes next indicated that he "Agrees," while adding that "As an original prop[osition] might be troublesome without Meyer,"[103] from which he had dissented two years earlier.[104] Two years after *Pierce*, in *Farrington v Tokushige*, where the Court extended the benefits of the right recognized in *Meyer* to aliens in Hawaii attending schools in which the primary language of instruction was Japanese, the vote was unanimous at the conference as well as in the published opinion.[105]

The same voting pattern occasionally occurred in cases involving criminal law and procedure. In *Linder v United States*,[106] for example, the Court unanimously reversed the conviction of a physician under the Harrison Narcotic Act by construing the statute not to apply to his conduct. The vote was unanimous,[107] with Brandeis and Sutherland voting to "Reverse," and Holmes stating "Rev if possible."[108] Van Devanter, who had voted to declare the statute unconstitutional in 1919,[109] asserted that the "Act [is] bad—but consistently with former decisions [the conviction] can be reversed."[110] McReynolds, who preserved a running constitutional objection to the statute,[111]

---

[99] *Meyer v Nebraska*, 262 US 390 (1923); Butler OT 1924 Docket Book.

[100] Butler OT 1924 Docket Book; *Adams v Tanner*, 244 US 590 (1917).

[101] Butler OT 1924 Docket Book.

[102] *Berea College v Kentucky*, 211 US 45, 68 (Harlan, J, dissenting).

[103] Id.

[104] 262 US 390 (1923).

[105] 273 US 284 (1927). Stone OT 1926 Docket Book.

[106] 268 US 5 (1925).

[107] Butler OT 1924 Docket Book; Stone OT 1924 Docket Book.

[108] Butler OT 1924 Docket Book.

[109] *United States v Doremus*, 249 US 86 (1919).

[110] Butler OT 1924 Docket Book.

[111] See, for example, *Casey v United States*, 276 US 413, 420–21 (1928); *Nigro v United States*, 276 US 332, 354–57 (1928); *United States v Daugherty*, 269 US 360, 362–63 (1926);

remarked, "Reverse—Would reverse the whole line." Interestingly, Taft, who spoke first, is recorded as stating, "Reviewed decisions and concluded 'affirm.'" But the Chief also voted last, and when the time came to cast his ballot, he joined his colleagues in voting to reverse.[112] In *United States v Daugherty*[113] the Justices unanimously criticized a fifteen-year sentence for three separate sales of cocaine as "extremely harsh" and unjustified by the circumstances disclosed in the record, and remanded the case for reconsideration of the appropriate punishment.[114] And in *Tumey v Ohio*[115] the Court invalidated as a denial of due process a scheme of compensation for certain judicial officers under which the officer received payment for his services only if the defendant were convicted.[116]

Of course, not all civil rights and civil liberties decisions that were unanimous both at the conference vote and at the final vote on the merits favored those who claimed that their rights had been infringed. This is illustrated by a series of cases arising in connection with enforcement of the prohibition laws. In *Dumbra v United States*,[117] the Court upheld a warrant to search premises for liquor as based upon probable cause.[118] In *Steele v United States*,[119] the Justices held that the description in a search warrant was sufficiently definite to satisfy constitutional and statutory requirements.[120] *Marron v United States*[121] upheld the seizure of account books and papers used in conducting a criminal enterprise during a search incident to a lawful arrest.[122] *Hebert v Louisiana*[123] held that conduct violating both state

---

United States v Behrman, 258 US 280, 289–90 (1922); *United States v Webb*, 249 US 96, 100 (1919); *United States v Doremus*, 249 US 86, 95 (1919).

[112] Butler OT 1924 Docket Book. The Justices also unanimously upheld the first section of the Harrison Act as a valid exercise of the taxing power in *Alston v United States*, 274 US 289 (1927). The vote in conference was similarly unanimous, with Sutherland absent. Stone OT 1926 Docket Book.

[113] 269 US 360 (1926).

[114] Stone OT 1925 Docket Book.

[115] 273 US 510 (1927).

[116] Stone OT 1926 Docket Book.

[117] 268 US 435 (1925).

[118] Butler OT 1924 Docket Book; Stone OT 1924 Docket Book.

[119] 267 US 498 (1925).

[120] Butler OT 1924 Docket Book; Stone OT 1924 Docket Book.

[121] 275 US 192 (1927).

[122] Stone OT 1927 Docket Book.

[123] 272 US 312 (1926).

and federal prohibition laws could be prosecuted by both state and federal authorities without violating the prohibition on Double Jeopardy.[124] And in *Van Oster v Kansas*,[125] the Court upheld a state forfeiture law as applied to property used in the violation of state liquor laws.[126]

Such mixed results can be seen as well in a broader array of civil rights and civil liberties decisions that were unanimous both at the conference vote and at the final vote on the merits. Though *Nixon v Herndon*[127] invalidated the Texas Democratic Party's "white primary,"[128] *Gong Lum v Rice*[129] upheld Mississippi's system of segregated education.[130] While *Ex parte Grossman*[131] upheld presidential commutation of a criminal contempt sentence imposed by a federal judge,[132] and *Hammershmidt v United States*[133] rejected a government attempt to characterize attempts to obstruct the draft as a criminal conspiracy to defraud the United States,[134] *Cockrill v California*[135] affirmed a conviction under California's Alien Land Law.[136] And just as *Cheung Sum Shee v Nagle*[137] overturned the Secretary of Labor's refusal to admit the alien wives and minor children of resident Chinese merchants lawfully domiciled in the United States,[138] so *United States v Thind*[139] held that a native of India was ineligible for naturalization.[140] Notwithstanding their seemingly variable policy valences, the norm of acquiescence was

---

[124] Stone OT 1926 Docket Book.

[125] 272 US 465 (1926).

[126] Stone OT 1926 Docket Book.

[127] 273 US 536 (1927).

[128] Stone OT 1926 Docket Book. Van Devanter was absent from the conference.

[129] 275 US 78 (1927).

[130] Stone OT 1927 Docket Book. Sutherland was absent from the conference.

[131] 267 US 87 (1925).

[132] Butler OT 1924 Docket Book; Stone OT 1924 Docket Book.

[133] 265 US 182 (1924).

[134] Butler OT 1923 Docket Book.

[135] 268 US 258 (1925).

[136] Butler OT 1924 Docket Book; Stone OT 1924 Docket Book.

[137] 268 US 336 (1925).

[138] Butler OT 1924 Docket Book; Stone OT 1924 Docket Book.

[139] 261 US 204 (1923).

[140] Butler OT 1922 Docket Book.

not in play in any of these cases. All of these were dispositions to which each of the Justices agreed from the outset.

III. Unanimous Cases with Vote Changes

Of the 1,028 unanimous 1922–28 Term decisions for which we have conference records, in 30% unanimity would not have been achieved had a conference dissenter not changed his vote to join the majority. In another 12%, unanimity would not have been attained had not a Justice who had expressed "uncertainty" at conference overcome his doubts.[141] In other words, 42% of the Taft Court's unanimous decisions for this period were not unanimous at conference. In these cases, the ultimate unanimity of the Court obscured differences that had emerged at conference. Consider, for example, *Radice v New York*,[142] which involved a challenge to a New York statute that prohibited the employment of women in restaurants between the hours of 10 p.m. and 6 a.m. The statute applied only to the state's larger cities, however, and it contained exemptions for singers and performers, for attendants in ladies' cloak rooms and parlors, and for those employed in hotel dining rooms and kitchens, or in lunch rooms or restaurants conducted by employers solely for the benefit of their employees. Sutherland's unanimous opinion upholding the statute as a legitimate measure for the protection of health dispelled any concern that the recent decision of *Adkins v Children's Hospital*[143] invalidating a minimum wage law for women had implicitly overruled the 1908 decision in *Muller v Oregon*[144] upholding a maximum working hours law for women. The Justices also were unanimous in their rejection of the contention that the limitation of the statute to larger cities and the exemptions for particular types of employment worked a denial of equal protection.

Felix Frankfurter later memorialized a conversation that he had with Brandeis about *Radice*, which he recounts as follows:

> July 6, 1924. I have said that I was certain that Ct would decide NY statute prohibiting night work by women favorably as it did (Radice v New York, 264 U.S.). L.D.B. took me aside and said "you might have been certain but

---

[141] Post, 85 Minn L Rev at 1332–33 (cited in note 2).

[142] 264 US 292 (1924).

[143] 261 US 525 (1923).

[144] 208 US 412 (1908).

it was not at all certain. That was one of those 5 to 4 that was teetering back
& forth for some time. The man who finally wrote—Sutherland was the
fifth man & he had doubts & after a good deal of study (for whatever you
may say of him he has character & conscience) came out for the act & then
wrote his opinion. That swung the others around to silence. It was deemed
inadvisable to express dissent and add another 5 to 4. The doubt as to the
statute turned on unequal protection, which now looms up even more
menacingly than due process, because the statute omitted some night work
& only included some."[145]

Butler's record of the *Radice* conference confirms this account in
most respects. The vote was 5–4, with McKenna, Van Devanter, Mc-
Reynolds, and Butler voting to invalidate the statute, though Butler
records McReynolds's dissenting vote as cast "Doubtfully." It also
appears that it was the equal protection issue that divided the Justices, and that Sutherland was decisive in forming the majority to
uphold the statute. Butler records Sutherland as stating, "Classification can be sustained."[146] It also is clear that the four conference dissenters ultimately acquiesced in the judgment of their colleagues in
the majority. It is not clear, however, whether the outcome was "teetering back & forth for some time." The case was argued January 17
and 18,[147] and the conference at which Sutherland cast the deciding
vote and defended the classification was held on January 26.[148] If there
was any subsequent vacillation, Butler's docket book does not record
it.

In *Brooks v United States*,[149] the Court unanimously upheld the Dyer
Act of 1919, which made it a federal crime to transport or cause to be
transported in interstate commerce "a motor vehicle, knowing the
same to be stolen." Seven years earlier, in *Hammer v Dagenhart*,[150] the
Justices had struck down the Keating-Owen Child Labor Act,[151]
which forbade the interstate shipment of goods produced by firms
employing children. The Court there had held that, unlike such pre-

---

[145] Melvin I. Urofsky, *The Brandeis-Frankfurter Conversations*, 1985 Supreme Court Review 299,
330.

[146] Butler OT 1923 Docket Book.

[147] 264 US 292 (1924).

[148] Butler OT 1923 Docket Book.

[149] 267 US 432 (1925).

[150] 247 US 251 (1918).

[151] 39 Stat 675 (1916).

decessor statutes as the Lottery Act,[152] which prohibited interstate shipment of lottery tickets, and the Pure Food and Drugs Act,[153] which prohibited interstate shipment of adulterated or mislabeled food and drugs, the Keating-Owen Act was not properly a regulation of interstate commerce because the goods whose interstate shipment it prohibited were "of themselves harmless."[154] Yet as a number of commentators have observed, Taft's opinion for the Court did not explain how there was anything in particular about cars that had been stolen that made them "of themselves" harmful.[155]

A private memorandum located in Taft's papers at the Library of Congress reveals that the Chief Justice himself struggled to distinguish the Dyer Act from the Keating-Owen Act. Taft understood the relevant line of cases to stand for the proposition that "[i]f the result of interstate transportation will be to spread some harmful matter or product, Congress may interfere without violating the Tenth Amendment. The facilities of interstate commerce may be withdrawn from those who are using it to corrupt others physically or morally." If, on the other hand, "the transportation is being used to transport something harmless in itself and not calculated to spread evil, like cotton cloth," Taft wrote, "Congress may not prohibit its interstate transportation, although its inception may have been in some evil which is the legitimate object of the police power, such as child labor." Earlier decisions could be distinguished from *Hammer* on this basis. The Chief Justice noted that "the interstate carriage of lottery tickets will communicate the gambling fever, of obscene literature will communicate moral degeneracy, of impure food will endanger health, [and] of diseased cattle will infect local cattle...." In each of these instances, interstate transportation of the item inflicted a harm outside the state of origin. The "justification" for the doctrine, Taft concluded, "must

---

[152] 28 Stat 963 (1895), upheld in *Champion v Ames*, 188 US 321 (1903) ("The Lottery Case").

[153] 34 Stat 768 (1906), upheld in *Hipolite Egg Co. v United States*, 220 US 45 (1910).

[154] 247 US at 272.

[155] See, for example, Melvin Urofsky and Paul Finkelman, 2 *A March of Liberty: A Constitutional History of the United States* 705 (Oxford, 3d ed 2011) (the Dyer Act "bore a striking resemblance to the Child Labor Law, which had also prohibited the movement of things that were not in themselves harmful"); David P. Currie, *The Constitution in the Supreme Court: The Second Century 1888–1986* at 176 (Chicago, 1990) (Taft "made no effort to show that stolen cars were harmful to anyone in the state to which they were transported"); Paul L. Murphy, *The Constitution in Crisis Times 1918–1969* at 61–62 (HarperCollins, 1972) (the Court ignored the "obvious similarity" between the Dyer Act and the Keating-Owen Act, both of which prohibited interstate transportation of "things not in themselves harmful.").

be that Congress can prohibit the interstate spread of an evil thing, although it cannot prohibit the spread of something harmless in itself in order to suppress an evil which is properly the object of state police regulation."[156]

Taft was persuaded that this reasoning sufficed to sustain the constitutionality of the Dyer Act, but he conceded that this conclusion might not be obvious. "At first I had a little difficulty with stolen automobiles," he confessed, "as the chief evil in connection therewith is the stealing and that of course is over before the machine takes on its character as a stolen automobile. This makes it look something like Hammer v Dagenhart." But the Chief Justice reassured himself with the observation that "a stolen automobile is a canker. It attracts shady and disreputable individuals and leads to secret and underhanded dealings. Certainly it is not ultra vires for Congress to prohibit the interstate communication of this canker."[157]

Taft apparently wrote this memorandum before the conference on *Brooks* that was held on January 31, 1925, because his presentation to his colleagues affirmed his belief in the Act's constitutionality. Butler summarized Taft's remarks as, "Thinks first section good. Distinguishes bet Caminetti & Dagenhart Case."[158] Holmes expressed the view that the defendant's constitutional claim was "not meritorious" and that the case presented "No substantial Const. qu[estion]."[159] Van Devanter also is recorded as taking the position that both the statute and the indictment were "good."[160]

Sutherland had been a U.S. Senator when the Pure Food and Drugs Act was passed, and had voted in favor of its passage.[161] He also was in the Senate in 1910 when that body approved by a voice vote the Mann Act,[162] which prohibited the interstate transportation of women

---

[156] *Brooks v United States*, Reel 614 William Howard Taft Papers, Library of Congress, 6–7.

[157] Id at 7.

[158] Butler OT 1924 Docket Book. *Caminetti v United States*, 242 US 470 (1917), upheld a conviction under the Mann Act for interstate transportation of a woman for an immoral purpose under circumstances that did not involve "commercialized vice." The "bet" case is presumably *The Lottery Case*, 188 US 321 (1903), in which the Court by a vote of 5–4 upheld a federal statute prohibiting the interstate transportation of lottery tickets.

[159] Butler OT 1924 Docket Book. In support of this view Holmes apparently cited *Purity Extract and Tonic Co. v Lynch*, 226 US 192 (1912).

[160] Butler OT 1924 Docket Book ("V Stat. good—Ind good").

[161] 40 Cong Rec 2773 (1906).

[162] 36 Stat 825 (1910).

and girls for immoral purposes.[163] And he still occupied a seat in the upper chamber in 1913 when Congress passed the Webb-Kenyon Act,[164] which prohibited the interstate transportation of liquor into states where it was intended to be received, possessed, or sold in violation of state law. Here Sutherland had voted against[165] and offered the principal constitutional argument in opposition to the bill.[166] Sutherland maintained that Congress did not have the power to prohibit the interstate shipment of liquor unless and until it had become "outlawed by the common opinion of the people."[167] Until such time as that occurred, Sutherland insisted, alcohol was "a legitimate article of commerce, and so long as it is recognized as such it cannot be denied the right of interstate transportation."[168]

The Court unanimously upheld the Pure Food and Drugs Act in *Hipolite Egg Co. v United States*,[169] and the Justices sustained the Mann Act in *Hoke v United States*[170] and *Caminetti*. In 1917 the Court upheld the Webb-Kenyon Act as a legitimate exercise of the commerce power, with Chief Justice Edward Douglass White writing that because of alcohol's "exceptional nature," it would be within congressional power to exclude it from interstate commerce altogether.[171] But despite these precedents, Sutherland was plagued by the very sorts of doubts about the Dyer Act that had troubled Taft. Butler records him as objecting that "Automobiles [are] not like liquor—[or] Bad food—[or] girls [transported for] immoral purposes—Transported as a [illegible] part." Both Sutherland and McReynolds apparently were not persuaded that stolen automobiles were "in themselves harmful," and when it came time to vote each of them registered their dissent.[172] But here again these Justices observed the Taft Court norm of acquiescence, and joined with their colleagues to make a unanimous Court.

---

[163] 40 Cong Rec 9037 (1910).

[164] 37 Stat 699 (1913).

[165] 49 Cong Rec 2922 (1913).

[166] 49 Cong Rec 2903–11 (1913).

[167] 49 Cong Rec 2906 (1913).

[168] 49 Cong Rec 2904 (1913).

[169] 220 US 45 (1910).

[170] 277 US 308 (1913).

[171] *Clark Distilling Co. v Western Maryland Railway Co.*, 242 US 311, 325–26, 331–32 (1917).

[172] Butler OT 1924 Docket Book.

Oliver Iron Mining Co. v Lord[173] was an important decision in the line of Commerce Clause authority distinguishing production from commerce.[174] There the Justices upheld a state occupation tax on coal mining, even though the coal extracted was to be shipped to points outside the state to satisfy existing contracts. "Mining," wrote Van Devanter for a unanimous Court, "is not interstate commerce, but, like manufacturing, is a local business subject to local regulation and taxation.... Its character in this regard is intrinsic, is not affected by the intended use or disposal of the product, is not controlled by contractual engagements, and persists even though the business be conducted in close connection with interstate commerce." In this case, he noted, "[t]he ore does not enter interstate commerce until after the mining is done." It was true that "[t]he tax may indirectly and incidentally affect such commerce," but this, he concluded, was "not a forbidden burden or interference."[175]

Only seven Justices participated in the conference vote taken on January 6, 1923. Justice Mahlon Pitney had retired a week earlier,[176] and Sanford had not yet been nominated to replace him.[177] Butler was not confirmed until December 21, 1922,[178] two weeks after the arguments had taken place on December 6 and 7,[179] and so did not participate at the conference. Butler records the conference vote as 4–3 to reverse the District Court, with Taft, McKenna, Van Devanter, and McReynolds opposed by Holmes, Brandeis, and Sutherland.[180] Ultimately, however, the Court was unanimous to affirm—the Justices in the conference majority were persuaded to join with the minority Justices in massing the Court. The decision was not handed down until May 7, months after Sanford's confirmation, and the published report contains no indication that Butler and Sanford did not participate. This suggests the possibility that another vote was

---

[173] 262 US 172 (1923).

[174] For later decisions relying upon *Oliver Iron* for this distinction, see, for example, *Carter v Carter Coal Co.*, 298 US 238, 302–03 (1936); *Champlin Refining Co. v Corporation Commission of Oklahoma*, 286 US 210, 235 (1932); *Utah Power and Light Co. v Pfost*, 286 US 165, 182 (1932).

[175] 262 US at 178–79.

[176] 260 US iii.

[177] Sanford was nominated on Jan 24, 1923, and took his seat on Feb 19. 261 US iii.

[178] 260 US iii. Butler took his seat on Jan 2, 1923. Id.

[179] 262 US 172.

[180] Butler OT 1922 Docket Book.

held with a full Court, that the two new Justices agreed with the conference minority, and that the four Justices now in the minority then acquiesced in the decision.

Coronado Coal Co. v United Mine Workers of America[181] involved a strike called by a local affiliate of the United Mine Workers (UMW) against Arkansas coal producers in which the strikers had deliberately destroyed company mines and equipment. The case involved two questions. The first was whether, under the circumstances, the UMW could be held liable for the property damage inflicted by members of the local union. The trial court had directed a verdict in favor of the UMW on this issue, and the Supreme Court unanimously affirmed this judgment. The second issue was whether the actions of the local union might constitute a conspiracy in restraint of trade in violation of the Sherman Act. The trial court also had directed a verdict in favor of the local union on this question, but here the Court unanimously reversed the judgment and remanded for a new trial. The Justices ruled that there was substantial evidence that the actions of the local union were undertaken with the intent to prevent interstate shipment of coal that would compete with union coal in neighboring states.[182]

This was precisely the position that Taft had taken at conference, and he was joined in that view by Van Devanter, Sutherland, and Butler. Butler records that Taft stated, "Af'[firm] as [to] United M.W. [and] Rev[erse] as to Local 21. I.C.C. [Interstate Commerce Clause] point for jury." Van Devanter is recorded "Same as 1[Taft]," and both Sutherland and Butler are recorded as "With 1." Holmes stated that he "Would affirm" as to both issues, and Brandeis is noted as agreeing with "O.W.H." McReynolds indicated that he "Would reverse all." There is no indication of any comment from Sanford or Stone. McReynolds apparently acquiesced at the conference: When the vote was taken, the count was 6–2 in favor of the disposition advocated by the Chief Justice, with Holmes and Brandeis dissenting, and no vote recorded for Stone. As Butler noted, "Brandeis and Holmes [voted] to affirm all." But between the time of the conference

---

[181] 268 US 295 (1925).

[182] In reviewing the verdict of the first trial in the case, the Court had held that the company had not adduced sufficient evidence of intent to restrain interstate commerce. *United Mine Workers v Coronado Coal Co.*, 259 US 344, 408–13 (1922).

and the delivery of the Court's opinion, these two Justices (and possibly Stone) acquiesced in the disposition favored by the majority.[183]

In *National Association of Window Glass Manufacturers v United States*,[184] the Court unanimously rejected a Sherman Act challenge to an agreement between union glass blowers and an association of window glass manufacturers to fix wages and seasonally rotate the labor force between two sets of factories. At the November 24, 1923 conference, however, Taft, McKenna, and McReynolds had dissented from the judgments of their colleagues.[185] In *Industrial Association of San Francisco v United States*,[186] the Court unanimously rejected the Sherman Act prosecution of building contractors who had agreed to maintain open shop employment policies by permitting sales of specified materials only to contractors maintaining an open shop. The price of that unanimity was Taft's suppression of the dissent that he had registered at conference.[187] *Dayton-Goose Creek Railway Co. v United States*[188] unanimously upheld the recapture provisions of the Transportation Act of 1920, but only because McKenna suppressed the dissenting vote that he had cast at conference.[189] *Panama Railroad v Johnson*[190] unanimously upheld provisions of the Jones Act authorizing injured seamen to sue their employers for damages, but only because McReynolds suppressed his dissenting conference vote.[191] And though the subject of intergovernmental tax immunities would become one of

---

[183] Butler OT 1924 Docket Book. Stone OT 1924 Docket Book contains no report of the conference.

[184] 263 US 403 (1923).

[185] Butler OT 1923 Docket Book.

[186] 268 US 64 (1925). This confirms the claims to this effect made in Taft's letter to Stone, Jan 27, 1927, quoted in Mason, *Harlan Fiske Stone* at 257–58 (cited in note 4) ("I voted against the decision of the Court in [the San Francisco case], but I acquiesced because I considered it, on the statement of Sutherland, a mere difference on my part in the matter of the significance of evidence, rather than any difference in principle between us.").

[187] Stone OT 1924 Docket Book; Butler OT 1924 Docket Book. McReynolds passed at the conference vote.

[188] 263 US 456 (1924).

[189] Butler OT 1923 Docket Book.

[190] 264 US 375 (1924). Sutherland did not participate.

[191] Butler OT 1923 Docket Book. That same Term the Court invalidated a federal statute that allowed state workmen's compensation laws to apply to certain work injuries sustained within the admiralty jurisdiction. *Washington v W. C. Dawson and Co.*, 264 US 219 (1924). The decision followed the precedents of *Knickerbocker Ice Co. v Stewart*, 253 US 149 (1920), which had struck down a similar federal statute, and *Southern Pacific v Jensen*, 244 US 205 (1917), which had held that New York's workmen's compensation statute could not apply to

the most divisive confronting the Taft and Hughes Courts,[192] in the 1926 case of *Metcalf & Eddy v Mitchell*[193] the Justices unanimously upheld the imposition of the federal income tax on the profits of a private contractor from performance of contracts with state governments. In a gesture that would be in short supply in such cases in the future, Sutherland abandoned his dissenting conference stance and acquiesced to make a unanimous Court.[194] On his return of Stone's circulated draft opinion, Sutherland wrote, "I felt rather strongly the other way, but I shall yield. You have written a good opinion, and if we are to draw what seems to me to be a rather arbitrary line, perhaps this is as good as any."[195]

Similarly, the result in *Trusler v Crooks*,[196] which unanimously invalidated as a "penalty" a tax imposed on options contracts in grain by the Futures Trading Act, did not receive the support of Van Devanter and Sutherland at conference.[197] In *Michigan Pub. Util. Comm'n v Duke*,[198] the Court unanimously condemned the state's attempt "to convert property used exclusively in the business of a private carrier into a public utility, or to make the owner a public carrier" as a deprivation of property without due process. At the conference, however, Holmes had passed.[199] Also divided at conference were two

---

work injuries sustained in the admiralty jurisdiction. At the *Dawson* conference, Holmes and Brandeis voted to uphold the federal statute. Butler OT 1923 Docket Book. Brandeis also dissented from the published opinion, but Holmes wrote separately that the reasoning of *Jensen* and the cases following it "never has satisfied me and therefore I should have been glad to see a limit set to the principle. But I must leave it to those who think the principle right to say how far it extends."

[192] See notes 260–66 and accompanying text.

[193] 269 US 514 (1926).

[194] Stone OT 1925 Docket Book. Stone placed a question mark next to the vote of either Sutherland or Butler, or perhaps both. The following year, in *Northwestern Mutual Life Insurance Co. v Wisconsin*, 275 US 136 (1927), the Court unanimously held that a state tax on the income from federal securities violated constitutional principles of intergovernmental tax immunity. The vote in conference was similarly unanimous, with the ailing Sutherland absent. Stone OT 1927 Docket Book.

[195] Justice Sutherland, Return of *Metcalf v. Mitchell*, Box 52, Harlan Fiske Stone MSS, Manuscript Division, Library of Congress.

[196] 269 US 475 (1926).

[197] Stone OT 1925 Docket Book.

[198] 266 US 570 (1925).

[199] Butler OT 1924 Docket Book. Butler records Van Devanter as saying that the company was a "Private carrier," citing "251/ US Pipe." Butler's notes clarify that Van Devanter was referring to the "Producer's Oil Case 251 US." The reference here is to *Producers' Transportation Co. v Railroad Commission*, 251 US 228 (1920), a Van Devanter opinion in which the Court had unanimously held that a pipeline had been devoted to public use and thus was

important land use cases. The decision in *Nectow v City of Cambridge*,[200] which unanimously invalidated a zoning ordinance as applied, received the support of only six Justices at conference. Brandeis dissented, and Holmes and Stone passed.[201] That same year, in *Washington v Roberge*,[202] the Court unanimously invalidated as repugnant to the Due Process Clause a zoning ordinance conditioning permission to construct a home for the aged poor on the written consent of the owners of two-thirds of the property within 400 feet of the proposed building. In conference, however, that disposition had garnered only five votes. McReynolds, Sutherland, and Sanford had dissented, and Stone had passed.[203]

Some significant civil rights and civil liberties decisions also followed this pattern. In *Whitney v California*,[204] the Justices unanimously affirmed the criminal syndicalism conviction of Anita Whitney, the niece of former Justice Stephen J. Field. Brandeis wrote a celebrated concurring opinion, joined by Holmes, in which the two Justices voted to affirm the conviction on the grounds that, at trial, Ms. Whitney had neither contended that the California statute as applied to her was void because there was no clear and present danger of a serious evil, nor requested that the question of the existence of such conditions be passed upon by the court or a jury. Because there was other evidence tending to establish a conspiracy to commit present serious crimes, Brandeis and Holmes believed that the Court was without power to disturb to judgment of the state court.[205]

Stone's record of the conference in the spring of the 1926 Term contains only an indication that the opinion was assigned to San-

---

subject to regulation as a common carrier. In dicta, the opinion had stated that "if the pipeline was constructed solely to carry oil for particular producers under strictly private contracts and never was devoted by its owner to public use, that is, to carrying for the public, the state could not, by mere legislative fiat or by any regulating order of a Commission, convert it into a public utility or make its owner a common carrier, for that would be taking private property for public use without just compensation, which no state can do consistently with the due process of law clause of the Fourteenth Amendment." 251 US at 230–31. Butler records Holmes as responding that the "Pipe line case right in result but no[t] reasons." Stone OT 1924 Docket Book contains no entry for the case.

[200] 277 US 183 (1928).

[201] Stone OT 1927 Docket Book.

[202] 278 US 116 (1928).

[203] Stone OT 1928 Docket Book. Other regulatory cases in which unanimity was achieved after conference include *Morris v Duby*, 274 US 135 (1927) (upholding regulation prescribing maximum weights for trucks and loads on state highways). At conference, Holmes and Sanford had passed. Stone OT 1926 Docket Book.

[204] 274 US 357 (1927).

[205] Id at 372–80.

ford.[206] The case was initially argued at the beginning of the 1925 Term,[207] however, and Stone's docket book from that Term provides some insight into events at the initial conference. Stone's notes indicate that the Justices unanimously voted to dismiss the case for want of jurisdiction.[208] The difficulty, as Sanford later explained in his opinion for the Court, was that the record contained no indication that Whitney had raised nor that the state courts had considered or decided any federal question. The lower court later entered an order certifying that it had in fact passed upon the question of whether the statute violated the Fourteenth Amendment, and that order subsequently was added to the record. With this addition, the Court concluded that it did have jurisdiction of the appeal, and returned the case to the docket for reargument in March of 1926.[209]

There is an ambiguity in Stone's 1925 Term entry that is worth lingering over. Stone also records a vote on the merits in *Whitney*, though it is unclear whether this vote took place before or after reargument. That vote was 7–1 to affirm the conviction, with Brandeis dissenting, and a question mark placed in the "Reverse" column for Holmes.[210] There is, however, another vote recorded, with "re-hearing" handwritten into the subject matter column above the vote tally. It is not clear whether this was a vote to grant reargument, or a vote on the merits following reargument. Stone lists the vote as 5–3, with Holmes, Brandeis, and Sanford voting in the negative column.[211] It may be that these three Justices simply saw no point in reviewing a conviction that the previous vote gave them good reason to believe would be affirmed. But if this last vote was taken on the merits after reargument, Sanford's vote to reverse would be remarkable for at least two reasons. First, he was the author of the 1925 decision *Gitlow v New York*,[212] which upheld Benjamin Gitlow's conviction under New York's Criminal Anarchy

---

[206] Stone OT 1926 Docket Book.

[207] 274 US 357 (1927).

[208] Stone OT 1925 Docket Book. McReynolds was absent for this vote.

[209] 274 US at 360–62.

[210] Stone OT 1925 Docket Book. Stone records McReynolds as voting with the majority on this issue.

[211] Stone OT 1925 Book. McReynolds is again listed as absent.

[212] 268 US 652 (1925). Unfortunately, we do not have a docket book account of the conference in *Gitlow*. The case was reargued on Nov 23, 1923, but Butler's docket books for the 1923 and 1924 Terms have no entries for the case. Butler's OT 1922 Docket Book lists *Gitlow* in the index, but contains no entry for the case. Stone OT 1924 Docket Book also contains no entry for the case.

statute for the publication of his "Left Wing Manifesto" in *The Revolutionary Age* newspaper. Brandeis there had joined Holmes's celebrated dissent, in which he maintained that Gitlow's "redundant discourse" presented no clear and present danger of an attempt to overthrow the government.[213] Second, Sanford ultimately wrote the majority opinion in *Whitney*, and it is with much of the First Amendment theory contained in that opinion that Brandeis implicitly took issue in his famous concurring opinion. Based on Sanford's opinions in *Gitlow* and *Whitney*, it does not seem likely that the 5–3 vote was on the merits. If it was, however, then Sanford may have performed the ultimate act of acquiescence, not only joining in a judgment from which he had dissented at conference, but also shouldering the responsibility for writing the opinion supporting that judgment. In any event, Holmes and Brandeis also ultimately acquiesced in the majority's disposition and, to a limited extent, its rationale. For many years, scholars have questioned why Brandeis did not dissent in *Whitney*.[214] Stone's record of the conference votes on the case shows that Brandeis voted to do so at least once, and perhaps twice.

In *Fiske v Kansas*,[215] decided the same day as *Whitney*, the Justices reversed the criminal syndicalism conviction of an organizer for the Industrial Workers of the World. Here again the judgment was unanimous, and this time there were no concurring opinions. At the conference, however, McReynolds had voted to affirm, and Stone placed question marks next to his own and Sutherland's votes to reverse.[216] In *Corrigan v Buckley*,[217] a unanimous bench held that the Court lacked jurisdiction to hear an appeal in a challenge to the constitutionality of racially restrictive real estate covenants, because the case presented no substantial federal question. At the conference, by contrast, Van Devanter, Brandeis, and Butler had voted against dismissal.[218] And in *Yu Cong Eng v Trinidad*,[219] the Court unanimously invalidated a law of the Philippine Islands prohibiting merchants

---

[213] 268 US at 672 (Holmes, J, dissenting).

[214] See, for example, Harry Kalven Jr., *A Worthy Tradition: Freedom of Speech in America* 164–65 (Harper & Row, 1988).

[215] 274 US 380 (1927).

[216] Stone OT 1925 Docket Book. The case was held over from the 1925 Term. The opinion originally was assigned to Van Devanter, and then transferred to Sanford.

[217] 271 US 623 (1926).

[218] Stone OT 1925 Docket Book.

[219] 271 US 500 (1926).

from keeping account books in any other than one of three approved languages. At the conference, however, this disposition had been opposed by Holmes and McReynolds.[220]

The same pattern can be observed in several cases involving criminal law and criminal procedure. In *Agnello v United States*,[221] the Court unanimously reversed a federal conviction for conspiracy to sell cocaine on the ground that the trial court had admitted evidence gathered during a warrantless search of the defendant's residence. At the conference, however, Taft and Holmes had not been prepared to join the majority.[222] In *Fasulo v United States*,[223] the Justices unanimously held that a scheme for obtaining money by means of intimidation through threats of murder and bodily harm was not a "scheme to defraud" within the meaning of a federal statute punishing the use of the mails for the purpose of executing any "scheme or artifice to defraud." The vote at conference was 7–1, with Taft dissenting and McReynolds passing, but each of them ultimately acquiesced in the majority's decision.[224] In *United States v Lee*,[225] the Court unanimously upheld the seizure and search incident to arrest by the Coast Guard of a vessel on the high seas, but only because Butler suppressed his dissenting conference vote.[226] In *Gambino v United States*,[227] the Court unanimously held that the Fourth Amendment barred introduction at federal trial of evidence seized by New York state police from the accused's automobile without a warrant and without probable cause, and then turned over to federal authorities for prosecution. At the October 22, 1927 conference, there were only two votes for this disposition. Butler and Stone were in the minority, while McReynolds

---

[220] Stone OT 1925 Docket Book. There is an erased vote to reverse in McReynolds's column, raising the possibility that he initially voted with the majority but changed his vote during the conference.

[221] 269 US 20 (1925).

[222] Dean Post records Taft and Hughes as voting to affirm. See Post, 48 Wm & Mary L Rev at 101, n 343 (cited in note 3); id at 134 n 442. Butler's record of the vote places X's straddling the "affirm" and "reverse" columns for these two Justices, which I read as placing them on the fence. Butler OT 1924 Docket Book. Stone records all of the Justices voting to reverse except for Taft and Holmes, in whose voting columns he wrote something illegible. Stone also has erased a vote to reverse in Taft's column. Stone OT 1924 Docket Book.

[223] 272 US 620 (1926).

[224] Stone OT 1926 Docket Book.

[225] 274 US 559 (1927).

[226] Stone OT 1926 Docket Book. Stone also placed a question mark next to Sutherland's vote with the conference majority.

[227] 275 US 310 (1927).

passed and Sutherland was absent. Moreover, Stone's vote to reverse the conviction was uncertain: he placed a question mark next to his own vote. When the Justices again met to discuss the case on December 10, however, they unanimously approved Brandeis's opinion for the Court reversing the conviction. The five members of the conference majority had changed their minds, and McReynolds and Sutherland joined the new majority.[228]

Similarly, in *Byars v United States*[229] the Court unanimously overturned a federal conviction secured on the basis of evidence discovered during a search underwritten by a defective state warrant. At conference, Taft, Holmes, and McReynolds had voted to affirm the conviction, but they ultimately acceded to the disposition favored by their brethren.[230] *Ziang Sung Wan v United States*[231] unanimously reversed a federal murder conviction obtained on the basis of a confession elicited under coercive circumstances. At the conference, however, McKenna, Van Devanter, and Sutherland had voted to affirm, and McReynolds passed.[232] Here the returns of Brandeis's draft opinion explicitly employed the language of acquiescence. McReynolds wrote, "I shall not oppose"; Van Devanter responded with "I shall assent"; and Sutherland replied, "This is well done. I voted the other way but probably shall acquiesce."[233] *Cooke v United States*,[234] which involved charges of contempt of court committed by a lawyer outside the courtroom, followed a similar pattern. The Court unanimously upheld the alleged contemnor's rights to be advised of the charges against him, and to be afforded the opportunity to defend or explain his actions, with the assistance of counsel if he so desired. But the decision was unanimous only because McReynolds again swallowed the objections that he had registered at conference.[235] And in *McGrain v Daugherty*,[236] a unanimous bench held that Congress has the

---

[228] Stone OT 1927 Docket Book. Sutherland also was absent from the Dec 10 conference.

[229] 273 US 28 (1927).

[230] Stone OT 1926 Docket Book.

[231] 266 US 1 (1924).

[232] Butler OT 1923 Docket Book.

[233] Post, 48 Wm & Mary L Rev at 160–61 n 537 (cited in note 3).

[234] 267 US 517 (1925).

[235] Butler OT 1924 Docket Book; Stone OT 1924 Docket Book.

[236] 273 US 135 (1927). Stone took no part in the decision.

power to subpoena witnesses and compel testimony. At the conference vote, however, Brandeis had dissented from this consensus.[237]

IV. Nonunanimous Cases

There were a number of major Taft Court decisions in which unanimity was not achieved. In some of these cases there was no notable movement—neither the votes of the Justices nor, to the extent recorded, the rationale of the decision changed between the conference and the published opinion.[238] This was true in both *Meyer v Nebraska*[239] and *Olmstead v United States,* in which a sharply divided Court upheld warrantless wiretapping.[240] It also was true in *Myers v United States,* a landmark decision on the scope of the President's removal power,[241] and in the four *Alien Land Law* cases of 1923, in which the majority affirmed judgments upholding the statutes while McReynolds and Brandeis maintained that there was "no jurisdiction" and voted to reverse.[242]

This was also the case in *Adkins v Children's Hospital,* which invalidated the District of Columbia's minimum wage law for women by a vote of 5–3.[243] In the four years following the decision in *Adkins,*

---

[237] Butler OT 1924 Docket Book. The case was carried over from the 1925 Term, where there was apparently no recorded vote, Stone OT 1925 Docket Book, and before that from the preceding Term, when it was argued on Dec 5, 1924. Butler recorded the 1924 vote reported in the text. He recorded Holmes as stating, "Was writ premature. Otherwise affirm." The follow-on unanimous decision in *Barry v United States,* 279 US 597 (1929), also was unanimous at conference. Stone OT 1928 Docket Book.

[238] *Moore v Dempsey,* 261 US 86 (1923), may fall into this category. The conference vote of Sutherland, who ultimately joined McReynolds in dissent, is not clear. Otherwise, everyone voted in conference as he would in the published decision. Butler OT 1922 Docket Book. See also *United States v Village of Hubbard,* 266 US 474 (1925) (upholding power of Interstate Commerce Commission to increase intrastate interurban railway rates), in which McReynolds, who wrote separately, registered the only dissenting vote at conference. Butler OT 1924 Docket Book.

[239] 262 US 390 (1923). Holmes and Sutherland dissented. Butler OT 1922 Docket Book.

[240] 277 US 438 (1928). Holmes, Brandeis, Butler, and Stone dissented. Stone OT 1927 Docket Book.

[241] 272 US 52 (1926). Holmes, McReynolds, and Brandeis dissented. Stone OT 1926 Docket Book.

[242] *Frick v Webb,* 263 US 326 (1923); *Webb v O'Brien,* 263 US 313 (1923); *Porterfield v Webb,* 263 US 225 (1923); *Terrace v Thompson,* 263 US 197 (1923). Sutherland took no part. At the conference, Van Devanter argued that the "cloud on title gives jurisdiction." Butler OT 1922 Docket Book.

[243] 261 US 525 (1923). Taft, Holmes, and Sanford dissented. Brandeis did not participate. Butler OT 1922 Docket Book.

the Court would twice invalidate state minimum wage statutes on the authority of that precedent. In the 1925 decision of *Murphy v Sardell*,[244] the Court per curiam affirmed the judgment of the District Court striking down the Arizona statute "upon the authority of *Adkins v Children's Hospital*." The brief report of the case continued, "Mr. Justice Holmes requests that it be stated that his concurrence is solely upon the ground that he regards himself bound by the decision in *Adkins v Children's Hospital*. Mr. Justice Brandeis dissents."[245] In the 1927 case of *Donham v West-Nelson Co.*,[246] the Court, again per curiam, affirmed the judgment of the District Court declaring the Arkansas statute unconstitutional "on the authority of *Adkins v Children's Hospital*." Brandeis again noted his dissent, though this time Holmes silently joined the majority.[247]

The conference vote in *Donham* was 7–1, with Brandeis dissenting and Sanford not voting, though Stone has an erased vote to affirm in the Brandeis column.[248] Two years earlier, in *Murphy*, the conference vote had been 8–1, with Brandeis noting a lone dissent, though here again Stone at one point marked Brandeis with the majority and then erased his vote to affirm. Stone's notes on *Murphy* differ from his record of *Donham* in one important respect, however. Next to the votes to affirm of Taft, Holmes, and Sanford—the three dissenters in *Adkins* (Brandeis had not participated)—Stone wrote "on authority [illegible] [illegible]." Stone also wrote this next to his own vote to affirm. The illegibility of the latter two words in Stone's notation makes it difficult to be certain, but it seems very likely that these four Justices indicated at the conference that they were voting to invalidate the statute only because they regarded themselves as bound by the recent authority of *Adkins*. If that is the case, then after McKenna's replacement by Stone in 1925, there was a majority of the Court that believed that *Adkins* had been wrongly decided. Four of those five Justices continued to strike down state minimum wage laws solely on the basis of a precedent that they believed was demonstrably erroneous. This no doubt frustrated Brandeis, whose solo dissents

---

[244] 269 US 530 (1925).

[245] Id.

[246] 273 US 657 (1927).

[247] Id.

[248] Stone OT 1926 Docket Book.

from these per curiam decisions might be read as opposing not only their results, but also the fealty to stare decisis that he soon would criticize in his celebrated dissent in *Burnet v Coronado Oil & Gas Co.*[249]

A similar pattern of postconference vote stability obtained in a series of lesser-known but important economic regulation cases. This was the case in *Williams v Standard Oil Co.*, which struck down a Tennessee statute regulating the retail price of gasoline;[250] in *Fairmont Creamery Co. v Minnesota*, which invalidated regulation of the prices at which dairy products were purchased and sold;[251] in *Di Santo v Pennsylvania*, where the Court held that a statute requiring that sellers of tickets for steamship travel to foreign countries secure a license and post a bond violated the foreign dormant Commerce Clause;[252] and in the domestic dormant Commerce Clause case of *Cudahy Packing Co. v Hinkle*, which struck down a state tax on an out-of-state corporation.[253] It was also the case in *Weaver v Palmer Bros.*, where the Court struck down a statute prohibiting the use of shoddy in the manufacturing of bedding;[254] in *Cement Manufacturers Protective v United States*[255] and *Maple Flooring v United States*,[256] two major antitrust decisions of the period;[257] in *Quaker City Cab Co. v*

---

[249] 285 US 393, 406–10 (1932) (Brandeis, J, dissenting) ("*Stare decisis* is usually the wise policy, because, in most matters, it is more important that the applicable rule of law be settled than that it be settled right.... But in cases involving the Federal Constitution, where correction through legislative action is practically impossible ... this court should refuse to follow an earlier constitutional decision which it deems erroneous.").

[250] 278 US 235 (1929). Holmes dissented, while Brandeis and Stone concurred in the result. Stone OT 1928 Docket Book.

[251] 274 US 1 (1927). Holmes, Brandeis, and Stone dissented without opinion. Stone OT 1926 Docket Book.

[252] 273 US 34 (1927). Holmes, Brandeis, and Stone dissented. Stone placed a question mark next to his own conference vote with the majority.

[253] 278 US 460 (1929). Holmes and Brandeis dissented. Stone OT 1928 Docket Book.

[254] 270 US 402 (1926). Holmes, Brandeis, and Stone dissented. Stone OT 1925 Docket Book.

[255] 268 US 588 (1925). Taft, McReynolds, and Sanford dissented. Butler OT 1924 Docket Book; Stone OT 1924 Docket Book.

[256] 268 US 563 (1925). Taft, McReynolds, and Sanford dissented. Butler OT 1924 Docket Book; Stone OT 1924 Docket Book.

[257] The same pattern was observed in *Lambert v Yellowley*, 272 US 581 (1926), which upheld a federal statute strictly regulating the amount of alcohol a physician could prescribe for medicinal use. The case was voted on at the 1925 Term, and the opinions were circulated, "but held up for some reason and carried over." The 5–4 conference vote was identical to the final vote, though Stone placed a question mark next to his own dissenting conference vote. Stone OT 1926 Docket Book; Stone OT 1925 Docket Book.

Pennsylvania, where the Court invalidated as a denial of equal protection a gross receipts tax that applied to corporations operating taxicabs but not to partnerships or individuals engaged in the same trade;[258] and in *St. Louis & O'Fallon Co. v United States*, where the Court annulled a recapture order of the Interstate Commerce Commission.[259]

Finally, none of the Justices budged in four closely divided decisions on the fractious subject of intergovernmental tax immunities, though the line-ups of the decisions differed. In *Long v Rockwood*,[260] Holmes, Brandeis, Stone, and Sutherland dissented both at conference and from the Court's published decision holding that a state may not tax income received from patents issued by federal government. Stone's docket book records question marks next to the conference votes of himself and Sutherland, but these two Justices ultimately stood firm with their dissenting brethren.[261] In *Panhandle Oil Co. v Mississippi*,[262] it was McReynolds who joined Holmes, Brandeis, and Stone at conference and in the published opinion in dissent from the majority's holding that a state tax on gasoline was unconstitutional as applied to sales to federal government instrumentalities such as the Coast Guard Fleet and a Veterans' Hospital.[263] In *National Life Ins. Co. v United States*, Holmes, Brandeis, and Stone held fast to their conference dissents from the position that a federal tax on the income from state and local securities was unconstitutional.[264] And in *Macallen v Massachusetts*,[265] these same three Justices dissented both at conference and from the published decision invalidating a state tax on the income from federal securities.[266]

---

[258] 277 US 389 (1928). Holmes, Brandeis, and Stone dissented. Stone OT 1927 Docket Book. Stone records a question mark next to his own conference vote. Stone's notes indicate that the case was carried over from the 1926 Term. It was argued Apr 20, 1927, and set for conference on Apr 23, but apparently not acted on. The note continues, "On Conf. List Apr 30—not voted on." "May 14 Conference List." The case originally was assigned to Van Devanter, but apparently he did not complete the assignment. It was "Left over at end of 1926 Term" and "Carried over to 1927 Term." The published majority opinion was written by Butler.

[259] 279 US 461 (1929). Holmes, Brandeis, and Stone dissented. Butler took no part in the decision. Stone OT 1928 Docket Book.

[260] 277 US 142 (1928).

[261] Stone OT 1927 Docket Book.

[262] 277 US 218 (1928).

[263] Stone OT 1927 Docket Book.

[264] 277 US 508 (1928). Stone OT 1927 Docket Book.

[265] 279 US 620 (1929).

[266] Stone OT 1928 Docket Book.

On the other hand, there also were a number of nonunanimous decisions in which the vote did change between conference and the announcement of the Court's decision. Although unanimity was not achieved in these cases, there often is evidence that the norm of acquiescence was at work. Most such vote changes involved a dissenter at conference joining the majority's opinion or judgment. These cases involved both acquiescence and nonacquiescence. One or more, but not all, of the Justices changed conference votes to join the majority. However, there also were some instances of defection, and in some cases instances of acquiescence by one Justice combined with defection by another. That is, in some cases Justices switched positions with one another between the conference vote and the final vote on the merits.

First, let us consider examples where we can see the norm of acquiescence at work. In *Chicago Board of Trade v Olsen*,[267] the Court upheld the Grain Futures Act of 1922.[268] The vote was 7–2, with McReynolds and Sutherland dissenting without opinion. Taft rested his opinion for the majority on the stream of commerce theory that Holmes had adopted in his 1905 majority opinion in *Swift v United States*,[269] and which the Court had applied to uphold the Packers and Stockyards Act of 1921[270] in the 1922 decision of *Stafford v Wallace*.[271] Holmes predictably had joined Taft's majority opinion in *Stafford*, but at the conference vote in *Olsen* he mysteriously voted with McReynolds and Sutherland.[272] Butler's docket book unfortunately provides no indication concerning why Holmes might have voted this way, nor why he might have decided ultimately to join the majority.

---

[267] 262 US 1 (1923).

[268] 38 Stat 803 (1922).

[269] 196 US 375 (1905).

[270] 42 Stat 159 (1921).

[271] 258 US 495 (1922).

[272] Butler OT 1922 Docket Book. McKenna passed at the conference vote. Mason, *William Howard Taft* at 201 (cited in note 4), erroneously reports that Brandeis wrote to Taft that he had "voted the other way" in the *Olsen* conference and that "the opinion has not removed my difficulties.... But I have differed from the Court recently on three expressed dissents and concluded that in this case, I had better 'shut up,'" citing Brandeis to Taft, Dec 23, 1922. In fact, as Dean Post has demonstrated, that letter referred to the case of *FTC v Curtis Publishing Co.*, 260 US 568 (1923). Post, 51 Duke L J at 1346 n 243 (cited in note 3) (citing William Howard Taft Papers, Reel 248). Butler's record of the *Olsen* conference vote places Brandeis with the majority from the outset. Butler OT 1922 Docket Book.

In *Jay Burns Baking Co. v Bryan*,[273] the Court struck down a Nebraska statute regulating the weights of loaves of bread offered for
sale. The vote was 7–2, with Brandeis and Holmes dissenting. At the
conference, however, the vote was 5–4, with McKenna and Sutherland joining Holmes and Brandeis in voting to uphold the statute.[274]
The decision was accorded a critical reception,[275] but the Nebraska
legislature soon enacted a revised bread-weight regulation designed
to meet the Court's objections.[276] The Court unanimously upheld the
revised statute in the 1934 case of *Petersen Baking Co. v Bryan*.[277] In
that conference, Van Devanter passed, but everyone else voted to
sustain the measure.[278]

In *Miles v Graham*,[279] the Court held that the salaries of federal
judges were not subject to the federal income tax. At the conference,
Taft pointed out that the 1920 case of *Evans v Gore*[280] had held that the
federal "income tax is a diminution" of judicial compensation in violation of Article III's prohibition. That case had involved a federal
judge confirmed to his office before enactment of the challenged
taxing statute. *Miles* involved a federal judge confirmed after the enactment of the challenged taxing statute. Holmes stated the he was
"Inclined to limit Evans v Gore," but that he had "no feelings about it"
and would "defer to [the] majority." Van Devanter indicated that he
agreed with Taft that the case fell within the principle of *Evans*.
McReynolds argued that the case presented a "Question of power."
There was "A stat[ute] prescribing compensation," he observed. "It is
paid at stated times. Then [it is] a tax on compensation." Brandeis

---

[273] 264 US 504 (1924).

[274] Butler OT 1923 Docket Book. Butler's tally is inconsistent with Felix Frankfurter's
record of Brandeis's account, in which Brandeis is quoted as saying that "The Burns case was
really 5 to 4, but Van Devanter 'got busy,' in his personal way, talking and laboring with
members of Court, finally led Sutherland and Sanford to suppress their dissents." Urofsky,
1985 Supreme Court Review at 328 (cited in note 145). See Post, 78 BU L Rev at 1501 n 77
(cited in note 3) (quoting a note from McKenna to Brandeis saying, "Disturbing doubts have
come to me. I am struggling with them and frankly I don't know whether they go to the
conclusions or to details and reasoning.").

[275] See, for example, E.M.B., Comment, *State Police Legislation and the Supreme Court*, 33
Yale L J 847 (1924).

[276] See *P. F. Petersen Baking Co. v Bryan*, 290 US 570, 572 (1934).

[277] 290 US 570 (1934).

[278] Stone OT 1933 Docket Book.

[279] 268 US 501 (1925).

[280] 253 US 245 (1920).

stated that he would reverse the lower court decision holding that the judge's salary was immune to income taxation.[281]

Brandeis ultimately dissented alone and without opinion from the published decision, but at the conference he was joined in dissent by Holmes and Stone.[282] The docket books thus confirm a claim that Stone made in a letter written to his sons in 1939, after *Miles* had been overruled:

> The Graham case was argued shortly after I came on the Court, and you will be interested to know that I joined Holmes and Brandeis in voting against the immunity of the judge's salary from income tax. The same principle as in the Graham case had been laid down in *Evans v Gore*, 253 U.S. 245 (1920), decided a year or two before I came on the Court. Holmes had written a dissent but he thought the Graham case indistinguishable in principle from the Gore case and therefore he and I concluded that we would not record a dissent. I have since regretted my action because it puts me apparently on record as supporting the majority decision which I thought then and still think wrong.[283]

The phenomenon of postconference acquiescence also occurred in some of the Court's more important rulings under the dormant Commerce Clause. *Texas Transport & Terminal Co., Inc. v New Orleans*[284] invalidated a license tax on an interstate and foreign shipping business by a vote of 7–2, with Holmes and Brandeis dissenting. At the conference, however, they had been joined in dissent by Sanford.[285] *Buck v Kuykendall*[286] and *George W. Bush & Sons v Maloy*[287] invalidated state laws requiring interstate common carriers to obtain certificates of necessity before using public highways. McReynolds dissented alone without opinion from the published decision in each case, but at the *Buck* conference he was joined by Sutherland and Sanford, and at the *Bush* conference he was joined by Sutherland.[288]

---

[281] Butler OT 1924 Docket Book.

[282] Butler OT 1924 Docket Book; Stone OT 1924 Docket Book.

[283] Mason, *Harlan Fiske Stone* at 790 n (cited in note 4).

[284] 264 US 150 (1924).

[285] Butler OT 1923 Docket Book.

[286] 267 US 307 (1925).

[287] 267 US 317 (1925).

[288] Butler OT 1924 Docket Book. See also *Shafer v Farmer's Grain Co.*, 268 US 189 (1925) (striking down a license requirement for the purchase of grain within a state where the grain sold was to be immediately shipped out of the state), from which Brandeis dissented alone without opinion. Holmes had voted with him at the conference, Butler OT 1924 Docket Book, Stone OT 1924 Docket Book, but suppressed his dissent and joined the published majority opinion.

When the Court invalidated a similar requirement for intrastate carriers under the Due Process Clause in *Frost & Frost Trucking Co. v R.R. Commission of California*,[289] Holmes, McReynolds, and Brandeis dissented. At the conference, however, they had been joined by Sanford, who ultimately acquiesced in the decision.[290]

In *Carroll v United States*,[291] the Court affirmed a judgment upholding a warrantless search of an automobile suspected of uses violating the National Prohibition Act. At the December 8, 1923 conference, Taft stated that there was "Ample evidence to sustain reasonable grounds for seizure. Adams case per Day, J."[292] It appears that the vote that day was 6–3 to affirm the conviction, with Sutherland, Butler, and Sanford in dissent. Butler's docket book indicates that the case initially was assigned to McReynolds. However, Butler later erased the vote to affirm in McReynolds's column, and added him to the ranks of the dissenters. It seems that on December 22, "McR brought [the case] up for further conference." Taft, Butler records, "suggests automobile differs from home." Holmes, who appeared to agree with Taft, is recorded as saying "Different principles." Brandeis also agreed, saying that the "Court could find business stopping & Arrest misdemeanor on suspicion." Following this Butler writes, "Common law right of peace officer to arrest," though it is not clear whether this was part of Brandeis's statement. It may be that these are the remarks of Taft at the March 29 conference held after reargument on March 14.[293] The remarks continued, "F. 294 page 776 what are reasonable grounds for belief of present commission. Must have ascertained facts. 'In presence of' = 'immediate knowledge'." Holmes is then recorded as saying, "Probable cause to surmise."[294] Following that conference, the vote was apparently 5–4, with McReynolds joining the dissenters from the earlier conference. When the published decision appeared nearly a year later, on March 2, 1925, however, only McReynolds and Sutherland dis-

---

[289] 271 US 583 (1926).

[290] Stone OT 1925 Docket Book.

[291] 267 US 132 (1925).

[292] Butler OT 1923 Docket Book. The reference is apparently to *Adams v New York*, 192 US 585 (1904). Butler OT 1924 Docket Book contains no entry for *Carroll*.

[293] 267 US 132.

[294] Butler OT 1923 Docket Book. The reference is to *Park v United States*, 294 F 776 (1st Cir 1924).

sented.[295] Butler and Sanford had acquiesced in the majority's judgment, while McReynolds remained resolute in his defection.[296]

Black & White Taxicab Co. v Brown & Yellow Taxicab Co.[297] involved a Kentucky taxicab concern that sought to enter into an enforceable exclusive service contract with a railroad. In order to avail itself of the favorable "general law" rule upholding such contracts that the federal courts applied when sitting in diversity, and to avoid application of the rule of the Kentucky state courts holding such contracts invalid, the company incorporated in Tennessee. The Court affirmed the lower federal court's application of the general law rule by a vote of 6–3, with Holmes, Brandeis, and Stone dissenting. At the conference, however, the dissenters were joined by McReynolds,[298] one of the principal expositors of what Holmes disparaged as the view that the common law was "a brooding omnipresence in the sky."[299]

In *New York v Zimmerman*,[300] the Justices upheld the power of New York to require the Ku Klux Klan to disclose to the secretary of state its governing documents, officer roster, and membership list. The Klan argued that requiring it to make such disclosure while excusing labor unions and other oath-bound organizations from such revelations denied the Klan equal protection, but only McReynolds dissented from Van Devanter's opinion maintaining that the classification was justified because the Klan, unlike labor unions, had a tendency "to make the secrecy surrounding its purposes and membership a cloak for acts and conduct inimical to personal rights and

---

[295] 267 US 132 (1925). The published opinion indicated that McKenna had concurred in the majority opinion before his retirement on Jan 5.

[296] The long delay in the production of the opinion may have been caused in part by vote changes after this last conference. Taft wrote to his brother that, after McReynolds had returned the case saying that he could not write in support of the seizure, "On a vote we lost once but McKenna came over so that I was able to assign it to myself." William Howard Taft to Horace D. Taft (Mar 1, 1925), quoted in Post, 48 Wm & Mary L Rev at 123 n 406 (cited in note 3). Butler's docket book, however, seems to record McKenna as with Taft from the outset. Taft earlier wrote his brother that "Brandeis was with me strongly before the summer vacation, but he went up to Cambridge and must have communed with Frankfurther [*sic*] and that crowd, and he came back with a notice to me that he was going to change his vote." William Howard Taft to Horace D. Taft (Dec 26, 1924), quoted in Post, 48 Wm & Mary L Rev at 125 n 406 (cited in note 3). Butler's docket book contains no record of such a vacillation.

[297] 276 US (1928).

[298] Stone OT 1927 Docket Book

[299] *Southern Pacific Co. v Jensen*, 244 US 205, 222 (1917) (Holmes, J, dissenting). McReynolds was the author of the majority opinion in *Jensen*.

[300] 278 US 63 (1928).

public welfare"; because it engaged in acts designed "'to strike terror into the minds of the people'"; because "its membership was limited to native born, gentile, Protestant whites" and its members took an oath "to shield and preserve 'white supremacy'"; and because "it was conducting a crusade against Catholics, Jews, and Negroes and stimulating hurtful religious and race prejudices."[301] The near unanimity of the decision was achieved only because the Chief Justice acquiesced, however. At the conference vote, Taft had been paired with McReynolds in dissent.[302]

In *Liggett Co. v Baldridge*,[303] the Justices invalidated a statute requiring that each of the shareholders of any corporation owning and operating a drug store be a licensed pharmacist. The final vote on the merits was 7–2, with Brandeis joining Holmes in dissent. At the conference, however, McReynolds had passed, and Stone had placed a question mark next to his own vote to strike down the statute.[304] Each of these Justices ultimately overcame his doubts sufficiently to join the majority opinion. And in *United Railways & Electric Co. v West*, the Court invalidated a regulation imposing a passenger fare rate that permitted a return "so inadequate as to result in a deprivation of property in violation of the due process of law clause of the Fourteenth Amendment."[305] Holmes, Brandeis, and Stone ultimately dissented, but at the conference McReynolds was with them as well.[306]

Sometimes persistent divisions on the merits masked acquiescence on issues of jurisdiction. In *Tyson & Bros. v Banton*,[307] for example, the New York statute regulating resale brokers of theater tickets returned to the Court. The Justices had upheld the statute's provisions requiring licensure of such brokers two years earlier in *Weller v New York*, but Taft and perhaps others had expressed doubts in conference about the constitutionality of the statute's price regulation provisions. The *Tyson* Court invalidated those provisions, and the vote on

---

[301] Id at 75–76.

[302] Stone OT 1927 Docket Book. The case was submitted on Oct 11, 1927, and was voted on in conference on Oct 15 of that year. The opinion was assigned to Van Devanter, who took over a year to get it out. The decision was announced on Nov 19, 1928. 278 US 63.

[303] 278 US 105 (1928).

[304] Stone OT 1928 Docket Book.

[305] 280 US 234, 349 (1930).

[306] Stone OT 1929 Docket Book.

[307] 273 US 418 (1927).

the merits in conference and the published opinion were the same: 5–4, with Holmes, Brandeis, Stone, and Sanford dissenting. But in conference there were three votes to dismiss the case on jurisdictional grounds: Holmes, McReynolds, and Brandeis. Sutherland's majority opinion disposed of the jurisdictional question summarily, and these three registered no dissent from the Court's resolution of that issue.[308]

Another price regulation case that came before the Court provides an illustration of quasi-acquiescence. *Ribnik v McBride*[309] concerned the constitutionality of state regulation of the fees charged by employment agencies. The case was ultimately decided by a vote of 6–3, with Holmes, Brandeis, and Stone dissenting from the majority opinion invalidating the measure. In conference, however, the vote had been 5–2: Stone and Sanford had passed.[310] These Justices ultimately resolved their doubts differently: Stone would write a lengthy dissent; Sanford would concur on the ground that he was bound by the authority of *Tyson*, from which he had dissented the previous year. An even clearer example of quasi-acquiescence is presented by *Bedford Cut Stone Co. v Journeymen Stone Cutters*.[311] There, over the dissents of Holmes and Brandeis, the Court held that a stonecutter union's boycott of stone quarried by members of unaffiliated unions violated the Sherman Act. At the conference the vote had been 5–4, with Sanford and Stone joining their dissenting colleagues.[312] In the published decision, however, each of them concurred separately only because they felt themselves bound by the authority of *Duplex Printing v Deering*,[313] an earlier decision that they were unable to distinguish.[314] As Taft wrote, "while Sanford and Stone concur in our opinion, they do it

---

[308] Stone OT 1926 Docket Book.

[309] 277 US 350 (1928).

[310] Stone OT 1927 Docket Book.

[311] 274 US 37 (1927).

[312] Stone OT 1926 Docket Book. This confirms the account reconstructed from intracurial correspondence in Mason, *Harlan Fiske Stone* at 255–60 (cited in note 4). Stone's docket book contains an erased vote to affirm in Sutherland's column, which raises the tantalizing but seemingly very remote possibility that there may at one point have been five votes for the Holmes/Brandeis position.

[313] 254 US 443 (1921).

[314] 274 US at 55 (Sanford, J, concurring); 274 US at 55–56 (Stone, J, concurring).

grudgingly, Stone with a kind of kickback that will make nobody happy."[315]

The Court's nonunanimous decisions also occasionally featured the phenomenon of defection. Perhaps the best-known instance occurred in *Village of Euclid v Ambler*,[316] a landmark decision upholding a comprehensive zoning law. The case was originally argued in January of 1926,[317] and then reargued in October of that year.[318] Two decades later, Alfred McCormack, Stone's clerk for the 1925 Term, reported that Sutherland had been writing an opinion in the case "holding the zoning ordinance unconstitutional, when talks with his dissenting brethren (principally Stone, I believe) shook his convictions and led him to request a reargument, after which he changed his mind and the ordinance was upheld."[319] On the basis of McCormack's brief report, Alpheus Thomas Mason offered a more elaborate account, claiming that Stone, along "[w]ith Brandeis and Holmes, who had also disagreed with the decision in conference ... carried on the argument with the opinion writer Justice Sutherland.... Under Stone's persistent hammering ... Sutherland began to doubt the correctness of his conclusion and asked for reargument. On the second hearing Sutherland changed his mind."[320]

This story has been repeated many times,[321] but elements of its accuracy have been called into question. Dean Post points out that nine months before *Euclid* was argued, Sutherland prepared a memorandum for Taft concerning another zoning case that the Court ultimately dismissed on procedural grounds. In that memorandum, Sutherland wrote that "[i]n the modern development of cities and towns, zoning laws are universally recognized as necessary and proper. The question presented by the law under review is a matter of degree,

---

[315] W. H. Taft to Robert A. Taft, Apr 10, 1927, quoted in Mason, *Harlan Fiske Stone* at 259 (cited in note 4).

[316] 272 US 365 (1926).

[317] Stone OT 1925 Docket Book.

[318] 272 US 365.

[319] Alfred McCormack, *A Law Clerk's Recollections*, 46 Colum L Rev 710, 712 (1946).

[320] Mason, *Harlan Fiske Stone* at 252 (cited in note 4).

[321] See, for example, David J. Garrow, *"The Lowest Form of Animal Life"?: Supreme Court Clerks and Supreme Court History*, 84 Cornell L Rev 855, 862 (1999); Samuel R. Olken, *Justice George Sutherland and Economic Liberty: Constitutional Conservatism and the Problem of Factions*, 6 Wm & Mary Bill Rights J 1, 70 n 329 (1997); Miriam Galston, *Activism and Restraint: The Evolution of Harlan Fiske Stone's Judicial Philosophy*, 70 Tulane L Rev 137, 162 (1995).

and I am not prepared to say that the judgment of the local law makers was arbitrarily exercised."[322] This would seem to make it less likely that Sutherland would have voted initially to invalidate the ordinance challenged in *Euclid*. Others have pointed out that because Sutherland did not hear the initial argument of the case, it is "unlikely" that the opinion would have been assigned to him,[323] and that "Sutherland was even less likely to have formed a negative opinion (or any other opinion) following the first hearing of the case—since he did not participate in it."[324] Some have maintained that the reargument was in fact suggested by Stone, who "as a new member of the Court ... was not fully conversant with the situation."[325] It also has been suggested that the reargument was ordered to provide the Court with more time to deliberate about the case and to permit an interested party to submit an amicus curiae brief that might better educate the Justices about the fundamentals of zoning.[326] Finally, it has been observed that "while the case was reargued, in order for a majority intending to strike down the ordinance to transform into a six to three majority to refrain from doing so, at least one other Justice (apart from Sutherland) must have switched his vote."[327]

Stone's docket books do not resolve all of these questions definitively, but they do shed considerable light on a number of them. Stone records that when the case was discussed in conference on February 13, Sutherland did participate in the deliberations. Stone records the vote as 5–3 to invalidate the ordinance, with Brandeis, Sanford, and Stone dissenting, and Holmes not voting. He records Sutherland in the majority along with his fellow Horsemen and Taft. Interestingly, however, Stone placed question marks next to both his own and Sutherland's votes, suggesting that each of them was un-

---

[322] Post, 78 BU L Rev at 1543 n 259 (cited in note 3) (quoting memorandum from Sutherland to Taft (Taft Papers, Reel 273)).

[323] Garrett Power, *Advocates at Cross-Purposes: The Briefs on Behalf of Zoning in the Supreme Court*, 2 J S Ct Hist 79, 87 n 39 (1997) (McCormack's recollection "is almost certainly garbled").

[324] Nadav Shoked, *The Reinvention of Ownership: The Embrace of Residential Zoning and the Modern Populist Reading of Property*, 28 Yale J Reg 91, 95 n 17 (2011).

[325] Arthur V. N. Brooks, *The Office File Box—Emanation from the Battlefield*, in Charles M. Haar and Jerold S. Kayden, eds, *Zoning and the American Dream: Promises Still to Keep* 3, 17 (APA Planners, 1989).

[326] Timothy Alan Fluck, *Euclid v. Ambler: A Retrospective*, 52 J Am Planning Assn 326, 331–32 (1986).

[327] Shoked, 28 Yale J Reg at 95 n 17 (cited in note 324).

certain about the positions that they had taken. This record, taken in combination with Sutherland's earlier memo to Taft on zoning, casts doubt on the notion that Stone was rock solid in his views and that Sutherland was brought around by Stone's "persistent hammering." It seems more likely that these two establishment Republicans discussed their own doubts with one another, perhaps only at the 1925 conference, and were sufficiently unsettled in their convictions to want to hear more argument. Moreover, though Stone typically signified opinion assignments by inscribing a large "X" next to the name of the Justice selected, his docket book record of the 1925 Term *Euclid* conference contains no indication that the opinion was assigned to Sutherland, nor to anyone else. Instead, on the same page of Stone's 1925 docket book, written in by another hand, appears "Rehearing suggested by Sutherland, J., and case set down for rehearing October Term 1926." This entry bears no date, but it was in all likelihood written by McCormack, and based upon information provided to him by Stone.[328] When the Justices met on October 26 to discuss the case again after reargument, Stone recorded the vote as identical to the breakdown in the published decision: 6–3, with Van Devanter, McReynolds, and Butler dissenting. Holmes registered his vote in favor of sustaining the ordinance, and both Sutherland and Taft abandoned their earlier positions and joined the new majority.[329]

Some instances of defection involved a Justice who had passed at conference deciding to cast a lone dissenting vote rather than to acquiesce and make a unanimous Court. Perhaps the most prominent of these involves Butler, at the time the Court's lone Catholic, who dissented without opinion from the Court's decision upholding Virginia's eugenic sterilization statute in *Buck v Bell*.[330] Yet Stone's docket book reveals that Butler did not register his dissenting vote at conference. Instead, he alone passed.[331] It was only after the conference that Butler resolved his doubts in favor of nonacquiescence. Similarly, McReynolds dissented alone from the Court's decision in *Foster-Fountain Packing Co. v Haydel*[332] striking down as a violation of the dormant Commerce Clause a Louisiana statute that sought to force

---

[328] Stone OT 1925 Docket Book.

[329] Stone OT 1926 Docket Book.

[330] 274 US 200 (1927).

[331] Stone OT 1926 Docket Book.

[332] 278 US 1 (1928).

shrimp producers to pack shrimp harvested in Louisiana within state. At the conference, however, McReynolds had merely passed.[333] *United States v One Ford Coupe Automobile*,[334] by contrast, involved an instance of defection from the majority to the dissent. There the Court upheld and interpreted broadly various seizure and taxation provisions of the Supplementary Prohibition Act. At the conference vote only Sutherland and Butler dissented. In the published decision, however, Stone concurred separately, and McReynolds defected from the majority to join Sutherland and Butler in opposition.[335]

There also were instances in which Justices passed one another crossing the line between majority and minority. In *Helson v Kentucky*,[336] for example, the Court by a vote of 6–3 struck down a state tax on gasoline purchased out of state and used to power an interstate ferry as violating the dormant Commerce Clause. The dissenters were Holmes, McReynolds, and Brandeis. At the conference, however, Brandeis had passed, Holmes had voted with the majority, and Stone had voted with the dissent. Holmes and Stone exchanged places between the conference vote and the final decision.[337] In *Louisville Gas & Electric Co. v Coleman*, a 5–4 Court held that a state tax imposed upon mortgages that did not mature within five years but exempting those that did violated the Equal Protection Clause. The dissenters were Holmes, Brandeis, Sanford, and Stone,[338] but Stone records that at the initial conference it was Holmes, Brandeis, Stone, and McReynolds who voted to uphold the tax, and Taft, Van Devanter, Butler, and Sanford voting to strike it down. Sutherland was ill and absent from the conference, so the equally divided Court set the case down for reargument. After the reargument, Sanford switched sides to vote in favor of the statute, while McReynolds shifted to the side favoring invalidation. Stone placed a question mark in Sutherland's column, indicating that at the conclusion of the second conference the Justices remained equally divided. Eventually, however, Sutherland resolved his uncertainty sufficiently to make a majority nullifying the law.[339]

---

[333] Stone OT 1928 Docket Book.

[334] 272 US 321 (1926).

[335] Stone OT 1926 Docket Book.

[336] 279 US 245 (1929).

[337] Stone OT 1928 Docket Book.

[338] 277 US 32 (1928).

[339] Stone OT 1927 Docket Book.

United Leather Workers v Herkert & Meisel Trunk Co.[340] may also fall into this category. There the Court held that a strike for a closed shop, conducted by means of illegal picketing and intimidation, did not violate the Sherman Act. Though the strike admittedly was designed to prevent the manufacture of goods to be shipped in interstate commerce, there was no evidence that the strikers had sought to interfere with the transport or sale of goods once they had been manufactured. Because the effect of the strikers' conduct on interstate commerce was therefore "indirect" rather than "direct," Chief Taft's majority opinion maintained that their activities lay beyond the reach of federal authority, and were subject only to state regulation.

This is precisely the position that Taft had taken at conference. There was, he stated, "No evidence of restraint of interstate commerce." Van Devanter, who dissented without opinion along with McKenna and Butler, argued at the conference that the "Restraint [was] direct." Yet the final vote of 6–3 belies the configuration in conference. At the conference vote, Butler records a vote of 5–4, with Van Devanter joined not only by McKenna, but also by McReynolds and Sanford. Moreover, Butler places himself in the majority. Thus, it appears that between the conference and the final opinion, three votes changed: McReynolds and Sanford moved from the minority to the majority, and Butler moved from the majority to the minority.[341]

Finally, among the most interesting instances of defection were those in which the unanimity of a conference vote was shattered by a Justice's later change of heart. For example, the vote in *Samuels v McCurdy*, in which Butler dissented from an opinion upholding a Georgia statute authorizing seizure and destruction of alcohol that had been purchased legally before the enactment of the statute,[342] was unanimous to affirm at conference.[343] And in *Toyota v United States*, which held that a Japanese national born in Japan was not eligible for naturalization,[344] the vote at conference was unanimous,[345] but

---

[340] 265 US 457 (1924).

[341] Butler OT 1923 Docket Book. This hypothesis must be advanced with caution. Butler's record of the conference vote is difficult to interpret, because he records the majority Justices as voting to affirm, and the minority Justices as voting to reverse, where in fact it was the other way around. In addition, Butler's entry has erased votes in the opposing columns for Taft, McKenna, Van Devanter, Sutherland, and Butler.

[342] 267 US 188 (1925).

[343] Butler OT 1924 Docket Book.

[344] 268 US 402 (1925).

[345] Butler OT 1924 Docket Book; Stone OT 1924 Docket Book.

the Chief Justice himself—the Court's great proponent of the acquiescence norm—dissented without opinion from the published
decision.

V. REASSIGNMENTS

Van Devanter was valued highly by his colleagues for his contributions to conference discussions[346] and his comments on the draft
opinions of others. But his "pen paralysis," as Sutherland called it, left
him notoriously incapable of producing written opinions promptly.[347]
During the nine Terms of the Taft Court, Van Devanter authored
only ninety-eight (6.07%) of the Court's majority opinions.[348] It has
been reported in a general way that "[s]everal times Taft was forced
tactfully to reassign to other Justices cases originally given to Van
Devanter so that they could be decided within a reasonable period
of time,"[349] but the extent and details of this practice never have been
documented. The docket books enable us to undertake such docu-
mentation.

For the 1922 Term, Butler notes that two cases were transferred
from McKenna, one each to Taft[350] and Brandeis.[351] Sutherland and
Sanford also traded cases in late April.[352] Van Devanter, who wrote
sixteen (7.11%) of the Term's majority opinions,[353] is not recorded as
transferring any cases. During the 1923 Term, Van Devanter wrote

---

[346] Charles Evans Hughes, *The Autobiographical Notes of Charles Evans Hughes* 171 (Harvard,
1973) (David D. Danelski and Joseph L. Tulchin, eds) ("his careful and elaborate statements in
conference, with his accurate review of authorities, were of the greatest value. If these
statements had been taken down stenographically they would have served with but little editing
as excellent opinions."); Harlan Fiske Stone, *Associate Justice Van Devanter: An Appraisal*, 28
ABA J 458, 459 (1942) ("At the conference table he was a tower of strength. When his turn came
to present his views of the case in hand, no point was overlooked, no promising possibility left
unexplored. His statements were characteristically lucid and complete, the manifest expression
of a judgment exercised with unswerving independence. Often his expositions would have
served worthily, both in point of form and substance, as the Court's opinion in the case.").

[347] Merlo J. Pusey, 2 *Charles Evans Hughes* 284 (Macmillan, 1951).

[348] Renstrom, *The Taft Court* at 99 (cited in note 4).

[349] Post, 85 Minn L Rev at 1295 n 86 (cited in note 2).

[350] No 330, *Dier v Banton*, transferred 4/28/23. Butler OT 1922 Docket Book.

[351] No 880, *Collins v Loisel*, transferred 5/6/23. Butler OT 1922 Docket Book.

[352] Nos 463–64, *Georgia Railway and Power Co. v Town of Decatur*, transferred from Sanford
to Sutherland, 4/29/23; No 237, *Rindge Co. v Los Angeles County*, transferred from Sutherland
to Sanford, 4/29/23. Butler OT 1922 Docket Book. Sutherland ultimately took no part in
Rindge. 267 US 700, 710 (1923).

[353] Renstrom, *The Taft Court* at 264 (cited in note 4). Van Devanter wrote no concurring
opinions during the Term. Id.

twenty (9.43%) of the Court's majority opinions, and two dissents.[354] That Term he released a case to Brandeis[355] and one to Sutherland,[356] but he also absorbed from McKenna a case in which the latter ultimately dissented.[357] That year McReynolds also gave up two cases to Taft.[358] During the 1924 Term, Taft became ill, and relied upon Van Devanter to run the conference.[359] Van Devanter's output dropped to twelve (5.22%) of the Court's majority opinions and two dissents,[360] as he gave up eight cases.[361] In January Van Devanter took on a case initially assigned to Sutherland, but by early April he had relinquished it to Brandeis.[362] Taft transferred one to McKenna[363] and received one from Brandeis,[364] Brandeis absorbed one from Mc-Reynolds,[365] and Holmes took one from Sanford.[366]

Van Devanter's output rebounded for the 1925 Term, during which he authored seventeen (8.13%) of the majority opinions and one dissent.[367] Stone's docket book contains no indication that any opinions were reassigned during the Term.[368] During the 1926 Term, however, Van Devanter's workload began a slide from which it never

---

[354] Id at 265.

[355] No 49, *Benedict v Ratner*, transferred 4/6/24. Butler OT 1923 Docket Book. *Benedict* was carried over to the 1924 Term. Butler OT 1924 Docket Book.

[356] Nos 324 and 336, *Idaho Irrigation Co. v Gooding*. Butler OT 1923 Docket Book.

[357] No 181, *Manufacturers' Land and Improvement Co. v United States Shipping Board Emergency Fleet Corp.* Butler OT 1923 Docket Book; 264 US 250, 255 (1924) (McKenna, J, dissenting).

[358] Nos 283–85, *Railroad Commission of California v Southern Pacific Co.*, transferred 2/16/24; No 117, *Carroll v United States*, transferred 5/24/24. Butler OT 1923 Docket Book. McReynolds ultimately dissented in *Carroll*. 267 US at 163 (McReynolds, J, dissenting).

[359] Clare Cushman, *Courtwatchers: Eyewitness Accounts in Supreme Court History* 150 (Rowman & Littlefield, 2011).

[360] Renstrom, *The Taft Court* at 266 (cited in note 4).

[361] Van Devanter transferred three cases to Holmes: No 47, *United States v The Coamo*; No 75, *Flanagan v Federal Coal Co.*; and No 177, *Stein v Tip-Top Baking Co.*; and one each to Brandeis: No 443, *Ray Consolidated Copper Co. v United States*; Sanford, No 64, *Endicott-Johnson Corp. v Smith*; Sutherland, No 187, *Grayson v Harris*; and McReynolds, No 53, *Miles v Graham*. Butler OT 1924 Docket Book. Butler also records Van Devanter as relinquishing to Brandeis No 49, *Federal Trade Commission v Hammond, Snyder, and Co.*, but the case was ultimately decided per curiam. 267 US 586 (1925).

[362] No 443, *Ray Consolidated Copper Co. v United States*. Butler OT 1924 Docket Book.

[363] No 147, *Davis v Manry*. Butler OT 1924 Docket Book.

[364] No 144, *Wells v Bodkin*. Butler OT 1924 Docket Book.

[365] No 229, *St. Louis, K and Southeast Railroad Co. v United States*. Butler OT 1924 Docket Book.

[366] No 130, *Yeiser v Dysart*. Butler OT 1924 Docket Book.

[367] Renstrom, *The Taft Court* at 267 (cited in note 4).

[368] Stone OT 1925 Docket Book.

fully recovered. That year he wrote ten (5.03%) of the majority opinions and two dissents,[369] while giving up ten opinions and absorbing none.[370] That Term Taft gave up one opinion to Holmes[371] and two to Brandeis,[372] and took two from McReynolds.[373] Sanford gave up two opinions to Holmes[374] and one to Brandeis.[375] During the 1927 Term, Van Devanter's production slipped to eight (4.62%) of the majority opinions and one concurrence.[376] That year Van Devanter gave up six cases and absorbed none.[377] Holmes gave one to Butler,[378] and he took a case from Sutherland[379] in which the latter ultimately dissented.[380]

The final two Terms of the Taft Court saw Van Devanter's written contributions decline even further. During the 1928 Term he au-

---

[369] Renstrom, *The Taft Court* at 268 (cited in note 4).

[370] Van Devanter transferred four opinions to Taft: No 312, *Ford v United States*; No 199, *Rhea v Smith*; No 202, *Messel v Foundation Co.*; and No 237, *Weedin v Chin Bow*. He also gave two to Stone: No 46, *Fidelity National Bank and Trust Co. of Kansas City v Swope*; and No 492, *Fox River Paper Co. v Railroad Commission of Wisconsin*. Four other colleagues absorbed one case each from Van Devanter: McReynolds, No 116, *American Railway Express Co. v F. S. Royster Guano Co.*; Butler, No 33, *Southern Railway Co. v Kentucky*; Sanford, No 48, *Fiske v Kansas*; and Sutherland, No 51, *Sacramento Navigation Co. v Salz*. Stone OT 1926 Docket Book.

[371] No 180, *Zimmerman v Sutherland*. Stone OT 1926 Docket Book.

[372] No 894, *Lawrence v St. Louis-San Francisco Railway Co.*; No 549, *Arkansas Railroad Commission v Chicago, Rock Island & Pacific Co.* Stone OT 1926 Docket Book.

[373] No 123, *United States v Shelby Iron Co. of New Jersey*; No 1, *Federal Trade Commission v Claire Furnace Co.* Stone OT 1926 Docket Book. McReynolds ultimately dissented in *Claire Furnace*. The case was carried over from the 1925 Term. The ultimate outcome is remarkable because the vote at the conference was 8–1 to affirm, with only Taft voting to reverse. Stone OT 1925 Docket Book. Eventually Sutherland and Butler took no part, and Taft was able to bring the rest of the Court over to his side, leaving behind only McReynolds, to whom the opinion was initially assigned. 274 US 160 (1927); Stone OT 1925 Docket Book. See Post, 85 Minn L Rev at 1311–12 (cited in note 2) (Taft "successfully diminished dissension" in *Claire Furnace*, citing "Brandeis Papers").

[374] No 766, *Westfall v United States*; No 983, *United States v Alford*. Stone OT 1926 Docket Book.

[375] No 257, *United States v McCarl*. Stone OT 1926 Docket Book.

[376] Renstrom, *The Taft Court* at 269 (cited in note 4).

[377] Van Devanter transferred two opinions to McReynolds, No 131, *Mellon v Goodyear*, and No 225, *Plamals v The Pinar Del Rio*; two to Sutherland, No 62, *Grosfield v United States*, and No 207, *Montana National Bank of Billings v Yellowstone County*; one to Butler, No 139, *Quaker City Cab Co. v Pennsylvania*; and one to Sanford, No 205, *National Leather Co. v Massachusetts*. Stone OT 1927 Docket Book.

[378] No 110, *Donnelley v United States*. Stone OT 1927 Docket Book.

[379] Nos 407–18, *Ferry v Ramsey*. Stone OT 1927 Docket Book.

[380] 277 US 88, 95 (1928) (Sutherland, J, dissenting). Stone noted that Nos 150–51, *Denney v Pacific Telephone and Telegraph Co.*, a case in which he ultimately took no part, 267 US 97, 104 (1928), was "assigned to Justice Stone by mistake" and transferred to McReynolds. Stone OT 1927 Docket Book.

thored four (3.1%) of the Court's majority opinions and three dissents.[381] It appears that Taft had determined to give him fewer assignments, as he gave up only two cases that year and again absorbed none.[382] The only other recorded reassignments for the 1928 Term were two cases transferred from Sanford, one to Holmes[383] and one to McReynolds.[384] The 1929 Term was marked by the retirement of Taft and the death of Sanford while in office, and their replacements by Charles Evans Hughes and Owen Roberts, respectively. Most of the reassignments of the Term thus involved transfers from Taft or Sanford to another Justice.[385] In addition, Brandeis took a case from Sutherland,[386] and Hughes took one from Holmes.[387] Van Devanter's output dropped to one majority opinion, one concurrence, and two dissents.[388] Indeed, it appears that he did not receive any initial assignments, for the one majority opinion that he did write was a transfer from McReynolds.[389]

VI. Conclusion

The Butler and Stone docket books provide us with a variety of valuable insights into the inner workings of the Taft Court. First, the docket books show that instances in which cases were reassigned on the Taft Court typically involved illness, death, a mid-Term re-

---

[381] Renstrom, *The Taft Court* at 270 (cited in note 4).

[382] Van Devanter gave up No 305, *United States v Fruit Growers' Express Co.*, to Taft and No 8, *Highland v Russell Car and Snowplow Co.*, to Butler. Stone OT 1928 Docket Book.

[383] No 513, *United States v American Livestock Commission Co.* Stone OT 1928 Docket Book.

[384] No 530, *Bekins Van Lines, Inc. v Riley*. Stone OT 1928 Docket Book.

[385] See No 31, *Gunning v Cooley*, transferred from Taft to Butler; Nos 15–16, *Wheeler Lumber Bridge and Supply Co. v United States* and *Indian Motor Cycle Co. v United States*, which on May 26, 1930 were transferred from Taft to Van Devanter and restored to the docket for reargument; No 104, *National Fire Insurance Co. of Hartford v Thompson*, transferred from Sanford to Butler; No 19, *Alexander Sprunt and Son v United States*, transferred from Sanford to Brandeis; No 248, *Nogueira v New York, New Haven & Hartford Railroad Co.*, transferred from Sanford to Hughes; No 356, *Lucas v Pilliod Lumber Co.*, transferred from Sanford to McReynolds; and Nos 10–11, *Powers Kennedy Contracting Corp. v Concrete Mixing and Conveying Co.*, transferred from Taft to Sanford, and then reargued after Sanford's death. Stone OT 1929 Docket Book. *Powers Kennedy* was reargued Oct 24, 1930, and was decided Dec 15 of that year in a unanimous opinion written by Sanford's successor, Owen Roberts. 282 US 175 (1930).

[386] Nos 443–45, *Campbell v Galeno Chemical Co.* Stone OT 1929 Docket Book.

[387] Nos 372–74, *City of Cincinnati v Vester*. Stone OT 1929 Docket Book.

[388] Renstrom, *The Taft Court* at 271 (cited in note 4).

[389] No 122, *Federal Radio Commission v General Electric Co.* Stone OT 1929 Docket Book.

tirement, a voting shift following conference, or the direct or indirect effects of Justice Van Devanter's increasing inability to discharge his literary burdens. Second, Stone's docket books help to clarify a series of questions about the deliberations in *Village of Euclid v Ambler*. Sutherland did vote in the initial conference on the case, and it seems that he was indeed the driving force behind the order for reargument. But Sutherland apparently expressed at the conference his doubts about his initial vote to invalidate the ordinance, and Stone also expressed at the conference reservations about his own vote to uphold it. Indeed, it is not at all clear that the opinion was assigned before the Justices agreed to order reargument. Stone's record of the deliberations also shows that it was Taft who joined Sutherland in defecting from the original conference majority and making a supermajority to sustain Euclid's zoning law.

The docket books also show that by 1925 a majority of the Justices believed that *Adkins v Children's Hospital* had been wrongly decided, and that the precedent survived two challenges only because of stare decisis. They disclose that *Frothingham v Mellon* and *Florida v Mellon*, two foundational decisions in the development of the national welfare state, were uncontroversial at conference. They reveal in addition that Brandeis, Holmes, and possibly even Sanford came close to dissenting in *Whitney v California*. And they demonstrate that none of the Justices voted to invalidate racially segregated education in *Gong Lum v Rice*.

We also learn from the docket books that the Court's published decisions are somewhat misleading concerning the civil rights and civil liberties views of Taft, Holmes, and McReynolds. Though he ultimately joined majorities favoring such claims in several cases, at conference the Chief Justice dissented from dispositions that he would publicly join in *Fasulo v United States*, *Byars v United States*, and *New York v Zimmerman*. Holmes likewise ultimately joined the *Byars* majority, but he was with Taft in dissent at the conference. And though both of these men were in the end with the rest of their colleagues in *Agnello v United States*, at conference each of them had assumed a posture that was at best equivocal. Similarly, McReynolds dissented at conference from positions that he ultimately would appear to endorse in *Byars* and *Cooke v United States*, and though he joined the published opinions in *Fasulo* and *Ziang Sung Wan v United States*, at the conference vote he had passed in each case. On the other hand, McReynolds took some surprising conference positions in cases involving questions of political economy. Though he ultimately joined majorities to invalidate the regulations challenged in *Liggett v Baldridge* and *United Railways & Electric Co. v West*, he passed at the conference on the former and dissented at the conference on the latter. Perhaps most notably, at the conference vote on *Black & White Taxicab Co. v Brown & Yellow Taxicab Co.*, McReynolds was with Holmes, Brandeis, and Stone in dissent.

The docket books also reveal considerable fluidity between the initial conference vote and the final vote on the merits among the Justices of the Taft Court. First, there were eight instances of defection to the minority in major cases. McReynolds was responsible for three of these, departing from conference votes with the majority in *Carroll* and *One Ford Coupe*, and from a passing conference vote in *Haydel*. Butler accounted for another two, departing from a conference vote with the majority in *Samuels* and from a passing conference vote in *Buck v Bell*. Taft abandoned a majority conference vote in *Toyota*, as did Holmes in *Helson*. And Stone departed from his passing conference vote in *Ribnik*.

Second, there also were shifts in voting that created majorities in favor of dispositions contrary to those produced at conference. In *Oliver Iron*, each of the Justices comprising the conference majority to reverse ultimately changed his vote to form a unanimous Court for affirmance. At the *Gambino* conference only Butler and Stone voted to reverse the conviction, but ultimately each of their colleagues joined them in the unanimous decision to reverse. And in *Euclid*, Taft and Sutherland defected from the initial conference majority to form a new majority to uphold rather than invalidate the Village's pioneering zoning ordinance.

Third, there were four instances of quasi-acquiescence. The published per curiam opinion in *Murphy v Sardell* stated that Holmes concurred only because he regarded himself as bound by the recent authority of *Adkins v Children's Hospital*. Sanford passed at the *Ribnik* conference, but ultimately concurred in the result on the ground that the case was governed by *Tyson*. And both Sanford and Stone cast dissenting ballots at the *Bedford Cut Stone* conference, but ultimately concurred on the ground that the case was governed by *Duplex Printing*.

Fourth, there was more than one instance in which Justices who had been in opposing camps at conference switched places before the final vote on the merits. In *Helson*, this movement did not change the ultimate disposition: Stone's acquiescence in the views of the majority offset Holmes's defection to the minority. Similarly, in *Coleman*, Sutherland's absence from the first conference and irresolution at the second meant that the postreargument exchange of places between McReynolds and Sanford did not meaningfully alter the deadlocked status quo.[390] Due to the difficulties of interpretation presented by Butler's docket book record of the *United Leather Workers* conference, one cannot rely upon that source for a definitive account of what transpired. But it appears that three votes changed between the conference vote and the final vote on the merits, with McReynolds and Sanford moving from the minority to the majority while Butler moved from the majority to the minority.[391]

The most common form of vote fluidity in major cases before the Taft Court, however, was acquiescence. Of the sixty-five unanimous decisions discussed here, thirty-nine (60%) also were unanimous at conference, but twenty-six (40%) were not. This observation is consistent with earlier studies finding that conformity voting is the most common form of vote fluidity.[392] The frequency with which each of the Justices acquiesced in the views of the majority is worthy of note. The notoriously cantankerous and disagreeable Justice McReynolds was actually the member of the Court who most frequently acquiesced in a major decision in order to produce unanimity. Of the

---

[390] Depending on the sequence of vote changes, one or the other of these Justices was presumably defecting from a newly constituted majority. But as the docket books do not reveal the sequence, they cannot inform us which of the Justices was the defector. Therefore I do not include this among the instances of defection listed above, though it might properly be added to the roster.

[391] Again, depending on the sequence of vote changes, these Justices may have been either acquiescing in or defecting from the majority. But as the docket books do not reveal the sequence, they cannot inform us which of the Justices should be characterized in which way. Therefore I do not include this among the instances of defection listed above, nor among the instances of acquiescence canvassed below.

[392] See, for example, Maltzman and Wahlbeck, 90 Am Pol Sci Rev at 590–91 (cited in note 4) (finding that Justices were more likely to move from a dissenting conference vote to the majority than to defect from the conference majority); Brenner and Dorff, 4 J Theoretical Polit at 198 (cited in note 56) (finding that movement from conference minority to ultimate majority is the most frequent type of vote fluidity); Brenner, 26 Am J Pol Sci at 389 (cited in note 4) (finding that 68% of the cases in which there was vote fluidity resulted in an increase in the size of the majority); Brenner, 24 Am J Pol Sci at 531, 534 (cited in note 4) ("justices are more likely to switch from the minority or nonparticipation at the original vote to the majority position at the final vote than to shift in the opposite direction. . . . Clearly, some of the justices, once they have lost at the original vote or failed to participate in that vote, are willing to conform to the opinion of the court's majority and vote with them at the final vote. Indeed, over three-quarters of the vote changes moved in a consensus direction.").

twenty-six unanimous decisions examined here that were not unanimous at conference, McReynolds acquiesced in eleven (42.3%). Holmes acquiesced in eight (30.7%), Taft, Brandeis, and Sutherland in five (19.2%) each, McKenna and Van Devanter in four (15.4%) each, Butler in three (11.5%), and Sanford and Stone in two (7.7%) each. Of these forty-nine instances of acquiescence, thirty-eight (77.6%) were of the strong variety and eleven (22.4%) were of the weak variety.[393]

With respect to cases that did not produce unanimity, McReynolds, Holmes, and Sanford acquiesced in four each, Sutherland in three, McKenna, Brandeis, and Stone in two each, and Taft and Butler in one each. The only member of the Court who did not acquiesce in any of these divided decisions was Van Devanter. Of these twenty-three instances of acquiescence, twenty-one (91.3%) were of the strong variety, and only two (8.7%) were of the weak sort.[394] Thus, of these seventy-two total instances of acquiescence in major Taft Court cases, fifty-nine (81.9%) were of the strong variety, and thirteen (18.1%) were of the weak variety. McReynolds alone was responsible for 20.8% of these instances of acquiescence, recording fifteen in all. Holmes accounted for twelve (16.7%), Sutherland for eight (11.1%), Brandeis for seven (9.7%), Taft, McKenna, and San-

---

[393] Nine of McReynolds's eleven acquiescences in ultimately unanimous cases were strong (*Radice, Brooks, Window Glass Manufacturers, Panama Railroad, Roberge, Fiske, Yu Cong Eng, Byars,* and *Cooke*), while two were weak (*Fasulo* and *Ziang*). Holmes's acquiescences in *Coronado Coal II, Yu Cong Eng,* and *Byars* were strong, and his acquiescence in *Whitney* was strong as to result if not as to First Amendment theory. His remaining four acquiescences were of the weak variety (*Duke, Nectow, Duby,* and *Agnello*). Four of Taft's five acquiescences were strong (*Window Glass Manufacturers, Industrial Association, Fasulo,* and *Byars*), while one was weak (*Agnello*). Brandeis's acquiescences in *Coronado Coal II, Nectow, Corrigan,* and *McGrain* were all of the strong variety, and his acquiescence in *Whitney* was strong as to result if not as to First Amendment theory. Each of Sutherland's five acquiescences was strong (*Brooks, Metcalf, Trusler, Roberge,* and *Ziang*), as were McKenna's four (*Radice, Window Glass Manufacturers, Dayton-Goose Creek,* and *Ziang*) and Van Devanter's four (*Radice, Trusler, Corrigan,* and *Ziang*). Butler acquiesced strongly in *Radice* and *Corrigan* but only weakly in *Lee.* Sanford acquiesced strongly in *Roberge* but weakly in *Duby.* And Stone acquiesced weakly in both *Nectow* and *Roberge.*

[394] McReynolds acquiesced strongly in *Black and White Taxicab, West,* and on the jurisdictional issue in *Tyson,* but weakly in *Liggett.* Holmes acquiesced strongly in *Olsen, Shafer,* and on the jurisdictional issue in *Tyson,* and though he expressed at the *Miles* conference his willingness to defer to the majority, his dissenting conference vote qualifies his acquiescence in that decision as strong also. Sanford acquiesced strongly in *Texas Transport, Buck v Kuykendall, Frost,* and *Carroll.* Sutherland acquiesced strongly in *Jay Burns, Buck v Kuykendall,* and *Bush,* while McKenna acquiesced strongly in *Jay Burns* but weakly in *Olsen.* Brandeis acquiesced strongly in the jurisdictional holding in *Tyson,* but weakly in *Helson.* Stone acquiesced strongly in both *Miles* and *Helson,* as did Taft in *Zimmerman* and Butler in *Carroll.*

ford for six (8.3%) each, and Van Devanter, Butler, and Stone for four (5.6%) each. Expressed as a percentage of acquiescences per conference vote in which he participated, McReynolds acquiesced in 12.9% of such cases, Holmes did so in 10.2%, Sutherland in 7.5%, Brandeis in 6%, Taft in 5.1%, Butler in 3.5%, and Van Devanter in 3.4%.[395] The fact that McReynolds and Holmes were the Taft Court Justices who most frequently acquiesced in major decisions echoes Professor Saul Brenner's finding that on the Vinson Court "extreme justices [were] most likely to be closer to the mean at the final vote than at the original vote," because "extreme justices are likely to lose more often at the original vote."[396]

---

[395] Van Devanter did not participate in the conference vote in *Nixon v Herndon*; McReynolds did not do so in *Miller v Schoene*; Brandeis did not participate in *Adkins*; Sutherland did not participate in the conference votes in *Panama Railroad*, *Frick v Webb*, *Webb v O'Brien*, *Porterfield v Webb*, *Terrace v Thompson*, *Gambino*, *Roschen*, *Alston*, *Gong Lum*, *Northwestern Mutual*, or *Whitney*; and Butler did not participate in the conference votes for *O'Fallon* or *Oliver Iron*.

The numbers for these major cases are generally consistent with Dean Post's finding of the total number of times each of the Justices changed his conference vote to join the Court's opinion. McReynolds was first with 99, Brandeis second with 95, Sanford third with 93, Sutherland fourth with 87, Holmes fifth with 80, Butler sixth with 60, Taft seventh with 48, Van Devanter eighth with 45, McKenna ninth with 38, and Stone last with 35. Expressed as a percentage of the decisions in which he participated, McKenna led the Court by acquiescing in 10.3%, McReynolds was next with 9.3%, followed by Brandeis, Sanford, and Sutherland each comfortably above 8%, Holmes well over 7%, Stone and Butler over 5%, Taft at 4.7%, and Van Devanter at 3.9%. As Dean Post observes, however, these percentages might be misleading for the reason that Taft and Van Devanter rarely cast dissenting votes in conference. When one looks at the rate at which each of the Justices was willing to change a dissenting conference vote and join the majority in the final vote on the merits, a different picture appears. McKenna again led the Court by doing so in nearly 90% of the cases in which he was a conference dissenter, but Van Devanter did so in 83.3%, Taft did so in 80%, followed by Sanford, Sutherland, and Butler each above 70%, Holmes in 60%, McReynolds in 59.3%, Brandeis in 57.2%, and Stone in 50%. Post, 85 Minn L Rev at 1333–34 n 203, 1377–78 (cited in note 2).

[396] Saul Brenner, *Ideological Voting on the Vinson Court: A Comparison of Original & Final Votes on the Merits*, 22 Polity 157, 163 (1989). An examination of these cases also provides some indication of the success of each of the Justices in preparing opinions that would attract colleagues who had dissented or passed at conference. In his study of all Taft Court opinions that became unanimous following a divided conference vote, Dean Post determined that Van Devanter did so at the highest rate and that McKenna was the least successful in doing so. Following Van Devanter in descending order were Butler, Sutherland, Holmes, Stone, McReynolds, Brandeis, Taft, and Sanford. Post, 85 Minn L Rev at 1334 n 203, 1388 (cited in note 2). If we exclude *Whitney*, which was unanimous only as to the judgment, there were twenty-five major cases that became unanimous after a divided conference vote. McKenna accounted for none of these, thus mirroring Dean Post's aggregate result. Similarly, though he wrote comparatively few opinions, Van Devanter accounted for three (*Oliver Iron*, *McGrain*, *Panama Railroad*), or 12%. Sutherland (*Industrial Association*, *Byars*, *Radice*, *Nectow*) and Butler (*Agnello*, *Fasulo*, *Roberge*, *Duke*) also again performed strongly in this category, each accounting for four, or 16%. Brandeis also accounted for three (*Ziang*, *Lee*, *Gambino*), or 12%, and Sanford's record of two (*Corrigan*, *Fiske*), or 8%, was consistent with his comparatively weak aggregate performance. Holmes (*Window Glass Manufacturers*), Stone (*Metcalf*), and McReynolds (*Trusler*), however, who were in the middle of the

These figures also speak to another debate in the political science literature. Some studies of voting fluidity conclude that "justices were no more likely to change their votes in important, or salient, cases than in those of lesser importance."[397] Others conclude that acquiescence was in fact more likely to occur in cases that were not "salient."[398] Dean Post has determined the percentage of all cases in

---

aggregate pack, each accounted for only one such opinion in a major case, or 4% each. By contrast, Taft, who was in the bottom third in the aggregate, was the author of six such major opinions (*Dayton Goose-Creek, Brooks, Yu Cong Eng, Cooke, Coronado Coal, Duby*), or fully 24% of the total.

This phenomenon also can be examined by looking at the percentage of unanimous opinions authored by a Justice that were not unanimous at conference. Overall, Dean Post found that Butler had the highest such percentage at 53%, followed by Holmes at about 50%, Sutherland at about 47%, Van Devanter at about 46%, Stone at around 40%, Brandeis at about 37%, McReynolds at about 36%, Taft at about 35%, Sanford at about 33%, and McKenna at 24%. Post, 85 Minn L Rev at 1334 n 203, 1389 (cited in note 2). When we examine the smaller number of major cases, we see substantial changes in ordinality. Here Van Devanter ranks first at 75% (3/4), Sanford second at 66.7% (2/3), Butler third at 57% (4/7), Taft fourth at 46.2% (6/13), Sutherland fifth at 44.4% (4/9), Brandeis sixth at 42.9% (3/7), Stone seventh at 25% (1/4), Holmes eighth at 20% (1/5), and McReynolds ninth at a remarkable 9.1% (1/11). McKenna did not author any major unanimous opinions.

These data also should be viewed in light of divided major decisions in which the author failed to increase the size of the conference majority. Neither Holmes, McKenna, Van Devanter, nor Sanford authored any such decisions; but of the twenty-two such cases, McReynolds was the author of six (*Meyer, Cudahy Packing, Fairmont Creamery, O'Fallon, Long v Rockwood, National Life*), Sutherland of three (*Adkins, Williams v Standard Oil, Macallen*), Taft of two (*Olmstead, Myers*), and Brandeis of one (*Lambert*). Stone was the author of two such companion cases (*Cement Manufacturers, Maple Flooring*) that were decided by identical votes and therefore might be more properly considered as one. Depending upon whether one counts the four companion *Alien Land Law Cases* (*Frick v Webb, Webb v O'Brien, Porterfield v Webb, Terrace v Thompson*) as four cases or one, Butler was the author of either eight or five. (The other four were *Di Santo, Weaver v Palmer Brothers, Quaker City Cab, Panhandle Oil*.) Thus, some of the Justices who were apparently most adept at attracting additional votes in major cases were also among those who most often failed to do so.

One should also consider cases in which the author of an opinion managed to attract additional votes, but failed to achieve unanimity. Sutherland did so in *Texas Transport, Frost Trucking, Liggett*, and *West*; Taft did so in *Carroll* and *Olsen*; Butler did so in *Jay Burns* and *Black and White Taxicab*; Van Devanter did so in *Shafer* and *Zimmerman*; Brandeis did so in the companion cases of *Buck v Kuykendall* and *Bush*; and McReynolds did so in *Miles*.

[397] Hagle and Spaeth, 44 Western Pol Q at 124 (cited in note 4). See also Maltzman and Wahlbeck, 90 Am Pol Sci Rev at 589 (cited in note 4) (finding that "justices are not less likely to switch in salient cases"); Brenner, Hagle, and Spaeth, 42 Western Pol Q 409 (cited in note 4) (concluding that the defection of the marginal member of the minimum winning coalition on the Warren Court is best explained not by the importance of the case, but instead by that Justice's ideological proximity to members of the dissenting coalition and, secondarily, to that Justice's relative lack of competence).

[398] Dorff and Brenner, 54 J Pol at 772, 773 (cited in note 4); Brenner, Hagle, and Spaeth, 23 Polity 309 (cited in note 4). Compare Brenner, 24 Am J Pol Sci at 530 (cited in note 4) (finding that percentage of total vote switches was no greater in "nonmajor" than in "major" cases, but that vote switches occurred in a higher percentage of "nonmajor" cases); Brenner, 26 Am J Pol Sci at 389 (cited in note 4) (reaching similar conclusions with a different data set).

which each of the Taft Court Justices changed his vote following the conference and ultimately joined the Court's opinion. With respect to those Justices who served on the Taft Court for the entire period for which we have docket books, a comparison of Dean Post's figures to those generated in this article produces an interesting result: some of the Justices were more likely to acquiesce in major cases than they were in cases of lower salience, whereas other were less likely to do so. Among the former category were McReynolds, Holmes, and Taft. McReynolds's overall acquiescence rate was 9.3%, but his rate in major cases was 12.9%. Holmes's overall rate was between 7% and 8%, but his major case rate was 10.2%. Taft's overall rate was 4.7%, but his major case rate was 5.1%. By contrast, Brandeis, Sutherland, Butler, and Van Devanter each had higher overall rates of acquiescence than rates of acquiescence in major cases. For Brandeis the figures were 8%–9% vs. 6%; for Sutherland they were 8%–9% vs. 7.5%; for Butler they were 5%–6% vs. 3.5%; and for Van Devanter they were 3.9% vs. 3.4%.[399]

For the Court as a whole, however, acquiescence was actually more likely in salient than in nonsalient cases. Overall there were 680 instances of acquiescence in 1,200 cases,[400] or a rate of 56.6%. In the major cases examined here, by contrast, there were seventy-two instances of acquiescence in 117 cases, or a rate of 61.5%. But when one looks at cases rather than votes, a different picture emerges. Whereas 55.6% of the Taft Court's decisions in major cases were unanimous, only 33.3% were unanimous at conference. By contrast, the Taft Court's overall rate of unanimity was 86%, and in 50% of its cases the vote was unanimous at conference.[401] At the same time, however, 58% of the Court's aggregate unanimous decisions were unanimous at conference, while 42% were not[402]—very nearly the same percentages (60%–40%) that we found for major decisions. Thus, while both conference unanimity and ultimate unanimity were significantly less likely to be achieved in salient than in nonsalient cases, the likelihood that a divided conference vote would ultimately be transformed into a unanimous decision was almost the same.

---

[399] Post, 85 Minn L Rev at 1333 n 203, 1387 (cited in note 2).

[400] Id at 1333 (cited in note 2).

[401] Id.

[402] Id.

The fact that two of the most senior Justices—McReynolds and Holmes—were those who most frequently acquiesced in the conference majority's judgment in major cases also indicates that newcomers to the Taft Court did not experience the kind of freshman effect with respect to voting fluidity that some scholars have found on other Courts. Though there is no agreed-upon period of judicial tenure during which to test for the freshman effect, the periods tested in the literature have ranged from one to five years.[403] Professor Howard, the first to identify the phenomenon, suggested that the freshman period was typically about three years.[404] Yet many of the instances of fluidity exhibited by these freshman Justices were produced well into their tenures on the Taft Court, and indeed persisted long after their freshman years had concluded.[405] Taft was the most mobile of the group, manifesting fluidity in ten major cases. The Chief Justice acquiesced in one major case (*Window Glass Manufacturers*) in his third full Term,[406] two (*Industrial Association, Agnello*) in his fourth, two (*Fasulo, Byars*) in his sixth, and one (*Zimmerman*) in his seventh. His one defection (*Toyota*) occurred in his fourth full Term. His three shifts from one conference majority to another occurred in his second (*Oliver Iron*), sixth (*Euclid*), and seventh (*Gambino*) full Terms. Moreover, at least some of Taft's shifts must have been prompted not by uncertainty, but instead by a desire to lead by example in cultivating the norm of acquiescence.

Two (*Jay Burns, Ziang*) of Sutherland's nine shifts in major cases occurred during his second full Term,[407] three (*Brooks, Buck v Kuykendall, Bush*) in his third, two (*Metcalf, Trusler*) in his fourth, and one (*Roberge*) in his seventh. His shift from one conference majority to another in *Euclid* occurred during his fifth full Term. Butler acquiesced in one major case (*Radice*) during his first Term, and one each

---

[403] Brenner and Hagle, 18 Pol Behav at 239 (cited in note 27).

[404] Howard Jr., 62 Am Pol Sci Rev at 45 (cited in note 24).

[405] See Barry Cushman, *The Hughes Court Docket Books: The Early Terms, 1930–1933*, 40 J Sup Ct Hist 103 (2015); Barry Cushman, *The Hughes Court Docket Books: The Late Terms, 1937–1940*, 55 Am J Leg Hist 361 (2015).

[406] As indicated in note 34 and its accompanying text, we do not have a docket book for the 1921 Term, Taft's first on the Court, nor for that portion of the 1922 Term antedating Justice Butler's accession to the Court.

[407] As indicated in note 34 and the accompanying text, we do not have docket book entries for that portion of the 1922 Term—Sutherland's first on the Court—antedating Justice Butler's accession to the Court.

during his second (*Carroll*), third (*Corrigan*), and fourth (*Lee*) full Terms. His two defections in major cases came in his second (*Samuels*) and fourth (*Buck v Bell*) full Terms, for a total of six instances of fluidity. Sanford acquiesced in one major case in each of his first (*Texas Transport*), third (*Frost*), fourth (*Duby*), and sixth (*Roberge*) full Terms, and two (*Carroll, Buck v Kuykendall*) in his second. His shift from one conference majority to another in *Gambino* came in his fifth full Term, for a total of seven such instances. Stone, who was on the Taft Court for a shorter time than his other freshman colleagues, acquiesced in one major case (*Miles v Graham*) in his first Term on the Court, in one (*Nectow*) during his third full Term, and in two (*Helson, Roberge*) during his fourth. His defection in *Ribnik* came during his third full Term, giving him a total of five instances of fluidity. Moreover, Stone and Butler were the only participants in the original *Gambino* conference to vote for the Court's ultimate disposition. By contrast, McReynolds exhibited nineteen instances of fluidity,[408] Holmes fourteen,[409] Brandeis eight,[410] and Van Devanter six.[411] The freshman Justices of the Taft Court were not markedly more likely than were their senior colleagues to change their votes between the conference and the final vote on the merits. Indeed, these five Justices together accounted for considerably fewer instances of fluidity in major cases than did the senior quartet of McReynolds, Holmes, Brandeis, and Van Devanter.[412]

---

[408] He acquiesced in *Radice, Brooks, Window Glass Manufacturers, Panama Railroad, Roberge, Fiske, Yu Cong Eng, Fasulo, Byars, Ziang, Cooke, Black and White Taxicab, Liggett, West*, and on the jurisdictional issue in *Tyson*; defected in *Carroll, Haydel*, and *One Ford Coupe*; and shifted from the initial conference majority to support a contrary disposition in *Oliver Iron*.

[409] He acquiesced in *Coronado Coal, Duke, Nectow, Duby, Yu Cong Eng, Agnello, Olsen, Miles, Shafer, Byars*, on the jurisdictional issue in *Tyson*, and in the judgment in *Whitney*; he defected in *Helson*; and he shifted from the initial conference majority to support a contrary disposition in *Gambino*.

[410] He acquiesced in *Coronado Coal, Nectow, Corrigan, McGrain*, and *Helson*, in the judgment in *Whitney*, on the jurisdictional issue in *Tyson*, and shifted from the initial conference majority to support a contrary disposition in *Gambino*.

[411] He acquiesced in *Radice, Trusler, Corrigan*, and *Ziang*, and shifted from the initial conference majority to support a contrary disposition in *Oliver Iron* and *Gambino*.

[412] Taft (10), Sutherland (9), Sanford (7), Butler (6), and Stone (5) accounted together for thirty-seven instances of fluidity. McReynolds (19), Holmes (14), Brandeis (8), and Van Devanter (6) accounted together for forty-seven. Other studies have shown that newcomers to the Taft Court did not demonstrate a freshman effect with respect to bloc voting. See Dudley, 21 Am Pol Q at 364–65 (cited in note 29); Bowen and Scheb II, 15 Pol Behav at 7, 11 (cited in note 29). Further research will be necessary to determine whether freshman Justices demonstrated greater degrees of vacillation in less salient cases than they did in the major

Of course, there are limits to what the docket books alone can teach us. Though they can document voting shifts between conference and published opinion, they typically do not reveal the reasons underlying such shifts.[413] Often they do not reveal the strength of preference underlying a conference vote, nor the force of persuasion required for that vote to change. The docket books typically do not reveal the extent to which a passing vote is explained by genuine indecision on the merits, a desire to see a draft of the majority opinion and its reasoning before making a commitment, or, as one might have reason to suspect in the case of McReynolds based on the assessment of one of his later clerks, a lack of preparation.[414] The docket books often do not reveal whether senior Justices, who spoke first but voted last, might have cast votes at variance with their expressed views in order to acquiesce in an emerging majority or, in the case of the Chief Justice or the most senior Associate Justice, to control assignment of the majority opinion.[415] For answers to these questions we must rely upon other sources or educated speculation, and to many of these issues we may never have satisfactory resolutions. But the information contained in the docket books permits us to answer a number of questions about the Taft Court, allows us to corroborate or confute a variety of scholarly claims, and opens avenues of investigation that previously had been obstructed or closed.

---

cases discussed here. Paul Freund reported that, "As far as I could make out, [Cardozo's] disagreements [with the majority in conference]—this being his first full term on the Court—derived from the fact that in New York he had been accustomed to a rather different set of procedural rules and substantive rules intermeshed with procedure, so that some things which werè decided one way in the federal courts would have been decided differently in New York," and that this is what may have accounted for the Justice's allegedly frequent changes of vote between the conference and the final vote on the merits. Freund, 26 Ohio St L J at 227 (cited in note 31). This suggests the possibility that in some instances a greater degree of freshman vote fluidity might be exhibited in less salient cases.

[413] For discussions of various possibilities, see, for example, Epstein, Segal, and Spaeth, 45 Am J Pol Sci at 372–73 (cited in note 20); Saul Brenner, *Minimum Winning Coalitions on the United States Supreme Court: A Comparison of the Original Vote on the Merits with the Opinion Vote*, 7 Am Pol Q 384, 391–92 (1979); Howard Jr., 62 Am Pol Sci Rev at 45–51 (cited in note 24).

[414] John Knox, *Experiences as a Law Clerk to Mr. Justice James C. McReynolds of the Supreme Court of the United States during the Year that President Franklin D. Roosevelt Attempted to "Pack" the Court* *vi (unpublished manuscript, Oct Term 1936, available at John Knox MSS, Special Collections, University of Virginia Library) (describing McReynolds as "genuinely lazy").

[415] See Johnson, Spriggs II, and Wahlbeck, 39 L & Society Rev 349 (cited in note 33).